'What is the use of a book', thought Alice, 'without pictures or conversations?'

Alice's Adventures in Wonderland

ARMAGH VOICES

Armagh Voices

A celebration of a century

Pamela Rea

Armagh Voices

Pamela Rea

Published by

Pamela Rea

11 Grove Terrace

Armagh BT60 1BX

Northern Ireland

ISBN 0-9529660-1-8

Printed by W. & G. Baird Ltd

Greystone Press, Caulside Drive

Antrim BT41 2RS

Northern Ireland

Design and layout by Caitriona Sherry

This book has received financial assistance from the Millennium programme of Armagh City and District Council

for Colette and Bill O'Brien

Contents

1940-1950

1950-1960

1960-1970

1970-1980

1980-1990

1990-2000

Acknowledgements

I owe my thanks to Ciarán Ó Maoláin who solved the aggravating and monumental task of finalising my text. With his vast store of knowledge, systematic approach and unfailing good taste, he edited this work to a standard I would otherwise have found it difficult to achieve. My sincere thanks also to Elaine Reid and Siobhán Lennon for their secretarial skills. By way of enriching a unique record, further kindly and generous sources of information were Kate Bond, Jim Campbell, Harry Carson, Louise Corr, Patricia Dakin (Queensland), Trevor Kirkpatrick, Catherine McCullough, Greer Ramsey, Betty McCann, Paul McAvinchey, Phyllis Mason, Bobby Moore, Kevin Toal, the Southern Education and Library Board, Lena Rafferty, Richard Burden and Stephen Richardson of the *Ulster Gazette* and Martin White.

The literary captions that preface each decade were capably and enthusiastically compiled by my friend, Colette O'Brien.

The production of this book was made possible by a significant subsidy from Armagh City and District Council, which decided to mark the new millennium by assisting in the creation of a lasting record of a selection of its past and present citizens. I should also record, with gratitude, that within broad guidelines the Council permitted me the freedom to select my subjects and to write without interference, and it follows that any opinions expressed herein should not be attributed to the Council. The staff of the Council, particularly Carol Kyle, Caitriona Sherry and Desmond Mitchell, were always helpful.

Finally I would like to record my gratitude to those who permitted me to tell their stories, many presented here for the first time and others adapted and updated from my 1996 work *Touching a Chord*. It has been a privilege to share and to record the recollections of so many who have contributed so much to the life of our community.

Pamela Rea
Armagh, November 1999

Foreword

There is, occasionally, one of those curious accidents of history when the name of a person perfectly communicates their character. In the case of Pamela, history cannot but be thankful that this 'ray' has been among us.

For Pamela Rea has brought to us what is, in a very important sense, an 'illuminated' work. In the great tradition of the early medieval scholars who occupied the hills of Armagh, she has, in a communal and utterly determined spirit, thrown light—not upon herself—but upon her subjects. And as one of those subjects, I must insist that her light is as kindly as it is sharp.

Though it is very much a collective, communal and civic work where the subjects are exhorted to define their own story under her transcribing hand, there is no doubt that her passion and dedication, combined with substantial editorial and writing gifts, have inscribed this compendium with a highly individual imprimatur.

I had the singular delight of teaching Pamela when she commenced her BA studies at Queen's University, Armagh. It was, indeed, a memorable experience, for Pamela was ever keen to be enlightened. We were, after all, conducting our literary 'operations' on the site of the old City Infirmary, which itself overlaid the locus of an impressive tradition of book-learning and book-making in a previous age. Archbishop Richard Robinson, who caused the building of the hospital and many other of the most beautiful and enduring buildings in the city—and who fought hard to have a university established—was an exemplum of 18th century enlightenment. Pamela was not slow either to understand or embrace the rich palimpsest of light and learning—coming as it did from both 'traditions.' She brought to her mature education a treasure trove of knowledge and skill, a wicked sense of humour, dedication and—most of all—the lucid excitement of the child for the sheer wonder of life and learning.

These qualities simply shine through the book. To be sure, it was not safe to be about Armagh when Pamela was upon her great enterprise. Citizens (and imports like myself) were flattered, fed, wheedled, cajoled and just plain ambushed. To turn a little quote from another one of her 'characters', Willie Nugent, "She is the girl who cannot be said no to". And how indebted should Armagh be for all her relentless bushwhackery.

The book is a little microcosm. Upon its canvas old soldiers paint their poignant histories of war, sportsmen score international victories, saxophone players and poets and playwrights and filmmakers engender a precious and consoling and challenging tribute to their city, politicians and public figures fret their sometimes tragic, sometimes comic hour.

It is a panorama worthy of Thackeray or Joyce. The famous are met—Liz Taylor, General Patton, President Clinton, the Queen—and well met by Pamela's heroes. For it is the ordinary as well as the 'great' who speak their piece.

The poignancy of many of the stories cannot but fail to move. Again and again, we hear not of the glory of war, but the human sacrifice. Joseph Proctor, veteran of the Somme, quietly computes: "Some 150 miles of territory regained cost three quarters of a million casualties." Who glories in strife, Joe asks: "Men who make war rarely do the fighting." His sombre question hangs compassionate over the many references to friends lost in our own 'Troubles'. But the Armagh spirit, somehow, soldiers on and many are the accounts of generosity between neighbours and communities.

Silver Bands and Foresters share instruments, soldiers sent to quell riots in Belfast lay down their rifles, Catholic and Protestant alike, leading unionists quote from Irish mythology, Armagh comes together to raise thousands of pounds for Romania in one day.

It is, nevertheless, a book that is rarely unduly earnest or sanctimonious in tone. Humour flashes through it like the ancient Hallowe'en fires at Emhain Macha. The stray dogs' pound is cleared in one day by a very large Dalmatian answering to the name of Willie. The same Willie Nugent's outrageous feats for charity include a 'convincing' impersonation of General Custer in a shop window, pushing a pea for 2 1/2 miles and being 'mugged' by Paddy Gallen's guide dog, Yale, who incomprehensibly devoured a chocolate egg destined for a round of the Mall on Willie's nose.

The 100 profiles are arranged chronologically, often by

decade of birth but sometimes just because a particular profile illuminates the era to which it is assigned, unfolding the living history of the city in a most effective way. The sense of time and its passing is perhaps nowhere so lovingly and kindly caught than in Pamela's concluding sentence to her account of the clockmaking works of James Stewart: "In the year of Our Lord, 1999, time can be forgiven for flying when told by such a beautiful face."

And while the past is saluted, so too, fittingly, are the present and the future. We hear of the new light of Armagh's young musicians, writers, artists and sportsmen; of the exciting work to come from this great city. The youngest speaker is Master John Maguire: "I live with my Mum, Dad and my dog Barney. I am five years old and Barney is six."The last word must surely go to a spirit echoing the enlightenment and generosity of Pamela Rea. Here is 19-year-old Joanne Bloomer, who happens to have osteomalacia: "In looking forward to the rest of my life, I am grateful for what has gone already. Not everyone gets the chance to say this in print or to mention great people like [paramedics] Darren and Stephen. Pamela told me she wouldn't have been able to produce this book without equally great people who helped by typing, proof-reading or just being there when the going was hard. It just goes to show—we all need each other."

Tess Hurson
Queen's University, Armagh, November 1999

Armagh Voices
a celebration of a century

1900 ~ 1910

When to the sessions of sweet silent thought
I summon up remembrance of things past

William Shakespeare

Armagh Old Boys' Silver Band

Since the beginning of time people have responded to music in the form of rhythm and melody. Music is a language that speaks to us all and a unique method of communication. Armagh Old Boys' Silver Band has held a place of affection within the community ever since its formation in 1895. Present chairman Ivor Stevenson inherited almost a century of information handed on from past members.

"To see our history in print was the wish of my late father, Bob, who loved this band and served as its conductor for 12 years. I visualise his pride when, instruments gleaming, we stepped out striking near-perfect pitch in a stirring march." Every study tells a story as Ivor deciphers early photography, which is carefully preserved at the Band's Music Centre on the Mall. "Our earliest group of 1st Armagh Boys' Brigade dates to 1895. Pinky Warrilow, band tutor, is standing in the background. Reliable memoirs of the late Dick Irwin, whose membership spanned more than 60 years, take us back to 1897 and our early beginnings as a melody flute band. The Boys' Brigade organisation, from whose ranks musicians were drawn, had been established by 1899.

"Another portrait taken in 1901 shows a group of Boys' Brigade members substituting wooden 'rifles' for drill practice. Many are wearing sailor suits and again, centrally placed, is musical director Pinky Warrilow. By 1908 our identity changed dramatically, from flute to brass and reed, almost a simplified form of military band. I know Dick Irwin contributed his skill at this crucial time. A special photograph recently donated to the Old Boys' collection includes Pinky Warrilow with St Malachy's Championship Flute Band, 1912. Armagh had long been a garrison town and research confirms Pinky Warrilow to have been an army musician who, for the sheer joy of this medium, trained both the Old Boys and St Malachy's Flute Band, a four-part harmony band, outstanding in quality of sound.

"A token of the Old Boys' popularity at the beginning of the century is that they then accompanied children and parents on annual Sunday school excursions. They often chose Warrenpoint as a seaside venue, travelling by train. After forming at College Street, the band paraded to the station, playing all the way. Arriving in Warrenpoint, the band played en route to a chosen venue where sandwiches and lemonade constituted lunch. Seaside visitors on the esplanade enjoyed a medley of popular music by courtesy of the band before they made the homeward journey. Day-trippers would have represented all faiths, Methodist, Roman Catholic, Presbyterian and Church of Ireland. Mrs Houston, who is now 102, nostalgically remembers how, when she was a child, she ran ahead of the band to ensure a seat with her best friend on the outward journey."

During both World Wars, instruments remained silent, laid up for safety in the vaults of several churches. Local solicitor and tenor horn player, Brian Dougan, introduces a poignant note to this narrative. "Old Boys escorted comrades leaving for World War I to the station, playing until the train disappeared from sight. Members left behind carried home the instruments of men who had gone." It is a scene that is easily visualised because of its powerful dual symbolism: the musicians have gone, and their silver lies silent. November 1918 brought the end of war. Now the musicians had returned, the band strikes up and steps out in celebration.

Ivor's father, Bob Stevenson, was a newcomer in 1921. "He'd pestered conductor Dick Irwin to allow him join. 'You may when you can play the opening bars of the march *Barvada* perfectly', commented Dick. Practising furiously, Bob chose summer camp in Kilkeel for an audition, calling at Dick's tent at five in the morning. It must have worked for Bob was taken on board." Taken at the Courthouse steps in 1921, another photograph includes Dick's brother, William Irwin, who played the cornet with Tommy Bennett and Sydney and Jack McVeigh (relatives of the late Wilfie McVeigh, proprietor of 'The Hole in the Wall' tavern). In the back row stands young Albert Rea who would leave Armagh in 1934, becoming, at the zenith of his career, Moderator of the General Assembly of the Church of South Africa and Rhodesia. Church influence is reinforced with the presence of the Rev. J.W.P. Elliott and the Rev. D. Graham. Ivor adds: "We are indebted to the late Harcourt Irwin who preserved photographs from the *Ulster Gazette* and *Armagh Guardian*. Harcourt, with Brian Lester, son of member David, documented much of this material. As a new century dawns, these records, which are crucial to the band's past, might easily have been lost."

A formal study of 1st Armagh Company Boys' Brigade Brass and Reed Band, 1925, shows a group of members assembled in the courtyard of Royal School, Armagh. Past musicians are listed as: Thomas Quail, Jack McVeigh, William Somerville, Alfie Rowan, Ernest Auld, George McKinney, Ed McCormick, William Rowan, Max Zwecker, Albert Auld, Bob Stevenson, Thomas Bennett, William Irwin, William West, Richard Irwin, William Bennett and Captain Robert McDonald.

"This photograph has special significance", Ivor stresses. "They had just won a prestigious competition when the opposition claimed these musicians were surely over the age limit! Nothing came of such protests but soon after 'Old Boys' was incorporated into the band's title. It cost one penny a week for music lessons; strictly no smoking was allowed and Dick Irwin had now stepped into place as tutor and conductor."

The 'Roaring Twenties' through to the early Thirties saw the Old Boys accompany Armagh Boys' Brigade to annual summer camp in Kilkeel. "They brought their music, slept under canvas and the fun was phenomenal! Winds of change now brought an amicable parting of the ways. The band became an independent organisation, agreeably performing at Boys' Brigade church services or parades whilst moulding a mature new image for themselves. Our principal cornet player, Gordon Stewart, is the only remaining member to transfer from the Boys' Brigade Bugle Band of the 1950s."

The musicians wore suits, until the early 1930s when second-hand uniforms and white cap covers became formal dress. "This was how the band appeared when playing at the formal opening of the Armstrong Primary School in 1931. It was 1952 before Armagh Old Boys dressed in scarlet and navy uniforms. Herron of Dromore supplied this handsome makeover and possibly another new identity. And yet we never lost that sense of fun or mutual trust which men in a group share. Call it sentimental if you like, it is nevertheless part of our commitment. Drum major Bob Proctor, who sees humour in every situation, is still with us. Bob once helped a friend, Billy Crabbe, move into a new home by sowing his new lawn. When it grew, so did a seam of turnips, right down the centre."

For a time during 1930s and 1940s, Armagh Foresters' Club, having their own band, shared musical instruments and players with the Old Boys. "It seems", Ivor contributes, "that the Foresters' Club owned an excellent rope-tension drum while ours was but a poor specimen and thereby hangs a legend that improved with the telling! Cecil Rowan's father, a sign-writer, is said to have superimposed the Old Boys title on the better of the two. I have no idea who had sufficient courage to return the impostor!

"Family ties are reflected in the number of musical brothers who were band musicians. Those that spring to mind are Percy and Stanley McCullough, Eric and Hampton Ewart, Jim and Gordon Stewart, Billy and Bertie West, Cecil and Billy Rowan and Albert, Harold and Eric Auld. Eric was Captain of 1st Armagh Boys' Brigade until recently, when this responsibility was taken over by his son, Gordon. Down the decades, Armagh Old Boys forged excellent musically based relationships, sharing a special anniversary celebration with Tassagh Silver Band in 1956. Such goodwill was a tribute to Dick Irwin's versatility although his musical expertise resulted in excessive demands on his time.

"Dick conducted every evening, in rotation, Armagh Old Boys, Tassagh Silver Band, Tullyvallen Silver Band, Breaghey Silver Band and Hamiltonsbawn Silver Band. One of our members, Alton Beck, and my father attended these practices with Dick", Ivor adds, "indeed the three were inseparable."

A delightful tradition, 'Carols by Candlelight', began at Armagh Methodist Church in 1963, motivated by the Rev. Thomas Woods and Harcourt Irwin. A photographed memento of that evening includes drummer Bert Mackrel, prior to losing his sight. "Bert's sense of timing distinguished him as a musician", Ivor comments, "his sight loss robbing the Old Boys of an excellent talent. Stretching into the 1970s, a highlight of Old Boys' Christmas celebrations was the Methodist Service of Nine Lessons and Carols. For this event we wore concert uniform, affectionately known as our 'ice-cream jackets', costing £19 each. Members who were present include Alex Stinson, Harry Carson, Jim Scott, Jim Hamilton, Tom McCracken, Kenny Lutton, Gordon Stewart, John Swift, the late Alan Wilson and Trevor Kirkpatrick. Favourite carols included *Mary's Boy Child*, *Once in Royal David's City*, *Silent Night* and *O Little Town of Bethlehem.*

I remember Methodist suppers as savoury sandwiches and trays piled high with delicious apple creams!"

Many will remember Christmas through the Sixties when Armagh Old Boys, conducted by Bob Stevenson, played seasonal melodies around the tree. "As the switch was thrown, a thousand twinkling lights flooded Market Square. The atmosphere was euphoric as parents bore children shoulder-high in a pulsing throng. Our fee from Armagh Urban District Council was then a modest £5. Father Christmas made a dramatic arrival, escorted by the Fire Brigade or straight from the Lennox Store in a large sleigh."

Conductor Harry Prentice, described by Ivor as 'The Wind Beneath our Wings', came to fill a void for three months and remained for 25 years. "Harry's arrival as conductor was the inspiration of the late Billy Rowan, during 1972. The appointment was quietly encouraged by Harry's father, the late Billy Prentice, a great supporter of the Old Boys' Band. Harry easily absorbed difficult pieces with his tremendous sight-reading skills, loved rhythm, calypso, one or two pieces from the Glenn Miller repertoire and an occasional jazz number. Harry was a motivating influence in the building of our new official meeting place, the Music Centre. Here", Ivor gestures, "is practicality demonstrated in bricks and mortar. Tabletops were made by Gordon Stewart, fireplace base and construction is the skill of Alton Beck. Bob Nelson carried out electrical wiring and plumbing. Jim Hamilton laid carpet tiles; Billy and Cecil Rowan completed ceramic tiling in the washrooms. Kenny Lutton laid outside cables and everyone gave of their best in assisting with the work. Our Music Centre provides a meeting place for friends and supporters in the relaxed atmosphere of a social club. That it runs smoothly is a tribute to members who rally to our cause in a voluntary capacity. Financial aid from Armagh Confederation of Voluntary Groups, the Apple Blossom Festival, Starplan and James Stewart and Sons, saw us host the Scheidt-Quintet from Nordrhein-Westfalen, Germany, in concerts of classical and modern brass music. Down the years the Music Centre has hosted some marvellous musicians", Ivor comments enthusiastically. "Amongst the best we've enjoyed pianist Barry Douglas, John Fletcher on the tuba, the Philip Jones Brass Ensemble, Budapest Wind Ensemble and 'Young Musicians in Northern Ireland'. World famous violinist Nigel Kennedy entertained us in the late Eighties, and Armagh Arts Committee are to be congratulated on such smoothly organised and memorable events."

Each Armistice Sunday it is an established tradition that Armagh Old Boys' lead a parade to the Cenotaph for the wreath-laying ceremony. "We changed our repertoire last year, playing a medley of First World War marching songs on the way to church. Along the route observers tapped their feet to the beat of *It's a Long Way to Tipperary* and *Pack up your Troubles*.

"It seems appropriate to pay tribute to many members and friends who have passed on, particularly Richard Irwin, Harcourt Irwin, Billy Crabbe, David Cloughan who was also a gifted singer, and George Allen. Possibly our proudest moment came in October 1998, when arts officer Kate Bond, on behalf of Armagh City and District Council, invited us to play for President Clinton at 'A Gathering for Peace'. We had 48 hours notice to put a programme in place. Following rigorous checks by the Federal Bureau of Investigation, we were seated behind our scores for a performance beamed live to the United States. We basked in the afterglow for hours and that event is one we will long remember."

In recent years Armagh Old Boys has invited many top bands in concert. "We've hosted senior grade, Murley Silver Band, Fivemiletown, Belfast 1st Old Boys, and Agnes Street which sadly no longer exists. Such events are a pleasure shared whilst raising the profile of music." He recalls the exceptional final concert of Armagh Music Week in 1987. "Goff Richards wrote a commissioned work, *Momentary—The Armagh Cantata*, appropriately difficult and something that will remain in the memory of all who truly love music. Richard McNicol conducted the Ulster Orchestra with solo performances from Paschal Allen, bass, and Romeo Forte on piano. A diverse programme was provided by Armagh Pipers' Club, Armagh Old Boys' Silver Band, Armagh City Choir, Portadown Ladies Choir, Portadown Male Voice Choir, Charles Ives and pupils of St Catherine's College and Royal School, Armagh.

"A quarter century is quite a time to have one person in charge of events", Ivor concludes. "Harry Prentice's retirement brought an evaluation of comradeship, achievements, events and downright good fun, ample reward for all members of the band. We recognise the ability of our present conductor, Derek Orr, to communicate meaningfully and sensitively with a vast

Back row (L to R): Gordon Stewart Snr, Alan Graham, Trevor Kirkpatrick, Norman Pollock, Brian Dougan, Ivor Stevenson, Brian Lester, Lisa Stewart, Michelle Baird, Alton Beck, Jim Scott.
Middle row: Stanley McCullough, Julie Ann Stevenson, Stewart Stevenson, Simon Cardwell, Gordon Stewart Jnr, Louise Graham, Sarah Jane Stevenson, Kate Megaw, Samantha Stevenson, Evan Downey.
Front row: Mervyn Watt, Neil Watson, Freddie Woods, Harold Prentice (conductor), Alex Stinson (chairman), Gillian Black, Caroline Stewart, William Stevenson.

Armagh Old Boys' Silver Band
Photograph by Michael Campbell, LBIPP

range of talent, be it that of musical arranger Goff Richards or the hesitant beginner. Ashgrove Brass Band owes much to the musical skills of Derek as its founder, and assuredly he will build on the firm foundations established by Harry Prentice and previous conductors."

Ivor Stevenson has been a science teacher for 23 years with Armagh High School, and three of his children are young band musicians. "Equal opportunities introduced the fairer sex to our ranks", Ivor says. "Cornet player Michelle Baird made history as the band's first woman member when she joined in 1982. My two daughters joined later, Julie-Anne playing the cornet, and Sarah Jane the trombone. My son Stewart is attempting to master the intricacies of the flugelhorn. We welcome and will train any young musician who wishes to play. With 105 years behind us, continuity is a vocation."

And so say all of us. Since the beginning of time people have responded to music, the language of the soul. So once again, strike up the band, and greet the new century by stepping confidently into 2000 AD... and well beyond.

Joseph Proctor

Armagh City and District's sole survivor of the Battle of the Somme, Joseph Proctor, died on 13 February 1995, leaving only four surviving veterans in Northern Ireland. Aged 96, Joe was the youngest of four children whose parents were Thomas and Mary Proctor of Kilmore, Richhill.

Joseph's memories were recorded in November, three months before his death. In the space of an afternoon that stretched until winter's darkness stole the daylight, he spoke of childhood and his part in the great battle of July-November 1916.

"Of my family, Edward was eldest", Joe explains, "then came George, Elizabeth, and myself, born on 16 October 1898." He remembers nothing of his mother who died when he was an infant. "My father served with the 62nd Regiment of Foot, now the Wiltshire Regiment, in India from 1858-79, during Queen Victoria's reign. His good conduct medal and discharge papers are today in the care of a grandson, Leslie Proctor, who lives in Australia, and are deemed exceptional collector's items. My own World War I medals were passed on to a favourite great-grandson."

Returning from India, Thomas Proctor became the local postman for Richhill, delivering mail on foot. "He was a good-natured man", Joe comments, "but due to the nature of his work, we children never saw him until after school. The task of bringing me up fell to my brothers and sister." Edward Ruddock was the teacher in charge of Kilmore Primary School when Joe left in 1912. As a boy of 14 Joe worked for Lambs of Richhill, picking fruit that was used to make jams and preserves. "I spent my days at the Sandymount branch of the factory where strawberries, plums, damsons and apples were grown. The Lambs were kindly people, members of the Society of Friends. You'll probably think conditions sound hard but it was work and we accepted the terms. An 11-hour day was paid at the going rate of five shillings for a six-day week."

World War I involved 30 nations and 65 million fighting men, eight million of whom died. It was on impulse that Joe, in common with many young men across the United Kingdom, volunteered for active service. Signing on with the Royal Irish Fusiliers at Portadown, he was dispatched to North Queen Street Barracks, Belfast, on a four-month training course.

"We were in such a jubilant mood leaving for Le Havre. Kitchener, then Secretary for War, inspired great enthusiasm massing and training an army but there was an unwillingness to use heavy artillery on the field. Men died by the thousand before the War Office grasped this fact." German armies were sweeping Belgium and France. For men in the thick of battle, a mood of jubilation swiftly changed. "Canadian troops had landed in October, the week before us. For a shilling a day we stood up to the waist in trenches of mud and slime. Reloading my rifle, I'd call over my shoulder to a comrade. If no answer came, I knew he was dead. The men lay where they fell until dusk. Decomposing bodies being eaten by rats was commonplace. At nightfall the dead were collected, and if possible identified."

"What passing bells for these who die as cattle?" wrote Wilfred Owen, outraged by the carnage of this war, which was foolishly prophesied to end all others. Owen's life drained away on the Western Front, one week before the 1918 Armistice.

"I was with 'A' Company, 1st Royal Irish Fusiliers", Joe continues. "We were a mixed division of Irish—Dublin Fusiliers, Irish Rangers from Munster, Leinster and Connaught Divisions—then men from the Royal Scots and Seaforth Highlanders. War news was usually distorted. We had no idea of the true situation. Those at home were lucky to receive a letter from us once a month." He is the last remaining veteran in this county to have participated in the Battle of the Somme. Few of his contemporaries are left in Northern Ireland and in view of this, a first-hand account becomes the more urgent.

"On 16 January 1916", Joe continues, "our unit tried to hold ground but rolls of barbed wire laid by an advance party up ahead had been badly cut. It was impossible to get through without being ripped to pieces. All the while, the Germans were bombarding us like there was no tomorrow. I caught it in the shoulder. Shrapnel lodged there has been my companion for 78 years. X-rays show it has moved, but I've lived with that. A French field hospital typified medical conditions then. Wounded men lay in agony and amputations were performed without anaesthetics. Those nurses were a remarkable breed of women, saving lives if they could, whispering words of comfort when they could not. The Red Cross carried out magnificent work under fire. If they got to a casualty, at least he stood a chance.

"On 1 July 1916, my division was diverted to the Somme, a 25-mile front. At first, the Germans who were not as well prepared as the French fell back. The next phase, the struggle for Thiepval-Combles-Maurepas ridges, took a heavy toll but was necessary for the September breakthrough. Slow progress in August allowed the Germans to prepare new lines to which they might retire. Bad weather prevented fresh assaults on these lines. To progress, we had to leave the trenches and run across open ground towards machine-gun fire. Suicide, you might say. Some 150 miles of territory regained cost three quarters of a million casualties. As with every war, what was it all for? My brother George enlisted before me, with the Royal Scots Regiment. We must have been in the thick of fighting at the same time, yet never did I catch as much as a glimpse of him."

George came through unscathed but Joe sustained injuries in November 1917. These wounds kept him hospitalised until the war ended. "I was brought by stretcher to England and placed in a military hospital in Yorkshire. One morning a ripple ran through that King George V and Queen Mary were visiting. They stopped by my bed to chat for a few minutes. He, if you recall, established the tradition of a Christmas Day Broadcast in 1932." To the last, the Germans resisted valiantly, but outmatched, surrendered to Marshal Foch, commander-in-chief of the Allied armies, on 11 November 1918. Wounded three times, Joseph Proctor was invalided out of the army while he held the rank of Lance Corporal.

Returning to Richhill in December 1918, Joe was stunned to find his father had died two years earlier. News had been sent, but never reached France. He resumed his old job with Fruitfield canning factory, then in 1926 opened a small shop in Barrack Street, trading as a grocer and confectioner. He married Elizabeth McBride from Keady and she later worked as his assistant in the business. When the local postmistress retired in 1935, Joe merged his business with the sub-post office.

"A hunting man then, I took great interest in following the beagles. Indeed I kept my own dogs at Barrack Street. Ned McCann was master of the hounds and off we'd go, several times a week, tracking hares on foot."

Joe and Elizabeth had two children, George and Eileen. George served with the Royal Air Force in the Second World War while Eileen works with the Southern Education and Library Board. Elizabeth Proctor died in 1954 and Joe continued his business and sub-post office until 1965, when George assumed control. That same year, Joe married Martha Stinson. His stepdaughter Lillian has taken charge and recently came runner-up in the 'Best Post Office in Northern Ireland' competition. Joe's second stepdaughter, Rosemary, is a nurse in Longstone Hospital. "Both families are exceptional in their kindness", he acknowledges. "I would say I was fortunate."

Joseph Proctor was honoured in December 1991, when a special medallion inscribed with his rank and number was presented by Lord Caledon, patron of Armagh Branch of the Royal British Legion. Joe remained in good health, attending the Belfast July anniversary of the Battle of the Somme in 1994. "I very much enjoyed the event. Charles Brady, president of the Armagh Branch, accompanied me as did Robert McIlveen, welfare secretary of the Royal British Legion. Lt-General Sir Roger Wheeler chatted afterwards during a reception in Belfast City Hall.

"Who glories in strife?" Joe asks, summing up this account. "Men who make war rarely do the fighting. The carnage of the Somme was laid at the door of the Generals, the Government, and the Germans. It began with the assassination of Archduke Franz Ferdinand but none of us thought of the Archduke when we buried our comrades at dead of night in a far country."

Joe Proctor is tired so we leave him with his thoughts. Around 45 million poppies are sold annually, in advance of Armistice Day. One in Joe's lapel shows he has not broken faith with 'you who lie in Flanders Fields'.

Joseph Proctor
at the Somme Commemoration,
Belfast City Hall, July 1994

Paul Harvey Jackson

Adapting his technique to best express the intensity of suffering experienced by men at the Western Front in World War I (1914-18), writer and editor Paul Harvey Jackson pays tribute to veterans such as Joseph Proctor. Powerful use of discordance and harshness equate war and hell. This is quite the most moving work of a poet and novelist, who was for 13 years with the Southern Education and Library Board at Charlemont Place, Armagh as information officer and editor of *Southern Board News* magazine. Circulation ran to thousands and it was received by more than 300 schools.

Paul began writing seriously in 1975, then moved to France with his wife Alfreda. In a Peter Mayle-style account, his story of two years spent in Nice and Cannes sold in serial form. *Stephen's Pigeon*, Paul's first children's book, made a tremendous impact and was followed by cartoon character *The Gobbly Goobcheck.* He was 'ghost writer' for *They Said It With Music*, the autobiography of Peggy Cochrane, wife of big band leader Jack Payne. Of his many short stories, a number have been read on air. His most recent work, a political thriller, *McCluskey*, was serialised in *Figments*, a literary magazine.

With 40 published poems, Paul was shortlisted many times by the British Poetry Society. In September 1997 he was awarded a bursary for a period of residency at the Tyrone Guthrie Centre at Annaghmakerrig, Co. Monaghan. Later that year he was shortlisted for the Brian Moore Short Story Awards.

Through the medium of *Southern Board News*, awards were made annually for the most inspiring school magazine. In 1995 Paul introduced a new short story competition, aimed at A-Level students. This valuable outlet paved the way for several aspiring young writers. *War... Terrible Bloody War...* is a new work that capably holds its own place in the 'war poets' arena.

War... Terrible Bloody War...

Dear God why is it
You allow greedy, stupid politicians
To create the perfect climate
For men to slaughter other men
Without guilt or contrition
At the flick of a finger
Or a signature...
The click of a rifle bolt
Some poor woman's son
Some sorrowing wife's man
Some young girl's boy
Consigned to eternity.....?

What is it all for
But to fuel empty political ambition
Or satisfy some hideous bloodthirsty tyrant?
To be sure there are no winners in war
Only losers...
The pain, the cost—the appalling waste
The thousand lives lost to gain one lousy acre of ground
To lose it perhaps the very next day
And the noise dear God—the noise
The screams—the never to be forgotten screams
Prayers
A million souls clutching rosary beads
Perhaps you cannot hear them God?

Slate grey observation posts
Field guns bogged to the axles in mire
No man's land
Putrefying flesh...
Low flying spotter planes
With machine guns
Low slung fat-bellied barrage balloons
Barbed wire—mile upon terrible mile
Nasty spirals of viciously rusted teeth
Spilling out ugly
Over an already devastated heath...

Paul Harvey Jackson, writer and poet
Photograph by Ian Maginess

Deep dark shell craters
Filled with muddy stagnant water
Like putrid pockmarks on some ghastly giant's face
Better by far they were filled
With
Politicians
Or
Generals....

The staccato rattle of maxims
The overhead roar of heavy guns
Nowhere to hide
Rats—thousands, crawling everywhere
Poor dead horses
Shell shocked soldiers
Some too young to shave
Pathetic confused deserters
Rounded up to await a firing squad.

Scurrying stretcher bearers
Field Hospitals
Barely more than tents
Overworked surgeons
Operating by emergency lighting...
Insufficient morphine
Makeshift bandages
Blood-a-plenty...
Padres doing their utmost
For the souls of the dying
Providing succour to the wounded
Injecting hope
Into fragmented bodies...

Insensitive arrogant senior officers
Strutting around in safe places well behind firing lines
Or on horseback
Like so many dim-witted turkey cocks
Full of their own importance.
Field glasses a-swinging
Hip flasks filled with rum—or something stronger
Lions led by donkeys...
Some Hun said
About old Tommy...

The greatest gift God has given us
Is
Not allowing us to see
Into the future
The inability to see...
Wars
Death
Famine
Plague
Or
Other human miseries...

Think about it
I'm sure you will agree...

Sarah Makem

We should attend to any sane voice, particularly that of someone who has flown specially from the United States of America. Tommy Makem shows no sign of fatigue, and is courteous in spite of a stringent schedule.

"I can always find time for Sarah", is his understated tribute to his late mother. The age of the century, Sarah was born in Keady in 1900 and there remained for the rest of her life. "She was the daughter of Thomas and Margaret Boyle, one of seven children, all endowed with a natural gift of music. Apart from Sarah, the other six emigrated to Dover, New Hampshire. Sarah's extended family, including her grandmother, were mill workers, carders, spinners and weavers. Keady and the Callan valley were punctuated with linen mills at the turn of this century. Sarah told us how her parents, on their wedding morning, after a simple ceremony in St Patrick's Church, immediately returned to work. It was then a sporting practice to trap singing birds and my grandfather kept linnets for their pure song. Times were not easy as Sarah's father, Thomas, died at the early age of 42. Her eldest sister Annie was first to emigrate followed by Johnny, Paddy, Tommy, Barney and Molly.

"The Industrial Revolution in England was established by 1850, when a representative of a wealthy American family named Sawyer came to study methods of production. Returning to the USA, he built cotton and woollen manufacturing mills in Dover, New Hampshire. The skills of one master weaver from Keady so impressed the Sawyer family that this man was asked to use his influence to persuading others, equally competent, to emigrate to the 'Granite State' of New Hampshire. Six of the Boyle children responded. In time they would encourage cousins to share new prosperity where the Merrimac and Cocheco rivers were said to turn more spindles and propel more shuttles than any in the world. Sarah's 16-year-old sister, Molly, almost refused entry because of a minor medical problem, found herself in charge of 16 looms within a week of being hired."

Sarah was left behind. "And there in Keady", Tommy contemplates, "she became their anchor—her home in Lirr Street a place to which the family constantly returned. The street name is derived, if I may air my love of Celtic mythology, from King Lír's palace, situated between Keady and Newtownhamilton, a place called Carrigatuke." With the compelling magnetism of an inveterate storyteller, he continues. "Here, it is said, a Druidic school flourished, inspiring young Patrick to found his church on the spot. Looking down the valley, Emhain Macha beckoned, a hypnotic force sufficient to draw Patrick to a fortressed green hill that became the first Christian site in Ireland. That was Armagh."

The Boyle family took their inimitable music to America. Sarah, at home, quite contentedly built on material she'd inherited combined with her own passion for song. "She was also privy to her grandmother's collected songs, learned at the knee. Peter, my father, worked in a Keady scutch mill. He played the fiddle, so for the remainder of her life, Sarah was absorbed in rhythm and melody, especially folk music. Famous Keady dancers were the Kelly family who owned the mill. Ned Kelly could stepdance at the age of 94. Once, when a young man, Ned was asked to demonstrate his skill. Composing intricate steps as he went along, the finale of this dance required he kick the apron of his partner over her head. A tribute to Ned's agility was the fact that he managed this easily. Keady celebrated the festival of Lúnasa, without knowing what it actually was, dancing at the crossroads each last Sunday in July and first Sunday in August—known as 'Blayberry Sunday' (a corruption of blueberry). Sarah danced and sang with young men and girls from our street.

"She was 18 when she married Peter Makem, moving to a flat over Mone's Forge. Of their five children, Jack and Peggy are dead. Mona lives in Omagh where her sons Tom and Jimmy Sweeney formed a professional folk singing trio called Barley Bree. Jimmy lives and sings solo at Halifax, Nova Scotia, while Tom, in Omagh, is a solo folk singer noted for children's concerts and folk music programmes on North West Radio. My youngest sister, Nancy Mone, remains in Keady.

"As Sarah's fame grew she became internationally known for her veritable treasury of songs and a capacity to retain both word and melody. Working in the mill, any new song was quickly absorbed, rippling along the rows of carders, spinners and weavers. I suppose Sarah's voice conformed to soprano scale, all who heard her deeming it natural, even beautiful.

"In 1953, Gloucestershire man Peter Kennedy (whose father Douglas began the English Folksong Society) was introduced to my mother by Seán O'Boyle, a teacher of Irish Language and Geography at St Patrick's College, Armagh. That meeting stretched into a fortnight, my mother singing hundreds of unaccompanied songs, which fascinated Peter. One ballad, *Barbara Allen*, moved him beyond description as Sarah's version was unique. Kennedy's recordings influenced the BBC who then made a programme for World Service transmission, using for its signature tune Sarah's song, *As I Roved Out*.

Much later I met someone who heard this in a bush hospital in Africa. 'I wept for the first time since childhood', that man admitted, 'and when my leg healed, I came to Ireland to tell Sarah myself.' David Hammond of BBC Belfast was another who appreciated her vast gift and promoted Sarah at every opportunity."

Sarah's LP of folk music, recorded for Topic Records, was reissued many times. "This inspired Jean Ritchie from Kentucky, Queen of American Folk Music, and her husband George Pickow to visit Keady, recording some of my mother's repertoire for the booming American folk market. Jean, profusely apologetic at disturbing my mother, was greeted with 'Come in! You're as welcome as the flowers in May!' Like most of her guests, they remained for days. Recently Jean commented on Sarah's warmth and stunning range of music when we were in concert at the Barbican, London.

Another American and top name in folk circles, Diane Hamilton, recorded many of Sarah's songs. Meeting these people whetted a curiosity for the States and Sarah visited New Hampshire several times during the autumn of her life. She never ceased to sing as she went about her work. Times we wanted some peace and quiet but still she sang... it was a compulsion, something she couldn't help. Sarah read quite a lot, loving the work of Annie M.P. Smithson.

"Sarah nursed my grandmother, who was paralysed, for nine years. Only when grandmother died was she free to visit her family. Dover, New Hampshire, now became 'Keady Revisited'", Tommy laughs. "Sarah inspired music from morning to late. My father, although he enjoyed every moment of it, considered they were all crazy. I visited home often, and once, weighted down with banjo and suitcase, had to pick my steps through an entire class of students together with their professor from America. My mother was attempting to make tea for everyone, between singing and discussing her brand of music. These students were furiously scribbling everything she said. My father, amused, commented 'There they were hanging on each word that I just took for granted!'"

By way of definition, Tommy describes his mother as a folk-singer, unlike himself whom he sees as a singer of folk songs. "She couldn't read music yet her contribution will probably prove her to be one of this century's greatest exponents. John Conway, who had a céilí band, taught the fiddle in and about Keady. Each evening our home reverberated to traditional music. I was a pupil of Keady De La Salle Brothers' School where, before my time, Brother Guildus had played the uillean pipes. My brother Jack was too young for this class, but never forgot the sound. I have such regard for this difficult instrument, and uillean players are rare.

When Canon Pentony came to Keady, he replaced an existing choir at St Patrick's Church with male voices. Joining the choir, I learned to read music and, in company with 50 voices, sang liturgical and Gregorian chant. It must have been 1941 for a far-off memory is the sky red with fire as Belfast shipyards were bombed by the Germans."

Leaving school, a young Tommy Makem worked as bookkeeper for Nugent's garage. "Evenings I played the piccolo in a céilí band and was vocalist with Brendan Hughes' Dance Band. Our range was drawn from the Top Forty, lightweight numbers such as *Sixteen Tons* or *Cherry Pink and Apple Blossom White*.

The stage mattered more to me than music so I joined Keady Dramatic Society. We alternated period drama with, perhaps, one of George Sheils' plays, bringing O'Casey's *Shadow of a Gunman* to Carrickmore Drama Festival, winning through to Ireland's prestigious National Festival at Athlone. Top societies enjoyed a week's performances at the Opera House, Belfast. Director of the Old Vic Company and adjudicator, Hugh Hunt, afterwards offered me an audition in London. I declined in favour of Keady's lavish production of Gilbert and Sullivan's *Pirates of Penzance*. When Micheál Mac Liammóir required extras at the Opera House, I chanced upon my first professional part at 30 shillings a week. I wasn't

Sarah Makem's welcoming smile, 1956
Photograph by David Hammond

mobile and Desmond Woods, nephew of local doctor John Woods, lent me his car so I could travel daily to Belfast."

New York and Broadway attracted young Tommy Makem, aspirant thespian, into 'summer stock', performing 11 plays in 12 weeks. "Method acting was in vogue and yet I auditioned successfully without benefit of this studio technique. Moving on to Chicago's Gate of Horn Folk Music and Jazz Club, I was offered 150 dollars to sing for a week, which was then an amazing amount of money."

Stage presence came easily to Tommy Makem, the crowd liked him, and for a time he collaborated with folk singer and actress Robyn Roberts. Tommy met Liam, the youngest Clancy Brother, in company with music collector Diane Hamilton. "Diane returned to Ireland with us, meeting and hearing Sarah Makem for herself."

During the Fifties, Tommy entertained an audience in Newry Town Hall while the McCusker Brothers took a short break. "I asked for a chair, sat down and waited for complete silence before singing *The Cobble*r. Liam Clancy and I later auditioned together in New York but it was 1956 before we teamed with Paddy and Tom as 'The Clancy Brothers and Tommy Makem'. Our first disc of selected Irish rebel songs, on Tradition Records, was called *The Rising of the Moon* and included *Kevin Barry* and *Kelly the Boy from Killane*. The cover won an award, launching us into our next album of folk and traditional, *Drinking Songs*. A new offer from Gate of Horn brought superb reviews in the *Chicago Sun-Times* and security for 43 years."

In 1963 Tommy married his American wife Mary, from Chicago, and they have four children. Daughter Katie works with the Physics Department of the University of New Hampshire. She and her brothers Shane, Conor and Rory are all musically talented. Tommy Makem holds American citizenship and freely admits he would hate to live anywhere else: "The States have been good to me and in any case, I couldn't afford to live here!" He parted amicably from the Clancy Brothers in 1969, embarking on a successful solo singing career.

It was the inspired idea of Tommy's nephew John Makem, careers officer at Keady High School, to found a humorous poetry competition entitled 'The Bard of Armagh'. After only a few years, entries arrived from all over the world, with an audience of six or seven hundred on the final evening.

"John inherited this skill from his father", Tommy says positively. "Humorous songs had a place in traditional music. I'd list *The Waterford Boy* as a fine example of such style. Comic verse such as *Dangerous Dan McGrew* or *The Green Eye of the Little Yellow God* had an avid following. The tradition relates to medieval times, when the bard sat next to the king and was served immediately after. A king was allowed to wear seven colours of clothing, the bard six. Bards were more fortunate for a king might be assassinated, whereas none dare slay a bard. The great skill of Irish bards on the harp was acknowledged everywhere. After the conquest of Ireland by Henry II, many chiefs maintained these minstrels whose songs and legends nurtured national feeling.

"I frequently return to my roots", insists Tommy Makem, and to prove it he intends to hold an International School of Song in celebration of the year 2000. "Mullaghbawn in South Armagh is my proposed venue as this area requires positive regeneration. I hope to entice musicians from every part of the world and attract cross-community participation. How wholesome if this area of outstanding natural beauty might become steeped in poetry and song. Irish poet Art McCooey is buried in nearby Creggan Church of Ireland graveyard. Historically this was once O'Neill territory in South Armagh, belonging to cousins of Red Hugh of Tyrone. A recently discovered vault contained ancestral bones of the O'Neill family. On examination, these bones bore signs of violent death.

Perhaps my venture might spur Navan 'fort' (Emhain Macha), the most important archaeological site in Western Europe, to pursue a similar idea. Armagh, with Barcelona and Rome, were described by medieval scholar, Arsène Dermesteter, as the three greatest cities and centres of learning and culture in Europe. Renowned for theology, poetry, music and literature, Armagh will, I am convinced, reverberate with greatness once more. We can make it happen if we combine in the name of things that are good, turning our backs on what is evil."

Sarah Makem died in 1984 but her talent, wit and invention live on in a new Makem generation. "Stephanie Makem, my great-niece, has collated Sarah's material which she plans to launch in 2000 AD. My mother was undoubtedly one of the greatest exponents of her craft so Stephanie's collection will prove a compelling memorial."

No higher tribute can be paid to a musical woman with

extraordinary power of recall. Hers was a story that begged to be written.

Through her son, Sarah Makem's intonations beckon us to share her life: '*Come in*', she is smiling, '*you're welcome as the flowers in May!*'

Ursula and Hugo McArdle

Funerals are for the living. A funeral provides family and friends with an opportunity to acknowledge and celebrate the life of the deceased. It is a ceremony that allows us express sorrow at our loss. Just as one life must make way for the next, it is fresh faces of a fourth generation who now capably control the family firm of J.J. McArdle & Sons, Funeral Directors and Embalmers.

Spring 1999 was a milestone for the family firm when Ursula McArdle became its first woman director. Now, brother and sister team, Hugo and Ursula McArdle, competently assume funeral arrangements in newly updated premises while offering that quality of discretion for which J.J. McArdle has always been known.

Ursula is a confident young woman qualified in Business Studies. She points out: "Many women now carry out the responsibilities of funeral directors. I agree it is a rather unique calling, one requiring sensitivity and genuine sympathy. The newly bereaved, often in a state of shock, are emotionally vulnerable. For the immediate family, those first few days following death are busy and confusing. We, as professionals, can advise as how best to make arrangements in keeping with personal needs. This can take place at home or here, in our funeral premises, and does involve a number of decisions."

Directors Hugo and Ursula know they themselves can draw on backing and support from their parents, Gerald and Patricia. A past president of the National Association of Funeral Directors in NI, Gerald McArdle has also been president of the Irish Association of Funeral Directors and chairman of the British Institute of Embalming in NI.

The funeral of Cardinal MacRory in 1945 set a precedent for the business of J.J. McArdle. Hugo can vouch for more than 100 years at 37 Thomas Street. "My great-grandfather, John Joseph McArdle, who founded the business, was born in 1864, not long after the Great Famine. He was a joiner. Some say he made a coffin for the child of a neighbour, transporting the family to the funeral by horse and cart. John Joseph became Armagh's first funeral director, his business sited on the corner of Primrose Hill and Upper Irish Street, now Culdee Street. John Joseph married Jane Boyle, a local woman, moving to Thomas Street at the turn of the century. They reared a family of eight children—Jack, Patrick, my grandfather Hugh, Michael, Joseph, Bridget, Vincent and Cissy. In the course of his life, my great-grandfather witnessed the rise and fall of 27 prime ministers, from Viscount Palmerston to Clement Attlee who was in power at the time of John Joseph's death. Closer to home, he followed the progress of Charles Stewart Parnell, 'uncrowned King of Ireland', and the founding of the Irish Free State under W.T. Cosgrave.

"Two of his sons, Patrick and Michael, with my grandfather, Hugh, assumed the running of the business in 1940. Hugh lived at premises now occupied by Oliver's fruit and vegetable store in Thomas Street. It was there my father, Gerald, grew up with his brother Ben and sisters, Frances and Mary." Gerald McArdle attended St Patrick's College as a boy, singing in the Cathedral choir. Joining the family business in 1966, he was the only person in Ireland to win a two-year scholarship to Eckels College of Mortuary Science in Philadelphia. It was then an outstanding achievement.

"I hadn't travelled beyond the British Isles", Gerald contributes, "so naturally, the prospect of going to America was thrilling. I set out from Dublin in an ageing Constellation aircraft. Refuelling brought us down at Gander in Newfoundland. Leaving for New York, we encountered a hurricane. Amid violent turbulence, passengers flung from their seats, I felt positive this award would bring my demise. Still we weathered it, landing safely.

"It was the beginning of two superb years", he recalls. "Philadelphia is cosmopolitan. Railroads and the mining industry had combined to produce a mixed workforce, Hungarian, Italian, German and Irish. I was based with a Jewish family called Levine. When I wasn't studying, I assisted at their funeral home. What wonderful people the Levines were. Jewish humour is distinct, infectious and intelligent. When a funeral took place on an overcast day, the senior partner would look skyward, gesture helplessly, commenting, 'Rain... I ask you? Who needs it?' Before long I was reciting Kaddish, the prayer for the dead, in Hebrew and acquiring an understanding of Jewish culture. After work we often ate at a kosher restaurant on Church

Directors Ursula and Hugo McArdle
of J.J. McArdle and Sons
Photograph by Philip Wilson

Avenue. The speciality was gefilte fish and chopped liver. I was happy amongst my Jewish fraternity and sometimes ponder the anguish their race endured. Rabbi Hugo Gryn survived the Holocaust to become a powerful voice with the BBC. He once said what the Nazis did was a denial of God. It was also a denial of humanity."

In handing over responsibility to Hugo and Ursula, Gerald adds some highly individual memories. "One Saturday afternoon, driving for Levine's, I encountered an unbelievably large crowd waving banners. A policeman ordered me to pull over and wait. Minutes later, President John F. Kennedy walked right by me. It was about that time he prevented the USSR from building nuclear missile bases on Cuba. Within the year he would be assassinated. Today I can hardly believe his own son, also John Kennedy, has just died, tragically lost at sea." Gerald graduated from Eckels College of Mortuary Science with an Honours Diploma, then the only person in Ireland to hold the award.

"Levine's business passed to Samuel Brodski and we remain the best of friends. I returned to London, working for a time with a funeral director on Holloway Road. It was a dismal place, none of the brightness of Levine's, Eckels College or, indeed, Philadelphia. News of my father's death brought me back to Armagh in 1962. Two uncles were running the business when I returned to Thomas Street. I more or less slotted back into the community, joining the Cathedral Choir and St Joseph's Musical Society. Performances were supported by all, not to mention the talent employed in productions. I enjoyed dancing and wouldn't have missed the Royal Showband or the Clipper Carlton. I was proud to meet singer Frank Patterson, but in my estimation, Count John McCormack will always remain Ireland's finest tenor."

Traditionally the McArdle family has been entrusted with funerals involving responsibility, such as that of Cardinal John Francis D'Alton, who died when returning from London in February 1963. "We were contacted immediately. It was a nerve-wracking experience", Gerald admits. "However my training in America gave me confidence and I knew we could comply with all formal requirements. Driving to Dublin, we brought the Cardinal's remains to Armagh. In O'Connell Street, our hearse was flanked by officers of the Irish Army who escorted us to the suburbs, with my Uncle Michael driving. At major towns along the route, a fresh escort met the cortege as people paid their last respects. Conditions were wintry and a blizzard made driving almost impossible. This was my first experience of a funeral on such a scale and one journey I shall never forget. Cardinal D'Alton had already designated his plot at the side of the Cathedral. After the protocol of lying in state, we completed the burial."

Gerald and Patricia, then a nurse, were married in 1964. "Patricia empathised in a special way with the newly bereaved and her contribution to the firm has been exceptional."

Weddings now became a major part of McArdle business, turning heads with a distinctive white Daimler or glittering Mercedes. Cardinal Conway's funeral on 22 April 1977 was, for Gerald, much less traumatic. "From Ara Coeli, we conveyed the Cardinal's remains to the Cathedral. It was hugely attended by Cardinals from throughout the world, President Hillary, An Taoiseach Mr Cosgrave, Lord Glentoran representing the Queen and Roy Mason attending as Secretary of State."

In May 1990, Gerald received instructions to meet the cortege of the late Cardinal Ó Fiaich at Dublin airport. "It was reminiscent of Cardinal D'Alton's death, but now older and wiser, I took it in my stride. We were waiting on the runway when the aircraft landed, and, for the fourth time, we bore a Cardinal to his final resting place."

In the world of sport, Gerald McArdle is past president of the Pearse Óg club in Armagh. Devoted to the GAA, he attends all Armagh county team events. Paying tribute to the late Joe Houlahan who was goalkeeper and played for the county, he comments: "Joe was a gentleman of the game, a loss Armagh feels acutely. Gerald, his grand-nephew, upholds the tradition and is a joy to watch on the field."

John Nichol from Railway Street, Armagh, was this city's only local fireman to die in the course of his duty, in 1976. "We carried the flowers in our hearse", Gerald recalls. "John's coffin was borne on the fire engine following behind. Details of this funeral were amongst records we managed to salvage after our premises were bomb-damaged. We particularly treasure what has survived."

Of the other McArdle family members, Liam conducts his own business. He and his wife, Jacqueline, have two children, seven-year-old Aoife, and Maeve, who is just three. Eldest daughter Anne-Marie is a teacher at Mount

St Catherine's School. She and her husband, Paul, have two children, four-year-old Conal and baby Caoimhe. Carmel, youngest daughter of the McArdle family, is a student.

Here, in the quiet confidences of this account you have met a family who are sympathetic to individual needs, capable of bringing solace to the most tragic situation. A family adept at taking over and looking after everything.

Vera Magee

Armagh-born wartime heroine Vera Magee, who died in May 1998, had an unfulfilled wish to see her story in print. Honoured by President Clinton in October 1997, Vera was later introduced to the First Lady at the University of Ulster at Jordanstown. At that meeting, Hillary Clinton requested that this account be sent to the White House.

On her 90th birthday, Vera Magee showed everyone how indomitable she could be. Just six weeks earlier she had undergone major surgery for cancer diagnosed in 1996, yet she celebrated with guests until the small hours. Vera's secluded room at Patrick's Fold reveals a collector. Books have outgrown shelf space, *objets d'art* cram every nook. A spice jar from Lille jostles with a plaster cast of Delacroix. "The dealer marked it down to 75 francs", Vera shrugs. "He saw me coming!"

Elegant, alert, hair stylishly bobbed, she speaks of an austere childhood. "I was born on 12 July 1907, one of four—Jack, myself, Molly and Eileen. After my father died of tuberculosis, mother eked a living by taking boarders. She died before my 11th birthday. We girls were sent to the nearest convent. I am trying to be fair but Irish orphanage existence at the time had overtones of Jane Eyre's hardship in Lowood Institution. Our clothing came second-hand, donated from outside, and convent food was unappetising. Winters were bitter and, unlike other children, we did not have boots to keep us warm. At once I was separated from my sisters and we rarely met again. Birthdays went unmarked and other than Mass, Christmas was not celebrated. None of us ever received a gift or card. A foster family took care of my sister Molly each school holiday but I remained within convent gates for more than six years. One morning just after my 17th birthday, Mother Superior summoned me to her office.

"'Prepare to leave for France tomorrow', she instructed crisply, 'you are to become governess to the Duprez family, near Lille'. She indicated a passport, one sovereign and a small suitcase. There was no time for farewells. As those tall convent gates swung behind me, I looked back frantically but not a glimpse of my sisters could I see.

"Most of my journey passed in a haze. I clutched that precious sovereign for it was all I had. You must understand we knew nothing of things worldly, nor the facts of life. A relative of our Mother Superior met me at Victoria Station where, in return for a night's lodgings, I handed over my precious coin. Don't people speak in terms of 'three car families' today? I possessed a cardboard suitcase and some faded clothing.

"Here I am on a train for the first time in my life, travelling to Dover. It is autumn, fields of ripening grain rushing towards me, swiftly passing to oblivion. Wheels and track seemed to clack in unison, a rhythm instilled in my memory for all time.

Only reapers, reaping early
In among the bearded barley,
Hear a song that echoes cheerly
From the river winding clearly.

"Admiration of Tennyson and his scheme of repeated rhyme was a happier legacy from Convent days. Besides", she reflects, "I felt I was, like his *Lady of Shallott*, travelling into the unknown." From Calais Maritime, Vera journeyed to Lille. "The family did not meet me as promised. I waited at the station until half-past midnight when a concerned passer-by saw my plight. Accompanying me by taxi to Tourcoing, I rang the bell of an imposing chateau and was admitted by a parlour maid. That young benefactor disappeared and we never met again.

"My unruly charges were the children of a wealthy industrialist and they lacked for nothing. I assumed total responsibility when they returned daily from lessons at Nôtre-Dame-des-Anges. Now extravagance ousted austerity for this family lived and entertained lavishly. Monsieur kept an impressive entourage of servants including an accomplished cook. I shall never forget that first meal at my new home, which began with mushroom vol-au-vent, salad with dressing and baguette. Cherry clafoutis followed and at a civilised interval, café noir. I enjoyed four hours freedom once a fortnight when I met my contemporaries at a street café. All of us were governesses from either Europe or England. Someone from Ireland was rare. Over coffee we'd discuss work conditions or jobs on offer. Back on duty I'd find the children had hidden my things in a spirit of good fun!"

Vera Magee meets First Lady Hillary Clinton at the University of Ulster, Jordanstown, October 1997
Official White House photograph

Vera's linguistic talents were such that within four years she moved to Lille and began private tutoring. As rumour became stark reality, France surrendered to invading German troops in 1940. "We knew General de Gaulle had escaped to England where he set up a Free French Government", Vera recalls. "Then, on 1 March 1941, an edict from German headquarters, the *Kommandantur*, ordered all British citizens living in the vicinity to assemble at Central Station. For the second time in my life I packed enough clothing for a few days. A similar order had summoned millions to their deaths, but, like my neighbours, I was unaware how grim a memorial this Third Reich was carving on the face of Europe. One German soldier called out names from a list and we were pushed unto buses, then taken by train to St Remychaussée. On that fearful journey, a soldier staring directly at me sneered, *'England kaput!'* Rashly I retaliated, *'Hitler kaput!'* 'You'll get us all shot', someone hissed. Our train thundered into a tunnel, distracting the guard so my crime went unpunished. We were to be taken east, bound for one of the camps, but, due to a misunderstanding, disembarked outside St Remychaussée. I was placed under house arrest reporting weekly to the area Commandant. Each partisan victory brought punishment deportations, so fear was a constant companion. It has to be said we were considerably better off than the Jews or thousands of French nationals. Radios were confiscated and war news suppressed until the Normandy landings, June 1944. After the Liberation, the American Forces formed the Railway Transportation Organisation, calling for skilled interpreters. Quite the happiest years of my life were those spent with the RTO.

"I had transferred to Metz, one of a team of 12, when the stationmaster called me aside. 'It's a special assignment', he whispered. He brought me to his office where Generals Patton and Bradley were present. I was required to translate details of urgent troop and munition movements. Towering over me, General George Patton asked if I'd heard of a comedy couple, popular then in the States, 'Fibber and Molly Magee'. 'Do you mind if I call you Magee?' he smilingly asked. To the Nazi regime, Patton was the most hated, most feared general of World War II. Ruthless as he was, we worked amicably and, our assignment complete, he presented me with a leather-covered box of chocolates. You can imagine the luxury of chocolate after five years of war."

Historically razor-sharp, Vera remembers de Gaulle's leadership restored in Paris, late 1944, the new National Assembly and Council of the Republic. Working in diplomatic circles brought knowledge of future Presidents Pompidou and Mitterrand. Vera's linguistic abilities next led to a post-wartime appointment with the British Consulate at Strasbourg. "I fell in love with a rather handsome French teacher and we married in 1952. Sadly our alliance didn't last. Still", she continues, "I had friends in the Council of Europe and remained there, working on a regular basis."

Returning to Armagh, the town of her birth, Vera's health is uncertain. "Of course there are aspects of 'La Belle France' which I miss", she adds, "a glass of chilled Sylvaner (a favourite white wine), the language that grew to be mine, or something as simple as freshly-grown endive."

In a life of novel dimension, Vera's wish is that this precious personal history be preserved after her death. As a Vera replies, drawing herself up regally, *"je ne regrette rien...* I regret nothing..."

Ulster Television presenter Pamela Ballantine met her, and described Vera's life as "the most memorable of my entire experience". Armagh County Museum has preserved this account together with Vera's portrait by local artist Jackie Connolly.

Kieran Grimley

"This evening represents a monument in our history", commented Kieran Grimley, president of Armagh Conference of the Society of St Vincent de Paul, when Archbishop Seán Brady unveiled a plaque on 16 October 1997 officially opening the new headquarters at Ogle Street, the birthplace of Malachy the Scribe. For more than 100 years the Armagh Conference has reinforced a vital principle on which this organisation is founded, *'I was hungry and you gave me to eat'*. Working quietly in the face of tragedy, most recently the plight of Kosovan refugees, St Patrick's Conference raised an emergency fund that amounted to an unbelievable £23,500 within a day! The appeal took the form of a church door collection and the money was handed over to parish Administrator Father Richard Naughton, who forwarded a cheque to the Sisters of Charity in that region.

Elected to the office of president in 1994, Kieran was introduced to the Society by fellow member Charles Brady. "I'd been working for my family butchery business but here I discovered my true vocation", he says, smiling broadly, "the collection and distribution of furniture. Visiting a home where hardship exists is a sobering experience, particularly the needs of elderly or infirm. All we are attempting to do, in our small way, is sustain the message of Vincent who, despite hardship and humiliation, went on giving. The Armagh Conference subscribes to the same spirit", affirms Kieran.

The Society was founded in Paris during 1833 and Armagh Conference has records dating to 1870. Kieran provides some necessary background. "St Vincent de Paul died in Paris, an old priest of 80 years. It was in the reign of Louis XIV and a lonely death for one who dominated the life of Paris for four decades. Where the poor were, St Vincent could be found. In homes, prisons, even on the battlefield."

Local greengrocer and vice-president, Joe Sherry, is affectionately described as 'Armagh's father of St Vincent de Paul'. "The poor teach us what true religion really is", Kieran acknowledges, "and Joe Sherry's private and humane input to the Society is beyond measure. Some 32 years ago, Greta Campbell asked him to join and Joe said he'd help in the background. After attending a meeting he saw how deeply the Conference cared for any less fortunate and signed on. Within a year, Joe became president. A term of three years in office can be doubled but the spirit of the Society never alters. All members try to lead decent lives. There is no law stating we must be saints but Vincentians should be conscious of their own standards if their aim is to help others. Joe, who is well known, makes a point of visiting as many as possible. He sings with Portadown Male Voice Choir and cross-community links with local businessmen are reflected in generous Christmas hamper collection and distribution. Joe and his wife Kathleen had their own personal sorrow. He understands more than most and makes a point of sharing a friendly word with all regular contributors besides conveying gratitude on behalf of the Society.

"Committee member Charles Brady has been with the Armagh Conference for 17 years", Kieran continues. "Charles had just retired and decided he would undertake voluntary church work. With its acutely Christian ethos, St Vincent de Paul appealed to him. Kathleen McCurdie, Briege McKenna and Charles were local hospital visitors. Each Sunday morning they delivered newspapers to Tower Hill and for many years Charles served on a team of collectors outside St Patrick's Cathedral. Armagh people", he would say, "are the essence of generosity. One man drops a ten pound note in my box weekly, going quietly on his way. Today we see the 'new poor' due to redundancy, perhaps a large mortgage to meet, therefore financial stress. At our Tuesday Conference meeting which begins with prayer, we open correspondence, considering requests for help in strictest confidence. There is no shame in being poor. Often it is a caring neighbour who designates a need. People still care."

Paying tribute to long-serving member, 76-year-old Joe Kelly of Ogle Street, Kieran Grimley says, "Like myself, Joe's forte was collecting and distributing furniture to families in need. While social deprivation may be less prevalent today, Joe would contend we are poorer spiritually. Many, he feels, are out of touch with God's laws. Lacking a moral code leads to lack of respect for civil law. Joe still attends daily Mass at St Malachy's and says he feels a personal sense of loss, if, for any reason he cannot be present. He resigned four years ago but St Vincent de Paul remained his chief interest. He watched almost as if he were foreman, when our new building took shape. That opening evening, on the site of St Malachy's birthplace, saw Joe's dream realised."

Committee members contribute individually to the overall success of this thriving Centre. "Jim McWilliams devotes his talents to furniture collection and restoration", Kieran points out. "People buy something new and rather than discard the old, telephone our Society which collects clean, presentable household goods. Jim probably will know a family or individual who will be glad of these items, perhaps as a temporary measure until finding their feet. His help can be counted on in times of need. When it comes to finance, a strict code governs donations placed in collection boxes. Allocated to the poor, this cannot be used for any other purpose."

Swift to acknowledge the work and input of women, Kieran as President points to Sister Margaret Ranaghan, a retired teacher from St Catherine's College and former member of St Vincent de Paul in Aberdeen. "Sister Ranaghan has been associated with the Armagh Conference since the middle Eighties. At any given time, over 100,000 Irish lives are touched by the Society in some respect. Sister Ranaghan has been a regular visitor, calling on the lonely or elderly, and St Patrick's Conference wouldn't be the same without her cheerful ways. Our Committee represents all occupations", smiles Kieran. "We have a hatchery manager with Armagh Fisheries Limited, Turlough Toner, who would describe himself as 'the money man'! Income must balance with expenditure or we're all in trouble. Workers contribute time and skills voluntarily so donations are all-found. Due to his financial expertise, Turlough was recently elected area president. Turlough's late father, the last member of the 1926 Junior GAA team, was a driver for James Trodden's Taxis—he took local priests to Mass each Sunday and taught the late Bishop O'Callaghan to drive. Turlough began collecting for St Vincent de Paul in 1976, advancing to book-keeping. With the aid of a second-hand computer, he kept finances in check. The voluntary post of treasurer came his way in 1987 and we are presently on an even keel. Our thrift shop should generate new funds, another source of help for those in need. Clean, new and nearly new bric-a-brac, toys and clothing are always gratefully received. Perhaps the public will keep children in mind as Christmas draws closer. Our financial boat is rolling on calm waters but the season of goodwill places a strain on resources."

Area secretary Victor Shaw, who runs Armagh Colour Copy Shop, has been with St Vincent de Paul for nine years. Victor copes with incoming requests. As government help is withdrawn from the most vulnerable in society, appeals for help increase. "Discretion attends each aspect of our business. I have seen those helped by the Society overcome difficulties, and in turn, donate to others", Kieran adds. "Conference members never disclose privileged information, and have a sixth sense when it comes to searching out those in need. We are non-denominational and it is a source of pride when those of other faiths ask for help or make donations. Conference secretary Damian Duffy keeps all minutes of meetings and constantly updates correspondence. Damian's speciality is the raising of funds by annually playing against the Lord's Taverners' Benevolent Fund. Most of our members have formed a team known affectionately as 'Red Ned's Tavern' of Ogle Street and we will attempt to bowl one over on the Taverners this coming Friday. Funds will contribute to the buying of a minibus for a children's charity."

Kieran returns to that evening in 1997, when 19-21 Ogle Street officially became the headquarters of St Patrick's Conference. "It was particularly eventful for deserving members who were presented with Vincentian Medals by Archbishop Brady. These were Joe McKee, Joe Sherry, Charles Brady, Brigín McKenna, Eileen Fitzgerald, Kathleen McAleavey (since deceased), Greta and Joe Campbell, Kathleen McCurdie, Paddy McArdle and Joe Kelly. I suppose the evening culminated in sheer relief for Brendan McGuirk who has served with the Society as project officer. Brendan's task in overseeing the building from inception to completion lasted three years. Contractor, Smalls of Dungannon, with architect Ivan Marshall and quantity surveyor Jarleth McAleavey, all worked on our behalf. Most importantly, Brendan identified funds. We never lose sight of the fact that support is paramount to progress and any need must be backed by facts and figures. Representatives of funding bodies that we had only known as names on a sheet of paper were present on that evening. Of prime importance to our cause, Graham Thompson, from the International Fund for Ireland, spoke of his pride on seeing a development project through to fruition. It was also

Kieran Grimley, President of St Patrick's Conference of St Vincent de Paul Society, receives a copy of Steps on my Pilgrim Journey from His Eminence Cardinal Cahal B. Daly
Photograph by Michael Campbell, LBIPP

revitalisation within an area of deprivation. Now the Armagh Conference continues its good work with a decent roof overhead and houses a Thrift Shop managed by Joe Sherry, a private Oratory open to those of all faiths, committee rooms and a small museum of artefacts."

Kieran Grimley gives an insight into his own life. "I was one of a butchery family, our name familiar to Armagh people for more than a century. At the time I was born, my father, Francis Grimley, ran the business in Thomas Street. Educated at Christian Brothers' School, Greenpark, Armagh, I then joined the civil service, working at Whitehall, London. It was 1967 when my father asked me to come home and join him in the business. Trading habits changed and for him it was a sad occasion when we closed the shop in 1987. I was taken on by the butchery department of F.A. Wellworths of Thomas Street where I was promoted to manager. It was in 1997 I became a traffic warden in Armagh, so I wasn't courting popularity", Kieran says with a wry smile.

Recently promoted to senior warden, he pays tribute to his team. "It's not a job for 'Mr Nice Guy' yet it is vital to the smooth running of traffic in the city. If everyone abandoned vehicles how and where they liked, mayhem would ensue. Indeed it often does. There is no pleasant way to tell someone they've been illegally parking for the last hour and an inventive public never runs out of excuses. One woman assured me she had lost her false teeth and, searching for them, forgot about her car. Another, clutching an empty cage, claimed the family guinea pig had escaped. Someone else met a former girlfriend and spent too long attempting to rekindle a former romance. His dalliance cost him £20! If we don't keep a check on allotted parking times no-one will find parking space. There are of course genuine reasons and we do try to be fair."

Returning to his great commitment as President, Kieran Grimley reminds, "We are one family under the umbrella of the Ozanam foundation, trying to live decently, helping where possible. May I express the Conference's appreciation of the vital role played by our local population, and that means every denomination. Without such generosity we would not exist." In each and every aspect, it is abundantly clear, the Armagh Conference upholds and honours the principles of St Vincent de Paul. Meeting Kieran Grimley convinces one that the true spirit of St Vincent lives on. With such a foundation St Patrick's Conference in Armagh cannot but do likewise.

Sheelagh Woods

It is a summer afternoon and peace pervades the garden at the home of Dr Sheelagh Woods, MB, BCh, BAO. A pioneer in her profession, Dr Sheelagh relaxes with friends Kathleen Bunting, Connie Lennon and Etta Mullan. With quiet contemplation she shares a cutting from the *Irish Times*, a report of the closing of Loreto Abbey, her old school, at Rathfarham, Dublin. Now approaching her 91st birthday, Dr Sheelagh was a pupil of the Abbey, leaving in the mid-Twenties.

"The Sisters were instructed to rule with kindness", she says. "Right from the mid-1800s they had a remarkable prospectus, offering European languages and extracurricular tuition on the harp, piano, vocal music and art. Many pupils went out as missionaries and that could mean leaving home forever. Social graces were strictly observed and no lady ever ran within the school. Talking in corridors was strictly forbidden. We were all quite docile, I suppose, conforming to a Victorian image of how young ladies should behave. The closure of Loreto Abbey does bring a certain sadness for here was a great tradition of empowering women through education."

Sheelagh was one of only five women to graduate in medicine from Queen's University, Belfast, in 1930. "Returning to Dublin, I undertook postgraduate work at Holles Street Maternity Hospital. My father, Dr Michael Deeny, ran a family practice in Lurgan, assisted by my brothers, Jim and Donnell. The practice had grown to such an extent that my father was overworked and he invited me to join them. It was he who influenced my decision to enter the medical profession and how right he was", she observes, "for I have loved my life." Caring passionately is an essential factor, bringing its own reward.

Anecdotes from Dr Sheelagh's life in the early Thirties may be of social interest. "My brother Jim owned an old sailing boat and with his fisherman friend, Hugh McAlinden, often went out on Lough Neagh before dawn. When part of the face of a bluff collapsed at Castor Bay, Lough Neagh, Jim was able to identify bones of red deer among the debris. This was right under an old house where John Wesley stayed and preached when he visited Lurgan. One of Jim's favourite recreations was Armagh Ramblers' Club, run by Museum curator T.G.F. Paterson."

A reference to T.G.F. Paterson is contained in James Deeny's book *To Cure and To Care—Memoirs of a Chief Medical Officer,* published in 1989: "...a most unusual man, pretty well self-educated, who ended up a great scholar. He was elected a Member of the Royal Irish Academy and received an Honorary Degree as Master of Arts from Queen's University. Apart from this, he was a thoroughly decent man, beloved by all. I used to slip away from the practice and go on outings with Paterson..."

"It may be of interest", she adds, "that my brother Donnell was an enthusiastic horseman and master of North Armagh Harriers for many years."

When her father introduced her to Dr John Woods from Keady, he little thought this eligible young man would become his son-in-law. "I came to Armagh, joining my husband's practice on the Mall", resumes Dr Sheelagh. "It was 1933, a difficult time in the profession, what with a mistrust of women doctors and any new or innovative methods. Through midwifery and antenatal care I came to know my patients. One doctor told me he attempted to count the number of babies he had delivered while a GP in Lurgan, estimating 300 a year. Nearly 60 years in practice, I hesitate to do likewise and yet the actual number would be interesting."

Harsh conditions prevailed in Dr Sheelagh's early days of general practice. "There was such poverty. Many homes were without running water, proper sanitation, heating or electricity. More than once I had to dig myself free of a snowdrift and during severe winters, brought a spade and sacking when called to homes in surrounding villages. More than once a new baby, taking its time to arrive, necessitated my staying, one occasion for the entire night. The family made up a settle bed for me in front of a turf fire."

Many of the babies Dr Sheelagh delivered are prominent citizens today. "I'd never embarrass anyone but smile recalling that I'd been first to hold this person in my arms. War came and went, heralding the National Health Service. Free medical treatment benefited the socially deprived as did antibiotics and excellent hospital care. From the Fifties, living standards began to improve; running water and sanitation changing for the better the lives of those who were deprived. Diseases of poverty—scarletina, diphtheria and tuberculosis—had virtually disappeared, while infant mortality was dramatically reduced. General practice care came under review, as did the grouping of dispensaries and clinics. With my husband, we worked as a team and, in turn, three of our four children embraced medical careers. Our son Oliver, who had studied at Queen's University, joined the practice during the early Sixties. Further change came in 1969, when city medical practices moved to new purpose-built accommodation at Armagh Health Centre."

Her accomplished playing of the cello and love of orchestral music constituted a major interest throughout Dr Sheelagh's life. "We used to have this pleasant little trio which comprised of Maud Stewart on piano, Peggy Herriot (who died in September 1999) played the violin, with myself on the cello. We'd meet alternately in each home, but, regretfully, this ceased with the passing of time. My daughter Sheelagh has carried on both family traditions of music and medicine. Sheelagh plays the harp, as did my mother, and is most accomplished."

An inspiring woman who could never bear to be idle, Dr Sheelagh became a founder member of Armagh Soroptimist Club. Dr John Woods was a keen golfer and Dr Sheelagh joined County Armagh Golf Club in 1933. She has the distinction of being its longest serving member. "I was lady captain in 1938, and exactly 50 years later, received a gold captain's brooch from lady captain Máire O'Neill. I still attend an occasional Club function and my 90th birthday party was held there on Thursday 3 September 1998. Current president, Jack O'Hare, was exceptionally kind to me in his historical work, *The Centenary Story*, a rather handsome history of County Armagh Golf Club, published in 1993."

Dr Sheelagh's many interests included serving on the Arts Committee, Armagh City and District Floral Art Society, the Bridge Club, Armagh City Orchestra, voluntary service with Dr Barnardo's charity shop and decades of enjoyable music shared with local operatic societies.

Dr Sheelagh and Dr John were joined at the inception of the National Health Service in 1948 by Dr Richard O'Reilly. When John died in 1972, Sheelagh continued in the family practice at Armagh Health Centre with her son, Dr Oliver Woods. Dr Patrick Kellett and Richard O'Reilly's son, Dr Gary O'Reilly also joined the practice, maintaining the level of care for which the Woods family was renowned. Continued expansion included medical, nursing, and secretarial staff who retained personal concern for each patient's welfare in a highly professional manner.

Of her other children, Dr Sheelagh explains, "Bronagh was a dietician in Portland, Oregon, but diverted to the world of real estate. Sheelagh is a consultant anaesthetist in London while Aiveen is a clinical psychologist in Bombay, India. Representing a third generation of Woods family in the medical profession, Cecilia and Oliver's son, my grandson John D., researched renal and heart disease in the United States and is now a consultant with Belfast City Hospital. My grand-daughter Kathy is an anaesthetist at Royal Gwent Hospital in Newport, Wales. I maintain family links by spending time with Oliver, his wife Cecilia and my youngest grandson Daniel, a student at St Patrick's Grammar School."

Beyond the garden of what was Dr Sheelagh's home at the time of this interview are the verdant greens of County Armagh Golf Club, and the Archbishop's Palace. "And yet the view isn't a patch on that seen from the music room upstairs", she informs. "Here, French windows open onto a small veranda, revealing the green heart of this city." *Le Cygne* by Camille Saint-Saëns remains Dr Sheelagh's favourite work, something she has often played on her cello. At the age of 75, Dr Sheelagh survived open-heart surgery. Following convalescence she returned to work for a further five years. By retirement she had completed more than six decades as a medical practitioner. It is significant that Dr Sheelagh is the last remaining member of her generation of the Deeny family. In October 1994, the *British Medical Journal* carried an outstanding obituary of Dr James Deeny. This 'ebullient doctor' held a central role in health services in the Republic of Ireland and the World Health Organization. Dr Sheelagh had always followed her brother's career with interest and retained excerpts from an appreciation of Dr Deeny in the *Irish Times,* dated 3 May 1994: "James Deeny directed projects for the World Health Organization for varying periods; national tuberculosis surveys in Sri Lanka in 1956 and in British Somaliland in 1957, and chief of mission in Indonesia 1958-60. Many times he was recalled on short-term consultancies to the World Health Organization in Geneva, Syria and the USSR. One of his most prestigious consultancies was his appointment as scientific advisor to

Dr Sheelagh Woods at the christening
of her great-grand-daughter Isabel Louise Jenkins

the Holy See for the years 1971-72. He was a member of a three-man team appointed by the Holy Father to advise on a scheme for the co-ordination of over 1,000 major Catholic charities throughout the world."

One of the last receptions given by Mayor Pat Brannigan in his year of office, 1997, was held in honour of Dr Sheelagh Woods. Mayor Brannigan commented: "Her contribution to the health and welfare of the people of Armagh has been outstanding."

One cannot help being won over by the ease and good-humoured charm of a woman whose professional identity was always 'Dr Sheelagh'. "If I've loved my life", she reiterates, "do say the most rewarding part was reaching out to people, connecting with them."

Armagh Voices
a celebration of a century

1910 ~ 1920

The Youth of a Nation
are the Trustees of Posterity

Benjamin Disraeli

Selwyn Tarleton

Investigations by Guinness Publishing in London have just established that Armagh-born Selwyn Tarleton, MBE, holds a world record, having 75 years unbroken service as a male chorister. Archbishop Eames paid tribute to this veteran of St Patrick's Church of Ireland Cathedral Choir on Sunday 25 September 1999, when Selwyn was appointed Honorary Lay Canon, one of a complement of six in Ireland.

A former director of Portadown Football Club, Selwyn has had a busy social life of late. At a gala civic event, this former organiser of Armagh Boys' Club was declared joint winner of the Contribution to Sport Award. To tremendous applause, Mayor Robert Turner presented him with an engraved gift of crystal.

If Selwyn's work bringing sporting opportunities to local youth accounted for half a lifetime, choral music and years of service to the Cathedral Choir made it complete. Asked to share his memorable moments, Selwyn doesn't hesitate: "Watching Glasgow Celtic win the European Cup during the Seventies. I've always organised my annual summer holiday around the European Cup so that Milan and Barcelona became familiar territory. If it's a question of music, two inspired works encompass my idea of perfection. These are *Awake Thou That Sleepest*—Sir John Stainer's oratorio from *Daughter of Jairus*—and Gounod's *Unfold Ye Portals Everlasting*, sung by the Mormon Tabernacle Choir."

Aged 89 on his last birthday, this very public figure, who now lives at Sunnymead residential home near Armagh, permits a rare glimpse into his private life. "My father, who came from Derby in 1889, was a professional chorister with the Cathedral Choir. After the death of his first wife, he married Alice Mary Ovens who became stepmother to his three children. Father worked as an assistant clerk at the Probate Registry, a redbrick building adjacent to the courthouse. Initially they lived on Vicar's Hill, moving to Victoria Street as his family grew, and there I was born in April 1910."

Selwyn began private lessons at Richmond High School, Victoria Street, managed by Miss Hogan. "Each denomination looked after the educational needs of its children, prior to the opening of Armstrong Primary School. My education continued at College Street National School, run by the Presbyterian Church. The Methodist Church ran a school hall in Abbey Street while St Mark's Church of Ireland parish held lessons at Church Walk, where the headmaster was Mr Whisker."

All in the Tarleton family were musically gifted. "My mother was a member of Armagh Philharmonic Society, playing the piano professionally and, indeed, quite beautifully. Alice, my sister, inherited her talent. In 1924, at the invitation of organist Dr Chaundy, I joined the Cathedral Choir, singing treble voice, and attended Cathedral Close Grammar School where headmaster James Fanning released the boys daily to sing at Choral Matins. A retainer of 25 shillings, paid quarterly, was then considered a fortune." Selwyn's acute memory recalls an occasion in 1932 when the Archbishop of Canterbury attended St Patrick's Day Service. "I also remember what we sang", he proudly adds, "Stanford B Flat *Te Deum*. It was magnificent!"

His first job in 1928 was the position of clerk at the offices of family firm, D.P. Martin and Company. "Income Tax and Rate Collection staff shared these offices. A bit Dickensian perhaps, but we worked agreeably. Summer evenings and weekends, I'd meet up with local boys on the Mall and organise a football match. To create a football we bundled paper into shape, wrapping it about with string. One evening, watching a game on the Mall just where Sainsbury's store is now situated, Sam Magwood from Milford and his son Jim, came over to chat. It was summer, 1936. During the conversation they asked if I would help to some extent in running of Armagh Whites Football Club, founded at the beginning of the Thirties. Already an ardent supporter of Portadown Football Club, I used to cycle in a group with others who hadn't the bus fare to matches at Shamrock Park. Within a matter of months I found myself representing Armagh Whites on the Mid-Ulster Football Association.

"The chill of winter 1936 persuaded us to look for a clubroom of sorts. My boss, D.P. Martin, rented us a loft behind the Seven Houses in English Street, for one penny a week. This germinated ideas for proper premises. War broke out and I left Armagh in 1940 to join the Royal Air

Force. Training at Hereford, then Blackpool, I remember seeing Max Millar in his prime at the Winter Gardens. Rarely missing a boxing match or wrestling match, I frequently attended variety shows at Blackpool Tower.

"There was an RAF base at Moreton-in-the-Marsh near Morecambe where I was assigned to special duties. Direction and range of aircraft were now detectable by short radio waves, or radar. Information vital to the war effort gathered from operation rooms was collated here, then passed to headquarters in the hope of saving casualties. I'd often meet tradesmen from Armagh who came to this area, earning good wages and sleeping rough whilst on emergency building programmes." With 238 Fighter Squadron, Selwyn served four years in Egypt and Italy, attached to Anti-Aircraft units in the desert. "The pace of life was frenetic. Men we saw today might well be tomorrow's casualties. It may sound gruesome, but personal belongings of dead pilots, especially garments of pure silk, were often auctioned and the proceeds sent on to relatives. One outstanding event for me was joining the United Forces' Choir at Cairo Cathedral in thanksgiving following the battle of El Alamein in 1942. I can still hear the voices of a thousand men, raised in unison, as we thanked God for safe deliverance. Clifford Harcour of Bristol Cathedral was organist. Throughout the war I retained choir attendance as a counter-tenor, never breaking my record which, on retirement, totalled 75 years. Five years of war was enough and I came home in 1945."

Love of sport, particularly football, led to post-war employment that would last for the remainder of Selwyn's working life. "Appointed by the Ministry of Education to manage Armagh Boys' Club in 1946, it was simply a case of taking up where I left off. Our old headquarters in Scotch Street is today Dr Barnardo's charity shop. Here youngsters freely participated in boxing, table tennis, snooker, an athletics team as well as competing in the Mid-Ulster Soccer League. Boys' attendance averaged more than 30 each evening, five nights a week. An example of forward thinking, this scheme prevented many from roaming the streets, teenage drinking or drifting into crime." It was a busy year in 1946, for, throwing his weight behind Armagh Whites, Selwyn also organised team training and fixtures, "wherever a field could be found. One outstanding player was Jim McParland from Markethill, who progressed to Belfast Celtic. Jim realised a dream in following his idol, Jackie Vernon, football hero of the Forties. Jackie played with Belfast Celtic, captained West Bromwich Albion and was capped 17 times by the Irish Football Association. Armagh Whites, Armagh Boys' Club and Armagh British Legion represented the city in the Mid-Ulster League. Armagh Whites also came up trumps as the first city club to reach and win the Irish Football Association Junior Cup in 1947. I found the strain of both organisations too much", Selwyn admits, "and resigned from Armagh Whites in 1949. Sad to say, the club closed in 1950."

He recalls Boys' Club member Raymond Hill who played for Bangor in the Irish League. "And his father before him", Selwyn emphasises; "Billy Hill made the grade with Glenavon from the late Forties until mid-Fifties. Another of ours, Maxie Patton, graduated from top division to play for Glenavon and Ards. Within the Irish Football Association, I had climbed from Chairman of the Junior Committee to the Mid-Ulster Council, becoming Secretary of the Mid-Ulster Youth Committee. Need I say, I hadn't an idle moment! What rejoicing there was when Armagh Boys' Club won the Mid-Ulster Shield in 1960-61. I had now become a director of Portadown Football Club but followed the fortunes of Sheffield United, knowing and admiring two Irish internationals, Billy Gillespie and Jimmy Dunn, who played for the team."

Organised outings were a part of Club life. "A typical summer holiday in 1948 was in Portrush, and then we graduated to educational trips. We became adventurous, taking a group of boys to London during the Festival of Britain, 1951. We were welcomed to Brussels in 1976 by M. Émile Grasser, an official of the Belgian 5th Brigade who served in Armagh during the Second World War. This was only one aspect of the Club. Arts and crafts appealed to many and we had great fun moulding lead soldiers which were then lacquered and sold for fund-raising."

Selwyn speaks affectionately of past members who made a positive contribution. "As a boy, John Creaney, later a QC, joined our discussion club. I like to think this influenced his future career. Ivan Baxter, one of the best I had, was a good all-rounder. Now, in the autumn of my life, Ivan remembers me in thoughtful ways. Desmond Robinson, another of our discussion group and a good musician, had great qualities. Sitting in the lounge at Sunnymead, my thoughts are my own and I'm miles away, recalling times past with nostalgia, all the fun and good-natured banter. My goodness", he shakes his head, "it would make a television series today! Always bright and breezy were Jim Scott, Alton Beck, the late Alan Wilson, Bill Lauder, W.G. Bryans and generations of the Stinson boys. Parents took an active part by forming a fund-raising committee. We bought equipment from the proceeds of beetle drives, jumble sales and sponsored efforts." For half a century, from February 1946 until February 1996, Selwyn's was a name known to generations of boys. Numbers declined and in 1988 membership was extended to local girls, Mrs Edith Webster volunteering to supervise activities. He deliberates. "Times have changed. I doubt if I could succeed today. The game of football is in decline. Players dictate policy and clubs seem unable to maintain discipline. A match no longer means skill on the pitch for the event is too often marred with undesirable elements of vandalism or violence. I am pleased however, to learn that two former Boys' Club members, Billy Irwin and Mervyn Calvin, have taken up the Club name with hopes of its continuity in the future."

Tireless efforts to extend sporting interests for Armagh city youth led to Selwyn's nomination and subsequent award of an MBE. "It was 1976 when I met the Queen at the Palace. 'How do you get on so well with the boys?' she asked. 'By keeping one step ahead of their pranks!' I responded."

From a lifetime of honours, Selwyn cites a triumph in his days a choirboy with St Patrick's Cathedral. "Expert training by Dr Chaundy gave us great confidence. I will never forget stepping up to receive first prize in the Boys' Open Solo at Dungannon Musical Festival when I was singing treble voice." As in Selwyn's youth, choirboys are paid a retainer today but no longer attend daily Matins. "Post-war conditions brought change. No longer were professional singers engaged, nor was it a paid occupation. Many of our choristers moved back to England. Ted Hetterley, a counter-tenor who'd married locally, was accepted into the choir of Christ Church Cathedral, Oxford."

From a succession of church hierarchy, Selwyn singles personal favourites as Dean Hamilton and the present Dean in Residence, Herbert Cassidy. "Our refurbished Walker organ makes Sunday services very special. St Patrick's Cathedral congregation really does appreciate and support the choir, especially lifetime member Joan Ensor. We sit together each Sunday and she has a kind word for everyone. Present choirmaster and organist, Martin White, in recognition of serving the profession with distinction, has recently been awarded the title of Associate of the Royal Academy of Music. Another young chorister, 12-year-old Robert Woods, a pupil of Martin White, recently won the Under-18 Section in the Organ Class at Portadown Music Festival. Now that is an achievement! It is traditional to take our choirboys on an annual treat and they've recently been to Paris and visited EuroDisney.

"In choir terms, the Reaney brothers, David, Stephen and Paul are worthy of special mention. Affectionately known as 'the three doctors', all have served the choir since they were boy sopranos. Stephen is a missionary doctor working in Tanzania, but takes his place in the choir stalls when home on leave. Singing brothers have always been strongly represented and presently in the choir are Philip and Andrew Fletcher, Nathan and Christopher Hawthorne, Marcus and Thomas Day, Robert and Ryan Woods. The Kellett brothers recently left for university and, down the years, our ranks contained three sets of twins!"

A favourite possession is a painting of important landmarks in Selwyn's life, presented on retirement from the Boys' Club. "Before coming to Sunnymead I donated this to our Church Music Hall on Vicar's Hill. There it hangs in acknowledgement of Armagh Boys' Club, the Mill Field where so many games were held, the Cathedral Church of St Patrick and the Cathedral Choir. Some of our present choristers were also Boys' Club members so for them it will always remain meaningful. Alice died in 1982 and in appreciation of her great musical gifts, my brother Denis and myself donated a tuba stop on the Walker organ in her memory."

Any literary aspirations he may have Selwyn attributes to his great-grandfather, Edward Rogers, born 1820, a chorister with the Cathedral Choir from 1830 and deputy custodian at Archbishop Robinson's library. "For a century the Tarleton family has shared a pew in the Cathedral. It's possible my love of music stemmed from Edward Rogers, who knows? I've often gone to the Cathedral alone, just to draw on the past, and watched sunlight flood the transept. I've told you of the contribution made by my ancestors but I am just as firmly rooted."

Selwyn Tarleton pictured in 1999 with the Choir of the Cathedral Church of St Patrick, Armagh following the presentation of new robes.

Front row (L to R): Robert Woods, Thomas Day, Jonathan Craig, Marcus Day, Andrew Fletcher, Ryan Woods, Russell Allen, Jamie Dickson.

Second row: Malcolm Leeman, John Humphries, Richard Craig, James Briggs, James Morton, Philip Todd, Wesley Brownlee, Jonathan Speers.

Third row: Martin White (Organist and Master of the Choristers), Selwyn Tarleton, Dr Paul Reaney, Peter Ferguson, Bill Lauder, Ian McGuckian, Dr David Reaney.

Back row: Stephen Burns, Tom Dawson, Stewart Anderson, Brian Wilson, Nigel Speers, Mark Speers, Philip McFarland.

Photograph by Jim Lyttle Photography

And sport has the last word. If Selwyn couldn't come to the Bass Irish Cup Final, then the Cup, in a manner of speaking, came to him. Portadown Football Club manager Ronnie McFaul, with club director, Ronnie Stinson and commercial manager, Bill Emerson, made a special visit to Sunnymead, bringing with them the glittering Bass Ireland trophy. As Armagh's 'Mr Football', Selwyn realised a wish by holding the Cup awarded to the Shamrock Park side.

In acknowledgement of a former director and life-long supporter, Portadown Football Club echoes the sentiments of past Armagh Boys' Club members. Merging metaphorically, they bear stalwart Selwyn Tarleton shoulder-high.

Lizzie Livingstone

Placing her amazing memory on record Mary Elizabeth (Lizzie) Livingstone registers her own particular claim to fame. Any pattern of a linear trail of past to future is knocked on the head when Lizzie sits back in her chair, and makes a reasonable comment: "Armagh is a city set on seven hills. Is it not something of a coincidence that I lived my entire life on seven hills?" Pausing to count on her fingers, Lizzie continues, "I was born on Banbrook Hill, went to school on Legar Hill, worked for 27 years on Vicar's Hill, moved from there to Richhill. I then found work at Buckhurst Hill Hospital in Essex, returning to a further 17 years at Tower Hill, Armagh and, *Deo volente,* will end my days at rest on Sandy Hill!"

A valued historian in her 85th year, Lizzie began life at Poplar Street, Banbrook Hill. "In 1914", she begins, "five streets ran parallel, forming a major part of Banbrook Hill. We had Poplar Street, Walker Street, Patrick Street, Shamrock Street and Walnut Street. Of course the original Banbrook has been rebuilt. Poplar Street was demolished and we moved to Banbrook Hill, home of my parents for 53 years. Those 'new' houses opposite, Columba's Terrace, were completed in 1936 by Cornelius Donaghy and James McGrath. Flats further down replaced a row previously erected by builders Peter O'Hare, McNally and McAvinchey."

Daughter of Elizabeth Toal and James Livingstone, Lizzie was an only child. "My mother's people were coachmen who came from Scotland, settling as tenant farmers, at Gosford Castle, Markethill. The home of my maternal great-grandparents is still there, at Carrick Lane. My father, James, was a coal carter with Turner's of Lower English Street, Armagh. Love of horses was ingrained in his family. My mother earned her living at Wilson's Mill, Moy Road, from the age of 18. Working as a rover meant she prepared yarn for spinners.

"James and Elizabeth married in 1911, moving to Banbrook Hill. Neighbours said she delivered every child that was born here. Once when I needed a reference, Armagh's best-loved woman physician Dr Sheelagh Woods, referred to my mother as a 'midwife of some standing'. She was a great lady and better looking than me", laughs Lizzie, "who nursed the sick and elderly, or if called upon, capably laid out the dead."

Her amazing memory comes into play when Lizzie recalls one of her uncles, Peter Toal, in his blue uniform, returning wounded from Egypt during the 1914-18 war. "I'm a walking street directory for I can recite the name of every neighbour in Banbrook Hill during 1919, at the time when I was five." And she does! "I'll start with Mrs Lyttle followed by Branken, Slevin, Wilson, McCreesh, Turley, Canavaghan, Loughran, Cravagan, two families of Donnelly, Halligan, McKee, Irwin, McGerrigan, Ryan, Lennox, McGurk, Livingstone, Mackle, two Miss Gribbon's, one taught in Bessbrook School, and last of all, Knipe. Now cross the street. Here you had Kelly, McConville, Haffey, Doran, Conway, Cusick, McKee, McCullough, Brady, McKenna, Toner, Hackett, McAuley, Keenan, McGovern, Gibbon, McDonald and Mr Smith, foreman at Simpson's builders.

"I attended Banbrook School, just across the street, my teacher then was Mrs Hughes, formerly Miss Martin. Everyone knew Armagh chemist, Jack Dougan, for human kindness was his way of life. He was born here. Jack's mother was a teacher at Banbrook School."

Rating top in class, Lizzie excelled at English and maths. "Due to my date of birth, I missed a scholarship opportunity of grammar school education at the Convent. How different my life could have been", she muses. "When my father took ill there was no alternative, I had to start work." Early 1928 found Lizzie enrolling for evening classes at Armagh Technical School. One teacher, Mr Martin, described her as "the most intelligent person in a class of 40 students".

"I was earning one pound a month at Wilson's mill and tuition in English, arithmetic and art cost two and sixpence a term. During second year we progressed to shorthand, typing and commercial correspondence and fees were set at seven and sixpence." Lizzie, who did not have seven and sixpence, was denied further education. "My father suffered a nervous breakdown, never working again. His only income was a small insurance of four and six a week. Wilson's factory closed so my mother too, was out of work. Nothing was handed over for free then! During that last year at Convent school in 1927, my books cost six and ninepence, exactly a week of my mother's pay. She received her money fortnightly and I remember how I cried because I needed the money to settle up next day. It was two weeks after my 14th birthday when my mother came home and told me I must now go to work with her. The mill closed three weeks later."

Lizzie's aunt, Lily Toal, who had been in service at 8 Vicar's Hill, unexpectedly came to the rescue. "Aunt Lily was retiring from the home of Mr Fanning, head of the Church of Ireland Cathedral School at Cathedral Close. He was a native of Tipperary, his wife from Wexford. Mr Fanning was severely arthritic so her husband required domestic help. Before the war, Mr Fanning's brother was manager of Harrods store in Knightsbridge. Once the family brought me a suit length when they returned from a short spell in London. I had my own room at the top of the stairs. Number eight Vicar's Hill is said to be haunted, yet never in 27 years did I witness anything untoward. There are however, interesting stories.

"The Music Rooms used by St Patrick's Cathedral are next door to number eight. This house had a spacious front door and was a popular venue for courting couples. Late one evening, my cousin, Tommy, took his girlfriend home to Primrose Hill and decided to take a short cut through Vicar's Hill. Passing the door of number eight, he was mysteriously knocked from the footpath. Few believed his story but never again did Tommy take that route. Once I was ill and a former employee, Mrs McAleavey, well in her seventies, returned to help. Sitting by my bedside, she told me how her husband late one evening was knocked from the footpath. He had the Sunday roast in a brown paper package. It fell to the street but he took to his heels, leaving it behind. Another resident, Miss Marks, was music teacher at the Convent. Her daily help came at seven each morning. From Navan Street, this woman took the steps leading to Vicar's Hill. One morning, a lady climbed these steps in front of her, melting into the wall. After that she refused to walk to Vicar's Hill alone and was accompanied by her brother.

"My next door neighbour in Banbrook Hill, Maggie Smith, reared in the country and accustomed to walking home late, had been to a wake in Irish Street. Taking a short-cut across Vicar's Hill, Maggie told me she saw nothing, yet felt a presence which joined her, remaining until she reached the Parochial House. By the post box Father Finnegan, later Canon at Donaghmore, was posting a letter. Maggie collapsed at his feet. I saw nothing in all my considerable time, 27 years with Fannings. My wage was one pound a week when I began. They were exceptionally kind but Mr Fanning did not have a huge salary. Tenancy of the house and ten pounds a month was his pension when he died, at the age of 90, in 1955. His wife had died in 1949. The Fanning family had resided at number eight for 59 years. Prior to that it was the home of Walter Ferris. Residents of Vicar's Hill were then Miss Wilkin, Mr Hamilton who worked in the Post Office, Mr Wilson, verger of the Cathedral, Mr Dean who sang in the choir, Mrs Scott, Mrs Egerton, Mrs Owens, Mr West, church organist, followed by Mr Carter, and singer Mr Roseigh." While resident at Vicar's Hill, Lizzie recalls a plaque unveiled in memory of liturgical composer, Charles Wood. "Born at number 12, he sang with the Cathedral Choir, progressing to become Professor of Music at Cambridge."

In her next employment, Lizzie nursed Miss Glendenning at Richhill. "Dr Spence recommended me and I remained until her death. Buckhurst Hill Hospital in Essex was my next step. I loved England, forming lasting friendships, but mother was lonely following my father's death in 1956 and asked me to return. That time in Essex is framed in my memory, the happiest of my life. I came back to Armagh nevertheless, finding employment at Tower Hill."

Distinguished by a beautiful soprano voice, Lizzie sang at parish concerts and acted with the Drama Club. "In a production of *The Lilac Ribbon*, Hughie Trainor, now Ireland's oldest band leader, was cast as my son Robert! Milford man and musician, Eugene Loughran, first heard me sing at the Minor Hall of Armagh City Hall. It was one of Moore's melodies, *I Saw From the Beach*, and Eugene advised I should follow a musical career. How could I?" she asks, "I still had to earn a living.

"Another of our plays, *The Down Express*, was taken to Armagh Prison in 1935, and staged, you could say, before a captive audience! Of the cast, Joe McManus, uncle of Joe from the *Observer* newspaper, Paddy McCreesh and Frank Campbell are now dead. Just myself left. I remember singing *The Lark in the Clear Air* at Tullymore School in January 1934, when the event was the retirement of Father Coyle who is himself remembered as a fine tenor. Again fate passed me by when George White, in 1937, deciding I had a pure soprano voice, promised to

Lizzie Livingstone with a boy
and his donkey at Rostrevor, Summer 1936

train me. He sang tenor with St Patrick's Church of Ireland Cathedral. It never came about. George had just built himself the first house in Duke's Grove when he fell ill, dying soon after. Organist George Minne was unable to admit women to the Cathedral Choir until after Vatican reform. Male voice and Gregorian Chant was church music as I knew it for most of my life.

"Each Christmas the Rev. J.C.M. Anderson called and brought me to sing for patients at Tower Hill Hospital. When Owen Webb from Railway Street asked me to entertain at the Chest Hospital, Mrs Blackwood, our local dentist's wife, was present. She invited me to perform at many concerts afterwards but I have never gone on stage without agonising", Lizzie confesses. "It added years waiting in the wings." Don't they say that is the mark of a true artist?

Now 25 years retired, only Lizzie remains of Banbrook's original residents. "I enjoy visits to the Community Centre and Tuesday meetings at Orchard Social Club for Visually Impaired People. Chairman Bert Mackrel, blind for 25 years, organises an enjoyable programme and members really care for each other. I deeply appreciate Dr Woods' practice and his staff at reception, especially Ann Daly with her cheerful and caring outlook. Far too often such wonderful people go unrecognised. Dr Oliver Woods, Mrs Dougan and Mrs McGrail administer the Sacrament now that I am housebound. Dessie Feeny used to call but has responsibility for another area. I thank all who do such work. Through such good people I maintain a fellowship with my faith."

In the vast mix of human experience, Mary Elizabeth Livingstone's contribution lies in what she knows. In any lifetime, each of us goes a particular way, finds a particular destiny. It is the last hill that shows the beauty of the valley. Content with that view Lizzie now rests. "I've run my race", she smiles. "Now it's time to stop and linger."

The McCusker Brothers' Céilí Band

The musical McCuskers of the last century had little idea that an equally musical generation of their descendants would greet the next century. Within weeks of publication of *Touching a Chord*, the story of nine musical brothers received mention on the Internet and world press. Today only three brothers remain, and Benignus, who is the youngest, acts as spokesman for the county's most famous céilí band.

"Our home was at Kilcreevy and we never really scattered. Those of us remaining, live nearby. There were 11 children, nine boys and two girls. John, the eldest, died some years ago, then Vincent in 1987. The deaths of Teresa and Barney were followed by Mary and Malachy. Brendan died in 1998 and Francis, earlier this year. Tommy, Kevin, and myself are left. The girls sang but never involved themselves with the band.

"My father could play the piccolo and mother, probably the better musician of the two, was an expert accordionist. The world they knew was one where men ploughed with horses and dug potatoes by means of a spade, lifting them by hand. For a time my father worked as a weaver in the local mill. As children he'd tell us of McCrum's factory whistle which was blown at six in the morning. Workers who were late had their pay docked accordingly. He walked home after a 12-hour day. For his toil, my father earned ten shillings a week.

"John, the eldest of our family, was born in Scotland. For a time my father worked in the coal mines there. Emptying sweat from his boots, he'd say working underground could kill any man not robust in health. At tea break he found enough energy to play the piccolo, greatly pleasing his workmates. Unexpectedly, news came to my parents in Scotland that a house was available for them at Kilcreevy. My uncle, it seemed, built this dwelling and then departed for America. So home they came.

"We were never taught to play", Benignus stresses. "If music is in your blood as it was in ours, you *have* to play. We were born into an era when entertainment was created at home. None of us read sheet music, and before starting school, we'd mastered our choice of instrument. John, Vincent and Brendan each played the violin. Kevin inherited my father's love of the piccolo. Tommy and myself were accordionists. Barney played piano. Francis played bass while Malachy took control of drums. My parents joined in rehearsals with an uncle, John O'Farrell, a brilliant accordionist."

News of the famous McCuskers' music spread throughout the country. "Malachy was appointed secretary and he dealt with the demand for bookings. By this time we were all working—John with the County Council, Barney and Tommy ran a grocery business, Vincent, Kevin and myself were farmers, Francis joined the building trade and Malachy collected eggs from rural farms for Bradford's of Dobbin Street. Brendan and his wife ran Mary Ann's Pub at Tullysaran. As our bookings increased we found ourselves constantly travelling to venues as far apart as Derry or Kerry. Radio Éireann gave us the opportunity to go on air during the late thirties.

"We had just finished a series of concerts, all live performance, when over the air came the announcement, *'...and as a consequence, we are at war with Germany'*. It was 3 September 1939. We drove back to Armagh in silence, not knowing what the future would hold. A wireless set was obtained and with the battery fully charged, we followed the progress of the war through the BBC." For nine musical McCusker brothers the future, had they known, held great promise.

Their fame began in earnest after 1945. "First we accepted London bookings, the Round Tower, Cricklewood, moving on to the clubs and ballrooms of Manchester. What with work, rehearsals and actually playing, we were rarely idle. Prior to St Patrick's Day in 1962, the band was invited to undertake a grand tour incorporating Chicago, Boston, Philadelphia and New York. We'd never seen such crowds", Benignus recalls. "In Chicago, following a USA reunion of the legal profession, the mayor presented us with a commemorative plaque to mark our visit. Looking back, it's almost funny. They begged us to extend the tour, promising to double our fee. We declined because we had to get back to work. Today's musicians would deal with it all so differently by engaging a manager and drawing up contracts."

During the Fifties, the McCusker Brothers' Céilí Band was a BBC household name. "We enjoyed series after series, live on the air. Our signature tune *Maid of the Mill* was chosen specially for my mother. It had long been a favourite of hers. Working to perfect our repertoire, there was no greater critic than my father. He had an ear for pitch and timing, nothing short of perfection deemed good enough. *The Irish Washerwoman*, a lively jig, heralded a further series with the BBC. Then Sam Denton and Havelock Nelson asked us to produce for the air a series entitled *Country Céilí*."

With their quiet genius, the McCusker Brothers held the musical platform for two decades. Then, in 1956, the band was invited to appear on the first televised programme from Northern Ireland. "That was *Come Dancing*, at the Plaza Ballroom in Belfast. We weren't really nervous", Brendan recalls, "after all, music was as natural to us as breathing or sleeping. Another televised show from Balmoral included the McCoy School of Irish Dancing. I remember the billing included Brendan O'Dowda singing *La Golondrina*. On reflection, the radio series I most enjoyed was our last, *As I Roved Out*."

RTÉ invited the band to celebrate the channel's opening night. Producer Philip Thompson requested a programme of everyone's favourite music. "When any particular style became tedious, we spruced up our repertoire, introducing old-time music for ballroom dancing. *The Cuckoo Waltz* and the *Blue Danube* were most frequently requested. It was a pleasure to perform both pieces."

John McCusker, father and founder of a musical legend, died in 1976 at the age of 96, having survived his wife Teresa by nine years. "He had never been ill nor spent a day in hospital during his entire life", affirms Benignus. The inimitable McCusker talent, however, lives on in a second and third generation. Vincent's son Benedict has an entirely musical family. Three daughters and two sons combine to play the accordion, whistle, fiddle and banjo. His daughter Donna competed with thousands to win the All-Ireland slow air on the tin whistle and the All-Ireland reel accordionist.

Benignus continues, "Local pop group Twice Shy is made up of Ben, Paul and Dermot who are my sons, plus Enda, my brother Kevin's boy. Enda owns a music shop in Abbey Lane. Their choice of repertoire is mostly taken from the charts. My brother John's son Brendan is an ex-member of Margo's famous band.

"The McCusker Brothers' Céilí Band finally retired in the early Eighties. Those of us who are left accept the dramatic change in popular taste and a younger generation's musical preferences. Whether Sinatra or Sinéad O'Connor, rhythm stems from the same source." Benignus pauses: "it's like a language that speaks differently to each of us, be it the feet, the heart or that part of the mind which is set aside for the appreciation of music. I have six daughters who sing in harmony at weddings. They steal the show with a beautiful interpretation of the *Ave Maria* by Schubert. In contrast, my 14-year-old grandson Stephen is continuing to do well as a member of Armagh Pipers' Club."

Three remaining brothers have to agree, this band was legendary. It is right that a self-taught family who communicated their traditional sound to three continents should be remembered. As they say, music is a language that speaks differently to each of us.

The McCusker Brothers in Chicago, St Patrick's Day 1962.
(L to R): Francis, Benignus, Brendan, John, Mayor Richard J. Daley of Chicago, Kevin, Malachy, Barney, Alderman Ben Briscoe (first Jewish Mayor of Dublin), Tommy and Vincent
Photograph courtesy of Brian Dougan LL.B

Maureen Corr

Eleanor, wife of President Franklin Roosevelt, had an international concern for all people: everyone's problems were hers. When her husband's career ended with his death in 1945, Eleanor's was just beginning. As chairman of the United Nations Commission on Human Rights, it was she who drafted the Universal Declaration of Human Rights. At three o'clock in the morning, exhausted delegates agreed the final text, and the UN General Assembly adopted the Declaration at the Palais de Chaillot in Paris on 10 December 1948. This would later be described by Secretary General U Thant as "the Magna Carta of mankind", and characterised by Alexander Solzhenitsyn in his Nobel lecture of 1970 as "the best document ever produced by the United Nations". In formulating a document that touched the lives of countless millions, former First Lady Eleanor Roosevelt required secretarial assistance of the highest calibre. This she found in Maureen Corr.

Maureen Corr, born in 1915, was a sickly child, the second youngest in a family of eight. Her parents, Mary Ann McArdle and Michael Joseph Corr, owned a small farm at Corr's Close, Magherarville, Co. Armagh. The Close was a little hamlet, chiefly a handful of whitewashed cottages and a sawmill run by the McKinney family. Michael Joseph had lived here since his birth in 1869. His daughter's health was of immense concern for she suffered severely from asthma. In the course of 17 years, Maureen spent only two of these at school. Confined to bed for most of the time, Maureen educated herself. An avid reader, she devoured information—and, importantly, retained everything she read. When Peg, the eldest of the Corr children, came home from New York on a visit she was struck by the plight of this intelligent teenager. Against the wishes of her parents, Peg brought Maureen back to New York.

"The family were sure their daughter, then 17, was much too ill to travel and would die before reaching America", contributes Maureen's nephew, Gerard Corr, who lives near Lisnadill, Co. Armagh. "And yet, Aunt Maureen astonished them all. She survived the journey, her asthma disappeared and she settled into school almost at once."

Maureen Corr's capabilities soon became evident. Catching up on the academic prowess of her peer group, she topped the class in most subjects. After graduating from college, Maureen became private secretary to a doctor, close to her sister's home in New York. When her employer moved, due to promotion, Maureen was invited to accompany him. At home with the vibrant rhythm of this great city, she declined. Somewhat regretfully her employer wrote a reference for Maureen. Handing it over, he added: "This will take you anywhere." How right he was! Within the year, Maureen Corr had moved to the White House where, over the course of the next 30 years, she fulfilled the role of private secretary, companion and confidante, and came to be looked upon by Eleanor Roosevelt as a member of the family.

Outside of the Corr family, Maureen's story is barely known. She took up residence in the White House at a time when the world was learning of the horrors of Hitlerism. In the post-war dream of uniting nations, of persuading them to turn their weapons into instruments of progress, a set of universally agreed propositions for assuring fundamental human rights had to be drawn up. Typical of her statesmanship, Mrs Roosevelt seized the moment to press for enactment of a Declaration. A commemoration of her uncommon concern for humanity came 25 years later with the publication of a personal album on her life, written by A. David Gurewitsch. Entitled *Eleanor Roosevelt: Her Day*, this work is as much a historical and visual record of the role Maureen Corr played in the life of the former First Lady. Beginning her 'long job' in 1946, Eleanor Roosevelt was appointed by President Harry Truman for a four-year term as the United States representative to the United Nations' embryonic Commission on Human Rights. President Truman, in his speech at the closing of the San Francisco Conference which created the United Nations, stated that under the Charter "we have good reason to expect the framing of an international Bill of Rights acceptable to all the nations involved". The newly formed Commission, comprised of 18 governmental representatives, elected Mrs Roosevelt as its chairman. Thanks to her effective leadership, she remained in the chair for the next six years.

The first issue was the international Bill of Rights and this had to be accepted by the governments attached to United Nations. In all Mrs Roosevelt's efforts at compromise and consensus with world representatives, Maureen Corr remained professionally by her side. Insisting that a Declaration of Human Rights should be easily memorised, Eleanor Roosevelt veered towards the terminology of the American Declaration of Independence and Bill of Rights, and the French Declaration of the Rights of Man. Only the views of the Soviet bloc, apartheid South Africa and Saudi Arabia stood in sharp opposition. At the final sessions of the commissioners' drafting committee the Soviet delegate, Professor Alexei P. Pavlov, proposed scrapping a project that had consumed 18 months of hard labour on the part of Eleanor Roosevelt. When a vote was taken, eight representatives comprising the Communist bloc, South Africa and Saudi Arabia abstained, but the Declaration was adopted by 48 votes to nil. Since she went out of her way to pay tribute to the Russians, it was then said that composure in the face of provocation was a hallmark of Mrs Roosevelt's conduct. In a speech at the Sorbonne in Paris in 1948, she delighted everyone with the observation that she had been mistaken in thinking that the limits of her patience had been reached in bringing up a large family: in presiding over the Commission on Human Rights, an even greater measure of patience was demanded.

Through all of this, Maureen Corr remained secretary, confidante and friend. After her husband's death Mrs Roosevelt settled in New York at Hyde Park, an impressive house with extensive gardens. She fervently enjoyed being with people she loved and her children often came to stay. Maureen Corr shared this elegant home with royalty, prime ministers, visiting groups of United Nations representatives, Russian jurists and American political figures. From this affluent world across the Atlantic, Maureen frequently returned to renew the bonds with her own family at Corr's Close.

"She held us and our nearest neighbours spellbound, while recounting world-wide travels and those she met during her career", recalls Gerard. "We heard how Mrs Roosevelt paid a tribute to her late husband each Memorial Day. One of her guests was President Lyndon B. Johnson who addressed her guests at the Rose Garden in Hyde Park, where Franklin Roosevelt was buried. Another year, Adlai Stevenson performed this duty, during the time he was Ambassador to the United Nations."

Maureen wrote home frequently. Her letters contained detailed accounts of what had become everyday experiences. She told of how Eleanor Roosevelt conducted tours around the main Roosevelt residence at Hyde Park, known as 'the Big House'. She particularly loved talking to children and would point out a rug that had been given to President Roosevelt by the Shah of Persia. Presidential nominee John F. Kennedy was invited to lunch at Hyde Park. Unsure as to how she would receive him, Kennedy afterwards told the press "I was absolutely smitten by this woman". With Maureen Corr by her side, Mrs Roosevelt visited President Khrushchev and his wife at their Yalta home. According to Maureen, Soviet hospitality "was excellent and extended to Leningrad where we were shown the Winter Palace, and Moscow where we saw Lenin's small, plainly furnished apartment, his tomb and the Kremlin". They watched chess buffs absorbed in this favourite game, within the chess pavilion at Moscow's Gorky Park. Some time later, Mrs Roosevelt reciprocated, inviting the Khrushchevs to Hyde Park.

President Tito of Yugoslavia shared his summer home on the Adriatic island of Brioni with the former First Lady and Maureen Corr, using this opportunity to exchange ideas on the difficult cold-war stalemate of international relations. When Emperor Haile Selassie visited Hyde Park, he had never seen himself before on television. Everyone had to sit and wait for his televised interview with a group of children, filmed the previous day. The Emperor insisted on visiting President Roosevelt's grave and paying his respects to the late President—a formidable wartime ally.

Maureen Corr spoke of Mrs Roosevelt's passionate involvement in the welfare of children. Singer Harry Belafonte, when he saw how genuinely she cared, hired a Jamaican musician who taught disturbed boys to play the steel drum. Agreeing to hold an annual concert for the school's benefit, these boys, when sufficiently accomplished, accompanied Belafonte in concert at the Carnegie Hall.

President Roosevelt had suffered from polio and Eleanor continued to support the research centre he had founded at Georgia's Warm Springs. Here the polio vaccine, which helped control the disease, was discovered. Eleanor Roosevelt delighted in showing Maureen places that she and her husband had visited and enjoyed in the past. One photograph in Gurewitsch's publication shows Mrs Roosevelt's bedroom at her Hyde Park home. One wall is entirely covered with family photographs, all neatly grouped, of those she loved most. Maureen Corr's picture is right beside that of President Roosevelt.

"Maureen accompanied Mrs Roosevelt on foreign travels and has retained snapshots of those visits captured by official photographer David Gurewitsch", says Gerard. "In newly independent India, they were guests of Maharaja Jam Sahib, at his palace in Jamnagar. The Maharaja was a colleague at the United Nations. Both women were then invited to a garden party given by Prime Minister Nehru, meeting his sister, Madame Vijaya Pandit. This visit culminated at Agra's Taj Mahal."

Of the spirited people in Israel, Maureen felt that Mrs Roosevelt was most taken by Prime Minister David Ben-Gurion, the three talking well into the small hours at his small house in Tel Aviv. Maureen Corr's first experience of an Iron Curtain country came when she accompanied Eleanor Roosevelt, at the invitation of Marshall Tito and his wife.

"Contrast Maureen's life with those of her parents or neighbours who rarely managed a day to Belfast by train", Gerard points out. "And yet she wore this role naturally, like a second skin. David Gurewitsch captured my aunt with the former First Lady, shopping for Christmas presents in Hong Kong. Again in Bangkok, attending a meeting of the World Federation of United Nations Associations, and in nearby Cambodia, they saw a jungle-bound city of 600 temples, most of them gripped by tree-roots."

Eleanor Roosevelt was revered as a wise and experienced diplomat. Visiting various countries where a dispute existed, she spoke with both governments, often averting hostilities. Cambodia and Siam were a case in point. In 1958, they agreed to re-establish friendly relations and place their dispute before the World Court. The Mufti of Samarkand welcomed both women to his legendary Asian city, once sacked by Genghis Khan and rebuilt by Tamerlane. This, with the Taj Mahal and the Khyber Pass, were three places Eleanor Roosevelt's father insisted she must visit. The World Fair in Brussels provided an opportunity to visit the Russian Pavilion, and here they stood in the shadow of Lenin's towering statue. Harry Belafonte and Maureen were later photographed chatting over a meal in the evening. During this stay, they watched and later met the Soviet Union's extraordinary Moiseyev dancers.

For many years Mrs Roosevelt ran a daily newspaper column entitled *My Day*. During a visit to West Berlin, she was sufficiently moved by a ruined synagogue—important to German Jews, and destroyed in 1938—that she wrote about this in her column. The resulting international publicity encouraged municipal authorities to begin an extensive publicly-funded programme of restoration. When Eleanor Roosevelt died on 7 November 1962, she was mourned in every continent and in particular, for her true spirit of humanity and selflessness. While her life illustrates the high standards of behaviour that are attainable by everyone she remains, for millions, the First Lady of the World.

But for Gerard Corr and his wife, Louise, none of this information on Maureen Corr would have found its way into a social history of Armagh and its people. Maureen is now 84 years of age, in good health and living near Central Park, New York. She has been the guest of every President and First Lady at the White House since the death of Mrs Roosevelt and recently attended a formal dinner given by President Bill Clinton and his wife, Hillary. Of Maureen's siblings, Peg, Tommy, Michael John, Rose, Harry and Kathleen are dead. Felix is presently resident at Greenpark Nursing Home and Maureen comes frequently to visit him. Louise and Gerard Corr live near Lisnadill, Co. Armagh, with their three children, Michael, Christopher and Maria.

The original home at Corr's Close, once the pride of Michael John, has fallen into decay. Is it not possible that when her story is told, Maureen Corr might become the 'First Lady' of our county and, in her honour, the Corr home a museum to a courageous young woman who went from here, met every world leader and assisted in formulating "the Magna Carta of mankind"?

Maureen Corr and Mrs Eleanor Roosevelt watch chess experts
playing at the pavilion in Moscow's Gorky Park
Photograph by David Gurewitsch

Annie Knipe

"Everything was different at the turn of the century", Annie Knipe observes, taking time to chat on her 89th birthday. As years of anecdote and fact unwind, Annie will touch hearts for while much of her story is typical of Irish life, in ways it is exceptional.

Annie's grey-green eyes and open face are as welcoming as her handshake. For four years she's been resident at Fairlawns nursing home close to Armagh. "We are an entirely happy lot", she declares. "My good friend, Joe Armstrong from Moygashel has a room down the corridor. Days pass pleasantly and of course my family visit often. Retirement can be carefree and Fairlawns is not so different from home.

"I was Annie Hughes", she begins, "the baby in a family of seven. Peter Hughes, my father, was a farmer, horse-dealing an important sideline. A century ago you'd have found him at Newtownhamilton Fair hiring extra, casual labour. There, Father insisted, were to be found the country's best workers. In Thomas Hardy's *Mayor of Casterbridge* such people were deemed 'bondagers'. Right up to the 19th century, women were bonded as servants, hired almost in slavery, for six months or a year.

"I was born in 1910 and remember only male hirings. These people worked at the heaviest tasks, carrying bales, hoeing turnips in all weathers or driving carthorses. My father's men were treated better than most. He allowed them to go home on Friday night and return Monday morning.

"Mother, I'm pleased to say, was also kind. 'Don't take your washing home', she'd insist, and stoking up the copper, saw to their laundry. They sat down to table with the rest of the family. In fact, we children grew fond of the farm hands, missing them sorely when they left. By the beginning of the last war, hiring came to an end.

"My mother, Susan Hegarty, worked as a governess in the United States for ten years. Her millionaire employers sent for each brother and sister in turn. Aunt Mary-Anne was their cook, Aunt Nell a maid, while Uncle Dan was chauffeur. This beautiful American residence came to be affectionately known as 'Hegarty's House'. Susan returned to Moy for occasional visits. My father Peter met her one afternoon when she was out walking. He, on horseback, had taken the Bog Road to Armagh. Besotted with her looks, Peter voiced his intentions straightaway. So began a three-year courtship. Susan, whilst in the States, had been acquisitive, her earnings posted home to the Moy for investment in what is now Clancey's pub. Two of her sisters helped run the business. She also purchased a small farm at Aughanlig. Upon marriage, Susan sold up, moving into Peter Hughes' home farm at Mullinary, the Moy."

For 23 years, from childhood until 1933, Annie worked on the farm, observing her father's excellent veterinary skills.

"He devised a cure for colic, a form of indigestion brought about by horses eating spring grass. This mixture", she leans thoughtfully forward, "was a combination of salt and soot. It worked too. Naturally he frequented Moy Fair. Farmers counted on a buyer for their stock but there was no guarantee of this. Money was scarce and we thought nothing of the many times he returned home, his animals unsold.

"Nellie, our mare, was shod by Jack McGuirk who ran the blacksmith's forge in Charlemont. Taking her there was my job. I'd climb onto one horse, Nellie trailing patiently behind. Before leaving for home, I'd say hello to Uncle Paddy Hegarty who lived at Corrdunavalley. He, too, was a horse dealer. Several times a year, officers from the Greek army came and bought up available stock, either for breeding or regimental use.

"Sometimes my father made poitín. Of course this was illegal but people said, like most things that are illegal, it tasted mighty good. After each bottling, Mother sterilised the still, putting it to dry in the sun. Made from corn, the brew took a week to ferment. Well, the idea!" Annie protests with a twinkle, when asked if she sampled illicit liquor, "but those Greeks did. Now and again the police carried out an indifferent search, shrugged apologetically and disappeared."

Suddenly she digresses. "With their beautiful accents and Southern European charm, Greek men were fascinating. They lodged at Laverty's Hotel in the Moy but oddly enough, never intermarried. Young women, mark you, were brought up with a bit of decorum then. No bunch of good-looking men would escape today's lot who seem altogether wild. My father wouldn't tolerate any such carry-on. I think not. We were a disciplined family.

"It was the task of my only brother, George, to fetch the weekly shopping. For this he took one of the ponies. 'Keep him on a tight rein going downhill', Father warned. Once, when George was only 16, he returned with the pony's knees badly lacerated. 'Father's going to kill me, Annie', he whispered. I loved my brother, so taking a tin of black boot-polish, covered up the pony's wounds. We didn't get away with the deception. On the nightly rounds, Father spotted the pony, boot-polish on his face from licking his sore knees. I pleaded for George and he escaped a walloping. That's what we did. Stuck up for each other time about.

"Mother made all our clothes. She'd buy material for skirts in Portadown, cutting bodices from laundered flour-bags. At Christmas my parents went off for the day and that was the year's big shopping. We produced our own egg, vegetables and pork that we salted down for winter. Free-range poultry provided ducks, geese and chickens. In all we were fairly self-sufficient. I remember nothing of the First World War. I was only four when it began, but many of the neighbouring men left to fight and never returned.

"As a family we did not escape our share of grief. My eldest sister May was just a little tot, when Mother, bringing tea to men harvesting in the fields' left her in care of our grandmother. Mother returned to find the child missing. May, unseen, toddled after her, falling into a pond where flax retted. At that stage, mother was expecting the twins, Lucy and Cassie. No-one knows how she bore this grief.' Pain flickers across Annie's face. "Such a good woman, to suffer the loss of her first little girl. I know it was our priest, Canon Quinn, who preserved her sanity.

"As the older children left home, my mother with her vast capacity for caring, visited Armagh Workhouse, now Tower Hill. Conditions were so awful that she scooped up two little orphan boys and brought them home. One was three years, the other six months. Paddy and Tony were soon calling her 'Mother'.

"She loved them", reminisces Annie, "and so did I, helping with the increased chores. My father brought us all treats each Fair Day. You could say that our home was more like an orphanage for when my brother George's wife died, mother took responsibility for his two children, Peter and Seán. She was a kind neighbour to all in need and I know bigotry had no place in her life. The role of local midwife fell to her and in times of death she was at one with the grieving.

"My idea of a childhood treat was visiting Aunt Mary-Anne Bowen outside Dungannon. She had seven children as well and that generation settled throughout Tyrone. I'd stand on a chair and sing for her. Hadn't a bad voice, you know. Indeed I later sang soprano in Clonfeacle Chapel choir where Mrs Curran was organist.

"We were better off than most for my father was always a good provider. Christmas saw roast goose on the table, an orange, apple and sweeties in our stockings. My mother set great standards", Annie stresses with pride. "Our home shone with cleanliness. There was nothing common about Susan. Her American life accustomed her to the best. Slovenly attitudes in Ireland caused her much frustration.

"Even though my parents wanted me to marry a farmer, in 1933 I accepted a proposal from Hugh Knipe who traded in poultry, moving to Armagh. I'd experienced enough of farming. Hugh and I had seven children, Mary, Pat, Hugh, Dan, Lucy, Letitia and John. Lucy and Dan live in England, the others are local.

"The entire district sorrowed when my mother died in 1942. Neighbours thronged to pay tribute, describing her as a gracious, capable woman. My father was to outlive her by 20 years.

"After Mother's death I recalled wonderful things she told us as children. My busy life didn't allow for writing any of it down. Later, we all regretted this. I often pictured the low thatch, apples weighing the boughs, rows of newly-baked currant buns on the kitchen table."

Annie's thoughts are apparent when she adds, "I am the last remaining member of that generation so this account will be treasured by those following after. I remember how mother described William McKinley, 25th President of the USA, inaugurated to a second term of office. She was in America when President McKinley was shot dead. Then came Theodore Roosevelt, one of the greatest presidents. When my mother came back to the Moy, she had newspapers showing photographs of work on the Panama Canal. Roosevelt supported that venture. Then", Annie adds thoughtfully, "he was awarded the Nobel peace prize for his part in bringing an end to the

Russo-Japanese war. History in the kitchen with us but we didn't realise."

From this shared afternoon, conclude that Annie Knipe's recollections are highly emotive, laced with humour and entirely personal. She settles back against her cushions. There are times when it's a privilege to meet such a person.

A wedding day study of Annie and Hugh Knipe, 1933

George Macartney

Presenting the spectacular life of George Macartney, MBE, Armagh City and District Chairman for three terms, is a daunting task. Many events during his dramatic years of office, 1992-94, are of social and historical importance. Immediately following his 1992 election, Chairman Macartney and his wife Iris received an invitation to represent Armagh, Northern Ireland as guests of honour at Armagh, Pennsylvania, where two weeks of bicentennial celebration had been arranged.

"Naturally this event took precedence in my Chairman's diary for 1992", George explains. "The Borough of Armagh is the oldest in Indiana County. Called after our own city and county, its first settlers were eight families from Armagh, who crossed the Atlantic, pioneering a new life in August 1792. They were James and Margaret Graham, Mr Parker, David and Mary Tomb, A. Fee, James and Catherine Anderson, Alexander and Elizabeth Carnathan, James Leslie, James Luke and Hugh Junkins. Until a treaty was formed with the native Indian population in 1795, their settlement suffered raids and it is recorded how all had to flee for safety, to East St Clair blockhouse near Laughlintown. This piece of history was a revelation", George admits, "but provided a marvellous opportunity to bring greetings from this ancient city of Patrick to our sister township in new Armagh, Pennsylvania."

Welcomed by Mayor John D. Varner of the Borough of Indiana, George and Iris Macartney, as Honorary Citizens, were presented with Keys to the City and commemorative lapel pins. That day of their visit, 25 June 1992, was proclaimed 'Councillor W. George Macartney Day' and celebratory events designated as 'Armagh Appreciation Days in Indiana'. The arrival of an Appalachian wagon train established a historical theme, followed in the evening by a formal dinner. Next day, gifts were presented at a special ceremony. One of these, an embossed silver tray, sits proudly in the Macartney dining room. George recalls a hectic programme of pageant, community family picnics and children's games with every evening given over to musical entertainment. "Sunday saw us at morning worship, and afterwards, a vintage car show, fashion show, outdoor crafts and quilting exhibitions. Each day brimmed with events, evenings culminated in music and dancing. It was wonderful but exhausting and went exactly to plan. Chief Executive Des Mitchell had previously set up superb arrangements, and Council secretary Wendy Geary, efficient and courteous at all times, finalised every detail. I know we fostered cross-Atlantic goodwill and we still exchange Christmas cards with many we met."

George Macartney's second year as Chairman carried equal significance when he hosted a civic reception to mark the bicentenary of the Royal Irish Fusiliers. Lord Caledon was present as Lord Lieutenant and Brigadier Naughton was guest of honour. Marking the 1550th anniversary of Patrick's coming to Ireland called for a year of celebration. "This was my final term as Chairman and our marketing officer Alan Hill designed a programme, Armagh Together, which left a lasting impression and involved community participation at every level. On behalf of the city I welcomed Jacques Delors, President of the European Commission, as a guest, and Sir Gordon Beveridge, Vice Chancellor of The Queen's University of Belfast, as chairman of the Armagh Together committee 1994-95. My association with the late Cardinal Ó Fiaich had always been excellent and his successor, Cardinal Daly, with Archbishop Eames, set a superb example of leadership throughout this commemorative year."

George was born in 1915 and first lived at Cathedral Villas, a terrace of four houses owned by his grandparents. "My parents, Tom and Rachel Macartney, farmed land that swept rurally from the Portadown Road", George contributes. "I was one of three brothers. Wilson and Leslie both worked for an uncle, who, with the consent of my grandfather, Robert Macartney, formed a partnership with Turners Coal Importers. Our branch of the family moved to Lindsey's Hill, where history would have us believe, a man named Lindsey was murdered in the grounds. Being surrounded by my father's land meant that after leaving school, I worked on the farm. I was only 16 years of age, and due to the amount of work we were asked to do, I constantly seemed to be at odds with our farm hands. For my own advancement I embarked on a business course at Armagh Technical College. When a local chap named Hadden left Messrs Lennox of Armagh, emigrating to South Africa, his vacancy in the menswear department provided an answer to my dilemma. Applying for the job, I was appointed by W.J. Lennox, founder of the business." Serving his apprenticeship with a soundly respected firm gave confidence to young George Macartney who had a natural intuition as to how a well-dressed man should look. "Two of my departmental colleagues then were Bertie West and George Richardson. When Tyson's, quality outfitters of O'Connell Street, Dublin, offered me a position at 30 shillings a week, Willie Lennox persuaded me to work instead for Sam Kells of Lisnaskea, rather than move so far away from home. The contrast between Armagh and this rural community was immense. Retail demands were more modest and I confess the rag trade wasn't nearly as satisfying without quality merchandise. 'Off the peg' hadn't been perfected and it cost just £1 to have a suit made. After six months I secured a position with Corbett's Menswear of Portadown."

Joining up in 1940 George, like most, believed war would be over in three months. "I favoured the Royal Horse Guards who were responsible for Changing of the Guard. This regiment wouldn't accept enlistments of less than three years, so switching allegiance, I joined the Royal Irish Fusiliers. It was Colonel Templar, father of Field Marshal Sir Gerald Templar, who presented me with my regimental buttons and cap badge. Soon after our meeting, the Colonel left Loughgall and with his wife, moved to Little Castledillon on the Portadown Road. His son, Sir Gerald, also joined the Royal Irish Fusiliers." Recommended for a commission, George declined. "I did however request that I be sent from Ballykinlar to a course at Catterick Camp." Whilst at Catterick, George learned a transfer was imminent. Remonstrating with the Brigadier, he was despatched to 22nd Armoured Brigade at Wiltshire.

Mussolini entered the war in 1940 and George's regiment was sent to Egypt in 1941. "Our convoy took over six weeks to arrive. Docking at Durban, I was granted shore leave. This gave a superb opportunity to visit the famed department store which Benburb man, John Orr, had established. Here I met acquaintances from home who were working at this magnificent emporium, with branches at Cape Town, Durban and Johannesburg. Business management intrigued me and I actually met and chatted to John Orr, expressing an interest in joining his company after the war." British forces fighting in the North African desert were facing an Italo-German combination under an astute German commander, Rommel. During this campaign George Macartney was mentioned in despatches. "Duty brought me back to the desert with the 22nd Armoured Brigade where we took heavy beatings from Rommel. I became part of the famous Long Range Desert Group, a reconnaissance unit operating over an area of thousands of square miles. Conditions were bad, army biscuits constituted meals, and as a consequence, men suffered dietary deficiencies. I contracted a blood disorder that resulted in serious skin trouble. For a time I soldiered with Captain Robert Blair Mayne, probably the most brilliant, fearless fighting man of our time, and later commanding officer of the SAS regiment. Fascism and Nazism produced monsters and confronted by either, Blair Mayne faced such problems squarely. Of course the war crimes tribunals were later established but Blair Mayne detested barbaric treatment of any vulnerable human being, so, when in a tight corner, used his own judgement. Such was the reputation of 'Colonel Paddy', as Blair Mayne was known, that Hitler ordered he be shot on sight. We continued to push our way through the desert until October 1942, when the Eighth Army under General Montgomery, reinforced with arms and equipment, attacked Rommel at Alamein. Breaking defences, Montgomery pressed the enemy back into Libya."

As the Allies moved toward Sicily, George Macartney was wounded by shrapnel. "I was treated at an army field station by Ian Fraser, an outstanding medical man destined to became head of Belfast's Royal Victoria Hospital. Upon recovery, I was ordered to go by motorbike and meet General Montgomery at a bridge near Taranto in Italy. Serving men fighting since 1940 had individual opinions of Montgomery. 'How are the men?' demanded the General. 'Not happy', I replied, 'mainly due to poor food and shortage of cigarettes.' 'They want a good kick', retorted Montgomery. I could well imagine Paddy Mayne's reaction to such a comment. 'Trouble is there are so many to kick', I answered looking skywards."

George Macartney was amongst the first to liberate the city of Brussels. "As the Germans retreated, those accused of fraternising with the enemy fell foul of their own people, paying a heavy penalty. After France and the Normandy landings, our unit was called to Arnhem in

Holland. Now serving with the Surrey and Sussex Yeomanry Regiment, orders came to join Russian troops at Lübeck in Germany. We found ourselves in Neustadt, at the site of a women's concentration camp. Waiting for the Russians to arrive, I cannot express our horror on seeing hundreds of starving women, Polish, Dutch, Czech, in rags, demented from treatment they had received. We drove into Neustadt and, from a large shop, bundled up all the clothing we could find. These garments were distributed amongst the wretched women at that camp."

With the ending of war, George was transferred to Düsseldorf. "Devastated by constant bombing, my job was now housing homeless German nationals. It was expected that I would help with a victory parade in London, but suffering an injury, I returned home instead. It was great to be home", he says with relish. "Corbett's of Portadown gave me my old job as department head of menswear after six weeks' rest." Now, contacted by Brigadier Nelson-Russell, General Officer Commanding at Northern Ireland Headquarters in Lisburn, George was requested to join 661 Field Regiment based in Portadown. He also learned of his promotion to the rank of Captain. Post-war there was an acute scarcity of clothing, and taking the matter into his own hands, George visited Londonderry, placing an order for shirts with Neely and Wilkinson's factory. Van Heusen and Vantella were quality trade names then, with prices ranging from five to 15 shillings. "In 1950 I opened my own menswear business at the former English Street premises of George Richardson. Assistant, Ernie Atkinson, was my first member of staff and Jim Speers joined the business as a teenager, remaining for 12 years. Jim had a keen interest in politics even then and was a member of the Young Unionists."

With encouragement from the late Captain Michael Armstrong, George joined the Unionist Party in 1952. "Sir Norman Stronge was Lord Lieutenant for Co. Armagh and Speaker of the House of Commons. He was also chairman of the Territorial Army Association while I served as a committee member. We became friends and I was often a guest at Tynan Abbey. Sir Norman's appalling death came in 1981, aged 84, with that of his son James, former MP for Armagh. These murders, as with every political atrocity, are a slur on the 20th century and humanity. Sir Norman and James Stronge were buried in Tynan Parish Churchyard. Last Christmas the Abbey itself, already badly gutted, was reduced to rubble, a sad ending for a dignified, 250-year-old country estate. Former rector of Tynan, the Rev. Tom Taylor, described Sir Norman as 'a perfect gentleman' and spoke of his sadness at the devastation of 'this beautiful place'.

"Since my father's death I had also been running the home farm with all its demands. Retiring from business, I stood for local government in 1980, serving for 12 years prior to my election as Chairman. Education deserved its proper place, and for 40 years, I served as a member of County Armagh Education Committee. With the late William Dawson, director of education, I supported the purchase of land for our present College of Further Education." George later became chairman, and was a member of the College board of governors when Hugh McIlwaine was appointed, remaining on this board for 40 years. Council representative on the Education Board for six years, George also sat on the boards of governors of Markethill High School and St Catherine's College.

Belgium has never forgotten those who took part in the liberation of her country and on the eve of Irish Day 1990, George Macartney in the presence of his wife Iris, was honoured as 'one of the brave amongst the good' at a reception in Brussels. Presenting George with a commemorative medal and the freedom of the city, Mr Vandroogenbroek, Chief of Protocol, commented with pleasure on the Cenotaph ceremony in Armagh when a plaque was unveiled by 5th Irish Brigade in honour of Belgian soldiers based in Northern Ireland.

Unhappily, during his term of office, Chairman George Macartney represented Armagh District Council at a litany of funerals. "For a time it was a daily occurrence. Often accompanied by Chief Executive Des Mitchell, I found the grief of wives, mothers and children unbearable. One day it was a policeman from Markethill, the next, Blackwatertown. Community relations were strained to the limits. The Royal Ulster Constabulary has paid an unfair and ultimate sacrifice, all too easily forgotten."

While George was recovering from a major heart attack in 1995, the death of his beloved wife Iris the following year was a devastating blow. "Iris was a niece of Loveday Poynton who ran an exclusive milliner's shop in Scotch Street. Loveday married Robert Johnston and their nephew, the late William Johnston who ran a business in Scotch Street, also served with the District Council. Iris came to assist at her aunt's shop and we met at the home

Chairman George Macartney and Mrs Iris Macartney *(seated right)* with guests in the Armstrong Room following the presentation of a Tyrone Crystal chandelier to Armagh District Council by the Northern Bank

of a friend. She was a constant support and I miss her dearly." He speaks with equal affection of their four daughters, Anne Hegan, an occupational therapist in Lisburn, second daughter Lyn Jackson who lives in Hillsborough, Karen in Portadown and Janet, the youngest, who was an officer with the Women's Royal Naval Service. He is grandfather to four, Lucy, Victoria, Claire and Christine. A proud moment in an exceptional life was meeting the Queen in 1998, when he became an MBE—a Member of the Order of the British Empire. He was accompanied by his three daughters, Lyn, Karen and Janet.

The face of the world has changed dramatically since George Macartney decided war would probably last only three months. Through him we have insight into men like his hero Robert Blair Mayne, a young solicitor from Ulster, who became the personification of Irish courage. Might not as much be said of George Macartney, businessman, farmer, soldier, educationalist and Council Chairman for three terms?

Phil McBride

"Make yourself at home, I'll be free in a moment", Phil McBride calls cheerfully. The room is high-ceilinged, logs crackle in the grate. *Grattan's Parliament* by P.W. Wheatley reflects in an ornate mirror above the marble fireplace. This house is a veritable museum, magnetically drawing on the past. About the walls, sporting personalities vie with Irish politicians, who sampled its hospitality for more than a century.

Trodden's Hotel in Irish Street was the home of James Trodden, originally from Tassagh, and his wife Brigid Doyle, a native of Armaghbreague. Both were born in 1878 and married in 1908 by Canon Corr. Silver-haired Phil McBride is the second of their three daughters. Now 89, she is known to the entire community and competently runs this large establishment on a day-to-day basis. "My parents lived in Downpatrick after they married", recounts Phil. "I believe my father took over an existing oil round, selling to neighbours by means of horse and cart. Astute in business, James brought his wife back to Armagh before long, establishing a little shop in Ogle Street opposite Bennett's the newsagent. Another short space and he moved to this address. I believe it was in dreadful repair when he took over but don't underestimate James Trodden's ability to make a home comfortable."

In the dull of a November afternoon, she unwraps sepia likenesses from yellowing tissue. "There were three of us, Molly, me, and Kathleen. My father's life was steeped in sport and politics. Before long, this house became a nerve centre for Armagh GAA. As a girl, I fetched buckets of hot water for teams cleaning up after a match. Young women today wouldn't dream of it. Sixty-five years later, board meetings for both players and supporters are still held here."

James Trodden acquired one of the first hackney cabs in Armagh. Phil has business records dating to 1917. A dusty ledger reveals this methodical man's way of conducting business. "He recorded the date, licence number of the vehicle, destination of fare and the driver's name. By now he had a fleet of cabs and most of the drivers lodged here. That's how we inherited 'hotel' status. Gilbert Slater, a garage proprietor of the time, sold vehicles to my father who kept the receipts." Turning a fusty page, she locates an entry whereby Dr McKee hired a driver to take him on a sick call in February 1917. A nameless RIC sergeant was driven to Milford, likewise a priest from the parochial house visited Tullysaran.

"We girls grew up in this bustling household. My mother was cooking for the family, our drivers, anyone who chanced by. Providing a meal following a funeral and a wedding breakfast were natural progressions. We have endless letters confirming how the local populace appreciated James Trodden's efficiency. My sister Molly was musically gifted. Mr Holden, the Cathedral organist, trained her, so she often sang at local concerts. I can rattle out a tune on the piano, but", she shrugs, "you certainly wouldn't *pay* to hear me."

Phil served her time with Charles Rooney, a quality outfitter in English Street. "It was my introduction to beautifully-made clothing. Such detail has its price today. Finishings and trimmings, velvet, fur or suede, were important. Peter McBride worked downstairs in menswear." Phil admits he was a pleasant young man who asked her out several times. "I wasn't interested in serious relationships. After all, the sporting fraternity was constantly coming and going at home. However Peter waited patiently and we married in 1938."

In common with her father, Peter had the ability to make business succeed. He acquired the Thomas Street premises, today carried on in the family name, making this one of Armagh's longest-established retailers. "Just as when we were single, Peter continued in menswear and I looked after ladies' fashion. You don't have to ask. It was quality stock, the best we felt people could afford. Times for many were hard, so accounts enabled some to pay on a weekly basis."

Women who have a way with fashion rarely change. In her sweater and smart skirt, Phil has retained all of her dress sense.

The McBrides raised a family above the shop in Thomas Street—Eamon, Moya, Peadar who died some years ago, Breige, Seamus, Sheelagh and Kieran. "I was happy in my own home but there wasn't a day when I didn't call at Trodden's. The place continued to buzz with the activity I'd know in my youth. Peter had a great fondness for my father, who, famous for his oratory, could hold a gathering spellbound. All his speeches were unwritten and unrehearsed. My father had a fine appearance. He wore a huge bow tie and possessed the ability to charm all he met.

"Michael Collins visited Trodden's Hotel when he was MP for Armagh in 1921. A child at the time, I remember the general stir this caused. The Ireland of his day was a sad place. I've kept a letter from Eamon De Valera dated February 1936. It is a reply to correspondence sent by my father, soon after the death of De Valera's child. Another close friend of my father was Charlie O'Neill, founder of Armagh Harps. Joe Houlihan and Gerry Arthurs attended GAA meetings at Trodden's Hotel a far back as 1933."

Phil and Peter enjoyed drama and both their names appear on programmes from the Fifties, when they acted in stage plays at the Pearse Óg Dramatic Society. When Peter died in 1961, Phil struggled to maintain the business. "I'll never know how I managed. We had already moved back to Trodden's Hotel, so to some extent, the cheery bustle lifted my spirits. The place may have been like Piccadilly but none was denied hospitality. My mother outlived my father by 15 years."

It is Trodden's that hosts Armagh County Camogie Board. Her encouragement and support led to Phil's appointment as county president. Groups of Armagh camógs dot the room. Here too is the 1985 team that won the Maguire Cup and the Ulster Junior Championship, becoming All-Ireland finalists. A vintage 1993 saw Armagh County win the Junior All-Ireland Final and in 1994, the Intermediate All-Ireland Final.

Phil's daughter Sheelagh takes after her mother. The same sporting fervour, excellent sense of dress, but above all, a desire to see continuity of the family business.

Phil McBride is the only woman to have been honoured by the county in that masculine preserve of the GAA. Known affectionately as the 'Mother of GAA' she received in recognition, a silver salver engraved with chased scrolls from the Hall of Fame. The Cú Chullain replica on her piano was presented by Armagh Civil Rights Committee which first assembled at Trodden's.

Beginning with James Trodden, this house has been a Mecca for the coming together of people in pursuit of an ideal. Ever open for hospitality, no-one turned away through lack of means. The doorbell rings. As much in demand as ever, Phil McBride will always be at the heart of Trodden's.

Her smile is slightly wistful as she recalls the past. "Such a pity you missed James. You would have loved him..."

Phil and Peter McBride with their family—
Eamon, Moya, Peader, Breege, Seamus, Sheelagh and Kieran

William Henning

As 'the most likely candidate', William Henning became Chairman of Armagh District Council in 1978, remaining in office for a three-year term. William, a farmer from Loughgilly, was eminently qualified for this post, having been a member of Armagh County Council for 12 years prior to serving another five as Vice-Chairman. His appointment coincided with a lack of enthusiasm felt by many in local government, a climate of political instability and unprecedented violence. During his term of office he would witness the deaths of more than 30 of his comrades in the Ulster Defence Regiment in which he held the rank of Major. William Henning topped the poll for three terms and received a standing ovation when he resigned.

"You succeeded where I failed through your temperament and approach", admitted Councillor Norman Creswell, Armagh's first Chairman in reorganised local government. "If all who follow you adopt this attitude, we can look forward to future harmony."

"I had no apprehension stepping into office knowing exactly what it entailed", asserts William Henning. "When I became an Ulster Unionist member of the County Council, I was replacing my uncle, Lindsey Henry, JP. My father had been a schoolteacher at Mullaghmore, now the electoral area of Cusher Ward." Indicative of his standing in society, William Henning was appointed Justice of the Peace in 1980. Dr George Fitzroy Gillespie of Tynan was similarly honoured at this time by the Lord Chancellor. A decade later William became a founder member of the Association of JPs, and is now its Chairman. Accepting the Chair of Armagh District Council, William Henning resolved to work on the principles of complete fairness— and this is how he was perceived.

"Norman Megaw was then Chief Executive of the Council and I found his administration to be first-rate. On my final evening in office, Deputy Chairman Douglas Hutchinson presented me with an official portrait, promising it would hang in the Council chamber. I was succeeded by Charles Armstrong, JP." On taking office, Chairman Henning shared the Council chamber with Seamus Mallon of the Social Democratic and Labour Party, subsequently Deputy First Minister Designate. "Seamus was a schoolteacher and, from all accounts, excellent in his profession. He admitted to being a reluctant politician in those days for we often stopped for a friendly chat after meetings. Subsequent to my appointment, June 1978 saw four political parties battle for the local Westminster seat. Unionist Party member Harold McCusker stood on the strength of his past representation of the constituency while Brian English, Alliance Councillor and Deputy Mayor of Craigavon, was a political newcomer. Douglas Hutchinson of the Democratic Unionist Party was determined to oppose Mr McCusker while Seamus Mallon was a rather reluctant candidate for the SDLP."

William Henning became something of a pioneer when, within his first months as Chairman, he attended a conference of local and regional authorities in Europe. "Here I discovered that my counterparts in other countries, including England and Southern Ireland, had council planning powers while all we could boast was a consultative role. About to leave Munich, it was a bitter irony to learn from my radio that Armagh, the ecclesiastical capital of Ireland, had been bombed and many of Scotch Street's historic buildings damaged. As the only representative from Northern Ireland, my voice was somewhat inadequate. The Republic of Ireland had at least 30 present at this symposium, all completely au fait with the workings of the Council of Europe. German industry had to be admired for its practicality. Munich, a city devastated during the war, was now restored to its former glory. It was a pleasure to visit Landshut, a beautiful little town in the Bavarian hills, and see what pride Germans take in maintaining their buildings. I felt strongly that NI government officials should have been present at this conference, as well as local authorities, for there was much to learn. The principles behind the European Charter called for reallocation of substantial national or regional budgetary appropriations earmarked for redevelopment and new construction which might foster architectural heritage. Looking back, I see just how futuristic were such concepts. Our agenda dealt with living conditions, and training of young people so that crafts threatened by extinction were safeguarded. European schools were nurturing an appreciation within young people for their architectural heritage as well as devising strategies for revitalising rural areas. That was 18 years ago and, in some respects, we in this country are only facing up to such matters today. I returned from Germany determined to initiate planning powers at local level.

"New Council offices opened at the Palace Demesne in Spring 1981. Resigning in June of that year meant I enjoyed only a few months at what has to be the best possible Council address! Negotiations on the purchase of this 200-year-old Georgian neo-classical country house and its lands began with Chairman Norman Creswell and were finalised during my term. It was the seat of successive Anglican Primates, but Archbishop George Otto Simms had now moved to See House in Cathedral Close. It seemed the Representative Church Body was finding the Palace financially difficult to maintain. Speculation as to its future was rife. Mr W.J. Dickson of the Southern Education and Library Board envisaged a joint venture between the Board and Armagh District Council, with the Palace as an education centre where youth leaders might be trained. We in the City and District Council were unanimous in our bid to purchase the property as reorganisation meant that Council departments had staff scattered throughout various buildings. The Palace had fallen into disrepair which necessitated a lot of work before we could move. This was well before the age of computing so masses of documents and files had to be transferred while normal administration continued. It must have been a nightmare for administrative clerk Ivan Baxter, and Irene Walker, his extremely competent secretary.

"On rare occasions when I visit the Palace, it is a source of pride to see this building so tastefully restored and preserved. The Armstrong Room—a former dining room at the Palace—was named for my successor who was brutally murdered. It is entirely carpeted and furnished from products manufactured exclusively in Northern Ireland. Tyrone Crystal walls lights and a centrally positioned chandelier were gifts sponsored by Tyrone Crystal and the Northern Bank.

"Some you win", William smiles wryly, "and some you lose. We made an unsuccessful attempt to purchase Gosford Castle, a 350-year-old derelict building with endless cultural and social possibilities, located at Markethill. An asking price of £100,000 was certainly a stumbling block so negotiations were abandoned. In January 1980, the property once more came onto the market, now at a giveaway price of £9,000. Harold McCusker, MP, raised the matter at Stormont. The property was eventually secured by a Belfast hotelier but I always felt that Council ownership might have seen the old castle restored for the mutual benefit of the community.

"While I was a member of the Education Committee, Markethill Primary School (now Markethill High School) came under threat of closure. With a wide catchment area, this meant local children travelling and little or no provision elsewhere. Leading a team in opposition, with the co-operation of head teacher, John McCartney, we eventually saved the day. This made headlines in every newspaper. The school has gone from strength to strength and my opposition recently admitted that closure would have been the wrong policy."

William Henning has a special empathy with border farmers who suffered immeasurably at the hands of terrorists. In addition, his military service as a Major in the Ulster Defence Regiment found him responsible for the security of a significant section of South Armagh terrain. Remembrance Sunday is a particularly poignant occasion when, in the past, he has placed as many as 14 wreaths in memory of men from his Company, all murdered by paramilitaries. When a UDR base at Glenanne was devastated by a massive bomb, three more lives were added to the toll.

"My own land spans the Council border, stretching from Newry and Mourne into Armagh. An example of what was happening on a regular basis was the killing of 38-year-old Harry Livingstone, a private in the Ulster Defence Regiment. Harry was shot dead in March 1980, while feeding cattle on his out-farm at Cortynan, close to the South Armagh border. My cousin, Charles Henning, was then shot dead nearby at Newry Cattle Market. Even closer to home was the shooting of my brother, Noel, at his Garden Centre in Sugar Island, Newry. He died a year later from a brain tumour. Sensing the outrage of that community, I made an immediate, impassioned public appeal to the community, church leaders and the government that each support our forces of law and order. These were heinous crimes and I felt church leaders were strangely silent when they should have been first to protest against the violation of taking life. Clearly cross-border security co-operation was inadequate. The British government needed to stress our plight with counterparts in Dublin so that Irish territory would no longer be a safe haven for terrorists. It's a tired statement", William agrees, "but our situation in 1980 would not have been tolerated on mainland Britain. Harry Livingstone had been a brother of Councillor Mary Huey and, at a meeting of Council, I expressed sympathy to the Livingstone family. Councillor Oliver Tobin of the SDLP, a technical college lecturer, added his sentiments and, in moving terms, told how Harry had been his pupil, describing him as 'a big, easy-going lad who wouldn't have hurt a fly'. Councillor Tobin was of the opinion that until men of violence sated their appetites for cold-blooded killing, it would continue. How right he was. I have newspaper cuttings that relate to the deaths of perhaps 30 men like Harry. For the press it was almost an everyday occurrence yet each fatality was someone's son. Retrospectively, I wonder how I coped with my farm, council business and my duties as a Major with the Ulster Defence Regiment.

"In a complete contrast of hostilities, following World War II, 25,000 young Belgians were trained in the Province after the liberation of their country from the Nazis by the Allies. Many were based in County Armagh where they formed a great affection for our area. This led to the twinning of Armagh with Messancy during 1975. More than 20 of these men were our guests in August 1980, a somewhat poignant visit led by two Regional Presidents. M. Émile Grasser, who had completed his training in Summerisland, Loughgall, represented the Federation of Brussels, Brabant, Flanders and Limburg while M. R. Lupcin represented the Federation of 5th Brigade, Namur. During this visit, M. Grasser placed a poppy wreath at the War Memorial in honour of soldiers from the Armagh area who died in the struggle for freedom in Europe. I hosted a reception in the Council chamber for our guests. Before leaving for Belgium, the party visited both Cathedrals and the Planetarium.

"It seems appropriate to add that I am a member of the Somme Association and have visited the war graves and museums of Ypres and Normandy. A year earlier, my neighbour from Glenanne visited Thiepval on 1 July, taking part in an annual memorial service. A second ceremony was to be held at the Ulster Tower later that afternoon. He decided to wait and attend that also. Passing the time, he crossed the valley to a cemetery at Thiepval Wood. All war dead are recorded in a memorial book placed in a wall safe. Taking out this book, my neighbour opened it at random. The first name he saw was that of 'William Smith Qua, Island Road, Loughgilly' (whose body was interred in another cemetery). This address was only a few miles from my neighbour's home yet the name was not familiar. I since established that William Qua was an only son who died at the Somme and whose family line has all but ceased. A year following I found his grave, well-kept in a nearby village and placed a cross there, in his memory."

While William Henning has been a Deputy Lieutenant for the county since 1981, the origin of his appointment is quite unusual. "Earlier on the evening on which Sir Norman Stronge was murdered he had written to me, stating his intention to put forward my name. This letter, bearing a second-class stamp, arrived at my home on the day of Sir Norman's funeral. On hearing this, Sir Norman's daughter smiled sadly, commenting: 'How like my father'. Given that Tynan Abbey was gutted by fire and Sir Norman's personal papers probably destroyed, I put all thoughts of the matter aside. A year later I heard of my appointment from Captain Michael Torrens-Spence (RN Retd), who replaced Sir Norman as Lord Lieutenant for the County. It seemed the matter had been discussed earlier.

"Lily, my wife, was a constant support during those 20 years I spent in local government. When I eventually stood down in 1981, so also did Mrs Huey, Oliver Tobin and Joseph Fullerton." Seamus Mallon paid tribute to all four commenting: "Politics have a loose edge if they don't have the cut, thrust and bite they should. I look forward to the day when we can grapple and fight elections on real issues. I wish the outgoing members all the best in the future but feel sorry that we will not have the benefit of their advice."

Awarded the Military MBE in the New Year Honours List of 1985, William Henning has also concentrated interests in farming and, in particular, his pedigree flock of Suffolk sheep. Past chairman of the Suffolk Sheep Society, he is also a member of the council of the Royal Ulster Agricultural Society. William is a former organiser of the Young Farmers' Clubs of Ulster and a lifelong member of the Ulster Farmers' Union.

Of three sons, Jim is assistant manager of Banbridge Creamery, Brian works as an executive with a construction

Chairman William Henning, JP, D.Lt., following the official opening of Poyntzpass Royal British Legion Hall hands over the Queen's congratulatory message to chairman Barry Gibson and secretary Harry Briggs

company in Belfast and Ivan continues the family tradition of farming. William and Lily have 11 grandchildren, most of whom live locally.

"My favourite possession is a grandfather clock which I was given in acknowledgement of 34 years as treasurer and member of the Kirk Session of Tullyallen Presbyterian Church. At present I am Clerk of Session. Like many people who have worked in public life, I have had to live on adrenalin and crisis management. I now consider being at home, or in a situation that is calm, to be life's greatest pleasure."

John Ward

Described by Archbishop Seán Brady as "Ireland's most prominent layman", John Ward was chauffeur to four cardinals for half a century. His funeral took place on 6 July 1998, exactly 52 years to the day from when he first arrived in Armagh.

A trusted employee, John enjoyed the confidences of Ireland's highest churchmen and his life resonates with the character of the black chauffeur played by Morgan Freeman, who struck a poignant chord in the film Driving Miss Daisy. Paying personal tributes to John, the congregation included the recently retired Cardinal Daly. During his oration, Archbishop Brady quoted from John's biography, which earned special mention at the Arts Council of England Awards in 1997.

Praise from Cardinal Cahal Daly has to be earned. Accepting John Ward's resignation after 47 years of service, the leading churchman commented, "It's like losing a trusted friend".

Chauffeur to Cardinal Daly and three of his predecessors, John has driven thousands of miles in the call of ecclesiastical duty. Silver-haired and fresh complexioned, at 74, he radiates a contentment many might envy.

"I was born in Castlepollard, Co. Westmeath, in 1919", John begins, conjuring an image of the times. "My father tilled the land to provide a living for a family of four children. The first real blow came when I was 14 and my mother died. It was essential that I make my own way in the world so I became a parlour boy at St Patrick's College, Maynooth, some 50 miles away. The job entailed serving meals to lay students training for the priesthood and I learned of the vacancy by word of mouth, there being no other means of communication."

He briefly ponders. "I missed my family. It was a sad time at first, for after all, I was little more than a child. I wrote home regularly, then watched longingly for a letter from my father in return. I hoarded correspondence from home, and once off-duty read and re-read each page a hundred times."

Students and academic staff at the College amounted to 600 at any given time. "My", he reflects, "we earned our keep."

At Maynooth, John acquired the skill that secured his lifetime of employment. He learned to drive. President of the College then was Monsignor John Francis D'Alton. Appointed Bishop of Meath in 1942, four years later he was appointed Archbishop of Armagh.

"I was called to his office and asked if I'd consider coming to Armagh with him as his driver." John smiles broadly. "I regarded the Monsignor as a father figure and went without a second thought. I was given my own accommodation in Ara Coeli, the Cardinal's official residence in Armagh.

"I met my future wife, Margaret Sherry, when inadvertently Cardinal D'Alton, as he now was, played Cupid. Margaret was helping with an important dinner and the Cardinal sent for me. I think he wanted me to drive one of the dignitaries home after dining. I was impressed by Miss Sherry's pleasant demeanour and made a point of getting in touch. She lived in Co. Monaghan and before long, I proposed.

We were married on 27 October 1954 in St Patrick's Cathedral—need I add, by the Cardinal, who also gave us a handsome cheque as a wedding gift, telling us to buy something for our new home."

Margaret Ward became matron of the boarding department at St Patrick's Grammar School, Armagh. John and she have five children. "Mary, our eldest, teaches in St Malachy's Primary School here in town. Jim is with a local timber firm. Seán, who came third, is a Professor of Biology at the University of Nevada, Kevin is a qualified nurse and representative for an American medical company in Northern Ireland. Clare, the youngest, holds a degree in Sociology and works for Health and Social Services."

John has privileged and personal memories of the various Cardinals for whom he worked. "They differed greatly in character", he agrees. "Cardinal D'Alton was 64 when appointed to office. I'd known him since my boyhood and he'd often confide in me as we drove along. In tranquil moments, I still hear his familiar bidding, 'John, we'd better be getting along.'"

He ponders a moment. "Ours was a world of quiet routine. Driving the Daimler through the leafy lanes of the county, we had no idea what was happening in Europe. Such a beautiful car that was! McAnerney's garage carried out the servicing and we never suffered a breakdown. It originally belonged to Cardinal MacRory and we used it for a further seven years.

"Cardinal D'Alton was eventually presented with an Austin Princess by the diocesan clergy. Sheer elegance of line made this car a pleasure to drive. Cardinal D'Alton loved his garden, particularly the rosebeds. He'd anxiously inspect the bushes for the first signs of greenfly or fungi. Herbaceous borders were utterly glorious during those days at Ara Coeli. The Cardinal sat in the garden reading or simply inhaling the peace and made a point of telling me when birds saw fit to nest there."

John recalls the death of Cardinal D'Alton in 1963. "Cardinals Cushing and Spellman of Boston and New York, respectively, came to the funeral as well as Cardinal Godfrey of London. Having had such care for my welfare—remember, I'd been in his service since boyhood—I found his death traumatic.

"There was a void until the appointment of Cardinal Conway in 1963. His personality was quiet and reserved and I soon adapted. A thinker and reflective, he did have a sense of humour. My employment continued much as before."

Following the death of Cardinal Conway in 1977, Monsignor Tomás Ó Fiaich of Cullyhanna, President of Maynooth College, was duly appointed. In June 1977, John, as chauffeur to the highest churchman in the land, accompanied Archbishop Ó Fiaich to Rome for his creation as Cardinal.

"We flew from Dublin to Rome, where, just imagine my thrill, a car was waiting for me! Now I was sampling the other side of the coin. I stayed at the Irish College within the Vatican City and during the course of the week, met Pope John Paul II. On various trips to England, we took the car by ferry and I twice accompanied Cardinal Ó Fiaich to Lourdes.

"I came to know him from an aspect few saw. He hated the strife that poisoned fair thinking and longed for peace in Ireland. Cardinal Ó Fiaich had the utmost regard for Archbishops Simms and Armstrong. When each held office, they exchanged cordial visits, often dining together.

"Cardinal Ó Fiaich was a sporting man with great affection for the GAA. I frequently drove him to matches in Croke Park listening to a running commentary on every player on the way there, then how they should have played on the way back. Gregarious by nature, he loved entertaining. His party piece was *The Aul' Orange Flute* which, if pressed, he would sing rather well."

John accompanied Cardinal Ó Fiaich to Dublin Airport for his last flight to Lourdes. "He hadn't been well and I had an unhappy feeling leaving him. 'John', the Cardinal suddenly requested, 'stay with me until I check in at the desk'. His flight was called and he made to leave. Then, as if in need of reassurance, paused and said 'You will be here when I get back?'

"He collapsed in France as you know, dying shortly afterwards. The Cardinal's sister-in-law specially asked I go to London and accompany his remains to Ireland. This I did with a heavy heart." John met Cardinal Hume, the Papal Nuncio and heads of state from all over the world when they attended the funeral on 8 May 1990.

"Our present Cardinal, previously Bishop of Down and Connor, was appointed Archbishop on 16 December 1990. I travelled to Rome for his creation as Cardinal in June 1991. Dr Oliver Woods, physician to Cardinal Daly, accompanied us as did Dr Woods' wife Cecilia and many of the Ara Coeli household staff. I met Pope John Paul a second time.

"During the week I was free most of the time and wandered through St Peter's gazing at the magnificence created by Michelangelo. The church of Sta Maria della Pace is very beautiful. Another day I climbed the hill to the walled town of Assisi stopping by the statue of St Francis in the church of Sta Maria degli Angeli. The little cell where St Francis died is within that church."

In his lifetime, John Ward has quietly worked through a World War, the Korean War, the Vietnam conflict and our own weary chronicle of troubles. He has also witnessed medical, scientific and educational advances. But he insists, "no-one in this land goes hungry today and that is the best advance of all."

Reluctant to cite a favourite, John has enormous regard for Cardinal Daly whom he considers "a dignified and scholarly man, who lectured at Queen's University for 21 years. He strove for peace, both he and Archbishop Eames. Mind you", John says, a twinkle in his eye, "the Cardinal has a sweet tooth and cannot always resist the beautiful cakes baked by Mrs Toner, his housekeeper.

"'Please don't break the link, John', Cardinal Daly requested, 'give up driving, but continue to visit Ara

John Ward, chauffeur to four Cardinals

Coeli.' So I attend to the post each day," John says happily, "or arrange the dining room for a special reception. I've done it so often, I can place guests with my eyes shut."

Faithful to the end, John Ward has proven himself a man for all seasons. One who will never break the link. On that you may depend.

Bob Carson

An array of congratulatory cards fills every available space in Robert Carson's comfortable living room. Proof, if need be, that hundreds share in the pleasure of his most recent honour, the Benemerenti Medal bestowed by Pope John Paul II.

One card bears a familiar sketch of James Joyce, an appropriate measure of the significance of this occasion. Joyce, by his literary ability, fitted a revelation of all life in a single day. Bob Carson competently unveils 200 years in one afternoon. "James Carson", he begins, "my great-grandfather, was a skilled tradesman who worked for Primate Lord John George Beresford in 1822. James Carson was employed in major restorative work on St Patrick's Cathedral. He married local woman Mary Ward, establishing himself in Lower Irish Street."

Snow falls softly outside Bob's home at Banbrook Hill where he is relaxing before a cheerful fire. Two of his daughters, Breege and Cora, have prepared afternoon tea. This is Carson hospitality at its best. At the very heart of his family, Bob has acquired a collection of mementoes, each inviting its memory.

"I was a war baby", Bob jests, "born in 1914. Phil Trodden is probably my best-known remaining neighbour of that era. My parents, Owen and Annie Carson, lived in Lower Irish Street. He bought domestic fowl from the farming community, selling these to Corrigan's yard, which supplied local butchers and markets. Annie's grandfather, Peter McGurk, occupied the last house in Jenny's Row and was employed as coachman by the Beresford Hotel."

Bob Carson is a modest man. Hundreds of congratulatory cards crowding this room bear witness to a life lived well and the massive esteem in which he is held by, and beyond, the Armagh community. Bob will place these in safe keeping with congratulatory letters including one from the then President of Ireland, Mary Robinson, on his 60th wedding anniversary. He has carefully filed a letter of thanks for hospitality extended at Cardinal Tomás Ó Fiaich's funeral from Ruairí Quinn, TD, Dáil Éireann.

Churchman and caretaker of St Patrick's Parochial Hall for more than 20 years, Bob is a connoisseur of past times, twinned with his own inimitable brand of kindness. Again he refers to his childhood where, from the tender care of Miss Rose Colgan at Mount St Catherine's nursery school, he advanced to Greenpark, where he remained until 1928. Bob remembers Brother Keeley as a devout and dedicated teacher.

"In flashes of the past I can recall great excitement surrounding Michael Collins' visit to Armagh in 1921. I had just left school to begin work at Wilson's Spinning Mill, later known as the Slipper Factory, on Loughgall Road. It was three days before my 14th birthday, which unfairly you must agree, marked the age of responsibility for us youngsters. In bare feet I attended experienced doffers and spinners, supplying new bobbins for each worker. Paid eight shillings a week, my day started at eight in the morning, finished at six. When Wilson's mill closed I was taken on by Corrigan's poultry yard. They were good people, the best", he adds with conviction. "No one went hungry. Any man without money received an advance on his pay at the office. Arthur McAnerney's haulage company at Lower Irish Street was my next employer. It was now 1934. Another good man, Arthur provided sick pay and food for many families in need long before social reform. Little is known of quiet deeds that meant everything to the deprived."

Bob married Miss Roseanne Burns from Derrygonnelly, nanny to the Eagleson family of Cathedral Villas. "Tuesday evening and you could guarantee I would be found at the Parochial Hall when traditional or céilí dancing took place. So, it seemed, was Roseanne. Each Tuesday, McCusker Brothers, my favourite band, were on stage and I never missed a chance to enjoy their music. That's how we met. Prior to our marriage, Roseanne went nursing with the Order of the Little Company of Mary at St Raphael's in Edinburgh." It was 1936 when Bob brought his bride to Primrose Hill.

"The Church has always been central to our lives, head of our home and a direct influence on all we did", Bob comments. "I never drank and both of us were Pioneers all our lives, in common with most of our family. Neither did we smoke. We observed Lent, annual Missions, the Corpus Christi June procession when Roseanne took every child without a guardian under her wing. Family Rosary was said at bedtime each evening. Roseanne's standards were high, she baked, was a great cook and skilled needlewoman. Raised on a farm, she cultivated our fresh vegetable and kept chickens.

"It was July 1938 when we moved to Banbrook Hill. No matter who called, Roseanne extended her special brand of warmth and hospitality. During the war, Belgian soldiers, far from home, coming or leaving the railway station, found a welcome and rested a while. It is worth mentioning that I remember General George Patton shepherding American troops en route to Europe, here in this street. You can imagine my thoughts when I read how the late Vera Magee, born and orphaned across the road, used her skills to assist Generals Patton and Bradley when Hitler was crippling half of the globe. My family are just now involved in a huge campaign to encourage neighbours from that era, living elsewhere, to 'Come Back to Banbrook' during August 2000 in special celebration of the Millennium. The main event will focus on Graveyard Sunday and every neighbour will be doing their bit to ensure success of this event. I'm looking forward to meeting up with friends from afar who shared life on Banbrook. Sadly Roseanne won't be here. She and I enjoyed 60 years of marriage and", tears stream down Bob's face, "I miss her dearly".

Councillor Charlie Armstrong, whose murder shocked all right-thinking citizens, was a great friend of the Carson family for decades. "Charlie worked at the Gas Board, collecting takings from our meters. Weighed down with coins, for homes had penny meters then—imagine, 240 in a pound—Charlie know he could safely leave this money with us overnight. Learning of this man's untimely death, like Christians would, we grieved for his family."

For more than 30 years, Bob fulfilled steward's duties at St Patrick's Cathedral. "In this capacity I officiated at the funerals of four Cardinals and am proud to retain the friendship of retired Cardinal Cahal Daly. On our Diamond Wedding Anniversary in 1996, Cardinal Daly sent a personal message to Roseanne and myself. One sentence I would like to quote, 'What changes you have seen in your life together since 8 September 1936: I am sure, however, that you felt both blessed and graced over the years, having been married on the Feast of Our Lady's Birthday.' President Mary Robinson also sent personal congratulations."

Bob and Roseanne as joint caretakers of St Patrick's Parochial Hall during the Sixties, were, for more than 20 years, acutely aware of this vital social venue. "Raised by funds from all four wards of the parish, there was never an evening free from activity. Dana sang here before she ever made a name for herself. Showband days brought the Capital, the Majestic, Dave Glover, Big Tom and the Mainliners, Tina and the Mexicans, Johnny Flynn, Dickie Rock and the Royal Showband. One dance advertising Big Tom, costing ten shillings admission caused concern for we didn't think people would pay. Well they did! 2,500 came. It wasn't my brand of music, I have to admit. I preferred McCusker Brothers' Céilí Band and dancing the 16-hand reel. Every time they were on stage, McCusker Brothers played the *Waves of Tory* just for me! St Joseph's Operatic Society staged performances at the Parochial Hall and I remember an exceptionally fine production of *The Mikado*. Dr Sheelagh Woods, who recently celebrated her 90th birthday, played a cello in the orchestra. Armagh Players held productions here and Roseanne had a lot of time for one young actor, Seamus Mallon. 'He'll go far', she'd say, always finding him 'a sincere and caring man'. Another marvellous person making excellent use of the Parochial Hall in those early days was Peggy McGarvey who taught physical education at the Convent Intermediate School. Peggy trained formation dancing, for as you know, *Come Dancing* caught and held everyone's attention during the Sixties. Couples like Roseanne and myself met here and later married.

"Organisations such as Scouts or the Youth Club utilised the hall on other nights so that it became a buzzing, vibrant part of Armagh. Everyone stopped for a cup of tea including little Joe Mullan who cycled by on his tricycle. Roseanne had a special affinity for those with special needs and learning disabilities and became a founder member of Longstone Hospital Support Group.

"To return to my present home", Bob continues, "when this property, considered spacious, became available, accommodation was scarce—94 families made application for tenancy. I had carried out substantial work at Sandy Hill graveyard so Bishop O'Callaghan declared it must come to me. It may be of interest that a previous occupant was Johnny Irwin, the shoemaker who ran his business from Jenny's Row. Close to the railway station, the Bradley family then kept number 112 as a boarding house. It was always a happy home, rooms rarely empty

Bob and Roseanne Carson
celebrate their Diamond Wedding Anniversary

and a haven for any traveller arriving late at the station. All our children except Jackie were born here. The other ten, Assumpta, Jim (deceased), Breege, Michael, Peter, Josefa, Rosemary, Margaret, Paul and Cora completed our family. Peter was born on 5 July 1948, the date our National Health Service commenced. He was delivered by Dr John Woods, who told us his practice was overflowing that morning, patients learning consultations were now free. Much later, my daughter Breege was to join the nursing profession, where in an English hospital she met Labour stalwart and Socialist, Bessie Braddock. Caring is in their blood for Michael is a nurse in St Luke's Hospital and a member of Armagh and District Talking Newspaper for the Blind."

A man for every match, Bob never missed one in his life. "I've always been an Armagh GAA supporter and consider Jim McCullough to have been an outstanding player. I found it heartbreaking, when three days after my father's funeral in 1953, I could not listen to the match. It was the All-Ireland Final between Armagh and Kerry. We observed a period of mourning and listening to the match would have been condemned as lacking respect. How times have changed! When Derry won the Sam Maguire Cup in 1992, the team stopped here at Banbrook Hilll and chatted to us for a time."

McAnerney's Haulage was absorbed into the Ulster Transport Authority during the late Thirties, moving to premises at the railway station. Bob remained an employee, continuing his service with the UTA for another 28 years. Daughters Breege and Cora say he was a strict father who led by example. "He set limits and we envied friends who could do whatever they liked. Today we feel privileged to have had such an upbringing. As for our mother, she herself was a woman of dignity who accepted everyone at face value. People in need or sorrow would ask her to pray for them and maybe, she being the person she was, her prayers were answered." Roseanne Carson, a woman of intense faith, loved by all who knew her, had a limb amputated shortly before celebrating her Diamond Wedding Anniversary. "We had a celebratory service at St Patrick's Cathedral on 8 September 1996", recalls Bob, "with our bridesmaid present! Afterwards the extended family was entertained at the Portmór Restaurant. It was our last important event together for Roseanne died on 14 June 1997. Eight of her brothers and sisters, all her children and grandchildren were with her at the moment of her death."

In savouring the joy of his latest honour, Bob Carson's only regret is that Roseanne is not by his side. "I know she's with me spiritually and I know she's happy so maybe I can be forgiven for mourning her loss." Such is the man. The language of James Joyce concealed as much as it revealed, and thus he created. It would be unforgivable to do less for Bob Carson.

William Johnston

At St Mary's Church, Bardon, Queensland, on 24 October 1998, William Johnston, MM, was laid to rest. Eighty-three years earlier, at St Mary's Parish Church, Aghavilly, William Johnston was baptised. Eldest son of Annie and William Johnston, he was born on 28 October 1915. Known locally as Billy, he seemed to learn without effort, having a good mind, good memory and an interest in everything around him. After Aghavilly National School his education was undertaken by the Christian Brothers at Greenpark, Armagh. His late sister Anna frequently commented on Billy's excellent reports and how often he brought home the class prize.

There were five children—Billy, Anna Elizabeth, Frances, Samuel and Kathleen. Billy, it was said, 'had his own brand of courage' and despite being the eldest, outlived the others. One neighbour, George Keys of Aghavilly House, now 88, remembers a spirited boy, described by Christian Brothers' teaching staff as 'brilliant rather than clever'. "Billy was a daredevil who inherited his father's gift for interesting conversation. Before we knew", George added, "he had gone. Joined the army. I chatted with him during war years, when home on leave. A handsome man, dashing even and always immaculate in uniform."

William Johnston's daughter Patricia Dakin, who lives in Queensland, continues this narrative. "My father ran away from home, joining the army when he was 16. His told us how his brother and sister had been brought up by a childless aunt and uncle at Ballyards, Milford, because my grandparents, like so many families then, were struggling to make ends meet. Dad was undoubtedly an achiever, his general knowledge and love of literature at another time could have been harnessed into university study. Poetry taught by Armagh Christian Brothers, my father could remember and recite up to his death. His was an alert mind, constantly testing our knowledge of capital cities or existing political situations throughout the globe.

"Dad was a historian, a great keeper of facts, so I can tell you something of his life since he left Armagh. We sailed to Australia from England in December 1949 when I was three years old, on a ship called *Austurius*. During the war he had married my London-born mother, Olivia. She served in the Women's Royal Air Force and had cousins living in Australia. One of them, a dairy farmer, nominated mum and dad as required by the migration authorities, so upon arrival they travelled to Kin Kin, north of Brisbane, near the gold mining town of Gympie. This dairy and bean farm was five creeks from Kin Kin. Can you imagine how my mother, a Londoner, must have felt? She couldn't cope with the conditions, and Christmas Eve 1949 saw them move to Brisbane.

"My twin brothers, Brian and Michael, were born on 15 November 1950. Following a series of jobs, Dad began his own roof contracting company, and in 1976 moved to Chapel Hill, a suburban area. This was home until their deaths last year. A keen golfer, Dad played every day, almost to the last, when lung cancer took his life. He frequently spoke of Armagh and childhood yet never returned.

"His war service will interest Armachians and there may yet be those who remember him. Down the years he spoke of contemporaries, the McCarragher boys, George Keys, Albert and Norman Watson, Johnny and Tommy Corr of Lislea and their sister who became private secretary to Eleanor, wife of President Franklin D. Roosevelt. He still has relatives residing in County Armagh but I doubt if they or many, knew of his wartime achievements. We have kept safe a letter from King George VI which accompanied his Military Medal, together with a citation from *The Times* (London) relative to action on the Italian front, 17 November 1944:

BOMBARDIER DEFIES CONDITIONS—It is announced that the Military Medal has been awarded to Bombardier William Johnston, Royal Artillery, of Battersea, for services on the Italian front. The citation states: 'During the advance to the River Cosina, this NCO was in charge of a party of signallers laying and maintaining telephone lines to the battery observation posts. During an attack on 17 November 1944, on a group of houses, the forward observation officer moved on foot with the company, and Bombardier Johnston laid the line with a carrying party as the attack progressed. The enemy mortared heavily. Two of the infantry were killed beside him and several wounded. The line was broken in several places and two Spandau posts directed fire on to the party at the same time. While the infantry and observation posts party deployed and took cover, Bombardier Johnston left a signaller on the end of the line and proceeded with his party to repair the cable which lay across the open ground behind. He succeeded in doing this under fire and kept communications open.

'During a counterattack on the same night the enemy mortared and shelled with continuous heavy concentrations for a period of an hour. Bombardier Johnston took his party and mended ten separate breaks in the area under fire and did not allow communication to fail for a longer period than 15 minutes at a time. In continued shelling during the night he remained on duty and repaired a number of breaks, although in the early concentrations he had fallen and been completely submerged in a canal. He was finally ordered to return.

'Bombardier Johnston showed an extremely high sense of duty and responsibility. By his personality and leadership he inspired in his team a state of mind which defied conditions and disregarded danger in order to carry out the job.'

"Prior to the Second World War he served in India, Palestine and China," continues Patricia. "One of the reasons for joining the artillery was a deep love of horses, acquired in childhood. His regimental horse was called Suzy Wuzy and he spoke of the wrench when, due to mechanisation, each man was ordered to shoot his own animal. He was indeed a daredevil in fair weather and foul, liked drinking with his comrades, was a man's man and capable of turning every lady's head. If he worked hard, he played hard!

"During the war, my father served with the 64th (7th London) Field Regiment Royal Artillery in North Africa, Italy, Yugoslavia and up to Germany. Because he was Irish his comrades knew him as 'Pat', a name that he liked and so it remained through life. His military association remained important and he was a member of Toowong Returned Servicemen and Women's League for many years. He enjoyed this comradeship and marching with them in the annual Anzac Day parade on 25 April. My mother died in May 1998 and we all mourned her, for Olivia Johnston was ladylike in every respect. When she died, in a sense, so did my father.

"In Australia we pay tribute to soldiers from all wars on Anzac Day (Australian and New Zealand Army Corps). This dates from Gallipoli, the First World War, when Australian and New Zealand armies went into battle under their own banner and not as part of the British Army. I should add that of course the British were there, fighting the Turks. That haunting song: *And the band played Waltzing Matilda...* tells how men were cut to shreds on the beaches. The singer is referring to the loss of his legs when he confirms in one evocative line: *'I'll go Waltzing Matilda no more...'*

"25 April 1915 is the actual date Anzacs had to withdraw from Gallipoli. Are Australia and New Zealand the only countries to honour men who had to retreat? They did so at dawn, hence the memorial service held at 3am, when veterans from the World Wars, Malaysia, Korea, Vietnam and other conflicts join with local areas to remember the fallen. This was a big day for my dad, who despite his distinguished record would have described himself as 'a good soldier—no more, no less'. When he was younger he would go to the dawn service with comrades from Toowong, usually with an Australian regiment, even though they had a British contingent. Mum prepared breakfast before they marched off through the city. Later they retired to the Irish Club for a few hours before returning to Toowong Returned Servicemen's League for an evening of reunion—need I say, one that ended merrily! In later years when a lot of dad's friends had died, he no longer participated. For some reason, last year, he asked my brother Michael, to take him. He said it would be his last and it was.

"On the night before he died, my father spoke of his late sister, Kathleen. I sat beside him and talked of family, his other sisters Frances and Anna, his mother and father. He shook his head when I said how sad it was that he had never returned. My brother Brian's daughter, Katrina, is currently in Manchester, England, running a sports programme for Adidas, having studied sports medicine at the University of Queensland. My hope is that I may one day come to Ireland, visit dad's old homestead and pay respects to our departed relatives at St Mary's Parish Church, Aghavilly, where he was baptised.

"I would say he had a fortunate life and this reflected in his choice of funeral music, *It's a Wonderful World* by Louis Armstrong. Dad knew he had approximately four months to live, and he did, to the day. By choice, his was a military funeral with The Last Post, The Ode, and Reveille. Because his sister Frances Johnston, who served

William and Olivia Johnston
at their home in Brisbane with sons Brian and Michael, and daughter Patricia

in the Women's Royal Air Force, had chosen as her final hymn, *The Day Thou Gavest, Lord, is Ended*, so did he. Some weeks later, half-way across the world, my second cousin Rachel, whom I have never met, placed a small cross at the Cenotaph in Armagh on Remembrance Sunday, symbolic recognition of one whose body is not in that place.

"In thanking you for my father's inclusion in this major work, I would like to think that some of you remember him. For he, the bright schoolboy and spirited young man who called yours his home town, *will go Waltzing Matilda no more...*"

Samuel Foster

Described as "one of the kindest men I ever met", Samuel Foster, JP, retained the office of Chairman of Armagh District Council for almost six years, from late 1983 until 1989.

In a sense, greatness was initially thrust upon him by an election called mid-term, following the appalling murder of Chairman Charles Armstrong. Samuel Foster, born in 1916, died in 1997 so his contribution to local government is recounted by his widow, Doreen. Speaking of the untimely death of Chairman Charles Armstrong she comments, "That fateful evening Sam had been to a meeting of Council at the Palace Offices. He drove straight home afterwards. We live rurally so it was the following morning before we heard news of Charlie Armstrong's appalling murder on the radio. Both of us were numb, we just did not believe what had happened."

Sam Foster, the eldest son in a family of seven, was born and lived close to Killylea, attending the village school. From there he turned to full-time farming. "We were married in 1951, settling at Lisnafeedy House where Sam concentrated on dairy farming. From 1967 he served with Armagh County Council, in succession to Sir Norman Stronge. His electoral district, together with that of Mrs Mary Huey, subsequently became the area known as Orchard Ward. Sam often canvassed at the Argory, thus forging an acquaintance with Mr MacGeogh Bond. I loved this Georgian country house and have visited several times since it was bequeathed to the nation in 1979 and then taken over by the National Trust. With Fourau's paintings of the family and the dining room set for tea, Sam said it remained almost exactly as in the time of Mr MacGeogh Bond. A Steinway grand piano dating to 1898 claimed great admiration, centrally placed in the drawing room where a marble fireplace was piled high with logs from the estate. The Argory has been put to excellent use, for on the afternoon of our visit, Armagh Art Club were exhibiting work in the courtyard, formerly the Argory stables. As with Ardress House, this is a beautiful place to visit and reminds us just how important a role is fulfilled by the National Trust.

"During the years Sam served as Chairman, I remember the official opening of Armagh Secondary School at Lonsdale Road. A previous Chairman, Councillor William Henning, was also present. This building became the City of Armagh High School and eventually a newly constructed building was opened in 1995, when the Queen officially visited, granting city status. Councillor William Henning and my husband were elected at the same time and remained friends for life. Sam often recalled how they exchanged a handshake whilst walking up the steps of the old County Council offices at Charlemont Place, Armagh. Education was one of Sam's compelling interests and he sat on the boards of governors of local primary schools including Killylea, Drumsallen and Benburb. He was also District Council representative with the former County Armagh Education Committee.

"Our home was something of a metropolis, people requiring assistance constantly came and went. Sam helped everyone he could and far as he was able. Wives of councillors attended quite a few functions but nothing on the scale of today when the office of Mayor is extremely high-profile, demanding full-time attention. In July 1985, while on holiday in Torquay with my sister, Irene, who had recently been widowed, we received an invitation to a garden party at Buckingham Palace. On that particular day, guests were permitted access to the Palace. For the benefit of anyone who has never been, each July three of these events are attended by 8,000 people who are representative of all walks of life. Tea in the garden was an English custom started by Queen Victoria in 1860, when guests came from what was then seen as 'polite society'. This particular social grouping has now all but vanished and it is impossible for the Queen to speak to everyone but she does circulate before and after, as well as chatting to those in the royal marquee. Cutlery is workaday stainless steel. Crested spoons were once tried but when 1,000 disappeared, the experiment was not repeated! In a similar vein, we attended several garden parties at Hillsborough Castle given by the Secretary of State. I recall Princess Anne, Princess Michael and the Queen Mother being present. Ladies always wore hats on these occasions as they were deemed an essential part of formal wear.

"We had our dark moments too", Doreen reminds.

"Sectarian murder has no place in civilised society and Sam could not accept any of it, nor the brutal killing of a young man from Grange who was just about to begin university. Following tragic happenings, in his capacity as Chairman, my husband visited bereaved homes and later attended funerals. One cruel event was the double murder of Sir Norman Stronge and his son, James. Latterly, Sam had Unionist Party contacts with James. Tynan Abbey, a historic landmark with its valuable books and furniture has now gone. We both felt acutely for Sir Norman's daughters who were present at his funeral."

A silver birch tree thriving in the ground of the Council offices at the Palace Demesne was planted by Chairman Sam Foster in July 1987. "It was the 250th anniversary of the founding of Belfast newspaper the *News Letter*, and Neil Alexander of Century Newspapers requested that Sam perform this duty on behalf of Armagh District Council. Trees benefit the environment so for 'Tree Week', Sam, with parks officer Patsy Campbell, was again invited to plant a sycamore at the District Council grounds. When Dr William Fleming became Moderator of the General Assembly of the Presbyterian Church, he and his wife were guests at the Palace. We were then photographed with Council finance officer Tom Millsop. I recall the launch of 'No Smoking Day' on behalf of the Ulster Cancer Foundation at Armagh Leisure Centre and soon after, in 1985, the retirement of Norman Megaw, Clerk of Armagh District Council. Administrative officer Ivan Baxter organised the event and I remember Sam saying it had been a pleasure to work with both men. To mark the occasion, Norman was presented with beautiful Waterford crystal glasses and a decanter.

"Travelling to Brussels, where 'Irish Day' is commemorated each September, was one of the most pleasant memories of time Sam spent as Chairman. Councillor Pat Brannigan and his wife Molly have a great fondness for Belgium and the strong link with the 5th Brigade. Our hosts took great pleasure in presenting Pat with several bottles of mineral water as he does not drink alcohol. The Belgians held special 40th anniversary commemorations in 1985 and it was there that I really came to know Councillor George and Iris Macartney. We were treated with such courtesy including a constant round of engagements, which gave us new insight into European life. As I said previously, the office of Chairman then was quite muted in comparison to now. I feel that Councillor George Macartney brought the position into focus and, since City status, each mayor now fulfils the civic role of 'First Citizen'.

"Sam often commented on the impeccable quality of work which secretary Margaret Mallon undertook for him. Margaret and myself were actually classmates, attending the old Armagh Girls' High School on the Mall, numbers 8 and 9 Beresford Row. I began in 1943 when our headmistress was an Englishwoman, the late Mrs Sylvia G. Kastell. Even then, she had a dream of a spacious new school and used say rabbits were freely running across the fields on which one day, a beautiful building would stand! Her dream was realised in 1954. Our upbringing was very different from children today and teachers were treated with the utmost respect. Speech Day was held at the old City Hall because we simply did not have sufficient room in Beresford Row."

Doreen and Samuel Foster had two sons, Allen and Keith, and a daughter, Sharon. "Both boys are farmers like their father but neither are interested in local government. I have six grandchildren who give me a great deal of pleasure. Michael and Matthew are Allen's children, Keith has Gareth and Samantha while Sharon's two are Stuart and Lauren. Sam often said if it hadn't been for the support of our sons, he could not have found time to carry out Council engagements.

"He was a stalwart member of the Ulster Farmers' Union, first chairman and then county chairman of the North West Branch and was awarded a certificate for long service to the organisation. We rarely missed their annual dinner and received invitations even when Sam's health made it obvious he could not be present.

" A devout member of Knappagh Presbyterian Church, Sam held the position of elder. He began Sunday School at the age of five, later becoming a teacher and finally, Sunday School superintendent. Drumsallen Primary School carried out a project in which Sam was referred to as 'The boy who never left Sunday School'. The church planned annual trips for the Sunday School excursion to the seaside but this has changed greatly as children are now more interested in exhibitions or theme parks. This year they visited the Ulster American Folk Park in Omagh.

"Sam sat on the panel when Chief Executive Desmond Mitchell was interviewed and accepted for the job he has held ever since. His abilities were held in great esteem by my husband and, when Sam died in 1997 after a lingering

Chairman Samuel Foster, JP, at the Cenotaph,
The Mall, Armagh with Councillor George Macartney

illness, Des Mitchell, in common with many of his colleagues from Armagh District Council, called to express sympathy.

"I often thought of Jean Armstrong in her grief and hold nothing but admiration for the hard-working wives of each successive Mayor who today, are constantly in the public eye. It was not nearly so exhausting in my era but from experience I can honestly say it is a juggling act, one that balances family, home and public demands."

Sam Brodison

Kosovo claimed grim headlines in the early months of 1999. At one emergency relief centre in Pristina, an appeal for veterinary surgeons and supplies now brings to life the story of Sam Brodison, MM. Of three Albanian veterinary surgeons hiding in a flat in Kosovo, one was a very old man, unable to come out. He indicated that Serbs had destroyed supplies and equipment, pointing the way to a state farm in Pec. Here animals lay dead or decomposing. Some were alive but beyond help and NATO soldiers were asked to put them out of their misery. Half a century ago, in Yugoslavia, a similar scene was experienced by Sam Brodison. His daughter, Mary, can remember living at The Clump, now Dobbin Hill Park, and attending Armstrong Primary School.

"For many years, my father was Regimental Sergeant-Major at the Territorial Army Centre, responsible for a training programme at Gough Barracks. Jean Reid, his niece, and a newsagent on Barrack Street, kept the family account of how Sam Brodison became saboteur throughout Norway and France, then airstrip controller in the mountains of Yugoslavia. It is strange to recall now, as Kosovo is torn apart, that this man from Armagh once befriended Marshal Tito and his partisan warriors while soldiering with writer, Captain Evelyn Waugh."

Providing the story, Jean begins, "Joining the Royal Irish Fusiliers in 1934, Sam volunteered for the Commandos. His brother William, my late father, described him as the daredevil in a family of 11, constantly itching for adventure. Or", she pauses, "maybe adventure sought him out. Leaving Gortnaglush National School, Sam worked for a local grocer until old enough to join the army. After two years training in England he found himself in Palestine where Jew and Arab were locked in conflict. From 1938, his battalion of the RIF garrisoned the Channel Islands. At the onset of war, they sailed for France. Sam was wounded in Belgium and on recovery, posted to Ballykinlar.

"In 1940 with so much happening in Europe, Sam found Ballykinlar restrictive. When commando volunteers were called for, he was first in line. The régime of 12th Commando 'A' Troop gave all the excitement he needed. In dead of winter they ran to Lough Neagh, dived in, swam a stretch and ran back for breakfast. Mock raids were organised, an Irish contingent pitted against the Welsh."

In early 1941, 12th Commando moved to England. "Sam had a superb memory for events", Jean discloses. "His first mission, a raid on occupied France was purely to capture German prisoners, thereby information. Eight commandos left in a motor torpedo boat after dark. One mile off the French coast, a small boat was lowered. The men flung themselves in, knowing they were perilously on their own. One remained behind in the boat whilst the others scaled a cliff. It was right beneath a lookout post where all shipping in the channel was reported to German naval command.

"From French intelligence they understood the post, held by eight men, had a battalion of German troops 500 yards beyond in the village. Sam told us later, 'It was our job to get in there, get a German, then get out before the alarm went up. When two sentries appeared, we lobbed a plastic bomb. A number of soldiers engaged us in hand to hand combat. We came out best. Grabbing every document in sight, we shouldered a wounded German and made for the beach. Vehicles revved in the village, lights were blazing and our time for tides was urgent. Reaching the boat, we found our prisoner had died.' Sam Brodison's face, seared by shrapnel was scarred for life. 'Nevertheless', he wrote later, 'we'd achieved something. Granted, we had no prisoner, but the lookout post on the cliff was obliterated. The Germans had considered that invincible.'"

His team effected 14 raids on the coast of France and a further three in Norway. One of Sam's more dangerous undertakings entailed a stay of four days on the Lofoten Islands, taking prisoners. For his part in this and raids on the French coast, he received the Military Medal. His account of the Normandy beaches reads: "Learning that the Germans were building defences, Intelligence needed to find out what was going on. One week before D-Day we set out from Dover: French, Polish and British commandos. The beaches were heavily mined, so that when the doors of the expected allied landing craft slammed down at high tide, men would be blown to shreds. We dismantled one, taking it with us, going inland on reconnaissance. Our ambush failed and the Germans opened fire." Sneaking along their flank, Sam flung a grenade, which fell, bull's eye. "There was little alternative", he recounted. "By running for it, we'd have been shot in the back."

For his Yugoslavian venture, parachute drops were essential. Training required jumping at 1,000 feet. Many agents were women of the French underground. In light of their courage, none of the men would admit to fear. Sam confessed, "It was the most beautiful thing in the world, a parachute billowing above, knowing you would land at a leisurely pace." Six practice jumps, a couple of night attempts and they were off to Bari in southern Italy. Seconded to the Yugoslavian mission, Sam, was dropped into mountainous region where he was quickly surrounded by partisan soldiers. "A wild-looking bunch", he observed, "but wonderful people with a great spirit." Next day he visited their headquarters, deep in the mountains.

'Brabizov', as Sam came to be known, was soon accepted as one of their own. The task of the British mission was to provide the partisans with supplies to aid war against the Germans. Sam controlled a rough landing strip at Daruvar. Over a small VHF ground-to-air radio, the voice of 'Brabizov' was often heard; his coded instruction always *'Clear to land on Piccadilly Pat'*.

Sam's wife, Trixie, remained in army accommodation with little knowledge of these missions. When war in Yugoslavia neared an end, Sam, now CSM Brodison, was dispatched to Dubrovnik. There he helped Captain Evelyn Waugh, already a famous author, set up headquarters. "Sam said wartime experiences changed Waugh but then", Jean considers, "war changed everyone."

Parachuted once more into Northern Yugoslavia, Sam found the partisan force even more effective. Germans, fleeing on all fronts, returning to the homeland, had to pass through this territory. Sam's unit arranged evacuation for 1,000 Yugoslav wounded, leaving Marshal Tito's brigades free to protect their people. Tito was almost captured when the Germans made a surprise drop. Sam wrote: "The Marshal withdrew to Italy, then set up a new HQ on the island of Vis, off the Adriatic coast. I was told to accompany him." He met Tito, a Croat, many times and they became firm friends. Sam spoke of the Marshal as a strong leader with tremendous personality. Colonel Mihailovic, the Serb leader, who was officially commander-in-chief and war minister, defected to the Nazis when the Allies switched their support to Tito in 1944.

In March 1945, war drawing to a close, his unit moved northwards to the Drava River and hence, the Hungarian frontier. Here they met the first of the Russian Army. A partisan commander halted to ask if all was well with *Stari Vojnik,* the old soldier, as Sam was now affectionately known. Granted three weeks leave, he returned to Southampton to be with his wife and baby daughter, Mary, whom he'd never seen. War in Europe ended, yet the Japanese held out. Sam did not tell his wife but he had volunteered for special duty somewhere in the Pacific. As he was about to leave, the startling news from a radio bulletin spread like wildfire. America had dropped the atomic bomb and Japan surrendered. The work of the entire Commando Brigade was over but Winston Churchill later said: "We may feel sure that nothing of which we have any knowledge or record has ever been done by mortal men which surpasses the splendour and daring of their feats of arms. Truly we may say of them, 'when shall their glory fade?'"

Returning to the Royal Irish Fusiliers, his former unit, Sam wondered how many of his comrades, not seen since 1940, were still alive. The main force was stationed in Austria as part of the army of occupation, but it was to Congleton in Cheshire he was sent. Being surrounded by the injured and unfit was utterly depressing to his vigorous persona. Sam resolved to leave the army. A visiting RIF Sergeant-Major promised a transfer to Austria and weeks later, he was patrolling the border with Yugoslavia. "Everything had changed", he commented, "Yugoslavia was entrenched within the Communist bloc and we now faced hostile Slav guards, once friends in the common war against Hitler." Acting as Regimental Sergeant-Major, he prepared a guard of honour for a visit by General Montgomery at Klagenfurt, Austria.

When the Army reduced numbers, Sam was appointed Company Sergeant-Major at Ballykinlar. As a permanent staff instructor he was then posted to the 5th Battalion RIF, Territorial Army, in Lurgan where he worked with Major Ronald Rosser and Captain James Stronge. West Berlin saw the last of his service abroad and it was there in 1953 he spent his first family Christmas with his wife and three daughters, Mary, Anne and Susan. He served with the Territorial Army in Armagh as Company Sergeant-Major

Sam Brodison, MM, in Yugoslavia,
October 1944

for ten years, most of this time at Gough Barracks. For bravery in the field, Sam was heavily decorated, winning seven medals including the Military Medal. These have been passed on to James, his only son.

It is hard to reconcile Sam Brodison's Yugoslavia with the ongoing Balkan crisis. From Pristina, Kosovo, an appeal for veterinary supplies reawakened this first-hand account.

At Sam Brodison's funeral in January 1986, representatives of his Troop, 12th Commando laid a wreath which simply said, 'To Sam, *Soldier Superb.*'

Norman Creswell

On Monday 11 June 1973, most of the 22 members of the new Armagh District Council took their seats in the Council Chamber based at Newry Road. It was a historic occasion and the first meeting of the corporate body which would on 1 October succeed the existing Armagh Rural District Council and the Urban District Councils of Armagh, Keady and Tandragee. The first meeting of the Council was taken by Harry Reid, former Secretary of Armagh County Council, and subsequently Norman Megaw was appointed to the position of Clerk of the Council from 1 October 1973. Colin Dawson was appointed administrative officer with Ivan Baxter as financial officer. Some may remember Colin's father, Jack, as Clerk of the Rural District Council prior to Norman Megaw's appointment.

Norman Megaw joined the Rural District Council in 1948, working from Tower Hill. Tommy Spence from Richhill was then Rural District Chairman. The following observations were made by retired Chief Executive Megaw. "Tommy was a popular man who enjoyed reading and talking. His abiding interest was that of a housing programme which would contain provision of water and sewage disposal for his beloved village of Richhill.

"Post-war Armagh was a busy market town with a population of approximately 10,000. Small housing developments had taken place but basically, the housing estates that are now part of our city were then a Green Belt. The new District Council was based opposite the police station at premises that had been occupied by the former Rural District Council. Originally three dwelling houses at Palace Row, these were developed by the former Rural District Council and are now occupied by the Department of Agriculture. The former Rural Council and the three Urban Councils had been responsible for all services in the new area of Armagh District Council prior to reorganisation in 1973. Reorganisation decreed that government bodies now assumed direct responsibility for specific services. Water and sewerage, roads and street lighting were undertaken by the Department of the Environment, education by the Southern Education and Library Board, and housing by the Housing Executive. Armagh District Council would now control refuse collection, street and road cleaning, parks and cemeteries, tourism and environmental health.

"With 26 members in the Rural Council and 20 members in the Urban Council, amalgamation meant shedding quite a few. After reorganisation, the new Councils in Northern Ireland formed an association to present Council views pertaining to local government. Norman Creswell was the second person appointed to the prestigious and much sought-after position as president of the Association of District Councils, confirming the high esteem in which he was held by councillors throughout Northern Ireland. In my relations with Norman Creswell, first Chairman of Armagh District Council, I found him to be agreeable and always interested in the welfare of all within the area. Mr Creswell owned a dental laboratory and was married with one daughter, Sandra, a former pupil of Armagh Girls' High School. Sandra Creswell qualified as a doctor, and, after her marriage, emigrated to the United States."

At the first meeting of Armagh District Council in June 1973, Mary Huey of The Tavern, Loughgall, was the only woman member to be elected. Fellow member Harry Mercer apologised for her absence. Ten Unionists chose to sit on the left side of the table; two Loyalist Unionist Coalition members were centrally seated, while Social Democratic and Labour Party members and Independents occupied the right-hand side. In all, there were 19 present and a declaration of office was made by each member. In thanking those who voted for him, the newly elected Unionist Chairman, Andrew Norman Creswell, stated that he hoped peace and prosperity would return to Northern Ireland for it was a turbulent time in our country. He assured members that he respected the right of others to their own opinion and would endeavour to conduct meetings with fairness and impartiality.

"We hope that our meetings will benefit all the people of Armagh, irrespective of class or creed, in the areas we serve," Chairman Creswell concluded.

This meeting was memorable for several reasons. Barney McManus from Cathedral Road, who fought the election on the SDLP label, now announced he was splitting from the Party by becoming an Independent. Barney had already officially resigned from the SDLP, due, he said, to a clash of personalities. At the inaugural meeting, Unionists voted en bloc with two Loyalist Coalition members and Norman Creswell was elected to the Chair. Unionist William Henning, a farmer from Loughgilly, was elected Vice-Chairman, proposed by Charles Armstrong and seconded by Isaac Crothers. Several SDLP members supported the Unionist nomination of William Henning for membership of the Southern Education and Library Board. Both Mr Hutchinson and Mr Creswell were nominated to the Group Committee for the Employment of Public Health Inspectors. Dan Magee and Joseph Reid were selected for the Committee for Building Control Inspectors.

First to his feet was Oliver Tobin, a lecturer at Armagh Technical College, who said he looked forward to a new era of give-and-take in local government affairs. He also registered dissatisfaction at this first meeting. "All appointments including membership of the two area boards have gone to the majority Party. Does no-one exist except the majority Party?" Seamus Mallon, SDLP, rose to his feet, making a similar point and asking councillors to "put people first". Mr Creswell then reiterated that it was not a matter for him to decide who went forward for office but a matter for the council.

"While not ideal in terms of political balance", Norman Megaw comments, "it was nevertheless a beginning."

Other business included a discussion on the possibility of holding future council meetings in the evening. Barney McManus described it as "ridiculous" that councillors should have to leave their work for daytime meetings. Support for evening meetings came from Douglas Hutchinson who agreed that it wasn't always easy to get away during the day. It was decided that fixing a time for future meetings would be the responsibility of the new Clerk on his appointment.

One of Norman Creswell's first engagements as Chairman was a presentation on behalf of the Ulster Savings Movement. On that occasion, badges marking 20 years of services were awarded to Mrs H. Quinn, BEM, Mrs H. Frazer, Mrs M. Laird, Mrs E. Bell, Mrs M.E. Lauder and Mr and Mrs G. Anderson.

Rioting, intimidation and loss of life cast an ugly shadow on Armagh's turbulent Seventies. A former Chairman of Armagh Urban District Council, William Johnston, had been murdered in December 1972. The distressing details of his death were recalled at the mid-June inaugural meeting of the successor Council. Councillor Johnston was a respected city businessman who had been abducted with one of his employees, Leeman Bratty, from a house at Drumarg housing estate. Mr Johnston had been a member of the Police Authority. He was later found dead in his car on the side of a road crater near Knockbane on the Middletown border. Councillor Johnston's death shocked the entire community and, for those in local government, emphasised a need for increased security.

Of Chairman Norman Creswell's time in office, Mr Megaw adds: "Norman Creswell set plans in motion which would lead to the District Council's purchase of the Primate's Palace. Our initial contacts were set up by the Rev. John Crooks of St Patrick's Cathedral, acting on behalf of the Representative Church Body. It was obvious that negotiations would take quite a time and, indeed, the actual move to the Palace did not take place until after Chairman Creswell had retired.

"The social calendar of a Chairman then had little in common with the high profile this position carries today. Norman and Mrs Creswell attended several garden parties at Hillsborough Castle, hosted by Lord and Lady Wakehurst. My wife and I were guests at one particular garden party when the Queen was present and stopped to speak."

Norman Creswell was re-elected as Chairman each consecutive year until his resignation in June 1978. He then gave support to the nomination of Vice-Chairman William Henning for the top office. On his impending resignation, Norman Creswell seemed thoroughly disillusioned with the lack of authority in local government. He is recorded as saying: "We are nothing. We do not even have the voice of a consultative body. All we seem to do is quarrel one with another. In truth this is a thankless job."

Andrew Norman Creswell, born in 1913, continued in his profession until his death on 30 June 1985. Ruby Creswell outlived her husband by 14 years. Following an accident at her home, she died in August 1999.

Thankless or otherwise, it remains that Norman Creswell was the first of 12 Councillors who would lead Armagh City and District through a turbulent quarter century.

Norman Creswell pictured with Armagh Urban District Council in 1970.
Front row (L to R): K.M. Hamilton, A.N. Creswell, Chairman J. Gray.
Back row: P. Agnew, R. Stinson, C. Armstrong, J.D. McCready, J.J. McGaughey, B. McManus, R. Johnston, D. Robinson, P. Speer, G. Proctor, D. Mitchell.

Diana Cowdy

A remarkable figure of this century, Diana Cowdy has known a life that is not easily portrayed. Distinguished by a spontaneous turn of phrase, growing up in the literary high ground of the Thirties, this highly individualistic woman evokes shades of the Bloomsbury Group.

"I suppose it began when James I pressed 3,000 acres of land in this county on Lord Saye and Sele, or 'Stay and Steal' as the latter was euphemistically tagged by my father. We have to admit times were dreadful. My ancestor, Sir Anthony Cope, bought Drumilly land near Loughgall. Here he settled his two younger sons, Anthony and Richard. It was", she calculates briefly, "circa 1610 when they sailed here.

"The Copes sustained a military tradition. On arrival, the brothers made particular reference to the crannóg, or artificial island, on the eastern side of the lake. That was the summer residence of the O'Neills, original owners of this land. Pottery and stone fragments unearthed down the years date to the Vikings."

Indulge in a little reverie and one can well imagine her accomplished oratory and humour keeping pace with that of Sir Peter Ustinov. "That is a compliment", she interjects, "but let us press on. Richard Cope was dining at Gregg's Mill on the evening of 22 October 1641, with Irish gentry, perhaps the Donnellys, who knows? The upshot of it was that Richard, his wife and their sons Walter and Anthony were taken prisoners. All escaped with the exception of Anthony, who was murdered in Portadown the following year. Walter had been renowned for enormous flair, doubling the Drumilly home in size and splendour. He duly became Bishop of Loughlin and Ferns, marrying the daughter of Sir Arthur Acheson, fifth baronet of Gosford Gate, Armagh.

"Sarah and Nicholas Cope succeeded him. The pair made a foolish decision to celebrate their accession by taking the Grand Tour. From apartments in the Place de la Concorde, Paris, frenzied shrieks of unfortunates being guillotined carried quite clearly. This conniving pair sent their pretty daughter to petition Napoleon I for the release of English persons trapped in Paris. Obviously the ruse worked, but civil unrest did not end there. Returning home, Sarah and Nicholas found Drumilly in a state of defence following the Wolfe Tone Rebellion of 1798."

Hardly an everyday story of country folk, but Diana pauses, beginning anew. "Drumilly, eventually my home, was a wonderful house. On the first floor, a corridor measured 174 feet, running from the drawing room to the dining room. The wallpaper was French, hand-painted damask. Drapes and hangings belonging to the house, from the Third Empire period, are to be seen in the Victoria and Albert Museum. An earlier visit to the house by Oliver Plunkett was seen as an important social event. Walter Cope wrote of this to his father-in-law, the Dean of Armagh. The antique turn of phrase is amusing provided one has only a small portion to read. 'I had to sup with me one Oliver Plunket, a Prelate, of gentle birth and much learning. A man of great character who to me commands the English tongue better than even I. My dear wife Jane heard with interest the work of Plunket, for the better instruction of the young, at a seat of learning at Drogheda and has mind that our dull son would there do better than with Mr Warren...'

"That excerpt is quite something, don't you think?" Diana comments.

Diana's mother, Vera Gordon-Wilson, was born at Abbey House, Armagh. "She was such a pretty woman. Her father owned a flax-spinning mill, for the linen industry was flourishing. She married Ralph Cope, my father, claiming he had a great sense of humour. Vera fell for him and the two eloped. Arriving in London there was a dreadful fuss. The Bishop of London was dragged out of bed to perform the ceremony in his night-cap. Afterwards they lodged with an uncle, James Princip Beadle, an artist. A painting of his, *The Ulster Division Going Over The Top*, hangs in Belfast City Hall. Back at Drumilly, half of the house was allocated to the young couple by my step-grandmother, whom Vera considered a most understanding woman. A generation earlier, at her own engagement party, a guest pointed to the prospective bridegroom gasping, 'Good God man, wasn't I at your wedding in London three months ago!' This woman didn't wallow in misery, simply married my grandfather who had been passionately in love with her all the time.

"Drumilly was a gracious house imbued with the

Past chairman Diana Cowdy
of the Southern Education and Library Board Library Committee

character of generations who shared it down the centuries. My sister Sibyl and I grew up in this quiet, rural landscape. Horsemanship was important for everyone rode then. Educated by French governesses, we were introduced to art at an early age. My love of painting is inherited. All Cope women were gifted in this fashion. Landscapes, animals, an occasional portrait and flora and fauna are my forte."

While at the Slade School of Fine Arts in London, Diana acquired the ability to capture mood, expression and emotion on canvas. As patron of Armagh Art Club, she presents the Summerisland Cup for an inspirational painting each winter exhibition. Her own works are often included in the displays. A Cowdy is highly collectable today but Diana insists "Show someone a well-known work of art, and, even if they hate it, they feel obliged to admire it."

Diana married near-neighbour Robin Cowdy when she was 21. They moved Summerisland House where she resides today. "It was an agreeable alliance. We matured together, remaining a couple for 53 years until Robin's death. He was a farmer but served the County Council and endless other committees. As a young woman, my new lifestyle was more relaxed than Drumilly had ever been for Summerisland reverberated with comings and going. Those who travelled were early foreign correspondents who brought news of politics, fashion and food to our isolated island."

A dedicated horsewoman, 150 equestrian stills confirm her abilities. "Jackie Stinson, our local saddler, always helps when I need advice. He understands horses and we share bloodstock as well as a passionate love of the animals themselves. I've always involved myself in things I liked, education, art, my horses, the farm. I cannot paint unless removed from noise and greatly value the rhythm of silence."

Down the century she remained in touch with many County families. As a visitor to Castle Leslie, Glaslough, Diana contributes something of this beautiful house. "Society beauty Jennie Jerome, Lady Randolph Churchill, was the mother of two sons, Winston and Jack. There was quite a strong Romanov connection for it was at a ball in Cowes, given in honour of the Tsar and Tsarina of Russia, in 1873, that Jennie met Randolph Churchill. Jennie's sister, Leoni, married Sir John Leslie, second baronet, and it is well known that Leo was Winston Churchill's favourite aunt. Sir Winston often came to Castle Leslie, extending his visits by travelling on to Dublin.

"A favourite possession is *The Traveller's Guide through Ireland* by George Tyner, published in 1794 by P. Byrne of Grafton Street, Dublin. It lists 'great roads from Dublin to every town in the Kingdom, the crossroads and description of the gentleman's seats near the road'. Of course the language is quaint, that's what I like about it."

Her son Ralph resides in Summerisland House, Diana occupying a suite of rooms to the rear. "I have my dogs and my painting. Just now I'm on my way to feed one of the horses." At the sound of her voice, a chestnut mare rushes to the fence and nuzzles her arm. They combine as a cameo, the rest of the world removed.

You may well say they're not making people like Diana Cowdy any more.

Dan McKeever

Last of the old brigade, Dan McKeever, MBE, sole remaining veteran of Armagh city fire-fighting team of 1930, died on 13 April 1999. Many were shocked to learn of his passing for Dan had remained active, often deep-sea diving, until his mid-seventies. One of life's achievers, he spoke of his fire-fighting role just a year earlier.

Dan McKeever is a private man. "I have never given an interview", he stresses, "but out of respect for social history would like to speak of my time as a fireman. Most firemen were also employees of Armagh Urban District Council. We are a poor match against the elements. Men worked helplessly as raging flames decimated an entire street. Rebuilt facades are architectural headstones to changing whims, the unreplaceable has gone, lost forever."

Dobbin Street Power Station was a great innovation for Armagh, generating its own current. "Unique to Northern Ireland, maintaining and installing cable which brought safe, clean, modern electricity to every home. I have my identity card, signed by the area engineer when I was a young man in 1931." Dan remained an employee until NIEB assumed control. From small beginnings, managing his electrical business in Scotch Street, Dan McKeever's status rose to that of major UK employer. During the Fifties, his signature on a weekly wages cheque was in excess of £40,000.

It is of his fire service that Dan speaks vividly. "During 1927, a workshop at the *Ulster Gazette* newspaper burned to the ground. Another fire at Barrack Street, when one woman resident died, convinced our Council that it was time to update an old handcart and pumps housed at the City Hall. This very basic system employed a town crier, who, by ringing a handbell, alerted the fire team. Modernisation manifested itself in a gleaming Thornycroft fire engine with solid rubber wheels. Manned by a driver and ten firemen, four to each side, we resembled a majestic swan transporting her young. Everyone rushed, crowding to see us. We almost imagined ourselves to be celebrities! Thomas McSorley, our first driver, lived above the new fire station in Dobbin Street. Thomas was previously groom, then chauffeur, to the late Cardinal Logue when the latter acquired a Fiat limousine. Following Thomas' death, Dominic McCreesh took control. The Stinson family have a long, prestigious history of fire service. James, grandfather of Jackie, the county's last saddler, was followed by his son James A. Stinson. The third generation was his son James W. Stinson. Another brother, Alfie, was awarded the MBE on completion of 36 years as a fireman. Of that original team, I recall the late John Cartmill who drove a steam-roller, essential to stone road servicing. Another was John Cunningham, uncle of Wilfie McVeigh who owned the historic 'Hole in the Wall' tavern. John worked as mechanic and fitter with a linen-making factory at Gillis.

"The brigade's range of call was extensive for our Thornycroft was the country's only engine outside Belfast and Derry. One photograph was taken following a serious fire at Clones in 1930. Could you imagine this today? Rattling along in the Thornycroft to Portadown or Lurgan, the likelihood was that a thatched building might burn to the ground before we reached it. Summers were often hot and a spring well was quite undependable as main source of water supply. When we extinguished a fire, assuming he survived the onslaught, a grateful householder provided steaming mugs of tea. A smoke alarm is deemed essential in every home today. Half a century ago, thatched roofs and open hearths were fire hazards, death-traps.

"Our team was alerted by the warning siren appointed on the old Municipal Technical College. This, with another later placed on the Courthouse, was utilised by authorities during the Second World War as air-raid warning."

Armagh fire station had a staff of six based at Dobbin Street in the early 1930s. Fire points were strategically based throughout the district. Break the glass and an alarm sounded in the station. An indicator pointed location, so firemen could be alerted by means of a bell in their home. "Mine was placed right over my bed and for some reason, shrilled in the middle of every pleasant dream. We were Council-employed, so fires during working hours counted as paid time. Outside a normal day we received six shillings for the first hour, four shillings for each thereafter. Team expertise was beyond comparison. Two worthy men were Joe McArdle and Frank Kelly, who off-duty, crafted a living as skilled roofing slaters."

One inferno at Tom Edwards' Joinery and Mill, Railway Street, Armagh, comes to mind. "A major employer during the Depression, Tom produced raw timber from which he manufactured distinctive Windsor chairs, exporting these throughout the UK. Late one evening, an emergency fire call came from his premises. A blaze had taken hold, streaking the horizon crimson and purple. Timber crackled, sparks shot like a fireworks display. We fought for days and while it was devastating, Tom Edwards was able to use his private railway siding to salvage a reasonable amount of his stock. An industrious man, he was back in production before long. Fittingly, Armagh has a street named after his family. Another catastrophic event taxed the brigade to its limits when machinery overheated at Umgola Linen Factory. Dry, flammable material ignited, tinder-box fashion. All able-bodied staff assisted so, mercifully, no lives were lost. Again in the Thirties, we were called to Moygashel Weaving Factory where a raging blaze turned dawn to streaks of livid purple. We trained our hoses and shafts of water leapt 30 feet in the air combating flames about to torch upper-storey windows. Thanks to an innate sense of survival, skill and judgement, none was injured.

"From Vincent Hughes, chief officer of the Fire Brigade and a graduate of the Institute of Electrical Engineers, I acquired enough knowledge at evening classes in the Municipal Technical School to open my own business. From my backyard in English Street, I eventually opened branches in Scotch Street, Armagh, Belfast, Dublin and Manchester. We undertook contracts, hospitals, schools, disposal works, employing our own accountant, clerical workers and a staff of 140. Naturally I had to resign from the Fire Brigade for my time was fully utilised with business demands. That was a sad day saying goodbye to colleagues and that important Thornycroft." For service and skills, Dan received his MBE at Buckingham Palace, presented by HM the Queen, some years ago.

Half a century ago, rose-tinted bowls suspended from gilt chains fringed his shop ceiling. "Retail merchandising had not been invented", admits Dan. "Customers browsed, usually buying from shelves carrying a comfortable mish-mash of cardboard boxes, kettles, or the latest small Baby Belling cooker with grill underneath. I began an important link, a 'wet-battery' service, charging current for old steam wireless sets." In a glimpse of Ireland past, he recalls brown-overalled bread salesmen collecting and distributing these on behalf of country customers. "*Children's Hour* ran from 5pm. County families had tea coinciding with the six o'clock news. Saturday night favourites broadcast on the Northern Ireland Light Programme were the *McCusker Brothers' Céilí Band* followed by *The McCooeys*. Customers chatted about the goings-on of *The McCooeys* as they now do of *The Archers* or *Coronation Street*. The onset of television can be attributed John Logie Baird's experiments at Crystal Palace. BBC transmissions were regularly sent from Alexandra Palace in 1936 but in Ireland it was not until the Fifties that enthusiasm grew. With it, we established a new rental service, engineers carrying out maintenance at the customer's home." In 1954, with the expertise of his sister, Kathleen, Dan's business, having sold the highest number of Philips products in the British Isles, won places for two on a Mediterranean cruise. He and his sister took advantage of this marvellous prize, travelling on what was the maiden voyage of the cruise ship *Arcadia*.

Dan's only son, Terence, who managed a major part of the business, was a victim of IRA terrorist violence in 1986. "We never reconciled to his loss", Dan confided. The irony of this dastardly act was the loss of almost 200 jobs. Despite his personal grief, Dan showed great strength of character and maintained close family bonds and was of immense support to his wife Claire and only daughter Karen. (Sadly, Claire was to survive Dan by only a few months, dying in September 1999.)

Some years earlier, a bomb placed outside McKeever's Scotch Street premises had torn the heart from his enterprise. "A warning was given", he recalls, "but this type of warfare was utterly foreign, we didn't taken it seriously. The incident was a herald of unmitigated destruction eroding the business heart of Armagh and with it, my enthusiasm." Today Boots Chemists trade where daily shoppers once visited McKeever's. "I occupied numbers 60-62", Dan recalls, "Lennon's pub was next door and below us, the hardware shop of Bertie Knipe."

Half a century of Dan McKeever's business life

Dan McKeever, MBE, and his sister Kathleen
at a presentation ceremony given by Philips appliances

included training young men for the industry. Many still manage successful business of their own. "A marvellous spirit existed throughout years of fire service and commerce. I am saddened", Dan admits, "considering that once buoyant atmosphere, customers I served, staff who worked with me. One local man, Leslie Fleming of Grove Terrace, was something of a technological genius. Leslie was sent by me on a course to Ecko, based at Southend on Sea, then to Pam or Pye, an important television factory in Larne. Easily the best in the profession, we remain friends. It is difficult to keep pace with modern advancement for a flash of technology achieves what once took days. Business acumen always fuelled my energies so to some extent, I make a point of keeping abreast with progress. Age doesn't really hinder for I still dive and enjoy a chat with friends. Perhaps it's indicative of my personal autumn but it suddenly seems important to lay down this history with that of the old brigade. Promise you will see to it?"

Douglas Hutchinson

Not everyone can take a blend of humanity and weave a coherent picture. Listening to Rena Hutchinson, widow of Chairman Douglas Hutchinson of the Ulster Democratic Unionist Party, is an insight into one man's exhaustive efforts towards conservation of Navan 'fort'.

"Ancient history mattered as much, if not more, to Dougie than politics", comments Rena. "When we married, it soon became clear that my life would become a combination of both. If Dougie found something in a book or magazine that grabbed his attention, he would read this aloud and whatever I happened to be doing, he'd insist I stop and listen. Fascinated by Ireland's richness in literature, legend and mythology, Dougie insisted that Newgrange in Meath proved an ancient and sophisticated civilisation had inhabited the land. From him I learned that Ireland's most famous archaeological site included a 5,000-year-old burial chamber that had its entrance placed in direct line with the rising sun. On the morning of the winter solstice when the sun comes up, a beam of light shoots to the very back of this chamber. How he marvelled at such ancient intelligence!"

Rena Hutchinson is a practical, busy woman, actively involved in the family business of apple production, and Woodview Nursery on Portadown Road, which is run by her younger son, David.

"Brian, my elder son, looks after our orchards and is a serving DUP member with the City and District Council. Brian is a third generation of our family involvement in local government", she adds with pride. "George Hutchinson, my father-in-law, had been a Unionist councillor and so was my husband from the time of his election to Armagh Rural District Council in 1953. I remember two other happenings", she says, laughing good-naturedly. "We had the Coronation of Queen Elizabeth II, combined with the 11th attempt to climb Everest when Edmund Hillary and Sherpa mountaineer, Tenzing Norgay, made it to the summit. Newspapers carried these stories for a week and cinema-goers flocked to the Ritz where the double-feature film of both events was shown in colour." Fruit farming is a third-generation occupation for the Hutchinson family who specialise in the famous Bramley variety.

"Dougie won successive trophies for his apples", continues Rena, a hint of sadness in her acutely blue eyes. "He was so proud of this skill. I remember when he first grafted Bramley shoots onto existing trees in the orchard fronting our home. We tried Cox's Orange Pippin but neither soil nor climate suited this essentially English variety. Brian has successfully experimented with the dessert apple, John O'Gold, which is delicious to eat and continues to thrive. Apple farming is a science and today's trees grow less high which makes for easier harvesting. Pruning, budding, grafting and fertilising is done seasonally and we never underestimate the importance of the honeybee, which pollinates a crop. It's always at the mercy of the elements—a late frost in May can wreck an entire harvest. Joiners say apple wood is a joy to work with and I am almost certain it was used to make the gavel that controls Council meetings at the Palace! Burning old apple wood creates a particularly aromatic scent so we try to save some for Christmas."

Serving local government for more than 40 years, Dougie Hutchinson witnessed social, political and economic change. Born in 1917, he was a member of the wartime Home Guard before joining the Ulster Special Constabulary, otherwise known as the 'B' Specials—a supportive security organisation whose Armagh headquarters were on the Mall. Within the USC, he rose to the rank of officer. When the USC disbanded in 1970, Dougie remained active in the ex-members' Association. Rena was present when Lady Brookeborough attended many commemorative events.

"The first civil rights march had just taken place in Omagh", Rena recalls, "and another was planned for Londonderry. This was October 1968, and a time of political unrest. The Minister of Home Affairs, William Craig, imposed a ban upon the intended route of the Londonderry march so that many stayed away. Gerry Fitt was Member for West Belfast and he brought several Westminster Labour Members of Parliament along to observe. Street violence erupted and the police, under attack, retaliated. When the Cabinet met at Stormont to discuss the situation, William Craig emphasised that the police had acted with restraint in difficult circumstances.

Prime Minister, Terence O'Neill, insisted Northern Ireland's standing had been seriously damaged and unionists came under attack. Dougie was enraged when they were accused of unfair practices. He felt that the real enemy was social injustice and class distinction. Protestant working-class families were as discriminated against as those from a Roman Catholic background. Londonderry had declined since 1945 when it was a principal base for countering the U-boat menace in the last war. It was overlooked in the Wilson Plan of 1965 and unemployment worsened. The University of Ulster, established in Coleraine, was another blow. You need to consider what was happening elsewhere at this time. There were demonstrations against the Vietnam War, and Black civil rights marches led by Dr Martin Luther King. Young, educated Roman Catholic graduates were taking to the streets here and this generated loyalist counter-demonstrators. Brian Faulkner was Minister of Education and strongly in opposition to reforms suggested by Prime Minister Terence O'Neill. While some unionists rallied to O'Neill, there was a breaking down of confidence. As the mood grew, Dougie followed the path of Faulkner and Craig and from unionism, Ian Paisley's political party emerged.

"As violence spread from Londonderry into towns all over the Province, a Civil Rights march was planned for Armagh during November 1969. Dougie and quite a few others thought it would be used as an opportunity for republican propagandists. They took a public stance in preventing the march, and the police turned a water cannon on the crowd. Dougie was arrested with Ian Paisley and subsequently brought to court.

"Both were sentenced to serve three months at Her Majesty's Prison, Crumlin Road, for their protests against O'Neill's activities. While serving his sentence, Dougie was detailed to duties in the prison gardens. Ian Paisley was set similar work but he lacked green fingers. Dougie set to, completing the quota for both. He was released after one month."

Having gone to prison for his politics, Dougie, disenchanted with the Unionist Party, now switched allegiance to the Democratic Unionist Party formed by Ian Paisley, and still in its infancy. Despite a lifetime of commitment to the Church of Ireland faith, he joined the first Free Presbyterian Church established in Armagh by Ian Paisley. Dougie remained religious throughout life, stringently honest in his dealings and reading his Bible daily. Everyone knew his beliefs and respected him for strict adherence to his convictions. Dougie was returned to local government throughout Armagh's difficult times. During two decades, loyalist and republican terrorists were trading blow for blow in a relentless register of death. Scotch Street was blasted top to bottom while buildings in Market Square were utterly destroyed.

Douglas Hutchinson was Deputy Chairman of Armagh District Council during the 1980s, when the Navan complex, Northern Ireland's most important historic monument, came onto the agenda. In 1985, a planning application for further extension of the limestone quarry situated to the east of the Navan was made. Many buildings in Armagh are of limestone taken from the Navan but, until 1985, the quarries were small and the scale of extractions modest. On the hills to the north are Neolithic tombs and north-east of the 'fort' is the ritual lake of Loughnashade, once much larger than now, where human bones and four bronze horns were found. One of these is the Loughnashade trumpet.

"Now Loughnashade was threatened", Rena continues. "Dougie was incensed at this violation, as was Councillor Pat Brannigan. Dougie came home and reaching for one of his books, read aloud of the exceptional status of Emhain Macha, political and spiritual capital of the Kings of Ulster and scene of the boyhood of legendary hero Cú Chulainn. Vowing that quarrying must stop, his supporters were a formidable section of society. Seamus Mallon, MP, enlisted David Warner, head curator of the Ulster Museum, who visited the site accompanied by Dr Gordon Beveridge, Vice Chancellor of Queen's University. Roger Weatherup, curator of Armagh County Museum, and Cardinal Tomás Ó Fiaich contributed to effective concern. Richard Needham, Secretary of State, began the longest public inquiry ever held in Northern Ireland and many of those concerned formed the Friends of Navan group. It was two years before the Historic Monuments Branch of the Department of the Environment rescinded the decision, and after a running-down period quarrying ceased on 30 September 1987.

"It was a time of constant comings and goings", Rena continues. "Meetings were held at our home and many in Dougie's party, not understanding the colossal significance of Navan, tried to denigrate his efforts. I said he was resolute", Rena reminds. "Well, he remained

A shared moment: Chairman Douglas Hutchinson
with Cardinal Tomás Ó Fiaich

resolute, steadfastly dedicated to safeguarding Navan, and a day came when quarrying eventually ceased. Unfortunately three or four vital acres of Loughnashade had been destroyed in the interim and Dougie bitterly resented the archaeological loss. Navan Fort Initiative Group was set up in 1987 by an independent group, while the Fort itself and the nearby King's Stables are owned by the Department of the Environment. I feel so proud of Dougie's contribution and would like to quote from George Priestley in his chairman's introduction to Navan: 'I commend it as a far-sighted and imaginative development, designed to present to our own community, the people of both islands, our neighbours in Europe and our friends in America, a monument of profound historical and symbolic importance.'"

One hundred thousand visitors have now passed through the Navan's award-winning Interpretative Centre. Quietly dedicated education officer Anne Hart welcomes schools and organisations, providing programmes and factual literature that stimulate an appreciation of the warrior aristocracy of the Ulster Cycle—the oldest heroic literature in Europe, and source of inspiration for later writers and artists including Synge, Yeats, Lady Gregory and closer to home, John B. Vallely.

In 1989, Douglas Hutchinson was elected Chairman of Armagh District Council. Of functions he attended, Rena treasures an invitation from Cardinal Tomás Ó Fiaich, requesting that Dougie and she attend Ara Coeli where those who had played a prominent part in the religious and cultural life of the country would be present.

"In this letter, Cardinal Ó Fiaich congratulated Dougie on becoming Chairman and wished him well. Brian, my son, tells a story of one meeting at the Council offices when Dougie was wearing a white linen hat. The Cardinal had been speaking to guests and he suddenly commented: 'Dougie, let me try on your lovely white hat'. Quick as a flash, Dougie retorted: 'You can have my white hat in return for your red hat!' This repartee shows that exchanges were pithy yet the Cardinal really loved a bit of fun. When Jack Dawson was Clerk of the Rural District Council, he and Dougie worked in harmony but meetings were stormy and Councillors much more aggressive than today. Thirty years of unrest changed the facades of this city. Something of an irony is surely that those who once brought Armagh to its knees now proclaim its lack of commerce! By the same token, under the Good Friday Agreement, prisoners are released with every form of rehabilitation support while the victims of these individuals go practically unnoticed.

"Dougie was an excellent constituency worker and this was reflected in letters and phone calls he received from every section of society. People knew he would work wholeheartedly for them. While the Chairman's role was not nearly as demanding as that of a Mayor today, he did write all his own speeches and kept a meticulous diary. Council secretary Margaret Mallon, BEM, was a tremendous help and he would not forgive me if I failed to compliment her outstanding efficiency. Saturday evening found Dougie visiting patients at Craigavon Hospital and residential homes and, in the event of death, sympathising with the bereaved or attending each funeral. As a Friend of Armagh County Museum he participated in arranged outings and took great pleasure in chatting to curator Roger Weatherup. When ill health forced him to retire, our son Brian stood successfully for Orchard Ward."

"I probably inherited my father's vote", Brian comments modestly. An ardent fisherman, Brian is vice-chairman of Armagh Angling Club. "We have a hatchery at Ednaveys from which we stock all our lakes including Seagahan Dam. I am also chairman of Blackwater Enhancement Association where all angling clubs on the Blackwater have one aim, that of improving the river system. We organise fishing competitions and I'm proud to say, enjoy cross-border membership. I've landed a 70lb shark on holiday off Gran Canaria and promise to frame the first salmon I catch that weighs over 20lbs! I enjoy local government and would like to build on another DUP seat. Our party leader is one of this country's three Members of the European Parliament working in harmony for the overall good of the country and that's what really counts.

"My father retired in 1993 due to poor health. He died two years later. Something of an irony is the fact that those who criticised him bitterly when he supported Navan are now effusive in claiming its importance but this, I suppose, is local government. You never reach the end of the battle but just go on fighting for what you believe."

That the Navan flourishes is the best tribute Douglas Hutchinson would have wished. Despite Rena Hutchinson's interests, there is no doubt that her husband always had—and, in the interests of his biography, always will claim her undivided attention.

Jean and Paddy Johnston

"I'd really hate to be famous", Jean Johnston confesses, dropping gratefully into a favourite chair. Jean and her husband Paddy had just finished an intensive afternoon of filming and horticultural interrogation. Paddy's garden would feature on BBC1's *Greenfingers* later in the week. The Johnstons are a stylish, relaxed couple who defy passing years by intelligent pursuit of various pastimes. Jean is slim, striking and noted for her excellent cooking. This is a devoted couple but not ostentatiously, they simply expand in each other's company.

"The washing machine has been giving such trouble", Jean says apologetically. Paddy leaves to see what can be done. She begins disclosures, compared to which, her garden rates a poor second. "I was born in Aberdeenshire. Paddy and I met early in 1945, at Dunbar, East Lothian. Everyone calls my husband Paddy, myself included, but his name is William. As the only Irish officer in an English battalion, he accepted the national nickname. Anyway, during the war I enlisted with the First Aid Nursing Yeomanry and was working in Dunbar. Paddy, newly returned from Burma, was training officer in charge of jungle warfare at the officer training unit. We met simply because both of us frequented the officers' mess."

Jean's organisation undertook work of a vital nature. "I mainly coded and decoded for the Free French underground movement. My unit was not linked to the army, but after the war, did integrate with the ATS. Most of what we did was top secret—even today I do not speak of it. Paddy and I became engaged in Dunbar and almost immediately were separated for 18 months. I was sent to Buckinghamshire, Paddy to Lincolnshire. We made a pact not to marry until the war ended. In fact we waited until 1947."

Chatting in the drawing room of Abbey House, a sense of history pervades. "This was the Johnston family home. I suppose it's something of an antique." There is a quality of delicacy about grouped oriental pictures or the unruffled fall of curtains. Plump chairs and a cheerfully burning fire contribute to overall comfort.

"This is a hobby of mine", Jean comments, picking up an original carving. "I take a piece of wood and simply allow a shape to evolve. It's something I enjoy."

Music has always been a major factor in her life. As a child she was encouraged to play the flute. "All six of us had our own instrument. We must have constituted a little orchestra. Anyway I learned to appreciate classical music at an early age. My favourite composers are Händel, Mozart, Schumann and *always*", she laughs, "Johann Sebastian Bach." Equally she enjoys operatic music, those considerable talents of Pavarotti and Domingo. Which does she cite as a best-loved piece? "Mendelssohn's Violin Concerto in D", Jean replies without hesitation.

A shared love of gardening has forged endless friendships. "We are members of the Gardening Club and have connections with the National Trust due to our own garden. Ours is totally screened by an enormous wall, so is aptly christened 'The Secret Garden'. Many of our acquaintance are not remotely interested in gardening, other than having to keep one tidy."

"It's fixed", Paddy announces triumphantly, having persuaded her washing machine against the folly of not working. Debonair and cheerful, he belies his age. Time spent in England represents a fraction of Paddy's wartime service. He remembers the gathering clouds. "British forces based in Cairo fought a ding-dong campaign in the North African desert, first against the Italians and then against an Italo-German combination under Rommel." In 1941, Paddy was involved in the siege and breakout from Tobruk. By the summer of 1942, the British had been pushed back into Egypt, but Paddy's unit had now been posted to India.

"India was menaced by the Japanese who had overrun Burma. I served for months behind enemy lines with the Chindit expeditions of 1943 and 1944." While he was leading a small outpost in the Chin hills, during the '43 expedition, posters nailed throughout the jungle offered 1,000 rupees for his capture. "Not a bad offer", he muses, "I suppose it would have been half a year's income for a Burmese hillman but I'm still here! Hard to believe it happened more than half a century ago." Paddy recalls the living hell of the jungle, disease, swamps, swarming with Japanese, hand-to-hand combat. "I found it impossible to reconcile the barbaric treatment meted out to prisoners-of-war and civilians by the Japanese considering the ancient culture and civilisation of that race." In 1944 Paddy was awarded the Military Cross.

"Leaving the army, I studied at Aberdeen School of Architecture. Jean and I lived in the little fishing village of Collieston, Aberdeenshire. Our elder son, Hunter, was born there and we have wonderful memories of that time." After a year in Ayrshire, Paddy returned to Armagh with Jean and his baby son. "My father, W.R. Johnston, due to the nature of his business, was affectionately called the 'seedsman' and everyone knew him. Complete strangers I met in Egypt, on learning my name would ask, 'Any relative of W.R.?' The family home became our base until we found a place of our own. My father gave me a room which I opened as an office within his home."

Memorials to Paddy's architectural skill permeate this ancient city of Armagh. He planned the Headmaster's House at Royal School, Armagh, and also the Reid Hall, redesigning the old gymnasium, then converting it to an auditorium. The Adam Gallery is a particularly pleasing example of Georgian restoration as is Studio 42 on the corner of Linenhall Street. Paddy is responsible for some of the more attractive housing complexes in local villages and neighbouring Portadown. The Johnstons had a second son, Alexander, but it was Hunter who followed his father's profession in London. Hunter's talents take him worldwide, and he is presently designing an office block for the ANC in Dar-es-Salaam.

Eventually Paddy and Jean moved into Abbey House, the family home, where every niche reflects style and devotion. Both love mountaineering and have in the past gone climbing in Africa. "Scotland will always rate highly with me", assures Jean. "Its climate is dramatic—one moment the air is fresh and invigorating, the next, black cloud and mist shroud the mountains. We dearly love England and go there often."

In addition to his Secret Garden, Paddy is an avid beekeeper. "This hobby provides honey for ourselves while the surplus goes to friends. I make my own beehives, which requires considerable precision. This wonderful insect teaches us much, conducting inside and outside business in a fashion that is an example to us humans. The hive is run like a city, kept in good repair. The bees clean and guard it, warm or cool it, stock it with food and rear their young. Fruit and flowers depend on pollination so the bee is essential to nature."

In his impetuous youth, Paddy penned his innermost thoughts. He kindly allows me to print one work which was later published by Arrival Press.

Floreat Armachia

Before thy golden streets, O Lord, I crave
Only the mire in a North country lane
Rigid and white with frost, to the heels ringing
Or dumb with long rain.

Instead of that bright tree whose fruit doth fall
For Nations' balm, give me a brambled hedge
Broken with lovers' nooks and the more happy they
For an old knowledge.

There are sweet birds in Heaven that sing all day
In harmony, unbroken, to Thy Majesty,
Through the long day that never falls in night they sing
In equability.

Leave me a robin in the young spring
To cheer more bravely for the day's inclemency
Or a gaunt thrush that sings, storm-pitted to the bone
In a tormented tree.

So Lord, in the inevitable day
When the last splendid sun falls to the last night
Establish where Thou wilt Thy New Jerusalem
But let my heaven abide.

Let there be seasons still, for hearts of men,
As for hedge blossomings and let the first loved star
Let sun and moon outcast from Heaven revolve
Above the green hills and the spired hills of Armagh.

William and Jean Johnston celebrate their Golden Wedding Anniversary, June 1997, with
Sandy, Vinny *(Lee)*, Amanda and Hunter

Cardinal Cahal Daly

Remaining active in retirement, His Eminence Cardinal Cahal B. Daly now resides in Belfast, at the home he once used whilst teaching at Queen's University. Dr Daly now speaks on a significant part of his life.

"I continue to accept lecturing engagements at home and abroad despite the fact that I am 82 years of age. This entails travelling and a host of interesting experiences. Since my retirement in 1996, I have spoken at a conference in Georgetown University, Washington DC, on conflict resolution in Northern Ireland. The Vendée, Western France, was the venue for another conference on the peace process in Northern Ireland. Christians and Jews and the roots of peace in the New Testament was our agenda at a congregation in Auschwitz. Cardiff hosted an ecumenical gathering under the auspices of *Cytun*, Churches Together in Wales, on a Christian vision for Europe. I then attended a special assembly of United States bishops in Tucson, Arizona, another conference on peace and reconciliation in Ypres as well as a number of venues in Great Britain and, naturally, in Ireland. The two visits that made the deepest impression were those to Ypres and Auschwitz. Exposure to war cemeteries in and around Ypres, where scores of Irishmen, Northern Protestant and Southern Catholic comrades in arms, lie together in death, was a powerful experience of the horror and tragedy of war. Visiting the death camps at Auschwitz and nearby Birkenau, the prisoners' blocks, crematoria; fields strewn with human ashes and charred bones, where no grass grows, only weeds, where no birds fly and no birds sing—all this was an overpowering and unforgettable experience of man's inhumanity to man.

"Retirement for me, all in all, has been a time of activity, of enriching experience and, I trust, of spiritual growth. I have also managed to write and publish memoirs under the title *Steps on my Pilgrim Journey* (1998). At the moment I have several other books in preparation.

"It seems I could read almost as soon as I learned to walk", Cardinal Daly comments, reflecting on his childhood. "Pears' soap was my mother's favourite brand. Saving coupons from each bar, I collected the specified number for a copy of *Pears' Cyclopedia*. During my life I acquired a veritable library of the Classics, but that book, my first, was precious. At the turn of the last century, my father left Co. Roscommon, taking up a teaching post in Ulster. Ours was a family of seven and education was of paramount importance in our home. I had no desire for any other career and a vocation to the priesthood constantly occupied my thoughts."

In company with three brothers, Cahal Brendan was educated at Cross and Passion College, Co. Antrim. "I loved reading", he says with relish. "My head was constantly in a book. 'You'll ruin your eyes', scolded my grandmother who'd been raised in the days of rush candles. 'You'll turn out just like John Joe', was another of her dire prophesies. You see, my father loved Zane Grey's cowboy stories, which he then passed these to our neighbour, John Joe. Trundling along in his horse and cart, intoxicated by *The Light of Western Stars*, both John Joe and his horse ended up in a ditch. As a little boy of six, I probably envied the possibility of any similarity."

Cahal Daly studied Ancient Classics, specialising in Greek and Roman Literature at Queen's University, Belfast. "I revelled in Virgil's *Aeneid,* composed in praise of Homer rather than imitation of his great mind." He ponders a moment. "Few in Ireland are more than a generation removed from the land. Horace, a Roman poet of middle age, spoke for me then. With Horace what is sound rather than *profound* acquires dignity." An Arts degree was augmented by an MA in Classics during his first year at Maynooth College. Three years later, in 1941, he was ordained. Another three years and Father Daly achieved a Doctorate in Theology. Recollections of Maynooth are austere. "Our numbers then were about 550, artificially inflated of course because the Irish College at Salamanca in Spain had closed, due to Civil War. Those students were evacuated, first to Paris, then prior to Hitler's invasion in 1939, to Maynooth. There were wartime restrictions on light, food and heat although a standing joke in Maynooth would have been *what heat?*"

Dr Daly lectured in Scholastic Philosophy at Queen's University for 22 years until 1967. "There I first met Robin Eames, now Archbishop of Armagh and Primate of Ireland. Never dreaming we would work together in our religious life, he was a fair-minded, logical man whom I

His Eminence Cardinal Cahal B. Daly

considered to have great potential."

Appointed Bishop of Ardagh and Clonmacnois, Dr Daly moved to Longford in 1967, where he would remain until 1982. A severe heart attack in February of that year led to six months' convalescence. "A year later I became Bishop of Down and Connor. North of the border 'the Troubles' were seething and almost immediately I became involved in problems relating to political uncertainty. I was in Glasgow attending an inter-church meeting when my sister telephoned with news that Cardinal Ó Fiaich had died. It was May 1990. The shock left me speechless for I assumed Cardinal Ó Fiaich enjoyed better health than I myself did. Cardinal Hume, the Papal Nuncio and heads of state from all over the world were present at Cardinal Ó Fiaich's funeral.

"While I was on a visit to Rome in October 1990, over breakfast Cardinal Gantin, president of the Roman Congregation for Bishops, broke the news that I was to become Archbishop of Armagh. Of course I protested! There was my health to consider, my age, now 72, nor did I feel I knew the diocese sufficiently." Pope John Paul II refused to accept any decision other than the affirmative and Dr Daly was installed as Archbishop in St Patrick's Cathedral, Armagh, on 1 December 1990. Seven months later, on 29 June 1991, having been called to a Consistory, he was ordained Cardinal by Pope John Paul II. Many distinguished church leaders were appointed on that memorable occasion.

"I vividly recall Cardinal Mahony of Los Angeles and Cardinal Bevilacqua of Philadelphia together with Romanian Cardinal Todea who bore scars of 14 years' imprisonment for his beliefs under the Ceausescu regime. Dr Oliver Woods, my physician, and his wife, Cecilia, travelled with me as did many of the staff from Ara Coeli, my new home in Armagh. A special privilege was having my family present, particularly my sister, Sheila, who had nursed my mother throughout her life. For such dedication, Sheila has always remained dearest to me.

"During my years as Primate I travelled extensively. Auxiliary Bishop Gerard Clifford was constantly on hand, substantially easing the pressures of commitment. Furthering peace and reconciliation led to a firm friendship with Archbishop Robin Eames and we often found common bonds. Both faiths joined in sharing the 1550th anniversary of St Patrick's foundation of Armagh in the same manner as sharing a common God.

"Balance this against moral progress, social awareness of world hunger, reconciliation in warring factions at home, in former Yugoslavia and the Middle East and a new awareness of our ecological responsibility. We know the planet will not support constant abuse and as various species come under threat, I admire the work of organisations such as the World Wide Fund for Nature."

His Eminence spoke appreciatively of Dr Seán Brady who contributed invaluable assistance as coadjutor Archbishop during 1996, Dr Daly's final year of office. "An exceptional moment during my life? Undoubtedly Queen Elizabeth's visit on 9 March 1995, when city status was conferred on our ancient capital of Armagh. I have great affection for my past residence, Ara Coeli, which translates as *the gate of Heaven*. It is a gracious house, steeped in atmosphere where, by courtesy of my library, I shared the elevated thoughts of philosophers, Cicero, Virgil, Dante and Homer. Traditionally a Cardinal becomes titular Parish Priest of a church in Rome. I was given St Patrick's, the Irish Augustinian Church which had been the titular church of both Cardinal Conway and Cardinal Ó Fiaich."

Nothing can ever replace the human touch. Asked if he envisages having time on his hands, Cardinal Daly smiles, shaking his head. "There is never a dull moment, never enough time to do the things I still want and hope to, if the Lord so wills, before I die."

Armagh Voices

a celebration of a century

1920 ~ 1930

Life well spent is long

Leonardo da Vinci

Peggy Trimble

One vital contribution to Armagh history has been narrated by Margaret (Peggy) Trimble, only daughter of Mary Quigg and Charles Delmege Trimble, editor of the *Armagh Guardian*. Peggy in her professional life combined health and community care for a population of 250,000. Her equally valid personal story begins retrospectively, on her return from Orsett, South Essex.

"It was 1982 and I'd retired as district administrative nursing officer for Basildon and Thurrock Hospital Group. Responsibility for ten hospitals and wider community services gave me little time to call my own. When I became matron of Orsett General Hospital, a recognised nurse training school, we considered ourselves lucky if a dozen young women made application at quarterly intervals. On leaving, the total student numbers had grown to 300 and training included plastic surgery, psychiatry and midwifery. That has all gone", she stresses, "and it would break my heart to go back!"

Through correspondence, Peggy is saddened to learn of what is happening to a general hospital that she helped to plan.

"I had a say in so many aspects and maybe made a nuisance of myself, but all in the name of patient care. I shared full-time nurse member management on a team comprised of two doctors, an administrator, treasurer and engineering services. We gave loyalty", she emphasises, "receiving the same in return. Our porters were a valuable team. Any good porter knows the exact workings of his department. Today it's a question of finance and this employee is switched here and there, to where the need exists, and so loses special value due to staff shortages. I know little of present National Health dictates but realise demands are greater. The waiting list for spare-part surgery, plastic hips for example, is enormous, and did not exist 20 years ago. Patients are often discharged too quickly and often aftercare can be scant. Part-time contracts do not allow patient-nurse care time to develop. As they say in Armagh, 'even the dogs in the street know' this must leads to nursing shortages. Someone balancing books dictated such a policy and we, the public, reap the shortfall. I keep informed to a superficial extent but I'm so glad I was there at that specific time."

Peggy embarked on a nursing career in Newtownards District Hospital in 1940, following her 17th birthday. "Nursing was then a socially-acceptable occupation for young women and, in any case, my parents could not have afforded to send me to university. Trainee nurses earned 15 shillings a month with one shilling taken out for use of a cape and our post", she recalls. "It was a time of shortages and my mother often sent me food parcels. I sat my State Final when I was 20, as opposed to 21, so for six months I worked as an unofficial staff nurse. I would never dream of pursuing this career today", she declares, "I'd much rather become an archaeologist or anthropologist. And yet in many ways I'm glad I was a nurse, for apart from enjoying the career, it enabled me to travel.

"My twin brother James was an air-gunner, 'a tail-end Charlie', with the Royal Air Force during the war, so you could say he also travelled at his employer's behest. It might be commonplace to jet off to Ecuador today, it certainly wasn't then! Although we have some of the empathy supposed to exist between twins, we do have vastly different attitudes and personalities. I like to start the day early while James burns the midnight oil. After leaving the RAF, he joined Camberwell School of Art in London. James is a good artist and George McCann was one teacher at Royal School, Armagh who encouraged him to further his talent. A career in advertising drew him into the commercial world but he continued to paint, exhibiting landscapes and still life studies in London, Italy and Armagh. Joining the Royal College of Art in 1976, as senior technician, he often took lectures and was appointed an Honorary Fellow."

The Armagh Peggy left behind in 1940 was not that to which she returned in 1988. "For 12 years I lived over the *Guardian* office in English Street and our big sitting-room windows allowed us a grandstand view of people passing by. Saturday evening with its bustle of crowded streets, was a colourful panorama of soap opera dimensions. Who was with whom? What were they wearing? Where were they going? We'd rest on our elbows watching it all happen. Whenever a procession took place, friends or relations gathered to share our vantage point. The City

Hall magnetically drew everyone to its entertainments, plays, dances or operatic works presented by Peter O'Hare, a local builder. I was cast as a page in Peter's production of Gilbert and Sullivan's *The Gondoliers*, a light-hearted parody of the real thing, brimming with mock-serious treatment of ridiculous circumstances and burlesque. Lavish costumes came from London as did the voice coach. Dr Ruth Lemon from Keady played the Duchess of Plazitora and in a magnificent, hooped gown, found herself wedged in the lavatory, unable to get out. We had full audiences for a week and I even received 'fan mail', my first fan letter from a boy who watched a performance from the gallery.

"For a time we lived in Dobbin Street and often climbed over the wall into the Primate's demesne which ran all the way down to the back of our garden. My father obtained permission for us to play here and we brought our chums along as well. 'Paddy's River' meandered through, flooding after heavy rain. From Dobbin Street corner it was great entertainment to watch cyclists negotiate the flooded street, hanging on to the nearest lamppost so they wouldn't fall in! Traffic-free, it was safe to play in the street. James, with help from my father, made a soapbox cart with pram wheels and I remember whizzing down from the Cathedral to the Shambles in this contraption, then coming to grief and spilling out at the bottom of the hill. We were a mixed bunch of kids, all neighbours, playing together and sharing good fun. For a time I lived in Abbey Street, near the County Infirmary, then a thriving community hospital with a respected staff under the direction of surgeon Hector Deane. Before the era of ambulances, serious casualties were brought to hospital on the roof of a car.

"At the hint of a catastrophe, we children used to run helter-skelter up the hill in our 'little horror' desire to see if there was 'much blood spilt'. A contribution towards upkeep of a hospital bed was often donated in memory of, amongst others, lives lost during the war. Many wards had a brass plaque paying tribute to young men of my knowing and generation. I'm glad to say these plaques have been preserved at Queen's University Outreach at Armagh and are displayed in a group on the first floor of the building.

"Abbey Street had its share of interesting neighbours to our childish way of thinking. There was Dr Chaundy, the Cathedral organist and his wife, an austere pukka couple who implied they would not stand any nonsense! When Father Finnegan stopped by at the Parochial House for his elevenses, we'd dash up, knock on the door, and recite the latest poem we'd learned. Our reward was a biscuit. Further down the hill lived 'Rosie' Davidson who fought in the Boer War. Later in life I worked in South Africa, and at Rosie's request, made a pilgrimage to the battle site at Ladysmith." There are memories all of us would wipe clean, were we able. Peggy recalls Workhouse children from Tower Hill joining the Armstrong School during the early 1930s. "I was already in Miss Mossman's class when they came wearing heavy boots, thick socks and tweed suits they'd 'grow into'. These children were bullied in the playground but we saw nothing amiss in that. When one girl was placed next to me, I went home and complained bitterly. My mother soon wiped out any superiority on my part. Years later I was asked to dance by a charming young man at Armagh City Hall. 'You don't remember me?' he asked. No, I did not. 'I was "Bertie the Bull"' (an orphan child at Tower Hill), he reminded me. Children's cruelty exacts a particularly heavy penalty and I still feel ashamed", she concludes.

"When my grandfather retired, we moved to English Street. My father now became editor of the *Armagh Guardian*. The Trimbles have been printers since William, my great-grandfather, began in Dublin in 1815. There was no free voice in Enniskillen to answer back to the *Erne Packet*, a pro-government journal at a time of controversy between landlords and Land League. William and his backers began *The Impartial Reporter,* which was read throughout Co. Fermanagh. Establishing this newspaper was difficult, inviting criticism and bankruptcy and yet he was greatly admired. Styled in broadsheet tradition, someone wrote of William at the time of his death in 1888:

He wrote as he felt, with the fire of a Celt,
And the rich and the great, and the power of the State
Were all treated alike, when old Trimble did write
For his great independence no foeman could buy.

"At the end of the last century, William's son, Delmege, bought the *Armagh Guardian* and left Ballyshannon for Armagh. After the death of his English wife and before he remarried a Dubliner, his young family were cared for by Brigid, a much-loved housekeeper from Donegal. My father often spoke of Brigid's tea, made at breakfast but continually topped-up so that it lasted all day. My great-aunts gave their redundant bonnets to Brigid but politely refused her offer of a cup of tea! Delmege used his newspaper as a method of raising funds and comforts for the 'Faughs', the county regiment, first in the Boer War and again during World War I. My grandfather, Delmege, epitomised the stern disposition and lifestyle of many Victorian gentlemen. He holidayed alone, and often ate sedately in another room removed from the family. No lady, in grandfather's estimation, ever smoked, drank spirits or wore sparkling jewellery early in the day. Etiquette required that a fruit cake be cut differently from a sponge cake! James and I were very young when every Thursday, which was publishing day, we went to see him. Suffering from severe arthritis, he remained in bed until late morning. Printers filed past, presenting proofs. Accuracy meant more than life itself and these men were required to leave the works, climb four flights of stairs, proffer their contribution to the newspaper and await his decision. James and I could hardly fail to be fascinated by this entertaining scenario. The uncles of Bob Humphries, one of our printers, walked from Donegal as young boys to find employment with my grandfather. Bob was a respected lifetime employee and so too, was Nat Orr, one of the best lino-printers in Ireland.

"In the street outside, newspaper boys from Callan Street swarmed at the works door awaiting batches of each week's edition which they sold for one penny. Enormous rivalry existed between the *Gazette* and the *Guardian* as to who would make it first unto the streets. We children loved the works and a whiff of printer's ink triggers memories of the linotypes and old handprinting machinery. Boxes of print and punctuation marks were stacked high. It was amazing to watch the speed at which a competent typesetter worked. Cultra Folk Museum has the original Eagle printing press on which first issues of the *Guardian* were printed. Charles Trimble, my father, joined the firm as senior reporter after returning from World War I. He had quite an adventurous time riding a motor bike round the countryside on 'stories'. He was a Reuters agent and copy for the English and Belfast press had to be sent on the evening train from Armagh. James or myself ran with this to the station where Mr Weir, the guard, looked out for us of an evening, before blowing his whistle and waving off the train. I would say my father retained that quality of exactness and accuracy from his early training. He firmly believed in the adage, 'Report the truth and keep your opinion for the editorial column'.

"The *Armagh Guardian* provided a life for young writers struggling to make a name in journalism. One of these was John O'Connor. It was O'Connor's association with Mill Row during the Twenties and Thirties which led to his novel, *Come Day, Go Day*, first published in Dublin, then later re-issued by a Belfast firm. John O'Connor had empathy and insight into lives of people and my father was proud to give him space. Charles Trimble's grounding in the writing business paved the way for promising young reporters who later joined national newspapers and BBC radio. He was futurist enough to employ women reporters at a time when the profession was male dominated. When I look back on the printing works it is easy to visualise the noise of machinery or that evocative smell of ink. Printers in overalls met deadlines while completing a hundred and one jobs in between. Mr Quinn, the 'father' of the works, typed my name and mounted this in a pad so I could stamp each new set of school books and by so doing, impress my classmates.

"My father loved the poems of Kipling", Peggy recalls, "often quoting from his *Barrack Room Ballads*. There is something forceful and memorable in this poet's phrasing that I, too, liked as a child. When my mother took us to church at First Armagh Presbyterian Church where the Rev. Alfie Neill was minister, I read Kipling during the sermon. It kept me quiet I suppose! We tend to recall times past through a rose-tinted haze of hindsight, but I remember being carried home by my father when a fight had broken out in Abbey Street. A young fellow had been set upon. My father made an effort to intervene but was restrained by my mother. I somehow doubt if he left it at that! I remember being driven by my great-uncle Charlie from Dublin when we were halted by a disturbance in Russell Street, just opposite the police station. Who was rioting or for what purpose, I hadn't a clue." When Peggy's father retired in 1961, a much-respected newspaper, the *Armagh Guardian*, was sold soon after.

"It is my firm belief that deprivation was class-related rather than deliberately political", she contributes. "Slums in Callan Street, now long-gone, had everything in common with slums of Navan or Irish Street. Repression and underprivilege caused hardship. While a student nurse, home on my one-day-a-month leave, I met a local woman who was pregnant, yet had walked to Portadown and back in the name of petitioning a councillor for a decent place to live. That woman then went to work at her cleaning job. Something had to change and dramatically."

Peggy Trimble reflects on her career
Photograph by Eric Smale, Kingston

Since returning to Armagh in 1982, Peggy describes herself as "a woman of unashamed leisure—but I did assist as secretary for the organisation of Armagh Music Week, a tremendous event that was a highlight of 1987. Three innovators from Armagh Arts Committee, Paul McAvinchey, Harry Carson and Seán Murray, brought together a special group led by Michael Doran and aided by the Arts Council for Northern Ireland, jointly planning a programme I will never forget. Armagh City Choir was a pleasing development of that exceptional Music Week when venues all over the city were used and filled. Over the years, a nucleus of young literary talent emerged from St Patrick's College, encouraged I would safely say, by Paul McAvinchey who has a visionary sense of what makes good drama. My affection for Armagh goes deep", Peggy admits, "and I am a Friend of the Cathedral Church of St Patrick often looking after the Cathedral shop. When I was growing up, a curfew bell tolled 99 times at 9pm each evening. We children were expected to be in bed by this time. Shuffling our feet and coughing was an attempt to drown out the sound. Bell-ringing ceased with the onset of World War II.

Peggy's travels take her worldwide and she has just returned from the Canadian Rockies and the Yukon. "I know *The Cremation of Sam McGee* backwards as our guide who drove the bus, recited every word Robert Service had ever written.

"I think back to the old printing works with its noise, bustle and evocative smell, compared with the same works now, computerised, silent and even busier. I know that my great-grandfather, who as a young boy in 1815 in Dublin wrestled with heavy, wooden-screw presses, would be amazed and delighted to see his grandson, Ted Trimble, continuing the family tradition so successfully. It astonishes when I think that my family's country newspapers published news of Catholic Emancipation, the Reform Bill, the Repeal Campaign, the deaths of King George IV, William IV and all the local, national and world events to World War II. These are images that please me greatly."

Bert Mackrel

That popular carol, *The Little Drummer Boy,* reminds William Albert (Bert) Mackrel of his fifth-generation military association. "John McCann, my great-grandfather, served with the Armagh Militia in the mid-19th century", Bert reflects. "In 1894 his son Robert joined the Irish Fusiliers as a drummer boy and was posted to Egypt. During the Boer War he met up with fellow Armachian Terry Devlin, a fife player in the regiment. Before a confrontation, Terry described how the men would yell 'For God's sake McCann stop polishing that drum... the Boers can see it for miles!'

"The two remained lifelong friends. Reminiscences at my grandfather's home in Lonsdale Street inevitably began 'Do you remember, Bob, when we were lying up at...' That was my mother's father. After the 1914-18 war, Bob McCann formed a cross-community flute band in Barrack Street, enlisting old comrades from the Fusiliers. The early Twenties saw Ireland in political turmoil and the demise of his beloved band. Armagh had lost a camaraderie that never returned. James Mackrel, my paternal grandfather, was employed at Belfast shipyard, graduating to chief engineer aboard several luxury liners. When James' wife died my father, also called Bert, was reared from the age of seven by his grandmother, a stern lady devoted to the Salvation Army. In ill health, she often remained in bed, her Salvation Army bonnet dangling from a peg overhead.

"Bert, my father, ran away to join the army at the age of 16. A recruit in 1919, he earned his first stripe within eight weeks. He met and later married Bob McCann's daughter Kathleen whilst billeted with the Royal Irish Rifles in Armagh. The establishment of the Irish Free State in 1922 altered the regimental name to the Royal Ulster Rifles. Ordered to quell conflict and rioting in Belfast, each man laid down his rifle, refusing to move. They were friends, Protestant and Catholic, not prepared to turn on their own people. My father's battalion was shipped to the Isle of Wight where many married local women." Returning to Victoria Barracks, Bert Senior went on a tour of duty to Colchester. Known as 'the glasshouse', it was here 'hard men' served detention. "I was born at Little Barrack Street, later moving to the old Goal Square. Christened William Albert after my father, I became 'Wee Bert'. My sight had always been a problem. To see better during lessons I was placed in the front row at the Armstrong School. I was seven, my sister Nancy only two, when the battalion received orders to leave for Palestine."

In December 1933, the RUR moved to Alexandria in Egypt. "From Armagh we joined my father, travelling aboard the P&O liner *Ballarat.* The wonders of a new continent were indescribable. I held my breath on sight of a camel train, slept underneath a mosquito net, learned the established drill of checking my shoes for scorpions each morning. Two years' tour of duty complete, Hong Kong was our next destination, a year on the island, six months at Victoria Peak, moving to Kowloon. We were living in China in 1937 when an Indian army doctor discovered I had a congenital cataract at the back of my eye." Surgery did not take place until Bert returned to Armagh.

"Nearing Christmas 1937, my father's battalion transferred to India. A two-day rail journey took us from Karachi to Victoria Barracks, Rawalpindi. With its population of 400 million, 30,000 troops held India, from Calcutta in the far east, Rawalpindi in the north-west, down to Bombay, as far as Delhi. On the rail journey to Rawalpindi, my mother bought boiled water for tea from the engine driver. Conditions at this hill station high in the Murree mountains (today Pakistan) were primitive. Jackals prowling nightly were a threat, so was disease. Like many, my sister Nancy contacted diphtheria."

Six years overseas, Bert's father now returned to Victoria Barracks, Armagh, as stores accountant. "I was 15 and began work as an apprentice in menswear with Lennox Brothers, Armagh. Willie and Jack Lennox ran this fabled store like clockwork. Department heads at the time were David Stewart in furniture, the late Jackie Speers had charge of linens, Miss Gilmour looked after millinery, Miss Herron had responsibility for lingerie, Miss Elliott and Miss Toms the glove department. Billy Bell was head of menswear. His assistant Billy McCall, who now must be 85 years old, went on to own two important shops in Lisburn. My sister Nancy, also a Lennox employee, modelled bridal gowns for mannequin parades held in the store. Her 'groom' was Tom Dale, our gifted window-dresser.

"Walking to work in 1943, I watched 25,000 American troops on the Mall, being addressed by General George Patton. Fired by enthusiasm I attempted to join the army under age but was turned away. A second attempt failed due to poor eyesight." Operations to both eyes gave Bert excellent sight for some years. He was then accepted by 5th Battalion Royal Irish Fusiliers (TA) on permanent staff, based at Gough Barracks.

Herta Genske, Bert's first wife, was East Prussian. "During the war her family escaped to the west from Tamau, a village close to Insterburg (now Chernyakhovsk) on the Baltic. Herta's brother, in the German Medical Corps, had been captured in France. Now desperate for reinforcements, Hitler ordered boys and old men, including her father, into the army. Russian troops had advanced from Poland, their guns could be heard only hours away. Herta's last memory of home was her father saying 'Look at this Christmas tree, it may be our last together'. Loading a cart they prepared to leave. Herta, a young woman of 18, wore her father's boots in the deep snow. Valuables, kept in an old clock on the mantelpiece, she wrapped in a handkerchief. The roads were thick with fleeing refugees and soon their horse was taken from them. Herta's parents ordered she go ahead, to look for lodgings. She would never see them again. Later Herta was told by the Red Cross in Berlin that her father was shot by the Russians and her mother died of typhus. Hiding in a ditch Herta escaped mortars, eventually finding her way to the Baltic. A sailor's uniform, flotsam in the water, Herta retrieved. From this, her self-sufficiency evident, she later made a skirt. At the harbour a vessel was loading only women and children. She could see a woman struggling with three children. Taking one in her arms, Herta was permitted on board. They sailed west. At a hospital in Hanover, she managed to find secretarial work. This hospital seethed with displaced persons and Herta became friends with Maria, daughter of a Countess, who introduced her to Dr Wilson from Ballymena. A regular pre-war visitor to Germany, it was 1950 when Dr Wilson asked Herta to return to Northern Ireland as his wife's companion. Maria accompanied them, she finding work in Ballymena."

On holiday at Butlin's, Mosney, across a crowded room, Bert spotted both young women. "Herta was fair-haired, quite petite. I asked her to dance and was impressed by her efforts to converse in English. We exchanged addresses, meeting for two years afterwards. I'd travel to Ballymena, and stay at the Clarence Hotel. We married in 1955." Bert brought Herta to Lonsdale Street, Armagh. "She was special in every sense", he agrees. "Herta worked as a machinist at the shoe factory and our mutual love of dogs resulted in rearing and showing the beautiful Samoyed breed." A natural progression was restoration of the long-lapsed Armagh Kennel Club.

The Little Drummer Boy kept time throughout Bert's life. Whilst on permanent staff at Gough Barracks with 5th Battalion (TA) he was Drum Sergeant with the Drums and Pipes. For 12 years he played side drum with Armagh Old Boys' Silver Band. "His talent was exceptional", today's members say, "none better." Bert smiles, and nods his head. "I joined Johnny Pickering's showband, The Bluebells, on drums and we played throughout the county."

Bert's sister Nancy had married Milford man Noel Hyde, and the two settled in Canada. "With 12 years' duty completed, I retired from the TA. Noel found work for me and it was my intention to emigrate. Before negotiations were complete, my sight failed. Canada was no longer an option." Worcester Valve opened a factory on Loughgall Road. Using Braille micrometers, Bert found work here in quality control. "I held this job until 1972 when my sight deteriorated. Herta insisted I apply for a guide dog. A year on, following training, I was appointed switchboard operator at St Luke's Hospital, Armagh. If you can imagine an old hotel switchboard with 100 extensions which I scanned by touch, that was how I passed each day. Candy, my guide dog, took me to work and brought me home each evening. We were living in Alexander Avenue when Herta's heart condition necessitated a by-pass operation. She died in the recovery room."

His difficulties unthinkable, Bert's 70-year-old mother now prepared an evening meal and Candy's food. "Candy and I continued to work for a further four years. Unknown to me, Lena, who became my second wife, had arrived from England and was living in Woodford. Realising she was lonely, her nephew brought her to a dinner dance at Drumsill Hotel where I too was invited. Our love of music saw us take to the floor and later we became partners for life. "I never saw Lena as my sight had gone completely

Bert and Lena Mackrel in Toronto

but through her energy, lived life to the full. Someone said we were like Siamese twins, always together. Herta was a wonderful wife who found me from the other side of the world. Lena now picked up the torch, and led me out of my darkness."

Bert is chairman of Orchard Social Club for Visually Impaired People, which meets fortnightly at Dobbin Street Community Centre. "Lena and I were founder members with the late Paddy Hamill and retired teacher Boyd Tweed. A decade ago as chairman, secretary and treasurer we enlisted 24 members. When we lost Paddy through ill health, Ivan Baxter ably filled the treasurer's seat." Orchard Social Club enjoys a summer trip and winter dinner dance with spot prizes awarded. Lena Mackrel would emerge arms brimming with donated gifts for this event. Tea lady at every meeting, her standards were high, trolley spotlessly set, herself immaculately dressed. Ellen Clements ably assumed this responsibility after Lena's death in December 1997—another unbearable blow for Bert.

"I have somewhat reconciled to my lot in life so give thanks for two wonderful women. Additionally Lena, for years an active supporter, collected donations for the British Legion Poppy Appeal and the Blind Centre, Belfast. Now my days are lightened when Ivan Baxter takes me shopping, to have my hair cut or visit the bank. We often disagree in the way good friends can. A pithy exchange makes us both smile afterwards! Joan and Seán Nugent never abandoned me. Gardening expert Charles Brady prunes Lena's shrubs. Her garden was a constant joy and Charles understands I maintain it in her memory. Jean and Bobby McMahon call for a welcome chat and I relish a visit from Jim Boyle, secretary of our Talking Newspaper for the Blind. Pamela Rea has taken the story of my life, lived on every continent, for transmission on the Talking Newspaper." Using skills of Braille, in his own home with his own equipment, Bert may be the only blind sound technician in the British Isles. He assists Armagh and District Talking Newspaper on two separate teams, enthusiastically awaiting the completed tape dropping through his letterbox each Saturday.

Longfellow's *Song of Hiawatha* asks, in haunting metre:
Should you ask me, whence these stories?
Whence these legends and traditions...

One answer says it began with a youngster polishing his drum in the Boer War, 1899. Bert Mackrel is the last of five generations whose lives fill more than a century.

A Tribute to Gerald Rafferty

The popular 'Rafferty Column' was integral to an earlier, broadsheet format of the weekly *Ulster Gazette*. Gerald Rafferty gave a clear impression of the scenes he wished to convey and his sudden death in September 1993 brought the demise of an excellent career.

Doreen McGrogan, deputy personnel manager of the *Belfast Telegraph*, offered the following information: "Gerry was a gifted raconteur and his death has robbed journalism of a highly-rated writer. A former *Ireland's Saturday Night* columnist, Gerry Rafferty's 'Listen Here Awhile' reflected old worthies of Ulster life. Born in 1925 at Drummanmore, near Armagh, he had his first contributions published while a teenager, by the *Armagh Observer*. Moving on to the *Irish News*, he later became a sub-editor with the *Belfast Telegraph* in 1962. Gerry wrote with authority on Irish folklore and country characters. His affection for *Ireland's Saturday Night* kept him on the sub-editorial team that processed sports news from all over the world. He retired in 1987 but continued to broadcast and to write for the *Ulster Gazette*. With more time at his disposal, Gerald completed a book of rural tales, *And The Band Played On*, published by Friar's Bush Press. This white-haired, softly spoken and unruffled journalist was a man of dignity and unbending principle..."

Gerald Rafferty also typed the script of *Come Day, Go Day* for Armagh author John O'Connor. Gerald's wife, Lena, now living in Lisburn, has selected excerpts from her husbands' work that will interest and involve many who appreciated his journalistic style. An article on St Luke's Hospital and its staff of the early Forties is supported by a photograph that was kindly donated. A further extract shows Gerald's intimate knowledge of Mill Row, and a piece on Armagh Great Northern Railway Station completes the trilogy.

THE ASYLUM DANCE *(wrote Gerald Rafferty)* was an important event in our social diary during the early and mid-Forties. These frequently held staff dances took place in the spacious dining room at the newly named St Luke's Hospital. Invitations were distributed by staff and it was difficult to procure one. My late brother Paddy, a former railwayman, worked in Armagh County Asylum *(as the Hospital was formerly known)* so I was sure of mine. As with the City Hall, the Asylum dances were great favourites and everyone was made welcome. Tea and sandwiches provided refreshments while leading dance bands supplied the music. Jim Bratten and his Red Shadows often took the stage at a time when Roy Kennedy was vocalist, a splendid singer. Patrons arrived steadily after nine in the evening, from Moy, the Grange, Blackwatertown, Keady, even Monaghan, most of them on bicycles, to be checked in by genial Sam Gillespie at the gatehouse entrance on Asylum Hill. Sam inspected each patron's invitation. Those he knew were admitted at once. The hospital then had its own dance band which included Rex Magill (violin), George Clarke (violin), Malachy McSorley (violin), Frank Corrigan (drums) and Larry Lee (saxophone). At this time all male nurses wore uniforms and were described as 'Keepers'. My other brother, Barney, was a Keeper at Castledillon before he joined the Great Northern Railway. My good friend, Willy John O'Hagan became a head nurse and John Harte's brother, Paddy, was also a Keeper, but is not in the photograph. William McAllister *(fourth row: fifth from left)*, in common with many of his era, left school at 14 years of age. He qualified in nursing, retiring with almost 40 years' service to his credit. William, who was in charge of the hospital's social club, organised dances, concerts and outings. Many times he took up a collection for a family in dire circumstances, due to the death of a staff member. Now 84 years of age, he is presently living in Scotland and not in the best of health.

Kathleen Johnston *(third row: third from left)* married Bob Whitcroft *(fourth row: second from left)*. Their eldest daughter, Elizabeth, is the wife of Canon Brian Bleaco who has the documented *Formative Years* of George Bernard Shaw (1856-1950) in which Shaw refers to his Aunt Whitcroft and his dislike of her. This, amazingly, was a distant relative of Keeper Bob Whitcroft!

We all enjoyed those dances at the Asylum where a great evening was assured.

Gerald concluded: There are surviving staff of those in the photograph and many may recognise familiar faces from the past.

A photograph showing many of the same staff (probably taken at the same time) appeared in the *Ulster Gazette* in 1988. This evoked the following response from Davina L. Mee (née Thompson): "I was the little girl in the front row of the photograph taken in 1940. My father was Dr Robert Thompson, medical superintendent of St Luke's from 1936-51. The steps on which this picture was taken were then the steps of my home, a lovely house of long corridors and hidden places for childhood games. Most of the staff and many patients were my friends. Long-term patients told me stories of their families—anecdotes from shell-shock victims of the First World War, to one patient with an amazing knowledge of history and Celtic mythology.

"Castledillon had imposing portraits of the Molyneux family in the front hall, a heavy old boat on the lake and miles of primroses and bluebells fringing the lawns in spring. Behind those walls walked not only the healers of today, but the inspiration and love of those, now gone, who lived and laboured to bring peace and comfort to troubled minds. They have gained a place in the history of psychiatric care. I remember my father's special interest in St Luke, the disciple who was also a physician. If I am right, it was his wish that the hospital be so named..."

We are deeply indebted to Kevin Toal, director of mental health services at St Luke's Hospital, for the following information relevant to that era of which Gerald Rafferty wrote. Kevin's uncle, Paddy Ferrity, is pictured *(fourth row: third from right).*

"In the early 1940s there were approximately 600 patients in St Luke's Hospital, with more males than females. Approximately 120 nursing staff represented a ratio of 5:1. Dr Thompson, the medical superintendent at that time, earned £1,000 per annum, plus allowances. The head store keeper was also an important member of staff and this reflects in his salary of £250 per annum. The Hospital had a local management team similar to the Trust management that has been brought into operation within the last few years. The management team had a number of functions including overall responsibility for patient care and maintaining financial accounts, as well as a local remuneration committee that made decisions on salaries of staff groups. The management team was accountable direct to the Northern Ireland Hospital Authority.

"Prior to the introduction of new drug therapies, social and work activities were considered an important aspect of treatment and the Hospital was recognised as a forerunner in this respect."

MILL ROW *(wrote Gerald Rafferty)* was a hamlet of 50 little houses built for the workers of Drumcairne Spinning Mill. Mill folk worked from six in the morning until six each evening and brought a modicum of prosperity to the Row. During the Twenties and Thirties, the mill periodically fell silent and times were hard. The Callan River flowing by on its way to the Blackwater would sometimes overflow, flooding most of the houses and driving families upstairs until the waters abated. Resilient people, even in these conditions, Mick and Paddy Murphy's accordion could be heard, although there wasn't a gondola in sight!

Residents took one day at a time and it was here that the boy John O'Connor lived with his family. They had a little shop where they sold sweets, cigarettes, tobacco, soap, laces and headache powders. It was 1932 when the O'Connor family moved to a brand new house in town. The early Forties came and John sat down to write his novel *Come Day, Go Day*, which was first published in Dublin, then re-issued by a Belfast publishing house. John did not live to see his work reprinted. He left Armagh in the Fifties, dying in Townsville, Queensland, Australia, in 1960. *Come Day, Go Day*, a gentle, evocative novel, charts the intricate relationships of the Coyle family, from the boy Neilly's viewpoint with all its wonders, dangers and magic of day-to-day living. Tyrone-born writer and critic, Ben Kiely, said: "This is a marvellous little book that could be classed among minor masterpieces." At the launching of its reprint, Belfast playwright and former BBC producer, John Boyd, said he would delete "minor" and describe the work as a full-blown masterpiece.

John O'Connor and myself were close companions and I knew the wonderful world of Mill Row also, living as I did less than a mile further down Loughgall Road at Reilly's Rocks in the townland of Drummanmore ('the high hills'). On my ancient Empire typewriter which I bought from a friend who was short of cash for a packet of cigarettes and the price of a cinema ticket, I typed out all of O'Connor's short stories and indeed the script of *Come Day, Go Day*, I worked late, often by candlelight in my bedroom. John O'Connor began writing in his teens, winning a short story in *The Bell*, a magazine edited by Irish writer Seán Ó Faoláin. Some of his stories were

Gerald Rafferty

St Luke's Hospital staff, circa 1942.

Front row (L to R): Jack Rice, chief male nurse; Kitty O'Brien, charge nurse; Charles Robert Cummins, engineer; Mr Cathcart, hospital secretary; Mary Alice Shields, matron; Dr Thompson, resident medical superintendent; Captain Ensor, chairman of committee; Mrs Thompson, superintendent's wife; Davina Thompson, superintendent's daughter; Dr Wright, assistant medical superintendent; Sam Boyd, storeman; Miss Reynolds, head nurse; Bob McFadden, head attendant, Castledillon. *Second row:* Bill Wilson, charge nurse; Bob Nicholson, charge nurse, Castledillon; Paddy Murphy, charge nurse; Cissie Callaghan, charge nurse; Rachael Warnock, charge nurse; Maggie Donnelly, charge nurse; Annie Reilly, charge nurse; Tom Cole, gateman; Paddy Hughes, charge nurse; John Kearney, charge nurse. *Third row:* Olive Symington, nurse; Mary McCrilly, student nurse; Kathleen Johnston, nurse; Sylvia McDonald, student nurse; Sadie Mitchell, student nurse; Violet Huston, nurse; Dorothy Moore, kitchen staff; Annie Rooney, nurse; Mamie Kirk, laundress; Ella Timmons, nurse; Miss Lyons, sewing room; Kathleen Connolly, laundress; Josie Gillanders, maid; Elizabeth Wright, mental nursing assistant; M. McKee, nurse; Sadie Murphy, charge nurse. *Fourth row:* George Wright, charge nurse; Bob Whitcroft, nurse; Jimmy Scarr, nurse; Jimmy McCauley, nurse; William McAllister, nurse; Billy Williamson; Paddy Mills, nurse; Larry Burns, nurse; Paddy Ferrity, nurse; Ernie Cathcart; William Coulter, tailor. Back row: John Hart, nurse; P. McCormack, joiner; Paddy Rafferty; Lexie Magill, engineer; Felix Fegan, nurse.

broadcast by John Boyd and Sam Hanna Bell.

Nothing remains of Mill Row today but re-reading the novel, pictures from the past reel back vividly. Men from the Row are gathered at the corner tossing a pair of halfpence or playing handball, engaged in a poker school or, more often, throwing bullets down the road past the Dead House, mortuary of Armagh Asylum, now St Luke's Psychiatric Hospital. From the Row would emerge a great bullet thrower, Jimmy Macklin, who on one memorable afternoon, defeated legendary 'Hammerman' Donnelly, a game that is still talked of amongst the road bowls fraternity from Armagh to Cork.

Life on the Row was light years removed from that of Georgian homes on our tree-lined Mall. Here cricket was played each balmy summer evening. By contrast, women of Mill Row sat outside their half-doors in a close-knit community where a genuine 'céad míle fáilte' was accompanied by a cup of tea. Many a cup I drank with philosopher Tom Withers, or Paddy Murphy who played the accordion or beat out a rhythm with drumsticks on a chair. Anyone with money in his pocket spent an evening at the Cosy Corner Picture House, City Cinema or the plush Ritz and, if the mill wasn't on short time, a pint in Francie Donnelly's, Vincent McMahon's pub or the 'Garden of Eden' in Castle Street. Children dragged buckets of water from the pump at the back of the mill, sure of a smack on the ear if they spilt a drop on their shoes or socks.

O'Connor painted his picture of old women gathering sticks for the fire, men at a procession of a bullet match, small boys plunging into the water in the quarry. These were characters and scenes I knew well, drawn from the immediacy of observation, not nostalgia. His quota included Wee John Lavery, Mahood Cairns, Big Ben Mallon, Wee Jack McCarthy, Big Matt McCarthy, Donal Quinn who made wireless sets, Sam Keenan the blacksmith, Ernie Richardson or Minnie Murphy, who organised dances on Mullinure Bridge where she played the accordion.

These Mill Row men could have stepped from a Damon Runyon story; hard men in a fight, gentle at home with their family. John O'Connor's uncle Tommy was a dapper, fast-talking, likeable man who wore a flat cap and smoked a fag which usually dangled from the corner of his mouth. Older women from the Row enjoyed a sniff of snuff from Sam Wright's shop or Maggie McKernan's at the station. Gallagher's snuff made in Belfast was a favourite brand. The late Cardinal Logue was said to enjoy his pinch of snuff on occasions. Alice, no-one knew her surname, from Mill Row, travelled the district with her pony and cart, collecting rags and bric-a-brac. Alice called at my house and my mother brought her in for a cup of tea.

John O'Connor and his literary disciples drank endless cups of coffee at Tommy McAvinchey's Rainbow Café when conversation ranged from writers and writing, bullet throwing or swimming in Drumman Lake. He was an all-year-round swimmer, tough as they come, who began life as a telegram boy with the Post Office, graduating to become a postman with a bike. Seasonally he pulled apples at Loughgall and perched up a tree, found inspiration for many of his stories. His works contained little or no plot but were concentrations of study or mood, calling for fine writing and expression. The Loughgall Road no longer echoes to Mill Row voice or a cheer for a bullet score. These former things have passed away.

A final passage from Gerald Rafferty details the staff of Armagh Great Northern Railway Station in 1937. Few who were employed when the station closed down in September 1957 remain, but Gerald had railway connections and close links with men who kept the trains running on time.

I KNEW EVERYONE who was employed at Armagh Station in 1937 *(wrote Gerald)*. That was a time when I used to walk up and down the track on my way to and from school. I left my bicycle beside Cabin South each morning in the care of signalmen, Bob Moorhead or Billy Friars. In Cabin North, Jimmy Taft and Paddy McKenna expertly wielded the levers and signals. Johnny Shannon from Banbrook, who retired to Portadown, wore several hats for he performed the duties of porter, signalman, guard and ticket inspector. Johnny's brother Jimmy was a clerk at the Station. Bertie McQuaid from the parcels office emigrated to Canada, followed by his brother Christie who was an official for the Prudential Corporation. Ticket collector, Davy Weir, lived in Railway Street. Larry Leonard and Alfie Rolston worked at the goods store, Larry living in Castle Street and Alfie on Barrack Hill. Signalman, Paddy McKenna kept goats on the railway bank, and Billy Lyness who operated the Wordie carts, lived nearby in Railway Street. Paddy, my brother, was a porter, Tom Pugh was station foreman while Brian Kerr and Davy Nelson were both in the parcels office. Teddy Megaw was chief ticket clerk, and later stationmaster. Mr McBrien was chief goods office clerk and A. Spence worked in the ticket office.

Armagh was a busy station and these men prided themselves on trains running smoothly. Every railwayman was given one or two free passes during the year and, thanks to my brother, I went to Dublin with my parents, leaving from Armagh and changing at Portadown. We had something to eat after arriving at Amiens Street Station and I can still picture thousands of cyclists speeding along O'Connell Street. Station men were the salt of the earth, like the good people of Mill Row or the staff of Armagh Asylum.

They may be gone but in my heart, will never be forgotten.

Phyllis Mason

"How many housewives such as myself absolutely loathe cleaning bedrooms? Perhaps it's psychological." Phyllis Mason, sitting at the opposite end of the table stops abruptly. "Are you sure about talking to me? After all, I've only been living here for the past 30 years." Didn't someone say *A pox on any incapable of perceiving themselves through a fresh retina?* "If you say so", Phyllis replies, shrugging good-naturedly.

Her persona brims with charm, the ultimate weapon. If you have it, you can do without any number of appendages. Phyllis Mason has got it, knows how to use it, and mercifully, the past 30 years have not contrived to diminish such an important quality. Her Honda City Express motorbike leans on its rest by the back door. "The only way to travel", declares this upwardly mobile senior in her distinctive Home Counties accent. "Unfortunately it's only 49cc so I can't take it on the motorway."

Phyllis and her husband Geoffrey with their daughters, Caroline and Jane, moved from Shropshire to Co. Armagh in 1967. "Goodyear International for whom Geoffrey worked had just opened a factory at Craigavon. I recall we booked into Drumsill House for a fortnight while finding somewhere to live. It was a frantic time, but eventually, everything fell into place. Visiting Vicar's Hill and St Patrick's Cathedral in our early days led to a chance meeting with Dean Lillie. We were fascinated by the sense of history pervading this building and the Dean kindly offered to take us on a conducted tour. The following Sunday we came to morning service and shortly after, enrolled as Friends of the Cathedral. Mrs Maud Love was treasurer and when she retired, Geoffrey was nominated to that office. I've never bored people about missing England, but allow me to say that during that hour at the Cathedral each Sunday, I feel utterly at home. The choir, under the guidance of Martin White, is magnificent, his interpretation of music second to one. Evensong seems to have a special tranquillity."

A young woman during the Second World War, Phyllis joined the WAAF in 1942, aged 21, training as a wireless operator. She was later to become an instructor at a radio school near Calne, in Wiltshire. "I met Geoffrey at an RAF dance in the local town hall. It just happened to be my birthday, so it's easy to calculate how long we've known each other. Sometimes I feel we should organise a plaque outside the building to commemorate our meeting!

"Meeting infrequently, we had such a lot of news to catch up with. One story I saved for Geoffrey might amuse readers. Our billets were absolutely freezing. We had no fuel, you see. I used the wooden lavatory seat from the least-used toilets to provide some heat. Geoffrey said only modesty prevented me taking the doors as well. Our orderly officer demanded the culprits stand up and be counted. Eighteen loyal WAAF jumped up. They couldn't put all of us on a charge so the matter dropped.

"Geoffrey has much more vivid memories as he was in Berlin immediately after liberation. We corresponded and so retained our relationship during those years. After the war, we married in Loughborough, where I lived. Something worth mentioning is the fact that as well as husband and wife, we're friends. That's so important. We avoided like the plague calling each other 'Mother' and 'Dad', something I find infuriating."

The family attuned to life in Armagh, and when Caroline and Jane were self-sufficient, Phyllis took a post as branch librarian at Tandragee, later moving to the Portadown division. She has an enduring love of literature. "Reading is a favourite relaxation and my personal preference is biography. I have never cared for crime nor romantic fiction. Hell", she laughs, "has to be paved with bookcases of Mills and Boon. I treasure Laurie Lee's *Cider with Rosie* as an intimate insight into the author's rural childhood. No-one seems to mention Robert Louis Stevenson any more, yet what sensitive poetry he wrote during his short life:

You too, my mother, read my rhymes,
For love of unforgotten times.
And you may chance to hear once more,
The little feet upon the floor.

"This little verse never deserts my memory."

When the factory at Craigavon closed after 16 years in operation, Geoffrey took early retirement. "We'd always been happy living in Northern Ireland and the family decision to stay was unanimous. Quite a number of factory personnel returned to England but Richhill became

Phyllis Mason, Women's Auxiliary Air Force, 1943

our established home."

"We visit my sister Sybil in Oakham fairly often. Her youngest son, Harry, works in Geneva where he's organising aid for Rwanda with the United Nations High Commission for Refugees. It's a nightmare. There are camps where camps should never have been, what with no water nearby and everything having to be trucked in. The UNHCR was trying to move a million refugees north of Kabale while, at the same time, encouraging them to return to Rwanda. It overwhelms but at least his team do all they can."

The Mason girls, Caroline and Jane, married local brothers, John and Charlie Nicholson. Caroline had obtained a degree from the University of Ulster and was then teaching full time. Jane ran her own page in the *Portadown Times*. She called it 'Just Jane' and featured up-to-the-minute happenings. Caroline and Charlie live in Carrickfergus with their daughter and the only grandson to carry on the Nicholson name. "When Geoffrey retired, Jane and John, who by now had four daughters, asked if we would care to convert part of their large home at Cranagill to suit ourselves. We did just that, utilising the old schoolroom and laundry, no longer in use."

"The original house built in 1760 has been constantly occupied by the Nicholson family ever since. We named ours *The Other House*. It's quite spacious with idyllic views of the countryside but what we like most of all", she lowers her voice, "it is blissfully *quiet*. We do not live in each other's pockets, a week may pass without family contact, then we share a meal. It's an arrangement that works well."

John is a partner in the film and television company Straightforward Productions, and co-producer of the highly successful BBC programme *Greenfingers*. RTE and Channel 4 have taken the series and a new run is anticipated this autumn. *Places Apart* was another series of theirs when Anne Gregg compared the complexities of distinctly differing attitudes throughout various towns and Northern Ireland. "Interesting people constantly come and go next door, so we're never short on stimulating conversation."

Phyllis is a volunteer member of a local Samaritans Group, but the confidentiality of such work precludes comment. As a skilled needlewoman, she enjoys quilting and tapestry. Delicate petit point is her speciality, however, and she's often engaged to carry out private commissions. "While I work, I listen to Radio 4. Call me a radio drama fanatic but *Afternoon Theatre* has to be the BBC at its best. With my sewing box I settle in a chair and hope the phone won't interrupt the crucial machinations of *Dombey and Son*.

"I am an avid collector of decanters but filling them is quite something else. Easily my favourite possession is a wedding ring belonging to my great-great grandmother. She was a teacher, born in Gloucestershire in 1812 and married before Queen Victoria ever came to the throne. I carry her name, Avery, which has been in the family since 1733, so does Caroline and one of my granddaughters. Hopefully the tradition will be sustained by future generations. I've threatened to haunt them if they don't.

"Geoffrey has been a dedicated radio ham since 1947. An avid reader, once a week he assists with the cataloguing of engravings at Archbishop Robinson's library on Vicar's Hill. We travel abroad for a major part of the summer. Both of us love France, returning again and again. I sometimes felt guilty about the happiness I've known. A major blow, for example the sudden death of someone in whom you have placed your confidence, must be shattering. I often remind myself that I am fortunate and give thanks for it all."

Her daughters say there is a teenager inside Phyllis, just longing to escape. She's never lost her identity or allowed a situation to swamp her, and mentally will never grow old. How many grandmas, I ask, would come flying down the swimming flume as she frequently does? Phyllis has a delightful adage. "It's better to travel hopefully than to arrive. Me? I'm still travelling."

Without fresh perspective we would have been denied this story and the irresistible magnetism of Phyllis Mason. Only 30 years input into the life of Armagh? I've forgotten who said *A pox on the long memory.*

One of 77 lives published in Touching A Chord *(1996), Phyllis Mason died on 24 November 1997. As her spirited interview suggests, those who knew her 'loved her well'.*

Robert Wilson

"During 37 years in Fane Valley management, my boss, Bob Wilson, raised a one-roomed hand-bottling store to the status of major Northern Ireland employer. He is worthy of mention..." wrote former Fane Valley employee, P.J. Connolly, MBE. Generosity of spirit is a rare trait and in deference to such a request, the life of Robert W. Wilson, OBE, JP came to notice.

"Fane Valley Creamery opened in summer 1904 at the Society's premises in Altnamackin", Robert Wilson says. "In our Diamond Jubilee Year, from Society minutes, I produced a history entitled *Sixty years of progress*. This work delineates the co-operative movement in Ireland, founded by Sir Horace Plunkett as the last century ebbed to a close. Realising Ireland suffered from widespread economic distress, agricultural stagnation and poor social conditions, Sir Horace persuaded farmers to combine in running their own creameries. The Irish farmer", Bob continues, "has always been a private individual, loath to betray his business, and 50 meetings were held before the first co-operative creamery in Ireland, Fane Valley, was registered on 7 April 1903. This highly successful Society was closed by the Ministry of Agriculture in 1942 under a wartime milk concentration scheme. Milk was then diverted to Tassagh, one of six new Ministry depots built in Northern Ireland. The Society reopened in Ballybrolly, bottling milk for schools and in 1948, moved to a new dairy at Railway Street, Armagh."

Since Bob Wilson joined Fane Valley management in 1951, he has steered the Society through an agricultural revolution. "I came from Glenarm where my grandfather was president of Deerpark Co-operative Society. Ours was a farming family and it was assumed I would follow the occupation. The opportunity of a scholarship to Larne Grammar School led to a degree course in Civil Engineering at Queen's University. War broke out within the year and I attempted to join the Royal Air Force but my eyesight proved a stumbling block. Back on our home farm and eldest of 13 children, my younger brothers were now earning a living and there was simply not enough to support us all. I found employment with Boyd's Dairy in Finaghy, where I bottled milk for a year. This experience nurtured thought of a career with the Ministry of Agriculture. An unexpected offer to study Dairy Science at University College Cork required thought for I now had my wife, Marie, to consider as well as obtaining an important qualification. Marie was supportive so I went ahead." With a diploma to his credit, Bob was committed to the Ministry of Agriculture. Posted to Ballyrashane Co-operative in North Derry, news of his abilities reached Alexander Smyth, general manager of Fane Valley Society since 1929. Offered a post in management, Bob moved to Armagh in 1951.

"At first I lodged with Mr and Mrs Sam Maxwell, people of extraordinary kindness. Words will not express how they supported me when my brother was killed in a farming accident. Fane Valley then engaged mainly in bottling one-third pints of milk for local schools. Only a small retail trade existed, milk coming directly from Tassagh Creamery. Fane Valley was a troubled ship at the time, under enormous pressure from the health authorities. Another problem was the balancing of milk purchased with milk sales. With depressing frequency I would find irate milkmen pacing up and down the yard because unreliable lorries had broken down. While the organisation was solvent, finance was not available for capital investment.

"My first resolve was finding a dependable fleet of vehicles of the same model, meaning easier maintenance, and this we achieved over a few years. To further investment, a committee decision invited additional shareholders on board. An individual investment figure of £10 was decided. Engendering capital in a small way involved a considerable number who now had the Society's interest and success at heart. Further funding came from a revolving loan scheme, where part of the annual interest and dividend would be invested as loan guarantee shares, repayable in five years. This new funding allowed investment in plant and machinery and, of course, expansion. It may be of interest that in 1950, shareholders numbered 253, average net profits over ten years were £2,378 with an intake of 65,000 gallons. A year later, net profits grew to £5,792 and our milk intake increased by over 10 per cent." At the time of Bob Wilson's retirement in 1987, shareholders numbered 2,563 and net profits were more than £500,000, with a milk intake of almost ten million gallons. Total turnover of Fane Valley and associated companies was now in the region of £50 million and they employed a staff of around 400.

"We obtained milk in bulk from Tassagh Creamery but it was obvious that more efficient use could be made if it came straight from the farm. Lobbying the Milk Marketing Board, permission was granted to pick up milk from farmers in the Richhill area, starting at eight each morning. Creamery cans were left out on the road. To help our venture, I myself drove a lorry and collected milk for almost two years. All milk was checked for quality on arrival by taste and smell. Whilst a grading officer with the Ministry of Agriculture I acquired this skill which I now passed on to our employees. Two decades later milk was collected by tanker from individual bulk tanks on the farm." Over the years a full range of Fane Valley dairy products began to appear in the shops.

Bob recalls important financial support given by the local branch of the Ulster Bank at a crucial time. "I enjoyed dealings with cashier Ken Lynn, a magnificent counter of notes, chatting while he worked yet always accurate. With a base in Altnamackin, our workforce came from South Armagh, Armagh itself, Keady and Newtownhamilton. Fane Valley has always been controlled by a management committee of members, mainly from the farming community.

"Quite a number of employees here when I began in 1951 were still on the payroll when I retired in 1988, as seen from our photograph. Those not included were Mrs Annie Knight who gave 60 years' service in the office at Altnamackin and Miss Phyllis Nugent, senior office clerk in Armagh, whose service extended to more than 40 years. Those photographed are: Jimmy Kissane, butter maker; P.J. Connolly, milk roundsman and latterly bulk tanker driver; Jimmy Compston, lorry driver, shop and delivery service; Stanley Cordner, mechanic; Leslie McKee, lorry driver; Paddy Leer, relief milk roundsman; Tommy Lennox, clerical duties; Sam Bartholomew, milk roundsman; Joe Blackwood, electrical and maintenance engineer, and Bobby Knight, milk process operator. Mr A. Smith, general manager, was my boss for 20 years and a tremendous source of support and guidance. Chairmen and committee members were receptive to suggestions for development, accepting that not every project started would succeed. Employees worked closely, even on the dairy floor, and were like one big family."

During the mid-1950s milk intake increased and it was decided to resume buttermaking at Armagh. Jimmy Kissane, who had been employed at Ballybrolly, rejoined Fane Valley. An employee since 1937, prize buttermaker Jimmy took more than 100 trophies during his career with Fane Valley and very often the Supreme Champion Cup at Balmoral Show or shows in London, Glasgow and Dublin. Bob remembers introducing Fane Valley butter to local traders. "I called on grocer Henry Emerson of Thomas Street and was delighted when he agreed to try four boxes each containing 28lbs. Some years later, Emerson's order with Fane Valley was one ton of butter a week.

"Providing a service to the farmer was essential and the Society tried to meet market demand rather than make profits. Most importantly, we prided ourselves on providing cross-community employment in areas where there was little work." In 1958, the committee embarked on an entirely new venture by acquiring an egg marketing business with a shipping licence attached.

"Adding the poultry farmer to our list of suppliers, the Society invested in a new store and modern packing and grading equipment, operative by 1960. That entire year was a milestone in Fane Valley development. Newtownhamilton had an important cattle fair and establishing an auction mart was the brainchild of our vice-president, Douglas Hughes. In keeping with Ministry stipulations and attestation, we acquired pens and accommodation, opening our mart in 1960. The Ulster Agricultural Organisation Society now approached Fane Valley asking how they might best assist Armagh and District Co-operative Society. This body was mainly comprised of consumers and Fane Valley took over the entire concern under a 'transfer of engagements'.

"An important year of Society history was 1963", continues Bob, "as Armaghdown Creameries in Newry, one of the largest milk intake centres in Northern Ireland, came onto the market. Fane Valley, with two other co-operative societies, combined in acquiring ownership, the greatest financial responsibility ever taken by our Society. A.J. Streahorn Ltd, produce merchants of principally egg and potatoes, was another takeover that year. By 1969 work commenced on a new factory for Armaghdown at Banbridge. Opening in 1970, this factory engaged in buttermaking and milk powder drying. Gradually

Members of Fane Valley staff at Robert Wilson's retirement in 1988 who were in employment when he started in January 1951.
Back row (L to R): J. Kissane, started 1937; P.J. Connolly, 1945; J. Compston, 1950; S. Cordner, 1950; L. McKee, 1942; P. Leer, 1949.
Front row (L to R): T. Lennox, 1944; S. Bartholomew, 1950; R.W. Wilson, 1951; J. Blackwood, 1939; R. Knight, 1943.

business expanded to cover a wide range of dairy products and world-wide exporting of milk powder. The next investment, in 1982, was in R. Sand Ltd of Newry, animal feed manufacturers. A fire in 1984 seriously damaged the factory, which reopened a year later and is currently a leading supplier of animal food. A further investment was made in Belfast during 1982, when the Society acquired Barr's Cash and Carry, a major wholesale grocery and hardware concern. Continued expansion saw Fane Valley embark on potato washing and grading at a store purchased in Dervock, North Antrim, in 1986. This provided a supply of washed and graded potatoes for our pre-packing unit in Belfast.

"I regret to say we suffered loss of life when our vice-president James McKee and his son Ronnie, Neville McConnell, manager of Fane Valley Mart, and an Altnamackin employee, Joe McCullough, were murdered whilst attending a meeting in Tullyvallen Orange Hall. Depression shrouded the factory for everyone regarded these men as comrades both at work and socially. Our Altnamackin premises were bombed and rebuilt too often to count. Indeed I remember lodging 27 simultaneous claims for bomb damage with the Northern Ireland Office. Once, while attending a meeting at Agricultural House, Knightsbridge, London, news came of an explosion in Armagh. I returned to find the dairy seriously damaged. Local residents assisted staff who worked through the night to clear debris. Thanks to all, we bottled next morning and delivered door to door. During 37 years with Fane Valley, we have never lost an hour's production regardless of bombing, strikes or work disputes. This is entirely due to a dedicated workforce who represent both sides of our community, working together as a team."

Involved with Armagh's commercial life and a past president of Armagh Chamber of Commerce, Bob Wilson recalls the Chamber's concern over inadequate provision for industrial development with the Armagh Area Plan. With Patsy McCoy, secretary of the Trade Union Council, he made representation to the District Council on behalf of the Chamber. "We feared for the town's business future as Armagh was then regarded as residential in relation to industrial Craigavon. A prominent Councillor claimed we were time-wasting, suggesting we seek government assistance. We did exactly that", he confirms. "Don Concannon of the Northern Ireland Office assured us he would pay heed to any sound proposal which would benefit Armagh. Following a series of meetings with interested bodies, and with the support of Adrian Stinson of the small business agency LEDU, we laid out a proposal to convert Bairnswear Factory into Armagh Business Centre. This, with a satellite in Markethill and an associate in Keady, provides workspace for up to 95 small businesses—69 are presently occupied."

Another voluntary and successful venture came about when he teamed with Patsy McCoy in establishing Armagh Community Projects ACE scheme in 1988. The scheme provided a major input into the Riding for the Disabled centre based at Longstone. At its peak, 32 workers were employed in a variety of schemes within its Armagh city catchment area. "To see an idea in operation gave great satisfaction", Bob states. He also served the Armagh area as a panel member with LEDU from the late 1970s to the mid-1980s. One of his first contacts was businessman John McKenna who today controls one of the city's thriving businesses. Sam Hughes of Redrock Engineering was an initial contact who made good of his investment. After retirement, Bob was approached by LEDU to act as a counsellor/advisor under their business start-up service for small firms. A further eight years in this capacity saw him assist prospective entrepreneurs.

In his spiritual life, as a member of the Mall Presbyterian Church Bob served on the Congregational Committee. Here he is remembered as inspirational in raising badly needed funding for church repairs and improvements. Bob describes a long-serving minister, the late Rev. J.C.M. Anderson, as "a tremendous congregational man". He was succeeded by present Moderator Dr John Lockington.

The qualities exhibited by Bob Wilson did not go unnoticed and he was elected a Fellow of the Royal Agricultural Society in 1984, amongst the first 12 in Northern Ireland to receive this honour. Bob served as chairman of the Society's Northern Ireland Panel from 1994 and describes his appointment as national chairman in 1997, for a two-year term, as "easily a highlight of my life".

Retiring to Kilkeel in 1994, he sits as director of Kilkeel Development Association and is chairman of Kilkeel Business Development Committee. His educational input includes a decade on the board of governors of Armagh College of Further Education and present membership of the boards of Kilkeel Nursery

School and Kilkeel Primary School. As a former member of Armagh Rotary Club, Bob was honoured with the Paul Harris Award. A Foundation Member of United Farmers in Edinburgh, he is proud to mention past employee, Uel Morton, who now holds managerial status there. Director and past chairman of the Ulster Agricultural Organisation Society, he is a life vice-president and still attends meetings.

"In all of this", Bob acknowledges, "Marie was a tremendous source of strength. We had seven children and 22 grandchildren. Today our eldest daughter, Rebecca, lives in Hillsborough. Stephen, her eldest son, provided Chloe, our first great-grandchild. Hazel, a teacher, lives in Australia and Sam, our eldest son, is transport manager with Fane Valley. John is principal of Newry High School, Colin runs a restaurant in Florida, Linda works locally at the Cake Shop and Paul runs a post office and general store near Tandragee. In addition to family responsibilities, Marie contributed to voluntary work at Tower Hill Hospital, retiring after 15 years' nursing service in Craigavon Hospital. A Marie Curie nurse for five years in Kilkeel, she was a volunteer with the HomeStart organisation and had a poem of appreciation written in her honour."

On his retirement, Fane Valley presented both Bob and Marie with travel vouchers. "This we used for a world tour lasting four months. Visiting 14 countries was the dream of a lifetime, comprising a Caribbean cruise and flying home from Miami in Concorde."

"He has worked tirelessly for the Society and Northern Ireland agriculture in general", wrote president W. Blackwood when Bob retired in 1988. P.J. Connolly, a modest man who initiated this story, was quite right. Robert Wilson's lifetime is certainly 'worthy of mention'.

Heather Black

Elected to the office of Mayor in June 1995, Councillor Heather Black is a member of the Ulster Democratic Unionist Party and the first woman ever to hold the office of Mayor within Armagh City and District Council. As Deputy Mayor to Jim Nicholson, MEP, in 1994, Mrs Black shared in the blaze of pageantry when the Queen conferred city status. She had also filled the position of Vice-Chairman to Pat Brannigan in the former District Council in 1993.

Mrs Black describes herself as "a unionist with traditional Reformation principles, with a life long interest in the politics of my country. Having become a member of the DUP at its inception, I support and endeavour to implement the principles of my party.

"My husband, the late Councillor Thomas Black, faithfully represented the electorate of Cusher for 16 years, being re-elected each consecutive year until his death in 1989. While I remained in the background, I found his political commitment interesting and, from Thomas, formed an understanding of the functions of committees within local government. Agreeing to stand for election after his death, I was returned with an increased majority. I am pleased to add that this increase has been sustained throughout my ten-year term. With the same cause at heart, I have endeavoured to participate in Council activities and continue the representation for the good of our area. It has been my privilege to work for the electorate of Cusher for the past ten years and I look forward to being given the opportunity to represent the area again in all aspects of the work of the Council.

"Elected to the office of Vice-Chairman in 1993, I became acutely aware of the value of common courtesy and consideration for others. I make a point of keeping in touch with young people, which is not difficult as I have two grandchildren, Hilary and Trevor, both of whom are graduates of Queen's University as well as having gained the Duke of Edinburgh Gold Award some Years ago. I had the great pleasure of being present when they were presented with their Awards at St James' Palace.

"Whatever the engagement, out of respect for those whom I will meet, I give a lot of thought to my standard of dress. Apart from the psychological pleasure of knowing that we look well, freshly-pressed appearance upholds the decorum attached to the office of Mayor".

Armagh is always glad to strengthen its links with the United States. One of the first major tasks Mayor Black had to perform, in June 1995, was to host a reception for Senator George Mitchell, then President Clinton's special advisor for economic initiatives in Northern Ireland, and the US Secretary of State.

"Following a meeting with church leaders, Senator Mitchell visited a number of historic sites and tourist attractions. The then Vice Chancellor of Queen's University, the late Sir Gordon Beveridge, showed Senator Mitchell the new Queen's University of Belfast at Armagh Outreach Project, which was under construction at the time in the vicinity of the cathedrals. It was my great pleasure to host this civic reception and welcome Senator Mitchell and other distinguished guests from the USA. Others at the reception included Sir Gordon Beveridge, Professor Mary McAleese, members of Armagh Economic Development Group, church representatives and Councillors. This visit was particularly significant as it closely followed the President's economic conference in Washington the previous month. The Council and its business partners were very pleased with the conference and their economic visit to Virginia and a number of important business contacts were made as a result. The Friendship Agreements signed by Armagh with the Cities of Richmond and Charlottesville have helped us to develop a lasting and mutually beneficial relationship with the people of Virginia."

Again reinforcing the US connection, Mrs Heather Black welcomed Dr Walter Witschey, director of the Science Museum in Richmond, Virginia, to a conference entitled 'Science Alive' at Armagh Planetarium, designed to highlight the benefits of increased understanding of science and technology in local economy and quality of life.

She also met author Jonathon Bardon, when his book *A History of Ulster* was included in an exhibition on the history of the Orange Order hosted at St Patrick's Trian in September 1995. "Jonathon included a detailed account of the Battle of the Diamond in this work", comments

Councillor Black, "so it was particularly important from that aspect.

"While I was Mayor, it was most pleasing when Armagh City and District Council took third place in the United Kingdom's 'Tidy Up Week' during October 1995. I later hosted a reception at the Palace when Mrs Irene Kempton, environmental health officer for the Council, received the award in the form of a framed certificate. Top places in the competition went to England with Lambeth Council, London, and Leicester City Council taking first and second prizes respectively. Credit must be paid to children from local schools and youth groups who carried out 'litter picks' beforehand. Many schools treated the event as an environmental exercise, later using collected litter creatively in the classroom. The Litter Order gives everyone increased responsibility and powers to deal with this menace. Every scrap of litter means we are departing from an image of cleanliness.

"Looking back across the millennium is one way of appreciating the changes that time has wrought. In this sombre context, I laid a wreath at the Cenotaph in November 1995, the 50th commemoration of VJ Day. Members of the Armagh Branch of the Royal British Legion were joined by St John Ambulance Brigade and members of the security forces. The parade was led by Armagh Old Boys' Silver Band. Somewhat sadly, this was the last event organised by parade marshal Mark Doyle, now in failing health. Mark conducted this duty with distinction for many years.

"A church service paying tribute to the sacrifice of all servicemen and women, and particularly those who were serving when Japan surrendered to the Allies, was held in St Mark's Church on 14 August 1995, conducted by the Rev. John McKegney with the Rev. Tony Davidson of First Armagh Presbyterian Church. It was also 50 years since the first atomic bomb dropped in Hiroshima and we held silence for all who died. I then stood while the salute was taken by Lord Caledon, Lord Lieutenant for County Armagh. Mr Charles Brady, president of the Armagh Branch of the Royal British Legion was also in attendance." In the same commemorative week, Heather Black was present when Prince Andrew laid a wreath in a solemn ceremony at the City War Memorial in Belfast.

"Everyone loves music", agrees Mrs Black, "and especially when it is performed by Armagh Old Boys' Silver Band. I was delighted to be guest of honour at their Centenary Celebration Night in the Music Centre. They played a medley that had to suit every taste and it was so enjoyable as to set everyone's feet tapping. I cannot envisage a world without music, nor Armagh without its Old Boys' Band!

"As a guest of the Secretary of State for Northern Ireland, the Rt Hon. Sir Patrick Mayhew, I met President Bill Clinton and the First Lady when they came to turn on Belfast's Christmas lights in November 1995. Van Morrison entertained and I chatted with Sir Patrick afterwards, when we were entertained to a marvellous reception at Queen's University Belfast. The atmosphere was euphoric, for everyone had high hopes of lasting peace. Unfortunately these hopes were shattered within a matter of months by the bombing of Canary Wharf in London, again with the loss of life.

"Comedian Patrick Kielty switched on our Christmas lights in December 1995. Young people seemed to enjoy the music and colourful sideshows, and chestnuts roasting gave a seasonal feel to a chilly evening. Arthur Miskelly, who is a member of the Council staff, donned his livery and I rode through the town in his gleaming open coach drawn by a pair of jet-black horses. Everyone stopped to admire Arthur's dressage. This is undoubtedly the only way to travel!

"A week prior to Christmas, we recalled the seventh anniversary of the Lockerbie disaster which occurred on 21 December 1988. A Breakfast of Peace was held at the Palace Stables Heritage Centre and I have never forgotten one guest, Lord Tonypandy, former Speaker of the House of Commons. We had a long conversation and his genuine sincerity shines out."

Mrs Heather Black's mayoral year continued busily into 1996, and in April she had the pleasure of welcoming the EU Commissioner Pádraig Flynn to a reception at the Palace. The purpose of the visit was to meet with members of Armagh City and District Partnership Board. The Commissioner was accompanied by members of the Northern Ireland Partnership Board and EU officials.

"I must confess, one of the most exciting events of my mayoral year was in May 1996, when I was invited to join Downtown Radio's Linda Jane for a trip in the 'Eye in the Sky' helicopter, as part of her radio show being conducted that day from Market Street in the city centre. Downtown Radio was celebrating its 20th anniversary by hosting shows from 20 major towns throughout Northern Ireland, including Armagh. This was a truly invigorating experience, with panoramic views over the city. I know that some lucky local listeners of Downtown Radio were also given the opportunity to enjoy a trip in the helicopter.

"My year as Mayor was a wonderful, if sometimes exhausting experience. It was also a great honour, and indeed, if I was called upon to do so again, yes, I would be delighted to fill the position of Mayor of Armagh City and District once more."

Mayor Heather Black
with members of Armagh City and District Council

Hughie Trainor

Stalwart dedication to the music business makes Hughie Trainor, at 79, the oldest active bandleader in Ireland. There was never a time when music did not feature in his life and he can vividly recall one concert in May 1951, "when the programme cost sixpence. On that evening, St Joseph's Light Orchestra entertained an audience at Armagh City Hall. I was then first clarinettist", says Hughie Trainor. "My brother Jim played with the first violin section while the *crème de la crème* of local talent sang in the mixed voice choir."

Born into a musical family, his background seethes with all the musical vitality of the Glenn Miller story. His band, although stylised as 'The Boys from the County Armagh', could be said to have its origins in Lisnagarvey, Co. Antrim, birthplace of Hughie's equally musical father. "In the early Twenties my father came to Armagh, establishing a music shop and newsagent's business in English Street", comments Hughie. "We were a family of ten children, living in the flat overhead. Violins my father sold were suspended from the ceiling and sheet music stood in a pyramid on the counter. Top quality needles for a wind-up His Master's Voice gramophone cost one shilling a packet. For his stock of musical instruments, he'd visit Tughan-Crane of Belfast. Sheet music came from Keith Prowse of Charing Cross Road: 70 years on, I am conducting business with this firm."

In keeping with the rest of the family, Hughie began music lessons at six years of age. "Miss Marks of Vicar's Hill taught violin. I kept an appointment with her, two mornings each week at 8.30am going straight to school afterwards at St Malachy's, Chapel Lane. My father played both violin and piano. We didn't fool him by pretending we'd practice. He listened downstairs until it sounded right to his ear. At one stage we had three pianos, a couple of violins, drums and a banjo thumping above the shop. My mother would look up, hold her breath and wait for the grand slam. The vibration was enough to land the lot of us in the middle of English Street. My favourite instrument was always the saxophone and she offered every encouragement. Although she didn't play herself, my mother was an excellent vocalist.

"Once my father took me to Belfast on a buying trip. I was only a nipper at the time. Walking along Royal Avenue, we came face to face with Stan Laurel and Oliver Hardy, who were there on a promotional tour. Both solemnly shook hands with us. Then Oliver winked and patted me on the head. It was a great moment for a small boy."

Leaving Armagh Technical School, Hughie developed sporting skills of football and hurling, playing for local teams. He did not take music seriously until his father retired and responsibility for the shop became his lot. "By now I was proficient on saxophone and ballroom dancing become the most popular form of entertainment from the Forties right through to the Sixties. I played at Armagh City Hall with Joe McBride and his band from the time I was 16. Remember Isaac Newton?" Hughie challenges. "A falling apple hits him on the head and he put it down to gravity. The same apple", he grins engagingly, "metaphorically speaking, dropped on mine, one afternoon in the shop. Why not form my own band? Newton never managed that, now did he?"

Within a few years, Hughie had established the Melody Makers. "We promoted ourselves thought the press as the first showband in Ireland to take to the road. From small beginnings, a trickle of bookings became a flood. Christmas dances at Armagh City Hall were followed by engagements with football, rugby and cricket clubs. Eventually we ran our own dancing class on Tuesday and Saturday night at Armagh City Hall. Kids then were so well mannered. It was the Brylcreme era, romance often blossoming on the ballroom floor. Confident young chaps would glide past, hair slicked down, and local girls in their wide skirts and stiletto heels were always impressed."

Hughie's original showband comprised Jim Bratten on drums, Pat Conlon and Jim Devlin on trumpet, Jim Trainor and James Kane on violin. Leo Trainor played saxophone and clarinet, John Warmoll piano and accordion, Jack Caldwell was accordionist while Hughie played tenor saxophone. "The boys looked good in black tie and tuxedo. We eventually built a reputation in Britain and were welcomed by top ballrooms in Glasgow, Birmingham, London and Coventry. This justified our name change to the Globe Trotters."

The Hughie Trainor Orchestra in 1959.
(L to R): Hughie, Eric Killen, the late Jack Caldwell, Francie Grimley, the late Tommy Houhilan, Seán McArdle, the late Mickey Keenan

A connoisseur of jazz, Hughie is a fervent admirer of Duke Ellington who expertly played every instrument in his own band. He met Nat King Cole when appearing at the Belfast Hippodrome in 1952, and Paul Robeson at HMV Recording Studios in Middlesex. "Robeson's music was in-built. He rippled through *Lazybones* and *Ole Man River*, then did up his tie and walked off. Yet it's Al Jolson, who, in my book, remains unrivalled. This chap arrived in America, a Russian Jew. Aged 12, he walked into a 'greasy spoon' restaurant and sang a song for a cup of coffee. By the time he'd reached 30, he was the undisputed star of Broadway, the Bing Crosby or Frank Sinatra of his day. Jolson was greater than Elvis Presley or the Beatles ever were. Now that has to be talent.

"I had a fondness for Eric Coates who is best known for a piece of music, *By the Sleepy Lagoon*, which he wrote in 1930. We still hear it as the signature tune to Radio 4's *Desert Island Discs*. What inspires a composer to write a piece like this, I've often wondered—was it a package tour to the South Pacific or simply his imagination?"

Appearing with Paddy Cole, who starred as saxophonist in *Hear My Song*, a film tribute to Josef Locke, was a highlight of Hughie's career. He has also played a musical miscellany with Gay McIntyre, top musician in Ireland for over 30 years. "Gay played with the best of them, Acker Bilk, Kenny Ball and his Jazzmen and the Dick Morrissey Quintet. Engagements kept coming, our band now appearing at annual Festival events such as Mary From Dungloe, the Galway Races, Puck Fair in Kerry, and the Mullingar Opera Company Annual Ball."

Emmett, Hughie's eldest son, died tragically in 1988, at the age of 38. "Jean, my wife, and I cannot reconcile ourselves to his loss. Emmett was an expert player of guitar, banjo, trumpet, piano and keyboard. He taught music to hundreds of youngsters who remember him fondly. Our other son Declan plays piano, as do our daughters Deirdre and Fiona. Fiona hopes to achieve the professional standard of a concert pianist."

Hughie was the guest of President Mary Robinson in 1991. "On that occasion I was the only person present from the nine counties of Ulster. She chatted in depth about music and what it means to her."

Big-time bands may come and go but, it seems, Hughie Trainor's ensemble just goes on. When dancing made a fashionable recovery, he persuaded Donal Gorman, then proprietor of Drumsill Hotel, Armagh, to launch an evening of ballroom dancing. The enthusiastic response led to Hughie hosting the *Ballroom of Romance*, a regular Saturday evening programme of dancing in the Navan Room at Drumsill. "We've always been given a free hand with our repertoire and the Melody Makers oblige with the old favourites, *Blue Moon*, *Sweet Genevieve*, *Moonlight and Roses* or *Red Sails in the Sunset*. My own favourites include the best of Glenn Miller's melodies, *American Patrol*, *Chatanooga Choo-Choo*, *Little Brown Jug* and *String of Pearls*. Presently I'm writing arrangements with harmony so one of these evenings my band will whisk you back to the Glenn Miller era."

He considers himself an authority on Irish history and takes more than passing interest in current affairs. "Travelling to GAA matches each Sunday, I enjoy listening to John Bennett's radio programme in my car. I hold a season ticket for Croke Park and never miss a match."

Hughie Trainor knows how to deliver, probably better and certainly longer than anyone presently in Irish showbusiness. His message is simple and comforting: *The Clouds Will Soon Roll By*, *I Dreamt I Dwelt in Marble Halls*, *I Can't Stop Loving You...* But until the dancing public sample his new Glenn Miller arrangement, he laughingly proclaims, "You ain't seen nothin' yet..."

Joe and Kathleen Sherry

There has to be amazing diversity in what is asked of us in life. Kathleen and Joe Sherry's only son suffered a hidden aneurysm in July 1994. When Stephen was pronounced clinically dead 11 days later, a hospital surgeon asked if they would donate his organs. The memory is racked with pain. "We said yes", Joe confirms, "so someone else might live." Months later a letter came from an anonymous source, a mother expressing her gratitude. "My son", she wrote, "would not be with me now but for you and your son. Not one day goes by without thanking God and you for being so selfless..."

Laying aside personal grief, Patrick Joseph Sherry can trace his forebears to the early 16th century. "Legislation then dictated that the eldest male of every family in Armagh could claim a burial plot in St Patrick's Cathedral graveyard. I am an only son", he smiles broadly, "and that's where I might have ended my days had it not been for men like Luther and Calvin. One morning I noticed a priest studying my name over the shop door. He came inside, began to chat and asked if I knew others with the same surname. I am last of my line but in my athletic days I competed against two brothers, Jack and Mickey Sherry, in Belfast. Jack went to Rhodesia but I had no idea what became of Mickey. 'I'm Mickey', informed the priest with a smile. He then produced some marvellous history. Centuries ago, a ship from Spain carrying a family named Jerez (Sherry) was wrecked off the Donegal coast. Survivors remained, gradually making their way to the south-east of Ireland, establishing the line. My predecessors lived in Lower English Street, plumbers by trade. One brother diverted to buying and selling cattle, opening his own butchery just across the road. In the mid-Twenties to early Thirties my father, also named Joe, was a major shipper of beef cattle to Glasgow markets. I was often sent as a child to tell Christy Dalton, our yardman, that a special train from Longford would stop at Armagh station to load these cattle. Our land ran from the old Bairnswear factory to Grange Church, providing employment for uncles George, Peter and Tom. Aunts Agnes, Lucy, Edie and Mary completed the family."

Of his own family, Joe followed seven sisters—May, Dolly, Lucy, Mildred, Belle, Eveline and Ita. "My father, who always got his priorities right, said I was born on Moy Fair Day, first of December 1927", he laughs. Joe's mother Elizabeth was an Englishwoman who had been nursing in Armagh City Hospital. "Grandfather Sherry, a businessman in every sense, expected my father, also named Joe, to help as drover each Fair Day. Besotted with Elizabeth, my father hid in the hayloft to avoid this. He knew the buying and selling would drag on and he'd never make it home in time to see Elizabeth that evening. She became private nurse to Mrs Lennon of Cathedral Road, leaving to be married from Senator Lennon's home. Her family in Winteringham, Lincolnshire, followed the Methodist faith. It seems her father, without any warning, announced he was converting to Catholicism so why not the whole family? Winteringham was without a local church, so until recently neighbours joined in Sunday Mass, said at my grandparent's home. When people comment on my love for singing, I say it must be the Methodist in me!"

Always dress-conscious, Joe attributes this to his father's influence. "His shoes were crafted at McAfee's in Royal Avenue, Belfast, while immaculately tailored suits were made by Ruben Payne and Ireland. My mother was a great homemaker, neat to a fault. A range of occupations beckoned and May, my sister, opened a hairdressing salon, Dolly and Mildred became nurses. Lucy, Eveline and Ita were civil servants while Belle worked at the Cake Shop which was owned by McNally's of Richhill. Belle was required to sign an undertaking that she'd never open in competition." It is of note that Belle Sherry married outstanding Armagh actor and Emmy award winner, Patrick Magee. Star of stage and screen Peter Bowles was among those who supported a move to have Armagh's new theatre named in memory of Patrick Magee.

A childhood spent at St Malachy's Terrace, Moy Road, meant Joe became pals with Jack Dougan and the Cush and McAvinchey boys. "Always a good runner, whenever we played 'Hares and Hounds' I was chosen as a Hare! We attended St Patrick's Primary School at Banbrook. For secondary education, boys moved upstairs, girls were sent to the Convent of the Sacred Heart. I do not consider myself academic but loved animals and especially sick animals, sufficiently to want to become a vet. It never happened for I joined my father's staff at his butcher's shop in English Street. Open-fronted, beneath a red-striped awning, a marble table piled high with meat was placed each morning. After this shop closed I moved to the branch run by my brother-in-law in Scotch Street." The 1930s brought the Depression, a nightmare time for the beef trade equal to today's catastrophic outbreak of BSE. "I remember my father stranded in Glasgow with 2,000 head of cattle that no-one wanted to buy. Somehow we survived, people do", he muses philosophically.

Schoolboy 'Hares and Hounds' introduced Joe to Armagh Harriers and considerable claim to fame. Running for Ulster, he won the Ulster Championship (400 metres) in 1953, followed by a gold medal for the 440 yards in Co. Monaghan. "At this time my future was undecided. I thought about leaving home, going to England. May, who all her life had a soft spot for her little brother, obtained premises in English Street and persuaded me to stay, and open a greengrocery business right below her hairdressing shop. Shelves bursting with fruit and vegetables including a colourful street display, the total cost £40. I shudder at the amount it would take now. Each Saturday we spit-roasted chickens, selling easily 150 during the day. Annual rates that first year, paid to collector Tom Frazer, were £90. Within a short time I had a staff of four including Stan Ellingham who shared my interest in greyhound racing. We did have modest success by travelling to Dublin, Navan and Belfast."

With Armagh Theatre Group Joe took a major role in *Many Young Men of Twenty.* Rehearsals were held at the old Police Recreation Room in Jenny's Row, performances staged at the City Hall. "Production manager Seamus Mallon was a stickler for detail. When it came to Brendan Behan's play *The Hostage*, where a British soldier is captured by the IRA, shots had to be fired. Seamus wouldn't settle for anything less than the real thing so during rehearsal, Maurice Steenson was sent up to the rafters to discharge cartridges from an old blunderbuss. Local councillors holding a meeting below, unaware of what was happening, ran terrified into the street. Seamus established another firm rule, no-one must indulge in alcohol before a performance. Armagh then had abundant talent and we next launched into *Joan of Arc,* Mary Lamb playing the part of Joan. A band of less-confident thespians waived Seamus' rule, fortifying their courage with a pint or two at the Beresford Arms. Joan almost had a lucky escape from burning at the stake, as none of us were sober enough to find the matches! Our enthusiasm was something else! When St Joseph's Choral Society was formed, I remember counting 120 at Sunday rehearsal in the Hibernian Hall, Castle Street, Father Coyle undertaking stage management. You wouldn't get 20 today! Ringing the changes for a time, we hired principal singers. The Mikado was entirely our own production however, and Tony Crilly, a magnificent tenor voice, took lead roles in Gilbert and Sullivan's *Pirates of Penzance* and *The Gondoliers*.

"The shop was a success and I had established a way of life, each weekend attending football matches with Joe McManus from the *Observer.* It was now the late Sixties. Going to work, I remember turning the corner one morning, meeting with total darkness. Ian Paisley and a mob had taken over the town intent on wrecking a civil rights march where every denomination and all professions were taking part. It was to be a peaceful protest, no vested interest except social justice for all, yet scores of farmers with machinery blocked the marchers' path. If you can imagine a toboggan hurtling down an icy run? Violence escalated as swiftly, and we are still paying the cost of a community that never healed. Accusations were rife, businessmen blamed for violent acts, many of which I know to be untrue. Evil influence has turned our world upside down."

A versatile musician, Joe is a founder member of St Malachy's Male Voice Choir. "I recall Fathers Murray and Kerr visiting myself and Jim Kirk, asking if we would recruit members. Seán Boylan was appointed organist. Male voices lead ten o'clock Mass with the ladies' choir at 11.30. We amalgamate for special events and some members sing with Armagh City Choir. Singing is in my veins, for Mervyn White, a good friend, easily persuaded me to join Portadown Male Voice Choir. Last year I held the office of choir chairman and can honestly say we enjoy harmony in its widest sense. I have sung at churches of almost every denomination, felt a competitive thrill at Cork International Festival and we expect to tour Canada during the summer. When our son died you will never know the comfort it brought Kathleen and myself that every member came to pay his respects. Stephen's funeral Mass was held at St Patrick's Cathedral and I specially requested the hymn *Be Still My Soul.*

Joe and Kathleen Sherry
at their home in Armagh, 1999

"John Betjeman produced a small book of poems in 1954. One, *A Child Ill*, spoke my thoughts in this writer's neat style:

Oh little body, do not die.
You hold the soul that talks to me
Although our conversation be
As wordless as the windy sky.

"All I could picture was our son taking his first steps. In another hospital room a family in anguish awaited our decision. How could we refuse? Just before Christmas 1994, Eleanor Donaghy, transplant co-ordinator with Belfast City Hospital, wrote to say she had a letter from the anonymous mother of a man who received our Stephen's heart. This young man maintained a good recovery and his mother writes each Christmas. That he lives", Joe adds quietly, "sustains my day. I hold my breath when I hear news of someone we will never know who carries part of Stephen."

Joe and Kathleen Sherry permit sight of a deeply private letter: "Fighting cancer took a heavy toll on my son's heart. He was waiting in hospital just after his 16th birthday, when on 19 July we heard there was a heart that might be good for my son. I know the grief you must have been feeling, your son fit and well one minute, the next deciding as to whether you should give away his organs. I am grateful for the decision you made. Not one day passes without thanking God that I have him. He also appreciates what you had to go through. Thank you for being so selfless. I am forever grateful. A Loving Mother."

Joe and Kathleen will always mourn the loss of their 21-year-old son. Daughter Caitriona, now their precious only child, a graphic designer, still sets a fourth place at the dinner table on Christmas Day for her dearly-loved brother.

We are grateful for this shared experience. There is undoubtedly a great diversity in what is asked of each of us in life.

Paddy McGarvey

The Irish are a fair-minded race; they never speak well of one another... may be an acerbic truth, but it entirely excludes the kindly nature of Paddy McGarvey.

"I arrived at Fleet Street in 1952 when the job had the aura of show business. Today the profession is at its nadir and the public has a low opinion of it." Raising his magnificent eyebrows, Paddy continues. "People used to say 'What an exciting life you must lead' and it was, but television put paid to all that. Performers with little or no talent are mobbed in the street while a good correspondent goes quietly unnoticed."

While writing for the *Sunday Dispatch*, sister newspaper to the *Daily Mail*, Armagh-born Paddy had his own show business column and legitimate access to the rich and famous. His own life has been studded with coincidences which he qualifies by stating, "If you travel as widely as I have and meet as many people, the planet suddenly becomes quite a small place. At the *Sunday Dispatch* I shared an office with columnist Godfrey Wynn. Women readers adored this chap, pouring out their troubles in thousands of letters he'd receive daily. Godfrey was rich beyond my dreams, but comically sad, coming to the office each day in a Rolls Royce driven by Jimmy, his chaffeur and companion. Godfrey would greet me some mornings with a deep sigh: 'Oh Paddy wherever did you get those divine eyebrows?' And I would snap in return, 'I got them in Northern Ireland Godfrey and none of your nonsense now, d'ye hear!' I was still raw, uncouth and decidedly heterosexual as would later become obvious when I met my English wife, Pamela, and become father of six children, plus 'one she made earlier' in a previous marriage."

A spotted bow tie, hankie spilling from his pocket, Panama at a rakish angle are the distinguishing marks of the now seldom-spotted McGarvey. "You make me sound like Ustinov in *Death on the Nile*", he accuses "but go on then, what do you want to know? Maybe I should start with Elizabeth Taylor. She was in bed in her luxury suite at the Dorchester when I called. I was standing there, notebook at the ready, when Mike Todd, her husband *du jour* grabbed me by the nape of my jacket. He'd shown me into her room because Elizabeth wanted to apologise for being unwell, thus cancelling my promised interview. We did have a little chat", Paddy sighs. "I have never forgotten those great violet eyes against a satin pillow. Todd however decided she'd said enough and in a fashion, encouraged me to leave."

To start at the beginning, Paddy was born at Railway Street, Armagh and educated at Christian Brothers' School, Greenpark. "My hand-writing was so bad that when I was 12 Louis Doyle, our Latin master, made me copy script from the infant classes. I was humiliated before tittering classmates but it didn't work. I do, and always will, write badly." Paddy was headhunted as a legal clerk by Vincent Mulholland, whose practice was then in English Street beside the City Hall. "Vincent", Paddy recalls, "was a gentle soul who died in middle age. Far too gentle to be a trial lawyer, unlike my father's cousin, Gerry Lennon, whom I admired all my life and longed to emulate. This was financially impossible as, at that time, a barrister could not hope to earn a sou until he was at least 35."

Vincent Mulholland taught Paddy to write land indentures, probate grants and wills. "Remember I said my handwriting was illegible? These were typed", interjects Paddy. What he recalls sadly was the spectacle of farmers squabbling over the line of a ditch or fence. "Family savings were squandered on such issues. Indirectly, Vincent gave me a head start in journalism because law writing was boring. If I prospered early it was because I had spent two years with a boss who had time to talk to me."

From newspapers in Cork and Drogheda, Paddy advanced to working at the Four Courts for the *Dublin Evening Mail*. He now found himself sitting next to famous barristers, John Costello, an impulsive Taoiseach-to-be who would take Ireland out of the Commonwealth. "Costello was an untidy man, frequently representing publicans and invariably he carried a huge map of his client's premises. Often I helped sort these into order, over a shared bench-table. Then there was suave and elegant Seán MacBride, who became Costello's 'Fo'wyn' Secretary. MacBride had a French accent, rarely practised at the bar and could always be found hovering around

Costello. Cecil Lavery from Armagh became head of the Supreme Court. Here I had a link with home. My father worked as head clerk for Cecil's father in a huge practice that moved from the Courthouse to the City Hall, finally resting in Russell Street when acquired by Vincent Toner."

During long legal vacations, a young and raw McGarvey met and worked with one towering Irish giant. Paddy's casual employment with the Dublin *Evening Mail* ended each law term. Few were employed due to newsprint rationing and he considered himself fortunate when taken on for part-time work with the Catholic Church's standard bearer, labelled as you might expect, *The Standard*.

"Editor Peadar O'Curry also came from Armagh and remembered a kindness extended by my father", Paddy continues. "I joined the newspaper as temporary news reporter. The man on the other side of my desk was a film critic called Pat. Film reviewing was the most difficult job on a newspaper serving the Counter-Reformation Catholic Church. Pat's liberalism landed him in constant trouble with the editor and sometimes we were threatened with intervention by that fierce fundamentalist, Archbishop Charles McQuaid. Pat, my colleague was about 40, old to a lad like me, just turned 20. He was also unkempt, crabby when intoxicated and sometimes he tied his overcoat with twine. Frequently, in a deep-voiced Co. Monaghan accent he would regale me with: 'Oh mighty man from Armagh, lend us half a dollar till Thursday and I'll get you a plenary indulgence for your sins when next our beloved Archbishop calls'. A dramatic flourish accompanied this plea but I always got my money back on Thursday, religiously you might say! Of course the Archbishop never called.

"We became great friends, had lots of laughs and six months later when I'd left Ireland, was dumbfounded to read that my office companion was the poet Patrick Kavanagh, his writing extolled in much the same context as Yeats. Today he is recognised as such. Pat had published his first collection, *The Green Fool*, in 1938. His fame faded due to wartime paper shortages but it was I who was green", Paddy ruefully admits. "When I first saw the wonderful, life-sized statue of Kavanagh at Portobello on the Grand Canal, I sat down beside him and wept. Partly for myself, I think. I felt both foolish and ashamed that I had shared his desk yet did not recognise the man's literary depths."

Before leaving for England, Paddy spent a last Saturday night in Armagh with a few pals. "I remember flaunting a new watch I'd bought for £2 from the 'Pillar Jeweller' in Dublin. Billy Weir, a gangly youth from Richhill affectionately known as 'Ritchie', and myself were all eating fish and chips from paper cones, watching the girls go by, when Billy Weir asked 'Paddy, what time is it?' A grand gesture accompanied a look at my newly acquired watch and simultaneously tipped all my chips onto the pavement. The boys roared with laughter, practically falling through the café window. A week later I found myself struggling to keep my job. The national press agency, knowing I had courtroom experience, sent me into the divorce court at Shrewsbury on my first morning. This was new ground as divorce didn't exist in the Republic of Ireland.

"Here I was, walking aimlessly through Shrewsbury Flower Show, the biggest in Britain. Again I was at a loss for Ireland had no garden culture to speak of and, after a fruitless search of the huge marquees, could not find a story of interest. I made a decision to go back to the office, apologise to my editor and resign. Too green for England, I would return to Dublin.

"As I was looking at my watch a big voice boomed over my shoulder: 'I see you still got yon watch ye boy ye!' I turned and there was Ritchie pushing a trolley full of roses. I gaped. What was he doing here? Ritchie was indignant. Drawing himself up (and he was already six feet three), he declared, 'Sure I work for Sam McCready now'. It was like finding an oil well. Sam McCready was the world's top rose-grower from Co. Armagh. Ritchie had to work hard because 'them roses wuz growin' in Portie-Down till after three this mornin' when we cut them and tuk them to Nutts Corner and flew them here in an RAF Anson'. This was Britain in the Forties, drab, run down, weary from rationing and shortages. The following morning my story shone out in twenty British newspapers under headlines bright in this aura of gloom, 'AN AIRLIFT OF ROSES FOR BRITAIN'. And I never looked back, thanks to a £2 watch and a boy from County Armagh."

By the age of 26, Paddy McGarvey was working on the *Daily Mirror*, the world's largest-circulation newspaper. Disappointingly his talents were diverted to the *Junior Mirror*, a separate weekly for children. Directors thought younger journalists ideal for this purpose, a serious error.

Paddy McGarvey
in Fleet Street days

"They should have used 'old codgers' such as I am now", laughs Paddy. "It was a Fleet Street fad for a year, the *Express* and others following our example." He describes the thrill when asked to spend a day at the Surrey home of Captain W.E. Johns, creator of *Biggles*. "Biggles was an all-conquering air ace and every schoolboy's hero between the wars, solving problems with his twin-gun Sopwith Camel. It was another big moment in my life when Marjorie Proops, First Lady of Fleet Street and doyen of agony aunts in Britain, asked me to be her 'leg-man' and trouble-shooter on hard case stories pouring into her office from readers. In a sense", he pauses, "this established a pattern for the rest of my career."

Three times Paddy McGarvey returned to Northern Ireland. "I felt I had something to contribute", he reasonably points out. "Standing as Labour candidate in the 1964 General Election I took a tilt at traditional voting. To no avail, like a candle in the wind my voice was promptly extinguished. Twice during the dark Seventies I came in voluntary assistance to the old Labour Party and the trade unions in job creation. *The Mirror* was in fierce problem-solving competition with other newspapers and had full-time solicitors on their payroll. I found myself back at my old job, liaising with six lawyers in Cambridge and working full time on readers' problems. You could call it a service but this was really free legal aid before there was free legal aid!"

Paddy's reputation at Fleet Street had grown and Lord Hartwell, owner of the *Sunday Telegraph*, requested he undertake a particular assignment, studying and comparing the living conditions of the Germans with those of the British. Instead of reporting to the Bonn office and living nearby, Paddy was ordered to submerge himself in local life. "I moved to Dettmold, a small town near Hanover, well away from tourist routes and traps. Dettmold might equate with Keady in relation to Armagh. The local factory where I found work made electrical connectors for industrial plant."

Paddy reported to British readers that an average German manufacturing director, his wife and family, live in a house inside the factory gates, whereas a British factory would have a gate lodge or watchman's hut. His British counterpart chose a much more sylvan setting. And there were subtle social differences. A German company director, seeing workers standing by the bus stop would stop and offer a lift in his executive limousine. Secretaries came to work at 7.15am. These reports were front-page headlines in Britain. Paddy's articles from the German industrial front explained the real ingredients of the *Wirtschaftswunder*—the economic miracle—while Britain languished in 'the English Sickness'.

Back in England, Paddy undertook a three-part series based on a lengthy study of the working of Heathrow Airport, 'Jungle Under the Jets'. "All was clockwork on the surface, anarchy underneath", he recalls. "It led to lunch in the boardroom of Rolls Royce a week before the company collapsed and an invitation to Henley School of Management as guest lecturer.

"A white monkey on my shoulder prompted me, every now and then, to return home. It was 1994 when I established the Irish Parliament Trust, a research charity examining new constitutional ideas for Britain and Ireland from a neutral standpoint." Paddy's work within the Trust came to the attention of the British-Irish Parliamentary Body. "My first thought was that peace is a male-only occupation, no women were involved at any level and I said so, out loud." Before long a group of women in Belfast founded a party which they named the Women's Coalition. A year later, Tony Blair appointed a woman Secretary of State, but with a wry smile Paddy observes, "she has not yet thanked me!"

His Trust made proposals for peace to the Mitchell Commission and the Decommissioning Commission, one of which is visible at the time of this interview—the 'amnesty without prosecution' clause. Last year and impressively, the Trust produced *(R)Evolution*, a magazine for 1,100 senior schools in Ireland. Supported by the European Union Peace and Reconciliation Fund and Co-operation Ireland, the magazine concentrated on thousands of Scots-Irish Presbyterians who fled from British religious repression in the 18th century. To all practical purposes these people became the real leaders of the American Revolution and founders of America.

"I hoped that focusing on this forgotten population might germinate a new approach to the teaching of Irish history in our schools. For tactical reasons, after five years of hard work, the Trust returned to England, based in Cambridge, where I shall shortly be living. It has more to offer and what it offers promises to be exciting."

Paddy McGarvey spent time and energy in an attempt to have Armagh's new theatre and Arts Centre named after local actor, Patrick (Paudge) Magee. Paul Scofield, who knew Patrick Magee well, supported this venture, writing in firm agreement with such an idea.

Paddy McGarvey, with his comical by-line, has given voice to many personalities. One was a young, black Welsh girl, who sang last in a variety show. Her name was Shirley Bassey. "This girl has talent", wrote Paddy. He accompanied Ruby Murray and her mother, both dressed in Sunday best, to Bernard Delfont's Piccadilly office where Ruby signed her first singing contract. Paddy has renown amongst journalist colleagues, who whilst hating to admit it, recognise talent when they see it. Honesty in our stagnant pond is unusual and it is rare to find one so entertainingly frank.

As Paddy McGarvey takes leave of Armagh an uneasy feeling lingers, that one day we may regret his going. As with Kavanagh there is a certain shame in having 'shared the desk' of a man without recognising his worth.

Audrey Pharoah

"Invisible strings tug and I have to come back", Audrey Pharoah admits in her precise South African accent. Gazing up at the top floor of Morrow House, Market Street, Armagh, she reverts to childhood and 1934. "I see myself looking from one of the windows of our flat above the old Co-operative. I'm seven years old and my family are about to leave for Africa in pursuit of a new life."

Audrey Pharoah was the eldest daughter of Albert Rea and Margaret Frazer of Scotch Street, Armagh. Events in her life, long submerged, gradually resurface. "My father was a cabinet maker. He'd been one of a large family, born at Railway Street. As a child he'd joined the Boys' Brigade, advancing to Armagh Old Boys Silver Band. I have memories of him studying hard, his head bent over a stack of books. Qualifying in Theology eventually led to his becoming ordained. As a family, with my sisters, Edith and Sheelagh, we attended the Mall Presbyterian Church in Armagh, and years later, on visits back home, Dad took services there. An Armagh businessman, H.M. Barbour, had earlier established a thriving store in Rhodesia, now Zimbabwe. My father was easily persuaded, and, deciding to uproot, established a new life in that country."

Audrey's first experience of South Africa was the Mazoe Valley near Glendale. "The climate and exotic fruits were something extraordinary. Eventually we came to think of the Valley as our home but Irish ties remained strong. My father's sister was Edith Maginnis of Railway Street, a woman who was both dignified and travelled. She'd wait anxiously for news of our progress abroad. Edith's letters to us were tucked safely in a drawer, my mother's panacea for homesickness. We treated the native population with respect and they us, but we mainly encountered whites in Glendale."

Five years later, Audrey's family returned to Armagh on holiday. "We stayed with Aunt Edith at Railway Street. It was 1939 and an anxious time. People queued for newspapers in the fervent hope that rumours of war were exaggerated. 'It'll be over by Christmas,' everyone said. We three girls were sent to the Armstrong Primary School for the duration of this trip. Mother wisely decided we'd do better to continue our education than run wild. I was 12 and my major concern was finding answers to the tricky maths set by Miss Whisker! My father returned to South Africa on 3 September 1939, the day war was declared. We were to follow later. As soon as dread became reality, all communications ceased. We would neither receive news of my father, nor he of us."

Audrey suddenly breaks off, "you could always count on mother who was such a resourceful woman. Borrowing the money for our fares, she packed our bags and before we knew, the lot of us arrived in Cape Town. Church Office cabled my father. I'll never forget the look on his face when we met up, travel-stained and weary, but alive and together."

The family transferred first to a congregation at Umtali Presbyterian Church, finally settling at St John's Church, Tuffontein, Johannesburg, in the Transvaal. "A poor area", Audrey states, "with a predominately white congregation. We had our own struggle, living on a small stipend. It helped that my mother was an expert seamstress and she even made my father's shirts." Albert Rea earned a reputation as a fine churchman and was eventually appointed Moderator of the General Assembly of the Presbyterian Church of South Africa and Rhodesia. This imposed much travelling and many diplomatic engagements.

"Through my father", Audrey recalls, "we made the acquaintance of Prime Minister Ian Smith and ever since, both families have remained friends. Dad died before black Africans, after 14 years of determined political unrest, gained independence in 1980."

Audrey married in 1948. "Arthur and I both worked for the Anglo-American Corporation who controlled the Kimberley diamond mines, Oppenheimer's and De Beers. Our first private venture, a citrus farm, was unsuccessful, so jointly, we undertook the running of an hotel in Duiwelskloof. Our three daughters were born there and still live in South Africa. My mother continued to visit Armagh until the time of her death, so ties with that branch of the family remained strong. After Arthur's death in 1980, I was invited to become a partner in the ownership of the hotel."

Audrey met her present husband, Stan, through his son Noel, who was her general practitioner. "Stan's wife had

Audrey and Stan Pharoah,
September 1994

died some time earlier. Finding out how much we had in common, our friendship developed and we married in 1991." They are obviously happy, each allowing the other space, but sharing the major part of each day.

"Audrey swims and plays tennis three times a week", says Stan, taking up the narrative. "I take life at a more leisurely pace." Brigadier Stanley Pharoah, South African Air Force, now retired, is the most charming of men. "May I begin by paying tribute to our hosts, George and Edna Doupe of Hillside Farm, Caledon, for a quality of hospitality which could not possibly exist anywhere else", Stan declares. "Edna is Audrey's cousin. Meeting the clan was quite an undertaking, but these are caring people. We've been completely at peace, surrounded by such beauty as this rural setting affords. Margaret Mallon, another cousin of Audrey's and her husband, Albert, showed us historical features of Armagh City. Margaret was a former secretary to the Chief Executive of Armagh District Council. We were impressed by the obvious efforts to preserve what is ancient and beautiful. Ireland is more modern than I thought. Perhaps I expected those 14th and 15th century cobbles, gables and mullioned windows which seem to defy time and which I recall from England during wartime service."

Stan's background could stretch to a credible blockbuster film. His grandfather was an Indian Army Colonel, serving in the day of the Raj, cashiered for non-payment of debts. His father, originally from Wales, joined the Dublin Fusiliers, going off to fight in the Boer War. "I was born in 1914 in the Transvaal", Stan continues, "a place named Christiana. As children we swam in a public bathing place on the Knysna Lagoon. One morning, an elderly man with a wispy beard joined us. He simply referred to himself as 'GB'. For six weeks he came each day and we found him highly entertaining. His wife, it seemed, was hospitalised nearby following an accident. Only later, much later, did I learn this was George Bernard Shaw, Irish dramatist, critic and social thinker."

As a young man, Stan worked for the Forestry Department, then in the gold mines. "I toiled all hours, investing my money in private flying lessons. When war broke out, I had a permanent appointment as Second Lieutenant in the South African Air Force Reserve. Cicily, my first wife, and I had been married a short time when a posting came as a bomber pilot, to the Middle East." In July 1942, then a Major, the equivalent of Squadron Leader in this country, Stan was shot down by an ME-109 fighter in the Western Desert, sustaining a shattered right hand. "I limped back behind the El Alamein line on half a wing and any number of fervent prayers."

A return to health, followed by tedious convalescence, took longer than he envisaged. With aviation no longer possible, Stan found his way to the Empire Central Flying School at Hullavington in Wiltshire. As one of a team, he researched fatalities of all-weather wartime flying. "Pilots survived the hazards of raids over Germany. Returning exhausted to base, they all too often crash landed. As many died in such a tragic manner as at the hands of the Messerschmitts." Stan's team dramatically reduced fatalities, saving the lives of vital young airmen. Colleagues included future round-the-world yachtsman Francis Chichester.

"It wasn't quite the end of that chapter", Stan continues, "for I taught my elder son Hugh to fly and he is presently a senior Captain with Air Singapore, flying mainly the Boeing 747. This is my first visit to Ireland and I can see why Audrey finds it impossible to stay away. Tonight we are having dinner with Audrey's relatives, Beverley and her husband Phil. Rarely have I experienced such kindness as here."

Miniature trains are his favourite pastime. Stan designs and builds his own locomotives, extending the range when the layout becomes familiar. "I love the rhythm of nature. Voltaire said 'Go and cultivate your garden' and I know exactly what he meant. A garden is a very spiritual possession." Stan held the position of Director of Training when he retired from the South African Air Force in 1974, but briefly returned for another spell at Strategic Planning HQ. Finally quitting at the age of 65 he had an aggregate of 40 years' service. Now 80 years of age, Brigadier Stan Pharoah is reasonably active, an intelligent and charming man. Audrey Pharoah has two, vastly differing, perspectives. "One is of a herd of elephant, pacing along as if keeping an appointment at the end of the world. The other creeps up unaware. Reed by dark water, the sound of a harp as 'the swan in the evening moves over the lea'."

'I am seven years and about to leave for Africa in pursuit of a new life...' her vivid narrative began. As one who constantly kept in touch, her story is of worth. Today she knows she will never completely come out of Africa.

Brigadier Stan Pharoah died on 16 June 1996.

Armagh Voices

a celebration of a century

1930 ~ 1940

The afternoon of human life must also have significance of its own

Carl Gustav Jung

Teresa O'Brien

A Countrywoman's Song

Derry and Antrim and Down
Fermanagh, Armagh and Tyrone,
Six counties' women all working together
And everyone proud of her own.

A familiar verse is sung at the end of each meeting of the Women's Institute. The first Women's Institute in the world was formed in Ontario, Canada, in February 1897. It is an organisation open to all women, irrespective of political or religious views, and includes women of all interests. It was Miss Dorothea Macausland who pioneered the movement in Northern Ireland and the first Institute in this country was formed in Garvagh, Co. Londonderry, during 1932. The Women's Institute is strictly non-political, non-sectarian and after six decades, retains the same sound base on which the organisation began.

War years slowed growth of this movement but hardships and privations also served to consolidate and strengthen those Institutes already in existence. The wartime fruit preservation scheme introduced by the Ministry of Food met with enthusiasm, and NI Institutes hold the record of 1,200 pounds of jam made on a single day. Here was an example of superb housekeeping, for every pound of sugar and fruit had to be accounted for. The Federation of Institutes met first on 24 April 1942, Her Grace the Duchess of Abercorn presiding. There are 22 area committees within the Northern Ireland Federation.

A talented and dedicated member, Teresa O'Brien is currently chairperson of Gosford Area which includes most of Armagh County, Cladymiltown, Collone, Drumsallen, Glenanne, Killylea, Milford, Mountnorris, Richhill, Saltersgrange and Wastelands. Teresa tirelessly promotes the organisation at every level.

The Institute motto sounds difficult to live up to: 'To unite in promoting any work which makes for the betterment of our homes and the development and improvement of conditions of rural life, by providing a centre for educational activities and social intercourse'. However Teresa O'Brien ably matches all these requirements. She herself stitched 'Gosford', one square of 22 in the Federation tapestry that commemorated the Diamond Jubilee of the WI in Northern Ireland. Teresa comments, "Gosford Castle itself was inspiration for our square and its tower and turrets were designed by Maisie McClung of Maytown WI."

A farmer's wife and mother of four, Teresa uses her expertise in crafts for the overall good of this organisation. She also spends much of her time in the classroom, assisting children who have moderate learning difficulties. Drawing inspiration from her home and family, Teresa holds impressive awards for exquisite handiwork.

"I particularly love the Irish flora and fauna design", she comments, holding up an example of rose and shamrock on linked, picot lace. For this she was awarded top prize at Belfast Flower Show plus the Fine Crochet prize at Harmony Hill Arts Centre, Lisburn. Delicate as thistledown is a veil Teresa worked in Carrickmacross lace. During 1989, she won the Hilda Stewart Trophy for lacemaking, presented by Lady Anthony Hamilton who is Federation President. The coveted silver spinning-wheel brooch, awarded for all-round proficiency by the Women's Institute, is easily one of Teresa's favourite possessions. On sale in many craft shops you may come across Teresa's individually crafted brooches, a lace flower or butterfly against a black background: an ideal gift for someone special.

Transporting us back to her own childhood, Teresa provides some background. "I am one of seven children who were brought up on the outskirts of Armagh city. Ours was a sporting family for quite a few generations. Jackie Vernon, my uncle, played for Belfast Celtic and captained West Bromwich Albion for six years. As a young woman I played hockey for Armagh Ladies' team and was a member of Armagh Badminton Club. If the new generation of O'Brien's is competitive, I suppose it's hereditary. My father set our standards. There wasn't a local swimming pool, so taking us individually on the bar of this bike to the Callan river, he taught us to swim. As a young woman, I served as secretary of Armagh Swimming Club from 1981 for nine years. What a debt we owe to Eileen Steenson and Brother Colm Carlin who promoted, trained and coached all interested, local youngsters, including mine. Inheriting the Vernon will to succeed", smiles Teresa, "and always a swimmer, Emma won the back crawl at the All-Ireland Schools Gala in 1984. By this date she had achieved 53 swimming awards, 26 dancing trophies and five athletic honours. With the guidance of Esther Graham, Emma took the Judy Lamb Perpetual Cup in Speech and Drama at Portadown Festival. Today she is an executive with the Association for Standards and Practices in Electronic Trade, based and living in London."

Teresa's children have always brought pleasure to her life, whether ferrying them to training sessions or lending support in their individual interests. "Our only son, Neil, swam competitively at Ulster level but cycling is his preference. After winning the Tour of Ulster, in 1991, he utilised his expertise by reporting the Nissan Classic on Irish Radio News for the past two years. Neil is presently a senior executive in Super Schools Ireland, a not-for-profit organisation that promotes health, fitness and participation in sport around the country."

Third in the family, Laura O'Brien, was a former head girl at St Catherine's College where her talents in public speaking were greatly encouraged. Joining the local drama group Metamorphosis, Laura was chosen in 1994 as Youth Leader of the Year by Armagh Rotary Club. Last November she graduated from University College Dublin and now works there.

Carla, the youngest, excels at Irish dancing. She first qualified for the World Irish Dancing Championships held in Mullingar in 1993 and currently holds fifth place in the World Under-16 Championships. News from America confirms that she has taken second place in American-Irish National Dancing Championships in Chicago. While in the USA, Carla will assist dance teacher Mona Lennon (née Ruddy) at workshops in Boston, New Jersey and New York. This will keep her occupied as she awaits GCSE examinations results.

Consistently making headlines for her own skills, Teresa's talents include the delicate craft of Carrickmacross lacemaking. From the cosy kitchen through to an elegant drawing room, embroidery and needlepoint add charming touches throughout this comfortable home. "It had long been my ambition to produce delicate hand-made Carrickmacross lace", Teresa says. "Discovering that Florence Nicholson was teaching the craft at St Catherine's College, I joined her class. Carrickmacross is appliqué lace, deriving its name from the town in Co. Monaghan. Mrs Gray Porter, wife of a local rector, saw examples of very fine lace when in Italy on holiday in 1820. She bought some and unpicking the work, discovered how it was made. Mrs Porter trained local girls in the skill for the area had little employment. When the Sisters of St Louis came to Carrickmacross they kept the craft alive. When I acquired the knack, Florence Nicholson, Josie Kirk and myself founded Laceappeal, our own cottage industry. We assembled a kit with simple instructions for beginners. Now anyone may conquer this absorbing art. I enjoy creating what is pleasing to the eye", she adds modestly. "Of course it takes time and patience. In my first job, a colleague could effortlessly crochet a tablemat during her lunch-break. Asking her to teach me, I was told 'Teach yourself, it's easy!' All weekend I wrestled with hook and cotton, until finally mastering the technique. By now I'd met Denis, and swapping town for country, was about to get married. Friends suggested I should make my own wedding dress. That would have been ultra-ambitious but I did design and crochet the bodice." The garment she holds up is patterned Irish rose dotted with pearls. Twenty-nine years later it's still fashionable and fits perfectly.

When Emma was born, Denis bought local and national newspapers of the day. "I saved these until she was 21; tied them with a red ribbon and gave them to her. It's an idea worth passing on." Teresa crocheted Emma's lace christening gown, little realising how important the garment would become. "Since then, 21 babies of relatives and friends have worn it. I embroidered the name and date of each around the hem. This, I expect, will become an heirloom for subsequent generations."

Special Education plays a vital role in Teresa's life and since 1995, she has been classroom assistant at City of Armagh High School.

"I must give you some background", Teresa explains. "Armagh County Secondary School opened in 1965, sharing a campus with Armagh Technical College. Hugh McIlwaine was principal of both schools. W.J. Craig became principal in 1985, presiding over the school's relocation at Alexander Road. When Queen Elizabeth awarded Armagh its City Charter in March 1995, she officially opened the new school building under the name of City of Armagh High School. Amongst the most modern in the Province, this school is equipped to the highest of standards by the Southern Education and Library Board. Mr Craig, a much-loved and respected principal, died on 14 November 1997. Brian Rolston, vice-principal of the school since 1985, was then appointed principal in 1998."

Of her duties as classroom assistant, Teresa says "I began by helping one boy who had special needs through our mainstream department. From a child with physical disabilities, I moved to the Special Educational Needs Unit. This department caters for up to 35 pupils of compulsory school age who have moderate learning difficulties together with statements of special educational needs. We have established a warmly supportive and hardworking atmosphere in this unit. As pupils increase in confidence they are provided with opportunities to integrate into the mainstream school. I thoroughly enjoy working with the children. My day is both challenging and utterly satisfying."

Returning to her responsibility for the Women's Institute, Teresa comments, "Within the Gosford Area, delegates from each Women's Institute meet to discuss and arrange a Spring Meeting, usually held in the Crozier Hall of St Mark's Church, Armagh. This is a highlight in our Institute calendar", Teresa agrees, "with an invited guest speaker. Each Institute performs some special duty, anything from stewarding, hosting the craft display, flower arranging, a competition, proposing the vote of thanks, helping with entertainment, supper or seconding a vote of thanks. Our audience held more than 200 when this year's speaker was Mrs Hilda Steward, MBE, world president of the Associated Countrywomen of the World, past Federation chairman and a member of Randalstown Women's Institute. Mrs Stewart spoke of her world travels, promoting the important work of the WI. We were deeply moved when she described living conditions for hard-working women in remote parts of Europe and Africa. In honour of sterling work with the Institute over the years, our own Doreen Dawson from Killuney, is a long-serving honorary vice-president."

What in life has given the greatest pleasure to this accomplished woman? "Family", she decides at once, "not just my own but the family in every sense. I love the way people link together, that indefinable well-being harmony brings. Just now, our country needs all it can accrue. Nor could I exist without music. The Carpenters were favourites of mine in the Sixties." Asked to cite a favourite piece of music, she doesn't hesitate. "The theme from the *The Thornbirds* by Henri Mancini which I found most evocative."

From her window we watch Denis across the field with Pipps, the family dog. "I may have grown up in Armagh city but I love the countryside. It matters that we conserve as we manage, fields, wild animals, flowers and trees and it is never too late to protect the environment. Time for myself is precious and that's when I read. Two favourite books were Alice Taylor's *To School through the Fields* followed by *Quench the Lamp*. These told of country living and I find Taylor to be a generous-hearted writer who defines changing times with poignancy, '...prosperity boomed and our teenagers grew up far from the shadow cast by the oil lamp and the plaintive call of the corncrake'."

In sharing a personal history of the Women's Institute, we've found many interesting aspects contained in one family—whether international footballer Jackie Vernon or world-standard Irish dancer Carla O'Brien. In wishing Teresa success as chairperson of Gosford Area Committee, somehow we know that is exactly what she will be.

Teresa O'Brien with officers of the Women's Institute.
(L to R): Patricia Oliver, Gosford Area executive; Hilda Stewart, MBE, world president ACWW;
Teresa O'Brien, Gosford Area president; Eileen Lawson, Gosford Area secretary.

Pat Brannigan

Making history for the third time, Councillor Pat Brannigan of the Social and Democratic Labour Party was elected first nationalist Mayor of Armagh City and District Council in June 1997. Previously serving as the first nationalist Vice-Chairman of the then Armagh District Council in 1989, he had become its first nationalist Chairman in 1993.

"On my election, I pledged to work equally for all of the people irrespective of their political views or religious affiliations. Despite a busy year filled with high points, it was also needlessly tinged with sadness", he recalls.

Pat Brannigan speaks with regret of the sorrow that manifested itself during his year of office. "It was a term which saw the murders in Lurgan of two policemen, one of whom, Constable John Graham, lived in Richhill. The cold-blooded murder of two friends in Poyntzpass, Philip Allen and Damien Trainor, was followed in Armagh by the callous murder of former reserve policeman Cyril Stewart. I also recall the devastation following the Markethill bombing, a mortar attack on Newry Road RUC Station and the discovery of a van bomb left outside the same base."

Asked if he had always been concerned with local government, Pat shakes his head. "My life changed completely in 1974 when two elections took place. Impressed by John Hume's vigorous efforts to promote social reform, I joined the SDLP purely as a member. Prior to that second election, I volunteered my services. A guest speaker at one of the meetings who spurred me to greater things was Tom Daly. His brother, Bishop Edward Daly of Derry, once coined the phrase 'Better to have tried and died, than never tried at all!' Deciding I could identify with that sentiment, straightaway I offered my services. Guess what they asked me to do?" Pat's laughter is infectious. "Paste election posters in strategic places! I was a painting and decorating contractor so party officials decided this was obviously the area to which I was best suited."

The warmth of his personality expands as he chats. Pat's efforts must have impressed for he found himself election agent to Seamus Mallon in 1975. In 1976 he became an elected member of the executive of the SDLP, then in 1977 made headlines for the first time. Taking a formerly unionist seat, Pat was elected to the District Council.

"Privately I sympathised with the defeated candidate", he confesses. "Losing is the greatest blow for anyone seriously committed to local government, the area to which I seemed best suited. As a young man, growing up in Charlemont, council representation for our neighbourhood was poor. I often thought that given the chance, I'd try to do better."

In every respect, he is community-minded and speaks confidently about the change of attitude that swept Armagh in the mid-1980s. "Ours had been a troubled land, and then suddenly came signs of an end to the warring factionalism. Like Martin Luther King, we also had a dream. King was fired by a vision of a country where his children would eventually be judged, not by the colour of their skin but the content of their character. There is no reason why we in Ireland cannot accept each other in the same spirit. And to some extent", he considers, "this was happening. Hopes of a wider understanding gradually filtered through to the electorate. It was a source of pride when everyone worked together for the common good."

Leading by example has gained Pat Brannigan the respect and admiration of the community. The spirited response of Armagh's first SDLP Chairman to invitations from every walk of life endeared him to those outside his Party. Pat read a lesson at the Festival of Nine Lessons and Carols in St Patrick's Church of Ireland Cathedral by invitation of the Dean of Armagh and, in an official capacity, attended the Cenotaph on Remembrance Sunday.

"Already there are memories of my chairmanship which I will treasure", Pat agrees. "At the official opening of St Patrick's Trian, after my official welcome, I spoke extempore, directing my thoughts to Prime Minister John Major. 'It was your birthday yesterday and today it is mine. You were given a present and so was I; yet neither of us appreciated the gift we received'.

"Everyone was patiently waiting to hear what I might say next. I reminded that gathering of the ceasefire for Easter, promising three days free of bloodshed. While not enough, I stressed the joy if this should become permanent. As we all know", Pat purses his lips, "miracles take a little longer!"

Mayor Brannigan recalls numerous engagements throughout Armagh City and District when his wife Molly was always supportively by his side. "As Chairman I carried out more than 400 engagements but the office of Mayor during 1997-98 probably involved more. It was a great pleasure to attend the opening of a new Youth Hostel in the City, which proved a welcome addition in relation to tourism. I was delighted with the announcement and subsequent work on the new Mall West shopping centre, Sainsbury's being anchor tenants. In company with Lord Dubs, we laid the first stone for a new bus station at Lonsdale Road. This was one of several visits by Lord Dubs and political development minister Paul Murphy. Both made private visits to Armagh to experience the wealth of tourist attractions now available.

"I was particularly pleased when Irish President, Mary Robinson, visited the Navan Centre shortly before she left office. Seven years previously, I was the first elected representative to welcome her to Northern Ireland when she visited the Observatory. Conversely, I was last to wish her well on her departure in 1997."

Highlights of his mayoral year included an invitation to be present at Dublin Castle for the installation and official banquet in honour of new President, Professor Mary McAleese.

"President McAleese then made her first visit to Armagh during Church Unity Week, attending an ecumenical service in St Patrick's Cathedral. Prior to the service, Molly and I were guests of Archbishop Brady at a dinner held in honour of the President. Others guests present on that occasion were Lord Caledon, Seamus Mallon, MP, and leaders or representatives of other main churches.

"August brought sadness following the tragic deaths of two of the 20th century's most famous women, Diana, Princess of Wales, and Mother Teresa, both of whom had visited Armagh in recent years. In October 1997, Molly and I hosted a reception for a remarkable 90-year-old lady, Vera Magee, who had worked as translator for United States General George Patton during the Second World War. I was honoured to present Vera with a surprise message of congratulations from the President and First Lady of the United States, Bill and Hillary Clinton. Vera died shortly after, in May 1998.

"During my year of office, I saw the opening of the vacant Armagh gaol to the public and the setting up of a design competition for its future development. Arts Council chairman Donnell Deeny was present when I cut the first sod at our new Armagh theatre development, which has received £3,670,000 from the Arts Lottery Fund. A chance meeting in Westminster at Arts Council awards between Hannah Williams of Basingstoke and a local author led to a spectacular St Patrick's Day concert organised at the Anvil Concert Hall in Basingstoke. Those hosted by Basingstoke Male Voice Choir were Armagh Girl Singers with their musical director Aubrey McClintock, and Armagh Pipers' Club with musical director Eithne Vallely. Molly and myself were honoured to be present.

"I had the pleasure of making a presentation to Armagh centenarian, Mrs Catherine Coulter, when Molly and I visited her home on the morning of her 100th birthday.

"We also received an invitation from our seven-year-old grandson, Mark, who lives in Omagh. Mark had been telling his teacher and classmates how his Grandpa and Granny were Mayor and Mayoress of Armagh. Soon afterwards we were invited to visit St Colmcille's Primary School, Omagh, and speak to Mark's class.

"Throughout the year I hosted many receptions at the Palace for community groups, sporting organisations, arts and musical groups and individuals who served our community in various ways. One of the last functions I held was a reception for Dr Sheelagh Woods whose contribution to the health and welfare of this community is greatly revered. Dr Sheelagh had also recently celebrated her 90th birthday."

Pat has been a driving force in constantly seeking to promote the lucrative development of this City and District. He serves with Armagh Economic Development Group and was part of a delegation visiting America for the Clinton Conference in his year as Chairman in 1995. Conference chairman George Mitchell announced a link-up between major US and Northern Ireland universities, including Queen's Outreach at Armagh.

Pat has since been part of another delegation to visit Staunton, Richmond, Charlottesville and Williamsburg, in Virgina, furthering cross-Atlantic links. He is former chairman of the North West Passage tourism marketing organisation, which promotes an area stretching from

Dublin through Meath, Louth, Monaghan, Armagh, Tyrone and Donegal. He still serves on the committee with representatives of the Northern Ireland Tourist Board, Bord Fáilte and local authorities of the North West Passage route. For him, an important joint initiative in which he plays a major role is the Blackwater Catchment Committee, which also promotes development.

Pat has served as vice-chairman of the Association of Direct Labour Organisations and is currently chairman of the Northern Ireland region of ADLO. His concern for public health matters sees him serve on the Southern Health and Social Services Council.

Carol Thatcher, daughter of former Prime Minister Margaret, said that all private life rushed past, eclipsed by the sheer pace of her mother's career. Mayor Pat Brannigan would agree that enthusiastically meeting commitments, in addition to the demands of his post as monitoring and reviewing officer with Armagh College of Further Education, left little time for home or family.

"We tried to balance a busy week by enjoying a leisurely Sunday lunch. Molly coped admirably with the demands of hospital visits, meeting dignitaries, opening art exhibitions and endless public functions. People welcomed us warmly and those beautiful bouquets Molly received were much appreciated. At times our home must have looked like Covent Garden. Our Ruby Wedding anniversary fell during my year of office and we found time for a celebration with our close family present."

If one suggests that Pat has surely achieved his main objective, he shakes his head. "My party enjoys the confidence of the people. If I've helped win any of that confidence, I'm simply on the way to realising an ideal. Communication doesn't come easily, but I gradually overcame any hesitancy I once had for public speaking. My grandfather, James Grew, born in the latter half of the last century, was by occupation a thatcher, and in his free time, a poet. A local author examined his writings and, deeming them worthy, published a representative selection. When I look for inspiration, who knows, it may well emanate from James. My rules are simplicity and confidence. And I always prepare. Addressing those from abroad, I strive to mention a connection, any link that may exist between their country and mine."

That he coped efficiently with public duties, Pat pointed out, was entirely due to flexibility of the board of governors at Armagh College of Further Education. "They facilitated me in every possible way and I reciprocated by meeting my targets."

Pat and Molly have a daughter, Colette, who teaches at Derrynoose Primary School, and two sons. John runs an oil business in Armagh while Paul teaches at the Christian Brothers' Grammar School in Omagh. Daughters-in-law Colleen and Una are held in great affection. "Family harmony means everything to me", he discloses. "Our four happy, healthy grandchildren, Mark, Rachel, Gavin and Nadine are frequent visitors. We cannot possibly forget their ages, eight, ten, 12 and 14 respectively. I spend every opportunity with them for life can be all too fleeting.

"My father died when he was only 58 and, almost immediately, my mother developed Alzheimer's Disease. For years she was barely lucid. Despite the fact that we felt excluded, the family continued to visit. People have always mattered to me. Here was one who mattered greatly but could not comprehend a word I was saying.

"On a personal note, as Chairman in 1994, I opened an exhibition of Jackie Connolly's art entitled 'Along the Callan'. Most of the paintings were well-known beauty spots, from the source of the river right to the mouth of the Blackwater. One watercolour of a fisherman, I told the audience, reminded me of my youth, when my father taught me to fish. My first catch was a handsome trout and, whilst part of me wanted to bear my trophy home, the higher self urged I return him to the water where he belonged. While I agonised over the dilemma, the fish expired on the bank. While I'd been speaking, I could see a tear glistening in the eye of a lady at the front. Meeting me recently, she confessed she never ceases to be moved by my boyhood struggle over the moral ethics of fishing. I assured her I couldn't reconcile myself to the sport and gave it up.

"I regard myself as a complete news print addict who cannot face the day without reading several papers. It's essential that I keep abreast of current affairs. I have my favourite columnists and feel deprived if a day is too busy to digest whatever topic they've chosen for general consumption. The most difficult question I have ever been asked is to nominate my favourite garden. As far as I am concerned, it must have trees. They are vital to the environment, maintaining the oxygen, which is essential to all human life.

"Traditional music is dear to my heart and I long for the day when Armagh City Choir will sing *Carrickfergus*

Mayor Pat Brannigan and Mayoress Mrs Mollie Brannigan
Photograph by Michael Campbell, LBIPP

especially for me. Had I not become so deeply involved with local government I can easily envisage a career devoted to teaching."

So all in all, Pat Brannigan summarises, "1997 was a very eventful and busy year. It was also a year when there was new hope. The holding of the referendum and great success of the 'Yes' vote is something to hold onto in the hope of new peace for our area, for Northern Ireland and throughout Ireland as a whole."

Roger Weatherup

"My waking thought on the morning of 9 March was 'haven't I an appointment to keep?'" Such a comment is typical of Roger Weatherup, lively, entertaining and after 43 years as a dedicated local historian, still busily occupied.

Roger indeed had an appointment that morning, 9 March 1995. At noon he would address HM the Queen and HRH the Duke of Edinburgh at the Primate's Chapel in the Palace Demesne. Tracing the route to this pinnacle of his life, it is safe to surmise if ever a man seemed predestined for his career, that man was Roger Weatherup.

"I arrived in Armagh all of 44 years ago", he recollects, "in the midst of a downpour. I, a relatively young man, walked up the steps to my new job at the County Museum. The building began life as a schoolhouse and was then the home of the Natural History and Philosophical Society. It came under the auspices of Armagh County Council in 1931. T.G.F. Paterson was honorary curator of the Society's Museum, then, four years later, full-time curator of what became the County Museum. I learned much from this erudite and generous man who researched tirelessly, wrote prolifically and lectured throughout the country. I believe in the role of museums", Roger observes with relish, "here preserved for future generations are constant reminders of previous ages. When someone donates a treasured possession it enriches the lives of all. Most of the exhibits have a tale to tell whether a four-barrelled shotgun, 20lb freshwater pike, railwayman's watch or 19th century watercolour of The Mall. It is the duty of a museum to capture and preserve what represents the history and ways of life characterising the country."

Roger, who spent most of his early years in Belfast recalls the atmosphere of Armagh in the mid-Fifties. "It was a county town, 'uppity' in tone and ethos. I had certain reservations as to my reception. Yet, with little difficulty, I slotted into place. Once, cutting short my weekend, I returned to conduct a tour and quite unexpectedly, experienced that surge of returning to things familiar. Akin to belonging, I had fallen in love with this place.

"My appointment preceded extensive renovations to the Museum. The Council appreciated Mr Paterson could not single-handedly pack and put to bed such a quantity of artefacts. Casting around for safe storage, we found sanctuary in Armagh Prison for the next four years."

From 1957 until 1961, Roger occupied a cell in the men's wing, his comings and goings overseen by a warden with a bunch of jingling keys. "Kate O'Brien, author of *My Ireland*, humorously spoke of our incarceration when she visited Armagh. Kate penned a delightful phrase, one I greatly admire, 'The people of Armagh, though they are not tedious about it at all, do truly love Armagh.'"

The entire contents of the Museum were eventually transferred back from 'B' Wing to the modernised and enlarged new building. "You can be sure it was a busy if challenging time", Roger continues. "Modern showcases brought a stunning transformation to our display. Eight years training in Belfast Museum and Art Gallery under such men as Alfred George and John Hewitt were of great benefit. With the hazy spectacles of hindsight I now realise there is always more to learn. Erudition is not how much you know, rather a realisation of how much you *do not* know.

"By far the most rewarding aspect of Museum work was meeting the public. Scholars, students, schoolchildren, farmers and housewives came to browse, mull over various exhibitions and stopped to chat. T.G.F. Paterson was a scholar, known and highly regarded throughout Northern Ireland and far beyond. His thrill was the chase rather than the kill and I think he published too little. As successor, I was privileged to bask somewhat in the goodwill he engendered. Sweeping changes came in 1973 when the County Council was abolished. It was voluntarily agreed to transfer Armagh County Museum to the trustees of the Ulster Museum. Our funding now came from the Department of Education. Administration was formalised and regulations were to be much more prohibitive. To be fair, the authorities were tolerant of the relaxed system under which I'd worked and to a great degree, permitted me freedom within the limitations of a large institution."

Maintaining good working relations with the Ulster Museum, Roger sustained continuity of his individual programme of events at Armagh County Museum. "Our facilities were now spacious enough to allow for a series of temporary exhibitions, usually from six to 12 a year. The retrospective *Art of James Slater* caused a lot of interest. Another I particularly enjoyed was a collection of paintings by the Ulster Arts Club. Each artist, on joining the Club in Belfast, donated a work so the selection was marvellously varied. Harvey's Wine Exhibition and another from Bushmills Distillery stand out as memorable events—I wonder why? Every ten years I displayed new acquisitions made possible by the generosity of the donors and the purchase funds of first the County Council and then the Ulster Museum."

Right from schooldays at Royal Belfast Academical Institution, Roger enjoyed stage management and lighting. Hill walking and a study of natural history were favourite outdoor pursuits.

"I found that I always returned refreshed, to things historical. Armagh of the early Sixties was in a depressed state. Development lacked vision and gave no consideration to the character or history of the town. A real appreciation of Armagh's buildings and the importance of using local building materials is due to our present Council and the fact that the city is protected by Conservation Order. One classic example of sensitive restoration is Castle Street. I share the derision of Prince Charles for characterless, ill-designed glass and concrete slab buildings. Consider the catastrophe of Craigavon, land carved up for motorways, the demise of our railway system and no conception of local character in housing estates. The city has withstood the unrest and destruction of over a quarter of a century of troubles. I was particularly saddened by the destruction of Armagh City Hall, which epitomised neutral ground. That building had happy memories for me. It was there, while a member of the Drama Club, that I met Anne, my wife.

"In the course of work I was privileged to meet statesmen, politicians, scholars and enthusiasts from many walks of life. People came to accept me, whether rummaging in their back yards or collecting discarded cans from The Mall in an effort to promote recycling. Working in the Museum I willingly gave time to students and where I had information they were welcome to it. Only when I retired did I find time for private research. The private man within me always had certain reluctance towards public speaking. Initially I would have brought notes when lecturing to clubs or societies but now I tend to speak extempore as I realise that reading a lecture is distracting for the listener. In acknowledgement, in those days I was frequently presented with an attractive box of Irish linen handkerchiefs. Just think what they'd be worth now!"

His is the authoritative voice summoned by the BBC, Radio Ulster, RTÉ or press offices throughout the UK. "Broadcasting is something I take in my stride, after all I don't face an audience. Meeting the distinguished is easy, it must be said, they have the ability to put one at ease."

Roger agrees that addressing the Queen was truly his finest hour. "Mr Mitchell of Armagh District Council approached me beforehand. He said the Councillors would like a brief description on the Palace and Armagh in general. It should be delivered to the guest of honour in the Primate's Chapel, while the Council members donned their robes. I was both honoured and overawed although initially this naturally was privileged information." In typical humorous fashion, Roger admits to being "shaken but not stirred". Anne and he had previously attended a garden party at Buckingham Palace and he had been awarded the Queen's Jubilee Medal in 1978.

Pressed to share his feelings at that moment, he shrugs. "I spoke in my usual extempore fashion but sitting down to lunch afterwards was a relief, even though Anne and I were seated at the Queen's table.

"When I married Anne she was a widow with an infant son, Daniel. We surprised everyone, for I wasn't exactly in the first flush of youth—here I was taking on a ready-made family. Yes it was challenging but also the most enriching part my life. I often asked myself why I hadn't done this years before. The answer was simply that I hadn't met the right woman! We had three children of our own but I automatically count my family as four. That Daniel refers to me as his father brings a quiet thrill of pleasure."

In retirement Roger continues to lecture when requested at St Patrick's Trian, Queen's University at Armagh and the Navan Centre, and his list of interests is daunting. He is vice-president of the Ulster Archaeological Society and Brantry Historical Society. Roger serves on several committees including the Armagh Diocesan Historical Society, the Ulster Architectural Heritage Society and Armagh Natural History and Philosophical Society. He is a member of the board of St Patrick's

A young Roger Weatherup outside Armagh County Museum
Photograph by S.H. Keown

Cathedral and a governor of Royal School, Armagh. He has been chairman of the Irish Museums Association, ICOM (Ireland) and a member of the Museums Association Council, the Continuing Education Committee and the Northern Ireland Museums Advisory Committee. Love of things rural saw him as a member of the Countryside Committee, Belfast Naturalists' Field Club, the National Trust and Craigavon Historical Society and has been honorary secretary and chairman of Armagh Field Naturalists' Society. Interested in art, he has served in Armagh and District Arts Committee and is an honorary member of Armagh Art Club.

In 1992 he was appointed as a heritage consultant to Armagh District Council and for almost 40 years has organised and led educational and historical excursions throughout the county. "I sometimes think that I should go back to work for a little ease", Roger smiles, "but while I remain mobile and vertical I shall continue to try to make the most every moment."

Roger Weatherup's drive and determination have certainly guaranteed the sweet aroma of success. And, as the family cat, aptly named Reilly, settles comfortably on his knee, I am bound to add the Queen's been to Armagh to listen to *him!*

Maureen McNeice and the Diary of Peter McSorley

"My grandfather's diary dates to 1878... would you like to see it?" enquired an unknown voice on the telephone. Maureen McNeice had certainly unearthed a find—a journal account of a voyage from Australia to Ireland lasting over two months and 23 pages of written detail kept by her grandfather, Peter McSorley, in 1878.

Peter McSorley had been raised at Collegelands near the Moy. Turning the pages, Maureen, an Armachian, discovered just how outgoing this man was. We visualise him, bent over the page in his small cabin, pen poised, humid air smacking of the Indian Ocean. A true diarist, he diligently logs each day's events, more than a century ago.

"This book", Maureen considers, "tells us as much of the man as it does of the times. Clear copperplate, upper-case letters scrolled and embellished. He writes compassionately, assisting the ship's doctor when fever strikes, deploring conditions endured by steerage passengers, the meat rancid following the slaying of a bullock. The corners are frayed, pages yellowing, but in view of such detail, I contacted the Ulster Historical Foundation. An extract from their reply states: 'No official records of emigration from the British Isles survive before 1890. You are therefore fortunate in having found this diary, a memoir of your grandfather's experiences in 1878.' They go on to explain that more may be learned of Peter McSorley from the Australian State Archives in Victoria."

Peter's grand-daughter, Maureen, is the sole remaining relative of his immediate family. Piecing the facts together, she produces a background scenario of this intrepid voyager. "Peter was the second child of Hugh McSorley and Catherine Tamney, from the parish of Donaghmore. His baptism appears on the church register, 2 June 1840, the family address given as Garvagh. Armagh Ancestry helped evolve a family tree. Peter's father is listed as Hugh McSorley, born 1794 in the reign of George III, dying at the age of 72. My mother, Catherine McSorley was the daughter of Peter and eldest of four children. The civil deaths register for Blackwatertown has a record of the demise of 51-year-old Peter in 1891. He was laid to rest in Collegelands Cemetery, the parish of his youth. Peter's wife survived him by a mere five years, so the children were orphaned when my mother was just 11.

"My mother often told how she and the other three children were claimed by various relatives. Peter had opened a hotel at Old Market Gate, Lisburn, several years prior to his death. From there, she and a little sister Annie, were despatched to Collegelands, into their grandmother's care. Catherine had an aptitude for maths and the same elegant hand as her father, but education after the age of 14 was out of the question. Mother remembered how they had servants in her old home so we can assume Peter and Jane McSorley were people of means.

"The diary was amongst my late mother's possessions. Two facts astonish", Maureen pauses: "Catherine was only 11 when the family divided, yet she clung to that diary, never parting with it during her entire life. While she had only a child's recollection of her father, everything she said tallied with the persona of my own brother, also called Peter." Maureen is the youngest in a family of six, Peter, Daniel, Gerald, Seán, Dermot and herself. Maureen is the last survivor. "Elderly neighbours confirmed my brother Peter bore a strong physical resemblance to our grandfather. Both were meticulous in matters of dress, possessed similar mannerisms and were equally fastidious. My brother Peter worked as a joiner, ornate carving his particular skill. He married a girl from Dún Laoghaire, eventually moving to London. After his death he was interred in Dún Laoghaire."

It remained a mystery why Peter McSorley visited Australia, so Maureen contacted the Genealogical Society of Victoria in Melbourne. Back came information. Peter's name did not appear on the index of assisted passengers 1839-71, so it must be concluded he arrived unassisted. If he arrived in Australia after 1860 it was too late for prospecting. Most alluvial gold had been mined by 1855. The Society suggested he may have come for the purpose of visiting relatives. When the National Maritime Museum in Greenwich was contacted, it expressed interest in publishing Maureen's diary for its archives.

Twenty-three pages of Peter's account remain intact. He began each day with the date, ending with the ship's reading, degrees latitude and longitude, knots covered since his previous entry. Neat phrasing suggests Peter was educated to a reasonable degree.

On 31 May 1878 (then 38 years old) he writes, *Wind light but still against us. Believe we have a 'Jonas' on board. Crossed the line at 10.00 am, the worst run since leaving Melbourne. Nights are very pleasant and cool on deck. Distance: 150 miles.*

1-2 June 1878: *Wind more favourable making sail likely. Passengers are beginning to get impatient not seeing land as we are nearly on the African coast. Distance: 100 miles. Kept up my birthday.*

6 June 1878: *Went on shore immediately after anchoring at Aden Point. Then to the Hotel de Orient kept by a Frenchman. Had brandy with ice for which we paid two shilling each with two Arabs to fan us while we were drinking. This is the most beautiful place were it not so dreadfully hot. Posted letters to Australia, sixpence each. Saw camels on the road at work, should say they are capable of carrying half a ton. There is a very large jail close to Aden enclosed in high and strong walls. Believe the Governor is a Scotsman but did not make his acquaintance!*

Two deaths of lady passengers occurred while I was on shore. Believe they were ailing since leaving Melbourne. A French priest said he would have the Catholic passenger buried in consecrated ground. Was not speaking to him, seemed a good man.

10 June 1878: *One of the engineers knocked down by the sun a few days since and I am afraid he stands a poor chance of recovery. Takes fits every few hours. A steward very ill and a stoker paralysed one side. The ship at present is more like a floating hospital. A steamer following in our wake this morning at daylight, passed us at 4.00 pm. Could barely make out her name with glasses. She is the Prince of London bound for there loaded with tea from China.*

12 June 1878: *In sight of the Asian and African coasts. Abyssinia on the port side. We are at the place where Moses and the Children of Israel crossed the Red Sea and Pharoah and his horsemen drowned. It came to my knowledge that a German passenger was robbed last night of twenty-five sovereigns, his box having been broken and the money extracted.*

Peter reached London on 29 June where he *conducted business*. Then, leaving Euston Station for Glasgow, he again *transacted some business*. He describes how on 10 July, he *took the train for Armagh and remained there awaiting luggage for the entire day.*

It is easy to detect exhaustion, reading between Peter's lines. *I would not advise anybody to make this trip unless they are reluctantly compelled to do so for I consider there should be different boats built before passengers will have pleasure in travelling by that route, frightful heat making it unpleasant.* He signs this with a flourish. Turn a page and a single line states, *Got married 8 October 1878 in Loughgall Chapel by Father Mooney, PP.* Loughgall Parish Register confirms Peter McSorley, a bookseller of Cordonvalley, and Jane Clancey of Aughanlig were bound in matrimony. Jane's baptism had never been entered.

Maureen's son, Adrian, is head of department at Coleraine College of Further Education. Her daughter, Geraldine, an art teacher, lives in Guernsey, Channel Islands. In true family tradition, Geraldine's son, Christopher Higgs, went travelling in Africa during 1997. "Instead of going straight to university", Maureen explains, "Christopher opted to take a year out, teaching at Marange High School in Zimbabwe. Everything was arranged by African Venture, a company that helps find vocational projects for students. School resources were limited and Chris took with him 30 hockey sticks given by friends. He is now studying physiotherapy but vows to return to this school. Rianna, his sister, plans to study dance at Surrey University, then use her talent to help the Third World in the same spirit as her brother. I believe their great-great-grandfather would approve!

"All my research was worthwhile", Maureen says on reflection, "and now I have something precious to hand on to my children. From various references, we assume Peter returned with a quantity of gold. What he did with that money is not clear. The Public Record Office have listings of his hotel at the Old Market Gate in Lisburn, today, almost certainly, the site of The Gaff Cutter."

"Do you agree the story was exceptional?" she suddenly asks. If I do, it's entirely down to her enthusiasm — but what else would one expect from Peter McSorley's granddaughter?

Maureen McNeice with Peter McSorley's photograph and diary
Photograph by Ian Maginess

John O'Neill

Rarely has there been a time in history when the human race did not have its medical men. Surgery was known to the Egyptians and documents from 3500 BC prove surgical operations were common. For his healing art and contribution to medicine during a crucial part of this ebbing 20th century, Armagh is proud to acknowledge gifted surgeon Mr John Joseph O'Neill, FRCS.

Originally from the lovely lakelands of Fermanagh, John O'Neill escorted his daughter, Patricia, to her wedding in Bristol, just two days before our interview. "I did feel a pang as we walked together up the aisle", he admits with a smile. "Not only did Patricia remind me of her mother that afternoon, but she is the last of our girls to fly the nest."

Setting his own particular trend, John O'Neill tells how he was born at home, one of triplets, with brothers Thomas and Ignatius. "Thomas died relatively young while Ignatius is now a retired pharmacist in my home town of Lisnaskea", John contributes. "My father, from Clonakilty, Co. Cork, came as head teacher to Moat No. 1 Primary School, Lisnaskea, where he taught my sister, my brothers and myself. Perhaps it was my mother who established the medical link, she having qualified as a nurse at the Mater Infirmorum Hospital, Belfast, in 1922. After a year at Enniskillen's Presentation Brothers, from 1947-52 I was a student at St Macartan's College, Monaghan, where I took the Leaving Certificate. Enrolling at Queen's University, Ignatius and I now parted company, as he was able to qualify in Pharmacy through apprenticeship with a recognised chemist. In fact he gained the gold medal award from the Pharmaceutical Society Northern Ireland in 1957. My year of intake at University was small, only 48 qualifying in Medicine. This number is in the region of 155 today.

"From 1958 I was houseman with the Mater Hospital for one year. Our scope was very different then, general hospital routine allowing a certain breathing space to experience and adjust to my chosen career. This century has witnessed marvellous medical advancement, from insulin, which relieved diabetes in 1922, to anaesthetics and asepsis, guaranteeing safer surgery. Medical operations have extended to such a degree that there is little a surgeon cannot attempt."

Now fully registered, John O'Neill became an assistant demonstrator in the Physiology Department at Queen's University. "This entailed teaching the function of organs and systems with their various interactions. It was in 1959 when I studied for the Primary Fellowship so I might undertake surgery. This was always my vocation. In the early Sixties general surgery included operations on almost all parts of the body and general surgical emergencies following road accidents or physical injury. Today general surgery is almost limited to emergencies while surgeons with a special interest deal in specialist areas such as orthopaedics, neurosurgery, ophthalmology, gastrointestinal surgery and plastic surgery.

"Negotiating the various levels involved working at many hospitals—Musgrave Park, Belfast City, Royal Victoria, Craigavon Area Hospital, Lisburn, Coleraine, Ballymoney and Altnagelvin. One step at a time, I satisfied the requirements of junior house officer, senior house officer, registrar, senior registrar and finally, that of consultant. While working as senior registrar in Musgrave Park Hospital, May 1971, I was appointed as a consultant to Craigavon Area Hospital, which was newly built but not entirely ready for occupation. Armagh City Hospital was destined to close as an acute hospital but for the time being, I was seconded to work there. The hospital's previous surgeon, Hector Deane, had retired and was duly replaced by Paddy Creighton. George Parkes succeeded Paddy in the fullness of time and after he moved to the Department of Surgery, I was appointed. From May 1971 until September of the following year, I covered emergency operations at both Armagh City and South Tyrone Hospital, Dungannon. With my wife Máire, who had grown up in Belfast, we established our home on the Portadown Road.

"Northern Ireland's violent era was making its impact. Deliberately inflicting hurt or harm is 'man's inhumanity to man' in the worst sense. Many were too badly injured to save and, when necessary, we operated right through the night. The plight of casualties remains with me, principally those injured in a serious Keady bombing, the massacre at Tullyvallen Mission Hall, a bomb blast at

Banbridge and many other serious incidents. Our 'major incident protocol' became operative at such times, all hospital personnel returned to work, remaining as long as the emergency required. I have seen four theatres staffed and operating simultaneously in an effort to save victims. Regardless of personal feelings, everyone worked objectively with those most seriously injured taking priority. Conventional training did not prepare us for the stressful reality of informing relatives when someone died and I welcome counselling for the bereaved in the humanitarian sense.

"It was then common to have small district hospitals with one surgeon in charge. This workload was evaluated as too strenuous and following the Platt Report, the appointment of a second surgeon came into practice in most Ulster hospitals. Medical advancement and development of sophisticated investigative techniques aided the diagnosis and treatment of patients. I am speaking of ultrasound, CAT scanning, magnetic resonance imaging (MRI), or laparoscopic surgery. Such expensive equipment has to be centralised as does the accompanying expertise, hence the closing of so many district hospitals. If you consider that any person may become ill any one of 365 days a year, requiring highly skilled attention, meeting such a criterion requires increased staffing. The Health Service", Mr O'Neill considers, "has existed this length of time thanks, in part, to the goodwill of medical staff and nurses. Many worked far beyond the call of duty but today everything is minutely calculated by financial management and the spirit of giving freely much less apparent. The teaching of junior doctors by qualified personnel was once undertaken not as paid work, but as a matter of course. This, I add, was in addition to clinical work and 'on-call' duties.

"I once attended a lecture given by former Minister of Health, Enoch Powell, who described the Health Service as 'limited means—unlimited demand'. Today's improved standards promote longevity and the burden inevitably falls on the taxpayer. At a time a career in medicine was a vocation but I would say for many today it is regarded as a profession. There is a difference."

Many of his medical colleagues were lured abroad but John O'Neill was never tempted to leave Ireland. "I found Co. Armagh not unlike my native Fermanagh. People were welcoming and friendly. As our children became independent, Máire undertook a Social Science course with the Open University, earning an honours degree. A founder member of Armagh City and District Floral Art Society, Máire gained a City and Guilds diploma in Floral Art and a teaching diploma. She now teaches this subject. We had five children. The eldest, Colette, became a pharmacist. Patricia went to Robinson College, Cambridge, in order to study medicine. Following her success in becoming a Member of the Royal College of Physicians, she took a year out in Australia. Patricia is now a general practitioner in Bristol and, as I said previously, just newly married. Nuala is a plant pathologist specialising in plant diseases with the Department of Agriculture in Belfast. My son Colm is a podiatrist with Foyle Health Care Trust in Derry and the youngest, Ciarán, is a chemist with St Malachy's College, Belfast. So, medically you could say, tradition lives on!

"I have experienced the spiritual leadership of Cardinal Conway who was quite a reserved man. Cardinal Ó Fiaich shared my sporting interest in Gaelic Athletic Association football. His remarkable memory amazed us all for he never forgot anyone he met. When I was a student doctor in 1956, Cardinal Daly, a Professor in Scholastic Philosophy at Queen's University, lectured on various aspects of medical ethics to us at the Mater Hospital. In a personal flashback of Cavan playing a GAA match against Fermanagh, Archbishop Seán Brady and myself were pitted in competition. Actually we drew", he admits.

A sportingly competitive young man, John O'Neill's accomplishments included being a member of St Macartan's 1952 McCrory Cup winning team and a member of the 1951 and 1952 winning Colleges' Interprovincial teams. He was also a member of a number of successful Senior League and Championship teams for Lisnaskea in Co. Fermanagh and won an Antrim Senior League medal with Queen's University in 1958. John O'Neill played with the Combined University Teams from 1955 to 1958 against the Rest of Ireland, winning in 1955 and 1958. John played in goals for the first Gaelic Football team at Queen's University which won the inter-university Sigerson Cup competition in 1958. He was also a reserve on the Ulster Railway Cup team in 1958.

"And", he recalls, not without a trace of modest pride, "I played in goals with the Fermanagh team, which won the All-Ireland Championship in 1958. There was a time in the Fifties, at county team level, when I thought nothing of hiring a car, picking up players en route from

Newtownards, Ardoyne and St Mary's Training College, driving on to Ballybofey or Irvinestown and playing the match. Afterwards we'd have a meal and then I undertook the trip in reverse, seeing each player safely home. From 1952-53 I played for Queen's on Saturday afternoon and then took the train home to Lisnaskea (before the railway closed in 1953) to play for the club or the county. Next morning a lift took me up the Clogher Valley in one of the lorries from Lisnaskea which collected grain in Belfast. Stopping in Scotch Street, Armagh, we had breakfast at Ma Mercer's restaurant, leaving me back at Queen's in time for a 9am lecture. Those were the days! I was a medical officer for the Ulster Amateur Boxing Association for ten years, from 1961. I look back on those as great times in my life.

"Golf has long since replaced Gaelic football except for reading about the game or watching a televised match. I enjoy sports coverage on television, attend international rugby matches and the All-Ireland Football and Hurling Finals. A seasoned member of County Armagh Golf Club, I've played on the Pierce Purcell Team and Junior Cowdy Team." Modesty forbids John's admission of golfing trophies he's taken, including Captain's Prize in 1973 or a hole-in-one at the famous Eleventh, known as 'The Shambles', the verdant background of which is recaptured in delicate watercolour by Joe Hynes.

Angling provides endless hours of pleasure, and, he agrees, requires a particular dexterity. "I was secretary and chairman of Armagh and District Angling Club in the past. The successful angler must understand the haunts and habits of fish and above all, have patience. I'd given up the hobby for 15 years but began again in 1969 when my interest was not in coarse fishing but fly-fishing. Retirement means I can indulge in a favourite pastime. Coming from Fermanagh as I do, the lakes beckon and I respond! Drifting in a boat on a fine day, idly fly-fishing, is a great form of enjoyment.

"Fermanagh waters attract coarse fish, salmon and trout and are patronised by anglers from Europe. I have fished many of the West of Ireland lakes and naturally, Co. Armagh local waters, Lowry's Lough or Seagahan Dam. A mounted display of salmon flies occupies a special place on my study wall where, colourfully grouped, you find superb examples of the *Durham Ranger*, *Silver Doctor*, *Goldfinch*, *Jock Scott* and the *Red Shrimp*. A special rod was given to me by the late Paddy Hamill, a great friend who enjoyed fishing. This rod originally belonged to the Bishop of Nottingham, and was made by Hardy's in 1913. On his retirement, the Bishop gave it as a gift to Paddy who passed it on to me. This will always remain one of my favourite possessions."

Family groups are an essential part of the decor in this pleasingly airy room. "Máire's father", John says, "was at a time, manager of the Northern Bank in Cushendall, so scenes which capture the peace and tranquillity of the Antrim coast in oils and watercolours are important to her. Máire admired a floral memento of her Lady Captain's Day in 1988, painted by Joe Hynes, and it seems to suit exactly, where it hangs. I amassed a collection of prints of famous hospitals such as Dublin's Rotunda and Lying-In Hospital, Westminister Hospital and Church, St Bartholomew's, the Royal Hospital Dublin, Edinburgh Infirmary, Bristol General or the General Infirmary, Sheffield, yet ironically, I do not as yet have a likeness of Armagh City Hospital."

A garden is important to the O'Neill family and effectively screens a very private home with mature trees and magnificent flowering shrubs. Máire teaches floral art so a constant supply of background foliage is essential for her classes. Artichokes cluster in groups around the border while an abundance of sorbus is particularly effective. "I get up early and cut the grass", John says, "and, as if we hadn't enough to cope with, moving the fence a few yards added considerably to the chore. Gardening programmes are television at its best and I appreciate the advice of Geoffrey Smith in *Gardeners' Question Time* on Radio 4. I would argue that one of the most practical and enjoyable methods of acquiring an education in plantmanship and design is by visiting other people's gardens. Some of the more interesting features here are probably taken from an idea I've seen elsewhere yet combines to look entirely different."

When surgeon John O'Neill retired in March 1998, staff in the theatre of Craigavon Area Hospital composed a humorous poem in his honour. Written in script on parchment, embellished with Celtic design and art, this work tells us everything of the man, his modesty, sense of fun and above all, total professional dedication. By contrast, one patient simply comments "If I am alive today, it is thanks to John O'Neill". The sensitive hands of a surgeon so well serving the cause of humanity are one aspect of this man's life.

Physician and surgeon
John O'Neill

In celebration of his quiet sense of humour, with a smile, he quotes from *The Litany* of Sir James Hutchinson (1871-1960), a verse that he feels is appropriate to all clinicians:

From inability to leave well alone;
From too much zeal for what is new
and contempt for what is old,
From putting knowledge before wisdom,
science before art,
cleverness before common sense;
From treating patients as cases;
and from making the cure of the disease
more grievous than its endurance
Good Lord, Deliver Us.

Mary Armstrong

On most topics, Mary Armstrong is philosophical. "Changes", she decides, "are seldom made, most are thrust upon you." She is chatting in the library at Dean's Hill, where an impressive backdrop of leather volumes bridges two centuries.

Mary dresses comfortably, suits her classical hairstyle and possesses an aura of serenity. "This house", she explains, "was built for Dean Hamilton in 1772, who on appointment, considered no other residence appropriate. Because of disestablishment, Dean's Hill had to be sold, and as far as I am aware, lay empty for some time. Eventually it was purchased by my grandfather, Henry Bruce Armstrong, and to date, remains in the family."

Dean's Hill is spacious, overlooking farmland and lush green hills that encircle Armagh. "Last Christmas we hosted 17", laughs Mary, "so I suppose you might say it's sufficiently roomy for the extended family. My grandfather was a legal man who had been called to the Bar in London during 1868. His appointment as High Sheriff of Armagh required that he reside there. One year previously, he had been appointed High Sheriff of Longford. Grandfather's wife came from Cork and they had eight children.

"It was something of a tragedy when his eldest son, William Fortesque Armstrong, was killed in a point-to-point accident. This unhappy event orphaned William's only child, Michael Henry. The boy's French mother, Madeleine (née Toucas-Massillon), had died soon after his birth. Michael Henry was brought to Dean's Hill and cared for by his aunt, Miss Margaret Armstrong. In later life, he became my husband."

Mary is the daughter of Robert, fourth son of Henry Bruce Armstrong. "My mother, the Hon. Kathleen Napier, was a keen horticulturist, studying botany at Kew. Immediately after the First World War, my father bought a coffee farm in Kenya. He had served with the North Irish Horse, and studied law, as did his father before him. A farm in Africa was a complete departure from any established pattern. I tend to think they were imbued with a pioneering spirit. Have you read *Out of Africa*? I can imagine my parents struggling with the difficulties experienced by Baroness Karen Blixen. Just think of losing a crop before harvesting, due to locusts or drought. With it goes three years of intensive labour. A full potential crop took up to six years maturing.

"Despite having five children, my mother assisted in management of the plantation during the Second World War. She didn't shrink from hard work, in many ways a very modern woman, but then, I expect she had to be." In 1946, Mary and her elder sister Frances were sent to Manor House School near Milford, Co. Armagh.

"Mrs Killen was headmistress, "Mary recalls. "She was kind to boarders who were often homesick and lonely. The quality of education was superb. Frances, my sister, eventually gained a degree in Archaeology from Cambridge. I however remained in Ireland, studying Economics at Trinity College Dublin."

Of childhood, Mary observes, "Although my parents were abroad, I had relatives in Armagh. Two sets of aunts and uncles, the Leader family of Hockley Lodge and Major and Mrs Boyle of Desart, often invited me to stay with them during half term or the long summer break. That is how I met Michael Henry Armstrong, my husband. Michael read Law and had been called to the Bar in London at this time. He was my cousin. Perhaps I should say the Armstrongs frequently married within their own family circle. Michael served in the 1939-45 war and due to his legal experience, was required to work for the War Crimes Tribunal. He took the defence for the accused. How long ago it all seems now."

Things were changing dramatically for her parents. In Kenya, the Mau Mau movement had risen, killing not only Europeans, but Kenyans perceived as opposing independence. "With enormous sadness my father and mother returned to Ireland. Fellow's Hall at Tynan was on the market and they bought that property with accompanying farm. My engagement party was the first family event to be held there."

Mary's wedding at Killylea Parish Church was a quiet celebration. "It was 1954 and things were much more subdued than today. If you were to ask me when I was happiest, it was then. For our honeymoon, Michael and I returned to Kenya, the beloved country of my childhood. It was daunting to become mistress of Dean's Hill but I quickly surrounded myself with activities of home, farm and my own children. We had five", she says, listing them in turn. "Anne Cooke lives near Templepatrick. Flora Stone, my second daughter, is in Tain, East Scotland. Edward and his wife Jill run the home farm. They have three children—William, the eldest, is a pupil at the preparatory department of Royal School, Armagh, Madeleine is nearly four years old, with Henry following after. That leaves Robert and Jane who both work in London. I see all of them frequently."

Captain Michael Armstrong, Mary's husband, died before any of his grandchildren were born. She recounts his fatal accident. "This happened in 1982. Michael was attending a meeting in Belfast. We said goodbye. A few hours later the police telephoned to say there had been a crash. He survived two weeks in intensive care. I don't know how we endured those terrible days... and yet with friends and faith, we did."

Adjusting to a life alone, Mary continued with those organisations dear to her heart. "The Mothers' Union is vitally important. Never underestimate a mother's influence on her family. I do wish today's women worried less about equality. In their role as enabler, they are equal. Without their support, few men would succeed. I have always involved myself with the local Ulster Unionist Party and act as delegate for them. During the early Sixties, I served on the board of governors of Manor House School. That has long gone but there are other schools and I am active on the Church Board for Social Responsibilities.

"My reading interests centre on biography and travel. I am an avid letter-writer, often corresponding with those overseas as we have relatives in Kenya. Apart from that, I am a member of the Scripture Union. Learning of missionaries serving in India, who desperately needed encouragement from home, I immediately put pen to paper in support of what they are doing. Indian nationals have taken up this vital work and the Kingdom of God thrives in that country."

Each month at Dean's Hill, Mary hosts an inter-denominational meeting of the Africa Inland Mission Prayer Group. "This is something I greatly enjoy and our numbers continue to grow. I admire empathy in a fellow human being. It's closer to the heart than sympathy. At the opposite end of the spectrum, I deplore violence, including what is verbal. An unkind word, with its attendant ugly ripples, is a chief destroyer of harmony. I remain optimistic about the future of Ireland, having faith that all of us will eventually come together.

"This cutting was found in my grandmother's bible, passed on from her mother, Florence Martha Napier. None of us know who wrote it but the words are rather beautiful, certainly worth sharing."

Don't lose courage, Spirit brave
Carry with you to the grave.
Don't lose time in vain distress
Work, not worry, brings success.
Don't lose hope, who lets her stray
Goes forlornly on their way.
Don't lose patience, come what will
Patience oft-times outruns skill.
Don't lose gladness, every hour
Blooms for you, some happy flower.
Though be foiled your dearest plan
Don't lose faith in God and man.

Mary Armstrong and faithful friend, Dandy
Photograph by Philip Wilson

Jackie Stinson

Displaying the zest of a man half his age, Jackie Stinson comes bounding down the stairs of his saddlery at Thomas Street, Armagh. Peering over half-spectacles, he gives a perfect interpretation of Siegfried Farnon, the stylishly rumbustious Yorkshire vet played by Robert Hardy in *All Creatures Great and Small*. "I'm full of energy", admits Jackie, "mentally at least, I'll never grow old."

The scent of leather permeates his shop. Saddle soap, heaped precariously in a pile, threatens to topple. A stand of glossy blackthorns waits by the door. The premises were originally those of Walsh Linton, when six-year-old Jackie was engaged to run errands. Walsh Linton's wife Kathleen had two sisters, Susie and Jean, then proprietors of one of Armagh's newspapers, the *Ulster Gazette*.

Jackie recounts his first meeting with Walsh Linton. "I was accompanying my Uncle Reggie to the saddlery. I remember him puffing under a weighty harness which required mending. Walsh Linton made a great fuss of me. Setting me up on the counter, he produced sixpence and sent me to buy some Bluebird toffee. The Lintons loved children but had none of their own. They asked my father if I might come each day after school. Kathleen Linton was a corsetière. One of my chores was escorting her clients upstairs, opening the door for them and offering a seat. It's an understatement to say times were more gracious. I was a regular 'Little Lord Fauntleroy'. Mind you, I was dying to know what went on upstairs over the chink of dainty teacups and hushed conversation. No-one explained the function of corsets", he laughs, "anyway it added to the aura of those days."

Jackie's home in Linenhall Street, Armagh, stood opposite Armstrong's pub. "Today this is a carpark in the scheme of things that metamorphose a city. Joe Johnston was a publican and another neighbour, Kate Riley, sold second-hand furniture. I was one of seven children. Apart from Jimmy who died, the others still live close to Armagh. My father was a hairdresser with Zwecker's of English Street. Once a month we got the treatment. Lined up, gown swept under our chins, he snipped and clipped until satisfied we looked presentable. They were good people, my parents", he adds, "perhaps not a lot of cash to spare but an abundance of care. I attended Drelincourt, Armstrong Primary School and finally Armagh Technical College. Charlie Bennett was a woodwork teacher second to none. Skills he taught stood me in good stead for the rest of my life."

Commercial momentum stilled, the shop is a place of shadows. The steady rhythm of a wall clock accompanies Jackie's dialogue. "That's my old pal", he comments, "a veteran of 125 years. It belonged to Kathleen Walsh's father, W.H. Greer, the founder of this business. If you look you can see where, around the face, it reads *Vanner and Prest's Compo Embrocation*. They were an English firm who made liniment for horses. Indeed, the preparation is still used for footballers sustaining injury on the field."

Kathleen Linton died in 1954, the year Jackie officially joined the business. "Since childhood, I'd been learning from Walsh, who was an expert craftsman, and I could hand-stitch using two needles. I continue to use his clamp when sewing harness. As you see, it's coated with the dried wax of a century."

He fingers the grain of an oaken stool. "This too, belonged to Walsh and dates to the 19th century. Money could not buy nor words express what these things mean to me."

Until the Fifties, the farming community ensured constant demand for harnesses, saddles and bridles. "Then when American forces were based locally", Jackie recalls, "we must have made thousands of leather belts." He offers a substantial choice of goods—suitcases, briefcases, schoolbags, wallets and purses. Hides come from Belfast tanneries, Robert Johnston of North Street or Presho and Sons, Talbot Street. He fingers a swatch of leather on the cutting-table. "It was something to work with material like this. Our patterns were exclusive and the product a source of pride. Appreciation of a job well done is a craftsman's chief reward. In the main, my customers are a pleasure to serve.

"A revolution in farming began quietly, the tractor usurping the great Shire or Clydesdale. Last of the working breeds to go was the Suffolk Punch. Walsh Linton", affirms Jackie, "saw the shape of things to come and substituted agricultural trade for the equestrian

Jackie Stinson sews a stitch in time
Photograph by Philip Wilson

equivalent." He suddenly produces a crook of tan leather: "It's a stand-up crupper dock. Walsh devised this method of displaying the tail of a horse attractively in the show ring. It's been accredited as ingenious." When Walsh Linton died in 1977, Jackie inherited the remaining share of his business and attendant goodwill. "I loved the man", he states simply, "and feel he's with me yet."

Jackie highlights one exceptional family from the equestrian world, the Woods' of Baltaran, near Milford. "As a boy, Patrick and John Woods taught me to ride. They then introduced me to local businessmen whose children had little interest in horseriding. Exercising fell to me. A favourite pony belonged to W.P. Ewart, the local chemist. Little Pippin he was called and with this strapping animal, I won the Northern Ireland Pony Championship at Lurgan when I was 14."

As a schoolboy, Jackie competed in every showring, achieving professional standards. Encouraged by the Woods family, whose friendship he esteems, Jackie graduated to the category of lightweight amateur jockey. At point-to-point and under National Hunt Rules, he won with Down South, owned by the late Andrew Gordon of Armagh and My Girl, owned by local veterinary surgeon Wilmer McCall. Jackie also rode for the late Dr Fitzroy Gillespie at the Maze and Down Royal racecourses. Well-loved names from county stables trip easily off his tongue.

"There was Star Beam, Straight Man, Inquisitive Bachelor and one beauty of a filly, Lady Geino. Kevin Woods remains one of Ireland's top amateur jockeys. I shall never forget how much work he channelled in my direction." Of his successes, he is specially proud to have come fourth at Navan to wonderhorse Arkle, ridden by Pat Taaffe. A beam, directly overhead in the saddlery, carries his favourite painting, an oil of Mill Reef with jockey Geoff Lewis, and Brigadier Gerard ridden by Joe Mercer. "And yet with all, I'm not a gambler", Jackie stresses. "Talking to you is the biggest risk I've ever taken!"

National Hunt breeding now occupies most of his time, selling on his young foals, unbroken as three- or four-year-olds. One of these, Chrisali, won at Clonmel the previous week and he is equally optimistic about her half-brother, a fine gelding still in the paddock. Watching his own stock make the grade, Jackie reckons, "surpasses any pleasure known to man".

Through his son John, the business will bridge another generation. John responds to a challenge and will create a specialist product if the need arises. He and his fiancée Donna plan to marry next year. Linda, Jackie's daughter, is a medical secretary, living locally with her sons, Jonathan and Simon. Once a choirboy with St Patrick's Cathedral, Jackie is a member of Portadown Male Voice Choir. "It was rewarding for our conductor, Gordon Speers, when the choir won outright at Cork International Festival earlier this year. Gordon accepts only one standard and we give of our best. For the Festival we sang in German, *Nacht*, a beautiful piece. Our coach in phonetics was a fellow choir member."

Siegfried Farnon, the Yorkshire vet he emulates so well, loved Sibelius and Nielsen. Jackie makes his own music, responding, if requested, with *The Fields of Athenry* or *The Blacksmith*. The similarities between both men are amazing. Jackie could play Siegfried as easily as falling backwards into a comfortable bed.

The world of Jackie Stinson will not change. He'll always exhibit that zest, love his horses, take joy from those he meets or stubborn pride in his craft. And yet his is an identifiable world, one you, the reader, may be reluctant to leave.

Evelyn Corry

How often, in a self-indulgent age, will you meet someone who consistently placed the development of children above personal interests? Such a person is Evelyn B. Corry of Farmacaffley, the MBE she holds a tribute to 42 years of youth work combined with her career in education.

As a young woman taking up training at Stranmillis College, social restrictions prevented her specialising in her first love of science. She accepts this may have altered the entire course of her future. "Stranmillis Training College encouraged me to specialise in music rather than science. After a tough fight, I was permitted to study secondary school Rural Science for a further year. Whilst I was on teaching practice at Armstrong Primary School, my mother died. That was a bitter blow for I had resolved to teach neither in a primary school nor in a school close to home. Suddenly everything changed. Now, eldest of three children, I felt it essential to teach locally and live at home. My brother and sister followed the same profession and are now retired teachers."

Renowned for dislike of euphemism and affectation, Miss Corry matter-of-factly recalls her first appointment, that of assistant teacher at Aghavilly Primary School. "Children today would never believe what primitive conditions existed in 1955. Thirty-three pupils worked from tattered, dog-eared textbooks. The schoolhouse itself was dilapidated, requiring massive repairs. Dry toilets stank to high heaven in summer. After my first day's teaching, I came home heart-broken, thinking, how do I endure two years of my contract in such a place? It soon came to light that the Education Committee planned to close down Aghavilly School.

"Aghavilly National School was established in 1876, the present building erected in 1896. Records show Mrs Hawthorne as having been principal of Aghavilly Primary Elementary School, during the war years with 11 children on the rolls. Mrs Knipe succeeded, followed in 1946 by Mrs Gillespie. Mrs Nancy Cunningham, principal since 1952, had as assistant, a young student who had recently left the Royal School, Armagh. This young man, William Johnston McAllister, held the post (locum tenens) for one year, September 1954—June 1955. William (Billy) McAllister had the rare distinction of gaining Northern Ireland Senior Certificate Examinations before his 16th birthday. Minimum entry age for Stranmillis Training College was then 17$^{1}/_{2}$ years on 1 September in any given year. William McAllister took Advanced Senior, and still too young for Stranmillis, was appointed to the post of untrained teacher at Aghavilly School. Employed by Armagh County Education Committee, here was his ideal opportunity to gain experience.

"A locum was then paid 23 shillings (£1.15) a day as opposed to weekly pay or monthly salary. It may not seem a lot but was quite reasonable for a young person. William spoke of his regard for Nancy Cunningham who gave good advice when it was sought. He learned quickly, and following a school inspection was given a first-class report. When he left, William handed the older children on to Nancy. His efforts should not be underestimated for classes in his care had been well instructed, particularly in the fundamentals of English. Learning a classical poem each week, many of the children could recite on request Byron's *The Destruction of Sennacherib*, Browning's *Home Thoughts from Abroad* or *The Burial of Sir John Moore* by Charles Wolfe.

"I took infant junior classes for two years, never my forte, so each year seemed to last a thousand days. By retirement I had the rare distinction of 40 years' experience of the dreaded 11-Plus examination. I also must pay tribute to Nancy Cunningham. Consideration for country children, walking miles each morning in bitter weather, saw Nancy make a huge saucepan of hot cocoa from supplied school milk. Pupils brought their own mug and warmed themselves around the pot-bellied stove at break time. Entirely at her own expense, Nancy established a Christmas concert and party afterwards when a tree was hung with a gift for every pupil. One child, now a grandmother, remembers being given a copy of *Little Women* by Louisa M. Alcott. It had 2/6d marked on the dust jacket and long remained a treasured possession. From such little anecdotes you can appreciate times were hard and families more or less equal in the material sense."

In 1958, Evelyn Corry was appointed principal of the school on Mrs Cunningham's retirement. Eunice Murray, newly qualified from Stranmillis Training College, now became teaching assistant. "We were still fighting to keep our jobs but structural improvements had taken place. A change of attitude in teaching methods allowed flexibility. I've always sympathised with the non-academic child, so right from the beginning of my career, introduced PE, art, crafts, singing, sport and later, swimming. Besides providing a happy interval on which to end each day, this gave a sense of purpose rather than psychologically dreading school. We brought living things into the classroom, hatching chickens, ducklings and providing water for the ducklings' first swim. Every Friday, children were loaded into our cars and taken to Orchard Leisure Centre when I taught them to swim. Each one was taken home afterwards. I love water but have seen so many dread deep water that I really wanted our children to master swimming as early as possible. It also meant they could go canoeing, banana skiing and yachting. Before we knew what was happening, numbers on roll increased, a trickle that grew to dozens."

Evelyn Corry's system was unique but still in its infancy. She organised trips, perhaps to Aldergrove Airport where the children were allowed to turn propellers on an aircraft, Blackhead lighthouse on the Antrim coast, or the newly opened Safari Park at Benvarden. Visits were essential to her teaching programme so annual major trips were planned to the Ulster American Folk Park, the Folk and Transport Museum and the museum at Gortin. "Such outings required we take out our own private insurance and always, the day ended with an enjoyable, recreational visit."

What pleases enormously is any past pupil remaining in touch. "Down the years I taught 11 Nicholsons: present MEP Jim Nicholson, his three sisters and his family of seven children. With sadness I recall meeting Sam McAllister at Aldergrove en route to Canada. Sam had been a pupil of Aghavilly School in the mid-Forties and was now taking a trip with his wife Margaret and daughters, Wendy and Vivien, to Ontario, before making a decision to emigrate. I'd been to Canada and we exchanged experiences until their flight was called. Sam died in a traffic accident in September 1984, on his way to Winnipeg, where his daughter was enrolling at university. Another past pupil, Bill Lyons, died suddenly. Twin brother of Tom, the two boys were inseparable."

In a happier vein, Miss Corry speaks of accomplished past pupils. "Brenda Patterson, daughter of Aghavilly Rector the Rev. Forde Patterson, realised her ambition to study law, later becoming Lady Shiel, wife of Lord Justice Shiel. Derek McAllister, a younger brother of Sam, is a fine arts investigator, in our eyes something of an *Antiques Roadshow* expert. Brian, youngest boy of that family, had an aptitude for languages, spending a short time at Moscow University. Graduating from the New University of Ulster, he is a Russian translator based at Cheltenham, Gloucestershire. It is unfair to be selective for every child possesses something unique. As with the song, 'It's not what you do, it's *the way* that you do it', that matters. Our children were drawn from a farming community and down the years, many contributed to Northern Ireland's principal industry, agriculture, and to medicine, education, sport, policing, business and commerce. And yes, I am human enough to feel proud of those who have already, or are presently, leaving an intelligent mark in society."

Miss Murray married Harold Black, continuing as vice-principal of the school. "She was held in great affection by the children", comments Miss Corry. "Her love of nature had a positive influence so from her, pupils learned respect for our environment and wild life. She too believed education worked best when object-orientated. Visiting the Argory or a museum, Mrs Black encouraged the children to think themselves into that era. Dressing in fashions provided helped our children to identify with history and social conditions. When Martin White, organist of St Patrick's Church of Ireland Cathedral, asked if any of our boys had an interest in becoming choristers, auditions were held. Quite a few enjoyed the experience of training and singing with the Cathedral Choir. James Morton and Wesley Brownlee are present members.

"As numbers at Aghavilly School increased, so did our staff. First came Mrs J.E. Baird, then Mrs L. Dunwoody and later, Mrs L. Lawson as a part-time teacher. When Mrs Black retired in 1993, she and I had shared more than 30 agreeable years as colleagues."

Rural life afforded children little by way of social interchange or entertainment. A blend of Miss Corry's commitment, help from parents and the RUC Community Branch saw Aghavilly Youth Club emerge in 1978. "It was important that the Club should offer something to both boys and girls. From humble beginnings and 13 children", she proudly states, "we have now increased to 171. We first met at Aghavilly Orange Hall, moving to the Rectory in 1980. Children are drawn from Killylea, Armagh and Milford, their ages ranging from five to 21. Weekly activities include uni-hoc, swimming, football, netball and badminton. Camping and camp holidays are an important feature of our Youth Club. As a group we visited Switzerland and several European countries. Travels within the British Isles drew us to contrasting towns as far apart as Edinburgh and Bournemouth or York and Westport.

"We urgently required transport, so with the help of parents, we raised more than £20,000 to fund our own minibus, which is driven by five volunteer parents. Forty leaders supervise activities that now include the Duke of Edinburgh Award Scheme. When our girls asked if I would start the scheme, I was at first reluctant. I relented and now 50 members are involved in the Award. Eleven qualified for the highest honour, the Duke of Edinburgh Gold Award, and travelled to Buckingham Palace in July. Needlecraft is not so essential to the curriculum so parents have asked me to teach sewing, crochet, knitting and quilting. Formerly, in the classroom, our children produced some excellent work and Armagh Show provided an ideal outlet. We took awards for exhibits of art and craft, immortalising our worthy winners in school scrapbooks. Held in trust, Aghavilly School has its own little museum of past history, including a wall sundial dated 1819, amongst local artefacts."

For Aghavilly Primary School's Centenary in 1996, Miss Corry and her staff organised a formal church service and series of events in celebration of an important landmark. Former teachers attending were Mrs Gillespie, Mrs Cunningham and Mrs Black. Past pupils came, paying tribute to a country schoolhouse and teachers who, by their dedication, contributed to the common good.

A favourite relaxation is gardening and she has a passion for scented flowers and herbaceous borders. "I read, mainly biography, but for sheer relaxation, enjoy playing the piano. Margaret, my mother, was an accomplished organist at First Keady Presbyterian Church and Samuel, my father believed her most accomplished piece was Handel's *Largo*. I was asked to perform the role of organist at Aghavilly Parish Church on a temporary basis but am there yet! Once I played the *Largo* at a funeral in Aghavilly Parish Church, unaware that my father was in the congregation. He stopped me afterwards, as I walked to my car. 'You played that just like your mother', was his quiet comment."

Miss Corry recollects the excitement of a letter from Buckingham Palace, asking if she would accept the award of MBE. "I was specifically requested to maintain silence until the presentation. That was difficult. Almost daily, I found myself biting my tongue. Three guests could accompany me, so I invited my brother Fred, sister Ida and stepmother, May. From Eileen Sterritt's fashion shop I chose a suit under the guise of 'going to a wedding'. The Queen smiled and murmured something humorous when, with difficulty, she secured the medal on a pin already in my jacket. Afterwards we posed for photographs, leaving to have our own celebratory lunch."

A highly alternative vision of a country schoolmistress now focuses on Evelyn Corry's zest for travel. "In 1980 I tackled Australia, touring the east coast to Mount Isa, then up to Darwin. Central Australia brought me to Ayers Rock and Alice Springs where I saddled up, riding into the outback, something I'd dreamed of doing. From Adelaide I boarded a train to Kalgoorlie. Half of my joy had to be the assorted wildlife. While breakfasting, I'd watch wallaby and kangaroo graze outside my window. Panning for gold in the mines, none materialised, but at least I didn't fall down the mineshaft like one unfortunate tourist! Ten weeks in all, acclimatising to home was very difficult."

Now, with time for herself, she looks forward to visiting Greenland. "I imagine it may be similar to Iceland with hundreds of miles of lava, hot springs utilised for various uses and rare mosses."

Having promised herself she'd retire when a third generation of pupils enrolled, that was exactly what Evelyn did. To mark her lifetime of dedication, parents, teachers and pupils planned a surprise party and presentation. "I hadn't an inkling of what was happening", Evelyn confesses. In addition to a Jackie Connolly painting depicting places of special significance in her life, Evelyn was given a travel ticket to the Somme.

"A group of our Primary Seven children won a trip in 1990, when their project was chosen by the Somme Association. The pupils had researched the live of four men from Aghavilly who died in the Battle of the Somme. These were Sam McClean, Sam Broomfield, Archibald McCammond and Albert Keys. I went back, paying respects to young men in their teens, simply marked by a stark white cross. Many, too young to enrol, had falsified their ages and lie in the green fields of France."

Retirement for Miss Corry does not mean knitting in an easy chair. "Always interested in politics, I was asked to stand in local council elections as an Ulster Unionist candidate and was delighted to win a seat in Armagh City and District Council. That was 1997. I also serve as representative on the Southern Education and Library Board. Without this I might have vegetated", she firmly declares.

Rarely in a self-indulgent age do we meet with someone so utterly dedicated. Asked to summarise her vast arena of interests, Evelyn B. Corry pauses a moment to reflect.

"In rare moments of nostalgia I picture an endless queue of children I've taught. If I've improved the life of even one of them... then I am well content."

Miss E.B. Corry, MBE,
at Buckingham Palace

Nan Allen

"I can picture my mother, a homely little woman in an apron sitting knitting by the radio. It was wartime and she made everything we wore." Mary Anne (Nan) Allen's words reproduce a scene of personal significance and social importance.

"In 1951, I was the eldest daughter of probably the county's largest family. Of 20 Rhodie children, 17 survived. Although a local newspaper took our photograph we did not realise our family was unusual. Looking at that picture today I realise it contains more than a personal story. From eldest to youngest, we had Bertie, myself Mary Anne (Nan), Victor (deceased), James (deceased), Eleanor, John (Jack), Jean, Edith, Margaret (Peggy), Isobel (deceased), Joe, George, Lynne, Joyce, Trevor, Donald and baby Kenneth (deceased). My parents, May and James, first lived in the old schoolhouse at Drumbeebeg, Kildarton, near Hamiltonsbawn. Solicitors Monroe and Anderson handled the legalities of our tenancy and today this dwelling is a listed building. James Rhodie originated in Edinburgh. Research by one of my brothers revealed his ancestors were Greek, from the Aegean island of Rhodes. Unable to find work in Scotland or England, James came to Armagh during the General Strike."

James Rhodie served in World War I with the Seaforth Highlanders. His regiment wore particularly striking tartan kilts and was distinguished for its contribution at the battle of the Somme. "A cook for the troops, he spoke of inhuman conditions which men had to endure, and food shortages at field stations", says Nan. "James was capable of making a good meal when my mother was ill or nursing an infant. At the time he arrived in Armagh there was work to be had as scores of men were employed in diverting an underground river from Scotch Street. This scheme prevented flooding of the Mall, prior to this an annual winter occurrence. My mother worked as housekeeper to the Allison family, famous for their photographic studio. May Rhodie's standards were high and our home scrupulously clean. When they married, James was 20 years senior to his wife.

"My earliest recollections are of 1936", Nan continues. "It took every inch of the old schoolhouse to accommodate so many of us children. James was a gardener and in summer we'd remain outside helping him until darkness fell. Moss roses and scented purple sweet pea, the frilled variety, grew against the wall. Old-fashioned forget-me-not and tulips made a fine show each spring. When I was five years old I enrolled at Wastelands Primary School, staffed by teachers Mrs Ebbitt and Mr Patterson. I remember both as kindly, caring individuals. Mrs Ebbitt made cocoa from powder that we ourselves provided. Winters were usually severe, so when break-time came, we stood around the stove enjoying a hot drink. The children numbered 50 in total so the Rhodie family must have provided almost half of that intake.

"Each Christmas my mother bought an orange for each of us, pencils, sharpeners and rubbers that she then placed in a row of stockings laid on the couch. We were delighted with whatever we'd been given, glad that each of us received something. Today's selfishness hadn't been born and people cared for each other. The Shillington family had a farm nearby and when they had surplus food, they shared it with my mother. Billy Megarity and Leslie Fleming were local children I often meet today.

"During the war years we carried to school gas masks which had been issued by the Ministry of Defence. I had a child's horror of attack as we placed these in a box beside our desks. Maybe it was the very idea of having to put Peggy, our latest baby, into a protective incubator! To avoid malnutrition, cod liver oil and orange juice was standard issue for every home with children." At the tender age of 14, Nan had no choice but find her way in the world.

"A week before my birthday I was sent to Taniokey, near Poyntzpass, where I became nanny to the child of our teacher, Mrs Cox, earning 15 shillings a week. This was work I understood for I had helped at home, rearing most of my brothers and sisters so that my mother could go out to work. Maud Pember Reeves wrote of pre-war times in her book entitled *Round About A Pound A Week*, a study of budgets in the lives of 30 working-class families in Lambeth. None of those families had more than six children. Had my mother been a writer, she could have told of rearing 17 on the same amount of money! For the article accompanying our photograph, my mother was asked how much food it took weekly to feed us. The reporter looked in disbelief when she said, 'I bake nine loaves of bread each day, so multiply that by seven, then add six cakes for the weekend'. Such domestic output required a hundredweight of flour weekly. When everyone was at home, a modest dinner required three stones of potatoes, six cabbages and 36 slices of bacon.

"To manage somehow on her income, my mother was first and foremost, an economist. After that came as much cleanliness and order as she could squeeze in. She knitted every jumper and cardigan, even made the skirts her daughters wore. I remember being invited to a Christmas party and she sat up all night finishing my outfit. She also instilled a respect for nature in all of us. Peggy and Edith once brought home the nest eggs of a thrush that had built in a laurel bush nearby. Both girls were told this should not have happened and wiping the eggs carefully, my mother returned them to the nest. She lived in a constant state of exhaustion. As each child was born, I left my job to help at home. No-one would dream of doing this now and of course I resented the unfairness, but such was the harsh reality of the times."

Only five feet two inches in height, May Rhodie remained cheerful while she washed, baked, laundered and cleaned for her enormous family. "I said she was scrupulously clean", Nan reminds. "Let me stress, May's surrounding were kept up to standard. She constantly painted and decorated our home. My father had an acre of land on which to grow vegetables and rear poultry. This helped feed his enormous family. Every time my mother went shopping, we girls were left a list of chores that had to be completed on her return. It rarely changed. We scrubbed the kitchen table until the wood turned white, dusted, brushed, swept and black-leaded the stove.

"By now I'd found another job as housekeeper with Mr McKenna who ran a bookmaker's shop in Dobbin Street. With his recommendation, the Hanna family asked me to become resident housekeeper. I also worked for their son Jim at St Mark's Place. My day off was completely taken up by helping at home. During the war hardship increased for my father went to work in Shetland and the Orkney islands. The burden of responsibility now fell on my mother and the eldest children. Once when he had an accident and was laid off for weeks, we discovered the meaning of hardship. Government aid didn't exist then and May was forced to work the clock round to provide for her children."

Nan remembers everyone clustering around the radio, listening to war bulletins. "There had been a continual series of hit-and-run bombing. How my father cheered when the announcer said Nazi aircraft attempts to destroy Forth Bridge in Scotland had scudded into the water. Greater London had taken a terrible pounding along with Coventry, Hull, Sheffield, Plymouth and Southampton. I was only ten when Belfast shipyards suffered heavy bombing. Terrible as these times were, Britain distinguished herself, everyone working together in a spirit of determination. My father had a brother, Jack, who also came from Scotland on a working contract. Jack married locally, living in Callan Street so we had seven cousins while they had the lion's share, with 17 of us! To ensure everyone had an equal share of food and clothing, ration books were issued. Mrs George of Barrack Street bought whatever coupons my mother could not afford to use.

"After the war, a Labour government was voted into power. By 1950, National Insurance eased the burden in times of sickness, unemployment and old age. The health service brought a welcome nationalisation of hospitals and free medicine. Children of working-class families now received free secondary education. A Welfare State meant no-one went hungry or experienced the hardship of my mother's generation. Fifty-five years later, I regret to say, a system set up for the poor is shamefully exploited by many who are well off, or just not prepared to provide for themselves. Earning a wage, however small, brought a dignity which is hard to define, but of which I was proud."

Updating her own life, Nan had now married and was living at Little Barrack Street. "When the McCann family moved, Marshall Ritchie became our closest neighbour. Marshall died in a tuberculosis epidemic that swept Armagh in the late Forties. Mark Doyle, who served in Korea with the Royal Irish Fusiliers, came to this house. All of us are saddened by Mark's ill health and grateful that Trevor Kilpatrick cares for Toby, Mark's faithful old dog. I had two children when the Rhodie family moved from Wastelands to Goal Square, Armagh. It was a somewhat unusual situation as their aunts and uncles (my younger brothers and sisters) were also attending Armstrong Primary School!"

For a time Nan worked as housekeeper at Vernon

College, Ballyards, once the lovely home of the Sinton family. "Converted into a private school for boys, fees were high and numbers limited to 100. I often chatted with the boys who were extremely polite but far from home and quite lonely. Mr Huggard, the English headmaster, quickly lost interest and Vernon College fell into bankruptcy."

As the Rhodie family left school they slotted into the workplace in a variety of ways. "Victor became manager at Wilson McCartney's coal business in Lower English Street. Transferring to Turners, general merchants, Victor remained there until his death at the early age of 45. Two of my brothers, Victor and Bertie, married two sisters, Vicky and Betty Watt from Newtownhamilton. James was employed by Fane Valley dairy as a milkman. He joined the army but became seriously ill, dying in 1968. Eleanor enrolled with the Women's Royal Naval Service, serving on HMS *Collingwood* in Scotland. Eleanor's husband was a Petty Officer on board the famous aircraft carrier, HMS *Eagle*. Jack worked for Louden's undertakers. Jean joined the Women's Royal Army Corps and, widowed at the early age of 39, now lives near Manchester. It may be of interest that her husband trained with the late Dan McKeever, his skill earning him a position with Hawker Siddley.

"Edith and Peggy both joined the army, Edith rising to the rank of warrant officer. Isobel's husband had his own driving school but she died at when only 34. Joe, a talented musician, has worked with Emerson's Supermarket for many years. Always a sportsman, Joe played for Armagh Cricket Club 1st XI. He and his wife Myrtle are exceptionally keen golfers. George lives locally as does Lynne. Living at the family home, Lynne has all my mother's good housekeeping traits. Joyce works for Social Services in Leicester. Trevor keeps occupied at Appleby Connections. That leaves Donald who lives and works in Ballymena."

May Rhodie died in 1979, aged 68. "She was laid to rest at Kildarton Parish Church. My father predeceased her, dying in 1963 at the age of 73. At her death, May Rhodie had 39 grandchildren and more than 100 great-grandchildren." Nan pauses: "I myself have 15 grandchildren and seven great-grandchildren. Only as we grew older did we realise how enormous our family was, therefore the extended family must be record-breaking! Unlike my generation who lived in harmony with everyone, my youngest son aged 31 has known a lifetime of tension. Human nature cannot have changed so much. I refuse to believe we are not capable of returning to a way of life where everyone saw and responded to their neighbour's need.

"I spoke earlier of the importance of wireless broadcasts during the war", Nan reminds. "I'd give a lot if we could have that quality of comradeship today but without the suffering. In blacked-out nights, millions of people were one as we soaked up Churchill, Roosevelt, Freddie Grisewood, Stuart Hibberd, Arthur Askey, Gracie Fields, Tommy Handley and *ITMA* with the catchphrases of situation comedy, such as 'Can I do yer now, sir?'

"That reminds me, I entered a fancy dress competition run by Poyntzpass Young Farmers' Club in celebration of VE Day. Dressed as 'Mrs Mopps' of the Tommy Handley show, I took first prize. For six years, every turn of the radio switch had a special significance for someone, somewhere. It was almost as if prime ministers or presidents had dropped into the front room. We only get that from a book today."

This account of Nan Rhodie, eldest girl in what may have been the county's largest family of the Fifties, makes fascinating reading. More importantly, she has fitted major pieces into the jigsaw of an ebbing century.

Nan Allen and the Rhodie family, 1952

Archbishop Seán Brady

Speaking at St Patrick's Cathedral, Armagh, on World Peace Day, 1 January 1999, Archbishop Seán Brady made a dramatic statement. Consider the example of Chile and Argentina, the Archbishop suggested; two countries, which after decades of conflict, finally reached agreement. To mark the occasion, they jointly constructed a 29-foot statue of Christ that was moulded from the metal of old guns and cannons. On it they put this inscription: *Sooner let these mountains crumble to dust than that Argentinians and Chileans break the peace sworn at the feet of Christ, the Redeemer.*

"Here in Northern Ireland", he continued, "we have been given another chance to build peace. We must grasp the chance and make sure that it is not lost again." Six months later, approaching a time of year when tensions run particularly high, Archbishop Brady urged calm reflection and objective assessment. His address at St Peter's, Drogheda, was given on the occasion of the annual pilgrimage to the Shrine of St Oliver Plunkett, Apostle of Peace and Reconciliation.

"The issue of the impasse at Drumcree is a mighty challenge, but overcoming challenges is the essence of the human spirit. Mighty challenges require mighty solutions. A resolution can be reached provided both sides commit themselves to working constructively towards community relations in Portadown, to understand each other's position, and to reach accommodation on the future of parades. This impasse could be resolved if both sides were to approach those talks in a spirit of good faith, mutual respect and generous acceptance of cultural diversity. May God grant that the last year of this millennium might also be the last year of such painful and damaging conflict."

Good sense is the essence of this deserving paragraph and such words are worthy of a public voice beyond that of a particular group. What a major contribution, if, as Archbishop Brady urges, we would 'turn our weapons into one great statue of Christ'.

A messenger for peace, Monsignor Seán Brady was ordained Coadjutor Archbishop of Armagh in February 1996. What time-honoured formula, we wonder, elevated a quiet man from Cavan to the top ecclesiastical post in Ireland? An impressive curriculum vitae reveals the scholar with a Bachelor of Arts degree in Ancient Classics from St Patrick's College, Maynooth, a Licentiate in Sacred Theology and a Doctorate in Canon Law from Lateran University, Rome, and a Higher Diploma in Education from Maynooth.

Cast to the people of Ballyhaise, Co. Cavan, where he served as parish priest. They say the appointment brought an entirely personal thrill of pride. If appearing possessive in laying claim to his affections, they are, as we say, entitled, for Seán Brady was Cavan-born—educated at, and later a teacher of French and Latin at, the College of St Patrick. These are his people in the deepest sense, sharing his joys and supportive in sorrow. Whilst vice-rector of the Irish College in Rome, he never failed to return to the rural setting of childhood.

"Con, my brother and his wife, Bernadette, run the family farm. Both my parents are dead but I retain a passion for this sweeping countryside. My father was a member of the County Council and chairman of the local creamery. He often exhibited pedigree cattle at Royal Dublin Show, once taking Supreme Champion with a favourite Aberdeen Angus. Mother helped on the farm in an effort to preserve what she loved. I imagine if she were alive, she'd be campaigning against worldwide destruction of this planet. Grief came in 1992, when three-year old Seamus, the son of Con and Bernadette, was killed in a tractor accident. We survived that tragedy in the way people do, with support and help from neighbours, indeed the entire community. It was a crucial time and the Irish College in Rome prayed for us unceasingly. The family asked me to say Mass. Thinking it would be emotionally beyond my capabilities, I asked for help. It came", he recalls, "in a great surge emanating from the congregation. I cited the biblical death of Lazarus when Martha said reproachfully, 'Lord, if you had been here it would not have happened...' I was only minutes away when the accident happened and we each tried to shoulder blame, yet ultimately none of us could have saved that little child. Now the grief of others touches me in a way I hitherto could not conceive."

Archbishop Brady's sister, Kitty, teaches in Dublin.

Archbishop Seán Brady

Sketching a family profile, she describes her brother as "impeccable... he is thorough in everything he does. Should I require a second opinion, he will give the alternatives, pointing out that ultimately the decision has to be mine. As a family we were close. When my brother was rector at the Irish College in Rome we visited him. Architecturally beautiful, crowds standing in awe at St Peter's Basilica, it was thrilling in every sense. He seemed part of it all, the Renaissance city ablaze with flower-stalls, tourists photographing friends amidst beauty and colour. People say he was more than rector", Kitty adds simply, "they see him as an ambassador for our land."

Major events festoon the life of the youngest Archbishop ever appointed to Armagh. Of student days, Dr Brady comments, "It was that exciting era of the Second Vatican Council. Pope John XXIII, a radical reformer, had flung wide the windows so the Church enjoyed a doctrinal spring-clean. John XXIII believed the essence of truth should be constantly restated in the light of the Gospel. You had to be there to savour the universality of it all, bishops of every colour representing the human race."

Dr Brady describes his happiest memory of his ordination to the priesthood, in February 1964: "Easily the arrival of my mother at the airport, that look on her face as she came towards me. It was evident that this was the most important event in her life. Naturally I appreciate the role of women within my faith. Half of the population have a right to be heard—in any case, theirs is usually the reasoning voice."

Asked to comment on a recent survey showing a majority within the Church has no objection to priests marrying, Archbishop Brady admits he is aware of a desire in some quarters for change. "I myself remain convinced that celibacy is a precious gift for Catholic priesthood to cherish." On the painful topic of divorce he reiterates a strong belief in the sanctity of marriage while accepting that annulments are now commonplace. "A Tribunal will advise in the case of irretrievable breakdown. When an annulment is granted, those concerned may remarry with the blessing of the Church."

He acknowledges that paedophile offences within the priesthood rocked the Church to its core. "Violation of a child's trust is probably the most serious moral offence in existence. Now allegations receive immediate attention, victims know they can rely on confidentiality and support."

It is the conscious aim of the Archbishop to foster the relationship so painstakingly built by Cardinal Daly and Archbishop Eames. "I was heartened to see the Archbishop and Lady Eames present at my Ordination in St Patrick's Cathedral, Armagh. We share the urgency of grasping the chance for peace thus avoiding a return to violence."

Of his many talents, Archbishop Brady is a man who makes things happen. When the papal visit to Ireland took place in 1979, he was assistant secretary of the national organising committee. He is a former editor of *Breifne*, Cavan's Historical Society journal, and played half-back on Cavan GAA senior county team. It was the sportsman in Monsignor Brady who set about arranging a papal audience for Jack Charlton and the Irish team at the World Cup in Italy, during the summer of 1990.

Armagh has extended the hand of friendship in every way. "I was fortunate in the extreme in that it was possible to draw from the vast experience of Cardinal Daly. If my appointment came unexpectedly, I was given both time and space to adjust." So if a quiet man from Cavan was chosen to fill the top ecclesiastical vacancy in Ireland, you may conclude it had much to do with his firm convictions. A natural communicator, he will read the road ahead, take advice, drive with skill, be solicitous for the welfare of his passengers.

Could there be a greater tribute to such as he, than 'turning our weapons into one great statue of Christ'?

The assistance of Diocesan Secretary Father Eugene Sweeney, who made relevant information available, is gratefully acknowledged.

Dean Herbert and Mrs Ann Cassidy

Beyond the sculptured stone of Cathedral Close is a microcosm of the Anglican Church in Ireland. Within this leafy precinct the secular merges with the spiritual—the strains of Stanford's Magnificat, the Dean and Chapter, Evensong, mullioned leaded windows and a newly-restored Walker organ. All professing the Christian faith, and those with alternative beliefs, are welcome at St Patrick's Cathedral. Guided tours during summer months may be conducted by its Dean, Herbert Cassidy. Now the Dean turns to his own background.

"It was 1989 when I came to Armagh, although my association as Vicar Choral with the Cathedral amounts to a term of 35 years. When Dean John Crooks, secretary of the General Synod, retired, I assumed both roles." A native of Cork, Dean Cassidy studied History and English at Trinity College Dublin. Following ordination in 1958, he came North. "I knew something of this part of the island because when I was a boy of eight, my parents brought me to live in Belfast during the war years. My father had been in the motor business and due to petrol shortage, all vehicles were off the road. We returned to Cork for my secondary education."

The young Herbert Cassidy was appointed curate of Holy Trinity Church, Belfast. "Vacancies were not easy to find", he recalls, "with 23 students in my year searching for curacies, huge competition existed. With larger parishes north of the border, experience here seemed to count for more." From Belfast, moving north-west to Londonderry he became Senior Curate of Christ Church Parish. "Those were happy years. I felt I had found my calling, all the choral music I wished, and now Ann, my wife. Ann had been a nurse at Royal Victoria Hospital, Belfast, but in truth, we'd met years earlier, while she was a boarding student at Dublin's Alexandra College."

Ann Cassidy exhibits such easy confidence one could almost accept clergy wives possess a built-in immunity that places them apart. "Not at all", she shakes her head. "I was born to this life. My father, H.F.O. Egerton, was Rector of Derryloran Parish, dying before I was two years old. With my mother and George, my older brother, we had six weeks to find alternative accommodation. Mother was a third-generation clergy wife and a Diocesan vacancy at Church House, Cathedral Close, Armagh, provided employment. From Armagh Girls' High School, where Mrs Castell was headmistress and Miss Lois Reid my form mistress, I boarded at Alexandra College, Dublin. Education there fitted us for life. At the annual College dance our partners were either medical or divinity students. My junior housemistress crisply informed me that Herbert Cassidy would make an excellent escort. Our paths crossed again when Herbert was a young curate in Belfast."

Ann Egerton now lived with her mother at 6 Vicar's Hill, Armagh, so her wedding in 1961 was held at St Patrick's Cathedral. "Such a happy and close-knit place it was. I recall my neighbours very well including Mr Fanning at number 8, headmaster of the Cathedral School. Lizzie Livingstone, the Fannings' housekeeper, was 'Lizzie Fanning' by my childish reckoning."

The Dean intervenes, "As Archbishop Simms had always taken a keen interest in my well-being when he was Bishop of Cork, it seemed natural he should officiate at our wedding. Dean Rennison was present, as was Canon Lillie, then Rector of St Mark's Parish. I have always passionately loved St Patrick's Cathedral, never finding it difficult to envisage congregations from medieval times in this holy place. I have never imagined, nor can I, becoming complacent in the face of its simplicity or beauty. Those who've gone before have stamped an identity at which I stand in awe. I also love music, see it as vital in worship, so Ann and myself enjoyed a full choir at our wedding."

In the early Sixties, Dean Cassidy recalls, "Derry City was a cauldron, quietly simmering. "It was quite obvious to all that only by gerrymandering was a unionist majority retained. My superior, Dean Griffin, spoke out strongly on the issue of parity of esteem. Not always popular for identifying this truth, time proved him right. On a personal note, the arrival of Nicola, our first child in 1962, made us a family."

One afternoon, while they were visiting Ann's mother on Vicar's Hill, Archdeacon Mayes called and if asked if Mr Cassidy would report to Archbishop McCann at The Palace. The Dean continues, "It seemed the parishes of

Aghavilly and Derrynoose had a vacancy. Satifying the Board of Nomination, I was appointed, succeeding the Rev. T.P.R. Kenny who moved to St Saviour's, Dobbin, Portadown. Aghavilly Rectory became our new home for the next three years. Thus, from the heart of Derry, we settled into a completely rural setting. It was here in 1964, Ian was born." As a young wife and mother, Ann dreaded her first meeting chairing the Mother's Union. "I spent the entire day, even when pegging out nappies in the back garden, reciting, 'On behalf of Aghavilly and Derrynoose Mothers' Union, I have much pleasure in welcoming Dr Hilary Mayes to our meeting.'" The evening went smoothly and, before long, Mrs Ann Cassidy was elected chairman of the Young Members Committee. "That was an exciting time in the organisation when we introduced child sex education, marriage and drugs as important topics. Confidence came with experience and I remember chairing meetings with attendances exceeding 300."

Another summons by the Archbishop presented Mr Cassidy with a daunting task. Portadown now required attention, as a new parish and a new church were to be established in that area. Taking charge required tenacity and purpose. "'Was I interested?' the Archbishop wanted to know. There was no guarantee this futuristic plan would work and I already had happy parishes of my own. Yes, it was a challenge but what should I do? Arriving home at Aghavilly Rectory I told Ann to start packing!

"Services began at the Church Hall in 1963", the Dean continues. "At that time celebrations marking 1,400 years since the sailing of St Columba to Iona were in progress. From this missionary Saint, a name for our new parish emerged." As priest in charge of a church he had fostered from its foundations, Mr Cassidy found himself constructing a new parish, fund raising, welding a community and subsequently, building a new Church and parish hall. "We now had Joanne, our youngest child, who was born in 1968. It was fascinating to watch the parish grow and develop its own individual character. Time passed and what began as a dream matured into 20 years of our lives, probably the happiest Ann and myself had known."

Love of children places Ann Cassidy central to the heart of her own family. To improve the quality of life for children around her, Ann took an important step in 1980, becoming a mature student. "I have always realised and respected the importance of nursery and pre-school playgroups and both were now coming into focus. A child gains confidence from the benefit of educational play in a community setting. I now had the necessary, formal requirements to establish a playgroup in Portadown. I decided to take a step further and become a nursery nurse with the Rupert Stanley College, Belfast, not dreaming that an important upheaval in our pastoral life was imminent." Dean Cassidy resumes the story. "One morning, as Christmas 1984 approached, Bishop Wilson of Kilmore, Co. Cavan, rang the Rectory doorbell. 'I require a new Dean,' he informed me crisply, issuing an invitation to visit. We did and fell in love with both Kilmore Cathedral and parish. Reminiscent of Aghavilly's rural setting, people were kind and supportive."

Proving herself a woman of substance and determination, Ann Cassidy continued with her work as a nursery nurse in Portadown. This involved considerable travelling on poor roads. "My youngest daughter, Joanne, also remained at school in Armagh as there could be no disruption to her education at a crucial time. Juggling church duties, home responsibilities and travelling was exhausting, but, like everything rewarding, wonderful when completed! I relished that achievement", she smiles. "Our children were now at university and every weekend the Deanery rang with laughter as they brought friends to share this idyllic home in the countryside."

Dean Cassidy recalls how, quite unexpectedly, a letter from the Archbishop announced the imminent retirement of Dean John Crooks from St Patrick's Cathedral. "It posed the same question, 'Was I interested?' I did not deliberate. Armagh is my spiritual home, here was the choir, choral music and unrivalled dignity. Remember I had been brought up in the cathedral tradition and this appointment was twinned with a tempting prospect, responsibility for Archbishop Robinson's Library. Because former Deans had little professional assistance, the Library was rarely open to the public. When I requested an assistant librarian, Mr Harry Carson, eminently qualified, was retiring from the Library Board. He was duly appointed. With an army of willing volunteers, books were cleaned, tidied, catalogued and computerised. Today we provide an invaluable source and link for members of the public who wish to delve into the past history of our country. A full-time assistant clerk now deals efficiently with both library system and visitors but I try to be there as often as possible. Cathedral matters

Dean Herbert Cassidy
and Mrs Ann Cassidy
Photograph by Ian Maginess

demand time, along with my work as honorary secretary of the General Synod."

Two centuries ago, Archbishop Robinson built his Library complete with residence. This fine Regency dwelling, unoccupied since Dean Lillie's residency, required energy and imagination to bring about its present transformation. Both qualities are reflected in Ann Cassidy's tasteful decor. Colours harmonise, pastel yellow, brilliant white and floral chintz.

"Much of this is a happy accident", she confesses. "My mother's furniture, large and loved, slotted handsomely with the character of our dining room." Deanery furnishings blend in seamless virtuosity. Ann Cassidy proves a welcoming hostess to a stream of visiting dignitaries. "I love flowers", she admits, indicating a cascade of old-fashioned blooms on a nearby table. "Perhaps by next year I'll have my garden landscaped", she adds, "and if I do it will have been achieved by hard work. Each time I've tamed a wilderness we've moved on", she adds wistfully. "Heaven will be someone saying, 'Here is an immaculate garden in which to relax and one you never need to leave'. I would add 'no more fundraising', which constituted so much of my life!"

Since becoming Dean of St Patrick's Cathedral, Herbert Cassidy met with Queen Elizabeth and Prince Philip when the City Charter was conferred on 9 March 1995. "For this event, we released from the Library, silver maces belonging to the original City Council. These occupied a place of honour at the ceremony. Prince Charles had preceded his parents with this special news. We were guests in 1994 when Prime Minister John Major officially opened St Patrick's Trian. During that year, President Mary Robinson attended an ecumenical service at the Cathedral and I met President Mary McAleese in her capacity as Pro-Vice Chancellor when Queen's University Outreach at Armagh formally opened. I have a treasured photograph taken in conversation with Mother Teresa of Calcutta, who graced our city with her presence. Personal and memorable occasions were the baptisms that I myself conducted, of our grandchildren Emma, James, Daire, Anna, Catherine and Maeve. Our daughter Joanne was always sportingly competitive. Her husband, Alan Bates, has a distinguished record in the world of sport. An Irish Superstar, Alan, as canoeist, was a former silver medallist in the Commonwealth Games."

On 25 July 1999, which was also his birthday, Dean Herbert Cassidy celebrated the 40th anniversary of his ordination to the priesthood. "As the date fell on Sunday, I returned to the church in which I was ordained a priest at the invitation of the Rector. The event marked a significant milestone in my life. Herbert, my father, died in 1985 and my mother, Frederica, aged 93, was able to attend. She was also present 40 years ago! Retirement crosses my mind but first I must see plans through for repairs and badly needed enhancement of the Cathedral in time for Millennial celebrations. Our architect has warned costs are phenomenal so a funding appeal will become necessary. Friends of the Cathedral are sponsoring a stained-glass window celebrating aspects of Irish Saints and Celtic spirituality and this is presently under commission. For St Patrick's Day, 2000 AD, Archbishop Eames has arranged a special Church of Ireland Conference concentrating on our primatial city. Visitors from all over Ireland will attend with the Archbishop of Canterbury being chief speaker. This distinguished guest will conduct our opening and closing services. In addition, a choral musical composition focusing on a new century will have its premiere in St Patrick's Cathedral next year."

While he subscribes to a belief that this Cathedral is a sacred building in which reverence for God is made manifest, Dean Cassidy has a longing that all in Ireland, while not agreeing on everything, might cultivate tolerance for other points of view and live in harmony. "This surely is the essence of Christanity, certainly from an Anglican point of view."

For such a traumatic parting as would be entailed in retirement, Dean Cassidy knows he must prepare in advance. "Leaving my congregation, St Patrick's beloved choir and our Walker organ will prove difficult. Now painstakingly restored, this organ has majesty, capability and historical tradition. I identify so entirely with its glorious sound that, banished to a desert island, in company with Shakespeare, the Bible and the Robinson Library, would it be too much to ask for a recording of Stanford's *Evening Canticles* in G, where a boy soprano solo takes us through the *Magnificat*?" An uncommon combination, yet weighed against the Dean's stewardship, one that balances perfectly.

Tom Canavan

As this century draws to a close so does the Christian Brothers' Community in Armagh City. By contrast, the first formal engagement Councillor Thomas Canavan attended as Mayor of Armagh City and District was a Mass of thanksgiving commemorating the educational commitment of the Brothers. At St Patrick's Cathedral an entire parish, together with representatives and friends from every school in the area, expressed profound gratitude for 148 years of dedicated service by the Christian Brothers.

"It was a solemn occasion", Mayor Canavan recalls, "for we were saying goodbye to a Community that gave selflessly to education since 1851. Outgoing Mayor Robert Turner had previously held a reception to mark the departure of four Christian Brothers working and residing in this parish—Bro. Leo Kelly, principal of St Patrick's Grammar School, Bro. Larry Ennis, Bro. Dermot McDermott and Bro. Des Young. On that occasion, a painting of St Patrick's Grammar School was presented to Bro. Kelly by Mayor Turner. Guests at the Palace included teaching staff and parents from St Patrick's Grammar School, the Christian Brothers' Primary School and head teachers from schools throughout the city.

"If I could speak for a moment on the concelebrated Mass, the chief celebrant, His Grace Archbishop Seán Brady, related how, in 1851, Archbishop Cullen issued an invitation to the Christian Brothers, asking if they would set up a school at Greenpark, Armagh. These schools were distinguished throughout Ireland, principally providing education for life. Encouraging the development of Irish culture, language and Christian inheritance, pupils left Greenpark confident in their ability to compete on equal footing with the best. It was a time when education was not free yet the Brothers never allowed lack of money to be an obstacle in the schooling of Armagh youth. If a family was known to be in need, the Brothers offered assistance in a discreet and respectful manner. With healthy emphasis on sport, Greenpark proved a nursery for many sporting clubs in Armagh, particularly the Gaelic Athletic Association.

"Non-Catholic pupils also attended the Christian Brothers' School at Greenpark and the story of one, the late William Johnston of Aghavilly, made local impact during the Second World War. Non-Catholic boys were made welcome, treated with respect, and ten of these past pupils became ministers of religion. They always spoke with gratitude of the quality education they had received.

"The music for this Mass was superb", concluded Mayor Canavan. "It was provided by the orchestra of St Patrick's Grammar School and choirs of the Grammar School, St Catherine's College and Christian Brothers' Primary School. A special Mass was composed by Father Liam Lawson and I have to say, there was also a certain attendant sadness. The century is drawing to a close and with it will go much that we once regarded as a way of life."

If a year is a long time in politics, this particular term of mayoral office, for Social Democratic and Labour Party Councillor Tom Canavan and his wife Roisín, includes the awesome civic leadership duty of greeting a new century. Glittering projects have been planned to provide audiences with lasting memories of talented musicians, choirs, artists, writers, producers and directors.

"Opening night at our new Theatre and Arts Centre promises to be a gala event", the Mayor comments. "Engagements are heavily booked for AD 2000 as it is possible to accommodate audiences of more than 350 in the main arena. Once again we hope to savour that legendary atmosphere associated with Armagh City Hall. Television is said to have usurped stage entertainment but many would disagree. Can you imagine the stage impact of a moment, voted to be the funniest in history, when a captured U-boat commander demanded the name of one of the Home Guard in *Dad's Army* and Captain Mainwaring yelled: 'Don't tell him your name, Pike!'"

Details surrounding the actual opening of the new Theatre remain privileged information but Mayor Canavan is positive of a return to elegant times when patrons dressed for formal or charity events. Bookings are guaranteed to stimulate demand for local services in a multiplicity of ways.

Hosting President Mary McAleese and her husband Martin at the Palace was a tremendous inception for any incoming Mayor. Having presented the President with the

Armagh coat of arms, Tom Canavan described the visit as "an exchange of friendship. We had met previously on matters concerning Queen's University Outreach at Armagh, a partnership of which the Council is justly proud. With our Chief Executive Desmond Mitchell and Council staff, guests were representative of this community and included Pauline Stanley, chief executive of Armagh and Dungannon Health Trust and Jack O'Hare, past principal of St Patrick's Primary School. President McAleese signed the Visitors Book, placing her name alongside famous dignitaries who have visited Armagh in the past. The President is always eager to receive positive news of Queen's University and it is a pleasure to mention Dr Tess Hurson, student support officer and lecturer at Armagh Campus, who encourages and draws results from her charges. Many are mature students who were unable to pursue earlier academic ideals. The President assured me that she was delighted to visit Armagh and we look forward to her return in the future.

"Restoration of Newry Canal is something I wholeheartedly support. Running as it does through the jurisdiction of Newry and Mourne, Portadown and Banbridge Councils, this would positively involve the villages of Jerrettspass, Poyntzpass, Scarva and Tandragee, creating a demand for accommodation, restaurants, fishing tackle, boats and chandlery. Following the Ulster Waterways Group annual conference, accountancy giant Price Waterhouse Coopers backed this ambitious scheme. Regeneration costs are significant but so are benefits. The original canal, built in 1740, was for the transport of coal from Coalisland to Newry. It was then taken by ship to Dublin and further. I visualise endless possibilities for increased tourism including the renting of narrowboats for holidays and trips. This will benefit schools, youth groups, people with disabilities or the elderly who might find this a pleasant form of relaxation. Five years ago, Ballyconnell Canal in the Republic of Ireland cost £35 million to restore and now generates £1 million each mile, per annum. We've conducted a hydrological survey and physically, it can be done. A real investment indeed, if we could achieve results similar to those of Ballyconnell."

Gerry Cosgrove, general secretary of the SDLP, wrote to Mayor Canavan following his election: "I often say the SDLP 'serves and leads'. You have served the community well over the years and now you have the opportunity to lead your community in true partnership..."

"My community is close-knit", Tom Canavan assures. "Poyntzpass village shares its joys and, equally, shoulders its grief. This was acutely evident when good friends Phillip Allen and Damien Trainor were murdered in my brother's bar. Described as an example to the rest of Northern Ireland, these lads were known and liked by everyone. I grew up and socialised with Damien's father, Seán. It was from Trainor's garage my first car was bought and we've enjoyed a business relationship ever since. I have equal respect for the Allen family. That evening of the atrocity I remained on call and at daybreak the following morning, was asked to make a comment by the BBC. It grieved when I offered condolence yet I was proud to say that we would not allow evil to divide us.

"It hasn't", he reiterates. "Poyntzpass, in terms of neighbourly respect, is an example to all. Good community relations were clearly evident throughout this dreadful time. Damien's funeral took place in the morning and all local Protestant clerics came to pay their respects. Our chapel couldn't accommodate the mourners so the service was relayed by loudspeaker. One ordeal over, everyone then attended Phillip's interment.

"Donations came from many, requesting a suitable memorial for these young men. We decided on a wrought-iron seat placed near the scene of this tragedy but the craftsman in question refused to take payment for his work. We now plan to invest the fund in a form of bursary, perhaps for the benefit of a child who deserves recognition. One excellent example in practice is the memorial to our late chemist, Donal O'Neill. Donal was friend and advisor to all and a great ally in times of anxiety or illness. Villagers contributed to honour his memory in an annual award for which local primary school children are nominated for some aspect of caring. The award takes place at Christmas during our Village Care for the Elderly Society dinner and the award is presented by Mrs O'Neill.

"I regret to say in times past we had two other sectarian murders. Seán McShane was killed in a bookmaker's shop. His family coped with the ultimate hypocrisy, a claim of mistaken identity. Another victim, Fred Morton, was a breadman on his way to work. I must have dealt with Fred in a business capacity for 20 years. I detest and deplore inhumanity and particularly that which reduces and degrades us in the eyes of the world."

Tom Canavan is essentially a family man and his

convictions are such that he joined the SDLP to set an example to his sons. "Parents must agree that children are easily drawn into wrong company. Juvenile crime is one of our afflictions and every parent should be asking *where is my child tonight?* The world is a dangerous place and parental control seems seriously on the decline. We are answerable for our children's behaviour and, brought up with guidelines, children are as capable of bringing joy as sorrow. By my politics I have shown that I support democracy obtained by peaceful means, abhorring intimidation and violence. Seamus Mallon, prior to becoming an MP, asked me to keep the electoral register for this area. I've now been involved in various ways for 26 years. When Seamus became a Member of Parliament, I stood for Cusher Ward. It can be fairly said that I represent our electorate on an equal basis and they are free to call on me at all times.

"Our sons, Declan, Cathal and Michael have all gone from home. They chose to marry in the same year, which proved to be rather costly! I run a farm, beef cattle mainly, and my wife, Roisín, was a nurse who originated from a farming background. She enjoys keeping fit, often walking two miles each day. I accompany her when possible. Roisín provides valuable support at civic functions and enjoys meeting people from every stratum of society. Whatever the occasion, we are always received with warmth and kindess.

"I enjoy involving and imparting information to the community and for this reason, was pleased to unveil *Insight*, a new glossy newsletter that will be delivered quarterly to homes in the area. This attractively produced magazine tells our public exactly what is happening within each council department as well as giving information on matters of local interest. It is compiled by a small team of officers, and we always look forward to the next issue. On the topic of magazines, Armagh man Paddy McGarvey, who had been a Fleet Street journalist for many years, founded the Irish Parliament Trust in Armagh during the early Nineties. Like myself, a man of mature years", Tom smiles, "Paddy had the courage to undertake publication of a historical magazine with secondary schools in mind. Supported by the European Union Special Support Fund for Peace and Reconciliation, his magazine delineated thousands of forgotten Scots-Irish Presbyterians who fled British religious repression in the 18th century. It was a quality work which 1,100 schools throughout Ireland received, and deserves mention. Paddy returned to England earlier this year and we miss his colourful presence."

In addition to civic engagements, Tom sits on the public liaison committee and committees associated with housing and planning, leisure and tourism, and policy and resources. Poyntzpass Development Committee is anxious to see the village shop restored and is acutely concerned about the lack of employment in rural areas.

"Customer loyalty is vital to the small shopkeeper, indeed they depend upon it. People have no qualms about driving over the border to buy petrol or food yet expect local shopkeepers to provide a service in emergencies. In the past, our youth had little choice but to leave rural areas to find employment but, should those enterprises I spoke of succeed, this pattern will change. Markethill benefited enormously from the International Fund for Ireland and Community Economic Regeneration.

"The town recently refurbished its derelict former courthouse and Johnston House on Fairgreen Road. Both offer a neutral venue where the community meets and develops relationships. Seamus Mallon, MP, was loud in his praise for the overall outcome and particularly the contribution of William Johnston, chairman of Markethill Development Enterprise. Markethill's commercial sector suffered setbacks from a massive bombing campaign but new initiatives such as this point to a brighter future for the whole area."

A sportsman in his youth and Gaelic footballer for Carrickcruppen, South Armagh, Mayor Tom Canavan was delighted when Armagh won the Ulster Championship for the first time in 17 years. Tom's stalwart reputation: *They Shall Not Pass*, is reflected by his nephew, Brian, presently team co-manager and a player when Armagh last won the Ulster Championship. Planning a reception for the team at the Palace, Tom comments, "It was a great moment for Armagh substitute, Gerard Houlihan, decidedly one of the old sporting brigade. Called onto the field shortly before the match ended, Gerard has gone out in glory, tasting a victory that has eluded him for 16 years, as his team outshone arch-enemy Down. I look forward to having a photograph taken with the victorious Armagh team for my grandchildren.

"In this book my children and grandchildren will have another memento, an authentic insight into a century of social history of Armagh county. Writing is what our culture does best and launching this work fills me with immense pride. It is a literary celebration that speaks of men, women and children whose roots are embedded in the tradition of this ancient City and District. Invisible strings connect us with Armachians throughout the globe who are not forgotten. Many have never or rarely enjoyed a public voice yet each person portrayed here proves they have not passed this way in vain. Ten decades provide a stage for the evolution of an amazing range of issues. You will find opinion, hope, fear, joy, sorrow, compassion, confusion, reflection and observation. It shows how lives were lived, is an excellent read and worthy of a place on every bookshelf.

"To be part of such history is to be immortalised. None of us would ask for more."

Mayor Tom Canavan

Catherine McCullough and Greer Ramsey

Did you realise the British Museum originated from a bequest given by Sir Hans Sloane, of Killyleagh, Co. Down? Catherine McCullough, curator of Armagh County Museum has this information easily at her fingertips.

"In 1753", she explains, "Sir Hans made available objects of history, works of art, books and manuscripts for a sum of £20,000, or two-fifths their original cost. His offer was accepted and the British Museum opened in 1759, George III presenting this institution with a collection of Egyptian antiquities in 1802. Sharing our inheritance with future generations has been a practice for centuries. Society without historical or material records is unthinkable."

Newly refurbished, Armagh County Museum literally sparkles. Present exhibitions indicate a rich and varied history afforded by this city and district. Catherine, who holds a Master's degree in Economic and Social History from the University of St Andrew's, has been its curator since 1992. "A branch of the Ulster Museum, we are now part of a new structure, National Museums and Galleries of Northern Ireland", contributes Catherine. "The outdated notion of a museum as a place of hush, everyone creeping on tiptoe, has radically changed. When the education curriculum becomes more object-orientated, a museum such as ours provides teachers and students with visual source material, a pick-and-mix that may include the dynamics of ceramics, maps, posters, our local railway and varied aspects of social history."

Deputy curator Dr Greer Ramsey, a graduate archaeologist, joined Armagh County Museum staff in 1993. Both Greer and Catherine are anxious to extend special exhibitions in liaison with the Southern Education and Library Board. "School bookings swell our numbers but more importantly, widen the child's concept of times past. Temporary displays change approximately every six weeks", he continues, "so donated artefacts are vital, extending and enriching the lives of a new generation." Costume pieces, both curators agree, demand most in terms of care, and storage space is a real problem. "This was the first county museum in Ireland and is affectionately considered the treasure house of Co. Armagh, housing exceptionally fine natural and scientific artefacts", Greer explains.

"This building serves as a meeting place for the Natural History and Philosophical Society which maintains a Reading Room. This body still owns the building but our local council assumed responsibility for a museum in 1931. Armagh County Museum presently hosts County Armagh Art Club, Armagh City and District Arts Committee and Armagh Field Naturalists Society. Historian T.G.F. Paterson was honorary curator of the Society's museum, a massive figure in terms of local knowledge and social history. He became a full-time curator for more than 20 years. Roger Weatherup followed in the footsteps of Paterson, serving this Museum as curator for almost 30 years."

Third in curatorial succession, Catherine assumes responsibility for overall administration, staff management, maintaining the fabric of the building, changing exhibitions on a flexible or seasonal basis, taking local events into account with professional caring and cataloguing of donated artefacts. "But", she stresses, "it is my opinion that a museum's usefulness should be gauged on the help it renders to students and general public." In terms of layout, Catherine and Greer have skilfully organised a visual representation of a people whose past was lived close to the land. Simple implements, a turf spade with narrowing edge evokes a farmer in a bog, eking out a living. Horse brasses, shoes and harness, once a blacksmith's trade, are now rare as the great Clydesdale who ploughed a perfect furrow.

For more than a century our population depended on linen and wool. Intricacies of carding, spinning and weaving are nostalgically preserved along with a redundant factory clock. Who, we wonder, obeyed its unspoken authority, checking in each morning or rushing home after a day's labour? Here too are the factory payslips, the identity card of a power station linesman and a gas mask from the last war. Local taxidermist Kenny Murphy contributes his unique skill in bird and animal collections, the countryside at home, tastefully arranged in glass cabinets. Needlework has its place and the Armagh Community Quilt, designed and made entirely by local needlewomen, symbolises a spirit of harmony besides celebrating the Armagh Together year in honour of St Patrick, 1994-95.

Church and State plays their historic parts. Here is a treasured family bible, a lace wedding dress, an afternoon gown, a beaded glove. Within this context, Catherine makes an interesting comment. "Armagh County Museum has always played an important role when a family home is being cleared following bereavement. At a loss as to how they might preserve old photographs, documents, militaria, or items difficult to place, they remember us. Museums in general operate a code of honour. Regardless of how desirable an artefact, should its history not fall within our specified area, we feel duty bound to hand it over to its ethnic origins. Naturally this is discussed with the donor."

Art, especially that of local painters, is paramount to any museum. Visitors to Armagh County Museum are greeted in the foyer by *The Old Callan Bridge,* John Luke's important landscape. Luke, when a boy, painted King William on a gable wall before enrolling for evening classes at Belfast School of Art. Studying at the Slade School of Fine Arts he won the Robert Ross scholarship. Luke was meticulous in every way and precision identifies his work. For a time he dwelt near Killylea, Co. Armagh, here completing many of his best-loved paintings. *The Old Callan Bridge* was chosen as cover art for Armagh man John O'Connor's colloquial writings, *Come Day, Go Day*, re-issued in 1984.

Every study does tell a story. James Black, a Scottish artist, spent time in Armagh during the early 19th century, completing a handsome oil painting of the city, now hanging in the main exhibition hall. Black shows our Church of Ireland Cathedral complete with spire in 1810, and the Market Cross in place before it was injured during a riot in 1813. "There are interesting theories on the disappearance of the Cathedral spire", Greer contributes. "Some say it became unstable and parishioners were reluctant to attend church in case it toppled over and came crashing down. As for the Market Cross, that was laid up for safe keeping in the crypt of the Church of Ireland Cathedral. On a rather sombre note, Black was said to have died from injuries sustained in coming to the defence of a woman during a domestic dispute. A poor reward for this man's chivalry!"

Museum staff are proud of a well-documented library and will gladly make books available for research purposes. "T.G.F. Paterson's writings are here", Catherine indicates a row of handsome volumes. "We have *Burke's Peerage,* ongoing from 1857. The son of an Irishman who settled in London, Sir John Burke was appointed Ulster King of Arms in 1853, keeper of state papers in Ireland and LL.D of Dublin in 1867. Sir John Burke published the *Peerage* annually from 1847. We're constantly augmenting our collection of *Who Was Who* and I believe a new book is presently about to leave the press entitled *Who's Who in Northern Ireland.* By the same token we retrieve features of local interest from daily and provincial newspapers. We've archived entire series from the *Ulster Gazette*, and pen drawings by artist Hampton Ewart."

A vital function of Armagh County Museum is assisting with intensively researched local history. "We regard this as a public service", Greer points out. "Topics do vary. Recently we had a spate of interest in the Vikings and were delighted to share substantial information with students. Naturally archaeological queries are dear to my heart but we deal with such a wide range of subjects. Using the Museum as a starting point can save time and energy for tourists for here is a glimpse of the county, neatly condensed. Group visits", he stresses, "are always welcome."

Museum staff work in harmony, setting up exhibitions or sharing research. Catherine and Greer acknowledge personal assistant Sarah Millsopp and attendants Brian Rooney, Roy Parkes and Seán Barden who keep a watchful eye as well as hanging exhibits or taking time to chat with visitors. "'Friends of the Museum' have our interests at the core of their organisation and are presently fund-raising to augment the collection."

A novel idea of 'Local Identity' is the chosen theme by which the Museum means to celebrate 2000 AD. "We will attempt to isolate what, in particular, distinguishes an Armachian from the rest of our island population", Catherine points out. "Culture we have in abundance, music, dance, poetry, needlework, art and crafts, and pertinent artefacts are sure to come our way. Important to the concept is a thesis donated by Darby Reid, a retired member of the teaching staff at Royal School, Armagh. A collection of photographs by Allison Studio, which was held in great affection by local people, tells a story in sepia."

The fabric of our past is woven with a master cord yet

the present makes an equally exciting statement. “An example of this”, Catherine suggests, “is the Millennium Quilt, under the guidance of quilt team co-ordinator Catherine Maxwell. Due for completion by the year 2000, this ongoing work, commissioned and funded by Armagh City and District Arts Committee, will augment our celebratory exhibition.”

The fabric of times long gone provides much to appreciate. By their painstaking efforts, Catherine and Greer are tastefully preserving our past for future generations. Before leaving, one visitor drops a coin into the donations box. A small price to assist future purchases and the preservation of this delightful ‘treasure house of Co. Armagh’.

Catherine McCullough, curator of
Armagh County Museum,
and deputy curator
Dr Greer Ramsey, arranging work for a
special summer exhibition,
Sources of Inspiration

Charles Armstrong

'Stop in God's name', was the stark headline, quoting Cardinal Tomás Ó Fiaich, which many newspapers carried on the morning of Tuesday 15 November 1983. Speaking from Maynooth, where he was presiding over the autumn meeting of Irish bishops, Cardinal Ó Fiaich said he was shocked and saddened to hear of the brutal murder of Official Unionist Chairman of Armagh District Council, Frederick Charles Armstrong, JP. Jean Armstrong vividly recalls the evening on which her husband died.

"We then lived at St Mark's Place on The Mall. As Charlie prepared to leave for Monday evening's Council meeting, he hurriedly kissed me on the cheek, pausing at the door to call over his shoulder, 'I won't be late'." It is almost 16 years since that evening but her pain is acute and the memory raw. "A few hours later when the children were in bed I heard an explosion followed by a second impact. Going outside, I stood listening on the pavement. It was a frosty night and in the unearthly stillness, something told me Charlie was in danger. Next door neighbours, Dr Patrick Kellett and his wife, Audrey, joined me and we exchanged a few comments before going inside.

"Moments later the bell rang. The experience was unreal. Police Superintendent George Harrison came inside, removing his cap. 'Your husband...' The look on his face said everything. I didn't need to be told. Charlie was dead."

Under cover of darkness, despite closed-circuit camera observation of the carpark at Council headquarters, terrorists fitted a device to Charles Armstrong's red Triumph Acclaim. Minutes before, inside the Council building, Chairman Armstrong had denounced the loyalist murder, which took place a week previously, of Armagh man Adrian Carroll.

The bleakness of that scene has nothing in common with the lifestyle Jean Armstrong has painstakingly recreated. And yet there are unchanging signs that say otherwise. Hands on a marble clock, once Charlie's pride and joy, indicate that it is twenty past four—the time it stopped on the night he died. "People say it gets easier", Jean says, "but it doesn't." Confronted with such deep-seated agony, it feels improper to tape her comments, but she is adamant that Charlie's life and contribution be included in a compendium of local history. Jean recounts nightmare events that followed:

"My home was suddenly full of people. Dr Cole arrived, putting his arms about me as neighbours and friends flooded through the door. The Rev. Ian Ellis was a tremendous source of strength in our sorrow and I will never forget all those who shared the burden by helping in the home. My children were deranged and I remember wishing these murderers had to face the aftermath of their own evil. Almost as much could be said of the media who showed no sensitivity whatsoever. Heather, my daughter, was watching television in her mobile home when *Hill Street Blues* was interrupted by a news flash. She sat stunned when they said an explosion had occurred at Armagh Council offices. To them it was simply one more in a violent litany regardless of the impact to family members unaware of his death. Heather had seen her father that morning when she called to share a cup of tea with us. He was outside, checking under his car—all part of the routine for a Major in the 2nd Co. Armagh Battalion, Ulster Defence Regiment. They exchanged a joke, saying it was 'well for some' who could turn up for work at 9.45am. For his personal safety, Charlie had to stagger working hours. When his death became known, the Ulster Defence Regiment stepped in, coping with all arrangements for his funeral."

Charles Armstrong was Chairman of Armagh District Council for three consecutive years, from 1981 until his death in November 1983. He also served as the last Vice-Chairman of the old Armagh Urban District Council, which was reorganised in 1973.

"Charlie was interested in positive aspects of local government", Jean comments, recalling that Sir Norman Stronge first proposed he stand for election. "We married in 1953, moving into Swiss House on the Newry Road which had been built by his grandfather. Charles was probably the most energetic person I've ever known. After a day as manager of the Gas Board, he'd take a short rest, then off he'd go, attending perhaps three meetings that evening. We lived for a time at Gas Lane where a house was provided as part of his job. A past chairman of the

Irish Gas Association, Charlie saw obvious advantages in bringing North Sea gas to the island of Ireland. With the late Harold McCusker, Member of Parliament for Armagh, he visited Westminster, presenting his proposal. Despite a valiant effort, there was fierce opposition from fellow members who insisted that paramilitaries would damage any pipeline linking North and South. It is something of an irony that consumers have paid excessively for energy ever since and now, a trouble-free link exists. Charlie was a long-serving member of the Junior Chamber of Commerce and seeing Armagh flourish was his greatest wish. Despite the fact that he had impartial and absolute respect for all sections of the community, rioters attacked our home in 1972. It speaks volumes for society at the time when I say mothers actually provided rocks for eight-year-old children to hurl. Within days of our leaving, the house was petrol-bombed. For six months our family was apart, living in four separate houses.

"Regardless of personal difficulties, Charlie consistently attempted to persuade fellow councillors to keep party politics out of debates. He also objected to the discussion in the chamber of a resolution calling for all loyalist detainees to be released. As a newly elected Party chairman in June 1981, Charlie told councillors that sniping, attempting to score political points and political wrangling would not serve the community. Within the remit of council business he served on the Southern Education and Library Board and management committees of several schools. Seeing the good sense of amalgamating two grammar schools—Royal School, Armagh and the Girls' High School—he voted against the Party on this issue. The establishment of Armagh Planetarium was of immense interest to Charlie and he furthered this initiative in every way possible. As a conservationist he was a dedicated Friend of Armagh County Museum. Regardless of how much work he had logged, Charlie saw it as a point of honour that he complete every task."

With eight children to rear, Jean Armstrong confined her interests to home and family.

"Charlie loved his children and I often felt he was taken from them at a time when they needed him most. Eldest to youngest we had Yvonne, Fred, Janet, Henry, Heather, Carol and our twins, Michael and David, who were just 14. We were numbed, desperately craving to have him back. That pain is just as intense but if I didn't have it, I'd have forgotten Charlie, and that I will never do. My mother lived in Victoria Street and I visited her that evening. She loved my husband as if he'd been her own son. Our eldest boys coped so well; they were marvellous. Council official Norman Megaw came at once, doing what he could to help. Administrative officer Ivan Baxter was close by the scene when Charlie died. He had the presence of mind to remove my husband's wedding ring, which he returned to me. It was Remembrance Sunday when Charlie carried out his last engagement, laying a wreath at the Cenotaph. Each Armistice Day anniversary since then, friends call with flowers or telephone to say they are thinking of us."

A congregation of mourners at St Mark's Parish Church included Chris Patten and members of Armagh District Council. In a glowing tribute, Archdeacon Fred Gowing, Rector of Mullavilly, contrasted Mr Armstrong's public service with the destructiveness of his killers. The Archdeacon described Mr Armstrong as a man whom any church would be proud to have as a member and his life, a testimony to all: "Charles was a devoted husband and a loving father to his eight children and everyone shares in their grief and loss. He had a sense of civic responsibility, worked tirelessly for the good of all sections of the community and was respected by political opponents and friends.

"His service with the Ulster Defence Regiment was evidence of his concern for others. Good relationships in the community are only possible when there are those prepared to risk their lives to protect the civilian population from wicked men who seem determined to destroy all that we hold sacred. Charles Armstrong was a reconciler, and during the years I have known him, my admiration for his courage and integrity increased. Evil men have destroyed the body of a gracious man of peace and goodwill but they cannot destroy his spirit, all that he stood for and lived for because it was the spirit of God which neither bomb nor bullet, Armalite nor mortar can destroy."

The Archdeacon then spoke of the sin of silence and called for those with information on this evil deed to speak out. Cardinal Tomás Ó Fiaich made it known that in all his associations with Mr Armstrong he had been impressed by his efforts to promote harmony and co-operation. Offering profound sympathy to Jean Armstrong and her children, Cardinal Ó Fiaich's message to the terrorists was clear: "Only a depraved mind could plan and carry out this foul deed. Stop in God's name before you leave our country in ruins."

Jean adds: "The congregation sang Charlie's favourite hymn, *Be Thou My Vision*. Speaking for myself, the entire service passed in a daze but many commented on the dignity in which it was conducted."

As evidence came to light, a mercury tilt switch was believed to have been the triggering device for the explosives, the same method by which his friend, Conservative spokesman on Northern Ireland Airey Neave, met his death as he left the underground carpark at the House of Commons in March 1979. An immediate call for additional protection of all public representatives was made to Secretary of State James Prior. It was also requested that council chambers be properly guarded whenever councillors met. Charles Armstrong, aged 54, was the third Official Unionist member of the Council to have been murdered. Councillor Sam Foster assumed the office of Chairman. Picking up the torch, he fulfilled many engagements on behalf of the late Charles Armstrong. One of the most emotional events was Mrs Jean Armstrong's unveiling of her husband's official portrait at Council headquarters. A special function room was then formally opened by Jean in memory of her husband and has been known ever since as the Armstrong Room. One hundred guests attended the ceremony. Chairman Foster related Charles Armstrong's association with local government in Armagh since 1973 when he was first elected onto the Urban District Council. He spoke of Mr Armstrong's devoted service as Chairman from 1981 until his tragic murder on 14 November 1983.

Guests crowding the main entrance hall to the Council Offices then saw the first official portrait of Mr Armstrong unveiled by his widow. A second portrait hangs above the fireplace of the Armstrong Room and Jean Armstrong was again invited to unveil a commemorative plaque. To mark the occasion, Mrs Doreen Foster, wife of the then Chairman, presented Mrs Armstrong with a Tyrone Crystal rose bowl.

Councillor Douglas Hutchinson of the Ulster Democratic Unionist Party commented: "It is a shame that a man like Charlie has been taken from his wife and family. I would extend God's blessing to her and her children." Councillor Pat Brannigan, on behalf of the Social and Democratic Labour Party, who was visibly moved, said: "This is a sad occasion. Not a day passes that we do not remember Charlie. If he is looking down from Heaven, how amused he must be to see his portrait placed so fittingly, between Queen Mary I and King William III." Former Council Chairman Norman Creswell referred to Mr Armstrong as a man of integrity and courage. Administrative officer Ivan Baxter paid tribute to Mr Armstrong, adding that they had been friends as young men. Responding on behalf of the Armstrong Family, Fred, the eldest son, thanked everyone concerned for the impressive memorial to his late father.

A year after Charles Armstrong's death, Jean and her children dedicated a radiant stained-glass window to his memory in St Mark's Parish Church. It depicts St Mark and St Patrick in an attitude of peace. It remains a bitter truth that eight children were robbed of a father and provider, Jean Armstrong of a husband and friend, and the community of an honourable citizen and leader.

"I have since had a cousin, Jack Megaw, murdered at the War Memorial in Enniskillen", says Jean sadly. "I find it hard to forgive either murders but have often asked that God may forgive the perpetrators."

Having moved from her home on The Mall with all its memories, Jean now lives quietly in a secluded home nearby. "My children remain in constant touch. In the early months after Charlie's death I spent hours reading letters and messages of sympathy and these helped so much at the time. There are many instances which would serve to pay tribute to Charlie's good nature but I'll use only one. An old chap used to call at our home, always with a sob story. He had previously worked for the Gas Company and what an excellent sense of timing he had, as Charlie was sure to be at home. If I answered the door he would ask if 'the Boss' was in. Always in need, we never gave him money for that would have gone on hard liquor. On these occasions my larder was raided and newly baked bread, butter and a packet of tea handed over, with perhaps a jacket or trousers to keep out the cold. I say this simply because Charlie always had time and a kind word for those less well off than himself.

"While I cope, I would not say I have come to terms with Charlie's death and probably never will. In this context, I must pay tribute to the Ulster Defence Regiment's Benevolent Fund which finances and arranges outings for widows and dependants and always remember us at Christmas."

Charles Frederick Armstrong, JP

Her dignity belies the jolt that accompanies unexpectedly coming upon a photograph or memento, which Charles may have given her in the past. A painting of Highland cattle which he chose for their former home brings a certain comfort or the marble clock which once belonged to her father, Joseph Megaw, a policeman at Russell Street Station, Armagh. Dating to 1898, this clock was made by West of Dublin. On retirement, District Inspector Lynn gave it to Jean's father. It next fell to Charles and winding this clock became a weekly ritual. It remains as he left it, both hands frozen at twenty minutes past four.

Such details serve to reinforce the fact that Charles Armstrong will never be just another statistic in a litany of horror. His death remains as acutely painful to those who loved him as it did that frosty November night in 1983.

A precious possession is a tribute to her late husband, written by a friend, Sybil Reardon. In thanking Jean for her deeply personal insight, she has also agreed to share this epitaph:

In Proud and Fond Memory of
Major Frederick Charles Armstrong

The noble task you set yourself was merely interrupted on 14 November 1983. May we who are left with prideful memories be ever mindful of the awesome responsibility which now rests with us. To increase our resolve to walk zealously for the cause of peace, for which, in such great measure of devotion, you gave so much. You have not died in vain for under God, the torch you held so high shall illuminate our road to a new birth of freedom, a new rule that will envelop us all in love, justice and brotherhood in our beloved country.

Sybil Reardon: 1983

Jackie Connolly

Gifted local artist Jackie Connolly has been perfecting his craft for 40 years. It was in 1994, however, that his name shot to fame, when he won the prestigious Royal Ulster Academy Award for Best Painting. Before he had time to wipe his brushes Jackie took, in quick succession, first prize for the Armagh Together Super Pro Loco Painting Competition, then the William Conor Award at the Royal Ulster Academy of Arts exhibition in Belfast.

To profile the artist as a young man, he began drawing while serving in the Merchant Navy. "'Join the Navy and see the world' is probably one of the best-known recruiting slogans", says Jackie. "I did just that—but could not afford a camera to capture its wonders. While a seafaring man, I travelled to every continent. By sketching impressions of harbour activity I was probably taking my personal odyssey. What a comparison there was—London on the Thames, wide-bridged Southampton, skylines of New York, Halifax, Nova Scotia, Adelaide, Melbourne, Hobart, Fremantle, the haggling commerce of Port Said and bustling Suez. Those sketches never survived—I gave them away. I suppose, to some extent, this served the purpose of perfecting a technique—using any type of pencil on any available piece of paper. Even yet I find myself resorting to methods which worked well then. Boglands and harbours of Ireland are amongst my favourite subject matter. A love of the sea in all its moods will find me painting harbour scenes in Donegal."

Jackie's passion for portraiture was stimulated outside a Fifth Avenue store in New York, when he watched five artists working in line at easels placed in the window of a department store. "Each was sketching a sitter. These artists had their backs to the street so that passers-by could observe the work of all five, identify one whose style they particularly liked, then go inside and become a sitter for a fee. The fee was beyond my means", Jackie muses, "but I resolved that one day, I would have my own sitters." Jackie realised his ambition. Seldom at home, he frequently travels to sketch and paint portraits in Spain, Greece and Norway.

Discovering the perfect pastel pencil for his style of sketching, the Schwan Stabilo, he wrote to the manufacturers who were based in Slough, Berkshire, complimenting them on its performance. Schwan Stabilo at once appointed him as their Northern Ireland demonstrator. "I made a promise that I would demonstrate my technique in two hourly sessions, absolutely free of charge, to any group of more than 20 people. This proved a great success. By 1989 I was demonstrating portraiture to a class of 60 A-Level students at Armagh College of Further Education. This College has a formidable reputation, with at least 95 per cent of its students taking top grades in art. Geraldine McKenna, head of the art department, and her excellent staff are to be complimented on this record. This College was the first institution to participate in my scheme and, to my delight, a number of students gained direct entry to colleges of art on the strength of their portfolios."

The William Conor Award, sponsored by Wellington Park Hotel, is a coveted prize for any artist who paints figures or portraits. Jackie Connolly's accomplishment now saw him join past winners Neil Shawcross, Tom Carr, Brian Ballard, Joe McWilliams, Basil Blackshaw, Rita Duffy, Cecil Maguire and Raymond Piper. It was a significant moment for the Armagh artist whose professional modesty is a particularly endearing trait. Commenting on the award, Jackie says, "I was truly delighted and honoured. This was a prize I had coveted for a lifetime, never imagining I'd actually achieve it. Suddenly, after a lifetime of painting, I find myself performing a hat trick!" His entry depicted aspects of Van Gogh and is entitled *The Life of Vincent*.

"I admire and empathise with Vincent", observes Jackie, in his quiet way. "He had a troubled mind and, perhaps for this reason, interpreted the universe in terms of brilliant colours. He makes use of Prussian blues, vivid vermilions and bright emerald greens. This gave the impression that his pictures seemed to dance and sway, almost as if they had a life of their own. He was a fine draughtsman whose pencil drawings reveal a delicacy, unexpected by those who know only the tempestuous brush-strokes of his painting. In attempting to incorporate facets of Van Gogh's character into settings with which he is associated, I felt at an advantage. Vincent had been a psychiatric patient shortly before he began some of his paintings in 1887. As a former nurse in a psychiatric hospital, I witnessed the distress and torment of many that felt they were outside a situation. Vincent's great gift was constantly interrupted by crippling depths of depression. In my career I found many such people amongst the troubled, the dispossessed or those with special needs. Most recognise his work in the *Sunflowers*, *The Chair, Bridge at Arles* and *Landscape with Cypress Trees*. I produced an amalgam of settings with Vincent to the forefront of my painting. He is wearing familiar garments—fur-peaked cap and buttoned coat. He has an elbow on the table, and friends and contemporaries of the artist are seated in contemplation. It is a café terrace fringed with cypress trees. Lighted windows imply it is evening. Somewhat ironically, these figures are looking towards Vincent, who stares, unseeingly out, and yet away from the onlooker. His expression is placid, concealing inner turmoil—the Vincent we will never know."

Attracting huge local interest, *The Life of Vincent* was exhibited at Armagh County Museum and the Royal Ulster Academy of Arts. The painting was then privately purchased by an art collector. A self-portrait of Jackie Connolly is presently being shown at the Royal Ulster Academy.

Shortly after the formation of Armagh Art Club, Jackie was invited to join by Seán Murray, then chairman. "I served as treasurer, becoming a member of committee for the next 13 years. Armagh Art Club and its members were always a source of encouragement and stimulus. We spoke the same language, helped each other with difficult techniques, commiserating over disasters or congratulating any member who achieved a triumph. Such special camaraderie is rare amid the cut-throat competition of today."

Jackie's daughter, Maria, qualified in nursing, moving to work in Norway. Here she met and married Gia Oga. Jackie visits quite often and a profile of him was recently published in the local newspaper, *Stavanger Aftenblad*.

"This land, defined by deeply cut valleys, glacial ice-caps and rocky inlets has provided me with an immense source of material", he observes. "When staying with Maria, I met Lea, a Polish Jew and a friend of Gia's family. Lea was a prisoner in Baden-Baden concentration camp, and is one of 300 survivors of Dachau. Her reticence about this, and its attendant horrors, is generally unyielding. When she came to know me a bit better, Lea talked of criminal 'medical' experiments, which took place in Dachau. Then a young woman, she was subjected to several operations by a camp doctor who, for fiendish reasons known only to himself, removed many of her organs, a lung and a kidney. Following liberation, Lea was taken to Switzerland for convalescence, eventually finding herself working in Norway. She speaks nine languages, and listening to her was easily one of the most moving experiences of my life.

"I suppose it was with Lea in mind that I visited the Anne Frank Exhibition at St Patrick's Trian, in January 1999, organised by Armagh Arts Committee. Deputy First Minister Designate Seamus Mallon described the story of Anne Frank as 'a lesson for every generation', drawing parallels between the Holocaust and our own society. Mr Mallon reinforced the harsh truth of evil flourishing 'when good people do nothing'. Anne's diary became a world, best-selling book, and Eva Schloss, stepsister of Anne, spoke of the degradation suffered by prisoners in German concentration camps. That evening, the South Ulster Oboe Trio provided solemn music, befitting the event. The Arts Committee in Armagh, and arts officer Kate Bond, are tireless in their attempts to bring major events to our doorstep."

It gives Jackie particular pleasure that his youngest son, John Paul Connolly, is a professional actor with the Royal Academy of Dramatic Art. "I have an ongoing love of the stage and an association with Armagh Theatre Group since its earliest days. Here I forged friendships with some great people—particularly the producers Larry Ryan, Stanley and Joyce Fitzgerald, James and Mary Lamb, Cecilia Woods, Robert Agnew, Marjorie Quinn and many more. Moved to admiration by the Theatre's first production, I asked if I might join."

As 'back-room boy', Jackie designed sets for countless productions, travelling with the Theatre Group throughout Ireland. Margaret, his wife, was stage assistant in all of this, although her interest lay in decor and the costume department. "Jackie Murphy took care of lighting while the late Paddy McArdle was stage carpenter. It may have the ring of a disintegrating pop group, but we three were affectionately tagged 'The two Jackies and Paddy'! I still attend Armagh Drama Group performances and remain the best of friends with founder members. A one-act play, *Adam's Children*, written by Seamus Mallon, went on to win an All-Ireland award. This symbolic glimpse through

Visions of Vincent
Jackie Connolly

the curtain was, undoubtedly, a small masterpiece. Perhaps my comments may inspire a new performance or, even better, encourage Seamus to stretch the script by adding another act. It is marvellous that this form of art survives constant challenges from cinema and television. Now, with the lustre of a new theatre, Armagh city may yet take its rightful stance in drama. It is vastly rewarding to watch a new generation carry on this timeless tradition." Tassagh Viaduct is one of Jackie's favourite subject matters. "This structure has everything to challenge an artist", he observes, "composition, perspective, shape, colour and, as the light changes, so does my representation on canvas. Damien Woods of St Patrick's Grammar School has one of my many paintings of Tassagh Viaduct, and I believe it has been used for the Channel 4 television programme *Watercolour Challenge*.

"Art is positively my favourite pastime while my wife would cite golf. Margaret has always encouraged me in my efforts to better my craft and it is pleasing to see her own skill in leaded glass designs. She and our six children—Maria, Eamon, Deirdre, Judith, Connie and John Paul—are the mainstay of my life."

To the last, Jackie Connolly retains a quiet, unassuming attitude—as good a reason as any for the special affection he has earned in the world of art, while remaining true to himself.

Fitzroy and Barbara Gillespie

When Dr Barbara Gillespie, MA, MB, BCh, BAO opens the door of her home in Tynan, she appears every inch the well-bred lady she is. "We've never given an interview before", comments her husband, Dr Fitzroy Gillespie, MA, MB, BCh, BAO, LM, JP, DL. "Once we did attempt to but the ill-prepared journalist's batteries were flat so she missed most of what we said!"

As events of a country practice unfold we step back to 1928. "My father, Dr Gillespie, established his surgery in what was once the home of the local curate. My mother, affectionately known as Queenie, performed the role of receptionist and registrar of births, deaths and marriages. Of four children, only I pursued a medical career and continuity of the practice. As my father seemed to survive the profession tolerably well, I imagined I might also", Dr Fitz adds cheerfully.

The family room in which we sit is warmly welcoming, its atmosphere conducive to a pleasant exchange of conversation. Art and textiles blend in Dr Barbara's impeccable, traditionally furnished home. She laughs heartily at the idea that it is somewhat unusual to find the kind of BBC accent straight out of the Third Programme in this quiet, country village. "I realise I've become three-quarters Irish when I go back to Hereford and find myself using colloquial expressions that once baffled me!"

As a child, Dr Fitz attended Miss Best's private school on The Mall, Armagh, and preparatory school at Castle Park, Dublin. "My secondary education was spent as boarder at Royal School, Armagh. Mr Hutchings was headmaster, and staff included Mr Jones, Mr Costain and Miss Maisie Hirsch, who incidentally was a celebrated golfer, twice winning the Swiss Ladies' Open Championship. Two of my contemporaries from those days, Edwin 'Buster' Holland and John Lowry, remain friends." Qualifying in medicine from Trinity College Dublin, young Fitz Gillespie embarked on his houseman's year at Sir Patrick Dunn's Hospital, Dublin.

Dr Fitz's intention to join his father's practice became a reality in 1958 "Patients had steadily increased since introduction of the National Health Service in 1948. When my name was added to the brass plate", he recalls with a smile, "my father was very generous in sharing helpful or wise advice and I was very proud to be his partner. Knowing many of our patients was a considerable advantage and although one of us was then on call day and night, I found my new role rewarding and pleasurable. It was a quite a different social climate then, unlike today's economic scenario. Recent governments have streamlined the National Health Service to quite a degree." With a catchment area including part of Co. Monaghan, this growing Tynan medical practice welcomed Dr Barbara in 1966. Describing herself as something of a 'trail-blazer', she surprised her Herefordshire family by embarking on a medical career.

"We all have our dreams and I envisaged this life as worthwhile and exciting. There was no one to warn me of endless repetition it involved or long hours of study. Yet I don't recall ever feeling resentful. Mind you", she ponders, "doctors were a scarce commodity then but we had some good times, more or less an antidote to the stress involved. My husband was qualified when we met. I was a second year medical student broadening my education at Sir Patrick Dunn's Hospital in Dublin. If, while assisting on the wards, you proved trustworthy, your houseman could manage a day's leave. Patients called us 'doctor' and yet", she smiles, "I looked all of 14! One evening I could see a patient required professional diagnosis beyond my remit. When I dashed into the corridor, Dr Fitz Gillespie was the first person I met. He came at once, thus averting disaster! We met afterwards and finding much in common, I was introduced to the Gillespie family. Having enjoyed Dublin with its diverse culture and bustling streets, Tynan was a direct contrast and yet I felt an immediate sense of belonging. We were married in England in 1959 and I assisted at the practice when called upon. At first we lived in Killylea but my father-in-law's death in 1964 saw us move here, this house becoming our established home. It was so difficult gaining the confidence of patients at first", she confesses. "I could see everyone in the waiting room with their gaze steadfastly fixed on the door leading to my husband's surgery!" Two Gillespie children, Patrick and Gael, were born in the following years. Before Dr Barbara became a partner in the practice, she undertook a refresher course for six months at Monaghan Hospital.

"Here I really enjoyed working with staff and patients. Returning to the family practice I found that it took a little time for people to accept a woman doctor, especially our male patients. Yet they did and soon I had no problem sharing surgery. Yes, I missed England but not consciously, as we were so busy. Tynan became my home and I hope I possess the good sense not to make comparisons. The Gillespie family had a wide circle of friends who, once introduced, became my friends as well. Families socialised a great deal in the era of the cocktail party. Guests came at 6pm, chatted over a drink, and left punctually at 7.30pm." The Gillespie family has long enjoyed the esteem of villagers and patients. Those who came to know Dr Barbara were soon won over by her engaging personality. She waves this comment aside. "It had much to do with the fact that I was wife to the local doctor. The ethos of a country practice contrasts enormously with that of town or city. Many of our patients are from a farming community and to them Fitz and his father were trusted friends. It was in such a spirit I came to be accepted."

Dr Barbara then turns to the Troubles, an epoch that would mark a third of this century.

"My husband attended every atrocity when a doctor was required, shielding me to some extent", she admits. "However I was taking surgery when the police station next door was mortar-bombed. I had just brought a mother and her sick child into the surgery when, without warning, the blast came. Our groom had left the stable yard for the evening, and the practice nurse and receptionist were clearing up to go home when, ten feet away, the mortars were released. Our elder children had left home but Rollo, the youngest, was here. Electricity blacked out as cables came down, but the village leapt into action and two badly injured policemen were rushed to hospital. We lost our police station and it was never rebuilt, Middletown Royal Ulster Constabulary later assuming responsibility for our care and security. When the crisis settled later that evening, a neighbour sent across a bottle of whiskey with the instructions, 'Take as directed'.

"You can equally imagine our revulsion at the death of Sir Norman Stronge and his son James who were close friends. All who undertake the Hippocratic oath have a duty to save lives. I cannot comprehend taking human life."

Both doctors acknowledge enormous social changes in Tynan village and the area. "No-one had a telephone when I joined the practice", recalls Dr Fitz, "now everyone has a mobile they take everywhere and many are linked to the World Wide Web! Church hall activities, drama, bowls, Women's Institute or keeping fit once occupied every night of the week and that seems to have gone. Standards of living in general have risen dramatically and most people recognise preventative medicine plays an important role in maintaining the health of the population at large. As regards spiritual health, we have been without a Rector for some time and that does reflect in a sense of community loss."

Ireland's climate is eminently suited to horse breeding, and the Gillespie stable is noted for thoroughbred stock. "We provide stud facilities while all aspects of the business are managed by our son Patrick, a professional trainer who manages and breeds steeplechasers", Dr Fitz contributes. "A racehorse is generally broken at 18 months and most are sold at the age of three. One of ours, aptly named Repeat the Dose, won the Cathcart Cup at Cheltenham Gold Cup Festival and Darton Ri, the name derived from the Irish for 'highway of the king', is another point-to-point veteran of ours. Bought by David Nicholson, Darton Ri continues to do well in England." In May 1999 the Gillespie stable was declared leading producer of point-to-point winners in Ireland, acknowledged by Weatherby's at Punchestown. "I was always interested in horses and rode with some success as an amateur in point-to-point and steeplechases all over Ireland."

Dr Fitz Gillespie is an acting steward with the Turf Club, a regulatory body for the integrity and reputation of Irish racing in Ireland and throughout the world. Speaking of his duties, Dr Fitz comments, "the Turf Club incorporates the Irish National Hunt Steeplechase Committee, both responsible for flat and national hunt racing and point-to-point racing in Ireland. Turf Club headquarters at the Curragh hold lists of runners for each individual race in the country, weights the horses must carry and a list of jockeys nominated to ride each horse. If you can accommodate statistics, last year 1,164,724 people attended race meetings in Ireland, watching 1,794 races throughout 32 counties. The running of every race in a fair manner is the responsibility of the Turf Club. Even the smallest fixture requires 16 professionals on site,

Dr Fitz Gillespie and Dr Barbara Gillespie

ensuring the integrity of every aspect of the meeting. When a horse arrives it comes under the protection of Turf Club security personnel whose job it is to ensure that only those with accreditation gain access to the area. A film crew captures every race using at least three cameras and a separate photo-finish camera is also critical. Horses are tested after racing for dope by the Turf Club veterinary officer. Charitable funds are administered by this body and include the Jockeys' Accident Fund and the Qualified Riders' Accident Fund. The Turf Club epitomises superb hospitality throughout the world. My wife is a Silver Pin holder. This entitles her to admittance, free of charge, throughout the world. We attend racing in the United Kingdom, Hong Kong, Singapore, Bangkok, South Africa and the United States."

Whenever possible Dr Barbara and Dr Fitz visit the Abbey Theatre in Dublin or attend the Waterfront Hall in Belfast. "Art exhibitions or the work of local artists are something we both enjoy", Dr Barbara emphasises. "Hunting scenes occupy a fair percentage of our walls but there are outstanding local painters worth supporting. One favourite is a horse study by Diana Cowdy, once a student at London's Slade School of Fine Art. We relax best at our holiday home in Sligo, a beautiful and rugged county. Everyone makes the association with Yeats but for me his work translates in a melancholy fashion. We know the water there very well and it's relatively safe for boating."

Dr Fitz contributes some interesting anecdotes relative to his family. "My grandfather, John, a solicitor, was a great friend of Sir Shane Leslie and it may be worth mentioning that John Gillespie's daughter, Doreen Gillespie Watt, was Ireland's first woman solicitor. On visits to Castle Leslie, my family have shared interesting evenings in good company. One frequent visitor was a young Londoner, Anthony Armstrong-Jones, who came over to take photographs of my sister's wedding."

When Tynan schoolhouse became vacant in 1992, the Doctors Gillespie decided to buy the building in the hope of re-opening the school. Numbers did not allow this to happen and in 1994 a decision was made to convert the building into a surgery. Dr Robert Carlisle became a partner and was joined by Dr James McMullan. "I am now retired", adds Dr Barbara, "and my husband job-shares with Dr McAlinden. A large staff of nurses and secretaries run the place like clockwork."

Tynan with a population of 90 souls has about it a sense of timelessness similar to nearby Killylea. It is quite the reverse each Boxing Day when thousands turn out to watch members of the Tynan and Armagh Harriers attend the traditional hunt. Dr Fitz Gillespie succeeded his father as master of the hunt. "Working in harmony with the farming community, I emphasise, our aim is not to kill the hare but participate in the thrill of the chase." Hunt dress is white and black but as master, Dr Fitz wears green. "Local solicitor Brian Dougan is joint master and a successful point-to-point jockey."

An avid gardener with a passion for roses, Dr Barbara declares, "We still have many of Sam McCready's superb varieties. My parents bought many fragrant species from Sam's uncle, another renowned rose grower. Probably inherited from my parents is a conviction that a garden should not depend on the beauty of flowers alone but how they contribute to an overall picture. I produce lilies for their scent but the exquisite orchid is undoubtedly my favourite bloom. When you consider how men risked their lives collecting and bringing this plant to civilisation—with its unusual shape and glorious colours, the orchid will always take pride of place in my home."

Bittersweet memories shared with Dr Fitz Gillespie and his wife, Dr Barbara, remind us of the crucial role a country practice performs. Such reflections provoke another truth, that a caring country doctor remains irreplaceable in the hearts of patients, friends and the wider community.

Michael Cairns presents Armagh Cricket Club

"I would say the game of cricket in Armagh is currently thriving", comments Michael J.H. Cairns, president of City of Armagh Cricket Club, "and undoubtedly the highlight of our 1999 season was the visit of the Lord's Taverners. Our Club facilitates a charity team known as the Armagh Taverners. Besides playing social matches against opponents drawn from a multitude of backgrounds, the Taverners have raised thousands of pounds for worthy cross-community causes. The Armagh Taverners have always maintained close links with their famous London counterparts, the Lord's Taverners. When the latter visited in September, their party included former England test match captain Mike Denness; three former England players, five county players and a host of local and national television celebrities. At a gala dinner held afterwards, a custom-built coach was presented to a local respite home for handicapped children. This was seen as a magnificent achievement for a small club."

In the world of sport, so many men and women have distinguished themselves that it is difficult to draw the line between 'famous' and 'well-known'. Asked to cite great cricketing names, Michael Cairns smiles broadly.

"There's no contest! Sir Donald Bradman will always loom large in cricketing annals, but Dr William Gilbert Grace (1848-1915) was something of a legend, even in his own lifetime, and for 40 years the best-known man in England. He was a giant-like figure with a big, black beard and his personality dominated any match in which he played. Gloucestershire was his county, but he captained England many times. In first-class cricket, Grace scored well over 54,000 runs, including 26 centuries, took over 2,800 wickets and, on three occasions, scored more than 300 runs in an innings. Grace's record of 126 centuries remained unbeaten until J.B. Hobbs (Sir Jack Hobbs, born 1882), the Surrey and England batsman, passed Grace's record in 1925. Hobbs scored a total of 61,221 (197 centuries)."

Conservative politician Lord Mancroft is recorded as having offered the definition: "Cricket—a game which the English, not being a spiritual people, have invented in order to give themselves some conception of eternity." If this is so, then The Ashes are probably the most sacred words ever uttered in competitive terms and came to be associated with the cricket test matches between Australia and England. If the game bewilders all who do not understand this, or the rudiments of cricket, Michael attempts to explain.

"When the Australian cricketers visited England in 1882, bringing one of their 'best-ever' elevens, they won the first two test matches. So everyone knew that if the Australians won the third match, they would win the 'rubber' (or best out of five) and be victorious in the series. After a fluctuating match on a rain-ruined wicket, the deciding day was Monday 29 August, and it seemed when the second innings of England began that Australian hopes of winning were at a very low level. But under the Australian bowling attack, it was English hopes that faded until, when Peate, the Yorkshire bowler, joined C.T. Studd, there was only one more English wicket to fall. England still needed seven runs to avoid defeat. At this point Peate, who should have simply tried to keep up his wicket, had a wild slog at the bowling and was out! Spectators, whatever their feelings, rushed on to the ground to cheer the winners, and the stumps disappeared. Afterwards a weekly newspaper (the *Sporting Times*) published an obituary notice: 'In affectionate remembrance of English Cricket, died on 29 August 1882. The body will be cremated and the Ashes taken to Australia.' The stumps which had been used in the match were afterwards burned. These ashes were then collected, and placed some time later in a casket which is kept at Lord's cricket ground, London. And this", concludes Michael, "is how the word 'Ashes' came to be associated with the cricket test matches between Australia and England."

Michael will take Armagh into another sort of century but it was against a Victorian background that the Cricket Club was founded. "The Club has a long-established tradition", he points out. "At one time it was the most famous in Ireland. For some years after its foundation, having no pitch of their own, Armagh was a guest on other pitches. The Mall Trustees were approached in 1861 and no objection was made to the playing of cricket on the Mall and here the Club remains. There was a hitch however. A few months after their request, the Club was cited as trespassing and involved in prosecution.

"The first meeting of City of Armagh Cricket Club is documented as having taken place in the drawing room of the house once occupied by the law firm, Monroe and Anderson. It seems the first game played was in 1859. On 2 September of that year, local newspaper *The Guardian* carried a report of a game against Monaghan Cricket Club in Caledon Demesne, and won by Armagh. The winning team was named as: Prentice, Allen, Turle, Darley, James, F.T. Foster, Bampfield, J. Stanley, A. Foster, McMatters and Kidd. From 1861, when the Club found its home on the Mall, matches were played against Banbridge and Monaghan—both games ending victoriously for Armagh. Since then cricket has been played on the Mall, the only interruption being two world wars.

"City of Armagh Cricket Club enjoyed its most successful term in 140 years of history during the period 1928-1939. Having teams of exceptional merit, they won the Senior League Championship three times besides challenging for the highest honours in those 11 years. The first league title to come to Armagh was won in 1928, when the team was captained by R. McKinley. Fifteen matches were played before winning the championship and of these, only one was lost. It was the first in the series, when Armagh lost to Lurgan. In 1931, the League Championship was won for a second time with much the same side as in 1928. Indeed this superb team had one more shot in the locker when they won the League again in 1939.

"Down the years, several Armagh players have achieved international status. Probably the most famous is Ivan J. Anderson, born in Armagh in 1944. Ivan is the holder of the highest Irish score in all international matches—198 not out against Canada in Toronto, in 1973. Ivan is still involved with Waringstown Cricket Club and his arm can still be twisted to turn out for the Thirds or Fourths. Other Armagh players to represent Ireland include: R. Lloyd, L. Armstrong, John H. Barnes, Robert J. Barnes, S. Wilfred McDonagh and Thomas Fitzgerald Ward. In 1982 Armagh Cricket Club took the decision to employ a professional and it has continued to do so ever since. The first 'pro' was Uday Joshi and several other superb overseas players have graced the Mall including Ashok Malhoha, Ashok Mankad, New Zealander Andrew Reinhold and Yashpal Sharma. Yashpal, a former Indian test player, who gained 37 caps and scored 2,315 runs for Armagh, is undoubtedly the best 'pro' the Club has ever had on board.

"Current captain of the side, Andrew Rennie, established his own unique record by skippering the First XI for the past six consecutive years, 1994-99. Another member of the First XI, Reggie Stinson, holds several records in the history of the Club. On 28 August 1999 Reggie took his 1,000th senior wicket for Armagh against Bangor and, earlier in the season, passed 7,000 career runs for the Club. Both of these records look set to remain long into the 21st century.

"Formal records of successive Club Presidents and Captains have been kept since 1920. They are listed in the table below.

"Our current First XI squad includes professional Ireland all rounder, Paul McCrum, Ken Mandair from India, South African Darren Hellwick, several students returning from university studies in Britain and, of course, local players. Twice in succession, the First XI has been runner-up in the Senior League, Section Two. The Second XI were second in their league last year and the Fourth XI won their league, and the Cup last year while retaining the Minor Qualifying Trophy this year. City of Armagh Cricket Club fields Under-12s, 13s, 15s and Under-19 XIs who play in League and Cup competitions. We are fortunate to have an excellent relationship with the Royal School, Armagh, an institution with a great cricketing tradition. Our professionals coach their pupils in summer while, in winter, the City of Armagh Cricket Club uses the Royal School's indoor nets facility. We share expensive equipment such as the automatic bowling machine, which was purchased this year. City of Armagh's cricket professional coaches at four local primary schools as well as junior and adult evening coaching on the Club grounds in summer. We organise and sponsor a mid-week League Competition, attracting up to ten teams drawn from a cross-section of backgrounds in the local area. It accommodates those who do not normally play or who wish to play only on a social basis.

"Current membership of City of Armagh Cricket Club—both adult and junior players—is thriving. Supportive corporate sponsors, club events such as summer barbecues and a healthy bar income all contribute to a sound financial position. The Pavilion was extensively rebuilt in 1992 and the grounds are well maintained. Much is owed to enthusiastic and hard-

City of Armagh Cricket Club First XI, 1999.

Front row: Andrew McCrum (professional's son), Paul McCrum (professional), Andrew Rennie (captain), Gareth Robinson and David Bullick.
Back row (L to R): Paul McCord (of sponsor Compaq), Darren Helwick, Reggie Stinson, John Briggs, David Robinson, Chris Cairns, Colin Russell, Ken Mondair and club president Michael J.H. Cairns.
Players not pictured: Alan Dundas, Timothy Cairns, Dean Lester, Jarleth McCready, Mark Elliott.

working members, the honorary club officials and the general executive committee, while Brian Weir has long been a dedicated scorekeeper. The ladies' committee provides cricket teas for all home fixtures and miraculously, makes a profit on this effort. It must be emphasised that the ladies' committee makes an invaluable contribution to City of Armagh Cricket Club.

"I have absolutely no doubt that City of Armagh Cricket Club will continue to prosper and, consequently, play a significant part in the social life of Armagh in the future. As president, I am honoured to lead an historic Club over the threshold into the new millennium and the new dawn of 1 January 2000."

Past Presidents

1920-26	W. McCrum
1927-42	M.Sinton
1943	no president (due to War)
1944-47	J.P. Best
1948-51	R.F.Forbes
1952-59	W.H. Dawson
1960-64	W. McDonagh
1965-69	J. Graham
1970-75	W. Elliott
1976-78	J. Elliott
1979-80	J.A. Baxter
1981-82	R. Neville
1983-84	J.A. Vaughan
1985-86	H. Ewart
1987-88	G. Elliott
1989-90	P.T. Homan
1991-92	R. Elliott
1993-94	Dr S.S. Duffy
1995-96	W. Williamson
1997-98	W.J. Briggs
1999-2000	M.J.H. Cairns

Past Club Captains

1939-40	W.H. Dawson
1941	W. McKinley
1942	T.W. Grainger
1943	no captain (due to War)
1944	W.H. Dawson
1945-48	T.W. Grainger
1949-52	L. Armstrong
1953-54	N. McKinley
1955	L.G. Spearman
1956	J. Graham
1957	L.G. Spearman
1958	J. Elliott
1959	W. Rowan & J.H. Baxter
1960	J.H. Baxter
1961-63	N.D. Graham
1964-67	G. Elliott
1968	I.J. Anderson
1969	T. Barnes
1970	R. Neville
1971	A. Stinson
1972-73	H. Deane
1974	O. Corvan
1975	M. McConville
1976-77	W.G.S. Parr
1978	K. Gordon
1979	R. Stinson
1980	T. Barnes
1981	K. McAuley
1982	G. Elliott
1983-84	R Stinson
1985	K. McAuley
1986	J. Walbran
1987	R. Stinson
1988	D. Lyttle
1989	A. Stinson
1990-91	R. Stinson
1992-93	A. Dundas
1994-99	A.W. Rennie

Armagh Voices
a celebration of a century

1940 ~ 1950

And Life is Colour and Warmth and Light
And a striving evermore for these

Julian Grenfell

Margaret Martin

Addressing pupils past and present at St Catherine's College Silver Jubilee Prizegiving, held in September 1998, Seamus Mallon MP, Deputy First Minister Designate, commented: "The pupils of this fine school are the future and it will be your job to mould with vision this society, a new society that is at ease with itself, having a sense of justice and reconciliation. I am confident that the values and excellent formation you received in St Catherine's College would have more than equipped you to build a new society."

Margaret Martin, BA (Hons), became principal of St Catherine's College, Armagh, in 1991. If a school is as good as its leader, the College has little to fear. Her responsibilities are daunting. An intake of almost 1,000 girls constitutes the largest institution of its kind in the Southern Board. Now, in its Jubilee Year, St Catherine's has been rated top non-selective school in the 1997-98 School Performance League Table. At GCSE level, 65 per cent of pupils obtained grades A-C against the Northern Ireland average of 31%. Such results pay testimony to a legacy of sterling work by Margaret Martin, her staff and pupils of this school over the past 25 years.

"I was born in Belfast", Margaret explains, "yet my roots lie in Tyrone. Mine could be classified as an academic family. Of seven, four, including myself, teach. Jim Herron, my brother, is head of modern languages at St Patrick's Grammar School, Armagh. Then I married into another academic family. My husband Mícheál and I met at Queen's University where we each took an arts degree, his in Celtic Studies, mine in English." Mícheál is presently a lecturer and director of student services at St Mary's University College, Belfast. He also lectures at the Department of Celtic Studies in Queen's University. Their home near Dungannon is accessible to both workplaces.

Margaret's spacious study reflects the status of a top executive. Despite a busy schedule, staff and pupils may freely knock on her door. Anglo-Irish writers cast a friendly eye from a vantage point above the marble fireplace. *Armagh*, a watercolour by local artist Bernard McWilliams, strikes a balance. "Bernard's sister, Patricia, was head of our art department and a close personal friend. Her death has been an enormous loss to St Catherine's. This painting is a constant reminder of Patricia's contribution.

"I grew up in the difficult Sixties, a pupil of St Dominic's on the Falls Road. Cross-community relationships, formed through school activities, made an intense impression on my thinking in those formative years. We had to widen our horizons simply to survive. What a tragedy this has taken so long and cost so dearly.

"I never cease to be grateful for the 1947 Education Act which gave such opportunity and provided free access to university education. My generation, that is, those in their forties, benefited most. Now the fruits of that education are evident and cultural diversity thrives today. You have only to look at the nearby enterprise of Navan Fort."

She is articulate, modern in her thinking and impeccable in a beige suit with crisp white blouse. Speaking of Navan, her face lights enthusiastically. "With a history, more or less fabulous, from the years 300 BC to 336 AD, few sites in Western Europe outshine us. Two thousand years ago, the entire land looked to Armagh for inspiration and was not disappointed. This is happening today. We are far more vital in the scheme of things than most realise and it is a fervent hope that differing cultures will eventually embrace. Waste any opportunity and history", she considers, "will judge if we are to be found wanting."

The Sisters of the *Sacré Coeur*, a French order, established the Convent of the Sacred Heart in Armagh during 1851. This international order has been characterised by a tremendous commitment to education. St Catherine's came into being on the present site in 1857. "If I feel overwhelmed by the complexities of life", Margaret admits, "I pause and draw on the benign spirit permeating this building. Help inevitably comes." Two of the Sisters whom she describes as "invaluable in their contribution to education" are Dolores Considine and Aideen Kinlen. "I feel privileged to have known both women who still live and work in Armagh.

"On 1 September 1973, many new members of staff joined pupils coming through the doors on that eventful morning when the Convent of the Sacred Heart Grammar School amalgamated with the Convent of the Sacred Heart

Margaret Martin, principal of St Catherine's College, with top A-Level achiever Debbie Lowe, and Professor George Bain, President and Vice-Chancellor of Queen's University Belfast

Photograph by Michael Campbell, LBIPP

Intermediate School. I consider myself privileged to be amongst their ranks. With Sister Considine we, the staff, set about the task of building a new school community, addressing ourselves to providing a life chance for each pupil, tackling issues of under-achievement and career opportunities for girls, and ensuring that we practice a policy of social inclusion. Our work has been supported by able, committed staff and the local community."

Among her numerous commitments, Margaret is vice-chairperson of the 17-member Council for Curriculum, Examinations and Assessment, chairperson of the BBC Education Committee, a member of the Sacred Heart's School Network Committee, a member of the Northern Bishops' Working Party on Catholic Education and a member of the Millennium Education Committee. Welcoming the Armagh City and District Council initiative that converted the old city hospital to academic purposes, Margaret comments, "My wish was realised when an Outreach Campus of Queen's University was established in Armagh. Students have taken advantage of this facility and now pursue third level education without the attendant stress of travel."

Literature is as essential to Margaret Martin as the air she breathes. "*Midnight's Children* by Salman Rushdie is exceptional reading. So too is Vikram Seth's *A Suitable Boy.* Add Cathal Ó Searcaigh and Máirtín Ó Díreáin to my list of favourite poets. I have long been drawn to the works of Seamus Heaney. In fact, he was guest of honour at the College, officially opening our new library. I treasure a signed copy of *Wintering Out* that he gave me. It's an account of political events in Ulster from 1963 to 1972, written in the tone of an urban journalist, at first bemused, then grimly prophetic. Heaney's most poignant poem, in my estimation, was written in Jutland on the first Sunday in September when the IRA ceasefire was announced: 'To make a new beginning and make a go of it, alive and sinning, ourselves again, free-willed, not bad.'"

A bell signals mid-morning break and footsteps echo in the corridor outside. Margaret, in addition to academic and pastoral responsibility, motivates 100 teaching and administrative staff. The school's development plan reflects aims that Margaret Martin has set in terms of its pastoral function. Key objectives are mutual respect and understanding, and it is a source of pride that in this Silver Jubilee Year, St Catherine's College won the Southern Education and Library Board European Award. True to her word, Margaret ensures that pupils will have the best access to the NI Curriculum. In eight years as principal she has spearheaded a £6 million building programme, funded by the Department of Education and the generosity of the Society of the Sacred Heart. She also co-ordinated the development of a state-of-the-art technology and information technology centre, a new examination centre and upgrading of the school restaurant facilities. Such was her interest that it was not uncommon to see this talented woman on the building site, equipped with hard hat, discussing plans with architect Dominic Carson.

If this school is dynamic, so is she. Margaret Martin is a born leader, in control, striving for success. "We are unique in Northern Ireland, being the largest single-sex academic institution in an area bounded by Craigavon, Monaghan and Tyrone. Academic life sits comfortably within my capabilities but peace of mind hinges on knowing my domestic world is smooth-running and I appreciate fully the rigours which beset a working mother." Mícheál and Margaret have five children. Ruairí is an accountant working with FPM Chartered Accountants, Conall is a third year law student at Queen's University, Lorcán and Páraic are students at St Patrick's Boys' Academy, Dungannon, while Caoimhe attends St Patrick's Girls' Academy.

"The boys are keen on sport, particularly football, and swim competitively. We seek solace in Donegal, walking the beaches in this wonderful wild place. All you need is warm clothing. It clears the mind and I return refreshed."

Her favourite time of day is sitting down to the evening meal. "It provides an opportunity to exchange family news and I relish that bonhomie on which we seem to thrive. I remain traditional when it comes to family values. As often as possible, I visit the National Gallery in Dublin. The best way to spend an absorbing hour is in company with Jack Yeats, Henry and Craig, great names from the Irish School of Art. Jeannie Minne, my personal assistant, is someone without whom I could not possibly manage. Her husband George is organist of St Patrick's Cathedral and a virtuoso. His breadth of vision is that of a European, a particular charm setting him apart."

Two thousand years ago the cultural world looked to Armagh for its inspiration and was not disappointed. Margaret Martin's *joie de vivre* is present day inspiration few can equal.

Kenny Murphy

Birds and woodland creatures direct their gaze from magnificent display cases at the home of Moy taxidermist Kenny Murphy. In a uniquely natural collection, owl, vole, squirrel and badger are grouped in silent company of raven, robin, starling and plover.

"First you must see my garden", Kenny invites, obviously proud of his creation. At one with nature, he is a wildlife site advisor throughout Northern Ireland. One portion of the strip garden is unspoilt, natural habitat for the bird population.

It's a morning made in heaven and Kenny raises his voice in an effort to compete with vociferous songsters. At least 25 species presently frequent this haven. "Listen", Kenny puts a finger to his lips. "That's the blackbird alerting his mate to our approach." Perfect peace encourages endless visitors, the robin, wren, greenfinch, goldfinch, hedge sparrow, redpoll, blue tit, coal tit, great tit. "The blue tit will only now begin to build", Kenny continues. "He has the good sense to wait until the caterpillar population hatches, providing food for the young." Kenny's tanned face fills with wonder. "The balance of nature is infinite. We humans know little when all's said and done."

Kenny was born in this secluded cottage which has remained his home ever since. "I worked first for the Topfield factory in Moygashel, then the carpet factory at Portadown. Becoming redundant meant I could now indulge my hobbies of fishing, shooting, bird watching and gardening, but more importantly, seriously concentrate on taxidermy. Susan and I are happy with our quiet life. Many trophies from various shoots were worthy of mounting so I made the acquaintance of Fred Gibson, now deceased, an expert taxidermist in Tandragee. Fred was busy and suggested I attempt to preserve these specimens myself. I began with a magpie. This particular bird is a menace to the smaller feathered population. He carries off the nesting eggs or helpless chicks, dramatically reducing their numbers."

Kenny's early effort at taxidermy was reasonably successful, "though not a standard I'd offer today", he admits. "When I became more proficient", he smiles, "I sold that magpie at a knock-down price." In 20 years of his craft he has handled almost every creature—fox, badger, squirrel, stoat, otter and an amazing variety of birds.

"Many species of wild birds are decreasing alarmingly, as the latest RSPB survey shows. The corncrake is now extinct in Northern Ireland with only one recorded sighting in 1998, near Lough Neagh. Other threatened species are nightjar, bar owl and ring ouzle while populations of grouse, cuckoo and yellowhammer are greatly reduced in number, mainly due to modern farming methods and the practice of removing hedges. This beautiful black Scoter duck came to grief on the motorway. He must have been migrating", Kenny explains. "They fly to Scandinavia or Russia in spring. It was raining when he was found. During rain or foggy conditions, birds often confuse a wet road for a river." Road accidents account for more than half of the work Kenny undertakes.

The Countryside and Wildlife Act 1985 requires taxidermists to register with the Department of the Environment, so no protected species is in danger of coming his way. "When a specimen is brought for preservation, I must list the cause of death, sex of the animal or bird and my supplier. Before selling any specimen, the finished product is numbered. I am obliged to pass this detail with a buyer's name to the DoE." Clinical conditions exist in the workshop where sterile surgical instruments are carefully placed. "Much of my work requires enormous patience and time. Charges levied depend on the animal in question. I pride myself on minute detail. Painting is usually necessary to complete a face. This is where taxidermists may differ. Examples from the Victorian era are regarded as superior. For the very good reason, I say, that the poor work was destroyed, only the best surviving. Nothing would please me more", he observes, "than to think my craft will also survive."

The Ulster Museum in Belfast and occasionally Armagh County Museum call on Kenny's expertise. He exhibits at the wildlife centre in Castle Archdale and the visitor centre of Crom Estate in County Fermanagh. "For the elegant country house, puffin or mallard look good under oval domes. The male pheasant is always in demand because of his outstanding plumage. I recently treated a yellowbill cuckoo, the first to be found in Northern Ireland, for the Ulster Museum."

Kenny has amusing stories from his repertoire of the last 20 years. "One morning I found a chap on my doorstep with a crocodile under his arm. Perhaps it would be wise to stress I never undertake work on reptiles, large heads, that is deer, antelope or stag, nor indeed on fish of any description. I sent the crocodile on his way so have no idea what fate befell him." Trips to the Ulster Wildlife Trust at Crossgar are an important part of Kenny's year.

"One of those beautiful days last week I went to a farm in Co. Down in search of the Holly Blue butterfly. I found the specimen I was seeking", he adds proudly. Under glass, painstakingly placed, Latin-labelled, Kenny has collected 440 specimen moths, practically every variety existing in Northern Ireland. "My friend, Robert Thompson, a member of the Northern Ireland branch of the Butterfly Society, is presently publishing a book and distribution atlas of moths in Northern Ireland, illustrated by his own photography of the live moth rather than using easily available photographs of set specimens. The difficulty here is finding a live moth of a rarer species! I have assisted in finding quite a few of the scarce species. An exceptional butterfly claims my attention, a cream lace-edged swallowtail from the Norfolk Broads. With the exception of museums no comparable collection exists."

The Forestry Service has an improved attitude to wildlife. With European biodiversity laws, organisations such as Forestry and Environment and Heritage are encouraged to allocate habitat for woodland creatures. Conifers offer no sanctuary for the nesting bird. "I do see change for the better in some areas. It would be unthinkable if wild flowers should disappear from our countryside. Weeds, as they are sometimes called, provide necessary food for moths, butterflies and other wildlife."

Creating a lasting, peaceful environment at his own home is paramount to Kenny. When he returned part of his garden to wildlife, little did he dream what pleasure this would bring. "I dug a pond as there were frogs in swampy land nearby. This morning, two green heads can be seen amidst the duckweed!" Marsh marigolds nod by the water's edge, tadpoles dart like minnows. A Painted Lady butterfly flutters unto a lilac-coloured buddleia bush. Kenny has ten different varieties of buddleia in his garden. "No-one really knows how, but her journey, 2,000 miles between Arabia and the Arctic Circle may be made in relays", Kenny informs. "The Painted Lady has a short lifespan, so some believe she hatches young, perhaps in Germany, and like a relay race, the cycle is completed by up to four of her species."

In tall trees, nesting boxes provide a sanctuary for the robin, tit and flycatcher. "My own cat once scaled a tree when a blackbird was feeding her young. It took one nestling but the parent birds abandoned their young so they died of cold overnight. To return to the nest having seen a cat there would have put their own lives at risk. Sensibly they decided to nest elsewhere. Now I place these boxes high in the trees so cats do not consider climbing up worth the trouble."

Apart from wounded creatures that he nurses back to health, Kenny keeps one gun dog for hunting expeditions. "Some days I lack the energy taxidermy demands but since I now receive less commissioned work, I am less under pressure at present." But what convincing work, especially his latest specimen, the long-eared owl. A swooping stance, imagination, and talons hook realistically about an unsuspecting field mouse.

Kenny Murphy
exhibits examples of his taxidermy

Anne Weatherup

Sister Anne Weatherup's early determination to pursue a medical career uplifts the lives of many elderly patients whom she visits daily. Quite by accident, the caring side of Anne's nature was also discovered, and since rewarded, by a little Jack Russell, sitting protectively at her side. "We found her abandoned on the M1", Anne says. "The children brought her home, christening her Belle, and now, as you see, she is firmly established as one of the family."

Clearly in control, Anne Weatherup is refreshingly free from self-importance with an eye for what is humorous. "Cold, tidy houses are an abomination", she affirms, leading the way to the lounge. This comfortable family room reflects what is important in her life. Family photographs, prints, watercolours and shelves sagging with books, each with a story to tell. The aroma of fresh coffee drifts from the kitchen. Pouring a fragrant cup, she proves an entertaining companion, as ready to ask questions as answer them. A lifetime of dedicated nursing she modestly attributes to doing what she always wanted. "As a teenager I spent some time in hospital", Anne recalls. "The quality of care I received then convinced this was the future for me."

Has she ever regretted that decision? "Absolutely not. My training began at Banbridge District Hospital, continuing in Middlesex, where I specialised in midwifery. I'll never forget the first baby I helped deliver, or its loud protest. The wonder of each new life never diminished during my career. With a view to increasing my skills, I next enrolled at Royal Marsden Hospital, which specialised in oncology. This important hospital will always remain special to me. African-Caribbean, Australian and European staff worked tirelessly for cancer victims, saving the lives of many. I consider Royal Marsden to have been the epitome in dedicated nursing care." Back in Northern Ireland, Anne secured a post at the Waveney General Hospital, Ballymena. Then, a young woman of 26, she transferred as staff midwife to the Carleton Maternity Hospital, Portadown.

"Experience gained gave me the confidence to embark on health visiting. By this time I had met Robin, whom I later married. Within a year tragedy struck. Robin died of an illness of which I was fully aware beforehand." Sadness shadows her memories yet she never regretted their short, entirely happy relationship. "What I did find hard to accept was the fact that Robin never saw our son Daniel, born two months after Robin's death."

Undoubtedly a woman of substance, Anne's courage carried her through this painful time. "It was more difficult than I ever imagined. My neighbours in Desart Lane were wonderfully supportive. The same must be said of my mother-in-law who took care of Daniel while I returned to work. As my son advanced at school, I often thought of Robin. How proud he would have been when later, as a young man, Daniel went on to read Law at Cardiff University."

For the next number of years, Anne continued to work in a visiting capacity as district nurse with the Health Board. Roger, her present husband, had been a close friend of Robin, and was at that time newly appointed curator of Armagh County Museum. The arts were a shared interest. During a drama festival at Armagh City Hall, Roger helped backstage while Anne assisted in organising the event.

"Our friendship deepened and eventually we married. It took a certain courage to begin again and little did I envisage finding such companionship and happiness. Many of us have fond memories of Armagh City Hall and cannot accept that where it once stood is now a car park. There was such excitement attached to those gala events of the Fifties and Sixties. Everyone knew everyone else in a friendly, companionable way. What a loss that was."

Anne and Roger had Diane, their first child, in 1972, then twins Catherine and Evan three years later. All four siblings have now completed third-level education, have 'flown the nest' and are working in various places—each following their individual interests. Fully occupied with her family, it was several years before Anne returned to nursing. With more than 30 years of dedicated nursing behind her, she glances at her diary, noting the next day's calls as district sister with Armagh's community clinic, then based at Dobbin Street.

"On my rounds I meet wonderful people. Most are senior citizens with an enduring spirit that brightens my day. Some have limited mobility yet they'll share a

Sister Anne Weatherup plans her busy day
Photograph by Ian Maginess

humourous comment or confide concerns for others, regardless of personal adversity. I cannot do other than pay tribute to the staff of Armagh Health Centre who are totally dedicated to the smooth running of each practice." Does having overcome personal difficulty enable her to cope with whatever life may deal?

"It is hard to have an independent sense of oneself", Anne admits. "I probably meet a problem squarely rather than fretting beforehand about something over which I have little control. I expect my life has given me self-respect and a sense of appreciation for good health. Violence is something that has always frightened me. For that reason, I deplore 'man's inhumanity to man' and, as a nurse, have too often dealt with the aftermath."

She is amazingly au fait with current affairs, crediting this to constant updating on her car radio whilst out on call. "Optimistic by nature, I savour good news and have you noticed", Anne pauses, "how much is achieved by women? Baroness Denton really worked to encourage investment in Northern Ireland. I was delighted when I heard that Rabbi Julia Neuberger had been awarded an honorary Doctorate of Literature from the University of Teeside. As well as being Chancellor of the University of Ulster, Julia is an author and lecturer. I had the pleasure of meeting her when Hillary Clinton gave the inaugural Joyce McCartan memorial lecture at Jordanstown. Closer to home, Lady Eames is one of the finest ambassadors we are ever likely to produce.

"I couldn't bear a world without music, whether a thrush in my garden or Andrew Lloyd Webber's evocative melodies. *Memories* from the musical *Cats* is a favourite piece. James Galway with his golden flute is, in my opinion, a truly polished performer."

She herself sings and is an alto in Armagh City Choir. Harmony in numbers is something Anne heartily recommends. "A choir is accessible to everyone, even those who doubt their own ability to sing. If you want to take the plunge and go for an audition, chances are you will find an appreciative ear, somewhere. Either you believe yourself to be a genuine singer—or you figure out how to act like one."

Travelling is one of Anne's favourite pastimes. She has visited Washington, New Orleans and Virginia in the States and has stayed in New South Wales. "Here the lonely beauty of the Blue Mountains was such a contrast to the bustling city of Sydney and the impressive capital at Canberra. A six-week sojourn in New Zealand, from North Island to Milford Sound in the South, gave a comprehensive view of that magnificent country. Europe, now so accessible, has always beckoned and, with Roger, I have explored many of its lands over the years. Perhaps the highlight was in 1998, when we visited New York, sailing out on the QE2 and returning on Concorde.

"Christmas is easily my favourite time of year—that lovely scent of spices, which seems to fill the house when cakes and puddings are brought from the oven. I am quite an exuberant cook and really try to make food look attractive." Deploring the ethics of factory farming, Anne admits, "I could easily become vegetarian."

Her children are vital to the life of this charismatic woman. "I think it's important to keep in touch with the young. Their company is what is marvellous. One of my treasured possessions is a gold-leaf hymnbook, given to me on my birthday by Diane. You see, she knew exactly what that would mean. It's as much for them I look forward and, equally essentially, assume I'll be there." Helen Keller who was blind and profoundly deaf, wrote "We differ, blind and seeing, one from another, not in our senses but in the use we make of them..."

It is impossible to share the company of Sister Anne Weatherup and not realise that here is a woman who uses all her senses for the common good and in the name of the highest calling.

Joe McManus

"My uncle was the village shoemaker, his workshop a nucleus of things seen and heard. As a boy, I'd slip into a shadowy corner, eavesdropping on half-understood conversations. Call it our 'Fleet Street' of the Fifties—pungent leather, forgotten tins of Dubbin, waxed-end of thread, a candle oozing grease. Men in flat caps called, idling away an hour but Uncle Joe seldom wasted a second. Tall and erect, he'd tap protectors on a farmer's boot or hold a lady's shoe, laces dangling, to the poor light, savouring fine glaze kid. I can see his hands, nails rimmed with mourning, as he burnished and stitched. Quiet, skilled as Michelangelo, earning a living, oblivious of his craft."

Joe McManus became a journalist, mid-1960, with the *Armagh Observer*, a job suiting his talent—the ability to structure a story. Joe is an authority on Milford, the historic red-brick village where he was born, and on the linen industry which for decades sustained its heartbeat. The main artery of any community is its characters and, of these, Joe has an index. What made him write?

"Words and a desire to communicate", he responds. "People fascinated me, so did conversation. I was educated at Greenpark School, staffed by Christian Brothers who, in 1999, left Armagh after 150 years' service to education. One of my favourite primary teachers was Brother O'Connor, who inspired my love, even at that age, of poetry and art. I can hear him read while we gathered around the classroom stove on a winter's morning... 'The North blind shall blow and we shall have snow, And what will the robin do then, poor thing?' I wrote my first story while a pupil at Greenpark when I was only nine. The words came easily, and reading it aloud was a real reward. Later I identified with the nature poets, Wordsworth, Goldsmith and Shelley." Asked to quote a favourite verse, he echoes George Pope Morris: "'Woodman, spare that tree! Touch not a single bough, In youth it sheltered me, And I'll protect it now.' Isn't it ironic to think that Ireland is the most treeless land in Europe?

"I developed a taste for parody whilst still a schoolboy. Once, when a barometer was accidentally broken, I laid down my thoughts. Recently, a friend bought a stack of books at an auction and found this little bit of satire on the back page: *Ode to a Broken Barometer*, by J. McManus. At the time, we probably resented a strict code of discipline but, with hindsight, appreciate how well prepared for life all of us were. The Christian Brothers taught courtesy, respect and purpose. That is how I will remember them.

"Our local 'poet laureate', a key character in Milford, was Paddy McCreesh, who eulogised in verse harmless gossip overheard on the factory floor. One of his epics, *The Pensioners' Seat*, took a tilt at village elders who sat there, puffing on pipes while setting the world aright. I was obviously striving to compete with Paddy! Television strangled the social badinage that filled long summer evenings, when senior citizens blissfully squandered time. When the first frost of the season lacquered the bare ribs of the old Pensioners' Seat, Paddy and his pals shifted to a neighbour's cosy fireplace." This famous bench was removed in order to make way for major road works. It will, I'm glad to say, be restored by Milford Community Development Association, of which Joe is vice-chairman.

"The McManus family came to Milford in 1920", Joe states. "I was born at 48 Hill Street, and that is where I remained. My home once served as the village shop, owned by the Armstrong family—Pastor Armstrong still resides in the village. At this little store, oil, soap or candles exchanged hands, and what essentially stimulates any community, the latest gossip. I've learned of old Milford from exchanges, which constitute a requiem for a way of life long gone. Here, in the shadow of a dormant mill chimney, is a rare link with the past. Milford and its population were envied by nearby Armagh. With a reputation for spotlessly kept homes, most village women worked. Having the means to dress well, they did. These were people with dignity who carried themselves with pride. Naturally there were village characters, like Bob McElroy, who visited my father and was affectionately known as 'Gunner' McElroy. In 'Black and Tan' days, Gunner ran a shebeen, peddling illicit poitín. Ironically, he also considered himself an authority on the Bible. Reluctantly going off to bed, I'd fall asleep to the familiar colloquy of my father and Gunner in the room below. Our next door neighbour, Betty Whitley, was a charmer with screen quality. She sang soprano voice, often accompanied by local girl Muriel Irwin. Betty entertained at village social events or accompanied dance bands on stage at the City Hall. She'd have made the charts today, easily outdoing many of today's entertainers."

Joe's heyday was the carefree, social scene of the Sixties. "The Rainbow Café, owned by Tommy McAvinchey, was everyone's rendezvous. I recall Jim Reeves' velvety hit, *He'll have to go*; Coca-Cola was the latest drink and local girls, in skirts with yards of frothy petticoats showing, perched on tall stools by the counter. It was also the advent of the Showband era with top bands, Larry Cunningham and the Mighty Avons, The Royal, Eileen Reid and The Cadets, or Joe Dolan and the Drifters playing in Armagh City Hall." Joe developed a love for big bands and country music, which has lingered until the present day. Of friends involved in country music he lists Margo O'Donnell (sister of Daniel), Gene Stuart and Philomena Begley. Joe has written a number of songs that were recorded, the best known of which is *Old Armagh*, recorded by various artists. "The lyrics of this song best express my feelings for my native city.

"Armagh has also seen the ugly face of anarchy, when a civil rights march, supported by people from all sides of the community, was organised. World press booked into the Charlemont Arms Hotel and the Beresford Hotel. I was covering this story for my newspaper next day. Making my way home, shortly after midnight, scores of farmers were preparing to take over the town, in a bid to prevent the march. The air was rife with hatred and I remember it as a terrifying experience. Men who enjoyed a reasonable standard of living were smashing up a peaceful protest—an attempt to highlight unfair allocation of jobs and housing. I've often wondered if those responsible for that escapade and subsequent violence, even gave a toss. Reporting almost three decades of violence was not how I'd envisaged my career. Ceasefires did bring a certain relaxation, yet we'd lost community harmony. I look forward to a time when we trust each other in friendship, socialising and working outside self-imposed ghettos.

"Respect and sharing is the only way ahead. A newspaper must report the truth or trouble ensues. National dailies seem to get away with almost anything, but not a local weekly. I never lose sight of how a life can be destroyed by insensitive reporting. Ian Maginess, a professional photographer, joined our staff in the Eighties. Respected by everyone, Ian's attitude typifies the press at its best.

"Personal experiences are a yardstick and for that reason I rarely judge others. My parents, John and Nellie McManus, had a simple philosophy. They didn't condemn anyone and I try to follow their example. After 30 years as the *Observer*'s 'man in Armagh', life is rarely dull, meeting and interviewing leading personalities or politicians who visit.

"My uncle, Malachy Sweeney, was also an uncle of the late 'Birdy' Sweeney. Malachy was known throughout Ireland as the 'Céilí King'. Playing frequently in my home, he awakened my love of céilí music. My sister, Jean, who has been in Australia since the early Sixties, played the piano for Malachy's band. Jean is musically gifted and expert at several instruments. My wife Margaret, a retired nurse, is always there for our three children. Encouraged in both their schoolwork and music, daughters Cathy and Jane both play piano and tin whistle. Cathy, aged 14, also enjoys the violin, and 12-year-old Jane the harp. My son Paul, now 15, is a historian, interested in drama, acting and antiques. Paul often says he loves the atmosphere of old houses."

A dedicated sportsman, Joe reports weekly on Gaelic Athletic Association football and with good friend, Joe Sherry, knows every pitch in Ireland. "The late Jim McCullough was easily Armagh's most-famous footballer and I produced a video film on his life. Joe Sherry, who doubles as my chauffeur, runs one of Armagh's longest established shops, sings with St Malachy's Choir and is a valued member of Portadown Male Voice Choir. Earlier this year, he travelled with the Portadown Choir on a singing tour of Canada." His village home occupies a special place in Joe's interests. When Robert McCrum, English author and great-great-grandson of Milford's founder, mill owner R.G. McCrum, came to Northern Ireland in the late Eighties to produce a television documentary, Joe contributed a wealth of information on his family, and both were guests on the Seán Rafferty BBC chat show. To further this history, Joe invited English soccer legend Gary Lineker to take part in a documentary on the penalty kick which was introduced into the game of soccer by William McCrum of Milford in 1891, and is used universally. "It was a good moment, bringing a

Joe McManus surveys the city
Photograph by Tom Conachy

Milford personality to recognition, as well as our village itself, and seeing both acknowledged by the world of sport", Joe offers.

"Everyone was saddened when the mill closed", Joe says finally. "Now a committee member of Milford Community Development Association, Gerard Mackle, has bought the McCrum Institute which he has re-named Callan House. Thanks to restoration, the Institute will again occupy an important role in village life. In time, he may also develop the site of Milford factory. It seems a coincidence that in 1912, William McCrum formed a committee to beautify the village. Now, nearly a century on, Milford Community Development Association is doing likewise. With the guidance of our chairman Stephen Hyde, son of Milford's best-loved entertainer, the late Cyril Hyde, we have withstood trouble and joy and, in that, remain unique."

Joe's editorial experience will prove invaluable in the Association's Millennium Project, a book recording the history of Milford village, the first of its kind.

"I love people, all people, and talking to people. In short, life's been good to me. There is no 'right' way to state a series of events", Joe concludes, "just your way. Another person would present things entirely differently. Ideas are rare, unless", he pauses, "you find a man like my Uncle Joe..." *A quiet man, earning a living, skilled as Michelangelo, oblivious of his craft...*

Amy Lyons

September 1999 saw the official opening by Lord Dubs of a new £1.7 million Ulsterbus depot at Lonsdale Road, Armagh. Offering the highest standards of comfort, this splendid new facility was designed by the local firm of Ian Donaldson Architects, and was described as a sign of the government's commitment to public transport. Mary O'Rourke, the Republic of Ireland's Minister for Public Enterprise, was also a guest. Unveiling a commemorative plaque, Lord Dubs commented: "This project is a tangible example of mutually beneficial, cross-border co-operation and a practical demonstration of the benefits of partnerships within the European Union. Each new bus station is an important part of improving links between Northern Ireland and the Republic of Ireland."

Mayor Tom Canavan of Armagh City and District accompanied dignitaries on a tour of the new complex. One of these, Joan Smyth, chairman of Translink, said Armagh bus centre was one of the most recently completed projects in Translink's long-term commitment to the provision of a comprehensive and modern public transport system. A £15 million investment programme will totally upgrade the bus fleet operating throughout Northern Ireland. Translink's managing director, Ted Heskith, accompanied guests on a guided tour of the premises, which he described as "bringing Armagh into line with the modern complex of Great Victoria Street, Belfast". District manager of Ulsterbus, Greg McLaughlin, promised that depot facilities would make every effort to sustain a customer-friendly image, and that an Inspector's information office would be centrally placed for easy access.

Standing in line at the enquiry desk of this modern complex, you can't help overhearing. "Do I travel directly to Letterkenny", a passenger is asking, "or must I go via Sydney?" "That depends on how much time you've got", smiles the clerk, pushing up one sleeve of her green cardigan. Patiently explaining the choices, she hands over a complimentary timetable. The passenger leaves, impressed. Eavesdropping can lead to better things. This little vignette is a prelude to Amy Lyons and her considerable experience of the Ulster Transport Authority.

Amy began her employment with Ulsterbus immediately after leaving Armagh Technical School. She'd been clerk for several years when she left to marry Brian Lyons, an electrician at St Luke's Hospital. "We live at Kilcreevy, close to Brian's home farm. With a family of five children—Andrea, Nichola, Jocelyn, John and Jayne—there was rarely a dull moment. As an only son, John may tell you he had to fight for his rights but believe me, he coped very well. When the girls were younger I relied on the talent of Brian's aunt, Lizzie Lyons, a seamstress in Milford village. Lizzie understood teenage fads and was capable of sewing from sketches they made and often implementing ideas of her own. Thanks to her they were always nicely turned-out for special occasions. Dressmaking is a skill that has all but disappeared and with it, the special atmosphere of a sewing-room where fabrics waited to be turned into summer, winter or evening dresses. The floor was strewn with discarded cuttings that made excellent patchwork quilt material or dresses for dolls. At fitting sessions, Lizzie marked each hem with chalk, and later, we had the joy of calling to collect the completed garment. In her quiet, competent manner, Lizzie was a craftswoman serving a vital need at a time when people could not always afford shop-bought clothing."

As soon as her family was self-sufficient, Amy returned to her job with Ulsterbus, which had moved from College Street to premises on the Mall. "Major revisions had taken place by then. With the Seventies came decimalisation, then computerised accounting. Personnel too, had also completely changed. My previous manager had resigned, and Bob Dormer, a driver whom everyone will remember affectionately, had retired. Doris Edgar was to be my colleague and we've worked together agreeably since. We are a team whose aim is maintaining a public service, efficiently and harmoniously. Long-serving stalwarts of the organisation were Inspectors Herbie McCarten and William McCartney who made my job a pleasure. Previously employed by the Ulster Transport Authority, both men worked in an era when weary cyclists paid half-fare to have bicycles transported on top of green and cream painted buses. During winter it was commonplace for drivers to plunge into snowdrifts.

Passengers then had to walk the rest of the way home. One-man buses came into vogue in 1965 then two years later, the UTA became part of the Transport Holding Company; a consortium of Ulsterbus, City Bus, Flexibus, NI Railways and Aldergrove Airport. Professor Chris Baines who campaigned for the Super-route concept now became the company's environmental advisor. You have to respect his thinking. Traffic congestion is one of our greatest sources of pollution. Trying to educate thousands of commuters to leave cars at home is not easy."

Amy agrees that litter dropped on public transport or ugly graffiti indicates a fall in personal standards. A hefty fine ended the anti-social habit of smoking on public transport and concealed video cameras have made detection of vandalism easier, but the problem still exists. Amy has sympathy for Ulsterbus drivers who may have to cope with less than courteous members of the general public.

"Remember that drivers are facing the hazards of chaotic traffic which is already quite enough. It's not just schoolchildren who behave badly—adults sometimes show little consideration for other people. If passengers would just remember that everyone else is going to work in the morning when they try to shove to the front of the queue. One or two buses still leave from the Mall and a town stop has been requested. The days of hundreds of schoolchildren massing on the Mall has gone as Ulsterbus has made arrangements to collect most directly from their schools. On my side of the counter we take the rough with the smooth. Of course our job is to assist, but a courteous member of the public extracts the best. This applies equally to the telephone, when a human voice has to be preferable to a dismembered one on tape. Surely I am not alone in questioning how much money, time and staff, this method of answering the telephone saves? Press-button-and-wait systems might suit a firm, but they are certainly not satisfactory from a customer's stance.

"Ulsterbus publishes a quarterly magazine, *The Express*, and it is surprising how many members of the general public write to say how helpful a driver has been, perhaps helping with luggage or giving directions for the remainder of a journey. Someone recently spoke to me in glowing terms of one of our drivers, Peter Macklin, who had shown tolerance in an extreme situation. Compliments come when we least expect them and are always welcome."

Ulsterbus employees enjoy excellent perquisites. In addition to a company pension fund, sickness pay scheme and free uniforms—in Amy's case, check skirt, white blouse, green cardigan and shoes—employees enjoy free travel throughout Northern Ireland, even after retirement.

"As a family, we travel with Ulsterbus. While I've not gone beyond the United Kingdom, I know that hotels for short breaks throughout the year or continental holidays are painstakingly selected by the company. So are the venues. We've visited Betty's Tea Rooms in Harrogate where founder Frederick Belmont, a Swiss confectioner whose policy is that everything be 'fresh and dainty', still survives. Tea at the Grand Hotel, Brighton, can be taken in the bright conservatory overlooking the sea or a cosy, Victorian lounge. An endless choice of little teashops is a welcome part of a relaxing holiday. They are to be found dotted all over England, Scotland and Wales. I recommend The Mad Hatter in Launceston, Cornwall, which has a menu to please Lewis Carroll fans and 'Eat Me' March Hare cakes. The Olde School Tea-room in Workshop, Nottinghamshire, has a blackboard menu, children's hand basins in the washrooms and old school bookshelves that display prints from local artists. I picked up a leaflet on my last trip to Scotland and was amazed to learn from a paragraph tucked away on the back page, that the man who gave us our homely cup of tea, Thomas Lipton, was born in 1850, in the poverty of a Glasgow tenement, to Irish parents who had fled the potato famine. His mother began a corner shop offering butter, eggs, cheese and ham sent from Ireland. When he was old enough to wheel a handcart, Tommy Lipton collected this produce from Broomielaw Quay each Monday. He became a cabin boy on the Broomielaw-to-Belfast liners, then learnt about business in America. The first Lipton store opened in Glasgow, again stocking Irish produce. By his 40th birthday, Thomas Lipton was a millionaire. An earlier generation in Armagh must have contributed to this, for a successful Lipton shop is part of our town's history. All information came free", laughs Amy. "Our programme for Millennium celebrations has not come to hand but, I anticipate, will be quite special."

July saw Amy's daughter, Jocelyn, travel to Buckingham Palace where she received her Duke of Edinburgh's Scheme Gold Award. "As a member of Aghavilly Youth Club, under the skilled direction of Miss Evelyn Corry, Jocelyn worked for years to achieve this, the

The official opening of Translink Armagh in September 1999.
(L to R): Mayor Tom Canavan, Mary O'Rourke, Republic of Ireland Minister for Public Enterprise, Lord Dubs, Northern Ireland Environment Minister, and Translink staff Doris Edgar, Amy Lyons and Eva Hill with managing director Ted Heskith

highest award of all. Miss Corry continued with her valuable youth work after retiring from teaching. How many would give so freely of their time in this day and age?"

Amy and Brian Lyons share a love of affordable antiques, old postcards, *Country Life* magazines and pottery. "Royal Doulton figurines are my weakness", Amy admits. "Once on holiday in Blackpool I saw a really special piece, *Lady Fayre*, dating to 1935. Her dress was green with flowers picked out in red and the model was moulded in the stance of a curtsey. The price was out of reach but, my, it was beautiful. I love dainty or unusual china plates, especially the cabbage-leaf design which Wedgwood made or Clarice Cliff's Art Deco, and I treasure all the pieces my children have given me over the years."

A typical homemaker, Amy used to make and decorate what she calls "passably good" wedding cakes. "I was taught the skill by Wendy Menary at evening classes that the College of Further Education ran some years ago. No-one appreciates what a time-consuming and painstaking pastime this is, and I certainly wouldn't have the patience to do it for a living." Her tapestry version of *The Last Supper* may have taken ages to complete, but is exquisite. Another favourite, *Little Boy Blue*, taken from a Royal Doulton design by Leslie Harradine, will hang agreeably in the living room. Doulton discontinued the pattern in 1973, which adds substantially to its interest.

Each day at Ulsterbus has the potential for an entertaining story. "We have a lost property department containing hundreds of umbrellas, school scarves, packed lunches and, once, a live hedgehog. After a few months, all are donated to a charity shop—not the hedgehog, though. It was claimed immediately. A favourite story is of Jake, a local collie, who managed to stowaway on a bus travelling to Dungannon. Bob Gibson, the driver, didn't notice him slip through a crowd of schoolchildren who were thronging the aisle. Inspector Joe Jordan spotted Jake in Dungannon the following day and arranged his return ticket to Armagh with driver Emmanuel Murtagh. I told you we had caring staff! Now, if you'll excuse me. I ought to be getting back to work."

Across the courtyard at the Ulsterbus complex, suitcases bake in this unusually lengthy spell of hot weather. Passengers queue patiently, then at the first rev of an engine, impassive faces brighten. Alphabetical destinations rotate, stirring our wanderlust. A Goldliner coach lazily pulls its half-load into the lane of traffic, everyone going somewhere.

"Do I travel directly to Letterkenny", another passenger at the enquiry desk is asking Amy, "or must I go via Sydney?"

Archbishop and Lady Eames

The Church of Ireland affirms the basic beliefs of the early Church—while taking care that she never denies truths. She holds to the threefold ministry of bishops, priests and deacons, subscribes to ancient creeds, and her teaching is rooted in Scripture and the tradition of the Catholic Church. In so doing, she claims a place in the tradition of Patrick.

The Archbishop of Armagh and Primate of Ireland, Dr Robin H.A. Eames, now ennobled as The Rt Hon. and Most Rev. The Lord Eames of Armagh, has committed his primacy to working continuously for peace and reconciliation between Ireland's two communities. Lady Christine Eames, wife of the Archbishop, now fulfilling her second term as world president of the Mothers' Union, is entirely supportive of her husband's work. Within her own sphere she is head of an organisation whose numbers are in excess of 750,000. Lady Eames was the first person from outside Great Britain to fill the presidency.

In 1994, His Grace received honorary degrees in recognition of his work from Cambridge University and Lancaster University. He was granted a life peerage in the 1995 Birthday Honours' List. On occasion Lady Eames accompanies her husband to the House of Lords, but both give priority to church responsibilities. An ongoing contribution to peace saw the Archbishop conferred with an honorary degree from Aberdeen University in 1997.

Most Sundays will find His Grace attending two or three services throughout Ireland. These may take the form of dedications, confirmations or anniversaries. Most weeks there are a number of Armagh diocesan meetings, which he must attend. Once a month, the Archbishop spends three or four days in Dublin at central committee meetings and must also find time for visits to the House of Lords, when Northern Ireland issues are being discussed. Dr Eames' private secretary, Mrs Roberta Haffey, keeps his diary of engagements and is much respected by a host of people who come into contact with the Archbishop's office. With rarely a free moment, his days are both varied and busy. In January 1999 Archbishop Eames spoke to the Literary and Historical Society of University College Dublin, on the topic 'Ireland: A State for the 21st Century'. In complete contrast, a week later he spoke and presented the prizes at Lisnagarvey High School, Lisburn. February found him attending the launch of the Children's Charter at Malone House, Belfast, meeting the Lord Mayor of Belfast with other church leaders, launching the *Irish Farmers' Journal* in Dublin and hosting 50 students from Trinity College Dublin, who were visiting Armagh. The next month included joining with other church leaders at Ballyclare Secondary School regarding the Peace Trail visit from St Joseph's School in Drogheda, speaking on BBC Radio 4 as part of the Daily Service and attending the Church of Ireland Youth Conference. The Archbishop considers *Any Questions* when it came from Omagh and the official opening of the Cardinal Ó Fiaich Memorial Library and Archive to have been of particular relevance.

Lady Christine Eames' list of engagements matches the strenuous itinerary of her husband. Checking the last few months, she has taken part in *Any Questions* on BBC Radio 4, spoken in the House of Commons to a group of parliamentarians and attended an international conference concerning the family in public policy. Following a series of interviews on television, radio and the press on the role of grandparents in society she then spoke in Wakefield Cathedral, at a service celebrating marriage. In June, Lady Eames opened the annual fête at Foster Green Hospital, Belfast, where her mother had been matron for 20 years. July brought a round of Mothers' Union visits in England and, in August, a meeting with members in Kenya. September's highlight was a Mothers' Union general meeting in Harrogate, when 2,000 members attended from all parts of the United Kingdom. The next general meeting will take place at the Waterfront Hall, Belfast, in September 2000.

It is rare to find them both with time to relax. When they are at home, The See House in Cathedral Close is an ideal sanctuary. With its neatly grouped seascapes and quiet decor, many of the rooms look over Armagh city and verdant countryside beyond.

"I began life in Dublin", Lady Eames says, indicating a silver-framed photograph. "My father, serving in the Army during the last war, was killed six weeks after I was born. My mother returned to work as a qualified nurse, becoming matron of Foster Green. She had a special quality, which captivated hearts wherever she went. In many ways, the hospital became an extension of our lives."

Educated at Belfast's Ashleigh House School, Christine was appointed head girl in her final year. "I particularly enjoyed our debating society and amateur dramatics, but, a head taller than my classmates, I was invariably cast as Brutus, Petruchio or one of Shakespeare's men." After visualising a career in medicine, an eleventh-hour decision changed the course of Christine's life. Opting instead for a law course at Queen's University, she graduated with an LL.B in 1965.

"I still had an unfulfilled compulsion to study medicine, so once more I enrolled for the appropriate course. I didn't complete, though", she pauses: "you see, I'd met a young curate called Robin Eames. His father was chaplain to Foster Green Hospital and naturally our paths crossed. Robin had also studied law, then rethinking his career, enrolled at Trinity College Dublin where he graduated with a PhD."

Following their marriage, Dr Eames was appointed Rector of St Dorothea's Parish on the outskirts of East Belfast. Christine has good memories of her first contact with a congregation. It was with St Dorothea's she enrolled as a member of the Mothers' Union. "This forward-thinking organisation accepts single parents and unmarried parents with children. Single men are also made welcome", Lady Eames assures. "Our common bond is spiritual health within the family. Such is the pivot upon which the church rotates. We are practical as well. Appeals for practical support are often launched in area suffering hardship or need.

"Our sons, Niall and Michael, were now at school. As I was busy with my family, there was something unreal about the violence which first struck Belfast, and tireless attempts were made by church leaders calling for restraint."

After seven years, Dr Eames was transferred to St Mark's, also in East Belfast, yet contrasting strongly with St Dorothea's. One year later came his appointment as Bishop of Derry and Raphoe. "We lived at See House in a beautiful setting on the outskirts of Derry. The years spent there, 1975 to 1980, were marked by political unrest and yet everyone made an effort to retain a semblance of normality. Life within the Church continued as before. Our sons were now students at Foyle Preparatory School. When my husband was elected Bishop of Down and Dromore, we returned to Knock on the outskirts of Belfast. It's always sad severing friendships but we'd become conditioned by now."

Niall and Michael became students of Campbell College and, for a time, Christine Eames taught Law at the College of Further Education. "Within the Mothers' Union, I was now vice-president of the diocese, besides being president of the Clergy Wives' Fellowship." It was in 1986 that Dr Eames was elected Primate of Ireland and Archbishop of Armagh. "I knew little of this city, but the prospect was exciting. The following year, the Mothers' Union celebrated its centenary in Ireland and I became diocesan president." This was a preparation for the world responsibility that she would later assume. "Our sons had entered university, both studying medicine. Today they are qualified surgeons." She herself continued to study and, in 1994, achieved a MPhil in Medical Law and Ethics.

As leaders of their respective churches, Archbishop Eames and Cardinal Daly worked to the point of exhaustion in the name of peace. That the first cease-fire came during the 1994-95 festival of Armagh Together was a source of joy, albeit short-lived. Now Archbishop Seán Brady agreeably fills the void left by Cardinal Daly who retired from the primacy in 1996.

"Church leaders", Lady Eames comments, "do not always agree on current issues, but grant each other a respectful hearing. Respect for differing cultures is constantly restated. If every person was genuinely dedicated to peace, then our land might once again experience stability and prosper as a result."

On 23 February 1995, Christine's Commissioning Service as MU world president was held in St Margaret's Church, Westminster. "Permitted my choice of music, I selected *St Patrick's Breastplate*, arranged by Cecil Frances Alexander, wife of a 19th-century Archbishop of Armagh. Good friends from Mothers' Union branches throughout the diocese were there. I was almost overwhelmed by this surge of goodwill." Her presidential diary found her representing the Anglican Church in Africa, America, Australia, Korea and New Zealand. Midsummer, she attended a conference in Australia while Archbishop Eames addressed the General Synod of the Anglican Church in Melbourne.

Elected to a second term of office, it is her experience that proves beyond doubt the efficiency of her work. As

His Grace Archbishop Robin Eames
and Lady Christine Eames

Lady Eames continues to fulfil her presidential duties, the relevance of the Mothers' Union throughout the world will, she believes, see her through this final three-year period. Capable of holding the attention of an audience on any relevant topic, she generally speaks without notes. Her Majesty the Queen is patron of the Mothers' Union and they have met several times.

In any given year, the number of guests visiting See House is enormous. "We have hosted the Archbishop of Canterbury, the Archbishop of the Sudan, Archbishop Desmond Tutu and a constant stream of church dignitaries. To implement decisions made by international leaders of the Mothers' Union, I make weekly trips to Mary Sumner House in London, where a lot of our work is carried out. I could not manage this without efficient secretarial support, and Mrs Eleanor Compston is my invaluable personal aide."

The Archbishop was introduced to the House of Lords on 1 November 1995, which Lady Eames as one of many exceptional moments in her life.

"I will always remember when my husband received his honorary degree from Cambridge, Betty Boothroyd, Speaker of the House of Commons, and actress Dame Maggie Smith were also conferred. We were guests of President Mary Robinson and later, President Mary McAleese, at the official residence, Áras an Uachtaráin. A possession which I treasure is my mother's Bible which I keep by my bedside."

If her life is strenuous, Lady Eames copes ably. Both are facilitators, and she will be as much remembered for her role in the Mothers' Union as Archbishop Eames for his challenging peace-making efforts.

The Vallely Family

'Another Yeats', critics say, observing the art of John B. Vallely. If Yeats had preferred painting people to landscapes, he might indeed have a disciple but Vallely's individuality is his own and unique. Believing the language of paint is texture rather than detail, he admires Rembrandt whose self-portraits showed more than just passing years—they told of the artist and his difficult life.

The personality of the man the art world knows as John Vallely is not easily interpreted—a man of dual but complementary identities, his canvasses are signed "J.B.V." though he is known to family and fellow musicians as Brian. His art certainly reflects a powerful and dramatic imagination. Many of his works are an antithesis, abstract yet strong in composition and tone. Presently showing at the National Gallery in London is *Rembrandt by Himself*, an extraordinary new exhibition of more than 60 self-portraits by this great man. One of these, *Self Portrait of the Artist as a Young Man*, was painted in 1628 when Rembrandt was in his early twenties. At much the same age, John B. Vallely, a young student in 1961, caught the attention of art critic Kenneth Jamison, with his first self-portrait. "Clearly", Jamison wrote, "this is a student of considerable promise."

Armagh was the place of John Vallely's birth in 1941. His early education began at old Blundells Grange Primary School where his father was principal for 44 years. From the Christian Brothers' School at Greenpark and St Patrick's College, he became a student at Armagh Technical School, attending art classes for two years. The first public showing of his work was here, under the direction of art teacher Peter McGirr, in 1958. One year later, winning a scholarship, John entered Belfast College of Art, where he studied drawing, painting and printing for a time. A model student, he won the Staff Association Prize in 1960, the Taylor prize for watercolours in 1961 and various awards at Royal Dublin Society for watercolours, landscape paintings and lithography. A diploma course at Edinburgh College of Art led to a postgraduate scholarship, part of which included use of a well equipped studio. Awarded the prestigious Andrew Grant Bequest travelling scholarship, John spent a year abroad, mostly in Spain and North Africa. This instilled confidence and he set up his own studio in Edinburgh where he worked for a further year. Returning home, John is based in Armagh where, in terms of talent, his is one of the most highly esteemed families in the county.

Eithne Carey, John's wife and mother to their five children, is originally from Donegal. Her inherited love of music she attributes to her Scottish-born grandmother, Catherine Slevin. Eithne's father Harry was raised in Glasgow, later moving to Beleek, Co. Fermanagh, where he lived with uncles John and James Slevin, both fiddle players. Eithne's childhood was steeped in music at home and céilithe at the local hall at Beleek.

"At the turn of the century", Eithne says, "everyone in my family played the fiddle. I represent the fourth playing generation, while my children are the fifth. School holidays and throughout summer we stayed at Kilcar, the home of my mother, where Seán Brady, once my school teacher, taught my children music on Clarke C whistles." Eithne recalls how Irish was the spoken language in her home and both parents sang in Irish. She perfected her knowledge of music, first at boarding school in Falcarragh, then St Louis Convent in Monaghan, learning classical violin, piano and song. "I studied Irish at University College Dublin in 1962", continues Eithne, "taking part in Dublin Pipers' Club, Comhaltas Ceoltóirí Éireann and house-sessions involving Seamus Ennis, Tommy Potts and Tommy Peoples. Through them I met Breandán Breathnach for whom I transcribed tunes. I was friendly with Helena Rowsome, daughter of pipe-maker Leo, and developed an interest in the uilleann pipes. Obtaining my own practice set, I took lessons. It was the following year, through our mutual love of the pipes, I met Brian at Milltown Malbay." Unaware of what significance the *Ceol Rince na hÉireann* collection would eventually have, Eithne, with Seán Keane of The Chieftains worked with Breathnach for subsistence money. "It was a good way of learning new work and since I had no grant, I transcribed a lot."

She began teaching in Dublin at 21, moving to St Louis in Monaghan in 1968, and taught music in Armagh until 1995. Eithne is one of this country's most respected musical authorities, deeply involved in the Northern

Ireland National Curriculum Planning for Music Education. The three eldest Vallely sons are professional musicians. Niall, the eldest, carried out postgraduate studies at Cork University combined with teaching music; Cillian has established himself throughout the United States as an accomplished player of pipes and flute. Caoimhín also studied music at Cork University and has toured professionally since he was 16. Lorcán is a student at Belfast College of Art while only daughter and youngest of the family, Máire, attends St Patrick's High School in Keady. When they are together, now a rare event, the family unites in music for pleasure.

Post-Impressionism was a revolutionary art form wherein its exponents, Van Gogh, Cézanne, Gaugin, Toulouse-Lautrec and Matisse experimented with new forms. Such vitality caught the imagination and interpretation of John Vallely who made an instant impact on the art world. Inspirational stimuli came from things that concerned him most—rural Ireland, its traditions, music, pastimes and sport. His own interest in traditional culture is almost vocational and total commitment is obvious in the originality of his work. Themes and hobbies interlock in John's painting; a sense of forgotten time can be detected in all these studies. He paints musicians and he plays and teaches music on uilleann pipes, concert flute and tin whistle.

John and Eithne Vallely founded the Pipers' Club in 1966, dedicating themselves to the promotion of a locally forgotten instrument. Now they play and are known all over the world. The Pipers' Club is a thriving cross-community organisation offering weekly classes in traditional music which 130 children presently attend. Since 1972, an important aspect of the Club has been the publication of tutors for traditional instruments. "We found from teaching", Eithne comments, "that some of the children could learn by ear while others wanted a written tune they might practise on their own. Thus the idea of duplicating sheets came about and the whistle tutor was born." The first of its kind, these books were a phenomenal success and huge numbers are now in circulation. Appletree Press commissioned a book and disc set which has been a best seller ever since. Neither the Vallelys nor the Pipers' Club benefit financially from sales but it is gratifying, Eithne agrees, "when we consider just how many have learned from our work, people as far apart as America or Australia. Many have written, or, meeting our children abroad, told them as much!" Traditional music is also taught in several local schools and, as an example, a quarter of the children who attend Saints and Scholars Integrated School are pupils of traditional music. The William Kennedy Piping Festival, usually held each November, dramatically increased local interest in the uilleann pipes. It is estimated that at least 3,000 people have benefited from this part-time teaching course.

Himself an avid athlete, sport occupied a major role in John Vallely's life and he participated in boxing, weightlifting, cycling and athletics. The latter was always his first sport and he has gone from competitive athletics to athletic administration as international secretary for the National Athletic Cultural Association of Ireland. Discovering the joys of travelling while attending the Rome Olympics, John was fascinated by Italian art which he encountered during a tour supporting Irish weightlifting. In 1969 he was awarded the Arts Council Major Subsistence Award and this enabled him to travel abroad. He agrees that reviewing the Irish situation from a distance has placed it in a universal context. Since then, new themes have appeared in John Vallely's work such as road bowls or bullet throwing, cycling and horse racing.

It is almost impossible to have lived in this county and not know of the talents of John B. Vallely and his gifted family. From his first exhibition, in company with Glasgow artist John Byrne, John's work is recognised and highly regarded throughout Europe and regularly across the Atlantic. Themes from Irish mythology, influenced by folklore and cultural definition, led to that which has dominated his work for 25 years, *The Musicians*. Many of the figures in his work are personal friends but are neither portraits nor caricatures. "They resemble de Staël's *Footballers and Jazz Musicians*", considers Brian Ferran, deputy director of the Arts Council for Northern Ireland. Nowhere, it seems, does John Vallely better express himself than in these paintings of musicians and music.

The Vallely family often performs together and represented Armagh at a gala St Patrick's Day concert in Basingstoke in 1997, when they with Armagh Girl Singers, Mayor Pat Brannigan and Mayoress Molly Brannigan were guests of Basingstoke Male Voice Choir. Organised by Hannah Williams—marketing officer for BMVC—a concert hall filled to capacity with an audience of 1,500 rose in admiration. Hannah Williams later

The multi-talented Vallely Family

commented, "people still speak of that event and like to think our Armagh friends will return to provide an encore."

Exhibitions of John Vallely's work have been held in Armagh, the Magee Gallery and the CEMA Gallery, Belfast, Molesworth Gallery and Hendricks Gallery, Dublin. More recently he has exhibited in Cavehill Gallery, Belfast and Jonathan Swift Gallery, Carrickfergus. John Vallely has contributed to major group in Edinburgh, Glasgow and Nottingham. Vallely collectors await these events with anticipation. In 1997, an Arts Council of England judging panel singled for special attention Vallely's jacket design for *Touching A Chord*, a book of Irish biographies. He has also designed compact disc covers for exclusive marketing. A.W. Boyer, art critic for the *Belfast Telegraph*, in his review of the Armagh artist's first exhibition, stated: "Mr Vallely already shows great capability as a painter and we can confidently look forward to a career for him and further pleasure for ourselves."

Today, in a mellow, mature light we see an artist at peace with himself and what he produces. His work is recognised at a glance and can be found in the foyer of Armagh City and District Council within the Palace Demesne, Queen's University Outreach at Armagh, the reception offices of the Southern Education and Library Board or the Servite Priory at Benburb. It was truly said: "He has a powerful and dramatic imagination, works best on a large scale, and has the technical skill to encompass his rich and barocco dreams in works whose depth and strength give great confidence in his future."

Gladys MacCabe, art critic and artist wrote: "John Vallely, an exhibition of whose recent paintings, drawings and watercolours is on view at the Arts Council Gallery, is an artist of rare ability. In this exhibition, musicians provide the subject matter for many of the works. There are works in this exhibition which move and delight one. This artist has conquered his idiom and enriched it with all the technical means which his instinct suggests: thick impasto, mixtures of tones, glazing, shading. Often his colours emit vivid glows, his canvases drip with light and are encrusted with warmth."

Perhaps this local artist, so frequently described as 'another Yeats', will one day exhibit at the National Gallery, and if our acceptance of this gifted family seems comfortable, it's simply because they fit so rightly into today's artistic firmament.

The author acknowledges material kindly supplied by Rachael Rea, Eithne Vallely and the Irish Section of the Southern Education and Library Board.

Tom Duncan

Record examination results were reported in September 1999 at Speech Night in the Royal School, Armagh, when chief guest was Dr Dawson Stelfox. An architect by profession, Dr Stelfox was the first Irishman to climb Mount Everest. Dr Patrick Kellett, chairman of the management committee of the board of governors, was chairman for the evening when parents, friends, governors and pupils heard of the Royal School's success during the past academic year. Headmaster Tom Duncan MA, BSc, DASE, reported that the 1999 GCSE results were far in excess of the average level for Northern Ireland. The pass rate for all subjects at top grades—A* to C—was 92 per cent, with 35% of grades being either A or A*. At A-Level, the results were also excellent, with a pass rate of 88% for grades A to E. In addition to the school's academic achievements, the Rugby 1st XV won the Subsidiary Shield at Ravenhill, the hockey teams had an excellent year and, on a high note, the school choir reached the final of Ulster Television's *Choir of the Year* competition and are presently making a compact disc for the Christmas market.

As end-of-term approaches, tentative sunshine falls across the quadrangle. The last students hurry off to class and mid-morning silence envelops the courtyard.

Tom Duncan has been headmaster of the Royal School, Armagh, since 1988, his appointment breaking with tradition. Each of his predecessors stemmed from the academia of Trinity College Dublin or Cambridge University. Regard for the past combined with modern innovation proved him to be an ideal candidate. Against a back-cloth of tradition he promotes tomorrow's world in a multiplicity of ways. A chemistry graduate of Queen's University Belfast, Tom later obtained a Master's degree in Education Administration from the New University of Ulster, as it was then known.

"I was educated at Methodist College Belfast and, on attaining my degree, appointed to teach chemistry at Dalriada School in Ballymoney. I held this post for 25 years, the last 13 in the capacity of vice-principal. Most of that time I was head of the Science Department. Roberta, my wife, is also from Belfast."

His comments on life in Portstewart and the north-west are tinged with nostalgia. "In the evenings, Roberta and I often walked three miles of Strand, right to the spot where the Bann enters the sea. Nothing quite substitutes for living by the coast. Tides and weather are constantly providing change. On that particular stretch you can virtually taste salt from an Atlantic swell. Ships and boats are my weakness so invariably I'd find my way to the harbour." Behind the headmaster's desk, witness to his comment, is a glassfronted showcase containing a model of *Capetown Castle*, a vessel of the Union Castle Line. "This ship was built in Belfast, when the city boasted the greatest shipyard in the world. As a boy, I spent my pocket money on annual editions of *Janes' Fighting Ships*. These books would be valuable today, if I knew where to find them.

"My interest in youth work began in Portstewart, assisting with the Boys' Brigade. The local Company was reconstituted and I took charge of the Junior Section. It was pleasing to hear they recently celebrated a quarter century of continuity."

With Coleraine Drama Club, Tom also undertook stage lighting for Ballymoney Drama Festival, an annual event of vital importance throughout the North. "During Festival week, when the curtain rose nightly, audience attention was devotional. Each drama group had its own supporters and an amazing range of talent. Afterwards in the lobby all waxed ecstatic whilst comparing notes. The same atmosphere attended the Ulster Drama Festival held in the Opera House." A continuing love of theatre is reflected in his frequent attendance at Armagh City and District Arts events or concerts at the Waterfront Hall, Belfast.

The Royal School was founded as a boys' school by James I in 1608, then granted the Royal Charter by Charles I in 1627. The site on College Hill came into being during the 18th century. The school acquired co-educational status following amalgamation with Armagh Girls' High School in August 1986. Major renovations were required to accommodate this increase in numbers. "Teachers and classes worked through the dust and din of cement-mixers and diggers", Tom recalls. "Eventually it took shape and the Duke of Gloucester performed the official opening ceremony in 1990. His Royal Highness the Prince of Wales visited the school in 1994 and it was then he declared that Armagh would have City status."

As present-day custodian of a 400-year-old establishment, Tom has a formidable task. "Our present intake of 650 is a comfortable number. There are another 50 children in the preparatory department. Ours is one of the few schools in Northern Ireland offering boarding facilities. This is a boon to families working on contracts abroad, diplomats or expatriates. Eighty boarders are drawn from Northern Ireland, the Republic of Ireland, Great Britain, Thailand, Zambia, Hong Kong and elsewhere. I am often asked how Asian families learn of the Royal School. This is usually by word of mouth. Children presently boarding return home, and discuss life as it is here. More and more Hong Kong and Malaysian parents are choosing to educate their children in the UK."

Maintaining the *esprit de corps* of any school is a tremendous responsibility. Tom Duncan successfully markets NI schools abroad, and was formerly chairman of the Northern Ireland Boarding Schools' Partnership.

"Upholding the tradition is daunting. It speaks volumes for our teaching staff that we go from strength to strength. We employ 43 teachers and 25 technical, domestic and administrative personnel. I am proud of this highly motivated team, their dedication and the reputation each strives to maintain. A general inspection highly commanded the standard of work within the Royal School. Our aim is chiefly the grooming of individual talents for higher education and the workplace. Well-prepared students should compete successfully. Children of this school represent the total socio-economic spectrum of society and I am confident, that with guidance, each will slot into appropriate employment."

In various ways, Royal School, Armagh, is integral to the community. "We provide a centre for Arts Council events, the Ulster Orchestra, sporting and coaching sessions, clubs and societies. There are also many summer activities held at the school—so gone are the days when the building became dormant as soon as lessons ended."

Tom Duncan's chairmanship of the inter-community committee forming 'Armagh Together', in celebration of 1,550 years since the coming of St Patrick to this island, was a natural progression. "This committee of local people was a blend of culture, background, opinions and skills based on the precept that we must advance together", Tom adds. He is also chairman of Armagh Marketing Initiative (AMI), Armagh District Scouts and a committee member of the Friends of St Patrick's Cathedral.

Royal School, Armagh, extends the hand of friendship to neighbouring colleges in the city. "We combine with St Catherine's College and St Patrick's Grammar School for cultural events and activities including an annual joint visit bringing aid to Romania. It is our fervent hope that a new generation's stewardship will advance fair political thinking and thereby the dawning of a pleasant, hospitable, no longer murderous land."

Summer vacation provides an opportunity to unwind. Tom and Roberta are both keen travellers and have recently returned from Australia. Roberta now works in the Southern Education and Library Board.

"As an avid reader of newspapers, I appreciate cryptic crosswords or well thought out opinion pieces. Our sons, David and Alan, attended Oxford University and now live in London. Alan works as a solicitor in the city while David is a computer consultant. Both boys attended Royal School, Armagh."

Blithe young voices cheer a distant match as I leave by the cloistered walk. There is precision in this grey stonework, sculpted witness to countless generations who passed this way and are now scattered about the globe. What makes him happiest, this unassuming scholar who ably undertakes his considerable responsibilities?

"That silence at the end of term", he unhesitatingly responds.

Headmaster Tom Duncan
of the Royal School, Armagh

Avril Paisley

Armagh College of Further Education is regarded as one the finest of its kind in Ireland. The courses on offer for the Autumn-Winter term 1999-2000 embrace a comprehensive range of subjects. One College tutor, Avril Paisley, is about to embark on her tenth year at the Lonsdale Street institution where she teaches the art of patchwork. Avril's contribution to the golden threads of history is significant for in 1993 she designed a masterpiece in quilting, one that symbolised the spirit of 'Armagh Together'. This was the concept of Armagh Arts Committee and Avril willingly assisted by creating a theme of united cultures.

"Today it hangs permanently in Armagh County Museum", says this pleasant and quietly spoken craftswoman. "For me the quilt is more than fine workmanship, it is a constant reminder of the fellowship enjoyed by the women who made it. Our team comprised Mary Dawson, Sister Casey, Margaret Oakes, Margaret Humphries, Catherine Maxwell, Rita Garvey, Brenda Loughran, Geraldine Joyce and Cecilia Woods. The quilt is a 'picture history' incorporating Celtic design against a background of stained glass and team spirit was sewn into every stitch. We spent hours bent over a table in a room allocated by the Golf Club and eventually produced a work which seemed to please everyone."

Avril and Niall Paisley's home suggests an almost forgotten era. Wild flowers and shrubs fringe a winding path leading to the front door. "We bought the cottage because of its exceptional location and the view", Avril comments. "From this vantage point, Armagh's skyline at sunset is constantly changing. After years of neglect, a lot of renovation had to be carried out, yet we've managed to retain something that is hard to quantify. Age makes for character and I have to say I would rather live here, despite the problems of an old house, than in one that is deemed modern."

Walking into the bright, spacious lounge there is a sense of timelessness. Each window overlooks the garden, which is carpeted with snowdrops in Spring. Avril provides food in winter for an endless variety of wild birds despite the fact that agile grey squirrels steal much of it. "Hedgehogs often seek refuge in the box hedge", Avril explains, "but they kept falling into the pond so we had to fill it in."

Avril Paisley is mother to three grown sons. "Jonathan, our eldest son, married last October. He met his wife Claire through his company, IBM UK, where he works as a consultant manager. After completing a degree in Economics from Southampton University, Jonathan travelled extensively through Europe and, with Claire, he still enjoys visiting far-off places. Our twins, Christopher and Niall, are now 27. Christopher lives in London where he is a systems architect with National Westminster Bank. Any free time and you'll find him working on his hand-built red Cobra car. My most memorable trip one where I sat beside him wearing dark sunglasses, my chiffon scarf flowing all the way from London to Burnham-on-Crouch! Niall has his own workshop in Hatton Garden, London, where he works on exquisite jewellery. He has career experience at the House of Fabergé. Go back a century in time and Theo Fabergé was designing exclusively for the St Petersburg Collection those jewelled eggs associated with the family of Tsar Nicholas. Niall has undertaken commissions for European heads of state but strict secrecy forbids disclosing details."

Both families originate from Banbridge where Niall's father was county medical officer and Avril's county welfare officer. "We knew each other from childhood and somewhat oddly, both families moved to Armagh when we were about seven years old. Niall boarded at Royal School, Armagh, and we became romantically attached as teenagers."

Disregarding his own love of precious stones, Niall studied as a pharmacist, opening his own research laboratory.

"I undertook a career in social work, mainly teaching Braille and Moon, a less known form of communication for blind. Technology gradually replaced both with a computerised system." Obviously genuine in her dedication to people with a physical disability, Avril dismisses those years by adding, "It wasn't a labour, I loved the work." Handicrafts formed a vital part of her training and Avril discovered she possessed a natural flair for quilting, sewing, knitting and tapestry, and for a time, she experimented with painting in oils.

"While the boys were growing up, I combined voluntary work with home commitments. A local playgroup claimed much of my time and, for ten years, I served as a member of St Mark's Church Select Vestry." Avril remains on the board of governors of Royal School, Armagh.

Classes in quilting first began as part-time day and evening courses on the syllabus of Armagh College of Further Education. Here, Avril found an outlet for her skill, with the double reward of 'a thing accomplished'. "In the early days I joined classes out of interest", she says. "Friendships made then were as important as the skill we were trying to master. As numbers grew, the administration at Armagh College of Further Education wanted to know if I would teach the craft. The College has grown impressively in academic terms. Now, in association with Queen's University, Belfast, it is possible for students to undertake a part-time degree course at Queen's University at Armagh."

From three groups of 16 meeting each Tuesday and Thursday mornings and Wednesday evening, Avril's quilting classes are now entering a tenth year. "Quite a number of students have been attending since the beginning so naturally, we have seen many changes, sometimes through illness or death. I am a member of the Northern Ireland Patchwork Guild which involves a monthly meeting with the added challenge of entering pieces for exhibition. Work exhibited at a special event to be held in December 1999 at the Ulster Folk and Transport Museum, Cultra, will then move to Armagh County Museum in the New Year of 2000 AD." The Guild's contribution to the Millennium is an exhibition with the theme 'Quilts in the Cathedral', which has been planned to take place in Dromore Cathedral, Co. Down, when the emphasis is based on aspects of Ecclesiastes iii, 1-8: *To every thing there is a season and a time to every purpose under the heaven: A time to be born—a time to plant—a time to dance—a time to embrace—a time to sew—a time to love and a time of peace.*

"Tapestry has always played an important role in church furnishings and I specifically mean the largest work of its kind in the world, *Christ in Glory*, which covers the wall behind the high altar in Coventry Cathedral. Weighing almost a ton it is 70 feet high and 39 feet wide. Craftsmen worked on it for four years and most impressively it is guaranteed to last for another 500 years."

Her own home is hung with lasting examples of stitching skills, colourful tapestries and delicate mosaic quilting. "As my sons left for college, I made a quilt for each one, using 'Courthouse steps', a design where intricate squares intersect in diagonal rows, with the emphasis on eye-catching colour." What she rightly imagines will become an heirloom is a quilt, which has taken over 20 years to complete. A snowflake pattern is made from many of the dresses she's worn over two decades. Each piece and pattern holds an association that is entirely personal. One particular framed work is extremely rare. Copying each family signature, Avril embroidered these, collectively, on to diagonal quilting. Her most prized work in colours of scarlet and gold is *Cathedral Spire* which she lent to Armagh RC Cathedral for a St Patrick's Day commemorative exhibition in 1993.

Avril also belong to the Quilters' Guild of the British Isles, where Northern Ireland is known as Region 17. "A suitcase exhibition of pieces 24" x 24" has been put together by each region. This suitcase will then travel around the other 18 regions finishing at the National Exhibition, 'Under the Covers', which is to be held during September at the Indoor Cricket School at Lord's Cricket Grounds in London.

"Niall and I still enjoy our travels and recently took a sightseeing trip to Italy. Before leaving, we discovered from the Commonwealth War Graves Commission that we were quite near to where a brother of my mother, the Rev. Cecil Henry Bingham of the Royal Army Chaplains' Department, had been buried after World War II. Cecil Henry Bingham was a Church of England chaplain and is interred at Montecchio War Cemetery in Urbino, Italy. This was previously the main Gothic line, a defensive German position. I have in my jewellery box a very beautiful dress ring that was bequeathed to me by this uncle at the grand old age of two! This ring was returned to his mother with a few belongings and his private communion set. We found the War Cemetery to be a very moving experience as no other member of the family had ever visited before. Here, I discovered my uncle had died on 31 August 1944, aged only 34. I felt privileged to represent my mother and write my name on her behalf, into the Book of Remembrance.

"A fortnight before going on holiday, we celebrated my mother's 80th birthday. Eleven of her grandchildren were present at a wonderful party for family and friends. Seven grandchildren had travelled from England and Scotland, the eldest bringing their wives, Claire and Sari.

"I love to visit the American Museum at Clamerton Manor, close to Bath. Domestic life in America from the late 17th to 19th centuries is interpreted and shown as well as the work of American craftsmen. What intrigues me most is a collection of very old American quilts. There are so many it takes days to see them all. Visiting our sons in July means a chance to see the largest United Kingdom quilt show at Olympia. Quilts and quilts and quilts..." she says with relish. "It's also a chance to have a spending spree at the craft stalls where glorious fabric and quilting cottons are piled high. Whenever possible, with the aim of keeping abreast of current trends in patchwork circles, I attend additional workshops throughout the year. This reinforces how much quilting has evolved from a thrift craft to that of a serious art form. Every exhibitor I visit has something creative and satisfying to offer as well as providing invaluable stimulus.

"I greatly admire the theatrical talents of Dame Judi Dench and 'was amused' by her role as Queen Victoria in *Mrs Brown*. Nor is it surprising that *Shakespeare in Love* took so many awards for this film was sheer entertainment. The televised series *As Time Goes By* is my favourite programme, as identifiable with life as slipping on a comfortable pair of shoes. I relax by listening to music and will automatically pick up whatever needlework happens to be on hand."

Having improved their home to such a degree, moving would be unthinkable. "It's just the garden", Avril points out ruefully. "We do our best but it still requires hacking every so often otherwise it becomes unworkable."

Avril Paisley can best be defined as someone preserving important skills of the past for future generations—a skilled needlewoman and an artist in her own right.

Avril Paisley with the commemorative 'Armagh Together' quilt
Photograph by Ian Maginess

Robert Turner

Good humour provides the best possible introduction to Robert Wolsley Turner. Shaking hands, he smiles engagingly. "We might begin by saying I'm a survivor. Two wives of Henry VIII lost their heads. I fared better. In a run-in with a razor I lost only my hair!"

Descended from farming stock and a man of tremendous practicality, Robert and his wife Barbara live in tranquil countryside mid-way between Tandragee and Poyntzpass. "Due to my father's ill health, I was forced to leave school at the age of 15", Robert states. "At the time, his was a smallholding, maybe 40 acres." By industry and commitment, the land on which Robert Turner farms beef cattle and specialises in milk production now extends to 250 acres.

"Loss of expendable income attributed to the beef crisis has adversely affected local commerce more than any other factor", he comments. "When a farmer has means, he changes his car, takes a holiday and his wife has money to spend on her home. From firsthand experience in terms of loss which this industry has suffered, Ulster's farming community is indebted to local Member of the European Parliament Jim Nicholson, whose sustained efforts helped lift the export ban."

Focused drive and determination brought Robert Turner to the top in local government when he was first elected Deputy Mayor in 1997, becoming Mayor the following year.

"Always interested in unionism, I was at one time a member of the Young Unionist movement and later, a member and secretary for Cusher electoral ward. A vacancy arose in 1981, when former Council Chairman Major William Henning, JP, retired. A selection meeting pressured me to put my name forward. Not remotely enthusiastic, I was nevertheless elected and have been returned to local government ever since. As mine is a predominantly nationalist area, it is a source of pride that I should consistently receive a majority vote. Respecting equal rights of all has remained my policy, one I strive to honour. When the unionist majority on the Council took a decision to share power with other parties, Pat Brannigan made history on his election as first Social Democratic and Labour Party Chairman. Now we rotate the office of mayor on an annual basis and believe me, one year is enough. It is fulfilling in one sense but it is also totally exhausting."

Somewhat ruefully, Robert Turner reflects on the greatest moment any city mayor could ever experience. This 'big fish' of an occasion might easily have slipped through the net, overshadowed by Omagh's grief in the wake of an appalling atrocity.

"A Book of Condolence was opened in Tandragee Methodist Church where right-thinking people, sickened by an unwarranted act of evil, thronged to sign. I wrote to the Mayor of Omagh at once, expressing sympathy on behalf of the people of this district. Books of Condolence were also opened at the Palace building and other venues for one week, allowing members of the public to record their own messages of sympathy.

"The visit of President and Mrs Clinton with Prime Minister Blair had been planned for months. World media looking on at our 'Gathering for Peace' on 3 September had no idea this visit could so easily have been cancelled as the President wished to visit and sympathise with Omagh's injured and bereaved. Desmond Mitchell, our Chief Executive, saved the day by suggesting President Clinton do both, spending somewhat less time in Armagh. Ten thousand onlookers cheered when I welcomed our distinguished guests. Two democratic leaders in the Christian Capital of Ireland presented us with a great opportunity and something unique on which to build. For Barbara, it was the crowning event of the year, and a moment 17-year-old local girl Sharon Haughey will never forget. Some time previously, her letter to the President moved him to ask if he might meet her in person. Sharon made a clear and impressive speech in which she asked for permanent peace in this Province. Ulster Television and the BBC followed every moment of the musical programme preceding our platform formalities. Next day I received a telephone call from a friend in New Zealand who saw me on television. Yes, it was the highlight of 1998", Robert agrees, quickly qualifying this comment with his stoic rationale: "Regardless of whatever the occasion, we earn our living as farmers. I am always aware of the fact that evening will see me return home to milk our cows."

Returning to 1981, Robert admits he had little idea of local government administration but a desire to learn all he could in order to contribute something worthwhile.

"My first experience and standard procedure, I imagine, for every newly elected Council representative, was serving on Armagh City and District Arts Committee of which Harry Carson was chairman. I am culture-conscious and will unhesitatingly promote drama, music, or literature in various forms. It is a joy to meet talented young County Armachians who rate with the best in the arts world. Whether it's jazz or James Joyce, I'd like to see better community support for these excellent events. Ballroom dancing is a favourite pastime of my wife, Barbara and myself. I suggest the showband era was a unique phenomenon that is woven into the souls of today's middle-aged citizens. We still take every opportunity to dance and perhaps like the Waterfront Hall, our new Theatre and Arts Centre will host a return to nostalgic evenings."

His increased first preference vote in 1984 was steadily repeated until Robert Turner was elected Deputy Mayor in 1997. "Pat Brannigan was Mayor that year and in every respect, a gentleman. With his support and agreement, I often took visitors on a conducted tour of the Palace or to our many tourist attractions."

Acutely aware that vacant business properties and commercial difficulties co-exist, Robert Turner shares the concerns of our retailing sector. "I reiterate that agriculture, in general, is the backbone of society. Lack of business stems from the farming community's lack of cash flow. Freezing district rates was a proposal and we presently run the Council on a shoestring, keeping district rates as low as possible. Regional rates are outside our authority. Grant aid from central government has been cut annually for some years, hence we have no choice to do other than increase district rates to maintain necessary operations. A thriving industry would ease the ratepayers' burden and in this respect, the Council has done everything possible to attract investment. Armagh and District is not an area where targeting social needs is recognised as vital or grant aid available. An investor will naturally seek a base where finance from the Industrial Development Board is accessible. I assure you we do all we can to change this situation. Ednaveys has an industrial estate, which remains unoccupied. Manufacturers must necessarily look at the infrastructure of our roads. The Department of the Environment has plans for a ring road to bypass Armagh, ending major traffic jams. We lobby the DoE to implement such plans and will continue to do so until they are in place. I presently serve on all committees and am chairman of the leisure and tourism subcommittee. I suppose this constitutes a total of five meetings each month."

As Mayor, easily his most moving experience was visiting Razgrad in Bulgaria. "This municipality has been technically twinned with Armagh since 1995. A number of projects led by Armagh City and District Council included assistance in obtaining European funding. Such funding helped overcome widespread poverty and a difficult transition from communism to a present democratic state. The exchange rate for the lev—the Bulgarian currency—at the time of our visit was 2,800 leva to one pound. To view the economics of this country in perspective, a top civil servant earns the equivalent of £48 a month. Winters are severe, temperatures often dropping to minus 20 Celsius, so he can expect to spend two-thirds of his salary on fuel. Following a previous visit to Razgrad and seeing what dire conditions existed in a Mother and Child Orphanage, Chief Executive Des Mitchell sought funding from those with whom we do business. His enterprise engendered sufficient means to install a new laundry. Visiting that orphanage was an experience I will never be able to wipe from my memory. Economics of Bulgaria are such that few families can afford more than one child and infants are often left behind in an orphanage. We saw babies—some only three days old—in rows and rows of cots. All they possessed were the clothes they wore. It was a warm, sunny day and some of the little ones were crawling on the grass outside. They tugged at our clothes and we picked up one or two. It was heartbreaking when they tried to follow us as we left. Asking to visit the kitchens, we discovered all cooking was done on a single ring of a very old cooker. In his year of office, each mayor supports a worthy cause. Right there on the spot I decided that proper cooking facilities for this orphanage would be my priority.

"Razgrad did not enjoy the benefits or hygiene of public cleansing and a Council decision agreed to donate to them one of our refurbished refuse collection vehicles. I presented the keys of this lorry to Council employees and drivers, Simon Allen and David Nesbitt, outside the

Palace. With Direct Services Operation manager David McKee, they set off on an eight-day trip—something of a nightmare I'd venture to add! From Armagh, crossing by ferry to England, another sea route saw them drive from the Hook of Holland through Germany, Hungary, Austria, Romania and finally Bulgaria, arriving in Razgrad town square, where, at a public ceremony, I handed over the vehicle. Former mayors Pat Brannigan and Jim Speers were also present with their wives. Our valiant drivers were only ten minutes late due to a delay at a border crossing. They coped with temperatures of 40 degrees Celsius, a speed of no more than 40 miles per hour and driving on the right hand side of the road."

Returning home, Robert pondered on a fund-raising theme. "In the middle of a Council function, I decided I'd have my head shaved and so raise sponsorship. When I asked Margaret Mitchell of Cut 'n' Curl hairdressing salon if she would undertake such an operation, she agreed. Palace Secretary Wendy Geary selected a date and I addressed all local councillors, asking if they could jointly raise £2,000 before I took this drastic action. Every councillor backed me handsomely. At Tandragee Leisure Centre, supported by Willie Nugent and local well-wishers, £8,500 came pouring in. I received eight knitted hats to keep me warm until my hair grew again. One came from the commanding officer and officers of 8th Battalion, Royal Irish Rifles based at Drumadd Barracks, Armagh. In addition to a new cooker, the children of Razgrad Mother and Baby Orphanage received a new heating system, vital in a country where winter temperatures are often below 20 degrees Celsius. I hope to visit Razgrad again before Christmas just to see how well administration is faring."

A member of North Armagh Motor Cycle Club with a passion for motorbikes, it was a great moment for Mayor Turner when top motorcyclist Philip McCallen launched Tandragee Motor Cycle Club Show in October.

"Philip has brought fame to the sport, to Tandragee and to Northern Ireland in general", Robert comments. "I have been a disciple right from childhood and 1999 saw the 43rd annual Tandragee 100 motorcycle race which takes place on the second Saturday in May. This race is preceded by a charity run when entrants and cycling supporters perform two laps of honour round the circuit, culminating in a huge display of machines at the Square in Tandragee. This year I donned leathers and helmet, joining in the spirit of the evening. I borrowed a bike from one Club member and, while it was all of 15 years since I'd been a biker, managed very well. Of 43 races in Tandragee, I've attended every one, marshalling the first when I was only 16. This year was exceptional for we erected grandstands at both starting and finishing areas. Televised coverage of the race undoubtedly promoted the area from a tourist perspective with possible future dividends. I look forward to meeting Philip again at the Ulster Grand Prix.

"Sainsbury's bright, new, centrally situated store opened shortly before Christmas. It was the first of a particular format in Northern Ireland and a great moment when Barbara and myself pulled a cracker with the store's first customer, Jimmy McEntee, and Sainsbury's manager, Sandra Derbyshire. Employing 230 staff from the local community, quality and merchandising was attractive and impressive. Sainsbury's have a commitment to use local produce and some meats on their shelves were supplied by Dungannon Meats from beef which originated on my farm. Hughes' mushrooms, local eggs and Bramley apples are also available and prominently displayed. Sainsbury's take an active role in our city Chamber of Commerce and have already become an integral part of local commercial life."

Every mayor looks forward to visiting the elderly each Christmas. During Robert Turner's mayoral year, he was invited to share in the 100th birthday celebrations of Miss Minnie Patton and Mrs Sara Jane Rainey. "Barbara was an exceptional aide on every occasion, but particularly at events such as these. She often represented me at functions when I found it impossible to be present and always in a caring, compassionate manner. Becoming a centenarian provokes the thought that anyone born in the late Victorian era, say 1899, who survives to 2001 AD will have the rare distinction of bridging three centuries. Of an annual round of perhaps 500 engagements, one of the last was the annual dinner for the Talking Newspaper for the Blind. This voluntary organisation comes close to my heart for I have a blind friend who receives a tape each Saturday morning. This comes through the letterbox, postage is free of charge and the tape can be returned by means of a reversible, addressed card. My friend will not speak until he hears both sides. 'I'm reading the newspaper', he'll say should I call."

Asked if he would again fill the office of mayor for Armagh City and District, Robert Turner contemplates:

Mayor Robert Turner with President Bill Clinton and Sharon Haughey at 'A Gathering For Peace', 1998
Photograph by Philip Wilson

"Not unless someone was managing my farm. I have my own interests as well as those of the public and am a member and former chairman of the Ulster Farmers' Union and former member and secretary of the Young Farmers' Club. Rural affairs concern me and, for that reason, I serve on the Rural Development Council. As chairman of Newry and Portadown Canal Joint Development Committee since the early' 80s, I have a wish to see this oldest man-made canal in the British Isles restored. Seventeen miles of this canal made navigable would represent a superb tourist attraction. When I retired as Mayor in June 1999, I slept for a week! My hair has grown back since I made that dramatic gesture. Unless I had completely retired from the farm, it would stand on end at the very idea of a second term!"

The Lennox Legend

One hundred and eleven years of history died on 11 April 1998, when Armagh's oldest department store, A. Lennox and Sons Ltd. finally closed. Supermarkets and hypermarkets are seen as the great shopping experiences of present times, demolishing in their wake the friendly butcher, baker and candlestick maker. It was the enthusiasm of Victorians, which founded a innovative retail experience—that of the department store. Pre-war London's Oxford Street was the epicentre of giant emporiums. Most of Oxford Street remains as it was with the exception of prestigious Marshall and Snelgrove (now Debenhams); elsewhere stores fell like ninepins over the years. A major casualty in Armagh was the loss of A. Lennox and Sons.

These unoccupied premises are a monument to our commercial past. The last managing director of this family firm, David Lennox, has outlined a history of his stylish department store, which served Armagh and its population since 1887.

Founder of the firm, W.J. Lennox, began trading at number 17 Market Street—later to become the menswear department. Before long, business expanded and he incorporated number 19, next door, into his premises.

W.J. Lennox lost a son, a Lieutenant in the Army, during the First World War. This young man was interred at St Mark's Parish Church graveyard. W.J. also had three daughters but none embarked on a business career, in keeping with social restrictions as to what women might 'respectably' do at the time. From his comments in the *Irish Daily Telegraph* of March 1913, W.J. Lennox faced economic problems similar to those which beset Armagh's business community today. He wrote: "It does no good to grumble about people going away to shop, neither is anything gained by well-meaning friends publishing abroad the shortcomings of Armagh and its people, for, as one man has said—'An enemy may injure a man, but it takes his friend to complete the disaster.' We do not shirk criticism, however, but insist that it be just and impartial, and above all things, that the wretched pessimism so general in some quarters today be not allowed to hang like a pall over the whole situation."

W.J. Lennox went on to advise: "What Armagh really requires in this particular respect is what all other local places require, viz., to put character, energy and enterprise into business, after adopting the best modern methods, so that a general high level of service will be secured which shall command the trade of the district; and with the foregoing advantage there should be no difficulty in keeping the major portion of the retail business at home."

Andrew Lennox, David's grandfather, ran a general drapery store in Cookstown. Andrew was second cousin to W.J. Lennox and he had two sons, William and Jack. In August 1929, Andrew commenced trading at 19 Market Street, Armagh with William and Jack assuming management. Ten years later and a month prior to the Second World War, Andrew incorporated 17 Market Street into his existing business, the merger resulting in a major department store. He had by now sold his store in Cookstown to the Hughes family who are still trading at the premises.

Having proved himself an entrepreneur, Andrew implemented every modern technique and, in November 1939, introduced the latest Lamson Pneumatic Cash System throughout the store. At a cost of £240, this was a time-saver. Instead of walking to the general office, each assistant deposited a customer's receipt and payment into a tube, which was carried by suction to the main office. If change had to be given, this was returned in exactly the same fashion. Besides his important seasonal sales, Andrew Lennox advertised his merchandise in the *Ulster Gazette*—gentlemen's tailored tweed suits, afternoon dresses in linen or bombazine, parasols, sewing silks and items of needlepoint or lace.

Because Jack Lennox, David's father, and his brother, William, were both forward-looking and innovative, the business continued to thrive during the difficult war years. William assisted in Air-Raid Precautions, and when Belfast suffered heavy bombardment by the Germans on 15 April 1941, he reported for duty. Post-war austerity brought rationing and only 66 clothing coupons per person per year was permitted. David Lennox recalls his mother's approval of this system. Describing it as "masterly", she added: "It kept the nation from consuming all it had."

Bert Mackrel was an apprentice in menswear during

the war. Looking back at a superior quality of service, it is now a matter of *Were you being served*? "Herbie Withers was a master tailor with six or seven assistants in his workshop, for 'off the peg' suits hadn't come into vogue. Selecting a suitable cloth, the customer was then expertly measured. Making a suit was a lengthy procedure, requiring several fittings", Bert recalls. "I was only a youngster of 17 and my duties included finding a chair for any customer who was being served at the counter—always addressed as 'Sir' or 'Madam'. When the transaction was complete, I carried brown paper packages tied with string, to whatever conveyance the customer used. A pony and open trap was common then or, rarely, a motor car."

May 1945 saw a succession of street parties as the country celebrated VE Day and the end of World War II. In addition to Renee's Fashion Shop, established in Belfast by the Lennox firm, they now looked to the future. In deference to a prophesied baby boom, they opened Babyneeds, a nursery shop in central Belfast.

Vigorous changes during the 1950s and '60s established the Lennox firm as an authoritative byword in trading. Mannequin parades were held with in-store merchandise modelled by the staff. Window-dresser Tom Dale, tall and dignified, provided a perfect figure for setting formal wedding attire off to advantage. Leading attractive fashion assistant, Nancy Mackrel, on his arm, his appearance was a prelude to the grand finale of each fashion event.

The firm's annual outing was usually a fun-filled day by the sea. Boarding a coach outside the store, the staff, with their spouses and children, enjoyed an all-expenses-paid trip to Portrush, usually dining at the Trocadero. Morning coffee and afternoon tea were the rituals of a relaxed, social era. Friends met at the fashionable Wheel and Lantern Coffee Shop within the Lennox store, first of its kind locally, where intimate confidences or small talk mingled with the fragrant aroma of percolating coffee. A lunchtime menu was gradually introduced and meals were served on occasional or seasonal late-night openings.

At the request of William and Jack Lennox, Billy Adair joined the firm as window-dresser in 1952, a partnership that would last more than 40 years. Spectacular window displays and interiors for which the Lennox store was renowned can be attributed to Billy's creativity and flair.

"Within a few months, Willie Lennox gave me complete control of window-dressing in the Armagh store as well as Renee's and Babyneeds in Belfast. Can you appreciate how it felt having freedom to exploit this new form of commercial art without hindrance?" Billy's displays were spacious and uncluttered. "It was a look I aimed for long before it came into vogue. My best windows were those which appeared to be uncontrived, or, if you like, carefully casual. If I couldn't find the right props, then I made my own in the workshop behind the store. I've always enjoyed working with my hands, loving the feel and texture of wood. Charlie Bennett taught me the craft of woodwork and, under his expert eye, everything had to dovetail."

Major stores throughout the United Kingdom made tempting offers but declining all of these, Billy remained with A. Lennox and Sons. When the town had its back to the wall in the turbulent Seventies and Eighties, he produced some wonderful displays.

"I remember a Christmas when", he demonstrates with one hand, "all six windows represented open railway carriages. The engine wore an enormous, beribboned garland. Couplings linked the carriages. From each spilled gifts, toys, followed by china and crystal, lingerie, men's wear, shirts, gloves and umbrellas. I appraise from a distance and this theme was totally effective. It probably evoked the most positive reaction of any before or since. Years later, a writer told me she included a description of my windows in a Christmas story, which was published nationally.

"The season of goodwill brought hard work but holds the happiest memories. We allocated part of the basement to Father Christmas and, again, a theme enhanced his fairytale grotto. I'd like to think this magical setting gave as much pleasure as the gaily-wrapped gifts each child received. Throughout the store we hung Austrian garlands of spruce, holly and pine. Seasonal music created its own special atmosphere. Crowds thronged the streets and the Old Boys' Silver Band played merrily as Father Christmas made his annual sleigh-drawn pilgrimage to the square." With his quiet style, Billy Adair will always remain synonymous with the Lennox legend. Whatever the display, scarves, photograph frames, crystal or china—every window bore his inimitable hallmark.

Those turbulent days of which Billy Adair spoke left a bitter aftermath. In November 1971, a bomb was placed at the rear of the store. Walking out to investigate, David

The staff of A. Lennox and Sons celebrate their centenary in 1987.
Front row (L to R): Sharon McNeice, Ronnie Dawson, Betty Rollston, Yvonne Watson, Janet Stewart, Elizabeth Reddick, Shirley Beggs, Hazel Johnston, Elsie Millar, Derek Campbell, Catherine Hughes, Winnie Watt.
Back row: Billy Adair, Derek Kerr, Lindsay McMullan, Ruth Wright, Imelda Smith, Muriel Hyde, Betty Cupples, Ann Murphy, May McClean, Sandra Blevins, Merle Lennox, Shirley Mitchell, Madaline Houlahan, David Lennox

Lennox, who had joined the firm in 1969, walked right into an explosion.

"The device had been planted in a workshop", he recalls. "It was mid-day and most of the staff were at lunch. I was about to go home for something to eat when I saw staff running from the building. I went to investigate. Caught in the midst of the impact, somehow I staggered out. I was brought to the City Hospital, which was then fully operational. Without the skill of theatre staff I would never have made it to Craigavon Area Hospital." David lost the sight of one eye and any peace of mind surrounding the future of his business. The Lennox premises were badly damaged on two subsequent occasions.

Through difficult political change, the Lennox store maintained a quality of individualism, which was unique. In 1987, a century of trading was marked by a week of celebrations. Staff dressed in Victorian-style outfits and had a group photograph taken outside the store. When directors David and his wife, Merle Lennox, decided finally to close down, it was with the utmost sadness, yet tempered with a certain relief. A. Lennox and Sons had become an institution, one that provided employment through all of the preceding century.

Long-serving members of staff, when the store finally closed on 11 April 1998, were Elizabeth Reddick, administration manageress, with 49 years' service, Derek Kerr, buyer in household linens, with 47 years' service and Betty Rolston, buyer in the lingerie department, with 43 years' service. Saying goodbye to 43 members of staff was fraught with difficulty for both David and Merle Lennox.

"They were friends", David adds, "but they understood we had made a decision. I am happy to say, we still remain friends."

The sun may have set on the Lennox empire but it is everyone's fervent wish that Armagh may again enjoy shopping at a store of this calibre.

Julia Maginess

"The shore in winter—at anytime, but especially in winter—is something I love. Miles of deserted sand, gulls wheeling above the breakers, my little dog by my side..." A wistful note creeps into Julia Maginess's dialogue. "Given the chance I'm off to Donegal, but don't get the idea that I am less than fond of Armagh. Living here since 1963, it's long-since become my home." Julia was born in the English Midlands, close to Wolverhampton, yet her memories are mostly of North Wales and Snowdonia, where she spent time with her maternal grandparents.

"My father was a district commissioner in Nigeria. He'd serve a tour of 18 months, then rejoin my mother and myself in England. Life in the tropics was not healthy, so my mother, from necessity, returned home before I was born." Julia, an only child, was educated at Christ's Hospital School in Hertford, where she boarded until the age of 17. "This was one of the oldest schools in England, founded by Edward VI in 1552. Previously, the sexes were taught separately, but recently, for economic reasons, the Girls' School joined with the Boys' School in Horsham, Sussex.

"My father had an exceptional sense of fun, yet as a scholar of Greek, also wrote the most sensitive poetry. I've kept old editions of *Punch* containing his reviews. From his enthralling stories, Africa, where native compounds were surrounded by jungle, became almost familiar territory. He was the first white man one chieftain ever set eyes on. It was a blow when he was invalided out of service while relatively young. Returning to England, he continued to write for the *West African Review*, as well as translating a Greek epic poem, which was later choreographed for ballet performances by the Manchester School of Dance. During this time he continued to write for *Punch*. Taking little heed of medical advice, my father sculled for City of London Rowing Club against Oxford and Cambridge. My interests reflect those of my mother who painted in oils—mostly floral studies. Women rarely worked outside the home then, but my mother often helped with various charitable organisations. To raise funds, I recall her sitting, head bent over a tapestry or making soft toys. Our home was a haven of peace and quiet which I probably appreciated all the more for having been to boarding school where the climate was one of constant noise."

Julia's father died when she was only five. "Years later my mother remarried a close family friend who worked for the National Westminster Bank. We now moved to Llandudno, living with my grandparents. I was 15 and totally unsure about this dramatic change. I needn't have worried, for Ray, my stepfather, proved to be a wonderful man, exceptionally caring. My mother died several years ago but Ray remains my stepfather, friend, and grandfather to my children. He enjoys opera so his visits invariably coincide with a special performance at the Grand Opera House. My stepfather is a keen birdwatcher and rarely misses the winter migration."

Finishing with Christ's Hospital School, for two years Julia studied at Blackpool School of Photography. "My first job was with an artist who'd studied under the acclaimed master, Van Dyke. To really learn, you must work for a perfectionist. The most wonderful traits were evident in this man's portraiture. World leader or a little child, he'd blend background and dress, wait until the sitter had sufficiently relaxed, then capture the moment. The world impresses an identity on each of us—just consider what compassion was to be found in the face of Mother Teresa. Tapping such character is indeed an art. The studio undertook professional work for five crowned heads of Europe. If I say I cannot bear shots out of perspective, buildings lurching drunkenly or branches of a tree appearing from someone's ear, it's all due to my training."

Julia moved on to the General Chemical Division of ICI in Widness where photographic duties ranged from excavation sites to accidents on duty. "My area included Blackpool, Liverpool and Birmingham. During the course of my working day, I met Terry Maginess from Northern Ireland. Our interests were shared and we had a lot of fun together. Eventually we married in England, afterwards establishing our first home in Canada. Barbara, our eldest daughter was born there.

"We have been told that my husband's people can be traced back to the Flight of the Earls. We traced Terry's genealogy and, sure enough, Lord Iveagh, an ancestor, escaped to Austria where he became a colonel in the army. Generations ago, the spelling of the surname changed to Maginess.

"Terry was appointed engineer manager of Armagh and Dungannon Water Board in 1963, a body subsequently incorporated into the Department of the Environment. We lived in the resident engineer's bungalow overlooking Seagahan Reservoir. Ballymacnab is beautiful countryside, which I soon came to love. I'd get up early just to catch the spectacular dawn. With a wide-angle spread of rural landscape before us, I thought of people in inner cities or high-rise flats, deprived of such a vista and never breathing air this pure."

Later the family moved to Ashley Park, Armagh where they raised two more daughters and a son. "Barbara studied nursing, then married Tim, a master mariner in the Merchant Navy. They have a little boy of eight. Heather, who came next, took a degree in Fine Art and Community Art, eventually joining Yorkshire Television. Her husband, Daniel, is an American, and worked on a film for the Royal Armouries. They moved to Portavogie, Co. alternative to visiting Donegal. This particular bay has a rugged similarity.

"Our youngest daughter, Fiona, studied architecture at Canterbury and at Queen's University Belfast. She presently works with Belfast City Council. Fiona and her husband, Brian, live in Hillsborough with their baby daughter, Aoife. Only son Ian, like myself, is a freelance photographer. We were so proud when he was commissioned by Pilgrim Press to capture various aspects of St Patrick's Church of Ireland Cathedral." Published in 1991, Ian Maginess's work, particularly the centrefold, *The Nave Looking East*, bathes the interior in golden light and is an exquisite example of photography.

Julia is a former President of Armagh Inner Wheel. "*Friendship and Service* is our motto—one we try to uphold. Each year the organisation supports worthy charities. The Inner Wheel of Great Britain and Ireland are presently funding a lifeboat in commemoration of the Royal National Lifeboat Institution's 175 years service of saving lives at sea. This lifeboat is to be named after our organisation. I enjoy ikebana, the art of Japanese flower arranging. Simplicity of line is my aim and a striking form can be achieved from a branch with perhaps one or two lilies.

"We are both Friends of Armagh County Museum and Terry is one of a team of bellringers at St Patrick's Church of Ireland Cathedral. When required, Terry or myself are happy to help with the Talking Newspaper for the Blind.

"I love Armagh dearly and wish we were more litter conscious. It has to be wrong to spoil what is beautiful." Julia enjoys cooking enough to have attended several different courses with Darina Allen at Ballymaloo, Co. Cork, where Madhur Jaffrey was a guest chef. "Darina now has her own televised programme and often appears as a judge on BBC *Masterchef*."

For their Silver Wedding anniversary, Julia and Terry visited Kenya. "Wild animals roam freely across great national parks. On safari we witnessed an unforgettable moment when we came upon a family of cheetahs at play. Aware of us, the parents attempted every stratagem to divert attention from their young. We could only watch in silent admiration. This was Africa and to some extent, I was treading in my father's footsteps."

Her love of nature includes visits to Strangford on bird-watching expeditions. "My stepfather counts for the RSPB and he estimates at least 6,000 Brent geese took flight from mudflats near Newtownards last September. The oystercatcher is a favourite of mine but I hold my breath in winter, when birds congregate on skeletal branches. Elgar, I imagine, could hear his own requiem in their song."

You may conclude that Julia Maginess has an acute eye for detail but a hint of mystery lingers beneath her smile. Placed as she is now in front of the lens, hers is a life where travel and insight combine to give a better balance. The camera doesn't lie. From where she sitting, the overall picture is one of pleasing perspective.

Julia Maginess
with her dog Trixie

Jim Speers

You may imagine that the achievements of a retiring Mayor are all too easily forgotten with the clearing of his desk. Ulster Unionist Councillor and former Mayor James A. Speers insists that this is not the case. "I prefer to think that one year of constant activity serves as catalyst for anyone seriously focused on politics", he says.

"As Deputy Mayor in 1995, I came to terms with the protocol of this office. It was also valuable experience. When elected to the office of Mayor a year later, I had gained the confidence to cope with the demands and dedication which accompanies the position. Each day in a Mayor's calendar differs and may hold as many as seven engagements. I remember meeting convalescent children from the radioactive zone of Chernobyl and then, later that day, presenting an award for a best-kept village. I am always mindful of my origins. Bearing that in mind, I had no desire to demean myself, those whom I represented, the protocol of the office which I now held and, not least, the political standpoint from which I came."

During his Mayoral year, Jim Speers stood down as leader of the Ulster Unionist group within Armagh City and District Council. He speaks generously of a kindred spirit existing in local government and, when elected, was pleased to receive a unanimous vote. "In my year as Mayor, I endeavoured to utilise the stature and civic role of the position. In every conceivable way, I brought the office to the population of our City and District by opening the Palace doors to many in the community.

"Knowledge brings perception and a milestone in Armagh's history was the achievement of university status. It had been a two-century dream, stemming from the wishes of Archbishop Robinson. Today, it is generally recognised that we enjoy the best educational system of any part of the United Kingdom. City status had already been accorded when I came to office and the fact that members of Council now wore robes on formal occasions added a certain dignity. Queen's University at Armagh was declared open on 17 February 1997 by Sir Ron Dearing, CB, chairman of the National Committee of Enquiry into Higher Education. Few realise how much is owed to the late Sir Gordon Beveridge who was Vice Chancellor of Queen's University and whose support continued in his ongoing commitment to our City and District. The highlight of my mayoral year was the visit of Prime Minister Tony Blair on 16 May 1997. This was his first visit to Northern Ireland as Prime Minister so I became the first elected representative he met in Northern Ireland. Elizabeth, my wife, was a constant support during the entire year but meeting the Prime Minister was equally exciting for our nine-year-old son, James. After signing the Visitors Book, Prime Minister Blair walked and talked to local people. It seemed as if the entire city turned out in welcome, lining a route from College Street to the Market Square.

"The mayoral chain of office was presented to Armagh Urban Council by the Royal Irish Fusiliers and bears both the city coat of arms and the royal insignia of that Regiment. Elizabeth was first Lady Mayoress to wear a newly commissioned Mayoress's Chain of Office. It was Sir Patrick Mayhew, then Secretary of State for Northern Ireland, who launched the Borough Charter and Ceremonial Mace, a culmination of our civic journey as a city within a Borough."

During his year of office, Jim and Elizabeth met and spoke with literally thousands of people at hundreds of events. "The advent of Christmas brought a caring aspect to bear and an important round of hospital and residential home visits. We met with the elderly at Lisanally House and nursing or residential homes at Greenpark, Sunnymead, Castledillon, Fairlawns, Hockley Lodge and the Retreat Care Centre. Seasonal goodwill surrounded these visits as we chatted to residents and staff. On Christmas morning 1996, Elizabeth and I went first to the home of Markethill lady, Mrs Brown, who was celebrating her 100th birthday. Resting in bed, she took such pride in showing us the Queen's telegram and a massive number of greetings cards. Switching on the Christmas lights at a ceremony in Market Square engendered a lot of fun, with crowds of children contributing to a seasonal atmosphere.

"For sheer dignity, I cannot forget the Royal Irish Regiment Beating Retreat in a ceremony at the Palace when I was invited to take the salute. Soon afterwards, plans for the Library of Cardinal Ó Fiaich were launched at the Palace with Cardinal Daly and other church dignitaries present. It was an important year with both cease-fires in place and optimism filling the air. A group of voluntary workers in Keady also played an important role by sending humanitarian aid to Romania. Drivers volunteered their services, taking food and essentials to people in need. The good that abounds in a community is a humbling experience, and each catastrophic event proved it was also unlimited. One lovely lady from Milford, retired teacher Mrs Nancy Cunningham, who has first-hand knowledge of Parkinson's Disease, wrote asking if I would give time to a new Support Group for this excellent cause. It was an invitation I could not refuse.

"During my time as Mayor, I was also chairman of the Northern Ireland Housing Council, representing this country at the International Federation of Housing and Planning congress in Japan. Travel arrangements met with delays. Aware that I could not possibly complete my engagement in Japan and meet Nancy's Support Group, I flew home early." Having given his word, he kept the appointment.

A Young Unionist in his teenage years, Jim is a committed party member, serving as a delegate to the Ulster Unionist Council in the Sixties. "I relish every aspect of politics", he says enthusiastically, "and allowed myself to be persuaded to stand for local government at the time of reorganisation in 1977. Our six wards then were Richhill, Markethill, Killeen, Poyntzpass, Tandragee and Laurelvale. Standing for Richhill and winning a local seat caused a flutter because I was considerably younger than any of my peer group. I hold on record the highest vote ever recorded by Armagh District Council in the 1981 local election." Jim barely recalls Prime Minister Terence O'Neill's leadership, except to say: "I would have preferred Brian Faulkner as party leader and really believe that, had he been elected, we may have avoided needless bloodshed. I will say in his favour that along with numerous bridge-building gestures, Terence O'Neill was the first Northern Ireland Premier to make reconciliation a central part of his programme.

"In Armagh District, 20 councillors had increased to 22, including Orchard Electoral Area, which I represent. I suspect it had some bearing on my influence when Eric, my brother, stood for election in 1985. Eric is presently chairman of the leisure and tourism committee."

An area of major importance to Mayor Jim Speers is his chairmanship of the Northern Ireland Housing Council. In 1995, the International Federation of Housing Planning congress theme, 'Accommodating Differences', reflected the NIHC's affiliation to the IFHP. At the congress, hosted by Northern Ireland Housing Executive and focusing on a strategic approach to regeneration, a brochure was launched promoting the tourist potential of the Province, with a striking photograph of Navan Fort as frontispiece. In this context, Jim Speers was highly commanded for his commitment, and has since attended IFHP congresses in Jerusalem, Helsinki and Edmonton.

"I also visited the United States, taking part in an economic conference initiated by the Prime Minister and President Bill Clinton, during Jim Nicholson's mayoral year. We were hosted in Washington, DC, furthering our American connection and fostering links with the State of Virginia. As elected representative for Orchard Area, I never miss an opportunity to promote that aspect. Before leaving home, I planned a visit to Winchester, Virginia a huge apple-producing area, with a group of the Armagh delegation. Here I investigated potential for promoting our own apple industry in the Armagh area. I also learned that Virginia holds an Apple Blossom Festival on a magnificent scale, drawing thousands from all over the United States. With a small number of the Armagh group, we met major producers in the apple industry. When I became Mayor, Elizabeth and myself were invited back in 1997, attending the opening of this Festival.

"As I said, politics are of prime importance in my life, and as we were travelling on the night of the Westminster election, it was not until our arrival in the United States that I learned Tony Blair was Prime Minister!

"Another major initiative in promoting educational and economic links with the United States came about in 1996. Mary McAleese, Pro-Vice Chancellor of Queen's University, Belfast, took part along with Tom Duncan of Royal School, Armagh, Brother Leo Kelly of St Patrick's Grammar School, the late Jim Craig of City of Armagh High School and Hugh McAleavey of Armagh College of Further Education. The world is not literally getting smaller; it's just becoming more accessible. Distance is no longer a problem and contacts with the wider world can only serve to promote the growth of our city and its economy. Heading up a delegation to the Blue Ridge Mountain area was, without doubt, the most taxing week of my life! We had meetings over meals, from breakfast to supper. Introductions and a final summing-up were my responsibility." He smiles ruefully, "So you see, I do have the stamina for politics!

"Back in Armagh, the Duke of Kent arrived to open and plant a tree at the newly built leisure centre at Tandragee. The Lord Lieutenant for Co. Armagh, Lord Caledon, was present on this occasion, with Michael Ancram, MP. Of great importance was the visit of Anglican envoy, Terry Waite, who came for the Apple Blossom Festival, delivering a moving address on his ordeal in the Lebanon.

"Throughout it all, I cannot stress how much easier my year was made by the efficiency of Palace secretary, Wendy Geary. She kept my appointment diary constantly updated and a rigorous timetable ran like clockwork. Her pleasant personality belied the pressure under which Chief Executive Desmond Mitchell and his staff constantly work.

"My memories as Mayor are entirely varied. Our Apple Blossom Festival continues to develop and typifies community spirit working for the overall good. Attending at least 80 events, which took place during May, I enjoyed the enthusiasm of participants. Promoting our youth and the arts saw me welcome the Charles Wood Choir to this city for magnificent choral performances at centres of every denomination. The best of our city is surely reflected in the talents of Armagh Girl Singers.

"My objective has always been impartial promotion of our area. In common with right-thinking individuals, it is also one of peace. Obviously, as a unionist, the absolute goal is maintaining the Union, but selling rather than enforcing the merits of such a concept is my aim. In this time of sweeping change, I agree that a Party should lead in such a positive fashion that a negative approach becomes the exception. If I could persuade my counterparts throughout the world exactly what it is which constitutes the positive face of unionism, greater awareness would surely exist. My wish, within the scope of my politics, is to create a society where one tradition is regarded as being as vital as another.

"If I might pay tribute to members of the Royal Ulster Constabulary who, in a troubled era, have borne atrocity after atrocity. Caught, as they are on many occasions, between opposing factions, they remain essential to our community. Similarly, the Royal Irish Regiment and serving members of the armed forces, many of whom so tragically paid the ultimate price. Easily my saddest memory is of the callous, obscene murder of Councillor Charlie Armstrong.

"In detesting begrudgery, however it may manifest itself, I see this as a shortcoming in our society. Try to remember that many strive for ideals in difficult circumstances and often without recognition. If only we were as swift to give credit as we are to judge."

In support of this comment, each function carried out by the Mayor of our City and District focuses on positive aspects of those deserving acknowledgement. It can be guaranteed that Jim Speers will appear immaculately dressed. To appear less than well groomed at any function is deemed by him to be discourteous, nor does this uphold the dignity of his office.

"In the context of awarding credit where it is due, I rarely comment on the Honours List but, in the case of our Chief Executive, Desmond Mitchell, his award of the MBE is richly deserved. I have met thousands in the course of my life, yet none more modest, more caring, professional or quietly industrious.

"Whatever may come or go, my family remains a constant source of support. Elizabeth and I have four children—Jill who attends Markethill High School, Dawn, about to go to Chester University, Jayne who has been accepted by Dundee University, and our youngest, James, who has just begun secondary level education at Markethill High School."

Gene Kerrigan, writing on our prevailing problems in the *Sunday Independent* surmised, "If only the extremists would shut up, go away, die or do all three, unionists might be shown to be reasonable, moderate people, *if* a little colourful." James Alexander Speers has demonstrated fresh perspective, courage to sustain his beliefs within his Party and the energy to stay the course.

"I love my city, my country and its people. I badly want to see growth industry come our way in the next century. And if ever called to do so, yes, I'd be honoured to once more fill the position of Mayor."

Mayor Jim Speers and Mayoress Elizabeth Speers
with son James, greeting Prime Minister Tony Blair

Gerry Oates

Awakenings, an anthology of new Irish writing published in 1995, was a celebration of work produced by creative writing classes organised by the Workers Educational Association in Northern Ireland. Maureen Campbell, an established local writer, was a past tutor of the Armagh Group and it is a tribute to her that Armagh achieved the highest number of accepted entries. One contribution, *Unsung Hero* by Gerry Oates, tells of a childhood encounter with Leading Seaman James Magennis, VC, who was posthumously honoured in October 1999.

For 27 years Gerry has been a lecturer in the Language Centre at Armagh College of Further Education. A gifted writer, he lives at Lisnadill, Co. Armagh. Gerry's entry was recently shortlisted from thousands submitted for the Fenner Brockway Peace and Reconciliation Prize. Gerry was a boy when newly decorated hero, James Magennis, returned to visit his old school in Belfast.

Unsung Hero recalls that Leading Seaman Magennis was the only serviceman from Northern Ireland to be awarded the Victoria Cross during World War II. He displayed outstanding bravery as a diver on HM Submarine XE-3, when an attack was carried out on the Japanese cruiser *Takao* at Singapore Harbour on 31 July 1945. Crewman Magennis crept beneath the boat and, with difficulty, attached mines to the ship in foul and murky water. He was also hampered by leakage of oxygen from his breathing apparatus. Despite this, Magennis remained, placing his full quota before returning exhausted. To the people of Belfast, he was a hero. When he fell on hard times, selling his Victoria Cross, it was later bought and returned. James Magennis left Belfast in the Fifties and died in England in 1986, without having been publicly honoured in any significant way for his wartime bravery. It was suggested this was due to the fact that he was a Roman Catholic from West Belfast although officials at Belfast City Hall vehemently denied the accusation...

Thirteen years after his death, on Friday 8 October 1999, at a ceremony which included relatives of the late James Magennis, Robert Stoker, Lord Mayor of Belfast, unveiled a six-foot high memorial to the hero, commenting: "It is now time for this city to acknowledge the courage and valour of one of our own. James Magennis was a very brave man and we are proud of him."

As with all WEA adult education courses, the central tenet is the learning process itself. By engaging in that process, individuals empower themselves to think and act creatively. Gerry Oates' short story widens our experience and delineates the double-edged prejudice that diminishes any society. Few will read *Unsung Hero* without shudders of recognition.

Unsung Hero

"What is the highest mountain in Scotland?"

"Ben Nevis, sir, 4,406 feet."

"And what is the highest mountain in Wales?"

"Snowdon, sir."

"How high, boys?"

"3,560 feet, sir."

"In England now. What is the highest peak in England?"

"Scafell, sir, 3,210 feet."

"Now, boys, the highest mountain in Ireland, name it for me."

"Carrantuohill, sir, in the Magillicuddy Reeks, County Kerry."

"Excellent! How high?"

"3,414 feet, sir."

"So you see, boys, that anybody in Ireland can be higher than anybody in England, any day."

A loud cheer burst upon the class as we rejoiced in our superiority over the English in the matter of mountains.

"Quiet now!" And silence fell upon the class as the master raised his open hand like a policeman on point duty. "Get out your spelling books. At once!"

And that was the end of the day's geography lesson on mountains and mountain ranges in the British Isles.

Another day we were learning the names of the English counties by heart.

"Now, boys, take a good look at the map of England", and he pointed to the large-scale wall map alongside the blackboard.

“Take a long look at the northern counties. The six northern counties: Westmoreland, Cumberland, Northumberland, Durham, Yorkshire and Lancashire. Now let me hear you repeat them...

“Westmoreland, Cumberland... That’s it. Study them carefully, boys, for these are the six northern counties that we shall partition off from the rest of England when Ireland gets her freedom.”

The class erupted into long and rousing applause, excited by the thought of getting one over on the ancient enemy, but equally eager to prolong the note of levity and find respite, however short, from the tiresome rigours of learning.

“Boys!” and at once a hushed reverence replaced the high spirits as the master raised his voice. “And now, some revision... Cassidy, what is the longest river in The British Isles? Quickly, boy!”

“The Shannon, sir, 224 miles long.”

“And where does it rise ? McKeown?”

“In the Cuilcagh Mountains in County Cavan, sir.”

“Excellent! And who can tell me which is the largest lake in the British Isles?”

A sea of hands went up, seeking to catch the master’s eye.

“You, Sweeney!”

“Lough Neagh, sir. It’s 21 miles long by 17 miles wide.”

“Very good, very good. And how many counties does it touch? Campbell?”

“Five, sir: Antrim, Tyrone, Derry, Armagh and... and...”

“Tell him, McLaverty, the remaining county that forms the shores of Lough Neagh.”

“County Down, sir.”

“County Down it is, well done, McLaverty. Now, how many provinces in Ireland? Donaghy?”

“Four provinces, sir: Ulster, Munster, Leinster and Connacht.”

“How many counties in Ulster? O’Neill?”

“Six, sir.”

“In the name of Ja... of all that’s holy! Come out here, boy!” And he went and hauled the unfortunate O’Neill out of his seat and led him by the ear up to the wall map.

“Now think again, me boy, and think hard. How many counties are there in the province of Ulster?”

The luckless O’Neill plumbed the depths of his memory for an answer. It couldn’t be six, that’s why he was in the predicament he was in. It must be more than six, he reckoned, for he had just heard that five of them touch Lough Neagh and Lough Neagh was definitely in Ulster. Seven was his lucky number, but it didn’t sound right, somehow.

“Eight, sir”, ventured O’Neill hopefully.

“Good God!” sighed the master catching hold of the victim’s ear once more. “And your very own ancestors would weep tears of blood to hear such an answer from the lips of an O’Neill.”

“Nine, sir, it’s nine”, interjected the young O’Neill in an attempt to rescue his ancestors’ honour and save his own hide.

“Nine, of course”, thundered the master letting go the boy’s ear, “border or no border, me boy, and always will be. Now, go back to your desk and never forget that.”

And the young boy quickly fled from the master’s grasp, grateful that he had been blessed with such an illustrious name.

When I first went to school in 1943 a big campaign was underway throughout the whole of Belfast to get school children to help with the war effort. An old bald-headed fella with a huge bushy moustache visited our school one day to promote a scheme for collecting waste paper. He talked for a long time in an odd accent about what we kids could do to support the boys at the front. We watched him with cool curiosity as he explained how would be rewarded with coloured badges denoting rank—sergeant, captain, major and so on: “Everyone will start off as a private with this white badge”, holding aloft a small, white cardboard disc, “but could end up, with the rank of field marshal”, he announced, certain that he had impressed his attentive audience. “It all depends on how much waste paper you can collect.”

The teachers were asked to co-ordinate the pupils’ efforts and award the commissions. It never got off the ground. The huge container for the waste paper lay empty until it was quietly taken away six months later. The same fate was destined for a similar campaign the following year to send old books and magazines to the troops. The unfortunate troops would be waiting still had they been depending on books from our school. The master said nothing about these plans, one way or the other, but we knew not to get involved.

A month or two afterwards, workmen arrived in the

school yard with cutting equipment and took away our railings and gate and any other fixtures made from iron. It was our involuntary contribution to Britain's war effort. We weren't the only ones to suffer: all buildings, public and private, were stripped of their iron fittings in a frantic attempt to provide raw material for munitions.

Then it happened—the unexpected—as it always does. A Victoria Cross was awarded to a Belfast man, the only one to come to Northern Ireland and, lo and behold, of all places, hadn't he been a pupil at our school and now that the war was over he wanted to come back and visit us all.

Able Seaman Magennis had received the highest military honour for exceptional gallantry during the Far East campaign. He had been one of a three-man team in midget submarines sent out to penetrate Japanese naval defences in Singapore harbour and plant limpet mines beneath a battleship. During the mission his comrades' subs broke collected his comrades' mines and put them, too, where they would count.

It was a cold November morning, damp with fog. The sun made a half-hearted appearance through lifeless, grey clouds then vanished giving way to continuous, seeping drizzle. The classroom window panes were sadly furrowed with rain, as the master recounted in detail how brave this young man, who had sat in these very seats, had been:

"Bravery beyond the call of duty, they describe it", said the master. "And when his task was done", he continued, "young Magennis went back and picked up his stranded comrades and brought them to safety. He is a brave man, nobody can deny that, and", there was a tremor in his voice as he raised it an octave, "he didn't do it for Ireland."

The class sat in silence, not a hand was raised to ask the usual questions. We sat there expectantly, proud and strangely sad at the same time.

An hour went by. At eleven o'clock there was a knock on classroom door and a party of four was ushered into the room: the Head Master, an elderly lady, an official of the Belfast Education Authority, a naval officer in full regalia with shining buttons and coloured service ribbons immediately catching the eye, and a shy, handsome young man in ordinary seaman's uniform with bell-bottoms and open-neck front; it was him, Able Seaman Magennis.

Nobody rose. We sat and we watched as the naval, officer told us in a swanky English accent what we already knew. Young Magennis smiled inoffensively and in very few words, uttered nervously, said he was glad to be back in his old school and the party left to visit another class.

A restless murmur ran through the class when they left: it wasn't an easy task to resume school work at once, so the master told us to read our story books and keep quiet.

I remember feeling proud that I was Irish and hadn't honoured the King by standing up. I was also proud that it was one of us who had shown the world how brave he was, yet there lingered an uneasy feeling inside me that I had hurt that poor, young lad Magennis in some way, and for years afterwards I could still see his kind, smiling face and his elderly mother by his side as we sat stubbornly in our seats.

Gerry Oates, language lecturer at Armagh College of Further Education, with students Patrick Kelly and Stephen McKenna
Photograph by Andrew Breakey

Jim Nicholson

In the royal calendar, 9 March 1995 was noted as a significant date. The day was similarly highlighted in the diary of Councillor Jim Nicholson. Following years of intense lobbying, it had been decreed that an Act of 1840 empowered the Queen to reincorporate towns in Ireland with a population of more than 3,500. Chief Executive Desmond Mitchell, on behalf of Armagh District Council, had campaigned vigorously to have Armagh legally and formally proclaimed a city. Jim Nicholson, Member of the European Parliament, was Chairman of the Council, when, on a visit in July 1994, Prince Charles announced the decision by Her Majesty Queen Elizabeth II to award city status.

"We were delighted", commented Councillor Nicholson. "Under the Local Government Act (NI) 1972, the geographical area of Armagh District Council included the surrounding towns of Tandragee, Markethill, Richhill and Keady and various villages throughout our district. There were obvious reasons for formalising our title as city. We are after all, the ecclesiastical capital of Ireland, having two cathedrals with the seats of Church of Ireland Primate of Ireland and Roman Catholic Primate of All Ireland. Armagh had been governed by Charter over a long period. In 1840, all Boroughs were dissolved and Armagh was then governed by City Commissioners instead of its Sovereign and Burgesses. It was something of a coincidence that I should be Chairman in this all-important year but it was also strenuous in terms of events, obligations, occasions and locations. Many of my appointments were rooted in history, others concerned educational or caring aspects of our society such as visiting schools or hospitals, hosting receptions for visitors from overseas or, for various reasons, the homes of the elderly."

Janus, the Roman god of gates, represents dual aspects, one face looking back, the other forward. Janus provides an excellent analogy for Jim Nicholson's Mayoral year and two-aspected role, that of the last Chairman and first Mayor of Armagh. Jim will never forget standing centre stage in the Primate's Chapel, during the conferral ceremony which lasted 15 minutes, or his address to Queen Elizabeth and Prince Philip: "It is a special honour for me as Chairman of the Council to welcome you both to the ancient ecclesiastical capital of Ireland. The Council is pleased to welcome so many distinguished visitors to share and witness this unique ceremony. We are overjoyed that Your Majesty has so graciously decided to confer on this historic town of Armagh the status of a city and to personally present the Royal Charter to the Council.

"We were delighted when we first received your decision from HRH the Prince of Wales during his visit to Armagh last year. The Council and its citizens have looked forward in eager anticipation to this important day for some considerable time. The dreams of many have now been realised. The rich history of Armagh has been inestimably enhanced. Thursday 9 March 1995 will be regarded by future generations as one of the most important dates in our long and significant chronology, as we celebrate the 1,550 years from St Patrick founding his first Christian church in Armagh. I can assure you, Your Majesty, that Armagh will take its place with pride as the third city in Northern Ireland.

"The new Armagh City and District Council will endeavour to pursue the highest ideals of public service and act in the best interest of all its citizens. Your Majesty and Your Royal Highness have our best wishes for good health and guidance as you continue your illustrious reign. It is appropriate, as we are gathered in this beautiful Primate's Chapel in the city of Patrick, that I now invite the Most Rev. Dr Robin Eames, Archbishop of Armagh and Primate of Ireland, to read an exhortation in which we seek the blessing of Almighty God on our City."

Looking back, Jim recalls: "When I became Chairman of Armagh District Council in June 1994, little did I realise what a momentous year lay ahead. The role of Chairman had practically assumed the identity of 'First Citizen' in recent years. It was more relaxed in political terms and a buoyant time when visitors were coming in strength as the City and District strove to move forward. I was determined to ensure this momentum continued right through my year in office. Encouraging development of the area was one part of that equation; attempting to secure outside investment constituted the remainder."

Recalling that moment when 100 invited guests were

seated in the Primate's Palace, Mayor Nicholson continues, "Naturally I was conscious of the presence of world media but this was a never-to-be-repeated moment in history and I was proud to be playing a role. Formalities completed, all our newly robed members of Council were officially photographed, then joined by the royal party. During this interval, Roger Weatherup, retired curator of Armagh County Museum, explained the distinguished history of the Primate's Palace where our conferment ceremony had taken place.

"Lunch followed and I retained my menu for the benefit of those not present. The meal was superb. Terrine of salmon and lobster was followed by roast sirloin of beef, Yorkshire pudding and creamed horseradish. Our guests enjoyed the cuisine and everyone chatted in a relaxed fashion.

"The Royal Charter is a work of art", Jim agrees. "It is made from calfskin vellum and inscribed with Chinese stick-ink and vermilion. Embellishments are in gold leaf and pure gold mixed with opaque pigments. It bears the Primatial Cross and representations of our two cathedrals are appended to the border ribbon in acknowledgement of the city's importance as the Primatial capital of Ireland."

The City's first Mayor recalls important highlights during this formal day. "Prior to her arrival, a crowd gathered, lining the Queen's route to the Palace. One woman, Eva Dillon, stepped out with a bouquet of red carnations. The Queen accepted this with a smile, and indicating her red coat commented, 'A good match'. I remained by the Queen's side as she shook hands and chatted to guests. It was also quite a moment for Margaret Mallon, BEM, of Drumadd Terrace and her husband, Albert, when the Queen spoke in a warm exchange. Margaret was former private secretary to the Clerk of the Council and an invaluable member of staff at both the City Hall and the Palace Council offices. My only daughter, Ruth, presented the Queen with a bouquet on her arrival while Elizabeth, my wife, handed over a gift of exquisite Irish-made linen.

"That afternoon was given over to the unveiling of a plaque by the Queen at City of Armagh High School, Alexander Road. This", explains the former Mayor, "was previously Armagh Girls' High School, which officially opened in 1954 at a ceremony carried out by Lady Wakehurst. Mrs Sylvia G. Kastell was first headmistress of the Girls' High, an establishment for young ladies. The school's last headmistress, prior to amalgamation with Royal School, Armagh, in 1986, was Esther Hamilton. Children lined the entrance of the newly refurbished school, waiting for the arrival of the Queen and the Duke who were accompanied by the Lord Lieutenant for County Armagh, the Earl of Caledon; Secretary of State, Sir Patrick Mayhew; and Education Minister, Michael Ancram. I'm grateful that headmaster Jim Craig, was able to participate fully in this momentous day for he was one of the most dedicated educationalists of our time. That afternoon, Mr Craig and deputy head Brian Roleston escorted the Queen and His Royal Highness on a conducted tour of the building where pupils waited for a glimpse of the royal couple. The board of governors was present and they spoke with the Queen, as did head girl Jennifer Zwecker and head boy Philip Miller. Gifts including Armagh crystal were presented to the Queen while the Duke received a commemorative book on the ancient spiritual capital of Ireland. Concluding this marvellous day, I would simply add a historical fact. In the famous inscription that is written into the *Book of Armagh* when Brian Boru, High King of Ireland, visited Armagh in 1005, is a reference that translates as: *the apostolic city which in Irish is called Ard Mhacha.* If we are such, then it was by virtue of the Archbishops' seats, having been governed by a charter over a long period of time and by right of ancient usage. It was also", he adds thoughtfully, "a dream fulfilled."

Jim Nicholson, MEP, has a farm of 120 acres at Ballyards. Involved in politics since 1962, Jim was branch secretary and later chairman of the Unionist Party. "I became a member of Armagh Constituency Association in 1968, then organising secretary in 1973, a position I retained for ten years. Everyone insists they were persuaded to stand for local government elections but I was co-opted as a member of Armagh District Council and, in December 1975, following the death of Councillor William Shilliday, stood successfully for the local area. I was successively re-elected until I retired from Armagh City and District Council in 1997. My interests were always allied to a political career and, as my family grew, education naturally claimed my attention. I served on the Board of Governors of Aghavilly Primary School where, a generation earlier, principal teacher Miss Evelyn B. Corry had taught me. Going the extra mile, she then succeeded me by taking my seat in local government! I represented Armagh District Council as a member of the Southern Health and Social Services Board during the years 1977-85. With my interest in agriculture I became a member of the Ulster Farmers' Union, remaining ever since. As Unionist Party spokesman on agriculture I travelled to the Continent. This undoubtedly helped in acquiring considerable understanding of European structures. At home I was elected to the Northern Ireland Assembly where I served from 1982 to 1986.

"Becoming Ulster Unionist MP for Newry and Armagh, I remained in office for three years. Even in those early days I realised I could integrate my efforts with those of Westminster Members of our Party, a requirement that became increasingly important as European decisions influenced our day-to-day lives. In addition to agriculture, Northern Ireland has other sectors of major importance including tourism and small manufacturing industry and I gave liberally of my time to each. Having been nominated, I stood for the 1989 European Assembly election and was voted into office as Ulster Unionist Member of the European Parliament.

"On a personal level, an attempt on my life was carried out in 1988—a terrifying experience for my family. We mention this as little as possible and, when we do, it is dispassionately referred to as 'the incident'. While we try to forget the implications, the memory does come back to haunt from time to time. Our experience was similar to that of many in three decades of unrest and upheaval."

In a spectacular year for Armagh, the City's first Mayor coped with an extremely busy diary of engagements. "I travelled to America as part of a local government deputation attending an investment conference in Washington. Our aim was that of establishing links with the most powerful nation on the globe. We met and spoke with President Bill Clinton who promised to give consideration to our proposals. Moving on to Virginia, meeting and talking with a vast number of people, we saw what could be engendered by foreign investment and still may be. American financial involvement has to remain a challenge for local government in Armagh.

"Events at home were just as demanding. It had been a pleasure to host the Prince of Wales in 1994. Coming in the role of ambassador, he paved the way for our principal event the following year. As the first Mayor of Armagh City and District, I was then a guest at a formal garden party held in Hillsborough Castle. One of the most enjoyable functions was the honour of being 'Chieftain of the Day' at a celebration of the Scottish Pipe Band Association and standing to attention as *Hail the Chief* was played. As the guest of Dublin's Lord Mayor, I attended the Mansion House and met President Mary Robinson. Celebrating the 1,550th anniversary of St Patrick's coming to Armagh, Archbishop of Canterbury George Carey and Dr David Sheppard, Archbishop of Liverpool, were both welcomed to a special service at St Patrick's Church of Ireland Cathedral, Armagh. Probably my most enduring memory is that of Hannah Hauxwell, *Daughter of the Dales*, who won the admiration of a nation when her story was first televised. She spoke publicly in Armagh, afterwards attending a special reception at the Palace. Hannah is one of the most genuine human beings I will probably ever meet and her spirit of humility combines with a great sense of humour. Throughout my year, a smoothly running itinerary was maintained by Chief Executive Desmond Mitchell and his staff at the Palace. Such assistance was inestimable.

"Elected as a member of the European Parliament, I devoted more time and energy to Brussels. In contact with representatives of the other 14 member states, it became imperative that I respond to new challenges and experiences. Coming from a strong unionist background, I had to face up to new challenges and understand that within the European context, one has to co-operate with other members from other states. This proved to be a serious learning curve as I sit in committee with members of the European Parliament from the Republic of Ireland, and I have worked closely with Irish EU Commissioner, Ray McSharry, who had responsibility for Agriculture. On many occasions I found we had much in common for we faced the same problems, suffered the same lack of investment and indeed, on many occasions, were able to co-operate for the benefit of all on this island, North and South. Agriculture is Northern Ireland's prime industry and main exporter, and is therefore extremely important to our economy. Combine this with assistance Northern Ireland receives from the European Union under Regional Development Funds and you may then appreciate how working for agriculture has been my priority within the European Union.

"The recent ban on Ulster beef, following an outbreak of BSE, showed exactly how important agriculture is to Northern Ireland and reflected in a down-swing in our

Mayor Jim Nicholson, MEP,
with Her Majesty the Queen

economy. Europe continues to play a major role in developing priorities within our everyday life, whether it be the air we breathe, the water we drink, food we eat or hours we work. I have always been conscious that we in Northern Ireland have an environment of a standard other regions would envy. We must do everything to protect our environment for future generations at a standard and level that is superior to any at this point in time. Enthusiasm for this worthy cause saw us embark on an Environment Awareness Week during my mayoral year. We invited Ken Collins, then chairman of the European Union Environment Committee, to launch the event. Issues presently crowding our agenda tend to be those of the acceptability of genetically modified foods or scientific cloning. I have reservations on both which will remain until thorough testing has been carried out.

"The European Parliament has resumed following our summer break and, again, I find myself on twice-weekly flights to and from Brussels. Less frequently in Strasbourg, I nevertheless discovered that an Armagh woman, the late Vera Magee, held a position of distinction there, at the British Consulate. I am pleased that her unusual story is preserved in Armagh County Museum.

"As another year of political engagements begin to crowd my diary, for sheer historical importance to Armagh City and District, 9 March 1995 is a date that will remain unmatched."

Desmond Mitchell

"It was a great surprise and privilege to be awarded the MBE in the Queen's Birthday Honours List for services to local government", comments Chief Executive Desmond Mitchell of Armagh City and District Council. Council business is administered from The Palace, one of Ireland's finest neo-classical houses. From the late 18th century until 1975, it was the home of successive Primates. Dessie Mitchell's office is south facing, commanding a stunning view. In serving the district, his 250-strong staff is responsible for corporate and technical services, leisure and tourism, community services, environmental health, building control and the management public monies.

Dessie Mitchell is a man who goes placidly amid noise and haste. He swiftly repudiates the present depressing consensus, that we sharing this island are incurably sectarian. "I've been in local government since 1962 and steadfastly refuse to lose hope in the human race or of finding acceptable compromise."

A graduate of the Open University with a Bachelor of Arts degree in Public Administration and Politics, it is as an old boy of the Royal School, Dungannon, he speaks fondly. "I'm convinced teachers have a vested interest in their charges. "I had the benefit of two headmasters, Alec de Gaudin and Dr Kincade. I met the latter at a public function years later. Conclude what you will, but he recognised me instantly."

From school, Dessie joined Dungannon Rural District Council as clerical officer. Five years later, in 1968, came his appointment as assistant Town Clerk in Armagh. "Maurice Fielding transferred to Lisburn, hence the vacancy. Don Ryan, a great friend and ever helpful, was Town Clerk. In essence, I transferred from a rural, market town environment to an urban county town with a sense of history and place. At Royal School, Dungannon, we developed sound appreciation of Irish history, thanks to an excellent teacher. In support of this, Georgian architects Thomas Cooley and Francis Johnston take their stance alongside, rather than diminish my early admiration for 'The Great O'Neill'. There were too, social and recreational adjustments. Rugby excelled in Dungannon. Armagh and cricket are as consistent as ballad and lyric.

"My father's family origins are in the Sperrins, their roots dating to the 17th century. A sound Tyrone adage which I equate with him runs, 'If you cannot do somebody a good turn, don't do them a bad one'.

Dessie continued to live in Aughnacloy until he married in 1970. "Margaret was a hairdresser whom I'd seen about town. Making tentative enquiries, I summoned the courage to ask her out. She had all the qualities I admire: spirited, strong personality and striking looks. Margaret is one of four women to mark my life with an individual, indelible impression. Both grandmothers and my mother, Queenie, who lives in Dungannon, make up the quartet. Margaret and I still reside at our first home in Lisnadill. I relish its serenity, escaping telephones and technology.

"During the cataclysmic Seventies and Eighties, Armagh underwent vast political and social change. A bomb warning came one busy afternoon during a meeting. Ordered from the City Hall, we watched the destruction of a building that held unparalleled memories. I'd been Clerk and Chief Executive with Omagh District Council since 1973, following amalgamation of urban and rural councils, returning to Armagh in 1988. Whilst in Omagh, the town hall had also been bombed. I might well have developed a phobia", he comments wryly. His experiences run the gamut of three decades. "Against a background of terrorism, there were the troubled Sixties, reorganisation of local government and the Ulster Workers' Council strike in the Seventies, hunger strikes for part of the Eighties, followed by an *Ulster Says No* campaign."

Dessie shrugs. "I coped, having served with many changes of party—Ulster Unionist, SDLP, DUP, Sinn Féin, Independents, Alliance, Republican Clubs. One party I have not encountered in the chair is NI Labour. Whilst remaining apolitical, I find the world of politics fascinating, whether it's the hype of an American presidential election or delving into Irish, British and European history. Nelson Mandela's biography, *The Long Walk to Freedom*, absorbed my attention more than any book I've ever read. What makes Mandela stand out in a crowd? Simply that his aura is enhanced by an ability to forgive, reinforcing my belief that fundamentally, nothing is achieved without self-sacrifice. We are victims of our society and upbringing but the secret is controlling one's preferences. Raised in the Methodist faith, I try to exemplify Wesley's maxim, 'To be a friend of all and enemy of none'. I've always striven to perform my job with integrity whilst walking an essentially diplomatic line.

"As professionals we ensure the Council is best informed to take decisions for betterment of the entire community. The 22 members invariably reach consensus. A vote is rare. July, with its attendant problems, has for the past few years brought a raft of accusation, mostly the inability of institutions to cope. Our Council made a mature decision, leading by example. What Armagh achieved must not be allowed to disintegrate. To improve quality of life and attract investment, we've worked to regenerate the city centre, and are concentrating now on rural areas. You can equate the summer setbacks with illness: a heart attack 20 years ago and one's chances of recovery were negligible. Medical science practically guarantees success today. Besides", he ruminates, "there is in all of us, a core of decency. Yes, we've lost ground but if we've the will, this can be recovered. In 1994-95, 'Armagh Together' was a combination of generously given time and talent. Some 250 successfully organised events showed exactly how great our combined potential. Who would set out to destroy such painstaking foundations?"

The visit of the Queen and Prince Philip visit on 9 March 1995, when the City Charter was conferred, demanded strenuous organisation by Dessie Mitchell and his staff. "Call it a vintage year if you like. Prince Charles had earlier announced that our Charter would be delivered by the Queen. MEP Jim Nicholson was Chairman in 1995, so he automatically assumed the role of Mayor. President Mary Robinson's presence gave an extra dimension to our celebration of this special year, the 1,550th anniversary of St Patrick establishing his church in Armagh. Prime Minister John Major had already performed the opening ceremony of St Patrick's Trian. George Carey, Archbishop of Canterbury, visited both cathedrals, as did Bishop of Liverpool the Rt Rev. Dr David Sheppard, and Archbishop of Liverpool the Most Rev. Dr Derek Worlock, whose death earlier this year saddened those of us who met him.

"Seeds painstakingly sown were rewarded when Queen's University chose Armagh for an Outreach Campus. Queen's has gone from strength to strength and President Mary McAleese, who as Pro-Vice Chancellor was so instrumental in setting up the Campus has since returned to Armagh as a VIP. Permit me a personal indulgence", he smiles. "1995 was also the year of my 25th wedding anniversary.

"Few appreciate how much members of Council give to the public. Endless demands on their time, visits to their homes, hate mail, aims misunderstood, abuse in the press. I do stress, most councillors are well intentioned. For the good of the community they develop understanding of beliefs they do not share, without compromising their own values. With successive Chairmen and Mayors, I visited victims of violence. At one home it happened to be the birthday of a child whose murdered father had planned to take him to on a special outing. We could barely speak." In 1984, Dessie was awarded a seven-week scholarship to the Federal Executive Institute in Charlottesville, Virginia. "This enabled me to take part in a senior management programme of training enjoyed by top federal employees in the US government. I gained insight into American opinion, and yes, travel invariably broadens one's outlook."

He applauds the new Church Forum, four main faiths discussing religious and social issues. "Respect for the person, tradition, beliefs and property has to be revived. Perhaps we should concentrate more on winning the people than winning the argument? Following Drumcree, we were swift to apportion blame. In itself, this represents immaturity. Called to account, which of us has ever demanded rights for those outside our camp, or peacefully protested against inequality?

"My work brings me into contact with wonderful people yet I met Mother Teresa when filling my car at the petrol station. Her death, like that of Diana, Princess of Wales, saddened many. Appreciating music at all levels, I equally enjoy Van Morrison or a musical. A new theatre, sited near the cinema, will realise yet another regenerative dream. Our desire is to create jobs, conserve what is historically precious and engender good feeling. The town has never looked better thanks to George Darling's sheer artistry and floral creations."

Dessie and Margaret have two children. Mark is 26 and a Mathematics, Statistics and Computer graduate while Carolyn is presently undertaking Psychology at Queen's University. "My family life is everything I might wish. Add a love of travel and gardening—colour,

Chief Executive Desmond Mitchell, BA, MBE
Photograph by Michael Campbell, LBIPP

profusion of blooms and neat lawns, somewhere to escape when work overwhelms. Margaret and I stood in awe when we visited the Great Falls of Niagara. Spray, spume and infinite power harnessed into electricity. Australia's Great Barrier Reef inspired as much wonder. The longest coral reef in the world, a series of atolls and islets, ever-changing. Indescribable beauty restores one's faith in the creator of this universe."

His favourite things include a framed Hebrew passage from Isaiah which Carolyn found in Israel, *Your God reigns...* and a Jackie Connolly painting of Armagh viewed from this executive office.

"With American assistance I researched the life of Sarah Mitchell, a paternal ancestor who emigrated to New York in the 19th century, at the tender age of 17. There she worked with impoverished and destitute women. Again", he gestures, "a strong character. Sarah, ahead of her time, comfortably offsets grandmothers Elizabeth Mitchell, who lived to be 98, and Emily Sawyers who at 96, remains the most tolerant person I've known."

"I would summarise my life as privileged. The beauty of this landscape, Armagh's majestic skyline of spires and turrets. Being here was always a pleasure, so was whatever part I played in its conservation and enhancement."

Desmond Mitchell, BA, MBE, Clerk and Chief Executive of Armagh City and District Council, speaks his truth quietly. None speak of him in terms other than glowing. A vast range of achievements in a remarkable life, decidedly a *Friend of all and enemy of none.*

Armagh Voices

a celebration of a century

1950 ~ 1960

Every decade of man's life possesses its own kind
Of happiness, its own hopes and prospects.

Johann Wolfgang Von Goethe

Tess Hurson

Queen's University, Belfast, opened its Outreach Campus in Armagh in September 1995. Now, more than 500 students are availing of higher education and 'lifelong learning'. Should any knock on a door marked 'Student Support Officer', Dr Tess Hurson warmly invites them in.

Once the old city infirmary, the building exhales the polished smoothness of a Vermeer interior. Dramatic black and white tiling sets a strong architectural mood. Soft tones of magnolia and white suggest prevailing calm.

The project has been described as an astonishing endeavour. Tess agrees her personal road to 'the bright city' contained its share of surprises. Part of the clockwork on which this academic dream rotates, Tess with her razor-sharp wit and expert turn of phrase proves a brilliant narrator.

"Armagh has a long and distinguished history of scholarship, stretching right back to the early Middle Ages. Two hundred years ago, Archbishop Richard Robinson conceived the vision of a university in Armagh. He had already moulded the city's horizon, establishing the Observatory, the Robinson Library, the elegant Palace Demesne and in 1774, the County Infirmary. Sir Gordon Beveridge, then Queen's Vice Chancellor, and Pro-Vice Chancellor Professor Mary McAleese, reflecting the enlightenment of Archbishop Robinson, set out to establish a university site in the city. Armagh City and District Council had the foresight and faith to offer a prime location. Poised between the Cathedrals, twin sentinels of this city, we are to be found."

Tess Hurson is finely built and finely featured. A burnt orange sweater, black trousers and neatly laced boots hint at Bohemia. Such down-to-earth attitude imparts the impression that she could hold court in a room full of professionals from any walk of life, and keep them entertained.

"I grew up on the Armagh-Tyrone border on a small farm where the meadows ran to the Blackwater River. My education at Kingsisland School, then at St Patrick's Academy, Dungannon, came during a time of overwhelming social and political change. Culturally, many like myself, from a rural background, suffered a great lack of confidence. Like shy gazelle in a forest, quite a few would take stock, gradually coming forward in the conviction of their own worth. Ideas once entertained as fond notions, now took definite form." She leans earnestly forward: "If, when I was 14 years old, anyone had predicted I would enjoy the advantage of university education after grammar school, much less a doctorate! Well, I'd have shrugged and said, 'Dream on!' Opportunities then were inhibited by practicalities. If the school was geographically inaccessible, that was sufficient to preclude further education."

Tess shone academically, becoming head girl at St Patrick's. But she was, as she puts it, "not idle" outside school. "I had one sister and no brothers so we did plenty of work round the farm, drenching cattle, drawing in hay, helping with vegetables. My father was an exceptional tutor and had a great knack of making fun out of the toughest jobs. He was an excellent mimic and my mother a fine singer, so many gifts were passed on to us. Always encouraging as parents, both had great faith in education. My history teacher, Brian Donoghue, passionate about his subject, communicated that fervour. He inspired enthusiasm while credit for rigour must go to my art teacher, Sister Anne McCartan."

Three impressive A grades gained Tess admittance to Trinity College, Dublin. "It was a relief to escape from Northern Ireland during the mid-Seventies. Good-natured raillery in shops and pubs challenged; 'So you're from the North? What are yez doin' up there anyway?' I must admit I loved every minute of those four years."

Achieving an Honours Bachelor of Arts degree in English, Tess returned to Ulster, signing up for a Master of Arts in Anglo-Irish Studies at Queen's University, Belfast. "After Dublin, the North seemed difficult and lonely. Still, I made great friends. From there I travelled to the great multicultural background that is Toronto. Whilst in Canada, I took my doctorate." The years that followed, she acknowledges, were challenging enough to provide experience in many new areas of work. Returning home, as director of studies at the Institute of Irish Studies in Dublin, she taught literature to foreign students and did just about everything else, from organising field trips to designing courses in ceramics.

She also began writing for the *Irish Independent* and organised an international symposium on Flann O'Brien who had been the subject of her doctorate. "As an undergraduate, I'd admired O'Brien's work, chiefly his experimental approach. Contemporary fiction is the genre I best enjoy. It was maybe a shade ironic, writing a thesis in the middle of Canada on an author from my own county."

Completing three years in Dublin, Tess moved back to Tyrone where Dungannon Development Association took her on as fundraiser. Before long she was running the communications section. "Workers on the ACE (Action for Community Employment) scheme were constantly changing, totally diverse in skills and yet we achieved many exciting things. By dint of trial and error, we produced two books of high standard on local history. This brought more meaning into ACE. We developed graphics, visual arts and obtained our first computer. Arts Council funding improved the DDA magazine and I began an Arts File, probably the only coverage west of the Bann. I recall interviews with writers such as Paul Muldoon and organising a competition to encourage creative arts. Judged by Michael Longley, among others, that engendered over 100 entries. We also produced an album of original songs from people living around Dungannon. In a way, I rediscovered what I had known all along—that the county is brimming with talent. But, unfortunately, people are so often not asked; what they have to give is not valued."

During this time Tess had been writing features, poetry and reviews, teaching, then back to helping on the farm. From this she evolved as freelance sub-editor, first with the *Irish News*, then the *News Letter*.

"I wrote features for the *News Letter* and have great admiration for editor Geoff Martin, who was always open to new ideas. I was allocated a double-page spread for my in-depth study of Newry's Travellers. My sister followed her own path, becoming a health visitor in Newry. She introduced me to the Travellers, with whom she was working, having established an on-site clinic."

Journalism and experience in community development and arts brought Tess to the Northern Ireland Voluntary Trust as a project officer. It was her task to assess applications for community arts funding. "What an interesting field that opened up. I visited projects all over Northern Ireland, where regardless of background, my welcome was always warm. The amount of work and energy that exists is astounding—and all done on a voluntary basis. I remember visiting the Dolly Mixtures Writing Group over in Craigavon who produced at least two anthologies. One of the group is now embarking on her doctorate, having started into higher education as a mature student."

When Fortnight Educational Trust engaged Tess, her duties included organising conferences. "We learned as we went along. Conferences covered a range of themes; emigration, the rural world, the built environment. They were, at the time, very important as a means of bringing all sorts of people together, community groups, funding bodies, and academics. A lot of skills and ideas were exchanged and a fair bit of good fun as well."

A natural progression was her post as information officer with the Rural Development Council, based in Cookstown. During this time Tess was appointed to the Arts Council of Northern Ireland and is now chair of the strategic development panel which covers areas like community arts, arts and disability and education.

Her poetry has appeared in *Fortnight*, the *News Letter* and *The Honest Ulsterman*. Polly Devlin, the well-known writer from Ardboe, was a massive source of support and encouragement as were many others like Damian Smyth and George Wakefield, fine poets themselves. Her first book, *Inside the Margins: A Carleton Reader* was published by Lagan Press in 1992.

The Calouste Gulbenkian Foundation in London approached Tess and asked her to conduct a review of their rural arts agency scheme. Two books ensued. A book of poetry and a collection of critical essays on Flann O'Brien (co-edited with Anne Clissmann of Trinity College) have been published. Tess also worked in collaboration with the artist Rita Duffy. Their particular blending of the visual arts and poetry can be seen in the Waterfront Hall, Belfast in a specially commissioned piece, *Shoals*.

"My father died in May 1995. He was a great source of courage and humour, bringing us all through many difficult times. I know he watches over us still. Just a few months after, I came to Queen's at Armagh and learned that my father had been a patient here many years ago. It was a kindly omen. Both sides of my family have produced a range of medics. Well, the only thing I have ever splinted was the leg of a heron crane, and my 'doctoring' there was none too parliamentary. Still, I believe that it is significant that the university has established itself in a place of healing.

"Local people now get the chance to come to university but there is not one that comes through the door empty handed. Every student brings a whole power of talent. *Educere*: it means, I think, 'to lead out'. So if we can lead out what is most definitely already there, we will be in the true sense, educating."

The enthusiasm and vision of the first director of the Outreach Campus, Gary Sloan, was "a major inspiration": with Professor Mary McAleese, he accomplished a huge amount in a very short time. "We have Masters students from all over Britain and the island of Ireland, degree programmes, certificate and diploma courses and an Open Door extra mural programme with subjects ranging from Astronomy to European Women in the 19th Century. The campus has ultra-modern technology and has 'beamed' as far as Richmond, Virginia, and California. During the first years of operation a very hard working small team has also organised exhibitions, conferences, inter-schools events and a whole range of cultural and educational events. Many groups from the local community use the building and it is fully accessible to those with disabilities.

"The City and District Council has been extremely supportive and the communities here have a lot of goodwill and encouragement to offer. New developments at the Council-owned campus complex in 1999-2000 include two centres for the study of religion, a centre for cross border studies and the arrival of the Irish Studies library, the Health Board training unit and other tenants. It will be an 'educational village' in the heart of the city.

"I have great faith in Queen's and the people of this place. Our new Vice Chancellor, Professor George Bain, part of whose family comes from Milford, near Armagh, has stressed the importance of access to high quality education. A short time ago, nobody would have thought it possible that there would be a university in Armagh. Do we not all have the right to hope?"

Dr Tess Hurson
Photograph by Ian Maginess

Robert Boyd

As the new millennium nears, so, it seems, do technological anxieties. Will aeroplanes fall from the sky? Can I use my cash card? Might I get stuck in a lift and miss the party? Chief Superintendent Robert Boyd, Divisional Commander of Policing in Armagh City and District and Newry and Mourne, is acutely aware of the vital part he and his officers will play as AD 2000 dawns. "Contingency plans are already drawn up for whatever may arise over New Year", he comments. "Organised public events require policing but special entertainment legislation, permitting 24-hour licensing, creates certain anxieties. Public consumption of alcohol, if not properly administered, leads to vandalism, traffic offences and domestic violence. Officers can expect to be on duty over the entire period, but that, as they say, goes with the territory!"

Chief Superintendent Boyd agrees that the protection of human rights is fundamental to the role of any police officer. He welcomes accountability within the Royal Ulster Constabulary and his objective is that of a good working relationship with all communities. Despite sustained controversy, policing goes on about its business. The denigration of motives, questioning of integrity and undermining of morale is hurtful for those who value the force's 30 years of counter-terrorist work, loss of life and injury. Can today's public actually close their eyes to the sacrifice of men and women who worked or gave their lives to bring about a climate in which society could move forward? *The Cost of the Troubles* was an impartial exhibition on tour in Northern Ireland during the year. In addition to civilian casualties, it was shown that these abnormal years cost the lives of more than 300 police officers, the injured totalling thousands. "Ours may seem a thankless task", interjects Mr Boyd, "but a record 2,701 appreciative letters from the public in the last year showed otherwise."

An articulate professional, Chief Superintendent Boyd has adapted to sweeping changes and modern demands. "I was born in this county, but", he smiles, "strayed for a time before returning in 1995. Like many of my profession, I waited anxiously for my 18th birthday and began training in 1968. Civil rights protests made headlines a year later, while I was serving in Coalisland. Austin Currie, Member of Parliament for the area, frequently called at the station and I found him to be a most reasonable man. A young constable then, my regular beat included the shores of Lough Neagh where fishermen told me about 'the one that got away' in friendly chats, or shared their catch. Caledon was my next destination and here, alleged housing discrimination by the local authority brought police into direct confrontation with protesters. Our profession does not make political judgements but parity of esteem might have considerably altered history. Reaping the whirlwind of history, appalling sacrifices have been borne by this force during three decades of impossible odds. It was in Caledon, bordering Co. Monaghan, I had my first raw experience of death. During a pre-Christmas lunch, news came that a private in the Ulster Defence Regiment had been murdered. The station sergeant and myself arrived at his home to be met by the dead man's parents. I spent the night with them, waiting for forensic experts to arrive. The agony of that family was almost unbearable for a youngster, which is all I was then."

Station conditions were poor when Constable Boyd joined the force. "We had worn linoleum on the floors, damp walls, and at Coalisland were without hot water. I remember buying an electric razor to avoid having to boil a kettle on the temperamental old stove in the kitchen. Baths or showers were unheard of and I seriously doubt if today's recruits would accept these conditions. My bedroom held the radio transmitter and I was expected to sleep through constant interruption. Four years' service and promotion to the rank of sergeant found me transferred to Dungiven. My introduction set the scene, the shape of things to come. An out-of-action army helicopter was being transported on a lorry and while attempting to help, three soldiers were brutally murdered. Sectarian violence was rife and yet, today, this is more or less a model town. English and Scottish regiments now moved into Northern Ireland and for our protection, we patrolled alongside these men.

"Another promotion, to inspector, brought me to Omagh and entirely differing social circumstances. Perhaps this bore some relationship to the fact that it was a garrison town. The first hunger striker, Bobby Sands, had just died and rioting reached fever pitch in Belfast. Omagh, in a controlled campaign, organised silent protests. In the surrounding countryside, terrorism was rampant so court appearances claimed a major part of my time, but many from the local population made it clear they wanted normality and resolution by peaceful means. Parades were already contentious in areas of the town and required strict policing. It requires only minimal intelligence to see that unseemly behaviour by some tarnishes the image of all. We took heart when the marching season passed off relatively peacefully this year. Mutual respect will achieve a solution and this is something positive on which to build.

"During my time in Armagh, the force has adapted to change at operational level. Our present Chief Constable, acutely media-aware, has frequently invited the public to state opinions on the police service they wish to see, and its future direction. Like no other leader, he has striven to determine community thinking and welcomes independent police accountability as essential to integrity. Our Annual Policing Plan now sets out objectives as agreed with the Police Authority. An Ombudsman will enhance the independent element provided by the Independent Commission for Police Complaints. On this topic, speculation on the Patten Commission is rife yet major unforced change has been implemented as normal, intelligent practice.

"Crime may not pay but detection is ongoing. As for offences against the person, or 'Class 1' in crime statistics, last year the number of murders increased from 47 to 71 as a result of the Omagh bombing. During a three-year period, 1996-98, 11 murders occurred in my area of command. All of these crimes, which included four terrorist-linked murders, have been solved. Intimidation in today's society is cowardly and dangerous. While an individual can do little, an entire community uniting discourages thuggery from gaining a foothold. Increased patrols considerably alleviated a recent spate of malicious violence.

"When I was transferred to Strand Road, Londonderry, in 1984, this was never a destination I would have chosen", he observes wryly. "As Operational Chief Inspector, responsible for policing flashpoints, searches and arrests, I worked in liaison with the army. The Bogside, Shantallow, Creggan and Waterside areas had sporadic outbursts of unrest. Bishop James Mehaffey was a great friend, soothing and urging calm at every opportunity. Bishop Edward Daly encouraged his curates in a similar vein, and he himself met for discussion with senior officers. I must stress how quickly I came to terms with Londonderry. Police officers were constantly coming and going, 15 or 20 at a time. Here was human nature at its best, in the form of steady camaraderie. We discovered the city's musical talent was unbelievable and in this context, I must mention Father Eugene O'Hagan, who conducted pastoral work in the Creggan and contributed immeasurably to our traditional Carol Service in the Presbyterian Church, Christmas 1993. This man's amazing tenor voice did justice to classical Italian works, which he sang so exceptionally.

"Saturday night brought riots as young people who had too much to drink left places of entertainment. Good solutions are usually the simplest. In this instance, we persuaded staff to open rear doors, permitting patrons to exit premises and avoid scenes of aggression. There are, too, the inevitable harrowing flashbacks. Several close colleagues were murdered and I must have attended 30 funerals during my career. Sadly it is not unknown for two generations of the same family to die at the hands of terrorists. A simple act of dignity, synonymous with this force, is the practice of saluting any passing cortège. During an Apprentice Boys' Parade, a funeral from Long Tower chapel passed by. All officers on duty stood to attention, observing the salute. The following week, a warm letter of appreciation from relatives appeared in our local press.

"To avoid any concept of alienation, the protection of human rights is fundamental in modern policing. We work with the newly created Northern Ireland Human Rights Commission so that parity of esteem governs all policing activities. To counteract unfounded allegations, interrogation of suspects is filmed and taped, often with a solicitor present. The general public may not be aware that all evidence is made available for a prisoner's legal defence. Terrorist charges are often met with blank silence on the part of a suspect so we rely heavily on forensic evidence.

"Approaching 1989, on promotion to superintendent, I was transferred to Strabane. There was an added bonus", he smiles, "my station was 20 miles up the road, so I did not need to move house. Strabane was a friendly town and we did not suffer animosity from a vast majority of the population. Its political climate was mixed as we were half a mile from the land boundary with the Republic of Ireland and pockets of terrorism were difficult to eradicate. Surrounding towns, where bombing and killing had left a mark, presented an opposing, hard front. Someone in Strand Road, Londonderry, must have liked me", he jests, "for within two years I was transferred back for a second stint. As Sub-Divisional Commander in 1990, I witnessed change for the better. Paramilitary activity and bombing had greatly lessened. The city boomed with commerce, excellent shops and facilities. I now look back, deeming this to be one of the most positive phases in my life. Radio presenter Gerry Anderson christened it 'Stroke City' to facilitate two cultures, but for a number who took their own lives by drowning, in the River Foyle, it carried a less happy tag, that of 'Suicide City'."

As Deputy Divisional Commander in 1993, Robert Boyd now inherited care of Waterside Sub-Division and Strabane Sub-Division in addition to responsibility for Strand Road. "The internet has bred a computer-orientated society. I probably sound like Captain Kirk of the Starship *Enterprise*, but this year we implemented an intelligence module of the integrated crime system. Now we exchange valid information with other criminal justice agencies. Information technology and statistics are meticulously updated and regularly reviewed. The RUC is dedicated to management and performance, with computer literacy as part of our training. Our structure reflects co-ordination with outside agencies and Community and Police Liaison Committees are an excellent way of remaining au fait with public issues of concern. Today we are accountable to the Independent Commission for Police Complaints which is something I welcome. We are always heartened by letters of appreciation. Following a serious road traffic accident, someone took the time to say: 'Your officers played a fundamental role in my life being saved by quick-thinking professionalism. While criticism is levied from all sides, it gives me a feeling of confidence that you have officers of such acumen and quality within the force.'"

Chief Superintendent Robert Boyd is highly supportive of the RUC Benevolent Fund which performs an invaluable service for the bereaved or dependants. Much of this work, by its very nature, must remain unsung. "Our patron is the Duchess of Kent who continues to visit Northern Ireland and has met the bereaved, the injured and their children, with a cross-section of officers. A remarkable woman, her compassion seems to reach out to all she meets. The Fund, as Topsy said, 'just growed'. In 1969, members of the public donated money for injured members of the Force. Our Central Representative Body decided that the RUC Benevolent Fund Management Committee should be set up and conducted on lines similar to those utilised by many English forces. This is now a recognised charity, funded by contributions from serving members of the force. Apart from providing assistance to widows and dependants, grants are available for those suffering intimidation. The Fund is vital at Christmas, providing fuel or necessities for pensioners, widows and children. Grants have assisted with school uniforms or fees besides remembering birthdays of children who have lost parents. Adventure holidays are organised for young people who otherwise might never enjoy the opportunity to go sailing, rock climbing or camping. The Fund has outings for police widows including a special visit to the House of Commons at Westminster, when they met Speaker Betty Boothroyd. Injured officers, many in wheelchairs, were brought to Clarence House as guests of the Queen Mother."

Typical of good unseen, funding for this, and other important causes, is often raised through quality performance concerts given by the RUC Silver Band, the RUC Pipe Band, the RUC Ladies' Choir and the RUC Male Voice Choir. For the first time in history, the RUC Silver Band performed at the Auld Lammas Fair in Ballycastle. Performing with colleagues in the Band of the Garda Siochána and Warrington Male Voice Choir was a spectacular event. The RUC Pipe Band's drum corps has taken first prize in the World Pipe Band Championships qualifying heat in Glasgow, and Champion of Champions in NI, having earned considerable success during the year. The RUC Choir excelled in 1998, winning the male voice section at Bangor Choral Festival, followed by record-breaking success at Cheltenham Competitive Festival. At Christmas, the Choir presented a cheque for £1,000 towards the building of a Children's Hospice for NI. RUC fundraising efforts for Mencap brought an award at Northern Ireland's charity 'Oscars'. An impressive fundraising total for the Blue Sky Appeal now stands at £245,000.

Armagh city, Chief Superintendent Boyd feels, has

Chief Superintendent Robert Boyd

greatly changed since he was a young constable based at Caledon. "I look forward to the new Theatre and Arts Centre which I believe has excellent forward bookings. The cinema and pedestrian zone has contributed to a brighter town centre. Sadly it seems to be a tale of two cities, west and east. Decent hard-working people in every community resemble each other—so, conversely, do the more destructive elements.

"My wife, Mary, would agree that sport is a chief preoccupation. Keeping fit has always been of paramount importance so I walked to this interview where most would have driven! I support our Athletic Association, which recently launched a 'Life Force' programme to promote physical and mental wellbeing. Angling is a superb relaxation, drifting idly in a boat with a line dangling over the side. It is easy to identify with the endurance of Ernest Hemingway's *Old Man and the Sea* where a Cuban fisherman goes fishing for marlin in the Gulf Stream. One fish for the table, for me, would have to be that silvery-skinned king of the species, the salmon."

Each neighbourly murder... Heaney wrote of sectarian atrocity. To ensure they have ceased, our political landscape has changed and must continue to change. The Royal Ulster Constabulary is not entirely sure what AD 2000 may bring, nevertheless Chief Superintendent Robert Boyd has permitted a detailed insight into his past and exceptionally varied career. His is an amazing capacity, for he speaks without rancour or bias of a time when outlandish demands were made on all who served this force. Assuredly there is a place in any organisation, at any time, for an officer of his calibre.

Lord Caledon

Country Life magazine has described the pretty village of Caledon surrounding the home of the Rt Hon. The Earl of Caledon, Lord Lieutenant of County Armagh, as "an admirable example of early 19th century planning". The present Earl agrees: "London's cosmopolitan bustle represents one aspect of life, yet inevitably I find myself returning to quietude and the Castle."

The demesne of Caledon Castle occupies a bend of the Blackwater River. Beech and Irish yew screen a winding drive. Cedars flank the colonnaded north front of one of the finest country houses in Ireland. A stone portico covers the main entrance and from here a flight of stone steps leads into an octagonal domed hallway, light-drenched from a central cupola. The hallway is an impressive entrée to the Regency Green drawing room, the dining room, Nash's exquisite oval drawing room and the library at the home of the seventh Earl.

This country seat, dating to 1797, has no oppressive sense of the past: a living, breathing house where fragrant wood smoke lingers and damask cushions are comfortably casual. Sèvres vases are re-filled with fresh flowers and Boulle desks dusted off as a matter of daily routine. Such order is a tribute to dedicated staff, who, according to the Earl, efficiently maintain these rooms while managing to avoid the fusty air of a museum. "If you've ever traipsed through the Hapsburg palaces in Vienna, you'll understand what I mean; a dispiriting experience. Perhaps we should look around", he suggests, "I'll give you background as we go."

In 1775, James Alexander, first Earl of Caledon, purchased the seat from the Earl of Cork and Ottery. At the same time he bought the Borough of Newtownards, paying £600,000 for both. Thomas Cooley designed and created the nucleus of the present house in 1779. Little is known of Cooley other than that he completed the Royal Exchange building in Dublin and was later associated with the construction of the Four Courts in Dublin. James Alexander was an enterprising young man who, by the age of 40, had acquired a substantial fortune working for the East India Company. The Earl participated in the famous Dungannon Convention in 1783 when Ireland, for a short space, appeared to stand united against English misgovernment. He died in 1802 at his Dublin house in Rutland Square.

Sweeping changes were made at Caledon Castle by the second Earl in the reign of George III. First Governor of the Cape of Good Hope, he was appointed His Majesty's Lord Lieutenant for County Tyrone. Returning from the Cape in 1812, he commissioned John Nash, later famous as the creator of Regent Street, the Haymarket Theatre and Brighton's Royal Pavilion, to add the top storey and portico. Thus the house was brought into line with the standards that the Earl had been accustomed to as pro-consul. The Ionic colonnades seen at Caledon predate Nash's similar work at Park Crescent and old Regent Street. The western dome surmounts and lights a magnificent library, probably the best preserved of any great room designed by Nash outside Buckingham Palace. Here hang full-length portraits of Queen Charlotte and George III by Sir Thomas Lawrence. After Waterloo, this second Earl of Caledon sailed around the world on a shopping trip. To grace his home he purchased china and porcelain from Holland, Empire furniture and Italian mantelpieces.

The present Lord Caledon is modestly proud of a collection of 7,000 books, the library of the celebrated Bishop Percy, sold by his executors to the second Earl. When he died in 1839 his son succeeded. The third Earl married the daughter of Lord Verulam and had a large family. The fourth Earl, his eldest son, succeeded in 1855, living until 1898. His widow was a daughter of the Earl of Norbury and mother of Eric, the fifth Earl. "My father succeeded in 1968. Sadly he died in St Thomas' Hospital, London, following a severe stroke. It was May 1980 and he'd been on a trip to Nepal exploring the foothills of the Himalayas. It was a shock as he was just 58 years old. I was living in London at that time."

The seventh Earl is adept at putting one at ease. Ask about his life and his personality expands as he discloses pertinent facts. "I was born in Rome, my father then working as a director with British Petroleum. It was there that he met my mother. Italy and Austria were familiar countries during childhood and English is my third language. I didn't come to Ireland or make acquaintance with Caledon until I was 13 years old." In common with Prince Charles, he was educated at Gordonstoun, taking the rigours of public school in his stride. "After the first year I actually enjoyed being there." At the age of 18 he embarked on a career with Lloyds of London, specialising in the insurance market. Two years later he embraced the world of banking at Dillon Reid in New York. "Almost immediately my father died and I returned to Ireland."

A country estate carries great managerial responsibility. "On a day to day basis, there is always something to be done", the Earl asserts. "My father renovated extensively in 1973 only to have his labour lost in a bomb attack almost immediately. Everything material was restored thanks to our staff, experts from Christie's and craftsmen with every imaginable skill. Many wall hangings in the Castle are Chinese, probably acquired through the first Earl, from his service with the East India Company. Most ceiling decorations are by Adam, prior to 1792, in classical Greek and Roman tradition. Replace something so precious? You can't." More recently, in 1991 another terrorist attack shook this beautiful house. "My son Freddie was here and asleep when it happened but fortunately no-one was injured. Wanton destruction lays bare something precious. I could sense how vulnerable villagers felt in the aftermath. We are fortunate to have here families who love the Castle as much as we do."

He speaks of his home with engaging modesty. "Each Earl endowed the house with an inimitable touch which we respect. Land surrounding the Castle is let on an annual basis to the farming community. The estate office in the village, efficiently run by Evelyn Beattie, buzzes with rural comings and goings." The Earl does not disguise his fondness for a workforce many of whom he has known since childhood. "Keith Willis is estate foreman and extremely capable. His brother Cyril was my official driver, sadly dying alongside two other policemen and a nun in a particularly grotesque killing. Our hearts went out to that family. If I could grant Ireland one wish", he says suddenly, "it would be that she mature as a land at peace with herself."

His concern for the community extends beyond platitude. "In August 1995 we opened our grounds for an organised fete, a means of raising funds for St John's Parish Church in the village. I often wished to make Caledon Castle available to the public previously but Ireland's political climate advised otherwise. With the ceasefire came an opportunity for people to see this place, simultaneously raising charitable funds. A committee comprising the Rev. Wilson, members of the select vestry and concerned parishioners planned the event. They worked, with a team spirit that does them credit, to ensure positive success."

The present Earl has an interest in history. "My maternal grandfather was Russian and chancellor to Nicholas, last Tsar of All Russia. A financier for the Romanov family, he managed to escape the Bolshevik revolution. I am fascinated by this dynasty, horrified to think of the family massacred at Ekaterinburg in the Urals. That brings me to conflicting theories surrounding the survival of Grand Duchess Anastasia. It serves only to make the tragic ending of a family all the more poignant. As an avid reader, *The Life and Times of Churchill* interested me greatly, especially those speeches for which he is famed."

Lord Caledon is both charismatic and swift to acknowledge qualities in those around him. "I meet some marvellous people, both as Lieutenant for the County and in the course of running the estate. It has to be said, this is inevitably where I return."

The Earl of Caledon

John Nixon presents Road Bowls

About to become one of the first mature students to graduate from Queen's University Outreach at Armagh, John Nixon has acquired some excellent material on social structures and cultural traditions within this county. John serves on the committee of the West Armagh Community Festival, or WestFest, a varied summer programme of events aimed at extending the hand of friendship to all neighbouring communities. At WestFest 1999, local writer Patricia Kennedy Patterson enjoyed a sell-out with a book of reminiscences that John helped her to bring to publication.

For the enjoyment of all who participate or follow the game of road bowling, John extensively researched and interviewed noted enthusiasts on the sport. He is generous in sharing these findings and comments made in the vernacular enrich the authenticity of his feature.

Road bowls, or 'bullets' as the sport is referred to *(John writes)* is synonymous with Armagh as apple orchards are with Loughgall. The game is also played in Cork and there has always been great rivalry between 'bullet men' of these two counties in All-Ireland and provincial championships. The organising body is Bol Chumann na hÉireann. It has been suggested that the origins of the game lie with Dutch soldiers who came to Ireland with William of Orange in 1689. Brian Toal has commented on the "relatively recent renewal of sporting contacts and revived bowling competition between Ireland and Holland, in Road Bowls and Moor Bowls". Another theory links the sport with the linen industry when mill workers, the weavers and scutchers played a game of 'long bullets', and suggests that the sport arrived in Ireland via linen workers from east Yorkshire and west Lancashire in the north of England. The basic nature of the bullets has not changed. Rivals pit their skill and strength throwing a 28oz (793.8 gram) iron ball along a stretch of road where the winner covers the distance in the least amount of shots. New rules apart, the game remains basically unchanged. You can't introduce new technology to road bowls. Patsy McCoy (see below) refers to the proximity of mills, which dotted the banks of the river Callan, to road bowling venues.

The popularity of bullets developed phenomenally in recent decades. In 1994 Armagh city hosted the first ever International Road Bowling Festival. This year the first World Championships took place in Armagh when over the period of a weekend thousands of enthusiasts took to the hedge-lined narrow roads on the famous Knappagh course to watch individuals and teams from Ireland, Germany Italy, Belgium and Holland compete at the highest levels. This was a major event, which Ireland won, Armagh man Michael Toal becoming world champion.

Because of the uniqueness of the sport it has been the focus of national and international media attention. Gender discrimination no longer exists and women, once regarded as the grass widows of the bullets, compete at all grades. Competitors of all ages participate: there is a veterans' tournament and even a vintage. Characters, heroes and events are an integral part of bowls culture and you'll hear stupendous stories wherever bullet men are gathered. Some family names crop up repeatedly. Bullets is a sport with dynasties.

The history of bullets in Armagh has been well documented. Dermot Hicks' *Road Bowls in Armagh* (1973) and Msgr Raymond Murray's *The Armagh Bullet Thrower* (1976) have been superseded by Brian Toal's *Road Bowling in Ireland* (1996), without doubt the most definitive account of the game to be published. Others who have written on the sport include the late curator of Armagh County Museum, T.G.F. Paterson, and musician Eithne Vallely.

Armagh bullet roads have been theatres for many memorable events. The first All-Ireland was staged on the old Moy Road in 1963. Danny McParland beat the southern champion Derry Kenny to win the first All-Ireland crown. Since then many Armagh men have taken home the laurels. Two men who have long been associated with bullets in Armagh are Patsy McCoy and Jimmy McEneney who was the first secretary of Bolchumann Ard Mhacha. The sport did not always enjoy the same level of legal tolerance as today and numerous cases were brought before the courts. In an interview, Patsy recalled how a consensus was reached with officialdom.

"A meeting was held one Sunday morning after ten o'clock Mass, in Frank Hughes bookie's shop at the

Shambles where the Cork players and Joe McVeigh's party arranged the rules and regulations for the score from Knappagh Angles. Joe Horan was one of the administrators at that time. People were saying it was the custom, as it was at that time, for the police to stop the bullets. So Joe and myself went to the sergeant in Russell Street barracks and told them about the score. I'd say that was the first time an official approach was made and I can mind well the sergeant in Russell Street saying that he was glad we had come up to him even though he couldn't give us permission to do it 'but we'll turn a blind eye'.

"Well, there's one case in the law books in Armagh of an outside judge who came along and stood in for the local magistrate. He didn't understand the game of bullets. He said: 'What are these boys doing? What do they do if they don't throw bullets, stand around corners?' He said 'I think that these men should get money rather than be fined' and he didn't fine them."

The rivalry between Armagh and Cork was intense and Jimmy recalls when the Corkmen's domination of the game was broken: "It was Danny Reilly who broke the myth of the Corkmen. Danny broke the myth because we thought the Corkmen were from another planet. Well, he played Dinny Murphy of Bandon down the [Moy] road and he beat him out of sight. But the Corkman came back at him and he played Danny up the road and beat *him* out of sight. But they still kept at Danny... that was all on the same day... on a Sunday and the next day. Monday was a Bank Holiday and the Corkman stayed over and Danny beat him out to the 'Cundy Corner' and back in again. It was the first time the Corkmen got a 'taging' in Armagh and it was the breakthrough."

One of the greatest exponents of the game was Red Joe Mc Veigh. His main rival was the famed Mick Barry from Cork. Both men played the game well into their sixties. Red Joe was the first Armagh man to throw in Cork when in 1956 the Cork-based Bol Chumann na hÉireann invited any Armagh man to throw in Cork against the great Mick Barry offering a bowl of odds. The stake was £25. Over 3,000 spectators watched the score which was played in the morning to avoid big crowds. Joe won the score by three shots, his last shot being stopped by a car. Jack O'Shea, Barry's handler, commented on the performance: "Joe threw bowls that morning that will never again be beaten."

Patsy McCoy remembers some of the old Meccas of the sport: the Loughgall Road, Killylea Road and the Milford Road. He recalls when the sport was played by Protestants and Catholics: "Not many think or know about the Loughgall Road. There were quite a lot of bullet scores threw on it. The Mill Row boys would come across a field along the mill path to throw the Moy roadmen. There were lads from Annaghcramph. There was the Scotts, the Orrs and the Georges, the Todds—mainly Protestant bowlers. Nobody was ever debarred from the sport because of religion. The reason why some Protestants never played so much was because it was played on a Sunday and they didn't believe like that. Actually, most Protestants, with the exception of Bill Hillock from Ballycrummy, played their scores on a Saturday. Saturday was very popular, there was nothing to distract you then."

Patsy also remembers some notable scores and skills: "Now one other major score played after that was a partner score down the old Moy Road between Mick Barry and fellow Corkman Dinny Donovan who played Armagh's Danny McParland and Aidan Toal. It was for the Convent Restoration Fund. Now I happened to be at eight o'clock Mass that morning and I came out and the Corkmen were practising from the Bridge. Now Mick Barry was playing the bowl from the Bridge and he was getting... and still going hard right up 'til what I call the 'Single Corner' and the first of the 'Doubles'. He was pegging it straight up and so was Donovan. But here Mick came up to this other part and Mick lofted right out over the Single and the Double and put it on the straight right up at Willie John Donnelly's."

Gambling on score is an important component of the sport, with a 'book' in which all bets are placed. One character who was the first man to introduce 'on course' betting was the renowned P.G. McQuaid. Patsy recalls him vividly: "P.G. was always a noted character but he put his board up and he could've given you the same bet in five different ways, maybe 15 different ways. It was the first time I saw a bookie at a score, he had the gift of the gab. He would get to listen, he could talk, he'd nearly make you take the money out of your pocket. He'd have something to say about every thrower. He'd shout '"Yous Armagh men, are yous afraid to back your own man, but sure don't be afraid if yous want to come and back the Corkman, sure come and back away. I'll tell nobody.'"

We finish with two poems by the late Paddy McGerrigan celebrating a famous bullets score, between

Red Joe McVeigh and Pat Coulter who was known as 'The Gentleman of Bullets'.

McVeigh v Coulter

In the year nineteen and forty six one Sunday afternoon,
A group of sportsmen left the town in most amusing
tune,
To see a score of bullets played between young
Joe McVeigh,
And the Ulster Champ, Pat Coulter, from the banks of
Plunkett's Bay.

With confidence they both began to throw with all their
skill.
The first shot, it was won by Joe, the townsmen cheered
their fill.
And as they went along the road the air was full of
jokes,
For Coulter was a shot behind going down by Bond
McGeough's.

They played on to McCready's with still a shot in hand,
Oh little did they think that Joe had met his bogeyman!
For Coulter smashed the record with a gallant
breakaway,
And brought home the Ulster title to the banks of
Plunkett's Bay.

The merry men from Dougan's Glen began to dance and
sing,
Young Anthony Smyth his trainer almost done the
Highland Fling,
And then they all departed on that dull October
day,
With the undefeated champion from the banks of
Plunkett's Bay.

Pat's song-vaunted victory was somewhat shortlived for young Joe McVeigh returned to take back his laurels from Plunkett's Bay. His victory over Pat Coulter was similarly recorded in verse by the prolific pen of "Angles", the *nom de plume* of Paddy McGerrigan.

The Answer

Attend you jolly sportsmen of high and low degree,
Just cast aside your troubles and listen unto to me.
I'll tell to all both great and small within this simple lay,
How Coulter met his Waterloo at the hands of young
McVeigh.

Now Anthony dear, be of good cheer, your voice is
sweet and low,
Your powers as a vocalist were heard not long ago;
In praise of Pat Coulter you gave a grand display,
But now we've turned the tables on your man from
Plunkett's Bay.

Not far from Cullen's Stone, the score it did begin,
While thousands lined the highway all bets were
taken in.
Mick Reilly led the champion and showed him
where to play,
Saying "Comrade Joe, strike hard and low, Remember
Plunkett's Bay."

Smith he speaks to Coulter, and whispers in his ear,
"Whate'er you do, play straight and true, and get the
corner clear."
But Coulter failed completely his promise to fulfil,
So cheers went in from Irish Street and the boys from
Primrose Hill.

John Nixon hands a copy of Brian Toal's *Road Bowling in Ireland*
to President Mary McAleese

James Stewart & Sons, Clockmakers

Alfred the Great calculated the lapse of time by the gradual shortening of a lighted candle. Time and its measure affects every aspect of our lives and, has as many references, both literally and symbolically. *It was the best of times, it was the worst of times...* began *A Tale of Two Cities*.

The clock is the invention of centuries and often a treasured possession. A particularly distinctive collection of grandfather and grandmother longcase clocks is crafted by the family firm of James Stewart & Sons. Skills being handed down to a third generation is rare in an age of mass production. Pride of craftsmanship has always distinguished this firm whose early clocks are now practically antique. Since 1952, Stewart clocks have provided their owners with a quality of elegance and solid worth. Distinguished by Westminster or other chimes, dials etched in Roman or raised, solid brass Arabic numerals, these timepieces are as personalised as Hepplewhite chairs or Sheraton tables. The comforting tick of a longcase clock suggests continuity. Finish and design are sheer inspiration, reminding us of a bygone age and gracious living.

Director Jim Stewart is a busy man. If we are speaking of time, life's governing force, here is an international business on our doorstep, where, in the space of an hour, several consignments of clock works arrive from Germany, a stockist telephones from Boston, Massachusetts, and a craftsman from the factory floor enquires if a distressed finish is what a customer has stipulated.

"We rarely advertise, engendering business at various exhibitions", Jim Stewart comments. "Three times annually we show our clocks at Birmingham's New Exhibition Centre, the Furniture Show and spring fair. James Stewart & Sons of Armagh was one the first companies to exhibit at that complex. I remember clambering over piles of wood on the station platform while attempting to find space for ourselves on the train—all in an effort to complete our stand for Sunday morning and NEC's official opening by Queen Elizabeth. That was 22 years ago. The firm has since opened a permanent showroom in Highpoint, North Carolina, furniture centre of the United States. We frequently travel to Germany and Belgium on sales trips and, twice a year, exhibit at Highpoint, designing and organising our stand right here in the factory. Lighting, background and selected pieces are planned to the finest detail. Even our floral displays, from Davidson's local nursery, are packed in containers, then transported."

Orders from the United States are faxed straight into the office at Stewart's out-of-town premises. "Export markets are crucial", Jim observes, "they help maintain a buoyancy of turnover upon which we depend. Our aim is to exceed expectations, whatever that may entail. Climatic changes require special timber tests before sending a clock to its destination. Yesterday, a customer from Dallas queried the moisture content of kiln-dried wood. Using mainly Brazilian mahogany for manufacture, we ceased exporting to Canada simply because the atmosphere is so dry. We buy French or European oak which can be used either in its natural state, or stained to co-ordinate with existing furniture in the customer's home. For this reason, our factory has a library of finishes used by leading furniture manufacturers: mahogany, mahogany distressed, oak, walnut, elm or yew."

Exquisite hand-painted clock faces have been perfected by a local artist—another example of specialist craft holding its own in a technological world. Clock dials are a matter of personal taste and are usually brass or silver. Following a Victorian and Edwardian fashion for colourful seasons and weather moods, James Stewart & Sons frequently produce a lunar-arched moon dial or brass corner spandrels. One handsome, satin-finished grandfather clock on display has carved swan neck pediments flanking a ball and eagle brass finial that is finished in brass scroll ends. The body, or trunk, has fluted columns, brass capitals and bases. Fretwork embellishment and roped columns have individual antique-waxed finishes. Chimes produce their own special resonance over a number of years and may mark the quarter hour, with a choice of three different chimes. If you can't stand noise, an automatic night silencer is the answer.

"Our customers are as varied as the work we produce",

Jim concurs. "Supplying Harrods of Knightsbridge carries a certain prestige, but one retailer, situated 30 miles north of London, outsells almost all United Kingdom competitors. I remember my first encounter with Harrods, which I initially used as a place to rendezvous with clients. Waiting for my colleague, I strolled into the clock department, where an assistant asked if I required help. 'No thank you', was my reply, 'I make them'. When he suggested I speak to the buyer, little did I realise that I would leave the store with an order. We are listed as stockists for the London area, but I take the attitude that business hinges on fair return and a customer is as good as his last settlement cheque."

Jim's father, also James Stewart, founded the firm. "He acquired a thorough knowledge in the employment of Albert Rea, a master cabinetmaker, whohad a small manufacturing company situated just off the Mall. I know another employee, Jack Houston, who worked there also. Albert Rea had a vocation for the church and, after studying for a theological degree, left Ireland to live in South Africa. When his business closed, Jack and my father found alternative employment. In time, James Stewart began his own cabinetmaking business at a corn mill owned by the Ulster Bank and situated behind the old 'B'-Special headquarters on the Mall. Aware that an academic life was not for me, I joined the firm at 15, straight from the Royal School, Armagh. Mr Hutchings was my headmaster then and training with the Combined Cadet Force was by far the highlight of my time at school. Eighteen months after I joined the business, my brother, Gordon, followed."

Beginning with veneering, Jim helped on van deliveries. "For this purpose, we had a custom-built, swop-body vehicle, legally the largest allowed on the road. It used to take five days to complete deliveries to the Republic of Ireland. At one time my father employed more than 50 men but, with too many firms chasing the same amount of business, the work eventually seemed unremunerative. The last government contract my father undertook was an order for 500 mahogany office desks. He had always nurtured a love of clocks, taxing the patience of my mother with a mishmash of works, cogs and cases, all kept in our kitchen. Canon Mortimer of St Mark's Parish, Dean Lillie of the Cathedral and many others were frequent visitors who, somehow, found their way to the kitchen. They lingered in conversation over these old clocks for hours. When James Stewart was urged to try making a clock, it proved a great success. His friend, Jack Thompson, from Lurgan, declared he could sell this item. And he did! Prior to Christmas that year, Jack sold four clocks. We began to produce in earnest, at first, selling only in Northern Ireland. Casey's and Keane's of Cork then became customers and at a time when import duty was 35 per cent. They rate amongst our best accounts. Casey's, like ourselves, are a family business and we've been doing business for three generations.

"There is enormous precision in weighting pendulums and after-sales service of these distinctive clocks. All movements are from German manufacturers, undoubtedly the best in the world. We have specialist stockists in Africa, America, Australia, Germany, the Czech Republic, Slovakia, Norway and the United Kingdom. When deliveries are made, weights and pendulum will be packed separately. On instruction, an expert completes the setting up of all clocks. We've had queries that really stretch the imagination. Someone rang from Wexford to say his clock was striking four times at 2pm! The solution was simple. We told him to move the clock hands to 4pm!"

Antiques Roadshow is a programme Jim cannot afford to miss. "I feel sure one of our earliest clocks is bound to appear in the hands of an expert. Stewart's clocks have been made now for 25 years. Well cared for, cherished perhaps by someone who has passed on, these have greatly appreciated in value. I am constantly asked to place a price on early models, which of course, hinges on their condition. Many have disappeared, so it pleases me greatly that something my father created will acquire antique status. From a customer's point of view, it increases confidence in investing in a Stewart clock—now seen as worthy of passing on to the next generation. Maybe a day will come when we can established a museum of our own collection."

The company produces a glossy catalogue that contains studies of the firm's past and present cabinetmakers at work, in a section prefixed 'Fine Craftsmanship'. Pointing to the first photograph, Jim explains, "Don Somerville was one of my father's employees. He is shown here using a knife to create fine marquetry, or inlay, on the base of a grandfather clock. Don died some years ago but we have never forgotten his tremendous contribution. All craftsmen working for James Stewart & Sons are local people, living within the vicinity of our factory. Most have a lifetime of experience and I like to think that this is obvious from the finished product. Kevin Harvey has been with the company all his working life. His intricate work involves assembling mechanism within the clocks. James Stewart, my son—a third generation of this family—joined more recently. Familiar with all aspects of cabinetmaking, his expertise lies in polishing. He developed the unique antique finish that makes our clocks distinctive. James is pictured working on the door of a Vienna wall clock. Robert Emerson and Ashdon Donnelly are lifetime workers whom we rate as invaluable."

"Our association with St Patrick's Church of Ireland Cathedral and its choir stretches to three generations. My father was a chorister, then myself and my brother Gordon. We were followed in turn by my three sons, James, William and Richard, and two of Gordon's sons, Alastair and Gordon. My wife, Myrtle, has been our office administrator since she left college. Her accomplishments include marketing and finance. She, with Gordon's wife, Ann, have made a great contribution to the firm. The skills of both have now given way to computation. Myrtle and Ann both retired recently, making way for technology—all part of the age of the new millennium. By way of celebration, we hope to produce a spectacular clock that will carry the city's name. Our firm may sell at international level, but we intend to continue operating from our present base for many years to come. Each of us has one son in the business with the same Christian names as Gordon and myself. This would surely have pleased my father, always a great man for tradition."

Horses matter to Jim who breeds a strain of hunting stock. Grazing outside his office window, with the rest, is a three-day old foal who will inherit the Stewart stable prefix, 'Folly Glen'.

A Belfast-based tutor helped Jim improve his conversational German—a language he deems essential for frequent business trips and telephone discussions. Spread across his office wall is a map of the United States. "I like to see the exact location when orders are being placed by American agents. As I said, the climate of the location must match the particular wood."

Also making excellent sense is a quote by John Ruskin, English art and social critic, which appears on the last page of the beautifully produced catalogue showing the fine clocks of James produced catalogue of Stewart & Sons. This affirms that quality is remembered when price is long forgotten. "All works of Quality must bear a price in proportion to the skill, time and risk attending their invention and manufacture. Those things called dear are, when justly estimated, the cheapest; they are attended with much less profit to the artist than those, which everybody calls cheap. Beautiful forms and compositions are not made by chance, nor can they in any material be made at small expense. A composition for cheapness and not for excellence or workmanship is the frequent and certain cause of the rapid decline and entire destruction of arts and manufacture."

One outstanding example of a Stewart mahogany carriage clock bears, on its dial, the scripted warning *Tempus Fugit*. In this year of Our Lord, 1999, time can be forgiven for flying when told by such a beautiful face!

Jim Stewart with his famous long case clocks
Photograph by Ian Maginess

Mary Corr

"My most recently acquired horse, Favour Royale, is something of a runaway success", observes Mary Corr. "He joined our stables in 1998 when I began his training. Successful in every County Show, we now expect him to take Royal Dublin Supreme Hunter in August."

As a little girl, Mary Corr bought, swapped or borrowed every pony book written by Christine Pullein-Thompson. "I'd fall asleep reading and clear every fence in my dreams", she recalls. Here, where County Armagh meets neighbouring Tyrone, this versatile woman manages Moy Riding School, her second-generation family business. Mother to four children, Mary is a lecturer in Equestrian Studies at Dungannon College of Further Education. "Hard work is the antidote to boredom", she considers, "but compared to other addictions, love of horses is entirely healthy."

Mary was born to equestrian life when her parents, Betty and Jero Laverty, established the county's first School of Riding in 1960. "I was the youngest to ride side-saddle in Ireland. The event was at Malahide, Co. Dublin, and Mrs Baker, presenter of the television show *Spotlight*, happened to be present. That evening I featured in her programme. For 20 years my parents ran Moy Riding School. After my father's death, I literally took up the reins. Presented with an ideal opportunity, we moved into premises adjoining the Argory two years ago. Horses were integral to this stately home in the last century so once again the yard echoes to clip-clopping hooves."

Riding out where trees meet overhead, hers is a world removed. Maintained by the National Trust, the Argory is popular with visitors who often arrange a riding lesson with their visit. The stables are busy this morning. Several students have arrived to further their skills. As tutor, Mary combines practical work in Moy Riding School with theoretical study taken at Dungannon College. "The course enables students to take British Horse Society qualifications or the HND in Horse Management. Mucking-out, feeding and grooming are nevertheless daily routine.

"Since early 1997 we've been running an indoor school at the stables. Here theory of riding, physical care of the animals, indeed the concept of a whole riding clinic means we offer an almost round-the-clock service." At this juncture our conversation is interrupted by the arrival of a local veterinary surgeon who has arranged to administer the stable tetanus jabs. Crossing the courtyard, he steps over several family dogs, snoozing in sunshine.

"I must introduce Desmond": Mary beckons her husband, a skilled joiner who was until recently lecturing at Lisburn College. "Now I'm more than adequately occupied", he affirms. Desmond designed and purpose-built his own transport, a step-frame lorry capable of accommodating seven horses, food and harnesses, besides seven of the family with attendant paraphernalia for up to two weeks stay at any showjumping event. He is an able horseman but swiftly admits, "not in Mary's league". "The stables wouldn't survive without his practicality", she responds. A partnership of equal commitment, theirs works well.

Horses have always featured strongly in Mary's life. "I was practically born in the saddle for my mother refused to give up exercising her favourite filly." Now Mary encourages her own children's interest. "Nicky, my eldest, has realised a dream, winning the trophy for his 15-hand working hunter, Kinnard Fair Exchange, at the Royal Dublin Show in August 1996. Jason favours cross-country events and hunting. Sarah has been extremely successful with her working hunter pony and is Ireland's youngest side-saddle competitor today. That, you might say, is maintaining family tradition." Jero, her youngest, now seven, is attending his second Pony Club Camp, run by his mother. His pony is affectionately known as Big Chief. "Jero shows aptitude and of course the older children enjoy helping him. I sometimes marvel we've enough animals to go round!"

Moving her school to spacious accommodation was a courageous step, justified eventually by a remarkable increase in pupils. "Our age range is elastic, from the four-year-old beginner to senior citizens who simply feel better for exercise." During a summer, she estimates, "I will teach at least 300 children to ride. What was once a middle-class privilege is now considered a healthy pursuit for kids on the long summer break. We are available for coaching from eight each morning until seven in the

Mary Corr on Favour Royal is presented with the 1999 Championship Cup at Bailieborough Show by Senior Judge Billy Connors

evening. Children turn up with a packed lunch and the day begins."

Mary rarely settles for second best. In 1993, with Ben Rush, she achieved international fame, winning the Dublin Champion Cob. "We bought him at a fair in Ballinasloe. It takes experience to judge a potential winner but he had it all—conformation, structure, a kind eye and pleasing temperament. Good stock, provided you work hard, will achieve Show standard. Horse and rider must blend as one. Ben Rush loved the accolade at Royal Dublin and Wembley. Well", she laughs, "so did I. A lap of honour is pure exhilaration. You can be sure European and American buyers are there too, seeking the best bloodstock. One of ours, Rising Rocket, an eventer, was bought by Alistair Hood who consistently produces a winner at the International Horse of the Year Show. Ben Rush took the Best Working Hunter again at RDS in 1995, carrying off a fabulous trophy. It was all or nothing that year."

Staking her reputation on Copper Star, Mary won both Reserve Heavyweight Champion and Four-Year Champion trophies. Copper Star is now resident at the English stables of Robert Oliver where he qualified for Wembley.

Rosettes and endless photographs of the family's successes line Mary's kitchen. Piled high, a stack of riding hats wait expectantly on a shelf. "A full-time nanny is essential", Mary explains, "given that we live and breathe horses. Competing sees us at Wembley, Balmoral, Bailieborough, RDS, and Ballivor, near Mullingar. Success in winter classic events helps finance our teaching programme in summer. Uniquely perhaps, I coach the children of people taught by my parents."

Given the luxury of time to herself, Mary finds a quiet place and a book. "At the moment I'm absorbed by David Ziegler's *Mountbatten*. Scathing reviews haven't discouraged me from reading *The Last Empress: Life and Times of Alexandra Feodorovna, Tsarina of Russia*. Regardless of the critics, I'll make my own judgement. Television has to be the greatest waste of time with the exception of David Attenborough's wildlife series."

The established Christmas tradition at Moy Riding School is a morning hack. "Everyone dresses for the occasion and the atmosphere is superb. We exchange greetings, then after mulled wine and mince pies, take to the saddle. An atmospheric dusting of snow on the hills makes it all the better. How better to work up a ravenous appetite for lunch?"

The bell clangs. Another student achieves a clear round. Thanks to Mary's hard work and horsemanship, the 'Sport of Kings' is placed affordably within the reach of all.

Tony Davidson

Another day, another death,
Another futile loss of breath...

"We are inclined to think that it is other people who have the responsibility for bringing peace on earth", commented Pam Rhodes, a presenter of *Songs of Praise*, when asked about her personal beliefs, adding: "Peace emerges from our hearts and into the community."

On the face of it, this is a simple ideal. Arriving in Armagh from Limerick in 1994, the Rev. Tony Davidson, BA, BD, was faced with the stark reality. "I was installed as Minister of First Armagh Presbyterian Church on 30 March 1994", he recollects. "Eight weeks later, we witnessed the violent deaths of many people within the space of a few days. On the morning of Sunday 22 May, at the last moment, I completely changed my sermon, addressing this crisis. Asking my congregation to open their hearts in prayer, I told them exactly what lay in mine. What I state as a sequence of events was in fact, the essence of my sermon."

Priorities are indicative of a person's age. The older generations tend to be absorbed by the past, while the young live for today and the future. It requires breadth and depth of character to be able to value tradition while empathising with modern times and with all who live in a particular diverse community. However painful this may be for his personal life, Tony Davidson is transparently honest, expressing his thoughts with shrewd and seamless logic.

"Limerick was an experience", he observes. "You must remember that I am speaking of the late 1980s when my joint Presbyterian and Methodist congregation comprised 70 families. I hope to dispel a myth for, in my experience, there was no evidence of religious or political discrimination while I lived there. Limerick itself was a thriving university city with a population of perhaps 70,000 people. It is not without its problems—there are areas of poverty, discrimination against Travellers, and drug dealing. When my wife Christine and I arrived in Armagh with our three children, Mark, Gemma and Ruth, it was exactly six months prior to the first ceasefire.

"My introduction to terrorism came within weeks. I keep office hours in my study at the rear of First Armagh Presbyterian Church. One Wednesday morning the telephone rang. Christine told me there had been a killing in Lower English Street. Grabbing my jacket, I went at once. Police and others at the scene were white with shock. Two teenagers, Gavin McShane and Shane McArdle, had been shot—one boy was dead, the other dying. My first reaction was one of helplessness, followed by anger that anyone could do this in the name of Protestantism. We are responsible for each other and, in the name of humanity, I needed to communicate my feelings. Walking up the hill to the Parochial House, I was warmly received. While I was expressing my horror, the telephone shrilled.

"'Who is dead?' someone demanded. 'Was it my son... is he safe?' begged another. I walked home feeling as if I were bearing the world on my back. That evening I left flowers at the scene of the killing.

"The Moderator of our Presbytery, the Rev. Bill Cameron, is a friend and together we visited the family of Gavin McShane. Despite their grief and shock, Gavin's parents, Maria and Matt, assured us we were welcome and brought us inside. We learned that Maria had been the victim of a terrorist bomb shortly before her son was born, costing her the sight of one eye. Her good-looking son lay in a coffin, physically perfect, save for a small bullet wound in his head. Matt told us of Gavin's passion for sport, the reason why his son was dressed in a hurling jersey. His teachers arrived, speaking in hushed tones of Gavin's zest for life. Maria invited us to say a prayer before leaving. A lump in my throat made this almost impossible but, somehow, the words came. On Friday morning, I visited the McArdle family who, weighed down with their own sorrow, were thinking of Gavin's people." Within days, an off-duty member of the Royal Irish Regiment, Reggie McCullough, was killed by the IRA in Armagh.

"There were so many deaths that week", Tony remembers. "Fred Anthony killed on his way to work in Lurgan, the murder of a soldier in Keady, Gerry Corrie and Eamon Fox from Maghery killed on a building site in Belfast, Eric Smith shot dead in his home in Salters'

Grange, and a pub doorman shot dead in Dublin. In essence, BBC and Ulster Television transmissions were the same—blast bombs, petrol bombs, nail bombs, bullets. Shane's father, haggard with grief, begged for the killing to stop. Little Emma Anthony had wires protruding from every part of her body. Her grandmother wept as she spoke. Viewers wept at the utter pointlessness of harming a three-year-old child." Tony Davidson looked at his three children, and he too wept.

"A seminar was held for sixth formers at St Patrick's Trian, as part of Armagh Together's international conference on Religion and Conflict", Tony continues. "Some of Gavin's friends were present and these young people talked frankly of their differences, similarities and hopes for peace. I was disappointed that more from the Protestant faiths were not present. I felt drained and dispirited. All this I recounted in my pulpit on Pentecost Sunday. 'Where is the Holy Spirit in all of this?' I recall demanding. 'Why,' I asked my congregation, 'did I leave the church study and go to the scene of Gavin's death? Why did I not stay safely within these walls? These were not, in the crudest of terms, our 'own' people. Why did I walk up the hill to the priests' house?' Pacing up and down, I gave my congregation the answer to all of those questions.

"I went because Jesus walked up the hill to Calvary, outside a city's walls, to identify with sin. I felt I had to walk up the hill, outside my metaphorical gates, to identify with the suffering of others. Jesus moved among the sad, the oppressed and the downtrodden. That, I decided is where the Holy Spirit is, and where I must be. The conquest of evil is an ongoing struggle that has nothing to do with unionist and nationalist, Protestant and Roman Catholic—but with right and wrong, good and bad. Strangely, in each house of those who mourned, there was a sense that God was present, that the unseen Holy Spirit was comforting those in sorrow. At the first Pentecost, the gift of tongues was given so that all could understand, regardless of language. So many deaths in so few days demanded a language that speaks across the sectarian divide—a language that communicates good news in evil times." As joint chair of the Armagh Church Forum and convenor of the Committee on Irish Church Relations for the Presbyterian Church in Ireland, Tony Davidson feels that we have a duty to work for the betterment of community relations.

By their lives, Maria and Matt McShane have shown a perfect example of good emanating from evil. "Maria was approached by Wave, a voluntary organisation offering counselling for victims of violence. She later helped establish a branch in Dobbin Street, Armagh, where the bereaved may discuss their problems with someone who has had similar traumatic experiences. She finds it difficult, yet Maria has spoken publicly at peace rallies and, with cross-community volunteers from Wave, met the President and First Lady of the United States at the Irish and British Embassies in Washington DC. Some time after the Omagh bombing, Maria and Matt were invited to come and share the grief of afflicted families. It is not easy", Tony emphasises, "for each occasion serves to open their own wounds. This has to be Christianity working for good in the worst circumstances."

Tony's wife Christine, as HomeStart organiser in Armagh, is making her own important contribution to the community. This is a voluntary organisation that supports young families under stress. Christine recruits and trains volunteers, and matches them to families who are seeking help.

In deference to the past, Tony refers to a local history examining three centuries of First Armagh Presbyterian Church, from 1673-1973, written by the late Dr G. Temple Lundie, Minister of the congregation from 1949-78. First Armagh Presbyterian Church holds a Session Minute Book dating from 1707-27. Thereafter we have little information until 1874. Committee minutes began in 1842. Dr Lundie comments: "There is a great deal of obscurity about the actual beginnings of Presbyterianism in Armagh. Mary Tudor had passed an Act preventing the bringing in, retaining or marrying of the Scots in Ireland but this Act was repealed by James I as part of his Plantation policy. The repeal led to the establishment of a large Scottish colony in Armagh and, especially, in surrounding country districts whereas the northern part of the country was mostly settled by families of English descent. The Scots brought with them the Presbyterian form of worship and church government which had, by the labours of John Knox and others, been firmly established in Scotland."

It is thought that the Armagh Congregation may have worshipped at the Old Meeting House at the Shambles. The Rev. John Hutcheson was then Minister. Another body of Presbyterians arrived in Armagh in the latter part

Rev. Tony Davidson
Photograph by Andrew Breakey

of the 18th century, known as the Seceders. The Old Meeting House was taken over by them and used until 1879. They were eventually known as Second Armagh Presbyterian Congregation. It is of note that John Wesley preached in the Seceders' pulpit in 1787. A church was built in Abbey Street, now the Memorial Hall, and worship began here during 1725, continuing until 1879, when it was passed on for the use of Second Armagh Presbyterian Church. In a Presbytery minute dated 7 November 1837, it was noted that a number of Presbyterians disannexed themselves from the congregation of Armagh. These petitioners formed a separate congregation to be called the Second Presbyterian Congregation of Armagh in connection with the Synod of Ulster. Approximately 60 families left the Armagh Congregation at this time and formed themselves into a separate congregation called the 'New' or the 'Mall' congregation. This group at first worshipped in Abbey Street and in 1838, the Rev. W.B. McAllister came from Ballygrainey as their first minister. During his administration, a church was built on the Mall, a Sabbath School was organised, a schoolroom started in Gosford Place and a manse purchased in the Seven Houses to which six acres of glebe were attached.

Fever was rampant in the district in 1851, and the Rev. Alex Fleming of the First Armagh Congregation is thought to have been a victim. He is buried at the old church in Abbey Street. First Armagh Presbyterian Church opened at its present site on 22 May 1879, 206 years after the setting up of the congregation. The Rev. Jackson Smyth was Minister of this new church, an exceptionally fine example of Gothic Revival, with its graceful spire reaching 185 feet skywards.

At this time, Mr McWilliams donated a field at Red Barns for use as a Presbyterian cemetery. Presbyterians in Armagh had been interred in Church of Ireland graveyards, mostly at St Mark's Parish Church, Kildarton, Lisnadill and Grange. The Presbyterian cemetery was known as 'The New Cemetery' and in January 1900, steps were taken to build a caretaker's lodge and entrance gates. National events are reflected in a resolution of November 1899, when a collection was taken up for the wives and families of soldiers who had gone to the Boer War. By 1911, 180 families were attached to First Armagh Presbyterian Church with 430 children on the Sunday School rolls.

The Irish Presbyterian Church had done much for education and in 1924 it was proposed in the Northern Ireland Parliament that churches transfer their schools to local education committees who would be responsible for their upkeep and the appointment of teachers. After considerable hesitation, First Armagh decided to transfer its school in College Street to the Regional Committee.

The death of James P. Irwin, JP, in April 1927 is recorded in Church Memorial Minutes. James Irwin was well known for the successful grocery business he established in Scotch Street. His sign, The Golden Teapot, was a trademark until the 1970s. One of his daughters married Mr Allison, the well-known photographer. The Wall Street Crash of 1929 shook the world and repercussions were felt in Armagh when the linen industry fell into serious decline. Farming was conducted at little more than subsistence level and unemployment was rife with few prospects for young people.

When King George V died on 28 January 1936 a Memorial Service was held in the Church at which the British Legion paraded under Captain Ensor. The parade was led by the Old Boys' Silver Band. War was declared in 1939 and soon the Army commandeered the Lecture Hall. Church organisations continued on a minimal scale due to the 'Blackout'. R.J. McDonald, who died in 1943, had been Captain of the Boys' Brigade Company for 40 years. A decision was made to sell the manse in Charlemont Place to Armagh County Council in 1958.

The Tercentenary was celebrated, wrote Dr Lundie, "against a background of turmoil and violence, and some of the approaches to our property are barricaded in the interests of security. One of our members, Mr William Johnston, was brutally murdered. Others have had property damaged by bombs, and the pattern of civilised living has been seriously disrupted. Our forefathers started this congregation in difficult days—their successors had to face many hardships and deprivations. They remained steadfast and unshaken and surely we too can say: 'Hitherto hath the Lord helped us; we will go in the Name of the Lord'."

Merging past and present, Tony Davidson recently recorded an interview with the oldest member of his congregation, Mrs Kathleen Huston, aged 102. "She now resides at Fairlawns nursing home and two generations of her family are members of our congregation. Mrs Huston and her husband once ran a jeweller's shop in Scotch Street. Visiting Mrs Huston is an exhilarating experience and, for this reason, I bought my taped conversation into the pulpit, sharing it with the congregation. We spoke of changes she has seen since 1897. This was her reply:

"'I was Kathleen Patterson, born in Thomas Street. My father was a grocer and we lived above the store, then on the Mall. A few pence bought a big bag of sweets then. My father delivered meal by pony and trap to customers in rural areas. I accompanied him each Friday, sitting up on the seat in front. At College Street National School, where I began my education, the girls sat in the front rows. Typically, the boys pulled our pigtails!

"'We skipped and played marbles at the War Memorial on the Mall, often risking our lives by jumping over the wall at the bottom of Russell Street. I joined the church choir when Miss Biggart was organist. Mr Maxwell was then church superintendent and, when he retired, my father took over. Our Sunday School excursion was the most exciting event of the year. After a prayer at College Street we were led by the Old Boys' Band to the station. I can still hear the train chuffing as it took us off to Warrenpoint. If I've reached my 102nd birthday, I think it has a lot to do with my guardian angel who watched over me in good times and bad.'

"Hearing her voice again was an emotional experience for many of our congregation. We then sang her favourite hymn: *What a Friend we have in Jesus*. The elderly have a contribution to make and this was hers."

The Rev. Tony Davidson has roused every emotion in a narrative where the impetus never slackens. This, and his work, shows exactly how valuable a contribution he is making.

Aubrey McClintock

When the Proms began in 1895, Queen Victoria had not yet celebrated her Diamond Jubilee, the Boer War had not begun and people were gossiping about a dispute between Gilbert and Sullivan. Henry Wood, then an up-and-coming young conductor, wanted to make classical music available at a price anybody could afford. A standing ticket for the first of his Promenade Concerts cost one shilling.

With similar aspirations, Aubrey McClintock, BA (Hons), LTCL, founded the first Charles Wood Summer School in 1994. Contrast the ugly political overtones of that July with a chorus of stunning reviews in August for exquisite performances given by the Charles Wood Singers. Music critics left us in no doubt that cries of *Encore!* were appropriate for Aubrey, and he has since delivered repeat performances on an annual basis. Community relations officer with Armagh City and District Council, he strives to make music, as he would out it, 'equally accessible to performer and listener'.

"Since arriving in Armagh in 1990, I had been searching for a way to celebrate church music, one that might involve those of all denominations. I've always relished the music of Charles Wood. This, incidentally, had been familiar to me from my earliest days as a chorister. It was only when I moved here that I discovered Charles Wood was born at Vicar's Hill, Armagh, and educated at the Church of Ireland Cathedral School in the mid-1870s.

"As well as singing in the Cathedral Choir, Wood showed early promise as both organist and composer. At the age of 17, he became a student at the newly established Royal College of Music in London. Charles Wood moved on to Cambridge where he spent the rest of his days as student, teacher, and finally Professor of Music. A prolific composer of liturgical music, his output included more than 30 anthems and a Latin Mass. At a planning meeting for the Armagh Together year, I came up with the idea of a dual celebration of liturgical music and of Charles Wood as a son of Armagh. Thus the Charles Wood Summer School was born."

Aubrey's enduring love of choral music was forged during his early years as a chorister in St Anne's Cathedral, Belfast. Undergraduate days saw him become a choral scholar at Norwich Cathedral while studying music at the University of East Anglia. Rather impressively, Aubrey in his final year was director of the University Chamber Choir that consisted of fellow students. During that year he conducted the choir in two concerts at Norwich Cathedral.

"Initially I'd been reluctant to take on the choir but the buzz I received from those performances led me to believe choral conducting was likely to become part of my life. My first appointment", Aubrey continues, "was teaching in St Michael's College, Tenbury Wells. This was a choir school, set up in the mid-19th century to provide a model for cathedral choirs all over the country, at a time when church music was at a low ebb. Apart from teaching I sang in the famous chapel choir. It was something of a coincidence that one of my first experiences of church music happened to be a recording, bought by my father in the early 1960s, of St Michael's College Choir. It was at St Bede's Preparatory School in Eastbourne that I gained my first experience of working with young voices. Imagine the thrill when my choir won the National Choral Competition at the Royal Festival Hall in 1988, going on to perform at the Schools' Promenade Concert held in the Royal Albert Hall."

His abilities shine out yet Aubrey wears his talent lightly. By nature he is agreeable and approachable. "Drawing from an abundance of young talent, I founded the Armagh City Junior Choir of 60 girls, aged from ten to 14. The older students later formed the basis of the Armagh Girl Singers. I audition every voice. None of the children find this easy yet if we are to maintain high vocal standards, it is essential."

His office is at the Palace Demesne where Aubrey's aim is one of encouraging and promoting cross-community contact and mutual understanding. "I hesitate to give the impression that all my time is dedicated to music but it is an excellent way of bringing people together, regardless of tradition and background."

The Christmas Gala Concert was Aubrey's brainchild and established an annual event when choirs from all sections of the Armagh community come together to celebrate the festive season, making a glad sound. Aubrey engenders a certain loyalty from his young singers who always give seem to give of their best in performance.

"Any new venture is daunting", he considers. "Yet the Charles Wood Summer School germinated quickly and, six years later, continues to thrive. The extensive programme covers all areas of church music and caters for organists, singers, choir trainers and composers. It is important that the Summer School is not perceived as elitist, and to that end there are events for those of all ages and musical abilities. The school attracts an impressive array of visiting tutors and performers. Internationally acclaimed organists such as Dame Gillian Weir and Thomas Trotter have performed, but rather than merely jetting in to give a recital and leaving immediately, they remained for several days, instructing aspiring local organists."

A thirst for learning has popularised the varied workshops dealing with aspects of choir training, conducting and composition. Notable facilitators include Professor Peter Aston, Malcolm Archer, Martin How and Dr Barry Rose. Each of these highly regarded musicians has brought a fragment of Aubrey's past to Armagh. "Peter Aston was my University Professor and taught me conducting. Malcolm Archer was assistant organist at Norwich Cathedral during my time as a choral scholar. Now an eminent composer, he was then relatively unknown. During the 1980s, I sang in the Southern Cathedral Singers, a choir directed by Martin How. Martin was perhaps my greatest inspiration as a choir trainer and it was my delight to have him attend the Summer School for two successive years. One of my enduring memories would be of Martin, a man in his late Sixties, dancing the night away with the girls from the choir, at the Charlemont Arms Hotel—they absolutely adored him! I recall singing under the direction of Barry Rose at St Paul's Cathedral in the late Seventies. Even then he was a living legend in the world of church music. However, it was not until 1993 that I came to know him personally. At that time, Barry was director of music at St Albans Cathedral. My brother, Nigel, was his organ scholar for a year and thus our acquaintance came about. My own style of choir training has developed from those trainers under whose direction I once sang.

"Ghislaine Morgan, the renowned English soprano, and Quentin Hayes, a principal baritone at the Royal Opera House, Covent Garden, both thoroughly enjoy visits to Armagh and are impressed by the wealth of local talent. Again I have known both for years as we sang together in the choir of St Bride's Church, Fleet Street, London. It is good to have such links with the past.

"Naturally some of our overseas guests have been concerned about civil unrest and our 1998 Summer School was undoubtedly overshadowed by the Omagh bombing. I asked them to trust my judgement, giving reassurance that I would not endanger their safety. Months of meticulous planning go into staging the Summer School. It is soul-destroying to think that our ongoing conflict adversely affects what is accepted as a beautiful medium. At the end of August, Armagh becomes a musical high ground, the place to be, and patrons will travel any distance to attend events of their choice. A Summer School committee has been established with the aim of strengthening community ownership while securing the future of this important annual event.

"My first love is church music of the late 19th and early 20th centuries. Elgar, Parry, Stanford and Vaughan Williams are composers whose music has impressed me ever since childhood. Charles Wood slots comfortably into this niche and I'd like to think I have increased awareness of both man and music. After all, until now and outside the Cathedral walls, Wood's music was almost unknown in his native Armagh."

Church music is considered by Aubrey to be a sound basis for musical training. "Andrew Davis, who conducted the Last Night of the Proms, began his musical career as an organ scholar at King's College, Cambridge. Stephen Barlow, who was the last musical director of Opera Northern Ireland, started as a chorister in Canterbury Cathedral and was then organ scholar at Trinity College, Cambridge. I first met Stephen 20 years ago on a music course at Canterbury. Meeting again some years ago led to a fair amount of catching up.

"I admire any musician who gives his time to assist young musicians. The late Yehudi Menuhin, virtuoso violinist and gifted conductor, created his own school for promising young musicians. Such was the celestial quality of Menuhin's playing that Einstein, on hearing the 12-year-old, declared, 'Now I know there is a God in heaven!'"

Asked to cite his favourite composers, Aubrey deliberates. "The answer I might give today is not necessarily one I would give tomorrow. Music, you understand, alternates and attunes to mood. Händel is a composer equally accessible to performer and listener. *Dixit Dominus* is, for me, Händel's finest choral work, acknowledged as one of the most demanding for singers in the choral repertoire. I look forward to the day when I shall direct a performance of this work in Armagh. I find I am increasingly interested in contemporary composers such as John Taverner whose *Song for Athene* was performed at the funeral of Diana, Princess of Wales.

"Our Summer School is unique within Ireland. I see it as equivalent to a combination of three major English festival events—Eton Choral Course, Oundel Organ Week and the Edington Festival of Music in Liturgy. It is appropriate that Armagh, with its two cathedrals in one city, should be capable of hosting a musical event of international standing—one befitting Ireland's ecclesiastical capital."

Despite a demanding lifestyle, Aubrey enjoys his own style of cooking, particularly Indian, Mexican and Italian dishes using fresh herbs and spices. "Pasta dishes, composed from whatever happens to be in the cupboard, are quick and tasty. This suits me very well. For a complete turnaround, I enjoy televised comedy, particularly the characters portrayed by Dawn French. *The Vicar of Dibley* is a superb example of easy viewing. I listen to Classic FM in the car and for sheer contrast, performers such as The Corrs or Mary Black."

Like Sir Colin Davis, principal conductor of the London Symphony Orchestra, Aubrey has succeeded in 'making the best music'. "I do not pretend that music can change the world but it certainly makes it a better place. For me it is the perfect image of life and the way we live it. It has a beginning, it goes through time and it has an end. And", he adds thoughtfully, "I can't imagine what would have happened if it hadn't become a major part of my life."

Aubrey McClintock with the Charles Wood Singers,
August 1999

Willie Nugent

What contributes to the success of Willie Nugent, MBE? He is not a comedian in any stand-up sense, yet in all his performances, a sense of good-natured humour shines through. However funny or impossible his undertaking, everyone wishes him well. And well is exactly what he has done, single-handedly raising to date almost £1 million for charity.

"It began by accident", says Willie, a most likeable man with dancing blue eyes. "Now I've twice been mentioned in the *Guinness Book of Records*, first in 1983 when I walked backwards for 81½ miles in 24 hours." Willie broke the world record, then 80 miles for such an accomplishment. Again in 1985 he received an entry by standing motionless for 13 hours, smashing the previous record of 12½ hours. "Guinness World of Records has a permanent exhibition at the Trocadero, Piccadilly Circus, London and here I qualified for my second mention in the midst of special Guinness anniversary celebrations."

Since 1974, Willie Nugent has undertaken one-man promotions for almost every good cause. "I'd just begun my job as a porter at Tower Hill Hospital when staff were invited to supply original ideas for a charity 'Fun Day'. I could hardly believe my ears when, out of the blue, I heard myself volunteer to cycle from Donegal town to Armagh. Somewhat difficult as I didn't have a bike! The idea expanded as I gave it some thought. Funds could be raised by asking people to guess how long I would take to complete the journey. As for the bicycle", Willie laughs. "My brother, Joey, found one that worked. We drove to Donegal and the Garda signed my starting time as 6am. Stopping only for drinks or a Mars bar to sustain energy, I arrived at Longstone Hospital by 4.45pm that evening. The event raised £500 which was considered a colossal amount and local newspapers carried reports on the event. Before my aches and pains had disappeared, I met someone who worked for a cancer research fundraising team who asked if I'd repeat the operation on behalf of this worthy cause." Willie shrugs, "I'm just a boy who can't say no! My next trip to Knock, Co. Mayo, and back was 302 miles, also based on guessing how many hours it would take me to cycle the distance. I arrived home at 4am when everyone was in bed. Local newspapers gave me excellent publicity and the late Winston McConville of the *Ulster Gazette* came round to take a photograph. Such a good-natured buzz has surrounding each event", says Willie. "If I'm honest I've always cared about people, especially those who seem to have a raw deal in life. My parents set an example including respect for others so this probably stems from their influence. I cannot understand why human beings should inflict pain on one another and that is why I never ceased trying to do the opposite. I'm not married so no-one is inconvenienced by seemingly daft undertakings in the name of a good cause. People often say I'm mad, or that I'll injure myself, yet", he emphasises, "in a quarter century I have never lost a day at work through illness."

One favourite stunt involved dressing up as a Dalmatian, Willie spending 24 hours locked up with stray dogs in Armagh Council animal pound. In support of the Royal Society for the Prevention of Cruelty to Animals, Willie hired a theatrical outfit made of white fur with black spots.

"Lots of families came the following day, bringing children who chose an abandoned dog. This saved the animal a dire fate on 'Death Row'. I was placed in a cage while the strays were exercised. By lunchtime every dog had found a home with caring owners. I love animals, particularly dogs, so this cause was close to my heart." Cycling events soon became repetitive and Willie decided to introduce new impetus to his campaigns. With each request for charitable help, he insisted on one proviso, the freedom to devise his own publicity stunt. "Inspiration always came and each event attracted a greater volume of attention from the general public", he agrees. "I took to walking with my Alsatian dog, Sheba. For people in Third World countries suffering devastating famine, I decided we would walk from Armagh to Belfast. Permission from the USPCA was granted with regulations for Sheba's welfare. The morning we set off, Sheba jumped up eagerly when I produced her lead. Next day she shook her paws and hid behind the settee!" That event was a sponsored effort, Willie and Sheba walking as far as Lisburn, then taking the towpath to Belfast. "Sheba was a star who helped me raise thousands of pounds", Willie recalls affectionately. When she died, he acquired one of Ben Simpson's famous cairn terriers. "I called this little chap Barney and what a great character he was! One idea that really worked was 'Pick A Bone Barney'. Barney's photograph headed sponsorship sheets and a prize could be won by an individual name printed on a bone-shaped biscuit. When we had 500 biscuits in a circle, I walked Barney round, then removed his lead. Naturally he grabbed the nearest biscuit. The name on that biscuit won the prize. Children thought this was great fun—some were convinced Barney could read! I was heart-broken when Barney died of old age. Having come to love this breed of dog, I replaced Barney with my present cairn terriers, Whiskey and Lady. From Joe Dean's Scarva kennels, both puppies were from the same litter."

Through charitable endeavours, Willie is known to everyone. Never dreaming he would extract close on a million pounds from our pockets, he lists some of his witty conquests. At a 'Dry Land Swim' of 50 meters freestyle, people laid a river of coins either side of this intrepid veteran. In 1981 he managed 16 miles on his knees, crawling round the Mall. "Despite being heavily bandaged", Willie says, "blood began seeping through protective knee pads and a doctor supervising the event insisted I stop. This was so disappointing for I was close to a world record.

"David Lennox allowed me use of a shop window in his department store. Dressed as General Custer, I relived the disastrous Battle of the Little Big Horn in 1876. I have pushed a pea with my nose for 2^1/2 miles which gained an appearance on *Kelly Live*. They asked me to demonstrate this feat along the floor of the studio, afterwards donating generously to my appeal." In the same vein, pushing an apple around the Mall, Willie was interviewed by Ulster Television personality Pamela Ballentine, and viewers all over the country responded generously. "To raise funds for the Blind Centre, Belfast, I decided to roll a chocolate egg around the Mall. Paddy Gallen, who works locally and is visually impaired, came to support me bringing Yale, his guide dog. Yale promptly ate the chocolate egg, bringing an end to that performance!" Willie's world record of walking backwards was performed on the Mall in 1983, again for the benefit of Tower Hill Hospital funds.

"And yet", he decides, "the most enjoyable atmosphere surrounding any event was when I stood motionless in London. Guinness personnel were present, saving endless authentication of documents. The world record to beat was 12^1/2 hours. I gave up when I reached 13, physically exhausted, but the crowd who gathered made it worthwhile. As world record-breaker, I was invited to appear on Michael Aspel's London regional television show and *That's Life* with Esther Rantzen. Esther asked me to remain motionless in Cornmarket, Belfast, while her team filmed. It was almost impossible not to laugh as everyone around me was doing just that. Then they asked me to appear on the show in London." Afterwards, at a special reception, Cliff Richard paid tribute to Willie's caring spirit.

"I really enjoy London crowds who gather quickly and give generously. Sitting in a rocking-chair at Leicester Square, I rocked around the clock and made lots of friends." For Children with Aids, labelling himself 'Birdman Willie', he crawled around Trafalgar Square with a tray of birdseed strapped to his back. Tourists flocked to watch and enjoying the fun, donated massively. Returning home, Willie was invited to the City Hall, Belfast and given a BBC interview afterwards. "Invitations come from every quarter", he comments. "Cavan and Monaghan Down's Syndrome Association asked if I would participate in a venture which again was massively supported and much appreciated by the organisers." Early fundraising days in 1980 would have been impossible without invaluable help from Tower Hill Hospital staff. "For their individual skills, it is important that I acknowledge and thank Isobel Matthews, Dorothy Haire, Kay Casey and Mildred Keenan."

Willie has always taken annual leave for his headline-grabbing events. Fundraising at weekends means no inconvenience to his employers at Tower Hill, now under the auspices of Southern Health and Social Services Board. Willie's duties involve sorting and delivering the post within the Board. Head porter John McGirr is tolerant of Willie's efforts and the staff are totally committed to many of these events. In 1998 they walked backwards with him around the Board building at Tower Hill, raising £800 for Children in Need.

"After each event, I best relax by taking a trip to Donegal", Willie comments. "When new ideas or inspiration fails, I walk and watch the sea in all its different moods. My mother, Annie Boyle, came from Donegal, another reason why I take such pleasure from this rugged county. The coast road is magical and never have I returned without fresh perspective. It is impossible to envisage a day when I will run out of material. John Wayne films are dear to my heart. *She Wore a Yellow Ribbon* or *The Quiet Man* guarantee relaxation after a strenuous day."

Willie's late father, Patrick was an employee of Armagh Gas House and was lamplighter for the city. "Our dwelling house adjoining the gasworks has been redeveloped and renamed Culdee Drive. Gaslight suggests mystery or Victorian theatre and an older generation may remember my father carrying a ladder and box of matches as he set out to light the street lamps each evening. From Irish Street corner he illuminated all the way to College Street. In winter lighting-up came earlier. One family in Russell Street called him 'the alarm clock' so punctual was he. There was a certain mystique in being a lamplighter, a figure immortalised in children's poetry or song. When Mount St Catherine's Primary School compiled a history of Armagh in times past, I supplied information for teacher Mary McCrave on my father's employment. I also contributed words and music which I had written on the much-loved theme of a lamplighter's occupation." The choir of Mount St Catherine's sang Willies song when Ulster Television highlighted the school on *The School Around The Corner*.

He speaks briefly on his less-known musical background. "As teenagers we formed a band, The Models, made up of my brothers, Joey and Jimmy who played guitar, Paddy on his harmonica and myself on drums. We filled engagements for Christmas parties and dances, playing popular tunes of the time. Presently I live with my sister Marian who is a nurse and extremely worthy of my thanks. Marian clears up after each 'Willie Nugent Extravaganza' and, take my word, costume-making can turn the most orderly home into a chaotic nightmare! My father died in 1980 and my mother in 1988, so they missed out on some of the greatest moments in my life. Receiving the MBE stands out as exceptional. Waiting to be called at Buckingham Palace I met and chatted with others who had been nominated. Bob Monkhouse and Dame Thora Hurd were two personalities to be honoured that morning. Before the actual presentation, someone reads a résumé of your life. When I came forward the Queen asked, 'How did you find time to do all this and work?' I replied that it wasn't a problem, fundraising simply became a way of life."

The list of enterprises undertaken by this incredible moneyraising maestro just goes on growing. Willie has eaten 70 lollipops in one hour, sustained a drum beat for 26 hours, walked 7 miles with a bucket of water on his head, eaten 1,500 baked beans with a cocktail stick at one sitting, and was buried in a bath of ice for one hour. Such undertakings are equalled only by the impressive list of personalities he's met.

"It was a special moment when past Mayor Robert Turner brought me to a reception at the Palace. The Mayor then spoke of his visit to a Bulgarian orphanage and how the plight of those children motivated him into raising £8,000. This amount was sufficient to heat the orphanage, install kitchen equipment and purchase a minibus. I felt at one with Robert Turner whose his heart is in the right place and whose reasons were genuine."

Willie Nugent leaves us with a highly personal insight. "No matter what I've done for any cause, I have evolved an established pattern. As soon as I reach home, up I go to the graveyard, now my parents' resting place, and for a few quiet moments, I tell them what has been happening. You see, they set an example, made me what I am. So if my dream is one of a world where we no longer inflict pain on each other or try to make life more bearable for those less fortunate—you may say it's all down to them."

Record-breaker Willie Nugent, with Yorkshire terriers Whiskey and Lady
Photograph by Michael Campbell, LBIPP

John McAllister

John McAllister came to Armagh in 1974 for two years, and stayed. He has his own accountancy practice in the city and is currently studying for a Master's degree in Creative Writing at Trinity College, Dublin.

John's work has been extensively published, not only in Ireland but in the Australian periodical Quadrant, and he has recently completed a novel. This work entitled *Neighbour John* is an acknowledgement of farmers past, an image that has all but disappeared in a technological age.

Neighbour John

He was an old man with trousers
nearly ready for the tub, carbolic
and the board.
Though designer stubbled,

he himself was clean, smelling
as he did: of the fields and fresh air
and the hosts of jobs he touched
but seldom lingered over.

For he was a man handy.
The one who ended up
behind the horse or at the wheel
or holding the post.

He would go to no end of bother
to give you a shot-out
but bored very easily
when money was involved.

With a shotgun in any hand but his
the rooks panicked; him
they ignored, he always missed.
And when he went poaching

the salmon landed him
and he ended up in hospital
with the police *making enquiries*.
The only thing he ever caught
was a stone with his head.

Poet John McAllister
Photograph by Michael Campbell, LBIPP

Dessie Feeney

Right places should fit like a garment and few are more at home in their particular niche than fashion retailer Dessie Feeney. It is doubtful that Harrods customers send Mohammed Fayed a postcard from Blackpool. 'Dessie's' has several, pinned as if they matter, behind the counter. Here, regular shoppers are greeted with warmth, tourists with courtesy. That he takes the trouble in an indifferent age is good enough reason for continuity of business in a tough economy.

"If you simply ask 'What sells?', quality will go out of the window", Dessie comments. In the space of a transaction, shoppers imperceptibly sink their worries into an enthusiastic engagement of conversation. Sliding a pair of denim jeans into a blue and yellow company bag, Dessie can recall with amazing clarity how, when you last shopped with him, you were moving house, going on holiday, had suffered a bereavement or had perhaps expressed a concern. If he seems caught up in events concerning his customer that's because his mind is focused on their importance. 'Shop talk' doesn't enter this relationship. Dessie has an aura of sincerity and is magnetically drawn to others with the same quality. If proof were needed, in a decade of difficult trading, this popular stockist has remained a local top shop, selling more Levi products in relation to his compact premises than many large-scale retailers in Britain.

"Success lies in relating to one's customer", Dessie insists. And he should know. Anywhere on this planet, the fragile figure of Mother Teresa would have been welcome yet, shortly before her death, she chose Armagh as a place for respite, founding a base for several nuns of her order, the Sisters of Charity. Mother Teresa once bought a pair of Levi jeans from Dessie. Somewhere in India, a child in up-to-the-minute denim is probably unaware that Dessie Feeney's method of business saw him strike a deal with Mother Teresa.

"Everyone expected I'd follow a career in industry but a visit to London changed everything. A job with Selfridge's was my initiation into the rag trade. Carnaby Street dictated new trends. Young Londoners had money to spend. There was a purpose to life. I may have worked hard but I felt I belonged and was part of it all. When I get the chance I go back often on business, and by walking the streets of London, reacquaint myself with places I know. The bustle of that great city is tremendous and yet I am always glad to come home."

An authority on world-famous manufacturers Levi, Dessie has brown eyes that dance mischievously in a healthily tanned face. "The first pair of jeans was made from tenting in 1850. A gold prospector panned a nugget in the Californian gold rush of 1849, nothing as dramatic as the Klondike strike, but enough to raise his temperature. Anyway, this chap was in rags so, ripping up his tent, he made himself respectable. He must have cut a dash", laughs Dessie, "for afterwards, Levi, an American-based company negotiated a cotton deal with the Deep South, beginning an industry that has never looked back."

Returning to Armagh, Dessie extended his experience by working as a fashion buyer. "When well situated premises became vacant, I jumped in head first." Product knowledge and a vital finger on the pulse of young fashion removed some of the risk factor. Ask what makes for success and he reiterates, "Relating to one's customer. Without that you won't succeed. I base my business on personal contact. Young men and women come here with money to spend and a clear picture of what they want. Designer-wear sells and anyone with an average figure steps easily into a garment. That, however, is not what the average shopper wants. Clothes ought to make the wearer feel special and, when a person feels special, it shows. My aim is to dress customers in whatever they want to buy, whatever does most for their personality or the particular image they wish to project."

Top brands, combined with the expertise of salesman Kevin Oates, helped Dessie's make instant High Street impact. "Ours is an informal atmosphere with background music that is relaxing rather than ear-splitting." Psychologists say shoppers instinctively return to wherever they last bought and it is hard to disagree. Dessie's business has permanence. Despite current trends, business has remained consistent. Given how many customers were travelling from Tyrone, it made sense to open a second branch. On 8 December 1994, Dessie's opened in Irish Street, Dungannon, trading as 'the small shop with the big selection'. Kevin Oates had already proved his worth during seven crucial years and he assumed control of the Dungannon branch.

"In order to be ready on time, we all lent a hand", Dessie continues. "A theme of stripped wood with blue and yellow decor identifies our trading image. It's modern, clean, and wholesome and everyone seems to accept it. Achieving a balance is tricky but a place people like to patronise soon become the place to be seen." Kevin's approach reflected Dessie's formula. Dressed in check shirt and Wrangler jeans, he mixes agreeably with his customers. Assistant Frances Currie discusses unisex clothing, currently in demand.

"Girl-fit jeans and shirts ensure female business remains at least 40 per cent of overall trade. I like the attitude of today's woman. She knows what she wants and cheerfully pays for a professional cut or name." Dessie's son David left St Patrick's Grammar School two years ago and joined the Dungannon branch full-time; he seems intent on making this his chosen career. "David is keen on all types of sport, and an ardent Liverpool supporter. I have always been a fan of Manchester United so there is quite a bit of rivalry as we watch our teams sink or swim in the tables. He has inherited my love of beautiful cars, although the latest seem, in terms of technology, to look more like the instrument panel of a jet plane."

Dessie's Girls' Fashions completed a trio of shops, opening three years later in Thomas Street, Armagh. This airy, attractive store appeals to young women who easily relate to Karen, Dessie's full-time assistant. Karen enjoys outdoor sports, playing for the local camogie team. Dessie's daughter Máire comes in to work after school and each weekend. Besides fashion clothing, Dessie's Girls' Fashions stocks school uniforms.

"Máire is a sixth-year student at St Catherine's College and presently studying for A-Levels. She loves tennis and is a great fan of Wimbledon, and champion Pete Sampras. Apart from open air concerts and discos, her taste is reflected in modern, trendy clothes and I do take her opinions seriously when I go buying." Fashion shows in London, Birmingham and Dublin ensure Dessie remains abreast of styles, yet he is most content when at home time with his family.

"I have come to love my present home and furnishing it was a labour of love. This is not just a house, it is a combination of furniture, carpets, colours, memories of friends in photographs dotted about the rooms; and it reflects the taste of my wife, Bronagh, who is a hairdresser. Both of us look forward to evening, away from the demands of a working day. Bronagh, in her agreeable way, gives me a free hand when it comes to buying pictures. If I get a certain hunch about a work of art, it usually pays off. That doesn't mean I'm a collector, rather I enjoy art for its own sake. *Blue Dancers* by Dégas is a painting I wouldn't mind owning because of its insight. Ballerinas seem so removed from the rest of us, but here they contort themselves to scratch their backs. Endearing, you might say. Local artist, Brian Vallely is by far the most collectable. Whether sporting, traditional or mythological, he captures harmony, balancing what he does with what he sees. Michael Houlihan, chief executive of the National Museums and Galleries of Northern Ireland, recently said: 'Artists use the language of creativity to describe their sense of place. We are privileged, therefore, to be able to listen in to the conversation between a painter and those he portrays.' I know exactly what he means for there is an emotional significance between an artist and what he portrays. Maybe I see a lot of Brian Vallely when I look at his canvasses. For me, this outer emotional statement, seemingly without effort, is eclipsed by Vallely's persona, that of the quiet, inner man.

"Bronagh and I both work hard so we have no qualms in enjoying an evening out. We intend to book a table at Castle Leslie in Glaslough. I understand they have planned a Millennium Event on New Year's Eve where dinner is followed by the Armagh Rhymers and a candlelit procession with music and dancing until dawn. You have to admit it's something entirely different!

"A leather-bound collection of novels by John Steinbeck have given me the greatest reading. I suppose *Grapes of Wrath* is best known but I prefer *Of Mice and Men*. Steinbeck can be ironic: 'Biography by its very nature must be half-fiction' is a great quote." He pauses to ask with a smile, "Hope you've taken that on board?" Deploring sectarianism, Dessie trawls nearer home. "I savour the comment, 'I'm always wary of those who believe their views on morals and faith is 100 per cent right.' A little doubt is a healthy thing. Caring", he quietly states, "is what our country used to be renowned for. Now a cry for help often falls on deaf ears. We look the other way, say 'It's not our business'."

If he makes it his business to keep in touch with the

needs of disabled children at Lisanally Special School, it's never bread cast on indifferent waters. Dessie, loved by every child, is the invited guest at school functions, particularly their Christmas party. He makes no apology for singling out one particular customer, Packie McGuigan from Duke's Grove, Armagh.

"Packie uses a wheelchair, and he is the most uplifting person to come through our shop door. As he engages my assistant Patricia in enjoyable banter, we tease him about the fortunes of Armagh GAA, although we had to sympathise in their recent unfortunate defeat by Meath, dashing high hopes of bringing home the Sam Maguire Cup. Old friends are best and in the past, I have enjoyed the support of Jackie Stinson, Armagh's saddler, who saw me through a difficult time."

Certain people seem ideally fitted to their circumstances. Few could envisage Armagh without Dessie's, a business focused on customer care. And somewhere in India, a child proud to be seen in up-to-the-minute denim may be nodding his head in agreement.

Businessman Dessie Feeney
Photograph by Michael Campbell, LBIPP

Mary Caldwell

Certain crimes are categorised by the press as worse than others. This particular hierarchy came tumbling down in August 1998, when Omagh was devastated by a massive bomb. World press descended on a close-knit community where 29 people lay dead with countless injured or maimed. That Saturday afternoon, Constable Mary Caldwell, press officer at Armagh RUC Station for the past 12 years, received a call to report to Omagh Police Station. In normal circumstances, Mary imparts daily information to a network of more than 30 newspapers and journals. Now she was facing international press bodies, Channel Four television, the pens and lens of CNN and Melanie Reid of the *Sunday Mail*.

They all had one objective, a new slant on the slaughter of innocent victims. Mary recollects the barrage, each demanding to know, "Where are the officers who were first on the scene? What was their reaction? How did they react to one dead mother and her unborn twins?"

Mary Caldwell's name is familiar to the media. The face behind the voice is strikingly Continental with her warm brown eyes and olive complexion. For a month following the Omagh atrocity, she organised press conferences and sat in on police interviews with world press and television. What she found hardest, describing it as a hiatus in grief, was liaising with bereaved families who were prepared to make comment or give interviews following each funeral.

"Omagh", Mary comments, "is remarkable in that it is considered non-sectarian. Warnings were not accurate and the sight of dismembered bodies was horrific. You might imagine that officers who have witnessed successive atrocities are casehardened to death. Sheer disbelief on every face told otherwise. Several commented: 'It could have been my family'. The dead were taken to a local army base where a temporary mortuary was set up in a gymnasium and soldiers who were helping added flowers and velvet curtains to give the place a certain dignity." Newspapers do not have a duty to support the peace process but now they united. Reports were diverse, ranging from the comments of President Bill Clinton to a Romanian family whose child was hosted by a bereaved family in Omagh. Every front page reported public outrage. Grief was felt worst by those who parted from relatives earlier in the day without a chance to say goodbye. "People continue to turn such punishing details over in their minds", Mary says quietly. "For many it is impossible to come to terms with so great a loss. Omagh Support Group and several self-help groups grew from the tragedy. The world sympathises and goes on its way leaving the bereaved to cope as best they can." Speaking on the tragedy, Mary was the guest of Orchard Social Club for the Visually Impaired. Members were deeply moved when she recounted poignant first-hand experiences. Chairman Bert Mackrel, in a letter to the Chief Constable, expressed appreciation of Mary's informed and compassionate talk.

Coping with the shift of political events, each morning produces a raft of media print at Armagh press office. "A fatal accident and our lines are jammed. Believe me, we run the gamut, from a paragraph on a stolen bicycle or lost spaniel to the more sinister, murder, riot, explosion or intermittent civil disorder."

If Mary and her colleagues in the press office enjoy media respect, this has been earned by courtesy and total impartiality. For the last quarter century, she played several roles within the Royal Ulster Constabulary. "I was educated in Co. Monaghan, my home overlooking Lough Muckno. If I speak passably good Irish and retain a passion for poetry, you may attribute this to my schooling. Robert Frost's *Stopping by the Woods on a Snowy Evening* gives immediate, visual pleasure. In absolute contrast, I can't forget the last stanza of W.B. Yeats' *Ballad of Peter Gilligan*, which refers to a weary priest during the Famine:

> *He who is wrapped in purple robes*
> *With planets in his care,*
> *Had pity on the least of things*
> *Asleep upon a chair.*

"By the same token, Patrick Kavanagh's reminiscences, *Spraying the Potatoes* or *To the Man after the Harrow* immortalise commonplace activities. Leaving school I worked for the local vet, coming North in the early Seventies. My intention was to join the Garda Siochána. William, my father, changed my plans by asking, 'Why not the Royal Ulster Constabulary?'" Mary recalls her squad of 44 recruits at Enniskillen Training Depot with a certain sadness.

"Young and impressionable, I little imagined that in the space of a quarter century, some would die violently while others were seriously injured or maimed for life. If two communities had contrived to live harmoniously, how differently my story might read. Now that the Patten Report has been made public, many feel that an expression of the intensity of suffering during three decades, should take the form of a suitable memorial."

In her early career, Mary served at Musgrave Street, Belfast. "Accompanied by a senior constable, it was still reasonably safe to walk the streets. My first traumatic experience was the bombing of the Abercorn Restaurant. Afterwards, people still in shock were coming to search in the debris for their belongings. The physical beauty of Ireland is mocked by gaping holes. We all inherited an unfair legacy, but individually, and if we had the serious intention, gaps can be repaired. During 1994-95, the Armagh Together project proved as much. Two Primates lit a candle with the core purpose of bringing people closer in understanding."

Alan, her husband, was based in Musgrave Street when they met. "We became friends, going our separate ways after six months. I transferred to Donegall Pass and drug squad duties before it became obvious how much we had in common. We then tied the knot in 1973." Within seven years, Mary and Alan had three sons, Geoffrey, Andrew and Jonathan. Returning to uniformed duties, it was suggested she take up a post with the press office.

"Despite certain reservations, I agreed. In Northern Ireland, three police departments provide public information—Knock, Derry and Armagh." Mary's team deals with newspaper editors, freelance correspondents, and television and radio news intake. "We, in turn, sift from the media those issues requiring investigation. Burglaries, thefts or serious assault come within this remit. A press release is generally prepared in anticipation of items of public concern."

Sifting from a grim catalogue, Mary recalls how the heart of Portadown was ripped asunder by a bomb in May 1993. Spotting a suspicious vehicle, one policeman sounded the alarm thereby saving countless lives. Sunday press throughout the country carried colour pictures of blitz-like devastation. One shot of an immaculately dressed woman striding purposefully through the rubble happens to be Mary. As the RUC's version of Kate Adie, she reported the scene first-hand for press office information.

Mary agrees that the rule of law has constantly suffered setbacks while expressing relief that July 1999 was relatively calm, unlike previous years, when police and their families were caught up amidst the fracas. "The parade at Drumcree and a majority of notified parades passed off fairly peacefully. Those who counselled peace and restraint were heeded and the Orange Order marshalled its followers, urging an avoidance of confrontation. It should be said that of 3,211 notified parades in one calendar year, most take place without incident. They become contentious where community relations are less than satisfactory. In a letter to the *Irish News*, Archbishop Seán Brady commented: 'It would appear that the solution lies in building new relationships of mutual respect and in improving the understanding of each other's position.' This is true. Television pictures are notoriously selective, as in past years, to our shame, the world witnessed Ulster striding headlong into the abyss. The Chief Constable said afterwards: 'People who demand rights should remember their responsibilities.' He reminded viewers that when the order to allow the march was given, stockpiled petrol bombs were in place to lob at his men. Television cameras showed a demonstrator hit by a truncheon. The public was not shown a colleague on the ground *beneath* the demonstrator. Rabbi Hugo Gryn, who died in 1996, survived Auschwitz concentration camp. Asked if he ever resented the religion that made him suffer, he replied grimly: 'It was other people's religion that made me suffer...'

"Before apportioning blame, let the accuser provide an acceptable alternative. If we simply ask ourselves what is happening to this Province? Assuredly the solution lies in building new relationships, particularly community friendships which have never been more important." She smiles. "I'm beginning to sound like my mother whom I love dearly. This proves the influence of one's upbringing and why we've always tried to be supportive where our children are concerned. Geoffrey, the eldest, at university in Scotland, has just taken an Honours degree in Business Studies. We were there in the audience watching, and I confess it was a marvellous moment. Andrew and Jonathan are both presently in the throes of third-level study."

Last year, in recognition of her efficiency within the RUC, Mary and her husband were guests of the Queen at a garden party at Buckingham Palace. "It was a wonderful event", she recalls, "especially as we met many interesting people." As press secretary for Armagh Diocesan Mothers' Union, Mary circulated relevant information when Lady Eames was commissioned as world president in 1995. "Attending St Margaret's, Westminster, I learned that Mary Robinson had been elected President of Ireland. Good news is far too rare in our society and both women have made an honourable contribution. In times of dramatic change, family life remains fundamental to society. Lady Eames makes her point with inimitable modesty and great dignity. I travel to various conferences on behalf of the Mothers' Union because it is time enjoyably spent."

Armagh District Scouting Council appreciates Mary's keen interest where, as badge secretary, she furthers the aims of this non-sectarian organisation. "Parading together on St Patrick's Day sets an excellent example and has brought an honourable mention in the *New York Times*. Tom Duncan, headmaster of Royal School, Armagh, is chairman of Armagh District Scout Council and must be acknowledged for his keen interest in the organisation."

Being constantly in communication with the public means she relishes quiet evenings. "I enjoy my garden and, just now, with a nip in the air, must get down to planting spring-flowering bulbs. Daffodils, snowdrops and crocuses need to be in position by September for good results. Friends and family matter to me as does occasionally eating in convivial company." A beautiful soprano voice is inherited from her mother, Sarah, who is an accomplished organist. Singing with her local church choir, Mary lists *Incline Thine Ear* by Himmel as a much-loved piece.

"Everyone enjoyed Patricia Routledge as Mrs Bouquet but this actress has a great sense of style, and can be seen at her best as Lady Bracknell in *The Importance of Being Earnest*. I have to be factually correct in my working life and enjoy the indifference of Miss Prism, telling of her crime in leaving the baby in a handbag on railway station. When asked exactly which line (of the London Underground) Miss Prism smartly retorts: 'The line is *immaterial...*'

"I admire the qualities of common sense and good humour in Betty Boothroyd, Speaker of the House of Commons. On a personal level, I will never forget clearing the way for Mary Peters when she was guest at a civic reception on her return from the Olympic Games. I was on duty in Royal Avenue and the atmosphere was tremendous." When Mary speaks of her father, who died in February 1998, it is with the utmost affection.

"He was an agricultural engineer, the most gentle of men and I miss him dearly. He prided himself on being able to devise a means to make everything work. The same enthusiasm on our part and, believe me, Ireland would work."

Mary Caldwell
Photograph by Francis McKinstry

Reggie Stinson

Few of us will fulfil our fondest ambitions but Reggie Stinson, hand on his heart, can say that he has done so. On 28 August 1999 Reggie took his 1,000th career wicket for Armagh Firsts at Bangor, Co. Down. A playing member of Armagh Cricket Club for over 20 years, it was his third wicket in the match that brought this unique record to an immensely satisfying figure.

"It was such a great feeling", Reggie says modestly. "At one stage in the season I thought it wouldn't happen until next year. I played badly at the beginning of the match, then suddenly seemed to bowl better than I have done all year. Conditions were favourable and the ball was moving in the air and off the seam." This is not Reggie's only record for he passed the figure of 7,000 runs during a recent match with Laurelvale. A wicket against Waringstown means he can now boast at least one run and one wicket against every team in the top three Sections in Northern Ireland.

Reggie Stinson is a sportsman, synonymous with the game of cricket. Yet Reggie *off* the pitch equally takes some beating. Physically fit, pleasantly agreeable, he applies a lively sense of humour to almost everything he does.

"Let me tell you about my early reputation as the 'Phantom Wrecker'", is Reggie's prelude to a commentary that includes many associated with his profession. "I'd just started my job with the Post Office and had this run of bad luck. It could happen to anyone", he warns, "so don't go making a big deal of it." Post Office regulation bikes and Reggie were incompatible. He wrecked several, colliding with things that just weren't there the day before. "Dogs caused most of the trouble. For a fact they hate postmen. Mercifully I became mobile just before Rotweillers came into fashion!"

He pours a mug of excellent coffee, then speaks of schooldays at Royal School, Armagh, where Jim Brennan was headmaster in the Seventies. Reggie had an aptitude for English, maths and history but excelled at physical education. "Johnny Hunter, who took us for games, advised me to make this my career but my mother required a lot of persuading. At five years of age, I'd suffered rheumatic fever and was found to have a heart murmur. As time passed and nothing untoward happened, she gradually stopped worrying. Cricket was my favourite sport from the moment I first picked up a bat."

An exceptional sportsman, Reggie was signed on by Middlesex Cricket Club in 1974, when he was just 17. "Trevor Bailey was then chairman at Lord's. Recommended by the Northern Cricketing Union of Ireland, I was given a trial match. They offered £65 a week, which in 1973 would have taken me into the surtax bracket! Overwhelmed by the sophistication of Lord's, I couldn't wait to return home. Ever since, when I've watched a game in Australia or the West Indies, I envisage possibilities the offer might have brought. There are compensations for I wouldn't have met Audrey, who, with my children, matters most in my life."

Reggie began work by training as an electrician with Elliott and Nelson. "They had taken over my father's retail business in Dobbin Street. Within five years I had City and Guilds qualifications, but the boredom factor set in. Learning of a vacancy at Armagh Post Office, I applied and was accepted for a postman's job." He speaks affectionately of colleagues from those days. "Pat O'Connor was head postmaster and a great guy. Eddie Lynas had charge of Royal Mail and he, poor fellow, tried to teach me to drive in order to banish my wrecked-bicycle syndrome. I simply could not pass my test. Given one last chance, an instructor beside me, we were motoring along the Moy Road in a 240 Ford Transit parcel van when a bomb exploded at Drumsill Hotel, lifting our vehicle six inches off the road. Despite the fact that he wasn't Catholic, my instructor crossed himself expertly, turned a whiter shade of pale, yelled, 'You'll do, you'll do...' followed by instructions that translated as: 'now get out of here and quickly'."

Reggie was at first allocated a rural postal route, then, taking post office examinations, he transferred to counter duties. Serving in various branches throughout the area, he eventually returned to Armagh. He sees the funny side and not a little irony in just about everything life throws at us.

"Armagh was then the place to be. Our postmaster was Bobby Pollock with Frankie McNamee as assistant. Seán

McCrory had charge of counter staff. What a great team they were. We were all saddened when Seán died during a snooker match at the Forester's Club. The late Bernie Cush was another stalwart. She worked in accounts, and loved the daft happenings in *Monty Python's Flying Circus* and in particular, 'Bicycle Repair Man'. 'Things can only get better', she'd sing as seriously overworked postmen struggled out of the sorting office laden down with Christmas mail. Frank Williams was an equally great character. I could recite a litany of names: Marcus Towers, Stanley Calvert and Billy Crabbe. Billy Elliott, whom everyone will remember as a gentleman, was fatally injured in a post office raid following his transfer to Newry. I cannot accept the logic of harming decent people or how the perpetrators live with what they've done. Sorting office staff since 1982 include postal executive Eddie Lynas, Tommy Edgar, Willie Monaghan, George Orr, Pat McCreesh, Harry Price, William Elliott (son of the late W. Elliott), Anthony McAneney, Derek Richardson, Ronnie Black, Frank Vallely, Arthur McCrory, Nigel Courtney and Jackie Kennedy. Postal staff find the going tough in winter or bad weather and for this reason it is less appealing to women, but we do have postal officer Audrey Strain, and postal cadet Diana Willis."

Privatisation consigned Armagh Post Office to sub-office category, three years after Reggie's promotion to manager of counter staff. "I was offered the franchise, so combining counter service with a retail outlet, opened my own business in November 1993. Henry Donnelly, who had 26 years' service to his credit, remained with me and counter staff include Eleanor Milligan, Simon Clarke and Barry Hyndes while Linda McIlveen looks after the shop and newspaper sales."

Quality service pays. Within the year, nominations from the general public brought Reggie and his staff first prize in the Best Post Office in Northern Ireland competition, and runner-up in 1995. "Each of our staff has favourite customers", Reggie acknowledges. "One of mine frequently requests 'Six second-hand stamps please'. Christmas has its moments. Someone once brought a live chicken, wrapped in brown paper and addressed with its head sticking out. 'It needs air,' we were told!"

His wife Audrey is a supply teacher and they have two children, Laura and Mark. The Stinson home is crammed with trophies, cups and plaques, all won by Reggie for top endeavour in football, cricket, table tennis, rugby, pool and darts. He also holds the Superstars Trophy awarded for skilled participation in a variety of sports. "I don't swim though, having a horror of deep water. Nor do I dance, so if anyone can teach me the rhumba, just call out. As for the children, Laura and Mark are both pupils of Royal School Armagh and Mark is already a cricketing fanatic."

Reggie's association with Armagh Cricket Club began at the age of 16 and his statistics take some beating. He had scored 3,000 runs by the age of 25, more than any Armagh post-war batsman, apart from Johnny and George Elliott and Leslie Spearman. In support of his dedication he has not missed a Saturday home game in over 20 years. Reggie's 6,000th run was scored at Cliftonville and by mid-1994 his score stood at 6,392, along with having taken 860 wickets. Brian Weir has kept a meticulous record of all scores and accuracy of these figures is entirely due to him. The highest tribute Reggie can pay goes to past Club president, the late Dr Seamus Duffy, whom he describes as "a father figure, loved by us all".

"In celebration of our refurbished clubhouse in August, 1994, West Indies test player Desmond Haynes and Mike Gatting of the MCC were both present. Our organised special event was a match, the Irish President's Select playing Armagh. Unfortunately the match was rained off after 45 minutes—typical, you might say!" Cricketing heroes in Reggie's estimation include Ian Botham and at local level, our own Harry McAuley. "What they have in common is not just skill but individuality on the field. I deplore the way confrontation and downright violence has crept into some areas of sport. Famous players should recognise the responsibility they carry as role models for youngsters. Golf seems to be the only sport to have avoided this deterioration in personal standards. Golfers show courtesy to each other, one of the reasons why the game is so special."

The lifeblood of any club has to be up and coming players. There are those, Reggie feels, who will make significant contributions to Armagh Cricket Club in the future. "Andrew Rennie, captain of Armagh Firsts for six years in a row, has kept the team together, arranged sponsorship and in short, is the backbone of Armagh Cricket Club. Chris Cairns has been with the Firsts for four years and makes headlines every week—by virtue of the fact that he is a sports reporter with the *Ulster Gazette*. Chris is a great all-rounder yet modesty forbids him saying so. In the Under-18s, Dean Lester continues to impress as does Under-15s' Michael Villiers who has represented Armagh Firsts. Captain of the Under-15s Andrew Bratten has played for Armagh Seconds. Mark Stinson and Stewart Lester, both aged 11, have surprised themselves by playing for the Under-15s. Our wives and friends continue to organise teas at matches, coffee mornings, suppers and fund-raising events, all of which is greatly appreciated by Armagh Cricket Club.

"I have only one regret", Reggie concludes. "Ideally I'd have like to take my 1,000th wicket on the Mall, but at the end of the day I was happy just to have achieved the score. Two more runs at the weekend would have secured runners-up places for the second successive year. For a club of our size, this is a terrific achievement." He will have an opportunity to extend his unique record before the season ends and in this, we wish him all the luck in the world.

Reggie Stinson brings an uplifting of spirit and sense of fun to a day. His attitude to winning and losing is one we could apply to life itself. He gift-wraps this philosophy in a final comment. "The last thing tennis players see before walking on to the centre court at Wimbledon, is a quotation from Rudyard Kipling, right above the door, *If you can meet with triumph and disaster and treat those two impostors just the same...*"

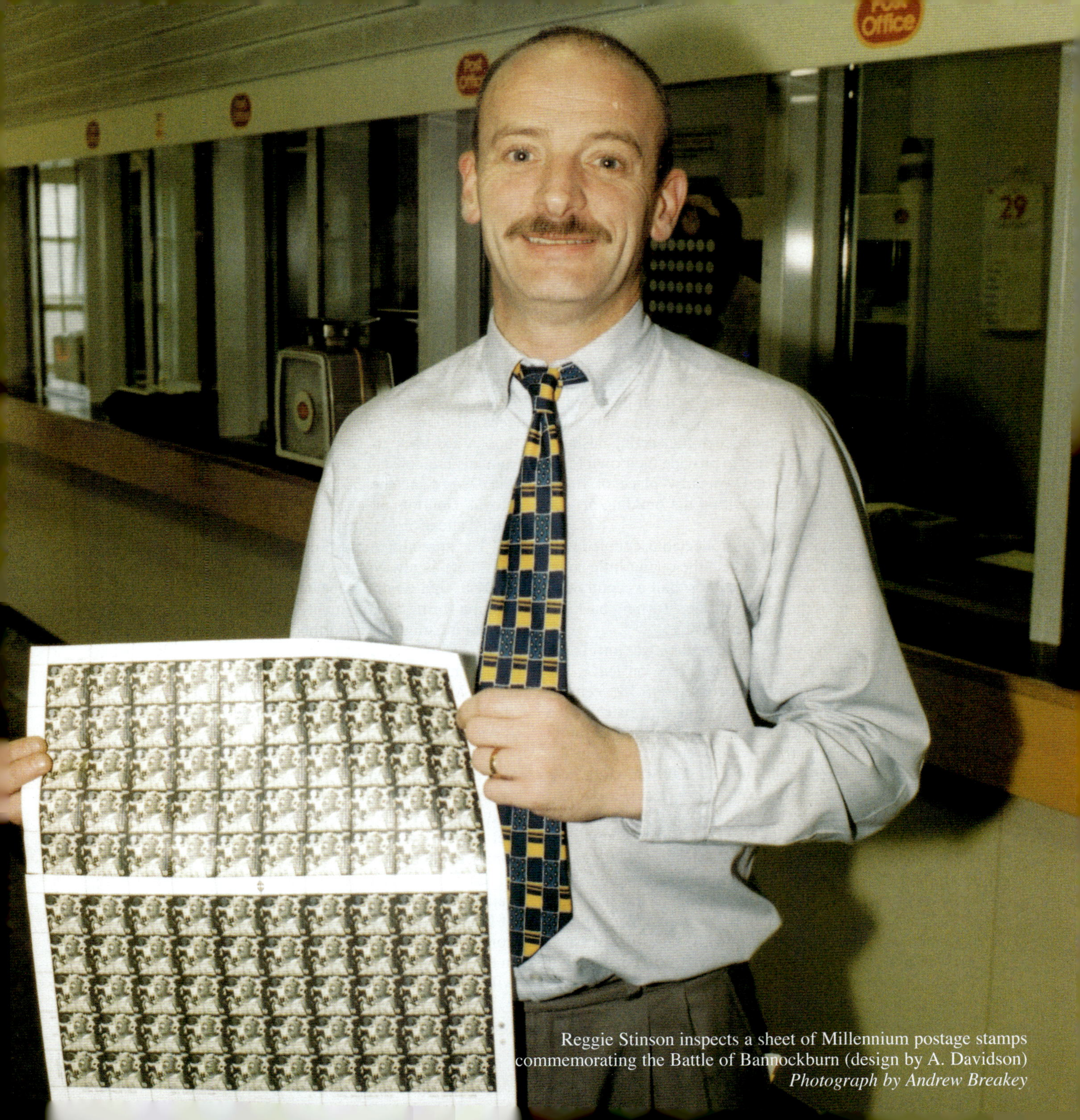

Reggie Stinson inspects a sheet of Millennium postage stamps commemorating the Battle of Bannockburn (design by A. Davidson)
Photograph by Andrew Breakey

Iona's Antique Shop

In a paved precinct leading to McCrum's Court can be found Armagh city's oldest antique shop. Since 1952, business has been conducted here—once the site of old Armagh jail. Casual customers browse over an assortment of bric-a-brac while the more serious collector concentrates on items of fine art. Television programmes like *Lovejoy* and the *Antiques Roadshow* have increased public awareness of what sells. Not every dusty painting is an old master, but Iona's antique shop, like its proprietor, has earned a respect that is entirely genuine. "I love what I do", affirms the proprietor—and it's plain to be seen.

This building, with adjoining licensed bar premises, is officially known as the Hole-in-the-Wall. The name was derived from a 17th century practice of transacting business close to a prison. Prisoners had to provide their own food, so they, or relatives, required a nearby place of trade. Traces of the placing of cells within the building are the only reminder of harsh times.

A growing fascination for the collectable, coupled with shrewd judgement, helped establish the quaint little shop. The proprietor's memories span almost half a century and are as rare at some of the items on sale. Turning back the clock, these are told with quiet dignity.

Eleanor Roosevelt's private secretary was originally from County Armagh. Once, when home on leave, she came into Iona's shop and purchased an 18th century Venetian glass and gilt candlestick, one of a pair. These had been bought at auction with a private collector in mind. Considering that one would come to rest in the home of the 32nd President of the United States, she was allowed to have it. Mrs Roosevelt was delighted and asked for the second. It was too late—a local collector had already snapped it up. Sotheby's say the story attending an artefact is as vital as the object. Most would agree!

Iona and her inimitable antique shop are widely known. Once, returning from Jerusalem in 1966, her flight was delayed. In order to make a connection, it was essential that she clear customs quickly. The official asked her surname and, when she told him, replied, "Isn't it Iona?" It seemed his wife came from Armagh and spoke of the shop a great deal.

Trends within the antique world are constantly changing. A Clarice Cliff Orange House pattern jug in good condition would probably fetch £500 on a good day—or given the revival in British pottery, any day! Irish cut glass decanters are highly collectable, particularly Waterford or by the Cork Glass Co. Here, annulated necks with three rings and a moulded mushroom stopper signify age and quality. Fine furniture in the style of Thomas Chippendale, Morgan and Sanders, or that enduring favourite, the Victorian spoonback chair, will be snapped up before it has gone on display. Children's toys, boxed and in good condition, are in constant demand. A collection of 35 Dinky die-cast cars dating from 1945-52 recently fetched far in excess of the reserve. Cowboy books are back in fashion while children's comics and annuals are constantly sought, particularly early issues of the *Dandy* and the *Beano*. Captain Hook Toby jugs by Royal Doulton or a Tiffany Favrile border lampshade excite attention but the proprietor has her own philosophy.

The attraction in this business is a gamble, she admits, and there is always an exciting possibility that one may make a 'find'. For her the business earns a living but each auction brings excitement and the remote hope that something might be unearthed—perhaps an antique of real worth. During the mid-Fifties, Iona bought a silver pepper pot at auction for a couple of shillings, selling it to the Ulster Museum for £20. The owner had not realised either the date or value of this 1727 George I item but Iona felt it was valuable.

Within this stone-flagged haven for the collector are row upon row of books, items of Sheffield plate, odd cups and saucers, crystal vases and inlaid furniture. Pictures and prints deck the walls, each imposing its own identity yet blending into an atmosphere and era of Mrs Beeton's famous cookbook.

Each successive auction will find customers waiting patiently for opening time outside the shuttered windows of Iona's antique shop. There is always the desire to fill a void in a collection, find a suitable gift or simply browse in the hope of something that catches the eye. Few, if any, will leave dissatisfied.

The late Kathleen M. Ferris, a much-loved Armachian, researched the history of the Hole-in-the-Wall building six

The Browser—a glimpse of the interior of Iona's Antique Shop
Watercolour by Joe Hynes

years before her death. The entire property once belonged to her great-grandfather, W.R. Ferris. One of Armagh's oldest buildings, access to the Hole-in-the-Wall used to be locked each evening. A right-of-way was created from Market Street, leading to Scotch Street. Kathleen Ferris established that the north tenement was formerly a prison. Part of the portion that is presently Iona's antique shop lay vacant until it was purchased by Lee McKinstry and used as a store. This remained in McKinstry possession after James Barnes purchased the other premises.

James Barnes' son, William, inherited the property from his father and, in turn, leased it to William Robert Ferris, who in 1872, purchased all of the property. Robert and James Whitsitt leased the portion known as 7 Market Street in 1879. From 1919, the late Jack Eagleson took it over. When William R. Ferris died in 1895, the property at 9 Market Street was inherited by his son Walter. Walter was Kathleen's grandfather and all his life he took great pride in the grocery and provisions business which was conducted at this address. Deliveries were made by horse and cart to outlying areas. On a June morning in 1889, Walter Ferris rode out to inspect two farms he owned which were situated on the Hamiltonsbawn Road. From the top of a hill, Walter observed the train disaster that has been extensively written of. Galloping back to Armagh, Walter warned the City Infirmary that Dr Palmer and his staff would be needed for this emergency. With his carters, Walter ferried relatives to the scene, bringing casualties back to hospital.

The Hole-in-the-Wall of this century was created in 1924, when the sale of intoxicating liquor was required by law to be separated from the sale of food. Walter Ferris made two separate departments, yet retained as much of the original interior as was possible. The new bar was, however, early 20th century and with alterations, did lose its concept of earlier times. Farmers in the past made their deals on market days, sealing the transaction over a drink in the Hole-in-the-Wall.

Walter Ferris died in 1938 and his son William (Kathleen's father) now assumed responsibility for the business. Kathleen remembered a member of staff, Joe Saunderson, who took charge of the bar. Joe was a second generation of his family to work for the Ferris firm. Joe Leeman, assisted by Bob Frazer, had charge of the grocery store. When Bob emigrated to South Africa in the mid-Thirties, Fred Keys filled the job until he volunteered for service in the Royal Air Force.

Cheap imports of wheat and grain from North America meant that farmers were less able to sell their grain locally. Armagh knew real poverty in the 1930s when there was neither social help nor work to be had. The workhouse at Tower Hill was a last resort. War years saw British and American soldiers frequent the Hole-in-the-Wall bar, and many across the Atlantic may still remember this friendly, atmospheric tavern. William Ferris sold the premises in 1965 to Marcus Martin, who in turn transacted a deal with Mr Proctor, Iona's father. Books, figures and statuettes of a post-Victorian era now replaced shelves once stocked with food and provisions. Stores to the rear of the property were bought by Willie and Jack Lennox, who converted these into a coffee shop and separate toy, curtain and drapery departments. The late Wilfred McVeigh was proprietor of the Hole-in-the-Wall public bar from 1960 until his death in 1996. A happy and genial landlord, Wilfie had great rapport with his clientele and set about transforming the interior. Now pewter tankards hang from stained wooden beams and, in winter, a log fire beckons patrons in from the cold. After Wilfie's death, his daughter, Lorraine, became licensee.

Stepping into Iona's antique shop, a little bell over the door rings. The worn flagstone floor and smell of beeswax polish is redolent of pleasant aspects from the past. Oblivious of noise and haste, the proprietor has created lasting friendships from customers who refuse to allow a week to pass without a visit. She has taken kindly counsel of the passing years, and the mere fact that collectibles on sale were chosen by her is an endorsement in itself.

Originality is scarce these days and yet the extraordinary in the ordinary does exist. Not every dusty painting is an old master but, unusually, it is the shop in this case that constitutes a 'find'.

Armagh Voices

a celebration of a century

1960 ~ 1970

O brave new world,
That has such people in't

William Shakespeare

The Realm of the Arts

Success is said to breed success. While working on a new play commissioned by the Royal Shakespeare Company, Daragh Carville was almost simultaneously appointed writer-in-residence at Queen's University, Belfast. His brief first-hand account serves as prelude, beckoning his many of his contemporaries earning critical acclaim by their contributions to the arts.

'What is it about Armagh?' someone asked, when what they actually meant was—*how has so much artistic talent emanated from this city and locality?*

"When I look back at my own family", Daragh ponders, "there seems to be a strong tradition of public service. Maura, my mother is a retired headmistress while Cyril, my father, still works as a psychiatric nurse at St Luke's Hospital, Armagh. We, that is, my generation, seem to be artists. Older brother, Conor, is a poet: a recipient of the Poetry Ireland prize a few years ago. Conor is a university lecturer, teaching at Goldsmith College in London. Barry is next youngest to me and a visual artist, working in various media—paint, print and etching. He has exhibited in various places including the Trian in Armagh. Barry also teaches. Youngest of the family, Gavin, is a very fine prose writer. His first published work was a short story included in *Shenanigans*, a successful anthology of Irish fiction, published by Sceptre in early 1999. He is currently working on his first novel. As I say, all of us are artists so maybe it has something to do with serving the community. It may also have some bearing on the fact that my mother is very artistic and Dad's a great conversationalist! Half of me suspects it has something to do with Armagh. We're just four to emerge from what has to be a real explosion of talent from this city and area."

Daragh Carville was born in 1967. Studying Drama and Film at the University of Kent he graduated in 1990, then lived in Paris until 1994. Returning to Ireland, he completed a Masters degree in Irish Writing at Queen's University Belfast.

Daragh's first play, *Language Roulette*, was premiered by Tinderbox Theatre Company at the Old Museum Arts Centre in Belfast, in May 1996. It depicts an intense, drink-fuelled evening in a Belfast pub during the first cease-fire, when a group of former friends and lovers gather together to welcome home one of their contemporaries. *Language Roulette* toured Northern Ireland, playing to huge audiences and attracting warm reviews from the local and national press. This play earned Daragh the 1997 Stewart Parker New Playwright Award and the 1998 Meyer-Whitworth Prize. It has since been presented in a new production at the New Art Theatre, New Hampshire, in the United States. The play is also included in a well-received collection of new Irish plays entitled *Far from the Land*, published in March 1998 by Methuen.

Daragh's second play, *Dumped*, was premiered by Tinderbox Theatre Company at the Reid Hall, Armagh, in September 1997, and afterwards played at selected venues throughout Ireland. Daragh describes this work as a revenge tragicomedy and an immorality play. A new production of *Dumped* was presented by the National Youth Theatre at the Pleasance Theatre, Edinburgh, in August 1998. The National Youth Theatre production next transferred to Battersea Arts Centre London, in April 1999, moving on to Paris and the Petit Hebertot theatre, where it was selected as Critics' Choice in *Time Out Paris*.

In March 1999 *Observatory*, Daragh's latest play, opened at the Peacock Theatre, Dublin. He describes the work as a Gothic time travel sci-fi drama, set in 1799 and 1999. Yet again, the reviewers were firmly in favour: "linguistically observant, emotionally eloquent and historically resonant"... "Daragh Carville's star is in the ascendant." *Observatory* is published by Methuen.

During his short time as arts assistant with Armagh City and District Council, Daragh's courteous, pleasant and helpful manner engendered interest in his career. He is swift to acknowledge the contagious talent that distinguishes fellow Armachians, a disparate group of successful performers and professional exponents of the arts. Many working in Ireland and throughout the United Kingdom made their debut in the 1980s and 1990s. Writers, musicians, artists, dancers, directors, actors and arts administrators characterise the broad sweep of ideas and concepts which were merely stirrings three decades ago. Evolution of the arts is seen by many as stemming from the inspiration of Paul McAvinchey, a senior teacher at St Patrick's Grammar School, Armagh. Creating an atmosphere where artists can meet under the aegis of a host inspires respect and confidence. Under Paul's scrupulous direction, school performances were physically and vocally compelling. Costumes and sets were deployed to such effect that every stage story made a stunning impact. This was one source: whatever the rest, the Armachian zest and enthusiasm within each chosen medium appears almost unrivalled in other parts of this island. These youngsters collectively weave the complex strands of the oldest arts into a narrative, which runs like the credits listing of an acclaimed production.

Conall Morrison from Armagh City is an associate director at Dublin's Abbey Theatre and an old boy of St Patrick's College, Armagh. Working as a director of student theatre in Edinburgh and Liverpool, Conall moved to Dublin in the early 1990s, quickly establishing himself as one of the most exciting young directors of Irish theatre. For the Abbey Theatre, Conall has directed (and adapted for stage) *Tarry Flynn*, which then went on tour to London. This won the *Irish Times*-ESB Award for Best Production in 1997, Conall winning the Best Director award. He directed the most recent Abbey production of *The Coleen Bawn* (which toured to the Royal National Theatre, London) and *Freedom of the City*. In 1999, this acclaimed production of a Brian Friel play toured to the Lincoln Centre Festival, New York. At the Peacock Theatre, Conall directed two Gary Mitchell plays set in Northern Ireland: *In a Little World of our Own* and *As the Beast Sleeps*. He directed the musical *Martin Guerre* for Cameron Mackintosh and in the United States of America. Conall is also a playwright and his *Hard to Believe*, which he directed for Bickerstaffe Theatre Company, toured to great acclaim throughout Ireland.

Jane Magowan originates from Mountnorris, Co. Armagh. She is an actress and a graduate of Bristol Old Vic Theatre School and Manchester University. A niece of James and Mary Lamb, founder members of Armagh Theatre Group, Jane is presently living and working in theatre in London.

John Paul Connolly is a professional actor and son of Armagh artist, Jackie Connolly. He began his acting career at St Patrick's Primary School and St Patrick's College, gaining valuable experience with Armagh Theatre Group and the Ulster Youth Theatre. After his role as Romeo, which he played for the Ulster Youth Theatre, he went on to the Royal Academy of Dramatic Art in London, where he presently enjoys a successful career on stage and in television. John Paul has taken roles in episodes of *Taggart* and *The Bill*. His career includes a tour of Scotland and Ireland in 1997, when he was cast as Saint Columba in a play by Ian Crichton Smith. It is worth noting that a contemporary of John Paul's at RADA was Richard Dormer, grandson of the late Bob Dormer, a well-known and respected Armagh character. Richard is currently playing Malvolio in *Twelfth Night* at the Lyric Theatre in Belfast.

Janice McAdam, another local woman, having graduated from York University in 1997, began a course at the Gaiety School of Acting in Dublin. Janice worked as a professional actress since 1992—both North and South of the border—and for television. With companies such as Red Kettle, Replay and Pig's Back, her theatre experience extends to the Abbey, the Gate and the Gaiety. She then embarked upon a career in public relations and administration, working for the Dance Council of Ireland, Rough Magic Theatre Company and City Arts Centre where she produced and a ran a late night comedy club entitled Stir Fry.

Janice is currently director of public affairs with responsibility for fund raising, marketing and public relations for Project Arts Centre in Dublin. This Centre in common with Armagh's Market Place Theatre and Arts Centre hopes to open a major new facility in 2000 AD.

Seamus McGarvey first came to public attention in Armagh when, as a schoolboy photographer, two of his photographic exhibitions, *Armagh Exposed* and *Eternity Where?* featured in Armagh Arts Festival during the 1980s. Since embarking on films, working as a trainee on Thaddeus O'Sullivan's production of *December Bride*, Seamus has gone on to work with some of the finest British film directors and is acknowledged as one of the most successful young cinematographers working in Britain today. He was Alan Rickman's first choice of cinematographer for his debut film as a director, *The Winter Guest*. Seamus McGarvey's latest film on release, *The War Zone*, was directed by Nick Roth.

Roisín Toal originates from Keady. She is a gifted professional operatic singer and soprano performer with the Irish Chamber Choir touring throughout Ireland and abroad.

David McGuckin, an accomplished organist and pianist, studied at Manchester Royal Northern College of Music, winning the Alice Shawcross and the Meadowcroft prizes for Organ. He was also a finalist in the John Ireland Piano Competition. David took a Postgraduate Diploma and from 1993 until 1999 was assistant organist at St Columb's Cathedral, Londonderry. He plays the harpsichord and organ with the Ulster Orchestra, and has given recitals in the North Wales Music Festival, the Two Cathedrals Festival, Derry, and the Ulster Hall. David presently teaches music technology at the North West Institute of Further and Higher Education and is director of Altnagelvin Hospital Choir. His father, David, is a retired honorary lay diocesan reader and lay vicar choral of St Patrick's Church of Ireland Cathedral.

David Revels began his singing tuition under the guidance of Aubrey McClintock at the age of 16. He went on study music at Christ Church, Oxford. In addition to concert appearances David has featured in many recordings including works by Palestrina, Purcell, Esteves, Pygott and Shephard, but is perhaps more universally known for the theme tunes of *The Vicar of Dibley* and *Mr Bean*. David will perform at the 12th Annual Young Musicians' Platform presented by Elizabeth Bicker in Armagh, in January 2000.

Niall Vallely followed his parents, John B. and Eithne, into the world of music, and is a professional traditional musician. He performs with Nomos and has issued a successful solo compact disc of concertina music. All five of the Vallely family are accomplished musicians with **Cillian** playing professionally in New York and **Caoimhín** in Limerick.

Brian Finnegan is a past member of Armagh Pipers' Club and has his own band, Flook. An expert flute player, Brian now tours throughout Europe with his own brand of modern and traditional music.

Stephanie Hughes is a freelance presenter and broadcaster with BBC Radio 3. An accomplished musician, Stephanie enjoyed a successful career as a solo pianist and accompanist. She is an authority on classical music concerts and was commentator on the *Last Night of the Proms*, the 1999 Sir Henry Wood Promenade Concerts held at the Royal Albert Hall.

Miriam Mone is a past pupil of St Catherine's College, Armagh, and one of Ireland's leading fashion designers. She is known for a look and style that is distinctively hers. One of her evening dresses was featured on the front cover of the Sunday *Observer* and she has taken the *Late Late Show* Fashion and Design Award several years in succession. In 1997, Miriam designed the outfit worn by Professor Mary McAleese for her Presidential Inauguration.

Drama is a genre unlike any other where the written word needs to be performed. For this reason it is open to interpretation—a challenge for Armagh's children of the Eighties and Nineties. Many who are presently making a mark in the world of theatre were earlier associated with Armagh Youth Theatre or Armagh Youth Dance, and hugely supportive of arts events and activities in Armagh. One of these is **Caoimhe McAvinchey**, scion of a well known Armagh family. Following her Master's degree in Performance Studies as a Fulbright scholar at New York University, Caoimhe was invited to Belfast in 1998 and given the task of organising the prestigious Belfast Festival Fringe at Queen's University. Her varied career in theatre has been that of director, producer, festival organiser and actress. Caoimhe had already taken her own company, Sticks and Stones, to the Edinburgh Festival Fringe in 1994, had directed the Signposts Festival for the Lyric Theatre in Belfast, and is director of the Lyric Drama Studio for which she staged *The Picture of Dorian Gray* in May 1999. Using many of her contacts in the world of theatre, Caoimhe organised the Radical Acts Political Theatre Seminar for the Old Museum Arts Centre in September of this year. A past pupil of St Catherine's College, for a time Caoimhe directed the newly formed Armagh Youth Theatre Group, and she now tutors students for the new drama degree course at Queen's University Belfast.

Paul Bosco McEneaney is an actor, magician and musician. He has acted professionally in the Lyric, Belfast, taking roles in *A Midsummer Night's Dream*, *Playboy of the Western World*, *Translations* and *Twelfth Night*. At the Abbey Theatre, Dublin, he performed in *Snaredrums and Toupees*. Paul has his own company, Shanakee Productions, which toured successfully with *A Quiet Night In*. He is also a member of the Magic Circle and a former drummer with rock band Heat the Beans.

Nicola and Matthew Curry are a talented duo. Since graduating from Queen's Unversity Belfast with LL.B (Hons), Nicola has worked as a freelance dance tutor and arts administrator. Earlier in 1999 she choreographed a

Talented young Armachians at an arts reception.
Back row (L to R): Barry Carville, Enda Hughes, David O'Toole,
M. Carville, Daragh Carville, Michael Duffy, Brian Kirk, Vincent McCann, Macdara Vallely and Colin McKeown.
Front row: Caoimhe McAvinchey, arts officer Kate Bond, Mayor Pat Brannigan, Mayoress Molly Brannigan and Janice McAdam

piece which was performed at the Waterfront Hall, Belfast. She worked for *Young at Art*, an international children's festival, in Belfast and was filmed in *Flying Saucer Rock and Roll* in 1997. Nicola formed a dance company, LOBE, who made their debut performance with *Fish Fingers* during the Belfast Festival Fringe. Matthew Curryworks in arts broadcasting public relations.

David O'Toole trained in Edinburgh and has acted with the Ulster Theatre Company in *Scrooge*, *Oklahoma*, *Godspell* and *West Side Story*.

Veronica Leer from Keady has been involved with Armagh Youth Drama Group, Armagh Youth Dance, Ulster Youth Theatre and Armagh Theatre Group. She studied drama at the Royal Scottish Academy of Music and Drama. Veronica is now a professional actress and constantly in work on stage and television. In Scotland she is regarded as one of the most talented young actresses on the Scottish stage. For her, 1999 began with *Beauty and the Beast*, a Christmas show at the McRoberts Arts Centre, Stirling. She also starred in *The Red Balloon*, a children's show devised by the Visible Fictions Theatre Company which toured to the USA and Canada. Following a most successful appearance at a showcase for children's theatre in Florida, she was invited to return to the United States in Spring 2000 for performances on Broadway and in Washington and Philadelphia. She is currently starring in a revival of *The Clearing* for Stellar Quines Theatre Company, on tour to Glasgow, Dundee, Edinburgh and Liverpool. When she finishes her role in *The Clearing*, Veronica begins another with *The Happy Prince*. This talented woman has appeared with all the major companies in Scotland and on television in episodes of *Taggart*, *Rab C. Nesbitt* and *Peak Practice*.

Brenda Jordan is a past pupil of St Catherine's College, Armagh, who recently qualified as a teacher. Brenda has just spent a year touring Canada and the United States as part of the *Riverdance* troupe. Other talented local dancers who have toured abroad with *Riverdance* include **Gemma Reid**, **Nicola Leonard** and **Damien Kirk**.

When the local cinema in Keady closed in 1978, brothers **Michael and Enda Hughes** from the village set about making their own brand of entertainment. Their father ran the local amateur dramatic society and it was he who supplied the boys' first camera. Both are passionate about the cinema and films. Their first, very low budget film, *The Eliminator*, was made on location in and about Armagh. This was enthusiastically received throughout Ireland and abroad in 1997-98. *Flying Saucer Rock and Roll*, where McAnerney's local supermarket permitted use of its warehouse as a studio, was televised. This short film—a pastiche on Hollywood—featured *Father Ted* star Ardal O'Hanlon, who had been so taken by *The Eliminator* that he wanted to become involved in the brothers' next film venture. While a student at Oxford University, Michael appeared in numerous productions and was cited in the *Sunday Times* as a most promising actor at the National Student Drama Festival. From Oxford, he went to live in Paris where he studied theatre production. Here, he trained for the theatre at L'École Jacques Lecoq. As there is already a Michael Hughes on Equity's books, he had to act under the name of Michael Colgan. Michael has appeared in Dublin's Abbey Theatre opposite Sorcha Cusack in Brian Friel's *Freedom of the City*, directed by Conall Morrison. Michael also toured to the Lincoln Centre Festival, New York, in July 1999 and appeared at the Abbey (Peacock Theatre) in Michael Harding's *Amazing Grace*. He has many other theatre credits in Dublin, Belfast, Britain and Italy. Younger brother Enda, a film director, is working on the script of *Frock Cop*, based on a cross-dressing policeman in Northern Ireland. The script has already been dubbed '*Dirty Harry* meets *Tootsie*' and with a television production in mind, Enda is working with Armagh co-writer **Michael Duffy**. Both Michael and Edna featured in a Channel 4 documentary *Revenge of the Little People* in March 1999. Enda undertook Media Studies at university but left after a year, totally disillusioned. As a promising young director, he was involved with the camera work in *Divorcing Jack* and invited to Hollywood where he saw, first-hand, the larger-scale film industry in action. He has a preference for 1950s and '60s B-movies and Enda is considered the finest cinematic talent to emerge in Northern Ireland in the last 20 years.

Say what you will, this has to be a mesmeric confluence of young talent focusing on the oldest medium of all. *So what is it about Armagh?* Many theatrical presentations deserve praise, a few command it, rendering the critic more or less redundant. Such a statement should apply to a future, major production, marrying this mighty force into a work that is locally written, directed, produced, choreographed, adapted, set designed and costumed. "Talent", wrote Goethe, "develops in quiet places." That's probably *what it is* about Armagh.

Ivy Hughes-Brennan

Papilio means butterfly. This gossamer insect inspired the concept that Ivy Hughes-Brennan chose for her Beauty Salon and Electrolysis Clinic at Rainbow House. Clients are convinced this highly motivated woman sets her own standards, and once attained, moves the peg up another notch.

"I have to", Ivy insists, "nothing stands still in the beauty industry. Each day brings another scientific 'miracle' or a new anti-ageing technique. Women are particularly vulnerable to propaganda and it is human nature to want to 'keep young and beautiful' for as long as possible. I'm constantly bombarded by cosmetic claims, 'Doctors have tested this', or 'we found, by using a new high frequency ultrasound technique on volunteers in their fifties, results resembled that of a 20-year-old'." Ivy deliberates. "Such claims may or may not be true. I hold ultimate responsibility for treatments carried out in my salon and will not attempt use of any new product without tested guarantees."

The desire to enhance our appearance is as old as civilisation itself. Cosmetics and perfumes discovered by Ancient Egyptians 3,000 years BC are still in use today. But what we call beautiful is surely open to individual interpretation? Ivy nods agreement.

"Everyone can't be Sophia Loren but you can do a lot with what you've been given", she states positively. "That 'skin-deep' cliché has no place in a scientific age. There has never been a more exciting time in the skin care industry, as beauty schools of the Nineties are becoming wellness-orientated. The image is highly specialised, health-based and altogether more professional. Not only are we able to achieve skin renewal and revival but we can reach out to the physical body, mind and spirit, with increasing numbers of holistic therapies. The world has indeed become our oyster as revolution meets evolution. Revolutionary skin care ingredients are growing, hydroxy acids for example, which for years were used to burn warts. 'Cosmeceuticals' are exciting products that combine the use of pharmaceutical ingredients, such as Trichesan, with skin care preparation. Such discoveries have made an amazing impact on acne and no longer need our general practitioners say, *Keep using soap and you'll grow out of it...* If we consider vitamin technology and what is happening there, once Vitamin C was big news in the war against collagen degeneration but now, hot on its heels is highly-acclaimed VC improving elasticity which strengthens connective tissue and is a superb exfoliator."

Dedication to her cause brought Ivy Hughes-Brennan confidence and trust from clients. In difficult days of commerce, she has a thriving business where none was before. Inside her salon, Ivy's love of Mediterranean shades is reflected in wheat and aquamarine decor. The atmosphere is tranquil and gracious. Soothing music induces a sense of peace. "I always knew I would become involved in a caring occupation", Ivy agrees. "As the youngest in a family of four, everyone busily occupied, I had to fend for myself. My imagination ran riot as I brushed and groomed our pets! Beauty therapy was a comparatively rare career when I left school in the mid-Seventies. Bronwyn Conroy of Dublin ran the only recognised course with acceptable qualifications in Ireland. Whilst it was a privilege to be selected, it also cost a great deal of money. I required lodgings and for the best reasons, my father chose a convent on the outskirts of Dublin where I boarded five days each week. I gasped when shown to my room. It held two iron bedsteads and cold-to-the-touch linoleum on the floor." Nevertheless, friends she made then remained associates for the rest of her life.

For the next year Ivy's studies were mainly anatomy and physiology, a course comparable to that undertaken by medical students. "Only when we thoroughly understood the internal functioning of the body, physical and chemical processing of its cells, tissues, organs and systems with their various interactions, were we allowed to proceed to the external. I enjoyed every moment, even what was arduous, never losing sight of the fact that this knowledge would safeguard myself and prospective clients. Leaving Bronwyn Conway School, I held a recognisable qualification in beauty therapy, including electrolysis, equipping me for my career. Having worked so intensely, I needed a break. Then came a brainwave, or so it seemed at the time. I decide to emigrate to America, not on holiday or for working experience, but go lock, stock and barrel!"

Securing a three-month visa, Ivy went to New York absorbing everything she saw in the luxurious beauty salons of Fifth Avenue. "I watched the therapeutic effect of massage. For at least an hour each client relaxed in restful surroundings. It seemed as if both body and mind floated away on wafts of aromatherapy oil. At one utterly luxurious salon, a client told me she felt like Alice Through the Looking Glass. Afterwards they could enjoy a healthy meal at the Orangery. America and I eventually parted company and home I came."

Armagh offered an opening and Ivy began her specialised work within the franchise of a hairdressing salon. "Treatments I gave then would be described as elementary today but nothing is ever lost, and I did establish client confidence which paved a sound basis for my future." Ivy's skills were entirely devoted to manicures, eyebrow shaping and tinting, and wedding and special occasion make-up. "Not nearly enough to stretch my qualifications therefore not fulfilling", she appraises. "I'd met my future husband Kieran at a private party and, apart from enjoying his company, respected his judgement. We discussed the possibility of my own business, and Kieran drew up a plan which brought financial approval from my bank manager." With faith, confidence and determination in her enterprise, Ivy had to succeed. "Perhaps you could say I identified with the idea. In physics, experiments respond to the mind of the experimenter rather than being blindly repeatable. There is hardly anything that can be done without love of the idea. On opening day in 1985, my entire stock, all I could afford, sat on two small shelves."

Ivy's efforts paid off and soon she was working from nine in the morning to midnight, six days a week. For a time her sister Hazel helped at the salon and when the appointment book overflowed, assistant Yolanda Malocca joined Papilio. "Within two years, the time allocated to succeed or fail, Papilio occupied the entire first floor of Rainbow Building. Today it feels good making appointments for daughters of clients who supported me then. Our range of treatments has grown extensively. Manicures, pedicures, waxing and eyebrow shaping are considered 'bread and butter' salon services. Electrolysis is an umbrella-word for the removal of unwanted hair by electrical current as opposed to constricting the hair follicle. Methods vary and there are obvious dangers when administered by unqualified therapists. From shows we attend in England, Dublin, France and Germany we have learned that finally, Guilded therapists are insisting practitioners declare their qualifications before setting up in business."

Laser use in beauty treatments is futuristic and timesaving, but, Ivy forecasts, "will be appallingly expensive. In any case it has not yet been fully researched so won't be introduced by me until I am confident about long-term effects. I prefer to use these", she says, holding up both shapely hands. "We live in an age of stress. Health spas promise it is possible to reduce tension and the waistline at the same time. I'll contribute to that. Clarins is the product I support because I find it works. Clients visibly relax from the mere description of a Clarins Paris facial." She unconsciously flexes both hands. "This face, neck and hand treatment is the Rolls Royce of the range. After an hour of smoothing and kneading, the application of creams and gels, a client feels as shiny and polished as Clarins promise! There is healing in the hands, a natural therapy that conducts a feeling of well being within those who try this particular treatment. Head massage for the scalp, shoulders and neck is another wonderful reliever of tension."

Our annual fortnight on the beach now carries a stern health warning. Ivy agrees. "Just as smoking restricts the flow of oxygen to the capillaries, prematurely leathering the skin, so will exposure to the sun. I agree we look better with a little colour but statistics don't lie. There is a direct link between sun rays and skin cancer. Ultraviolet light can be suppressed by sunscreen, applied at least 30 minutes before going out, then re-applied every two hours and after swimming. Dark glasses and a sun hat are attractive forms of protection. Drink plenty of water when the weather is hot to avoid dehydration. Babies under six months should never be exposed to sunlight."

Newest and most dramatic of all the treatments that Ivy Hughes-Brennan has introduced to her salon is Carole French's technique known as pigmentation. "This concept from the Far East works beneath the skin surface following an injection of colour. Any feature can be enhanced or reduced, lip lines, eyebrows or implantation of beauty spots. We introduced pigmentation three years ago and clients come from every part of Northern Ireland to avail of its benefits."

People on this part of the island, Ivy insists, suffer inhibition or low self-esteem. "Many feel guilty, even

Ivy Hughes-Brennan

unworthy spending money on themselves. Others hesitate to discuss problems from an acute sense of embarrassment. Our service is personal, therefore confidential, and we pride ourselves on sensitivity. As client demand grows, my wish is to find larger premises on ground level, thereby easier access for handicapped or elderly clients. It remains a dream", she shrugs, "as massive rents do not encourage change."

"Our city is presently undergoing a time of cataclysmic change which is proving difficult for all in business", Ivy concludes. "Hillary Duncan, commercial manager of Armagh City and District Council, does understand the concern of our local Chamber of Commerce, and devotes time and talent to augmenting any positive suggestion."

Ivy's husband Kieran is a committee member of Armagh Round Table, annual hosts of the formal May Ball. "All proceeds from this event of the year go to a worthy local charity", she emphasises. "This year, with children in mind, they chose the Gateway Club. When our son Adam developed a serious disease, two years ago, Dr O'Brien at Craigavon Hospital detected the symptoms of renal cell carcinoma and his swift reaction saved Adam's life. During Adam's convalescence we came in close contact with the CURE organisation. Subsequently we have worked to support research into this vital area."

Juggling career and family life takes efficiency, a quality not lacking in Ivy Hughes-Brennan. "My twin sons Adam and Alex certainly added a new dimension to my perspective. As you see pregnancy changes our shape, system, and skin. Our newest addition is due in September, something of a shock after seven years!" Ivy considered this an ideal time to introduce a programme for mothers-to-be at the salon that will support wellbeing from conception to birth, concentrating on muscle tone, exercise and appearance.

Alex and Adam are hardworking pupils of Lisnadill Primary School. "I keep for posterity drawings they bring me or stories they've written during lessons. One day these will form part of our family history so they are important. My idea of a free day is simply relaxing at home. Something special for our sons will be an afternoon at the Planetarium. Alex heard they have a piece of rock from Mars so we must investigate this phenomenon! Kieran and I enjoy music in all its forms, particularly Sixties and revival bands. My mother Frances is an avid Cliff Richards fan and we hope to attend his concert in June. When it comes to reading, P.D. James and Ruth Rendell enhance the status of a thriller, my favourite category of fiction. I'm also a woman driver who loves the open road. Personally I never want to look under the bonnet but expert Jeremy Clarkson does say the more you know about how an engine functions, the better. Women in Ireland have come a long way", she decides. In this context she has played a significant role. It's true that we can't all be Sophia Loren, but thanks to the skill of Ivy Hughes-Brennan, each of us can make the best of what attributes we have!

Richard Stewart

Everyone looks forward to the local newspaper. Buying and reading the *Ulster Gazette* is, for many in this county, a weekly ritual delineating the importance of remaining au fait with local events. At 36, Richard Stewart is one of the country's youngest editors working for one of its most senior newspapers.

"I had no intention of becoming a journalist", Richard freely admits. "Only when I answered an advertisement for a junior reporter with the *Ulster Gazette* did I think on those lines. Accepting the job meant saying goodbye to pharmacist Shannon Stewart, for whom I'd worked since leaving school." Richard's first term with the *Gazette* lasted ten years. Now he has returned to the newspaper of his origins, having been editor of the *Dromore Leader* since 1997. Within two brief years, his newspaper has acquired a keen reputation with a focused emphasis on accuracy. "Writing for a newspaper is highly specialised", he points out, "in fact it is the most difficult form of communication. People think that because a newspaper is 'popular', the writing is of a lesser calibre. The opposite is true. The more popular a paper, the more demanding it is to write for. Broadsheets allow their articles to ramble but tabloid press just hasn't the space. Hard news items are pared to the bone, written to a formula and this means sparingly.

"Editor William Greer introduced me to the news desk in 1980", Richard continues. "A daunting prospect for a beginner but William had a theory that writing obituaries instilled a pro forma for life. By that he meant facts correctly presented and names properly spelt. Irate readers soon let us know when they were otherwise. After a short time I could compose an obituary in my sleep! A welcome diversion to sports reporting upheld my sanity. I'd been a member of Armagh Boys' Club run by Selwyn Tarleton, playing Junior League football each Saturday. With Selwyn's encouragement, many of our boys advanced to Irish League or further afield. This gave me an edge and I was asked to cover the Armstrong Cup, a summer soccer competition, played province-wide. Now I learned to switch technique, developing a style that suited the subject. It was our present sports editor, Stephen Richardson, then a freelance journalist, who first took me along to court, opening up another major area of reporting. A local specialised correspondent can make a good living using daily newspapers as potential customers. Not everyone has time to sit in a court room yet a major trial is of prime importance and these accounts guarantee a wide readership."

Richard lists his *Gazette* team of the Eighties. "Ruth Loney and myself worked as reporters with Billy Morton from Bessbrook who left to join the church. Our staff photographer Winston McConville drowned tragically while fishing in 1993. In a switch of ownership during my first term with the *Gazette*, Alpha Newspaper Group assumed control and now Eric Villiers became editor. Titles in this group now include the *Tyrone Courier*, *Larne Gazette*, *Carrickfergus Advertiser*, *Ballyclare Gazette*, *Rathfriland Outlook* and the *Tyrone Constitution*. From Eric Villiers I learned the technique essential to producing a local newspaper, headline writing and the importance of pursuing the exclusive feature.

"At the same time, Eric invited Ivan Lambert to join the team. Vast experience on the *Belfast Telegraph* and *Daily Mail* distinguished Ivan as one of the best writers Northern Ireland had ever produced. A good journalist keeps in touch with his reading public who are generally found on the street, at a football match or relaxing in the local pub. The temptation of dropping in for a pint is an antidote to a stressful job and the demands of constantly meeting deadlines. Ivan Lambert's demise may have been accelerated by his lifestyle but he always remained master of his craft."

Established in 1844, *Gazette* headlines told a grim story. Millions were dying of hunger or were forced to leave Ireland as a parasitic fungus rotted successive potato crops. A century later this same journal proclaimed the end of World War II. "What differs then and now", Richard concedes, "is the way information pours in. Newspaper staff are tempted to remain behind a desk as opposed to going out in search of a human interest story. Formatted press releases are usually prepared before an event and utterly impersonal. I regret that the caring image of, say, Alastair Cooke's *Letter from America* has been lost and my ambition is to return to a hands-on style of reporting. Stories stem from being in the right place at the appropriate time or a whisper when important events are about to break. A tip-off that Prince Charles was about to conduct a border visit led to an exclusive story which Eric Villiers and I wrote jointly. It wouldn't have the same impact now as then, a decade dominated by terrorist violence. Even our offices were devastated, so that for a time, we worked from a makeshift tin shack!"

Headline horror stories of the Eighties made equally grim reading. Richard recalls Mountain Lodge at Darkley where worshippers were machine-gunned, Sir Norman Stronge murdered with his son James, the torching of Tynan Abbey and Councillor Charles Armstrong's horrendous death in a car bomb. "No matter what a reporter may feel, his capabilities should reflect in a balanced and reasonable report. How many", Richard demands, "could look at unmitigated carnage and remain impartial? My heart went out to all clearing this aftermath, ambulance crews, security forces and particularly the police. One morning shots were heard in the office. Ruth Loney and I rushed out to find a body lying in Dobbin Street. Bleeding profusely from the head, the man died in agony. He was a civilian, it was an IRA killing, a case of mistaken identity, the greatest insult any family should have to bear. Ruth practically collapsed. That image, repulsive and evil, remains with me still. This man was one of more than 3,000 victims of the Troubles. Police on the scene were in danger themselves and yet were expected to inform relatives, collect evidence, and, in the face of deliberate carnage, remain impartial. Few remained impartial following the Omagh bombing", he states emphatically. "If good men persist in remaining silent, propagandists will attempt to wipe out all traces of valiant police work, unrecorded acts of courage and humanity which were conducted throughout every obscene loyalist and nationalist atrocity."

Whilst a senior reporter with ten years' service, Richard Stewart decided he needed a fresh challenge. "An acquaintance, Richard Elliott, moved to become editor of Lisburn's Ulster Star, creating a vacancy at the *Portadown Times*. *Times* editor David Armstrong telephoned to say I was just a little late, the job had been allocated. David suggested the *Lurgan Mail*, also part of the Morton Group, and editor Bill Ireland took me on at once. I found the Lurgan community similar to Armagh—it too, regrettably, a society divided. The *Mail* had a good team. One colleague was Ian Malcolm, son of Louis, who recently retired as 'Roamer' in the *News Letter*. Lurgan had its fair share of grim headlines. One massive bomb blitzed the entire town. A civilian, a policeman and two off-duty Ulster Defence Regiment soldiers were gunned down at Castor Bay, Lough Neagh. The men had gone regularly to this spot, shooting wild duck. Four more deaths were now added to a senseless toll and we witnessed another litany of funerals and broken-hearted relatives. Good people of every creed endangering their lives by speaking vehemently against evil. Such were the depths to which terrorism had sunk."

Within the Morton Group, the need for a separate edition of the *Dromore Leader* had been identified. Two years as their senior reporter and Richard became the newspaper's Banbridge-based editor. "One difficulty was not knowing the territory or local people. Knowing one's readership is paramount so I went to schools, called on business people, chatted with those frequently in the news. Circulation affects every periodical from the *Beano* to the *Financial Times*. Daily newspapers constantly claim scoops, and many tabloids depend on scandal. Provincial weeklies, answerable for every printed word, tend to rely on a recognised and trusted news team. As a new title we were faced with a challenge. Watching our circulation grow was, I admit, rewarding." Circulation of the *Gazette* has increased appreciably since Richard took the chair of editor. "I can say that I had no intention of returning to this newspaper", he admits, "in fact I really enjoyed my job in Banbridge which was one of very few towns to escape terrorist violence. If you get a buzz from imparting good news, then the *Leader* office was the place to be.

"Much had changed since my first term with the *Ulster Gazette*. Eric Villiers had moved on and his successor, Karen Busby, transferred to Dungannon creating an editorial vacancy. Offered the job by our current directors, I accepted." Provincial readers do not readily subscribe to a tabloid culture and yet Richard Stewart has brought community news back to its rightful place in this long-established weekly. "I have a superb team", he acknowledges. "Sports editor Stephen Richardson competently fills ten pages on athletics, bowls, cricket, darts, GAA, hockey, rugby and swimming. His role extends to news, features and sub-editing. Deputy editor Richard Burden has developed a distinctive style, his knowledge of Armagh and its people essential to hard

Editor Richard Stewart and Ulster Gazette staff.
(L to R): Philip Wilson, Chris Cairns, Richard Burden, Melanie McIvor and Stephen Richardson

news stories that may break. Richard is a specialist in news reporting and frequently enjoys a well-deserved by-line for exclusive stories. Junior reporter Melanie McIvor shows excellent potential in presenting women's features, and is a favourite with readers. Chris Cairns, youngest of our team, has a sporting background and makes great use of this knowledge in preparing reports. Reminiscent of myself in bygone days, Chris is carving his own niche in journalism. Staff photographer Philip Wilson remains cheerful whatever may come."

Advertising funds editorial, and Alan Houston provides the professional impetus behind each promotion. Office manager Ruth Wilson is the *Gazette*'s longest-serving employee while downstairs at reception, Eva Homan deals efficiently with the general public. Geoffrey Glenny is popular and helpful as shop manager. "One factor unites us", Richard agrees, "that of achieving greater circulation. It also means a clear identity. Our readership ranges demographically from ten years to 90-plus, so can you imagine the range of material this requires? Reports on Women's Institute meetings matter to WI members, a surprisingly large number of readers. A feature we considered to be of passing interest was the instigation of correspondence for many weeks. Regardless of living in a computer age, newspapers are a valuable way in which we may source information. An old photograph of St Malachy's Flute Band, taken in 1912, brought a return of endless information from every part of Northern Ireland. President Clinton's visit last October was probably one of the most exciting news events to come our way. When again will we see a President walk across the Mall?

"We are frequently asked to withhold names in court cases and I cannot comply. My answer is invariably, 'keep out of trouble and you'll keep out of court'. By the same token I always endeavour to report the truth. Dishing the dirt is not our newspaper's policy. Unlike the tabloids, local newspapers are accountable so I refuse to publish private lives of public individuals. I once remember reading that Elton John, returning from holiday, was pounced upon at Heathrow Airport by a barrage of reporters. 'Did you enjoy lying in the sun?' one asked. Quick as a flash Elton replied, 'No, I leave that to you lot!' We do have an outcry when a feature displeases but some unhappy quirk in our nature prevents applause for exceptional reporting. When this does happen, it's gratefully welcomed. Any unexpected tribute will brighten the day of most."

Richard and his wife Eileen were romantically attached from schooldays. Achieving secretarial qualifications at evening class led to Eileen's appointment as financial administrator for Armagh Business Centre. A photograph of their children, Nicola and Darren, sits on Richard's desk. "Obviously my family is special to me. Nicola is a talented little artist but I suspect Darren may follow my career", Richard says with a smile. "He already attempts to read the *Gazette* or should I say, looks at the pictures! To really relax I play hockey and presently captain City of Armagh Mens' Seconds. Formed five years ago, we've just taken the cup", he adds proudly. "I'm an avid sportsman as well. Last year Eileen and I went to Old Trafford and watched Manchester United draw with Leicester City. I garden a little but my chief joy has to be the vista of a lush, green lawn."

Most writers are first of all readers. From half a dozen newspapers a day, who is his favourite columnist? "Undoubtedly Ian Wooldridge of the *Daily Mail* for a particularly witty style. I suppose it's a question of preference but David McKittrick from the *Independent* is another writer who leaves a good impression on the reader's mind." The most personal and intriguing comments are often made at the end of an interview. Richard Stewart, one of the country's youngest editors working on one its most senior newspapers leaves an impression of a good mind, stark honesty and sound judgement. From where the reader stands, Wednesday—*Ulster Gazette* publishing day—can only get better!

Jack O'Hare

Poet Laureate Ted Hughes, judging the W.H. Smith Children's Writing Awards, said of all entries those from St Patrick's Primary School, Armagh, possessed "a rare freshness and originality." At the time Jack O'Hare, as principal of St Patrick's, was in London to receive a Certificate of Excellence for work of exceptional standard, on behalf of the school.

Born in Derry, Jack came to Armagh in 1956 when he married Eithne O'Neill, also a teacher, from Middletown. Jack taught first in Gilford, then St Malachy's Primary School, Armagh, moving to the newly established St Patrick's Primary, on the Loughgall Road, in 1969. Becoming vice-principal in 1978, he held that position for 12 years. Thereafter he was principal until retirement, which coincided with the 25th anniversary of the opening of the school. St Patrick's provided Jack with many lasting memories and the achievements of his pupils remains a source of pride.

Jack's interest in and contribution to education extended far beyond the environment of the school classroom. He involved himself with the Irish National Teachers' Organisation, fighting firmly for rights of women teachers. Another educational coup in which Jack featured was the establishment of the Teachers' Resource Centre at Newry Road, where professional facilities are available to schools in the Southern Education and Library Board Area. Supported by the then SELB chief executive, Gerry Kelly, this Centre proved an enormous success.

Outside education, Jack has many other interests and commitments but dearest to his heart is time spent in fostering the Credit Union movement, a non-denominational, self-help organisation which originated in Germany. "If you can remember Armagh city before the Credit Union", he says, with a twinkle in his eye, "then you're on the wrong side of 50!" Perhaps the greatest success story in Ireland in the second half of the 20th century has been that of the Credit Union movement and synonymous with its development in Armagh has been the name of Jack O'Hare.

"Nowadays", says Jack, "the Credit Union is accepted as a normal part of life. That wasn't always the case. It is difficult to appreciate a situation lifted out of context, but in the '50s and '60s, only 30 per cent of the population had access to banking facilities. If you weren't among the lucky few your options were very limited—unless you had savings you used hire purchase or borrowed money from a moneylender. That may sound dramatic and Dickensian but for many in Armagh, it was a fact of life. Hire purchase I could understand. Most people used this in some form. The moneylender was a different matter. Apart from charging exorbitant rates of interest, often realising over 1,000 per cent, the demeaning of an individual's dignity was its most unedifying aspect. Women bore the brunt of this method of borrowing, as they were usually given the task of managing household finances."

Even now, 30 years on, it is possible to see the empathy with which Jack recalls relevant factors in those early days of the movement. "Until I became involved in Credit Union I wasn't even aware of what was going on around me. Only when my attention was drawn to it, did I realise what was happening. Saturday morning was a popular repayment time with part of Friday night's wages changing hands through the open window of a strategically parked car. Tuesday was another popular day with women collecting their Family Allowance and handing over both money and book to the shadowy figure in the driver's seat. Sordid as it may sound, the moneylender was probably a necessary evil of the time. At any rate, I think it important that these aspects of social history are recorded while still fresh in our minds.

"President John F. Kennedy's inaugural speech... *ask not what your country can do for you...* seems old, hackneyed and full of clichés. But hearing it for the first time it was quite inspirational, motivating many in Ireland to respond. With perfect timing, the Credit Union movement became known. Strangely, it wasn't new, and had originated in Germany in the mid-19th century, evolved by a man named Friedrich Wilhelm Raiffeisen, a German Protestant. The movement spread over much of Europe and in 1900 crossed the Atlantic where a Canadian Catholic, Alphonse Desjardins, started a Credit Union in Quebec. The first Credit Union in the United States was established by Edward Filene, a Boston Jew, in 1909. I mention these religions deliberately to emphasise the broad denominational origins of the movement, something that we cherish and promote at every opportunity. Incidentally, anyone who has been to Boston will be familiar with the famous Filene Stores."

Jack's enthusiasm for his subject is infectious. Listening to him it is easy to understand how the Credit Union in Armagh was acknowledged in those early days as one of the leading Credit Unions in Ireland. "What surprises me", continues Jack, "is that it took so long for the movement to come to Ireland. It wasn't until 1958 that two groups, one in Dublin and one in Derry, interested in community development, wrote independently to the National Association in the States, asking for information. On this being forwarded, CUNA put the two groups in touch with each other and so the Credit Union Movement in Ireland was born.

"Pat Quinn, a local Armagh business man, heard what was happening in Derry. He gathered a group to study the whole idea, and the Credit Union was launched at a public meeting in October 1962, only the second Credit Union in Northern Ireland. In those early days there was very little help or advice available from outside so naturally, a degree of trial and error existed prior to gaining knowledge from our own experiences. I became totally convinced of the value of Credit Union to the community and it gradually took over my life. I also saw the Credit Union as a practical way of expressing the Christian philosophy."

The imposing Georgian-style facade of the Credit Union building in Russell Street blends decorously with its surroundings. In keeping with the character of the city itself, one can hardly fail to be impressed. An older generation may remember the Cosy Cinema, as it was known, and one often hears tales of Saturday matinees with their celluloid heroes, Gene Autry, Roy Rodgers, the Lone Ranger and Tonto—so much for gender equality! The building had lain idle for many years after the cinema had gone out of fashion due to the advent of television. This proved to be the perfect location for a rapidly expanding Credit Union office. "I hope you don't think for one moment that we bought this place to start with", laughs Jack. "Life's not as simple as that. Big oaks from little acorns... No, the Credit Union started with a room in Handel House as an office—open on Sunday mornings from half-past 11 until half-past 12. As 1963 neared an end, increased membership and volume of business merited a move from Handel House. Rented premises in Market Street became available from the Forester's Club under a three-year lease. By then shares had risen to £7,000, loan demands were increasing. A big decision to provide longer opening hours and appoint a part-time manager was taken. From then onwards, growth was dramatic. Full-time staff were appointed and the search for permanent premises began. Initially, the purchase and refurbishment of Market Street was considered, even to the extent of protracted discussion with Armagh Urban Council and the Ulster Architectural Heritage Society. However, the constrictions of developing a listed building were too limiting and fortunately the Cinema site became available. We negotiated a keen price and were able to demolish, rebuild and equip the premises for £30,000—a fairly sound investment, one would have to admit!

"A week of celebrations was held in the city at the end of April 1971, heralding the new premises and our move to Russell Street. There were sports on the Mall for schoolchildren; a ten-mile fun walk for both adults and children, with almost 300 taking part; and a dance at the City Hall where St Patrick's College art students had mounted a display in the foyer, the centrepiece of which was an 11-foot space rocket. Our grand opening on Friday was followed by a civic reception in the City Hall and a concert by the City of Armagh Youth Orchestra. All main churches were represented and civic dignitaries present at the opening ceremony, jointly performed by His Eminence Cardinal Conway and His Grace Archbishop Simms. Those were indeed inspiring days, something positive in a community already beginning to suffer the effects of sharp division which was to blight our society over the next 30 years."

Jack's role in the development of the Credit Union movement is well known throughout Ireland. He and fellow directors travelled all over Ulster and further afield to form study groups and set up other Credit Unions. He was in great demand at seminars and public meetings where his commitment and enthusiasm often provided the vital spark needed to ignite a group into community action. His own Credit Union in Armagh was put firmly on the map when he was appointed treasurer of the Irish League of Credit Unions in 1973. Measured in statistical terms, the growth of the movement has been phenomenal. Armagh has now almost 6,000 members, over one third of the area's population, who have amassed £6.5 million in

The official opening of Armagh Credit Union in 1971:
Jack O'Hare, His Eminence Cardinal Conway and His Grace Archbishop Simms

shares. In Northern Ireland there are 257 credit unions while in Ireland as a whole there are 535 credit unions, with 2.2 million members and £3.3 billion in shares. Not even the 'starry-eyed visionaries from Armagh', as they were called, could have envisaged such progress.

Cardinal Conway in his address at the official opening ideally expressed the role of the Credit Union. "It would be impossible to measure the good, in human terms, which has accrued to so many families and individuals, the quantity of worry and anxiety which it has spared so many people... and, more important still, the contribution which it has made to their sense of self-reliance. I think the secret of that success has been the sense of dignity of the individual that is so central to the Christian Gospel. Fostering and strengthening that dignity in the community as a whole has been the foundation stone on which the movement has been built."

As the Credit Union became professional, the burden of voluntary work began to ease. A new cause beckoned and Jack, with his deep concern for those in need, was prompted to campaign for a local branch of the Citizen's Advice Bureau. Playing a major role in establishing the Armagh branch, he holds the office of trustee and keeps in touch with the Bureau.

Jack is currently president of County Armagh Golf Club, an honour richly deserved in view of the contribution he has made towards the development of the Club down the years. He had been elected captain of County Armagh Golf Club in 1984, so his organisational skills were well known. As the all-important year of 1993 approached, the Club Council appointed Jack as convenor of its centenary committee. He hands laurels to several members, particularly Bee Gordon and Damien Woods, who researched material for his book *The Centenary Story*.

"It was essential that this be a genuine story rather than collated facts", Jack explains. "This work addresses the game of golf, with the history of Armagh over the past hundred years woven into the development of the Golf Club. Ian Dawson was captain in 1993 and he cut the cake on the evening of our book launch. A 'Great Antiques Hunt' for competition prizes was particularly enjoyable. We tracked rare items of silver, porcelain, linen and prints from the last century. Tyrone Crystal designed and donated an exclusive glass replica of the historic obelisk monument which stands in the Palace grounds adjoining the golf course as a permanent memento of the occasion."

By way of recreation, Jack assisted the formation of a Chess Club within the clubhouse. A spectacular achievement was the acceptance of an invitation by Russian Grand Master, Victor Korchnoi, to Armagh where with two other members, Jack played Korchnoi in a televised match on the Gloria Hunniford Show. "We were annihilated!" Jack confesses. "Korchnoi then played at Drumsill House Hotel, simultaneously matching 40 skilled players from Northern Ireland. Frank Coll from Armagh emerged as the only victorious competitor. I am glad to say my fondness for chess has been inherited by my family."

His family will always remain the most important factor in Jack O'Hare's life. He and Eithne—now both retired—have five children and five grandchildren whom they visit frequently. Jack's community work continues through the Armagh Church Forum and the Parish Pastoral Council. Despite retirement his dedication remains unabated; so does his love of books and, in particular love of Jonathan Swift. "*Gulliver's Travels* is my favourite." With a twinkle in his eye he adds, "I'm still looking for that elusive first edition."

Central to Jack O'Hare's life is the Christian philosophy of love God and love thy neighbour. He has always given willingly in unconditional terms and this is reflected in everything he does. With that air of quiet and temperate humour, his work has enriched the lives of many in our community. His contribution to the fabric of our society in Armagh has been immense.

Gerald Rath

In these islands one in five of us buys at least one cookbook a year, spending an annual £100 million. Early food habits set a pattern for life so it makes sense to involve a child in preparing food as soon as possible. This is exactly what happened in the case of 30-year-old Gerald Rath from Armagh, now management chef with Salty's of Cape Cod, Massachusetts.

Gerald has earned a glowing report in the Good Food Guide of the *Boston Globe*, a gourmet feature written in terms that most people understand and enjoy. The *Globe* commended Gerald's ability to produce dishes sparkling with European and Italian flair. His French cuisine is described as "a tonic for the jaded palate". Four years ago, Gerald was head chef at Castraberti's, the restaurant of a Boston Italian family with associations reaching back to Sorrento. When Arthur Castraberti and his wife Rosa decided to retire, Gerald Rath was immediately offered the position of assistant banqueting chef at the Hawthorne Hotel, one of the most prestigious in the area. A year later he was promoted to another department outside the hotel at the Essex Peabody Museum in Salem. This elegant restaurant is French-inspired in terms of food, decor and fine table linen. Fifty patrons can be accommodated inside with 40 additional seats in the Chinese garden.

"Here I could be as creative as I wished", Gerald comments. "That the menu changed every day is just a small example of how meticulously this restaurant was organised. A typical dinner comprised: *Appetiser:* Escargot en croûte—fresh snails sautéed in garlic, cognac and cream, baked in a puff pastry shell with caramelised brulée finish. *Soup:* Roasted lobster and corn chowder. *Salad:* Mini crabcakes with a cucumber roulade topped with alfalfa sprouts and lemon. *Entrée:* Rolled salmon stuffed with crabmeat, drizzled with citrus yoghurt dill sauce and braised asparagus bundles served on an Asian noodle pancake. *Dessert:* Home-made cheesecake tartlets topped with fresh wild berries soaked in Grand Marnier with Chantilly whipped cream and two dessert sauces.

"All ingredients were fresh with nothing 'made earlier'."

Gerald's mother, Joan Nugent, formerly Joan Rath, speaks of his background from her home in Armagh. "Of my three sons, Gerald is the only one to take an interest in cooking. When my first husband Patsy died, I remember coming home from work one Sunday shortly afterwards, utterly exhausted. Patsy had always cooked Sunday lunch and, wondering where I would find the energy to make something, I pushed open the door. The table was attractively laid with glasses and napkins. Gerald was only 13 then. 'Sit down, Mum', he said, drawing out a chair, 'everything's ready.' I had to bite back the tears. He had prepared roast potatoes with chicken, which I'd left ready to go in the oven. The potatoes were tough as old boots and the vegetables soggy but just as every mother must have done at some time, I chewed my way through. Ask me about my most memorable meal? That was it."

Encouraged by Joan, the aroma from the Rath kitchen grew more delicious by the day as Gerald advanced from quiche and chocolate cake to mullet in vine leaves followed by lemon soufflé. "Even John and Paul began to take notice of their brother's expertise. Now they cook as well but not on such a grand scale."

She heaps all credit for her son's success in America on his training at local schools and colleges. "Gerald was educated at St Patrick's Primary School. Coming home after his first day, he announced that he was in love with his teacher, Mrs O'Hare. Today he says Jack O'Hare was the most caring, capable teacher he ever had."

In 1984, Chairman Sam Foster and Armagh District Council announced that young people from the area had been invited to visit America as part of the Ulster Project. Schoolchildren from each tradition were to be given an opportunity to mix in a relaxed, American family environment.

"They say everything looks different at 20,000 feet", Joan laughs. "For those children the confines of our troubled land melted in the excitement of winging across the Atlantic. Gerald described his trip to Maryland as pure magic. It certainly laid a foundation that changed his entire life. For two weeks he was guest of an American family who treated him as if he was one of their own. They retained a friendship and in 1986 they invited Gerald to visit again. Seán, my husband, and I always knew how impressed he was by the lifestyle of Boston and its people.

Leaving St Brigid's Secondary School, Gerald took a pre-catering course at Armagh College of Further Education. When he left Newry Catering College with City and Guilds qualifications, he could have undertaken any function whether a casual lunch or formal wedding.

"He has never forgotten teaching staff who helped along the way and will gladly cook a meal for any who may pass through Boston", Joan promises.

Gerald gained experience with the Northern Bar Hotel in Armagh where a busy lunchtime trade flourished. His next stop was the Charlemont Hotel. Prior to leaving for Boston, he had gone to work at Conway House Hotel in Dunmurry. And yet", she recalls, "he never stopped talking about America or the harbour based on Massachusetts Bay with its colourful, constantly changing traffic.

"Gerald was working at Conway House Hotel when news came of a vacancy for a sous-chef at The Landing Restaurant, Marblehead, Mass. He seized the opportunity. I was pleased his world was opening up in this marvellous way and yet it was sad saying goodbye. When your children leave, part of yourself goes with them."

Joan visited the USA in 1992, staying with her son. "Naturally my first formal meal was booked at The Landing. Built on a jetty, the dining room overlooked the sea. From our table we watched marine life in the bay below. I should have been accustomed to Gerald's cooking but each dish, presented by a smiling waitress, outclassed everything I'd ever eaten."

Joan recalls a mouth-watering medley of shellfish, crab, lobster, prawns and shrimp combined in a mousse, and spectacular salads accompanied by piquant vinaigrette dressing.

There was another important aspect to Joan's visit. "I met Connie, Gerald's fiancée, for the first time. Nanny to a professional family, Connie had a happy, bubbly personality. They were married soon after in Danvers, Mass., and I returned for their wedding."

"If I could take up the story from here", says Gerald who has more than a hint of Boston in his accent. "While with Castraberti's I catered for my own wedding, very hard work so I don't recommend it! We had a buffet appetiser table set with fruit, vegetable sticks, assorted breads and muffins with fruit, toasted mini bagels with dips and sauces. Hors d'oeuvre and assorted canapés were also passed around. In the centre was an ice sculpture of a leaning tower. I should add that Castraberti's was contained within another restaurant, which was humorously named The Leaning Tower of Pizza. My wedding dinner menu consisted of vichyssoise soup with crème fraiche, marinated green salad with a roasted pepper balsamic vinaigrette topped with chèvre cheese. Entrée was Surf and Turf: pan-seared medallions of tenderloin, wrapped in bacon with smoked shitake mushroom jus. Seafood casserole completed the dish with shrimp, scallops, lobster and crab legs in spiced Newburg sauce. Julienned spring vegetables tossed in pesto and parmesan cheese were served in a rice timbale with piped and baked potatoes which were stuffed with stewed Roma tomatoes and roasted garlic cloves.

"We finished our meal with slices of wedding cake and chocolate coconut truffles. And no, I didn't have time to make the cake! Our wedding was a huge success but it was also a lot of work. After toiling all day in the restaurant, I set up the function room, finishing at 3am. Returning at 6am, I prepared the food for my big day, managing to be in my tuxedo by noon, and was married two hours later. How it came together I will never know but I love to think I had a $30,000 wedding with 140 guests for a fraction of what it would have cost commercially.

"Moving on to the Essex Peabody Museum, I remained for two years. Connie, my wife, had become front-of-house manager. Here we had five function rooms where we catered for weddings and parties. Only the rich and famous could afford to eat at the Essex Peabody as it cost $5,000 just to hire the ballroom! Just over a year ago, someone familiar with my work approached me with an offer to run Salty's, his restaurant on Cape Cod. Included in the package was a four-bedroom house and six months' vacation time. Connie and I jumped at this deal and are now into our second season at Salty's. I am restaurant manager running all aspects of the business. This involves doing whatever it takes to maintain a quality restaurant and so I am liable to be boss, waiter, bartender or dishwasher but my main job is running the kitchen. Salty's is very different from my usual style of preparation with a menu that concentrates on laid-back, home cooking but I still make some of my gourmet dishes on the special board and these sell well.

"Connie is my backbone, always encouraging me to strive for the best. We work well as a team at Salty's and look forward to October when we close. Our season is

Chef Gerald Rath

from 1 April to mid-October. This may not sound strenuous but I am serving 1,000 meals a day—we don't take reservations! If any of you would like to come and visit we are five minutes from the beach, the pub and Salty's which easily seats 180. This is quite an update on my previous story. Maybe the next time we meet, I'll have my own restaurant. That is my dream and we never know what the future holds."

Gerald and Connie live at Yarmouth, one town over from where the Kennedy wedding was to be held when John Kennedy Junior, his wife and sister-in-law so tragically died. Asked if he has ever cooked for the Kennedy's, he smiles and replies, "That's privileged information."

Joan's other sons are teachers and both married. Paul and Anne have two children, Ciara and Aisling. Paul is an instructor in physical education and head of the boys' department of Drumcree College, Portadown. John and Patricia also have two children, Sarah and Aaron. John is a senior teacher at Abbey Christian Brothers' Grammar School, Newry.

How handsome a dividend for local schools, past teachers and the Ulster Project which invested in Gerald Rath. Recognition from the *Boston Globe* is a bonus, which allows us all to bask a little in the success of this talented young man. Perfecting his art may have been Gerald Rath's recipe for success but for Joan it all began with a 13-year-old boy saying: *Sit down, Mum, everything's ready.*

1970 ~ 1980

Life, like a dome of many-coloured glass,
Stains the white radiance of Eternity

Percy Bysshe Shelley

The Arts in Armagh

Thirty thousand spectators once fought their way into the theatre of Dionysus in Athens, where Greek audiences watched and listened with devotional intensity. Closer to home, Vincent McCann, administrator of the new theatre and arts centre, The Market Place, will be more than happy to fill the main auditorium of 400 seats. Each day brings this elegant building a step closer to completion and, with it, the realisation of a dream for all who cherish and promote the arts.

Armagh-born Vincent is adequately prepared for his responsibilities. He holds a degree in Drama and Theatre Studies from Trinity College Dublin and a Master's degree in Irish Theatre Studies. Art is everyone's concern and human existence cannot be imagined without it. Vincent has already subscribed to the medium as administrator of Dubbeljoint Productions and the Lyric Theatre. He founded his own Metamorphosis Theatre Company in Armagh, staging several local productions including *My Fair Lady* and *The Importance of Being Earnest*.

Vincent comments, "The aim of the theatre is to make available a platform for the arts as well as providing community access to marvellous new facilities. Following an official opening in March 2000, we have planned a number of performances by leading companies—the Lyric in Belfast and the Abbey in Dublin. A major proportion of my time will be dedicated to local productions and, hopefully, generating new initiatives. Armagh Theatre Group will also stage a number of local events in The Market Place. We estimate 280 performances within the year and, of course, a licensed restaurant will be another attractive feature of the theatre."

Human manifestations of art are expressed through architecture, sculpture, painting, music, poetry and drama. The ability to identify talent in others is a gift. In all of these areas the Council's arts officer, Kate Bond, relied on her own extensive experience. Skilfully interpreting what is best from each genre she, in conjunction with Armagh City and District Arts Committee, compiles a programme which reflects art in all its aspects.

"The benefit of a full-time arts officer cannot be overestimated", says Harry Carson, honorary secretary of Armagh Arts Committee. Paying tribute to Kate's competent, informed approach, he continues, "She addresses herself professionally to a task, which has doubled in volume since her appointment."

Kate is originally from Londonderry, and studied English Language and Literature at Queen's University Belfast. "While at Queen's, I used my spare time to work with a whole range of arts organisations", Kate comments. "These varied enormously. I was administrator for *Theatre Ireland* magazine, press officer for the Northern Ireland Symphony, a member of the public relations team for the Belfast Festival at Queen's and a member of the Fringe Benefits Theatre Group. After graduation, I worked with the renowned Field Day Theatre Company (with board members Brian Friel, Seamus Heaney, Stephen Rea, Tom Paulin, Seamus Deane, Tom Kilroy and Davy Hammond) as press and publicity officer, promoting two plays with them over the space of two years—*Saint Oscar* and Heaney's *The Cure at Troy*. I also worked with a whole range of organisations on cross-community and cultural activities."

Kate's literary background and practical commitment led to her appointment as arts officer with Armagh City and District Council in 1994. Within a short time her name had become synonymous with defining and bringing art in its myriad forms to audiences in Armagh. A popular figure with Armagh Arts Committee, Kate assists with its programme and Council arts initiatives. Recently her work has been concentrating on the exciting development of the new theatre complex.

Shakespeare said the purpose of drama was and is 'to hold the mirror up to nature'. "Actors and spectators share a particular unity", Kate agrees. "Many productions deserve praise and, while envying Dionysus and his 30,000 patrons, it is my aim to fill our seats from the community and far beyond. So much will be happening in this new Arts Centre including programmes for the young. Children are intensely bound up with what they are doing and make-believe is the pattern for drama. If we can release their imagination, they then have access to a story with words, perhaps music and actors.

"Other work includes organising the Summer Fun programme of street entertainment, and developing a range of classes including youth theatre, patchwork, stained glass, creative writing and other topics. The views of the public are most welcome. One excellent suggestion has been that of a weekly afternoon tea dance for the over-50s. There has been a revival of ballroom dancing to strict-tempo music. As well as providing exercise in a pleasant form, here is an opportunity to foster friendships for many who live alone."

The opening of The Market Place theatre and arts centre will provide a central focus and location for all activities: everything from traditional music, lunch-time concerts, and summer schools, through to film festivals, 'Music in Armagh' performances, writers' workshops, festivals and visual arts exhibitions.

Within the building, there will be a main auditorium seating almost 400 people, a studio theatre to seat 150, a gallery for visual arts activity, a bistro-style restaurant, coffee house and three bars, as well as three multi-purpose rooms for workshops and classes. The Market Place will play a key role in celebrating the district's tradition of culture. Arts officer Kate Bond will now assume the title of manager and there is little doubt that she and her team will provide a plethora of millennium highlights.

Armagh City and District Arts Committee must take a bow for undiminished loyalty that has kept the flame burning since 1974. Honorary secretary Harry Carson has compiled notes from Committee minutes. These proved invaluable in an overall appreciation of the arts in Armagh.

During 1973, local government reorganisation set up 26 local authorities. The Local Government Order contained a small clause that each authority be responsible for cultural and recreational activities. The Arts Council of Northern Ireland, anxious that this cultural element should not be overlooked, persuaded each Council to form an Arts Committee. Drawn from members of Council and the local community, the Armagh Committee was founded in 1974. Three original members are still serving: Seán Murray, Lois Reid and Harry Carson. As chief librarian of the Education and Library Board, Harry was deemed a suitable honorary secretary and he still retains that office. The first chairman of Armagh Arts Committee was Wilfred McDonagh, a former member of the CEMA Committee. He moved to Bangor, Co. Down, and in 1975 Seán Murray was elected chairman, a post he has ably held since.

This voluntary committee began with assistance from Arts Council staff. Drawing up a constitution, the aims and objectives were defined as promotion, co-ordination and encouragement of the arts in the district with the emphasis on a broader understanding and appreciation of the arts. Despite this brave endeavour, local apathy was most disappointing.

"Those early years of the Committee were fraught with difficulty", recalls Harry Carson. "It was a time of terrorist activity, which meant many were reluctant to leave home at night. A neutral venue for events was another factor to overcome. Eventually the local Technical School permitted use of its gymnasium. This became our 'Theatre'. Imagine George Geordias, playing music for an audience of 37 in the Tech? Well he did, and this was one of the first events staged by Armagh Arts Committee. At another, the Ulster Orchestra was playing in the Hall when a bomb exploded somewhere in the city. *The Rocky Horror Picture Show* appealed to an entirely different audience and was quite an experience! The Committee used a classroom for film shows but had to change to a different room at the Tech because more turned up than expected. That evening they were short of chairs and the film reel was too big for the projector to turn. Necessity begs invention so it was wound by hand.

"And yet it was all good fun", Harry reminisces. "Sound advice and much-needed help from the Arts Council in those early years cannot be over-emphasised. Thanks to their expertise, we found a varied selection of artists.

"The structure of the Committee in those early years was representative of existing cultural organisations, district councillors, and those of the general public who were interested in the arts. The Committee elected its own office bearers and, for ten years, held an annual meeting, open to members of the public and from whom they would elect four members to serve on the Committee for the ensuing year. I realise many are reluctant to serve on committees but, without the work of the Arts Committee, there would be a much-reduced arts programme in Armagh. When the Southern Education and Library Board found this work had increased beyond what was reasonable, Armagh District Council was asked to help. We were allowed an ACE worker followed by part-time clerical assistants. We progressed to a full-time clerical assistant, and professional administration is today undertaken by an arts officer and a clerical assistant. Paul

McAvinchey joined the Committee in the late 1970s and his enthusiasm and knowledge helped further an excellent cause in the name of the arts. Due to pressure of work Paul, unfortunately, had to resign some four or five years ago.

"Like most committees", Harry continues, "those in Armagh Arts had many responsibilities—for programme content, booking artists, press releases and administrative tasks which accompany each event. Chores on the evening of a performance involve lifting tickets, seating patrons, refreshments for the performers, answering queries, putting out chairs and clearing up afterwards. Committee involvement grew as a pattern of events emerged. We were now holding an annual Arts Festival in October, and a chamber music series of six or seven concerts which ran from September to May. A successful youth drama scheme operated for several years and flourished until its demise through lack of available tutors. A visual arts programme, drama events and a film club kept the Committee stretched to its limits. In recent years, with tourists in mind, the Committee embarked upon a series of lunchtime concerts on the last two Saturdays in July and four Saturdays in August when a pleasant hour could be spent at the Bishop's Palace enjoying good music.

"Over the past 24 years, personnel and members of the District Council changed. The status of the arts in Armagh has grown and the fortunes of Armagh Arts Committee changed. We now enjoy 100 per cent funding from Armagh City and District Council and often as many as seven councillors are willing to sit on the Arts Committee. Backing comes in many forms. We have a fully staffed arts office and facilities where the Committee may meet. We attend the Leisure and Tourism Committee of the Council once a quarter to present a report on arts events in Armagh, and once a year to present a copy of the annual report. The Committee is funded by a direct grant from the Council and financial assistance in the form of grants for individual events from the Arts Council.

"Another landmark in the story has to be Armagh Music Week. This took place in May 1986 and was a wonderful tribute of music. The Ulster Orchestra came to town, playing in small groups at every imaginable venue, schools, supermarkets, shops and cafes. I am proud that many still remember that remarkable week. The support of Armagh City and District Council for the Arts Committee must not be underestimated. While supporting the arts directly, they finance other events. One that may be familiar is the Annaghmakerrig Bursary. Annually, without hesitation, bursary money has been made available and many Armagh recipients proved their worth by making a name for themselves within the arts world. Conall Morrison, at present with the Abbey Theatre in Dublin, has won the *Irish Times* Theatre Award. Daragh Carville was joint winner of the Stewart Parker Drama Award and has since received a Lottery grant, and more recently a university appointment, to continue full-time writing. A major sculpture project was undertaken in 1995, in conjunction with Benburb Heritage Centre. Over two sessions, 16 artists from Europe and America were resident in Benburb and worked on pieces of sculpture that became part of the heritage of the site. This was jointly funded by Armagh and City District Council, the Arts Council and Benburb. Another exciting project was two pieces of sculpture, commissioned for the Garden of the Senses at the Palace Stables Heritage Centre, again funded by the Council and the Arts Council Lottery Scheme. Summer Fun was an experiment in street entertainment, funded directly by the Council. This proved most successful. Money was also made available for the Apple Blossom Festival that takes place in May. Be in no doubt that the City and District Council is a keen supporter of the arts.

"Conscious that most events were scheduled for Armagh city, some years ago, the Committee made a decision to take the arts out into the District. 'Music on the Move' it was called and, after two years, we clearly saw this was not a success. Thereafter it was decided to stage all events in Armagh itself. A major problem was accommodation. The City Hall had been destroyed in 1972 and not replaced. Arts events were held at schools or church halls with their inherent problems. The local silver band had built a new music hall, and this proved an ideal location for most events with a maximum audience of 150. Legislation in the form of the Licensed Clubs Act put an end to holding any event there which attracted Arts Council funding. The community owes a debt of thanks to schools who generously opened their premises to the arts over the years. Without them, it would have been nigh on impossible to run any programme.

"In 1993, the Arts Committee worked on a strategic plan for the arts in Armagh. When complete, they had it

Armagh Arts Committee with arts manager Kate Bond and theatre administrator Vincent McCann
Photograph by Ian Maginess

Founder Members of Armagh Arts Committee:
honorary secretary Harry Carson, Lois Reid and chairman Seán Murray

adopted by the City and District Council in 1994. It confirmed the pattern of specialist sub-committees, drama, music, etc., and listed the duties of various officers and of course, listed objectives. These included ambitious moves such as a three-year audience building plan, developing arts events for community groupings, a survey of other town within the District to ascertain their various arts interests and, of course, prepare a business plan. The only objective we can say we completed was that of persuading the Council to have an arts officer in post by 1 April 1995. This was undoubtedly our *pièce de résistance.* Kate Bond's persona and ability encompasses all the Arts Committee had envisaged—and more. Soon we will have a new theatre. The remainder of the objectives and the strategic plan were shelved because it was realised that we were facing a completely new scenario", he says, concluding his excellent summary.

The urge to create is both universal and timeless. Art is everyone's concern and for a quarter-century, Armagh Arts Committee kept alight the flame. If the celebration of sculpture, painting, music, poetry and drama have survived in this city, it is they who crystallised the germ and nurtured the seedling. A new Theatre and Arts Centre is their 'grand design'. Perhaps this small group would step into that time-honoured circle of spotlight and allow the theatre-going descendants of Dionysus to warmly applaud you!

Gareth Williams

Presenting the fresh face of our future is a pleasure when the aspirations are those of Gareth Williams, BMus (Hons). Thoroughly delighted with the outcome of his degree course in music at Queen's University, 21-year-old Gareth, who lives outside Richhill, agrees performing live has always been the best aspect of his chosen career.

"My parents provided each of us with an opportunity to study music and our interests do vary. While brother Ryan was less than enthusiastic about piano lessons, my sister, Sian, undertook Irish dancing and has done exceptionally well. I studied music at primary school level, under the guidance of St Patrick's Cathedral organist, George Minne. The flute was an instrument I greatly wished to master and Eithne Vallely, my tutor at St Patrick's Grammar School, arranged lessons with various tutors working for the Southern Education and Library Board." Taking music and its various aspects seriously, Gareth joined his school choir and the school orchestra. "Ulster Television's sponsorship of 'Choir of the Year' had not begun when I was at grammar school but it is well-presented and a superb recognition of singing talent in Northern Ireland."

Generous in his appreciation of quality education, Gareth singles out two past teachers as particularly supportive. "Mr Seamus Savage made Ancient History come alive. With this added dimension, the subject became one of my chosen A-Levels. Form teacher Mrs Colette O'Brien, who taught French, was recognised as superb at her craft. She was also an excellent judge of character", he jokes, "appointing me a First Year prefect! A school trip to Romania, when we combined with students from Royal School, Armagh, and St Catherine's College, is a harrowing memory. It was post-Ceausescu regime and media coverage was focusing on the plight of abandoned, orphanage children. With cheaper costs in Romania, we bought badly needed items for these children after our arrival there. The sadness emanating from one little girl remained with me so, on my return home, I wrote a song about this child, setting it to music. I still play the piece, entitled *Standing Alone*, from time to time."

Many remember Gareth Williams' televised performance when Cardinal Daly officially retired in 1996. "Seán Boylan, choirmaster of St Malachy's, asked me to provide a flute solo. Seán's daughter, Lois, played the oboe and we both accompanied the Choir of St Patrick's Cathedral with my former tutor, George Minne as organist. I was again asked to play the flute at Archbishop Seán Brady's Ordination on 19 February 1996. The piece requested, *Keep me Safe*, was a favourite of Archbishop Brady." In a switch of mode, Gareth has taken the Guinness Entertainer of the Year Award at Warrenpoint, playing the guitar and singing his own compositions. "That evening I was accompanied by my friend, bass player, Hugh Gribben. Comedian Patrick Kielty was a previous Guinness winner. A studio recording was an addition to the main prize." Gareth then took top award at a talent competition in Monaghan, the finals of which were televised. "I was still a student at St Patrick's College, when one afternoon a team from RTÉ came to interview me in the middle of an Ancient History class taken by Seamus Savage. If it's a question of success or Socrates, well", he grins engagingly, "there's no competition, but the cameraman made sure Mr Savage wasn't forgotten!" Gareth is a founder member of Kilmore Folk Group, composing a brand of music suited to group performances. Fit and sporting, as a keen swimmer, he represented St Patrick's Grammar at Ulster and All-Ireland level.

Achieving the required grades in Religion, Ancient History and Music, Gareth began Music Studies at Queen's University in 1996. "Entirely new aspects of this medium were part of our coursework. We also explored the role of new technical combinations in presentation—a range of electronics, composition and electroacoustics (new sounds with computers). I love the quote and it seems correct to use it here, 'Mathematics is music for the mind and music is mathematics for the soul.' Composing lyrics and melody into music with a message made way for contemporary work. I suppose I was really seeking an individual form of expression. For my finals at Queen's University, I had to write a selection of orchestral pieces lasting 25 minutes, based on the use of many combinations of various instruments. One lecturer, Piers Hellawell, encouraged incorporating specific systems and techniques into compositions. Last year, as part of the Sonorities (strange sounds) Festival, myself and three friends took part in an experiment in celebration of Stockhausen, the composer of the century, who, incidentally, was featured on the cover of the Beatles album, *Sergeant Pepper's Lonely Hearts Club Band*. A musical piece called *Goldust*, written in 1968, had never been premiered and the work's prose stated: *Live alone for four days in complete silence, eat nothing, think nothing, sleep as little as possible and, without communicating, play the first thing that comes to mind.* We did this, finding the experience meditative. Oddly enough, when we began to play it was audibly unified, if in a somewhat discordant way."

Mozart is Gareth's favourite classical composer. The opera-lovers of Prague were among the first to recognise Mozart's genius and for them, he wrote *Don Giovanni*, which Gareth selects as "Mozart at his best". While he was at University, the student body elected Gareth as president of Queen's Music Society. "I organised a weekly recital and concerts at Spring and Christmas. Programme planning involved all music students and as diverse a range as possible, Beethoven, jazz or even traditional music."

With a view to the future and studying for a Master's degree in Music, Gareth applied to the Royal Scottish Academy of Music and Drama in Glasgow and London's Guildhall. Both made unconditional offers but September will see him off to Scotland. "I expect to fund myself as I've done previously, playing my guitar and singing. Every weekend I've enjoyed residency entertaining at Duke's Hotel and Bonnie's Café in Belfast. It's good to be able to cover my own fees in this way."

Citing James Joyce and Homer as favourite authors, Gareth qualifies his interest in the latter as arising from the stimulus of Ancient History. "It's probably Homer's way with words, or as Mr Savage would say, linguistic arrangement, that defines him as an artist in my estimation. The *Iliad* is particularly important literature and perhaps loosely based on an actual Greek-Persian trade war of long ago. I've a vested interest in reading the works of James Joyce, particularly *Portrait of the Artist as a Young Man*. This autobiographical novel contains moments, which broken down, convey a story within the story. I'm interested in isolating certain paragraphs, identifying the mood and then composing the music that might reflect Joyce's thoughts when he wrote that scenario. I may eventually teach music and already coach a few pupils in piano when I'm at home."

Schubert as a young man was similarly inspired, taking up a copy of Goethe's work *The Erl King* and dashing down the song as we know it. The kingdom of music has no limits and Gareth may well breathe his own gift into this art. "You might be interested to know that the piano on which George Minne taught me was once owned by Leonard Bernstein. There I was running up and down scales on this great composer's instrument. For all we know, Bernstein may even have tried out lyrics by Stephen Sondheim for *West Side Story* on those very keys! I mentioned this to George who simply replied, 'Get on with your work!' Writing background music for films would appeal to me. I'll reinforce that comment, it would be my dream! I really admire the work of John Williams who wrote themes for *Jaws*, *Star Wars*, *Superman* and *The Phantom Menace*.

"Wherever I am, I like to come home. My family has always backed me and anything I've achieved was worth it, if only for the joy it gave them. That evening when I won the Guinness Award, my Uncle Conor and Dad were in the audience. I'm convinced it meant more to these two supporters than to me. Conor's a generation removed but more like my own brother in that we share the same zany sense of humour, people like John Cleese or Michael Palin. My parents are both involved with Special Education. Mum, alias Marie Williams, is principal of Lisanally Special School. I often go along to sing or play my guitar for them and the children show their pleasure by joining in. It refreshes to be involved with music, and I mean any kind of music."

One of the things that never cease to fascinate is the immense diversity of human beings in terms of what they can do. It refreshes to meet one of today's young men who knows exactly where he's going. Gareth wouldn't be the first *Williams* to make world-renowned music. While we await his contribution, let us wish him well.

Gareth Williams at the piano
Photograph by Ian Maginess

Joan Burney

It takes only moments to discern that 25-year-old Joan Burney, MSc, BA (Hons), MRS, ALCM, is indeed a woman of the Nineties. Working within the communications department of the BBC at Broadcasting House, Belfast, where she is events organiser, Joan utilises her public relations and event management skills in programmes such as *Children in Need*, *Making A Difference*, *The Patrick Kielty Show*, *Let me Entertain You*, *Town Challenge* and *The Hole in the Wall Gang*. In an abundance of major moments one takes precedence. Indicative of good looks and a pleasing personality, Joan represented her home county as 'Armagh Rose' in the 1994 Rose of Tralee competition. Impressing judges with her obvious intelligence, she proved that beauty and brains are compatible. Joan holds a Master's degree in Communications, Advertising and Public Relations from the University of Ulster at Jordanstown.

"The Rose of Tralee has established itself as a classic event but it was also a marvellous experience", Joan recalls. "For three days I attended various functions while representing County Armagh. Countless invitations have come my way ever since, including a 'Funday' for children with learning difficulties." Speaking fluent German and French, Joan is widely travelled and devoted two years to gaining valuable stage experience with the Ulster Youth Theatre. She is also an avid sportswoman who enjoys hockey. A former captain of the Royal School, Armagh, hockey team, she currently plays for BBC Northern Ireland. A participant in water sports, Joan happily admits that a new Jet Ski has become her latest toy. Little wonder this versatile young woman has become a vital member of the communications unit at BBC Broadcasting House, Belfast.

No stranger to the high life, Joan enjoys the somewhat unusual thrill of flying helicopters yet it was her christening that introduced her to Armagh County.

"I hadn't much to say in the matter", laughs this tremendously likeable young woman. "Five babies christened at one ceremony was a historic event for the Rev. J.H. Rankin and First Markethill Presbyterian Church. It was exceptional for our family as well. Present on that occasion were four generations of the Burney family, including my father Ronald, my grandfather Lindsay, and my great-grandfather."

Joan Etta Elizabeth Burney may have made family history as an infant but an advertisement in which she appeared during 1996 captured media headlines throughout Northern Ireland. A valiant attempt by Lisburn Borough Council to highlight the disgusting and health-threatening incidence of dog fouling encountered both opposition and applause.

"This came about while I was studying at university", Joan explains. "Part of my course in Business Studies found me on a year's placement in public relations and marketing with Lisburn Borough Council. The company making this controversial advertisement asked if I would provide a shot of my legs and feet, the implication being that I was mother of a child squatting in the park. Previous subtle efforts at reducing dog fouling had failed and this poster carried a blunt message: *Shocking, isn't it? You wouldn't let your child do it... so why let your dog?* When the poster appeared on boarding in Linenhall Street in May 1996, every newspaper in the country focused on this no-nonsense campaign. In a 'for and against' survey, Lisburn Council was congratulated for its hard-hitting technique to prevent the spread of disease. Looking back I'd do it again, particularly if it meant saving a child from serious illness or loss of sight."

By the time she reached the age of ten, Joan was an accomplished pupil in the world of speech and drama. "I was a pupil of Mrs Esther Graham who throughout her career worked single-mindedly for success. We competed at Portadown Festival where I remember taking the Yeats Senior Irish Poet Award. I could hardly have imagined that one day I would teach this subject. Now I enter my own pupils for the London College of Music examination every year. Given that one child recently achieved top marks in the county, my only regret is that I haven't more time to spend in local productions." Of her own happy childhood, Joan recalls returning from a trip to Disneyland, California, while a pupil at the Armstrong Primary School. "My tastes were eclectic even then as I remember adding a 200th novelty eraser to a record collection while the bedroom overflowed with at least 50 dolls in national costumes." Unable to recall a time when drama did not claim her attention, Joan agrees that love of the stage inspired an audition with the Ulster Youth Theatre while a pupil at the Royal School. "Soon after, during Belfast Arts Festival, I was involved in two televised productions as well as landing the part of an extra in the BBC production *Underbelly*, filmed at Armagh Prison in 1991. My most recent role is a part in *Eureka Street*, a four-part adaptation based on the highly successful novel by Belfast writer Robert McLiam Wilson. His first novel, *Ripley Bogle*, is said to have achieved cult status and helped earn his literary reputation in Europe. Filmed on the streets of Belfast, *Eureka Street* is about to be screened and has already received critical acclaim."

Her early years were spent at Collone, where Joan joined the local Young Farmers' Club. Oratory and clear diction were combined factors in securing second place in County Armagh and second place in the Northern Ireland Finals.

"Public speaking is probably one of the most underrated opportunities afforded by Young Farmers' Clubs in general. Having attended elocution lessons for 15 years, I recently obtained my Performing Arts and Teaching Diploma (ALCM). I am constantly challenged by what is just beyond my reach, studying as I am now for my ALCM (TD), the ultimate academic achievement in elocution. While I was still a pupil at Royal School, Armagh, my mother, Doreen, who had a natural flair for designer wear, began a fashion shop in Scotch Street, Armagh, which she named First Choice. I really enjoyed trips abroad when she visited German fashion houses or attended fashion shows at Harrogate. That was a marvellous experience for a teenager and I was eventually drawn into the business by helping out in my spare time. Customers came from Dundalk, Monaghan or were English visitors to Armagh city. Tower Hill Hospital's hydrotherapy pool was my mother's favourite charity and throughout her career she put enormous energy into engendering funds through charity fashion shows.

"With her keen business brain, Doreen extended the business by adding in a beauty salon. A specialist range of European cosmetics encouraged 300 guests to attend our launch. All of these events made life pretty exciting for a teenager."

If Joan has a caring disposition, she credits this as "entirely due to my mother's influence. Through her awareness, I became a fundraiser at an early age. Children and adults with learning difficulties are worthy causes and will always come first in my priorities." Joan has played a prominent part in voluntarily assisting many children with Down's Syndrome while raising funding for wheelchairs for people with physical disabilities.

"It was something I enjoyed", Joan comments, recalling how on each successive New Year's Eve she undertook a sponsored water ski at Lake Muckno, Co. Monaghan. "It was an innovative sport then and we took well over £1,000 following my first attempt." BRACE 2000, an offshoot of Blackwater Rural Agency for Community Enhancement, benefited from this versatile woman's expertise in 1996, when Joan's task involved organising a 64-event programme that would involve both sides of the community in a North-South experience. "Drawing ideas from every age group, the year was deemed a success but it was particularly rewarding to learn recently that some of these initiatives continue. Glaslough Chapel hosted a combined Harvest Thanksgiving attended by all faiths within the area. Flowers, fruit and vegetables created a theme on the continuity of seedtime and harvest with appropriate music and anthems. I feel modestly proud that this service has become an annual event."

In August 1999, when France played a friendly against Northern Ireland in a soccer international, Joan arranged for Damien McCorry to appear as team mascot. "Damien won the BBC competition 'Young Sports Reporter of the Year', and I will never forget that look on his face when I told him he could carry the World Cup onto the pitch at Windsor Park. Sharing the grandstand with television professional, Jackie Fullerton, completed the evening which I know, for Damien, will remain one to remember."

Joan Burney is a high performer who is not frightened to take a risk. Recently flying R22 helicopters, the next step is undertaking a convergence course, which will enable her to fly Jet Rangers. "Both my parents were rally drivers so I probably inherited a daredevil streak from them. My mother went solo because she said she was tired of standing watching in the sidelines! Her first competitive race was the Longford Rally in a new Ford Mexico. On finishing, she was presented with a crystal cup. Asked what the fascination was, she commented: 'the thrill of a fast-moving car—that kick from correcting a skid and the competition of racing time and weather. It gets into the system.' My father didn't interfere because he knew she would enter with or without his support." Ronald Burney was no pushover in the rallying world either, earning the title of NI Navigation Group One Championship in 1976. Such was the background into which Joan was born so is it surprising she should channel her energies into improving her performance in every aspect of life rather than worry about seeing off competitors?

Described as a 'face to look out for' by the BBC in its magazine *Airwaves*, she is commended for sheer enterprise, working all week, then teaching speech and drama at weekends. "I am keen to further develop my existing skills in public relations, media and event management, and am equally anxious to gain experience through travel or working on international projects. I really enjoyed my recent involvement in the London launch of an interactive CD-ROM entitled *A State Apart*, a chronicle of the Troubles in Northern Ireland. We are currently organising a similar launch at the European Commission in Brussels, which will take place in October."

Joan Burney may be a woman of major accomplishments but she is also refreshingly modest.

"I take nothing for granted and feel I have been lucky in my career. So much stemmed from the support and encouragement my parents have always given. I have a great set of close friends and wherever life takes me, I cannot imagine thinking otherwise." Such potential should not be underestimated. Certainly no stranger to the high life, she has used her vast experience in helping to improve the lives of others. Promising she won't be 'leaving on a jet plane' in the immediate future is the answer we all want to hear.

Joan Burney, former 'Armagh Rose'

Mark Blair

The short story *After the Match*, an exuberant insight into the Leinster schools' rugby final, achieved a literary award for Irish writer Mary O'Donnell. One phrase, "The opposition had been trounced in a stunning display of muscle and airborne muck..." neatly defines the prime factors in a charismatic game. 'A stunning display of muscle' perfectly describes rugby forward, Mark Blair. "I'm 26 years of age, I've been playing since I was five and a half", he grins, "so now people expect results!" And his expectations? "To pull on the green jersey for Ireland", Mark replies without hesitation.

A prophet may be short-changed in his own country, but Armagh is united in support of Mark Blair, an outstanding young sportsman. In the first-ever Coca-Cola Sports Awards, Mark received a special award for reaching European Cup heights. Sponsored by Bog Oak Productions and presented by television sports personality Adrian Logan, the award remains a moment to treasure. "Rather poignantly", Mark comments, "it was something similar for Selwyn Tarleton, manager of Armagh Boys' Club, who contributed a lifetime of enthusiasm to sport. Selwyn is 60 years my senior and our categories differed but we both relished the honour in our respective ways. Now retired, Selwyn is looked after by Helena, my mother, at Sunnymead residential home on the Portadown Road."

One short step from the Irish team, Irish A player, Mark Blair, at six foot five, weighs 17 stone and is startlingly blue-eyed with a brimming personality. Sports writers and commentators are hard individuals who have heard it all before, yet they constantly prophesy stardom for this likeable young man. Mark's career stemmed from Armagh Rugby Club with encouragement for his game from past president Des Fitzgerald and coach Wendel Magwood. "My early years were spent at Lisnadill Primary School where Mrs Mavis Crozier was principal. We still keep in touch and a marvellous letter I received from her, after the European Cup Final against Toulouse, invited me to come and meet present-day pupils. I was pleased to accept. Lisnadill brings back great memories of childhood.

"I never felt particularly gifted but rugby was always a consuming passion. When I'm not actually playing or training, I watch it on television. Willie Anderson, director of rugby for Dungannon, came to coach at Royal School, Armagh, during my time there. Willie was my hero with his record of 27 internationals for Ireland, three of which he captained. My father, Billy Blair, was head of the computer studies department at Royal School. It was RSA physical education coach Richard Maxwell who first intimated I had some potential. That mattered less at the time than being in the thick of things on the pitch." By fifth form, Mark, playing on the First XV, enjoyed a good season. "This determined our team for the Schools Cup which Armagh Royal had not won since 1977. In my final year I captained our side without success, as we were not particularly strong. From representative rugby, I was given a trial for the Ulster Schools League but suffered an injury early in the match and didn't play well. Putting it mildly, Richard Maxwell wasn't pleased!"

During a year at Armagh College of Further Education, Mark became a member of Armagh Rugby Club. "I'd known Des Fitzgerald and most of the players for years. I appreciate how they provided an anchor and some stability until I graduated to men's rugby. Placed second row with the Senior XV, I gained experience at a new level. I consider Armagh my home ground and it always will remain so. Beginning a civil engineering course at Heriot-Watt University, close to Edinburgh, it was almost by accident that I formed an association with Currie Rugby Club." After a season Mark made it to the First XV, gaining a worthy reputation in sporting circles. Local newspapers ran a story stating "Mark Blair, like Mr Micawber, just turned up, looking for a game..." "It was true I suppose", he shrugs. "After leaving home, I badly missed playing and wandering into Currie Rugby Club, found no-one there. The barmaid told me to return the following evening." Mark enrolled and proving his worth, played at Malleny Park, for seven seasons. His powerful contribution led to captaincy of Currie in the Premiership last season.

Resident in Scotland for three years, Mark, whose goal has always been to play at international level, was contracted by the Scottish Rugby Union. Split loyalties didn't enter the equation. "If by pulling on a blue jersey I

Mark Blair

could realise my dream", Mark asserts, "that's exactly what I'll do." It was his year. An offer came his way from superteam Edinburgh Reivers who are a combination of players from the Scottish League, competing in the European Cup. Was he tempted to accept? Mark considers for a moment. "Well, yes. Here was a place with top players, but when I studied the contract, there were uncertainties I didn't care to risk. In the balance, it was possible to do better at home. Ulster Rugby Football Union had already approached me so I had options. Obviously I want to participate in rugby at the highest level and Ulster will permit my playing in the European Cup. Going back to Ballymena, who came up with a tempting proposition, makes good sense. Dungannon were keen to sign me on, but I've decided, once the paperwork is complete, I'm Antrim bound. IRFU offered more money than Scotland, but whatever you might think, that's not nearly as important as access to play at international level."

"Ireland's gain is Scotland's loss", the Reivers' coach commented, "Mark had begun to develop in the last year and would have made a great member of our squad. I'm particularly disappointed to lose him."

Now living in Belfast, Mark rarely misses a workout, since keeping in shape depends on a daily routine "We train as a team, one gym session each morning, and afternoon training during the season. Diet is basically common sense, protein balanced with carbohydrates plus fruit and vegetables. Fitness was never more fashionable, leisure centres, gyms, health hydros or naturopathic clinics. Staff at the more luxurious places are genuinely enthusiastic... but they cost. You can keep in trim just as well with a daily swim at a modest outlay.

"I really enjoy a good film and am impatient to see *Star Wars Episode One*. Satire is for savouring, but I consider unmatched a scene from Steven Spielberg's *Saving Private Ryan* where two terrified children cower in a pile of rubble. Private Carpazo expresses an opinion that the decent thing to do is take the children to the next town. 'We're not here to do the decent thing,' Captain Millar snaps, 'we're here to follow orders!'"

With fiancée Kim Walker, Mark is happy to relax at home. "I don't like clutter so the house I've bought is best described as minimalist—rush matting, stone and old floorboards. Kim is a podiatrist, that is the science of foot and leg care. She is presently based at Hollywood Arches Health Centre. We hope to become a duet in June", he proudly discloses. Like every sportsman, his ambition is simply to be the best. "That's why I spent time in Canada and New Zealand, gaining experience and expanding match technique. Meeting and sharing with other nationalities expands our vision, helps offload what is small-minded. Back home, I'm happy to encourage kids with promise. I've tried talent spotting and see Gary Brown of Royal School, Armagh, as a lad with potential. Gary plays for the First XV and the Irish Schools League." He describes his greatest personal moment of glory as that 15-13 win over Toulouse at Ravenhill. The next day's newspaper headlines described lineout heroes Mark Blair and Gary Longwell as "two giants who epitomised the effort throughout the game. Blair proves, yet again, he is a wonderful all-rounder with athletic ability."

"Nothing inspires me as much as sport", Mark admits. "I play a little soccer, tennis when time affords, a game of snooker and", he grins, "I'm really a child at heart and a serious PlayStation fan. Should I participate in any game, be it only Snakes and Ladders, I set out to win. Call it a competitive streak, firmly rooted. Maybe that's essential to a sportsman."

"I've always loved Armagh", he states fervently, "and wish to see it take its rightful place in a cultural sense. Visiting my parents at Sunnymead is a metaphorical shot in the arm, should that be what I need at the time. I'm one of five children and we are all in our 20s: Nicky, me, Johnny, Sally and Peter. We've strong family bonds. Half of the point of doing well is the pleasure it brings my parents, Helena and Billy. I appreciate what they've done and especially how they've taken Kim into the fold."

Some players react to praise, others require challenge. "Each match brings tension", admits Mark, "a sense of something imminent. A prize worth having is within reach but so, too, is the menace of strong opposition. Rugby is based on technique and professionalism. That's what makes it such a satisfying game." Do we really need to ask his ultimate ambition?

"To pull on the green jersey for Ireland, of course", Mark Blair reiterates.

Armagh Voices

1980 ~ 1990

Make me a beautiful world for doing things tomorrow;
for that surely is a great and blessed invention

George Bernard Shaw

Shea Campbell

Chelsea Football Club director Ken Bates permitted his team to play a charity match at Omagh on 28 July 1999. This was a fund-raising event on behalf of victims of the town's bombing atrocity a year previously. Brian Kidd, as Northern Ireland scout for this Premier League team, was well known for appearing on the sidelines if ever there is even a hint of another George Best. Such was his dream.

Football, whether soccer or the Gaelic code, is the enveloping love of Shea Campbell's life. Attacking is a winger's duty and this sharp teenager has invited sufficient attention in Gaelic football circles to warrant an invitation to Philadelphia, all expenses paid, for six months on trial.

"I'm really looking forward to crossing the Atlantic", comments Shea, who will celebrate his 18th birthday this month. Acutely aware of how much he will miss his parents, Liam and Rosaleen Campbell from Newry Road, Shea comments, "Since I could walk my Dad has taken me to every match of interest." Although a supporter of Armagh City, formerly Milford Everton, Liam played and holds medals for Armagh Harps, A and B teams, and St Luke's, where he works as pharmacy technical officer. "I sleep and dream the game, so Dad gives every encouragement. In any case, he recognises that America is a chance in a lifetime.

"I played Gaelic football, beginning with the Under-10 League, and to prove it, have a room full of silverware from Pearse Ógs." Progressing to every league and championship up to Under-18, Shea won through, participating in the All-Ireland Under-14s. A former student of St Brigid's High School, Armagh, during 1996 Shea travelled to Holland with Potters Football Club, Portadown, South Belfast League, as guests of Amsterdam Junior Side Football Club.

"The opening part of this competition was played on a league basis. After four gruelling matches against tough European sides, Potters came out on top. Everything takes on that special lustre when you win... and we won", he grins. "What an experience. International competition provides opportunity. That rarely happens. This visit to Amsterdam outshone expectations and Holland was very interesting. Land reclaimed from the sea has been developed scientifically for agriculture. It is a great diamond and banking centre. Our teachers stressed the importance of European art and Rembrandt but training and playing left absolutely no time for Rembrandt or galleries! It was marvellous to see houseboats along the canal banks, and trips in glass-roofed boats. People I met were just great and we keep in touch."

Shea speaks proudly of his uncle, County Minors player Tommy Martin. "Tommy is secretary of Pearse Ógs Club, holding a plethora of GAA medals and trophies. He was delighted when I joined this club at junior level. Playing Gaelic with the Schools' League, right from primary level, I then found myself drawn to Orchard Youth Football Club, a cross-community team, along with several friends. This brought me into contact with Portadown Boys FC—they signed on my friend Kevin as goalkeeper and soon afterwards, took me as well." During two seasons, Shea won League and Cup two years running. From Portadown Boys, he was sent to trials, then chosen to play in the Milk Cup, the world's biggest youth tournament. Shea's footwork must have impressed for immediately Potters Football Club invited him on board. "With them I won the League Cup twice visiting Holland, then playing Farnborough Town in the final."

Shea heaps credit on Armagh City Football Club for an attitude where only the game matters. "Seán Daly (Dingle to us) was manager. He told me I had potential and to work on it. Near the end of the season, Armagh Firsts brought me in, playing big games against Ards Firsts and Portadown. I gained valued experience but was still very young. Having watched Armagh against Dungannon Swifts Reserve Team, Terry McCrory approached me, asking if I'd sign for them. Always an Armagh man, naturally I had reservations. My Dad helped me decide. Here was an offer of experience besides a chance to play in the Irish League." The transfer took place, Armagh signing Shea over to Dungannon. Didn't they want to hold on to this talented young striker? "Well yes..." he modestly agrees. "But they also stipulated they wouldn't stand in my way. Isn't that the mark of a good club? In at the deep end, we had a Saturday league match against Portadown within the week. The routine involved going across each Thursday evening to train and I did score a few goals

Shea Campbell

before the season ended. Three special men, Stephen Uprichard and Mark Neill of Armagh City FC and Colin Jeffers of Swifts, inspired me to give my best and I'll never lose sight of that fact. Indeed Mark encourages me each time we meet.

"During school years", Shea admits, "education came well down my list. Had I scored points for maths and English, equalling PE and games", he purses his lips, "I would have been something to reckon with!" Bowling was another skill and a newspaper clipping from 1994 tells how he captained St Brigid's second and third year boys at a tournament in Centrepoint, Lurgan. The game hinged on Shea, champion the previous year, who had only one remaining bowl. This he sent straight and true, a magnificent strike, earning 'Champion Bowler' for the second time.

Leaving St Brigid's, Shea became a trainee, specialising in butchery with qualifications in health and safety, and food hygiene. "I earned a good salary and bought my first car, a Renault Clio, but this is not where my heart lies. Recent news from a friend, Jason McCarron, may now change the entire course of my life. Jason, a fellow Swifts team player, was selected last year for Gaelic team Donegal Philadelphia. At a conference Jason recommended me. Team manager Louis Bradley checked my sports curriculum vitae, liked what he saw and before I knew, a ticket arrived for America. I fly out next Wednesday."

For the coming six months, Shea will eat, breathe and sleep Gaelic football. America has its own 'All-Ireland' League and should he make the grade, this young man has the world at his toe! "I've been on holiday to Disneyland, Florida", comments Shea, "and loved the climate. Now I can visit again. In itself, Philadelphia is a huge adventure, all expenses paid."

Dundee United has expressed interest in his talents but to trial for talent scouts like , Brian Kidd is an impossible dream. "Unfortunately I have an injured toe on my right foot, a hairline crack which heals naturally. If they take me on, you'll be first to know!"

If they take you on, Shea Campbell, all of the county will want to know!

The South Ulster Youth Band

Striking exactly the right chord, 63 energetic young musicians who form the South Ulster Youth Band have won the affection of concert audiences while enjoying glowing press reports throughout LaGrange and Newnan, Georgia, in the United States. Nine of these youthful ambassadors from local schools and colleges in Armagh City and District are Colm Campbell, Cathy Devlin, Stephen Gribbon, Jonathan Hoey of Royal School, Armagh, now studying Modern Languages at St Andrews University, Dave McAvinchey studying at Trinity College Dublin, Aisling McVeigh of Drumcree High School, David Moore, Kieran O'Connor and Ronan Scullion. An opportunity to bring their brand of music across the Atlantic came with an invitation from the committee of LaGrange International Friendship Exchange. Host families provided accommodation while LaGrange committee arranged the use of instruments and concert venues for the Band. After tearful farewells, all nine agree, Georgia will remain on their minds for years to come.

"We intend to return to America and probably individually at some future date for a visit to our exceptional host families", comments Dave McAvinchey who plays tenor saxophone. "Four years ago we visited Europe but America must rate as our most memorable trip yet."

By their individual skills and overall contribution to the musical tradition of Armagh City and District, these nine young musicians came to the attention of Mayor Tom Canavan who agrees theirs is a special talent and that all have a promising future. Chief executive of the Southern Education and Library Board, Helen McClenaghan, commented: "We are justly proud of all young people in the band. They are a credit to their families, schools, colleges and universities. We thank them for being wonderful ambassadors." Before they left on their trip, Northern Ireland First Minister Designate, David Trimble, MP, sent his message of congratulations. This was fully endorsed by the then Deputy First Minister Designate Seamus Mallon, MP, who wrote: "Music is an art and a discipline, but above all it is a wonderful means of communication."

South Ulster Youth Band is the senior band of the Southern Education and Library Board's Music Service, based in Portadown, and draws membership from more advanced pupils. Ages range from 14-21, young musicians having been trained to a minimum requirement of the recognised British examination standard of Grade 5. Many are of Grade 8 standard and above. The band is conducted by Uel Falkner, assisted by Luke Burke—two SELB tutors whose enthusiasm and dedication to high standards of musicianship have been rewarded by the band's success and popularity. Weekly rehearsals centre on the twin goals of achieving challenging musical standards while at the same time providing topical interest for young players who enjoy the latest chart songs.

Councillor J.K. Twyble of Craigavon Borough Council, the Sister City International Committee, and LaGrange co-ordinator Lewis Porter all deserve a particular word of thanks for setting up the necessary links with LaGrange prior to the visit.

"Our repertoire was well-chosen", says trumpet player Jonathan Hoey, and all nine gratefully acknowledge the professionalism of Eithne Benson, head of SELB Music Service, and Martin White, head of performance, in composing a superb programme. *An Irish Rhapsody*, a setting for symphonic band, contained six Irish songs—*The Minstrel Boy*, *I Know Where I'm Going*, *Shepherd Is Lamb Reel*, *Cockles and Mussels*, *Rakes of Mallow* and *Kathleen O'Moore*. "The coda returns to *Cockles and Mussels*", Jonathan explains, "then the tempo broadens as the horns and woodwind add their counter melodies in an impressive ending."

"I particularly liked a medley we played from *The Hunchback of Notre Dame*", is the comment of Colm Campbell. "This animated feature hit from Disney was inspired by Victor Hugo's novel. An arrangement by talented John Moss followed *Colours of the Wind* and included *The Bells of Notre Dame*, *Hellfire*, *Out There* and *Someday*. I agree it was a stimulating experience for both band and audience."

Michael Flatley made the stage his kingdom with his show *Lord of the Dance*. "We liked this music", says Kieran O'Connor, "and began our selection with Richard Saucedo's arrangement, a haunting statement of the theme on piccolo." Aisling McVeigh continues, "This builds into a swaggering rhythm with a jig-like feel, leading to the Celtic dance beat. The intensity builds to an abrupt but riveting ending."

"Sousa's *The Thunderer March* was dedicated to the Knights Templar of Washington DC, and it seems, was Mrs Sousa's favourite march", contributes Stephen Gribbon. "It was certainly an important part of our performance with *Titanic*, where *My Heart will Go On* was played by the solo oboe, then joined by the rest of the band, gradually reaching a dynamic conclusion."

The *Symphonic Beatles* enjoyed a *maestoso* introduction leading into *A Hard Day's Night*, allowing the woodwind to introduce Yesterday and the trumpets for *I Want to Hold Your Hand*. "During this particular concert in Newnan, lightning struck a power transformer and all the lights went off", Jonathan adds. "Undeterred, the band played on. It was David Moore's big trumpet solo and he gave a magnificent performance. Had he done otherwise, under the circumstances, the rest of us would have collapsed."

Georgia On My Mind by Hoagy Carmichael is a lovely swing ballad. "It perfectly fitted our location", Jonathan comments, "and we dedicated this performance to our superb hosts at LaGrange and Newnan."

"Nothing gets in the way when it comes to making a good sound", all nine emphatically agree. "There's no such thing as division in the world of music", Dave McAvinchey reiterates. "We've been members for years, meeting for three hours on Saturday mornings in order to practice. It's dedication that really matters."

We will have their best interests on our minds and without doubt, all nine will have 'Georgia on their minds' for years and years to come!

The South Ulster Youth Band with conductor Uel Falkner

Armagh City and District musicians from the South Ulster Youth Band. Front row (L to R): Kieran O'Connor, Aisling McVeigh, Colm Campbell. Middle row: Stephen Gribbon, Dave McAvinchey, Jonathan Hoey. Back row: Stephen McNally, David Moore

Joanne Bloomer

Nineteen-year-old Joanne Bloomer has chosen to tell her story in her own words. A young person of courage, this account is a tribute to all who cope with adversity, and to the work of the Northern Ireland Ambulance Trust based at Tower Hill, Armagh.

"From the day I was born I have suffered from osteomalacia, a disorder which causes softening, weakening and demineralisation of the bones due to vitamin D deficiency and lack of calcium or phosphate. My symptoms include bone pain or tenderness in the legs, spine and pelvis. Skeletal deformities accompany this illness such as shortness of stature. I am only four foot nine inches.

"When I first began to walk, my parents felt something was wrong and took me to our local general practitioner, Dr Fitzroy Gillespie. He agreed that I had a problem and at once referred me to the Royal Victoria Hospital for Sick Children. An attempt to straighten my legs when I was 11 years old resulted in an operation, which, I regret to say, was unsuccessful. Soon after I was referred to Musgrave Park Hospital where, following an examination, surgeon Mr Michael Laverick decided he would perform two operations, which might, hopefully, straighten my legs. I had the first of these in December 1994 and remained in hospital for three months undergoing physiotherapy with the help of Sarah Beattie, my hospital physiotherapist. The outcome of this operation was good. Soon it was time for the next. Ilizarou frames were now to be placed on my tibia and fibula. This operation took place in August 1997 and it was expected that I would wear the frames for a year. I did not have to remain in hospital all of this time, although I attended outpatients every two weeks, keeping appointments with Mr Laverick and Sarah Beattie.

"Throughout that year I also attended physiotherapy at Armagh Community Hospital three times a week where I obtained enormous professional help from physiotherapists within the department. They were really helpful when the time came to walk again. I would like everyone to know how good they were. It can be traumatic coming and going to hospital but it was always made easier by Darren Wilkinson and Stephen McComb, two paramedics who are employed by Northern Ireland Ambulance Service Trust based at Armagh Community Hospital. Darren and Stephen were great fun, yet well aware that it was painful for me to move my limbs. Each time they took me to hospital, they had a joke to share so that, before I knew, the ordeal was over. My parents have coped so well with my illness—right from the beginning. Two good friends, Gillian and Stephen Bruce, were always there when I felt downhearted.

"My last operation was a great success and now I am walking straight. Some time in the future I hope to go to university, studying for a degree in social work. This has been made possible by Dr Gillespie at Tynan surgery, his staff and all the wonderful people I mentioned already.

"To be included in this book makes me feel special. In looking forward to the rest of my life, I am grateful for what has gone already. Not everyone gets the chance to say this in print or to mention great people like Darren and Stephen. Pamela told me she wouldn't have been able to produce this book without equally great people who helped by typing, proof-reading or just being there when the going was hard. It just goes to show—we all need each other!"

Joanne with paramedics Darren and Stephen

Sarah Elizabeth Mawhinney

Her pragmatic attitude to life helps Sarah Mawhinney cope with an allergy that inflicts a seriously restricted diet. From her comments it is clear that Sarah's grandfather, Norman Mawhinney, occupies a special place in her affections.

For a lifetime, Norman was a professional photographer with the Allison Studio. His story was the last interview taken by the late Gerald Rafferty of the *Ulster Gazette*. Due to Gerald's unexpected death, this account was never written. Norman's long-awaited moment of glory is entirely by courtesy of his grand-daughter Sarah.

"My name is Sarah Elizabeth Mawhinney and I was born on 8 August 1988. People think I am lucky to have a date of birth like this (8.8.88), but when I consider that my little sister was born exactly four years later, and I have to share my birthday with her—maybe I'm not really so fortunate!

"I missed sharing my birthday with my grand-dad by one day. His is a day earlier. We always share our birthday cake and he likes to take a picture of my sister and me on this day. Grand-dad has done this ever since I was born. He first began taking photographs when he was only 14 years old and started work in Allison's Studios, Armagh. This year he was 92 and we hadn't enough room to put all the candles on the cake!

"I love my grand-dad very much. He has a great sense of humour. Each time I call to see him, he slips me some toffees from his special tin. Unfortunately I have to wait until he's not looking so I can then sneak them back again. You see, since the age of five, I have known that I am severely allergic to peanuts and cannot risk eating anything that might be contaminated. A reaction could prove fatal.

"Everything I eat has to be checked beforehand, in case it contains any nut traces and, unfortunately, most sweets do.

"I have been a pupil at the preparatory department of the Royal School, Armagh, for the past six years. I enjoyed studying there and made lots of friends. My favourite pastimes are swimming, playing the piano and reading. All this sounds very serious, but I also have fun playing Nintendo 64 with my sister, going to the cinema and looking after our pet guinea-pigs who also have to do without pet treats that contain nuts!"

Sarah Elizabeth Mawhinney
Sarah's grandfather, Norman Mawhinney

Armagh and District Talking Newspaper for the Blind

Imagine how vital, and valuable, the spoken word is for those who cannot inform themselves through newsprint. The completely free Talking Newspaper for the Blind in Armagh originated from a presentation that Isobel Holmes, of Dungannon Talking Newspaper, gave to Armagh Community Council. This worldwide phenomenon was inspired by Gwynn Prosser, editor of a Welsh local newspaper. In 1950, Prosser and his reporting team began taping news from their own paper. He then brought the tape to a home for the blind where 70 people gathered to listen. In 1958, the local Rotary Club took over this work, calling it the South Wales Talking Newspaper. By 1968, Talking Newspapers had been established in several localities.

Armagh made its debut in 1981, when local man Paddy Grimes chaired a series of discussions as to how the project might work. A publicity campaign was planned to stimulate public interest, financial backing and prospective contributors and organisers. First treasurer John Doogan went ahead in an attitude of faith, having considerable expenses yet absolutely no means. Such an undertaking required technicians with sufficient knowledge to purchase recording equipment and demonstrate its use. Local businessman Henry Emerson, with John Watson, undertook this responsibility. From tentative beginnings that important aspect of the project ran smoothly.

Armagh and District Talking Newspaper next recruited teams of newsreaders. Organisers were, however, at a loss as to how they might edit and present news from local newspapers, the *Ulster Gazette* and *Armagh Observer*. This work entailed selecting cuttings suitable for readers who, when they gained sufficient confidence, must read these in a clear voice. Eventually a system evolved and many memorable voices have emerged on air!

Side B of the tape, providing a topical magazine, presented another set of difficulties. Listeners, it was assumed, had varied tastes, so how could a team envisage what might, overall, constitute an interesting programme? Each side of the tape required 45 minutes of material presented by natural voices from an untrained group, meeting at regular intervals. It was also important that interesting features be presented. Volunteers were required to visualise material rather than simply reading it.

The late Sylvia Kastell was a member of the first committee of the Talking Newspaper. Within two years her sight deteriorated and she became a recipient of the tapes. As a listener, Sylvia was occasionally critical but always highly appreciative of work voluntarily undertaken by all who contributed to the Talking Newspaper. It was a link, she stressed, "for others like me, cut off from the printed word".

Armagh Community Council decided to promote a Talking Newspaper by way of contribution to the Year of the Disabled in 1981. With chairperson Paddy Grimes, the first committee members were G. Burns, Henry Emerson, Betty McCann, John O'Neill, Bert Mackrel, P. McCrory, P. Grant, Rosemary Reid, Pauline Mortimer, A. Hadden and John Doogan. Co-opted members were K. Spence, Carol Walsh, Brigid Finnegan, Rose Hoy, Irene Knox, Paddy Gallen, Mary McVeigh and John Watson. Paddy Grimes remained chairperson from 1981, being succeeded by Rosemary Reid from 1985, Tommy McKinney from 1988, Paddy Gallen from 1990 and Betty McCann, who still holds office, from 1993.

Generous funding came from schools, statutory bodies, and youth and voluntary groups representing all sections of the community. Permission was granted by the *Ulster Gazette* and *Armagh Observer* to record articles while the Southern Education and Library Board agreed to undertake reproduction and presentation of the cassettes. At a practice evening on 16 April 1981, tapes were produced and sent out to the first recipients.

It was decided that the magazine side of the tape should be recorded each Tuesday with news added on Thursday, which was then publication day for both newspapers. Seven teams providing the news tape were formed, each made up of two editors and six readers with an optional number of contributors responsible for magazine content. Armagh Girls' High School and St Luke's Hospital were venues for early recordings but from November 1981, Royal School, Armagh became a permanent venue. For many years, one team met at the home of Bert and Lena Mackrel. Bert, who has been blind for a quarter century,

The committee of Armagh and District Talking Newspaper for the Blind, 1999.
Front row (L to R): Bert Mackrel, Ellen Clements, Chairman Betty McCann, Paddy Gallen.
Back row: honorary secretary Jim Boyle, Patricia Mackle, Mary Hamilton (SELB), Rose Hoy, Norah McCabe and honorary treasurer Tony Clements

fulfils the role of team technician. Although Lena died in 1997, this team continues to be hosted by Bert. A room specifically fitted for recording the Talking Newspaper was a dream that became a reality in 1997, at Dobbin Street Community Centre. New equipment, financed by the Macan Trust for the Blind in 1998, has considerably enhanced the quality of production.

The *Elizabethan Serenade* has preceded news items every week for 18 years. Recipients have never complained, but readers and technicians feel they have been serenaded to death, and a welcome change is on the cards! From experience gained, magazine teams now work to a theme which may be triggered by seasonal stimuli; festivals, Christmas, childhood, war, travel, holidays, music, songs, childhood, the cinema or grandmother's delicious fruit cake. Questionnaire distribution resulted in valuable feedback as to individual tastes, favourite authors or musical preferences. Social outings for volunteers and subscribers have included a visit to the Ulster Museum Exhibition for the Blind and Partially Sighted, and trips to the Ulster American Folk Park at Omagh, the Share Centre in Lisnaskea, Bangor and several other seaside resorts. After 1988, the summer outing gave way to a social evening when dinner is followed by dancing and entertainment. This was preferred by the majority of Talking Newspaper subscribers.

Students in the area expressed their interest, and Royal School, Armagh, provides a news team. Talks promoting the aims and interests of the Newspaper are given regularly at schools or to various organisations by the present chairperson or members of committee. A special 10th anniversary booklet was produced in 1991 and is freely available. Anyone who is blind, partially sighted or suffers from a disability, which makes reading a strain, is entitled to receive the Talking Newspaper. Applications are made through the secretary, or through Southern Health and Social Services Board. If necessary, a cassette player will be provided by the Talking Newspaper.

Outside agencies play a vital role in completing production of this service. Staff of the Southern Health and Social Services Board publicise the service, encouraging blind and partially sighted people to avail of it. They deal with applications, deliver tape recorders and provide operating instructions. Audio-visual staff in the hospital and associated services department of the Southern Education and Library Board fast-copy and package the tapes. They also undertake some administrative work, such as recording changes of address. The Library Service amends records accordingly so that the Talking Newspaper list is always up to date. The recipient list is highly confidential and available only to Social Services or the Library Service.

Without a free postal service, the Talking Newspaper could not afford to operate a tape service. Tapes are delivered each Saturday morning to 120 homes in the area.

The Armagh operation is a member of the Northern Ireland Talking Newspaper Association and the Talking Newspaper Association of the UK.

Almost 20 years on, Armagh and District Talking Newspaper continues to thrive. Volunteers and subscribers have come to share a caring relationship that has much in common with a rather large family. Feedback confirms that listeners are satisfied with the original format of Headlines, Court News, Weddings, Council Business... Recipients may freely comment or criticise by placing remarks on a slip and inserting this behind the returns card. Production teams are drawn from every walk of life and so match the interests of listeners, even in the near-impossible task of providing a constant flow of stimulating material. The work is undertaken quietly and unfailingly. Today's committee comprises Betty McCann (chairperson), Maura McCarten (vice-chairperson), Tony Clements (treasurer), Jim Boyle (secretary), Ellen Clements, Paddy Gallen, Elizabeth Gallen, Bert Mackrel, Nora McCabe, Patricia Mackle, Josie Kirk and Rose Hoy.

All who devote time and energy in whatever capacity to Armagh and District Talking Newspaper do so on a voluntary basis. That recipients look forward to the postman's visit with a fresh tape each Saturday morning is, they say, a pleasing reward. Knowing where to end is as important as beginning and reinforces that volunteers are as crucial today as they were in 1981.

This is a precious service and worthy of continuity, as a co-founder put it, "for others like me, cut off from the printed word".

Armagh Voices

1990 ~ 2000

Bliss was it in that dawn to be alive
But to be young was very heaven!

William Wordsworth

Niamh Ó Maoláin

Because I Can See

Simplicity is so much,
Although often taken for granted.
But some people are not content until they have seen the
sights of the world,
The prettiest things.
We can see the rainbow miraculously placed by nature.
A world of colours surrounds us,
The Cathedrals standing tall and proud,
The sun a torch in a cloudless sky,
And the waves crashing on the rocks.
I am so lucky because I can see the immaculate raindrops
fall to the ground.
I am blessed because I can see myself.
Yes, I am blessed because I can see.

"My name is Niamh Ó Maoláin and I am ten years old. I live in Armagh with my Mum and Dad, Ruairí, my elder brother, Sinéad, my sister, and the youngest of the family, Cormac. My Dad is from County Derry whereas Mum is from Armagh. I have two pet gerbils, Philadelphia and Eimear.

"My favourite subjects at school are creative writing, art and maths. I go to St Malachy's Primary School and enjoy it a lot. This year I will be entering Primary Seven and am looking forward to that. I wrote my first poem when I was in P3. I enjoy writing stories but like poems best because you don't have to make an awful lot of sense and are able to write your own way without having to abide by rules. My advice to any young writer is to enter all the competitions you can because you just might win and get noticed. Enjoy yourself when you are writing and remember that with a bit of will power, you can be anything you want to be..."

"Our poetry competition has become the highlight of the year for members of Orchard Social Club for Visually Impaired People", comments chairman Bert Mackrel. During the 1999 Apple Blossom Festival, a silver trophy in memory of Bert's late wife and former Club Treasurer, Lena, was presented to the winner, Niamh Ó Maoláin of St Malachy's Primary School, by Armagh City and District Councillor Sylvia McRoberts. The theme of the competition, Because I Can See, encouraged original reflections on the responsibility which accompanies the gift of sight.

Commenting on the excellent response to the competition in May 1999, Mrs McRoberts said: "Each primary school in this city submitted entries which amounted to more than 300 in total. These were imaginative and impressive but Niamh's poem looked beyond obvious or easy options. It was confidently written: 'I can see the immaculate raindrops...' is a phrase worthy of a winner. How proud Niamh's parents and teacher must feel, seeing her take the Lena Mackrel Perpetual Trophy for the first time, indeed the only time in this ebbing century."

Second place in the competition was awarded to Rebecca Murray of Mount St Catherine's Primary School with third prize won by nine-year-old Hannah Taylor, the youngest competitor to enter. In thanking the Council for financial support, Bert also acknowledged parents and teachers who encouraged such impressive entries, and Anna Logan and Des Walsh of the Armagh Confederation of Voluntary Groups, who helped to organise the highly successful Apple Blossom Festival.

Mrs Eileen McDermott, Principal of St Malachy's Primary School, has a final word: "Niamh is a wonderful pupil with talents galore, creative writing being only one of them. May she be a shining light far into the new millennium."

Niamh Ó Maoláin,
first winner of the Lena Mackrel Perpetual Trophy

John Maguire

"My name is John Maguire. I live with my Mum, Dad and my dog, Barney. I am five years old and Barney is six.

"I think I want to be a rally driver when I grow up. Dad took me to a rally on Saturday and the cars made a lot of noise.

"Last Christmas, Santa Claus brought me a PlayStation and I am good at the Colin McRae rally. Usually I can manage up to first place!

"Books are my favourite thing. I have lots of them—all full of words. I am trying hard to read all these words. Dad takes me to the library each Tuesday night and this is what happens. I choose a book and hand over my ticket. The lady at the desk scans it and off we go, taking Barney for a walk. If Mum has finished washing up she comes as well.

"My Uncle Bryan sends me lots of books. He is very funny and so are the books, except sometimes they are scary like *The Haunted Planet*, which has holograms.

"I am going to Deirdre O'Reilly's party tomorrow. Next I hope to go to my cousin Gareth's party. Auntie Marie always has nice things for supper.

"I jumped on my bed and stood on my head when I heard I was going to be put in a book. Imagine—me in a book!

"Goodbye from John."

John Maguire's enthusiasm reflects what pleasure the written word holds for him. Literacy is a building block in the developed world and lending libraries are vital storehouses of old and current books. The British Library in London is entitled under various Copyright Acts to a free copy of every work published in the United Kingdom and presently holds more than five million books. John borrows from the Armagh Branch of the Southern Education and Library Board. For the elderly or housebound, a mobile library service brings books to the doorstep of many living in villages and towns throughout this district.

Every book had to be written. Long before television or radio came the storyteller, the poet, the philosopher, the historian, the scientist and the novelist. These were the giants of an earlier age who placed words on papyrus, then paper. While it was not always so, modern critical tastes tend to value fiction above other kinds of prose. Readers down the centuries have enjoyed creations credible enough to be real: Beowulf, the Wife of Bath, Shylock, Jane Eyre, Heathcliffe, Becky Sharp, Mr Micawber, Tess of the D'Urbervilles, Dorian Gray, Molly Bloom, Professor Higgins, Miss Jean Brodie, Paddy Clarke, Matilda and Harry Potter.

In the near-sacred hush of the library, alphabetical classification undercuts distinction save that of genre, and great works are placed cheek by jowl alongside those of simple authorial vanity. Library facilities continually face financial cuts. Avid borrowers help to ensure that impending threats remain only a threat.

A new book giving voice to 100 chosen members of this community has now found its way into our local library. It delineates a prolific host of memorable characters, all of them real. These are people who stand out in a crowd, as worthy of becoming established in a reader's memory as the inhabitants of great novels—if only we possessed the magic eye of Dickens to perceive this. Some like Dr Sheelagh Woods have lived for almost 100 years while John Maguire has experienced a mere five. Such combined experiences are of novel dimension and yet are true.

I cannot imagine a world without any one of them.

John Maguire
with Armagh Branch Library Assistant Jacqueline McArdle